LONDON'S LOST THEATRES OF THE NINETEENTH CENTURY

INTERIOR OF ASTLEY'S IN THE EARLY XIXTH CENTURY

From a coloured print in the British Museum

LONDON'S LOST THEATRES OF THE NINETEENTH CENTURY

With Notes on Plays and Players Seen There

BY

ERROLL SHERSON

" We are not done with the days that were
as soon as their sunsets have faded, but a
light remains from them and grows fairer and
fairer, like an afterglow lingering among
tremendous peaks above immeasurable slopes
of snow."—*Chronicles of Rodriguez.*
—LORD DUNSANY.

BENJAMIN BLOM  New York/London

First Published 1925
Reissued 1969 by
Benjamin Blom, Inc., Bronx, New York 10452
and 56 Doughty Street, London, W.C. 1

Library of Congress Catalog Card Number 70-81200

Printed in U.S.A. by
NOBLE OFFSET PRINTERS, INC.
NEW YORK 3, N. Y.

12, Portland Place, W.1.

To   August 3rd, 1925.

ERROLL SHERSON, Esq.

What is " Acting " ?   Like shadows, like a dream, a
distant voice, a pleasant memory : nothing more.   Acting has
no standard.   Certain forms may guide it a little—but
Imagination and Instinct are its principal movers.   Art is
simplicity : simplicity *is* Art, but Actors have one great
privilege above all others.   In *their* moments of triumph,
they *live* and the public live *with* them !

All men and women act—whether on or off the stage : so
do all little children : in the nursery they are seldom their
real selves—but a Mrs. Smith with a large family, or a Mr.
Jones—a confirmed bachelor.

I hope that in one of your lost theatres, some great genius
may have left his spirit,—his ghost of the days that are no
more,—and send forth Art and Inspiration for the theatres
of the future.

Yours faithfully
Madge Kendal

To the Memory of my dear Mother, Lady Anne Sherson, who loved the Play and knew many of the Players, and to my Sister, Grace Sherson, whose life has been one long self-sacrifice for others, with no thought for herself, this, my first book, is conjointly dedicated.

CONTENTS

FOREWORD BY MRS. KENDAL

CHAPTERS   PAGE

I.   LOOKING BACK   I

II.   THE GRECIAN THEATRE : WITH NOTES ON MELO-
         DRAMA AND PANTOMIME   9

III.   LONDON'S LOST THEATRES OF THE EAST END...   37

IV.   ASTLEY'S   52

V.   THE OLYMPIC THEATRE   77

VI.   THE PRINCESS'S THEATRE (I) FROM THE EARLIEST
         TIMES TO THE END OF THE MANAGEMENT OF
         CHARLES KEAN   121

VII. THE PRINCESS'S THEATRE (2) FROM 1860 TO THE
         FINAL CLOSING OF THE THEATRE   144

VIII. THE TWO THEATRES IN HOLBORN AND THE
         PANTHEON THEATRE   185

IX.   THE QUEEN'S THEATRE, LONG ACRE   201

X.   THE OLD STRAND THEATRE : WITH NOTES ON
         BURLESQUE   211

XI.   THE " RICKETY TWINS " : THE GLOBE AND THE
         OPERA COMIQUE THEATRES   237

XII. THE PHILHARMONIC THEATRE : WITH NOTES ON
         OPERA BOUFFE   262

XIII. THE MARYLEBONE THEATRE AND THE TWO
         ALEXANDRA THEATRES   278

XIV. THE IMPERIAL THEATRE AND TOOLE'S THEATRE...   295

XV. THE BOWER SALOON AND OTHER MINOR THEATRES   314

XVI. RICHARDSON'S SHOW AND OTHER BOOTHS   ...   329

XVII. THE PRIVATE THEATRE AT CAMPDEN HOUSE,
         KENSINGTON   339

XVIII. THE LOST THEATRES OF TOYLAND   346

XIX. AUDIENCES OF THE PAST AND AUDIENCES OF THE
         PRESENT   352

LIST OF ILLUSTRATIONS

INTERIOR OF ASTLEY'S IN THE EARLY NINETEENTH CENTURY *Frontispiece*

Facing Page

INTERIOR OF OLD ROYALTY THEATRE, WELLCLOSE SQUARE.. ..	44
ASTLEY'S ADVERTISING CART	52
EXTERIOR OF ASTLEY'S ROYAL AMPHITHEATRE	52
ADAH ISAACS MENKEN AS "MAZEPPA"..	62
MAZEPPA BOUND TO THE WILD HORSE	62
WYCH STREET, DRURY LANE	63
CRAVEN HOUSE, DRURY LANE, IN 1800..	80
REMAINS OF CRAVEN HOUSE, ABOUT 1806	80
EXTERIOR OF THE SECOND OLYMPIC THEATRE..	81
INTERIOR OF THE SECOND OLYMPIC THEATRE	81
EXTERIOR OF THE THIRD OLYMPIC THEATRE	84
F. ROBSON AS JACOB EARWIG IN "BOOTS OF THE SWAN" ..	85
F. ROBSON AS DADDY HARDACRE	85
HENRY NEVILLE AS BOB BRIERLY IN "TICKET OF LEAVE MAN"..	98
KATE TERRY AS VIOLA IN "TWELFTH NIGHT"	99
KATE TERRY AS BLANCHE DE NEVERS IN "THE DUKE'S MOTTO"	99
KATE TERRY IN "THE SERF"	102
MISS KATE TERRY	102
EXTERIOR OF PRINCESS'S THEATRE, OXFORD STREET, 1851	103
SOME AMERICAN PLAYERS (CHARLOTTE CUSHMAN, LAURA KEENE, GEORGE JORDAN AND J. W. WALLACK, JUNR.)	126
"A WINTER'S TALE": TWO HERMIONES (MRS. CHARLES KEAN AND MISS MARY ANDERSON)	136
CHARLES FECHTER	146
FECHTER AS ROBERT MACAIRE	146
FECHTER AS "HAMLET," "BELPHEGOR," "OTHELLO" AND "IAGO"	150
MR. AND MRS. CHARLES KEAN	156
MR. AND MRS. DION BOUCICAULT	156
MRS. JOHN WOOD	160
INTERIOR OF THE PANTHEON OPERA HOUSE, OXFORD STREET ..	198
HENRIETTA HODSON (MRS. LABOUCHERE)	204
J. L. TOOLE IN "TROVATORE" (BURLESQUE) AND "THE STEEPLE-CHASE"	206
MADAME CELESTE AS CYNTHIA IN "FLOWERS OF THE FOREST" ..	214
MR. AND MRS. KENDAL IN "AS YOU LIKE IT"	254
MISS EMILY SOLDENE	264
EMILY SOLDENE AS DROGAN IN "GENEVIEVE DE BRABANT" ..	264
MISS SELINA ("DOLLY") DOLARO	268
THE GARDENS AT HIGHBURY BARN	290
AMATEUR THEATRICALS AT CAMPDEN HOUSE	342
"THE CONNAUGHT JIG" AS DANCED BY LADY ANNE SHERSON AND MR. JOY..	344

LONDON'S LOST THEATRES

CHAPTER I

LOOKING BACK

" Difficilis, querulus, laudator temporis acti
Se puero."

THE Lost Theatres of London ! How many delightful
evenings in the past do these words recall to the old
playgoer ! Where are they all, and when and why
were they lost ? Some were swept away by the besom
of " modern improvement " ; some sacrificed to the demand for
Cinemas, a cheaper and much less intelligent form of entertainment ; some were burned down and not rebuilt ; some fell before
the greed of profiteers. Few old theatres remain which can afford
stories of great actors and great plays, and the green-rooms and
wings of such as survive must be haunted by many a sad shade.
There are, perhaps, half a dozen left which have a history—
Covent Garden, Drury Lane, Haymarket, Adelphi, Lyceum and
St. James's, to which may be added the Surrey and the Old Vic,
and not one of these but has been reconstructed at least once.
So when I set out to put down some stories of the lost London
theatres and some of the players who trod their boards, I had to
make up my mind which were really lost. Not, perhaps, those
that are only turned into Cinemas—they may possibly be resus-
citated in the days to come. Therefore, Sadler's Wells and
Marylebone are not yet lost. This might clear the way for me
and make my work the lighter, but my conscience was not easy
and told me that I was shirking what I ought to do. For those
two old homes of the Drama were among the most famous of the
day, keeping the flag of " The Legitimate " flying when other
places were given over to burlesque and weak adaptations from
the French and even, to their shame, to men-flies and performing
dogs as once were Drury Lane and Covent Garden.
So, although the Marylebone might conceivably be one day among
the living theatres, I have included it in the list of the lost. But
Sadler's Wells, though it has not been used as a regular theatre for
a considerable time will not, I hope, be numbered with the " lost

for years " yet and will assume the position in the North of London that the Old Vic has attained to in the South.*

But there is still another house with a great past which, though, I believe, still standing, is probably one of the lost. This is the Princess's Theatre in Oxford Street, left to the rats and the spiders now for nearly a quarter of a century. It cannot be omitted, for its boards saw the transition from the old style to the new, from the ponderous Macready to the more natural school of Fechter, Boucicault and Barrett, with Charles Kean as a connecting link between the two.

The younger playgoer of the present day, whose range does not extend much beyond the neighbourhood of the Strand and Shaftesbury Avenue, has little idea of the number of theatres which have been "lost" in the last forty or fifty years, or of the tales connected with them and the companies acting there. He has heard, perhaps, of the Olympic, Globe and Opera Comique, which were swallowed up in the improvements of the Strand ; he may be acquainted with some traditions of the old Strand burlesques and of the horsemanship at Astley's ; but he knows little or nothing of the story of those playhouses in the central and outlying districts which had their successful seasons, but are now totally lost to all save the memories of the oldest playgoers. Their records and traditions are buried beneath files of ancient theatrical programmes and newspapers and between the covers of Memoirs and Reminiscences of actors dead and gone.

There is nothing left, beyond the mere name, of the Lyceum to recall the glories of the Vestris, Fechter and Irving regimes. Excluding the Opera House, perhaps the Haymarket, the St. James's, the Adelphi and the little Royalty are the least altered from what they were in the sixties of last century. Let us see what has become of the rest. The remains of Sadler's Wells, one of the oldest places of entertainment in London or perhaps in the world, has been cast to the Movies for a very long time, if it be indeed used for anything at all now. The once famous Opera House, Her Majesty's (the old King's Theatre) has been reduced to a much smaller His Majesty's and surrendered half its body to the Carlton Hotel ; the Prince of Wales's (*alias* Queen's, Regency, Fitzroy or " Dust Hole ") has been transmogrified into the beautiful, high-brow and rather dull Scala, and handed over to Amateur Clubs. The Grand, Islington, built on the site of the Philharmonic (with its memories of Soldene, Dolaro and the *noceurs* of the seventies), the Surrey, Marylebone, Britannia, Standard, Pavilion (each with

---

* Since writing the above, Sadler's Wells has been saved by public subscription, and is being entirely re-constructed.

a history especially the two first-named) and other less important places are now Halls for exhibiting disembodied shadows on a screen. The Princess's—the theatre of Booth, Charlotte Cushman, Charles Kean, Fechter, Boucicault and Barrett—has been derelict for nearly a quarter of a century : a dusty mouldering vault, peopled with who knows how many ghosts of the past ! The Grecian now re-echoes to the Hallelujahs of Salvation Lasses. The famous Olympic, with its memories of Vestris, the Wigans, Robson, Brooke, Kate Terry, Henry Neville, Ada Cavendish and a dozen others, is gone. The old Strand, Alma Mater of burlesque, is gone. Astley's of Philip Astley, Ducrow, Batty and Sanger, with its unforgettable reminiscences of the beautiful Menken, is gone. The Queen's, Long Acre (Labouchere's toy), the two theatres of Holborn, the Globe, the Opera Comique, the Folly, the Imperial and many outlying houses, are all gone. More modern theatres named after some of these may help to recall their former triumphs, but they have not hitherto produced anything or anybody which the theatrical history of a future generation will care to note with more than a few passing words.

I therefore, who have been an enthusiastic playgoer since the sixties, have thought it worth while to jot down some recollections of delightful nights at those playhouses which have been either swept away entirely or have abolished flesh and blood drama for the soulless mechanism of the Movies, and to collect in one volume as much of the gossip and tradition of such places as can be gathered from personal reminiscence and scattered records.

I was at first induced to attempt this by certain young friends of mine who are devoted to the theatre and wish to hear all that I can tell them about it out of my playgoing experiences. These are full enough, for they extend from the sixties to the time of the disappearance of the theatres concerned, with the exception of two absences from England in the late eighties and the beginning of the present century—gaps easily filled by younger playgoers.

I must needs confess to being an old fogy, seeing that I can clearly remember theatrical events of so long ago, but, besides being an old fogy who sighs over the productions and performers of days that are gone, I count myself of that number who can find very little to like or praise in the theatre world of to-day, though one is bound, of course, to recognize a few bright exceptions standing out here and there from the rest. I venture, moreover, to exercise the privilege of an elder, and to suggest one or two reasons why there is such a dearth of really good acting as compared with my younger days, though I am quite aware of my rashness in so doing.

First, and perhaps this is the chief reason of all, there appears to be an engrained idea in the minds of the younger generation of actors and actresses that it is not really necessary to study or work hard at their profession : that, if you are good-looking, dress well, can learn a certain number of lines, and can be pushed by well-known actor-relatives or assisted by outside finance, you have the right to a huge salary, to the " centre of the stage," and to an *entrée* to the best society off the stage that London offers to-day.

Mr. Cosmo Hamilton in his very amusing book of Reminiscences (*Unwritten History*) alludes to this question of the young ladies who are quite ready to undertake an important part in a play at a moment's notice without any previous experience. He has written many successful pieces for the theatre himself, and says : " Lately it has become quite the fashion for debutantes—how soon conventions die !—to apply for the leading part in any play that I may have ready. It must, of course, be the leading part. Condescendingly enough, they inform me that they like my kind of stuff, and being fed up with dancing and the same old giddy round, are ready, the salary being high, to make the stage a career without ever having been nearer to it than the second row of stalls. And they often wind up by saying : ' I am a very beautiful girl, with a priceless voice and the most wonderful sex charm. ' "

In the same connection I have noticed a review of an important production at a West End theatre which must have cost thousands to put on. It was withdrawn after a very short run, and a leading dramatic critic thus speaks of the actress who was cast for the chief rôle :

" The heroine is played by a young lady who, to judge from recent appearances, is to enjoy the singular good fortune of learning her business while playing leading rôles. At present her equipment is too amateurish to call for criticism."

These young people should read, mark, learn and inwardly digest the accounts of the theatrical careers of their famous predecessors whose shoe latchets they are, in most cases, not worthy to loose ! Irving, the Bancrofts, the Kendals, the whole family of Terrys (I am not going farther back than the sixties), Toole, Wyndham, Alexander, Tree and others began their career early and worked for salaries so small that our budding Keans and Siddons would turn up their noses at the amount, even as " pocket money," on which their predecessors (and betters) had to live.

When I first saw the late Sir Charles Wyndham, he was playing a dancing and singing smuggler in Burnand's burlesque of " Black Eyed Susan " at the little Royalty, and this was not his first appearance. The late Kate Terry began at eight years old and her sister

Ellen almost as early, and they went through much drudgery before obtaining that recognition which the young people of to-day claim, as a right, at once.   It is true that Kate Terry, by reason of her extraordinary genius, achieved success sooner than most, for she was the Cordelia to Charles Kean's Lear when not fifteen years of age.   Tree, after he left the ranks of the amateurs, began in an East End theatre—one of the lost ones.   Mrs. Kendal served a long apprenticeship in provincial stock companies, playing several different parts every week, which involved immense study and left no time for garden parties by day or cabarets by night.

The young aspirants to dramatic honours should take to heart the lines of old Geoffrey Chaucer :

> The lyfe so short,
> The crafte so long to lerne,
> The essay so hard,
> So sharp the conquering.

Secondly, abnormally long runs, though doubtless very satis-factory from the managerial point of view, give no opportunity for the younger members of the company to attain front rank. A single production may run for years if it happen to hit the public's fancy, and what chance does that afford to such as really desire to be able to act ?   Another drawback of somewhat the same kind is that some get known for their ability to shine in a certain type of part.   Unfortunate ones !   They are labelled for life.   I know one extremely clever character actress, with years of experience behind her, who is invariably cast for the " slavey," generally of the lodging-house kind, and will never be thought of in connection with any other rôle.   The revival of Stock Companies such as used to flourish at Nottingham and under Sarah Thorne at Margate, and still do, I understand, under Greet and Benson *passim*, would do much to do away with the disadvantages of long runs, besides affording the younger members of the profession opportunities of experience in various kinds of parts.   The dramatic world owes a great debt to Sir Frank Benson and his charming wife for their work in this direction, and it is good to see that signs are not wanting that they will have successors in the same field.

Thirdly, the prevailing unhappy taste for what are called Revues (which they are not !) is probably another reason for the lack of good acting to-day.   A pretty face, a fair voice, a dancing knack, a good figure, a cheeky manner, may bring the lucky owner the offer of a weekly salary which in former days would have kept an actress in comfort for months.   Even in these times of high prices for everything, it is enough to provide for many pretty frocks, suppers at the Savoy and week-ends at Brighton.

But the well-being of the theatre does not depend on the stage alone.   The public must do its part.   After all, it is very natural that those who run the theatres should wish to do so at a profit, and if literary skill and dramatic intelligence are at a discount they must fall back upon " legs," mannequin fashion displays, and bed-room scenes—to say nothing of American crook plays !   It may be that the most intelligent class of audience has been greatly reduced since the war and its predatory after-years.   Educated people and those who enjoyed the first-class acting of former days can no longer afford to go to the play as often as they did.   Those who can afford the luxury belong rather to the half-educated, half-illiterate " must-be-amused " set, many of whom earlier in the century, had been more accustomed to the Music-hall Saloon and the Gaff !

I should not omit one other point tending to make a poor show in these days.   I allude to the gross miscasting of plays, which is obvious to any playgoer.   Young girls trained for Revue and good for nothing else, and actors who have made their names by dancing through " buffoonery parts," aspire to serious rôles in high comedy or even in Shakespeare's plays, and, glancing down the columns of the *Era* or the *Stage* or the Drama page of the *Daily Telegraph* on Thursdays, you will see many names of fine actors and actresses who have proved their worth, among the " resting " ones, while youths and young girls who may happen to be sons and daughters of well-known members of the profession, or have influence of some other kind, are shoved into the front rank and given good parts.   They fail, accordingly, time after time.   Notwithstanding, occupants of the stalls and boxes on first nights applaud loudly, murmuring " How perfectly sweet "—or " Just like her dear mother " (or father as the case may be).   It is not good for the " sweet thing," for she promptly thinks she has " arrived " when she is only just setting out !   Nor is it altogether good for the management, for the audience (or at least the intelligent part of them), in despair of finding a standard play, or even a new one, properly cast, fall back upon the " Chu Chin Chow " sort of piece, in which they can, at any rate, admire a lot of pretty girls, hear lively tunes, see gorgeous spectacle, and need not be too exigeant about the quality of the acting, or the intelligence of the performance generally.

Notable exceptions there are, of course, in the ranks of the managers and producers and the performers themselves ;   many will at once occur to the average playgoer.   On such exceptions rest the whole responsibility for restoring to the British Stage some of the cachet and distinction the absence of which old fogies like myself are bemoaning to-day.

Comparisons, we are told, are odious.   Yet, those old enough to remember the Prince of Wales's, Lyceum, St. James's, His Majesty's, Haymarket and Criterion in the days of the Bancrofts, Irving, the Kendals, Alexander, Tree and Wyndham, to go no farther back, will agree that nothing as good (with one exception perhaps) is now to be found.

Is it possible that what is required is the return of the Actor-Manager ?   I suspect that will prove to be the solution, provided he be an actor of the first rank, with really artistic ideas, a capacity for choosing, and managing, a good team, and a backing to start with.   There is said to be one on the horizon.   He has my fervent prayers.

A book of this kind must inevitably, at times, take on the form of a mere chronicle of productions and casts, but I have tried to avoid as much as possible anything like a continuous list of names *et præterea nihil.*   I have occasionally omitted names of plays and actors of slight importance, while striving to include all that would be of interest to the general reader, and in the accounts of the more important theatres I have included some short notes on the personality and careers of the chief players who have appeared there.   In the endeavour to ensure the accuracy of my script, I have ransacked the records of the Past.   I have hunted up old programmes and searched through dusty files of old newspapers, I have rummaged in the published Lives and Reminiscences of theatrical folk no longer with us.   The writings of Blanchard, Henry Morley, Clement Scott, Dutton Cook and others who wrote from " before the curtain " and the Lives of and accounts furnished by Macready, James Anderson, the Bancrofts, Kendals, Toole and others " behind the scenes " supply an old playgoer with dates and names and bring back vivid memories of the joyful nights of bygone years.

Constant playgoer as I was, I had, through occasional absences abroad, to miss many productions of note in London, and these lost opportunities can never be renewed.   The years are erased from my Calendar.

What Horace says is :
Eheu fugaces
Anni labuntur, Postume, Postume,
Years glide by and are lost to me, lost to me.

So can I also sing in company with old Barham of Ingoldsby in the words of his slightly altered quotation from Horace.

I doubt, however, if many of the plays produced to-day or the players in them, need be regretted by a future theatre enthusiast born too late to see them. He can certainly hope for, and look forward to, better things later on. For us, the old fogies, there is only the " looking back."

Perhaps, I have been unduly discursive and garrulous and sometimes inclined to repeat myself ; but these are faults pertaining to old-age. I hope that my readers (if I have any !) will forgive my sins of omission and commission and find something to interest them in this gossip of the Past.

Since writing the above, Terry's Theatre has "joined the majority," having been destroyed to modernize the Strand, and make it more respectable ! Under the direction of the actor whose name it bore, several notable pieces were produced, among which the best known is perhaps " Sweet Lavender." But its story belongs to very recent days and contains little of interest to the student of theatrical history.

I am indebted to the proprietors of the *Stage* for permission to include in the following pages the material of a slight sketch of " The Lost Theatres of London " which appeared in that journal in 1923.

CHAPTER II

THE GRECIAN THEATRE
WITH NOTES ON MELODRAMA AND PANTOMIME

THE old Grecian Theatre, in its earlier days, was known sometimes as the Olympic Saloon, sometimes as the Eagle Saloon, sometimes as the Grecian Saloon, and sometimes to frivolous youth as " The Bird." It made the usual start in life as an adjunct to a tavern. James Ritchie, in his " Night Side of London," remarks, somewhat sourly, that it was, appropriately enough, not far from a Lunatic Asylum and contiguous to a Workhouse ; but, then, he did not approve of such places.

It was a gay enough rèsort for the working classes of the day, who spent their money freely at the Eagle Tavern to which the Saloon was attached. The old jingle recurs to one's mind:

> Up and down the City Road,
> In and out the Eagle,
> That's the way the money goes,
> Pop goes the weasel !

The explanation of the last line is said to be that workmen, spending so much money " in and out the Eagle," were compelled to pawn their " weasels," a slang term for some kind of tool. I cannot vouch for the truth of this, but give it on the authority of my old friend, the late Mr. Hibbert, who knew so much about the inner life of the theatre.

The Olympic Saloon was a very lively place. It occupied the site of the old Shepherd and Shepherdess Tea Gardens, and there were grounds belonging to it with a dancing platform and arbours for refreshments, adding, of course, to the prosperity of the adjacent hostelry. The shows were varied enough, for, besides the ordinary programme of the week, there were special concerts of sacred music on Sundays.

The refreshments served at the Olympic Saloon were very different from those in favour at the present day. Brandy and water (and brown brandy at that) was the staple drink at taverns far into the nineteenth century, as we know from Mr. Pickwick, who never seems to have taken anything else—except rum punch ! Whisky was as yet unknown. Beer could be had—a vulgar drink—

and tea for the more moderate ones, but not, I think, coffee, which was looked upon as a " furriner's drink." A very favourite, rather syrupy drink appears to have been " Capillaire " said to be made from the maidenhair fern, and we should not forget the coarser spirituous drinks like shrub, rum, peppermint and gin. Enormous piles of the thickest sandwiches, and mountains of pork pies were nightly consumed at the Grecian, as they were to a much later date at the " Britannia, the Great Theatre, Hoxton."

In the thirties of the nineteenth century, before Rouse had built the first real theatre at the Eagle, there were Gardens and a Rotunda for concerts, with an organ, and a platform for dancing, and arbours for refreshments, all much enjoyed by the inhabitants of the neigh-bourhood and of North London in general. We can gather a very good impression of what the place was like in those very early days, when it was always called simply " The Eagle," from an account of a visit paid by one Mr. Samuel Wilkins, a journeyman carpenter, who was keeping company with Miss Jemima Evans (usually known as J'mima Ivins). He came to tea one Monday afternoon at the house of his lady-love, in his best attire, with a pint of shrimps " neatly folded up in a clean Belcher," as an extra zest for the tea, and Mrs. Ivins, the lady of the house, contributed " two ounces of seven and sixpenny green, and a quarter of a pound of the best fresh." Miss Jemima was upstairs "cleaning herself," and the two youngest Miss Ivinses were poking bits of lighted brown paper between the bars of the grate to make the kettle boil for tea.

" I wos a thinking," said Mr. Samuel Wilkins, during a pause in the conversation—" I wos a thinking of taking J'mima to the Eagle to-night." " Oh my ! " exclaimed Mrs. Ivins. " Lor ! how nice ! " said the youngest Miss Ivins. " Well, I declare ! " added the youngest Miss Ivins but one. " Tell J'mima to put on her white muslin," screamed Mrs. Ivins, with motherly anxiety ; and down came J'mima herself soon afterwards in a white muslin gown carefully hooked and eyed, a little red shawl plentifully pinned, a white straw bonnet trimmed with red ribbons, a small necklace, a large pair of bracelets, Denmark satin shoes, and open-worked stockings ; white cotton gloves on her fingers, and a cambric pocket-handkerchief, carefully folded up, in her hand—all quite genteel and ladylike.

And they sallied forth down the Pancras Road (I think they must have lived in Camden Town or Somers Town or one of those rather dreadful " Towns "), and met a friend of Jemima's and her young man, also going to the Eagle, and paused to have some shrub at the " Crown," and so to the Eagle in haste lest they should be too late for the beginning of the concert at the Rotunda. " How ev'nly ! " said Miss Jemima Ivins as they passed the gates and were fairly in the gardens.

" There were the walks, beautifully gravelled and planted, and the refreshment boxes, painted and ornamented like so many snuff-boxes, and the variegated lamps shedding their rich light upon the company's heads, and the place for dancing ready chalked for the company's feet, and a Moorish band playing at one end of the gardens, and an opposition military band playing away at the other. Then, the waiters were rushing to and fro with glasses of negus, and glasses of brandy-and-water, and bottles of ale, and bottles of stout ; and ginger-beer was going off in one place, and practical jokes were going on in another ; and people were crowding to the door of the Rotunda ; and in short the whole scene was, as Miss Jemima Ivins, inspired by the novelty, or the shrub, or both, observed, ' one of dazzling excitement.' As to the concert-room, never was anything half so splendid. There was an orchestra for the singers, all paint, gilding, and plate-glass ; and such an organ ! "

The two gentlemen drank rum and water " with," and two slices of lemon, and the two ladies had a pint of sherry wine and some sweet carraway-seed biscuits. Somebody in white satin sang " The Soldier Tired " and the overture on the organ was pronounced by Miss Ivins to be " solemn."

This short account of the visit of Miss Ivins and her friend and their two young men to the Eagle took place about 1835 or 1836, and if you want to know more about it and its disastrous finale, you must consult Mr. Charles Dickens in his *Sketches by Boz.* Incidentally it is of interest to this chapter as giving one a glimpse of the kind of audience at the Eagle concerts. It likewise lets us into the secret that green tea, " neat," at 7s. 6d. a pound was drunk by the lower middle class, that shrimps were carried in handker-chiefs of the " Belcher " kind usually seen round the necks of the costermongers and prize-fighters of the day, and that young ladies of that class imbibed sherry wine by the pint !

In the very early days, the programme was mixed with a good deal of individual song and dance, and the pieces were sometimes styled burlettas, sometimes operettas and sometimes " Original Operatic Spectacle." All London theatres but two were still under the heavy hand of the Lord Chamberlain and the iniquitous Walpole Law, so that a certain amount of music was obligatory in every piece.   An early effort of Blanchard's was "Arcadia or the Shepherd and the Shepherdess" produced at the Olympic Saloon in 1841, and its cast, is notable for the names of many who distinguished themselves later in the Profession.   The sisters Harriet and Jane Coveney were in it—well known in fairy plays and pantomimes and in all sorts of dramas in the West End far on towards the end of the century.   I shall refer later on to the efforts of Rouse (the proprietor) to popularize good opera at the Grecian, but I am tempted first to digress from the gossip of the Grecian itself, and speak of Melodrama as it was known in those days and for some years to come.

For Melodrama, accompanied by appropriate music, was the chief fare set before the Grecian audiences right up to the time of the theatre being taken over by the   "Hallelujah Lasses"— and it was the fare they appreciated the most.   It is not generally recognized that the derivation of the word "melodrama" is from two Greek words—"melos" and "drama," that is, a play with music.   All such plays were invariably interspersed with music at the critical points of the action.   "Don Cæsar de Bazan," a good example, ended up with a concerted number sung by the strength of the company.   Though songs by individuals and concerted pieces eventually dropped out of the scheme, the incidental accompaniment of the orchestra remained, and it is quite impossible to conceive a performance of a play like "The Red Rover" or "The Miller and His Men" without music to fit the action, while "The Ghost Melody" in "The Corsican Brothers" is a classic example that will never be omitted as long as the play holds the boards.   Nor will the tune ever be changed.   It was composed by Stoepel, brother-in-law of Vincent Wallace and afterwards leader of the Lyceum orchestra under the management of the Batemans.   Melodramas at the outlying theatres were often fearsome shows.   At that celebrated "Temple of Thespis," the Coburg, which is not a "lost theatre" but more flourishing than ever now as the Old Vic under the ægis of Miss Lilian Baylis, there was produced in 1827 a drama called "The Horrors of War."   It was a dreadfully bad piece, or else (as reported in a newspaper of the day), the audience was an "extremely vulgar one, for they kept on throwing orange peel and other rubbish on the stage, so that all the actors and the musicians had to play with their hats on!"   The Old Vic audience was also very free with its comments on occasions.   It protested once sarcastically against the unfinished condition of the scenery, a gallery critic calling out, as it would seem more in sorrow than in anger, "We don't expect grammar at the Wic, but you might jine your flats!"

Melodrama should not be confounded with what was known as the " Legitimate " : that, in reality, consisted of the plays of Shakespeare and other standard authors, though John Hollingshead rather neatly defined the " Legitimate drama " as a drama whose authors were dead, and whose copyrights were expired !

Very bloody indeed was the fare at the Grecian, Old Vic, Surrey, East London, and other such houses.   A popular drama was founded on " Oliver Twist."   At the Vic, the representative of Bill Sikes was one E. F. Saville, a brother of Helen Faucit (Lady Martin). John Hollingshead thus describes his business in the scene of the murder of Nancy, which was the *clou* of the play:

" Nancy was always dragged round the stage by her hair, and after this effort, Sykes always looked up defiantly at the gallery, as he was doubtless told to do in the marked prompt-book.   He was always answered by one loud and fearful curse, yelled by the whole mass like a Handel Festival Chorus.   The curse was answered by Sykes dragging Nancy, twice round the stage, and then like Ajax, defying the lightning.   The simultaneous yell then became louder and more blasphemous.   Finally, when Sykes, working up to a well-rehearsed climax, smeared Nancy with red ochre, and taking her by the hair (a most powerful wig) seemed to dash her brains out on the stage, no explosion of dynamite invented by the modern anarchist, no language ever dreamed of in Bedlam, could equal the outburst.   A thousand enraged voices which sounded like ten thousand, with the roar of a dozen escaped menageries, filled the theatre and deafened the audience, and when the smiling ruffian came forward and bowed, their voices in thorough plain English expressed a fierce determination to tear his sanguinary entrails from his sanguinary body."

The father of Helen Faucit and this Mr. Saville was one Saville Faucit, who was a playwright as well as an actor by profession. He was also the writer of publications which were known as " Penny Dreadfuls," generally published on a Saturday, presumably for Sunday reading—like the Sunday press of to-day with its verbatim reports of sensational trials.   They were very grim publications in addition to their cheapness, and horror was piled on horror.   One of Faucit's most successful Dreadfuls was called " The Heads of the Headless."

A celebrated melodrama was one founded on the murder of an Italian boy, Carlo Ferrari, which horrified all London in 1830. The lad was done to death for the sake of the money which his corpse would fetch from the surgeons.   Bishop and Williams, his murderers, were but poor imitations of the original body-snatchers, Burke and Hare, but they were equally callous, and in order to give the poor boy confidence induced him to play with their own children before proceeding to murder him. Williams turned King's evidence and was released. It is said that, in revenge for this, his eyes were put out by some pals of Bishop's, and that, blinded, he stood outside the National Gallery for many years to beg for charity, being escorted to and from his post every day by a respectably dressed woman who frequently showed one, or two, black eyes !

The best representative of the Italian boy in this play is said to have been Marchant, later a leading actor at the Britannia, Marylebone and other theatres.

Fearsome melodramas were " The Pirates of the Flowery Land " ; " The Gamblers " (based on the affair of Thurtell and Weare with the real original gig used by the murderers brought on to the stage) ; " The Man Cat " ; " The Bride's Death Leap " ; " Jonathan Bradford " (the first play to show a section of a house with four rooms seen at once) ; " Pedlars' Acre : or the Wife of Seven Husbands " ; and a very famous drama, played all over England for many years, called " Susan Hopley : or the Vicissitudes of a Servant-Girl," with a scene in which the mouldering remains of a corpse fell out of a cupboard—an incident used by the " Grand Guignol " in recent years. "Sweeney Todd " ; " Maria Martin : or the Murder in the Red Barn " ; " George Barnwell " ; " The Bleeding Nun," were also among the most favoured of these plays of horror. It was all very strong meat for the stomachs of playgoers, and I doubt if any of them would be possible in these days, though with the recent productions of the British Grand Guignol in our memory, " You never can tell," as the great Shaw says. As a rule, the audience insisted on the execution of the murderer taking place on the stage. The greater the realism, the more murders committed, and the more blood seen (if only in the form of red ochre) the better pleased they were. They also took a real and personal interest in the actors themselves and followed the dialogue of the play very closely indeed.

Many amusing stories are told of the ejaculations and interruptions shouted from the gallery as a piece progressed. At the Coburg, on one occasion, a character in the play had to mutter in a loud aside, " Should I be discovered, I am lost ! " He was promptly but civilly corrected by one in the gallery who called out to him, " No ; should you be discovered, you are found ! " If I am not mistaken, this was afterwards annexed to the dialogue of " The Private Secretary "—but it was in print years before that play saw the light. On another occasion, the great Siddons, when touring in the North of England, was taking poison in her most deliberate, tragedy-queen manner, and was suddenly encouraged by a voice from the gallery :

"That's a' reet, Molly ! Soop it oop, ma lass, soop it oop ! "

But the most delightful interruptions would come from those who were so engrossed with the action of the play that they would entirely forget it was all make-believe. They could not refrain from expressing their loud sympathy with the persecuted heroine, and their detestation of the villain and all his works. In the celebrated Adelphi drama, "The Green Bushes," Madame Celeste as the heroine has to shoot her husband who has deserted her. In the revival of 1872, a woman started up in the pit and called out "Serve him right. He's just like my monster ! " But I think the best story of all (and there are many such) is that of the sailors at the Greenock Theatre who, on seeing the captain of a ship knocked down by smugglers in the course of the play, made their way at once to the stage, knocked over all the smugglers and, putting their feet on their prostrate bodies, dared them to move for having presumed to hit a ship's officer !

Sometimes the management, especially in the provinces, were hard put to it to provide a sufficient number of supers for the due presentation of a play. Even Phelps at Sadler's Wells had recourse to shifts and fakes to deceive the audience as to the strength of his company. When he put on " Henry V," he wished to have as large an army as possible on the stage at once, so, for the march past before Agincourt, he arranged that the troops should defile behind a set-piece which rose breast high. He got Madame Tussaud's people to model eighty wax heads, which were fitted on dummy figures of wicker-work clad in the costumes and armour of the period. Every man of the forty supers—which was all they could muster—carried two of these figures, one on either side, attached to a sort of framework lashed to his waist, hence it seemed as if they were marching three abreast. As they tramped past, banners streaming, trumpets braying, the stage appeared to be crowded with soldiers, and the illusion was so complete that the audience never discovered the artifice.

As time went on, playgoers became more educated, more sophisticated, less prone to give way to primitive emotions. The appetite for blood-curdling pieces abated. Melodramas were more artistically put together and with effects far less crude. The outlying theatres, however, like the Grecian and some of the West End ones also, still liked a good deal of real sensation, and Sala has given in his theatrical notes in *The Illustrated London News* an amusing account

of the plot of a very sensational drama called " Mankind " produced
at the Globe Theatre in 1882:

" Messrs. George Conquest and Paul Merritt concocted a kind
of sensational bouillabaisse containing all kinds of strange fishes.
The recipe for the ingenious medley might run practically thus :
Take a witches' cauldron and set it over a blue fire : strangle
a disreputable junior partner of a money-lender and throw into
the pot : hang the other money-lender for murdering his colleague
and throw him in likewise : half drown a virtuous young married
lady and in with her ; beat a small clever child in black stockings
very hard to make her tender, and pop her in : add a cup of coffee
well poisoned : flavour with a stolen will, a Chubb burglar-proof
safe, several forgeries, a good deal of genial humour, an old woman's
gingham umbrella, some seaweed from Ramsgate sands, some gravel
from a garden on the Thames Embankment, a rasher of bacon from
a coffee tavern, a quartern of gin, a Gladstone bag, a small quantity
of blood, a pinch of gunpowder, and any amount of vigorous acting,
and then you have your bouillabaisse—your 'Mankind.' Make
the gravy very thick and slab and serve very hot."

A melodrama, in those early days, however long it might be,
was always preceded by a farce or a burletta or both. A favourite
farce in early times which was given year after year, and may be
still given in the provinces for all I know, was " The Secret," also
sometimes called " The Sliding Panel," and it had other names.
I am of the impression that the original " Charles, his friend "
was one of the characters in this old *lever de rideau*. At Christmas
there was always a pantomime to follow the blood horrors of the
melodrama. At some houses, the drama at Christmas was year after
year of a special kind. One very popular blood-and-thunder piece
was founded on the exploits of Jack Sheppard which up to the
sixties was allowed by the censor without remark. Then a virtuous
period seems to have set in at the Lord Chamberlain's office and
when the housebreaking play was brought out at the Queen's it
was in the form of a camouflaged edition and called " Old London "
—with Henrietta Hodson as Jack. At the Surrey Jonathan Wild
was played by the handsome John Neville, father of Henry Neville.
At the Adelphi in 1839 Mrs. Keeley was the Jack. At the Haymarket in 1852 Mrs. Keeley was again the Jack, with O. Smith
as Jonathan Wild. At the Surrey in 1856, Paul Bedford was the
Blueskin and Mrs. Billington also in the cast. The O. Smith
referred to was Richard John Smith, who was known as O. Smith
after his successful performance of " Obi Smith " in a lurid melo-

drama.   Born in 1786, he was destined for the legal profession, but, as he did not like it, sailed to West Africa, where he got into trouble for helping some slaves to escape.   Back in England he worked for Macready at Sheffield in various ways and was paid 12s. a week for it.   His London first appearance was at the Surrey under Elliston.   He was a man of varied parts, especially good in such uncanny rôles as Zamiel in " Der Freischütz " and " The Bottle Imp."   This latter was a very favourite blood-curdler of old days.   It was, I believe, written originally for Mr. Keeley, who played a terrified German servant.   O. Smith was the Bottle Imp, in a tight-fitting sea-green skin dress with horns on his head, and a demon's face and wings.   It was produced at the English Opera House (Lyceum) in 1828.

The latest Jack Sheppard that occurs to the mind is the famous burlesque at the Gaiety in 1885—one of the very best produced in the light of the " Sacred Lamp."   Nelly Farren was Jack ; Fred Leslie, Jonathan Wild ; David James, Blueskin ; Odell, Sir Roland ; Marion Hood, Winifred Wood ; Tilly Wadman, Thames Darrell ; and Harriet Coveney (who must have been about seventy years of age) Mrs. Wood.   Such a cast has never been brought together for a burlesque before or since.

A curious feature of the pantomimes in those early days was that they were not built up on the foundation of one of the well-known fairy tales but on a story specially made up for the occasion and generally having some topical allusion in the title, thus giving the cast unlimited opportunity for " gag."   This was really following the tradition of the earliest times, when the entertainment dealt solely with the adventures of Harlequin and Columbine who were the hero and heroine of the whole show, Opening as well as Harlequinade.   But for more extended notes on the origins and history of Pantomime see the close of this chapter.

It is high time I returned to the chief subject of this section of my book—the Grecian Theatre itself.   The original theatre, or, rather, the Saloon attached to the tavern, and which was called by various names, was built early in the nineteenth century by one Thomas Rouse, a bricklayer who had risen to be a master builder on his own account.

Rouse was a man of taste and discernment such as one would not have expected to find in a man of his trade and bringing up.   He was very devoted to musical entertainments and prided himself on the production of operas that were a credit to his establishment. They were, in fact, of a very high-class character and much in advance of the time as regards scenery, appointments and company. It is said that he lost some thousands yearly on these operatic attempts, but " what he lost on the swings he made on the roundabouts," for his tavern recouped him for all the deficits of the theatre, and left him a handsome profit to boot.

The following is a copy of one of the first posters issued by Rouse in 1838, when the saloon was opened with great ceremony to celebrate the Coronation of Her Majesty Queen Victoria :

ROYAL EAGLE CORONATION PLEASURE GROUNDS AND GRECIAN SALOON, CITY ROAD
Proprietor : Mr. T. Rouse.

Unrivalled galas with brilliant fireworks and splendid illuminations, and a series of superior amusements every Monday and Wednesday. To attempt a description of the numerous and varied sources of entertainment at this unrivalled establishment would be vain. Concerts in the open air, dancing and vaudeville in the Saloon, set paintings, cosmoramas, fountains, grottoes, elegant buildings, arcades, colonnades, grounds, statuary, singing, music, combine to render it a fairy scene, of which a due estimation can only be formed by inspection. Open every evening. On Thursday a benefit for the " Laudable Pension Society," Bethnal Green (See bills). The whole under the direction of Mr. Raymond. Brilliant discharge of fireworks by the inimitable British artist, Mr. Brock. A band will play during the evening. Admission 2s. Doors open at 5.0 p.m.

It is pleasant to come across the name of Brock as a purveyor of fireworks so long ago as 1838. Another noticeable item in the foregoing bill is the announcement of opening at 5.0 p.m. As there was no Licensing Act in those days to restrict the liberties of the public, they certainly got enough for their money. I notice also the word " vaudeville," probably one of the earliest if not the very first use of the word in connection with an English entertainment. The derivation of the expression is stated to be from " Vau (or Val) de Vire," a valley in Normandy where light musical entertainments with dances, songs and satirical allusions were given perhaps as long ago as the early part of the fifteenth century. The word, anyhow, came from France, and it is not surprising to find it used by Rouse at the Grecian when we remember that he delighted in producing versions of light French operettas and that many of his dramas were translations (with or without acknowledgment !) from French originals of which he had a vast stock.

Rouse would sit in his private box every night, keeping order with a big stick in full view of the whole house. He liked to be recognized as the " Boss," and ruled as the most autocratic of autocrats until the theatre was taken over by George Conquest in 1851.

The admission charges were low, the Saloon was most luxuriously fitted up and the entertainments were on the most liberal scale. There was an organ (chiefly, I imagine, for the decorous Sunday concerts), a " mechanical piano " whatever that may have meant in those days, and other extra attractions. The place held about 700 persons, and the seats were arranged with little shelves in front of them on which the visitors could place their pies or sandwiches or bread and cheese or other refreshments, which appear to have been provided here for the first time at a theatre.

One of Rouse's dreams was to popularize Opera with the masses. In 1840, he produced Bellini's " Sonnambula," the first of a series of similar works brought out by him, many of which were thus heard in England for the first time. He selected them chiefly from the répertoire of the Opera-Comique in Paris, and the list is a long one : " Masaniello," " Fra Diavolo," " The Crown Diamonds," " The Siren," " The Ambassadress "—all by Auber ; Rossini's " Gazza Ladra " ; Adams' " Postillon de Lonjumeau " ; Boieldieu's " Dame Blanche " ; Donizetti's " Elisire d'Amore," " Don Pasquale," " Figlia del Reggimento " ; Balfe's " Bohemian Girl " ; John Barnett's " Mountain Sylph " (produced under the direction of the composer) ; Weber's " Der Freischutz," " Abou Hassan," and many others. It is truly a great record, and Rouse's management of the old Saloon in the City Road must never be forgotten when reference is made to the development of opera in London for the education of the people.

In 1851, the house was taken over by George Conquest who, like other wise men before him, came from the East ! His father had had much to do with the Garrick Theatre in Whitechapel, and he was, so to speak, born in the buskin. 1851 was, of course, the year of the very first Great Exhibition that was ever held, a year when every one was feeling perfectly sure that a new era of Peace and Prosperity was dawning for the world, or as Mr. Lloyd George might put it, the commencement of a " harvest of rare and refreshing fruit ! "

For the first night Blanchard wrote the opening address, which was delivered by Conquest himself. It was as appropriate and as witty as all his lines were, and some of it is quite worth quoting :

> Shakespeare has told us of the drama's feature,
> To hold, as 'twere, the mirror up to nature.
> While such reflections here before you pass,
> You see your drama and you have your glass :

Both which I promise, with some conscious pride,
Shall be the best that London can provide.
This year all hope to better their condition,
And THIS is my Industrial Exhibition.
Although no glass this lofty roof contains,
Who looks for pleasure will not care for PAINS.
May crowds attend each night as we progress,
My 'pinions being the 'pinions of the Press.
And while I trust your pleasure to increase,
Hope, after CONQUEST, you will like a PIECE !

The programme on the opening night consisted of a Farce, Shakespeare's "A Midsummer Night's Dream" and a Ballet arranged by Mrs. Conquest. Among the dancers were clever Caroline Parkes (an excellent dancer and pantomimist and a favourite at the West End for many years), the sisters Gunniss (better known on the South side as *premières danseuses* in the ballets at the Surrey and South London Palace, but also seen at Drury Lane), and three of the talented daughters of Conquest himself—Amelia, Laura and Isabella—with also a male dancer without whom no ballet would have been considered complete. Lizzie Conquest, the cleverest of the sisters, was much the youngest of the family and was not born till eight or nine years later.

Mrs. Conquest had been a famous dancer in her day, and after she married Conquest she set up a Training School which turned out many great artistes. Among these were Milano, afterwards one of the best of all Harlequins and a renowned teacher of dancing. His wife, *née* Thérèse Cushnie, was a professional dancer of the first class who, in her early days, fulfilled many engagements at the Surrey, Grecian and Astley's. After a course of severe training in Paris, she made her debut as *première danseuse* at the Royal Italian Opera in company with her husband and a sister. Other pupils of Mrs. Conquest—their name was Legion—were Flexmore, the celebrated clown and dancer, Deulin, the Leclercq family, Miss Lingard and Kate Vaughan.

It is not generally known that Kate Vaughan was Scandinavian by birth. Her father's name was Candelin and he was one of the musicians employed at the Grecian. Besides learning to be a dancer, Kate Vaughan played under her own name in serious drama —as Little Em'ly in a version of "David Copperfield," for instance. Conquest himself—an actor of all the talents—was the Peggotty for a time ; and then the part was taken up by a Mr. Gilbert Hastings, afterwards better known as a music-hall singer under the name of the "Great Macdermott," the singer of "We don't want to fight, but, by Jingo, if we do," who added a new word (Jingoism) to the English language.   His real name was Farrell, and he had begun life as a bricklayer, later joining the Royal Navy as an A.B., where his talents for acting induced him to get out as soon as possible and go in for the profession in earnest.

The Leclercqs were a family of pantomimists and dancers who performed together in the pantomimes of the fifties and sixties much in the same way as the Vokes Family did later at Drury Lane.   At the Haymarket in 1859, the Christmas show was " Undine or the Spirit of the Waters."   Louise Leclercq was the Undine ; Arthur Leclercq, Harlequin ; Charles Leclercq, Clown. They remained regular members of the Haymarket company for several years, acting in pantomime, comedietta and extravaganza. Carlotta Leclercq, Fechter's leading lady at the Lyceum, and Rose Leclercq, whom living playgoers remember as an incomparable *grande dame* in Wilde's plays, were of the same family.

George Conquest pulled down the old Saloon of many memories, built a new and elegant theatre nearly as large as Drury Lane, and opened it in October, 1877, with a drama by himself and Henry Pettitt called " Bound to Succeed : or the Captain's Log-Book." It may be interesting to note that the real name of this talented family was not Conquest.   The father's name was Oliver, and he started life as a journeyman bootmaker !   After his success as a manager in the East End of London, he took the name of " Conquest " in a spirit of pure swank.

Like the old Bower Saloon, the Grecian was a regular nursery for the theatrical and musical professions.   Many artistes destined to make a name in the future earned their early recognition at the City Road Saloon.   Sims Reeves sang there in early days in the chorus under the name of Johnson, but he did not like the smoking and drinking element and left.   In 1844, the Great Little Robson made his first London appearance there and stayed there five years. Macdermott appeared as Quasimodo in a version of " Notre Dame " ; Harry Nicholls, Herbert Campbell, Arthur Williams, Harriet Coveney (who played Macheath in " The Beggars' Opera " when she was only fourteen), Mary Anne Victor, and a host of others came out at the Grecian.   Miss Victor made an excellent Martha in a revival of the Lyceum " Faust," and was also in the original cast of " Sweet Lavender " and with Brookfield at the Haymarket.   Other well-known names were Miss Tunstall, a ballad singer second only to Mrs. Waylett at that time, Mr. and Mrs. Caulfield (parents of Lennox Grey the opera bouffe artist, a beautiful woman), Harry Boleno and Deulin, Pantomimists, Flexmore, the clown and dancer who used to run the Christmas pieces for Kean at the Princess's, and a Miss Smith, who in after years was the incomparable Mrs. Raymond of the Swanborough company at the Strand Theatre.   Two others, now more forgotten than any of the above, were associated with the Grecian.   These were Henry Howell and Robert Glindon, both writers of popular comic songs.   Glindon wrote " Biddy the Basket-Woman " and " The Literary Dustman," frequently sung in those days.   He was really a scene-painter by trade and painted a great part of the huge Diorama, " London by Night," which made such a sensation at the opening of the Colosseum in Regent's Park.   He also painted for Drury Lane.

Conquest was a great writer of melodramas.   There was, as I have already noted, an extensive library of French plays at the Grecian, from which, with the help of Shirley, Petitt and other collaborators, he evolved many stirring dramas for the Grecian and Surrey theatres.   When " The Ticket of Leave Man " was first brought out, he at once spotted it as having been adapted from a French piece called " Leonard."

Now and again the management drifted into Shakespeare, as, for example, when " The Merchant of Venice " was put on in 1859 with one Arthur Young, a quondam reader of Shakespeare, as Shylock and the versatile sisters, Jane and Harriet Coveney (veritable general utility !) as Portia and Jessica.   But it was the annual pantomime that used to lure playgoers to make the long journey from the West End to the neighbourhood of the " Angel," Islington, and in after years across the water to the Surrey, in the same way as Soldene and her opera-bouffes used to entice them to Islington in the seventies.   Both the Conquests, father and son, were famous for wonderful flights from spring traps and dives through the stage, which came to be known as " Phantom Flights." A speciality of the elder one also was his wonderful make-ups as various kinds of animals—crabs, spiders, flying fish, not to mention the " Bottle Imp."   I remember him myself particularly as an oyster, but that was after he had migrated to the Surrey in 1882. All the family were notable members of the profession.   The mother was a great ballet mistress, whose pupils appeared all over London and in other countries as well ; the sons were clever actors ; the daughters all good dancers and pantomime artistes.   One was Mrs. Thomas Beard, but she died when only eighteen years of age ; another married Charles Dillon, the tragedian, the best Belphegor ever seen.

All things come to an appointed end.   When Conquest crossed the water to take over the Surrey, the old Grecian which had seen so many happy nights, and contributed so much to the pleasure of the London playgoer, passed into the hands of the Salvation Army.   It is a humorous thought that General Booth, a professional Pussyfoot, was obliged by the terms of the lease to take over the adjacent public-house, and keep it open for a time with a full licence.   Prices of admission at the Grecian in early days were : Stalls 1s. 6d. ; Boxes 1s. ; Pit 6d. ; Private Boxes 21s., 15s. and 10s. 6d., or 2s. each person.   The performances began at 7.0, but the doors were open long before " for the good of the house," *i.e.* for the sale of drinks !   This was in 1875.

The form of entertainment known as " Pantomime " which in modern days we associate with Christmas, was first introduced to Londoners by Rich the lessee of Covent Garden Theatre, the same man that brought out " The Beggars' Opera," which made Gay Rich and Rich Gay !   He produced in 1717 at the old Lincoln's Inn Fields Theatre (the site of which is now occupied by Soane's Museum) an entertainment called " Harlequin Sorcerer."   The idea was borrowed from the Italian Arlecchino, which was originally a speaking part, but Rich, being unable to speak on the stage, conceived the notion of a silent Harlequin, and it is said that by his mere dumb action he rivalled the most eloquent and pathetic tragedian.

Harlequin was at first the knockabout person, something like the Agouste of the modern circus.   Addison, in the *Spectator*, writes :

" Harlequin's part is made up of blunders and absurdities.   He is to mistake one name for another : to forget his errands : to stumble over Queens : to rub his head against every post that comes in his way : this is all attended with something so comical in the voice and gesture, that a man who is sensible of the folly of the part can hardly forbear to be pleased with it."

But Rich's pantomime was not all a knockabout show.   It was described as a species of dramatic composition, consisting of two parts, one serious and the other comic :

" By the help of gay scenes, fine habits, grand dances, appropriate music, and other decorations, Mr. Rich exhibited a story from Ovid's Metamorphoses or some other fabulous work.   Between the pauses or Acts of this serious representation, he interwove a comic fable consisting chiefly of the courtship of Harlequin and Columbine, with a variety of surpassing adventures and tricks which were produced by the magic wand of Harlequin, such as the sudden transformation of palaces and temples into huts and cottages, and of men and women into barrows and joint-stools, of trees turned to houses, colonnades to beds of tulips, and mechanical shops into serpents and ostriches."

The fertility of Rich's invention in devising these entertainments was very extraordinary. Of all the pantomimes he produced between 1717 and 1761, scarcely one was a failure. It continued to be a popular kind of show all through the century, for in 1798 we find the pantomime still on the same lines. This was called " Harlequin's Return " and the plot was something as follows : Harlequin, the hero, has returned from a voyage, having been struck dumb by a Witch in Lapland (more or less *terra incognita* in those days). The parents of the lovers are represented by two pantaloons and the clowns are the parents' servants. The programme gives full details, so that there shall be no misunderstanding of the piece, and it warns the audience when to look out for the marvellous trick changes introduced. Thus, Milkmaid changes to milkmaid's garland and Jack in the Green ; bottle changes to tarantula which bites Harlequin, who is cured by music, etc. In the last scene but one (a dragon's cave) the power of the dragon is counteracted by the Sylph (like the good fairy of later days) who then sings : " Hither haste, the young, the gay "—and changes the scene to " The Bower of Constancy." Here can be traced the germ of the Grand Transformation Scene of modern times.

On the occasion of the production of this pantomime, the evening's programme opened with a musical piece called " The Raft : or Both Sides of the Water." The pantomime was the centre attraction of a triple bill, and the evening's show ended up with nothing less than Shakespeare's " Comedy of Errors " in its entirety. Truly, a Gargantuan entertainment.

Harking back a little in the eighteenth century, we find that tricks and changes were always the principal attraction in pantomime. Rich was unrivalled in this line, and, at Drury Lane in 1723, brought out " Harlequin Doctor Faustus " with much more elaborate effects than he had attempted at the Lincoln's Inn Fields Theatre. In the thirties Garrick was himself the Harlequin, who was then a speaking character and was the impromptu wit of the piece, just as Stenterello and the other Maschere are in Italy to this day. This was, of course, a reversion to the real Italian type of Mask after the silent Harlequin of Rich's earlier pantomimes.

It has been maintained by some authorities that the " Opening " of the British pantomime is derived from the Masques of Elizabeth and the Stuart days, but it appears to me more likely that the Opening in early days was arranged for the sake of providing some sort of story to give an air of probability to the changes and transformations effected by Harlequin, who, with Columbine, provided the love interest of the plot. The clowns and pantaloons were, as I have said, the heavy parents and servants, the butts of the lovers in both parts. I believe Grimaldi was the first clown to evolve the purely comic business with indispensable songs and jokes, sausages and red-hot poker.

In 1820, Vestris appeared under the management of Elliston in a pantomime called "Shakespeare versus Harlequin," a version of the older one, "Harlequin's Invasion" produced by Garrick, which in turn was a version of an older piece still brought out at the Lincoln's Inn Fields Theatre. The 1820 show was described as "A Christmas Gambol in the manner of the Italian Comedy." Harlequin invades the realm of Poetry and Shakespeare and is finally expelled.

Curious were the plots on which the pantomimes of those days were built up. In 1840, the one at Covent Garden was founded on Walpole's "Castle of Otranto." It was nearly all a Harlequinade with tricks and changes and perhaps preceded by a sort of panorama instead of the regular Opening as we know it now, and the whole show could not have been very long, as the evening programme generally included a long standard piece by Shakespeare or Knowles.

All this time, in other countries as well as in England, the tricks and transformations were the chief features of the pantomime.

At Franconi's Cirque in Paris in 1839, there was produced a really wonderful spectacle called "Les Pilules du Diable" which Sala says ran a thousand nights ! The most ingenious tricks were introduced. Men were changed to turkeys ; children to cats ; hovels to jewelled palaces. Razors, suspended over barbers' shops, opened of themselves, cut off the heads of the passers-by, which clown substituted for the heads of the figures of an Italian statuette vendor. Engine cut a man to pieces and he was put together again ; beds were turned into baths of iced water, and a cotton factory into a lunatic asylum of four stories, with a lunatic looking out of each window.

Magloire was the clown in this production. When he ordered a bottle of wine at the Cabaret of "Le More Couronné," the sign itself became animated, jumped on the table and emptied the glass ; huge frogs issued from a neighbouring pool and carried off the bottle ; he dined at a cook-shop ; lo, roast pigeons flew up from the dish into the gaping mouth of a giant painted on a wall and raised pies burst asunder disclosing wondrous animals making fantastic grimaces. Sala, who saw this pantomime when he was young, says that it was revived at the Chatelet in 1874, but that the

management had done away with most of the tricks and transformations and substituted "legs." The piece gained in actual
splendour, but lost in fun, and had no long run.

In 1851, the year of the first Great Exhibition in the history
of the world, when London was full of visitors of all nations, many
gorgeous pantomimes were produced. At the old Princess's in
Oxford Street, the title was "Harlequin Billy Taylor." Flexmore
was clown—that same Flexmore who had graduated at the dirty
little Penny Gaff in King's Road, Chelsea, the Manor House
Theatre (*see Chapter XV*). Paulo, who used to work at the
Albert Saloon (another cheap Gaff) was the Pantaloon, and the
Columbine was Carlotta Leclercq, in after years a charming
emotional actress, leading lady in Fechter's productions and one
of the best, if not actually the best, Ophelia ever seen on the English
stage. But she was not the only young lady in the cast to achieve
the front ranks of the profession in years to come. At the end
of the Opening, a representation of a man-of-war was on the stage.
After "Rule Britannia" had been sung amid much coloured fire,
the figure-head of the vessel (a tiny child) descended to the level
of the stage, and, waving a wee wand, produced the Grand Transformation Scene. That tiny tot was Kate Terry.

Very odd titles were given to pantomimes in those days. At
the New Royalty Theatre in Dean Street, Soho (then called the
National Opera, and surely a very small house to produce a pantomime of any kind), the pantomime in 1850—51 was "Harlequin
Alfred the Great: or the Magic Banjo and the Mystic Raven,"
a curious concatenation of ideas. At the City of London Theatre,
under Nelson Lee, the title was "Knife, Fork and Spoon: or
Harlequin Breakfast, Dinner, Tea and Supper." At the Pavilion,
Whitechapel, it was longer still : "Sugar and Spice and All that's
Nice : or Harlequin March of Intellect and the Fairy Queen of
the Blissful Regions."

Grimaldi is generally recognized as having been the chief of all
clowns since that personage became a regular institution. His
Life has been written by more than one person, including Charles
Dickens, and I need not make a long reference to him here. His
father was Giuseppe Grimaldi, an Italian, who came to England
in 1770 in the capacity of dentist to Queen Charlotte. In his
own country, this royal tooth extractor had been a professor of
fencing and dancing ; and, having a decided preference for dancing
over tooth-drawing, he got permission to resign his post as Royal
Dentist to become Maître de Ballet at Drury Lane and Sadler's
Wells.

Joe Grimaldi, his son, the great clown, was born in Clare Market near the site of " Jo's churchyard," in 1778. He was first usually cast for cats and dogs and monkeys. By the year 1822 he had attained fame as a clown of great humour combined with pathos. In that year he was the clown at the Coburg (Old Vic) then under the management of Glossop, when the Harlequin was Howell, the Pantaloon was Barnes (one of a long series of pantaloons of the same name), the " lover " (a character of the Harlequinade afterwards done away with), Widdicomb, afterwards Ringmaster for years at Astley's, the Columbine, Madame Leclercq, mother of so many famous artistes. Grimaldi was also sometimes Harlequin ; as, for instance, at the Haymarket under the elder Buckstone. His pathos was remarkable in odd scenes. When he sang " An Oyster Crossed in Love," sitting between a cod's head and a huge oyster that opened and shut its shell in time to the music, it is said (though it is hard to credit) that touches of real pathos were apparent through the grotesqueness of the scene, and moved the audience to tears ! How he sang " Tippitywitchet " and " Hot Codlins " and " Me and My Neddy " and other songs, has often been told by those who had the good fortune to hear him, but I suppose that none of these performances would go down with a British audience nowadays. We have grown out of so much, and lost so much in the process.

It is interesting to note that pantomimes in Grimaldi's day were not confined to the Christmas season. That one at Sadler's Wells which was the cause of such loss of life, owing to a fire panic, was in October. More curious still is the fact that in July, 1823, there were three separate pantomimes brought out in the space of four weeks at the Old Vic (then the Coburg) and Grimaldi was clown in all three. These were (1) " Salmagundi : or the Clown's Dish of Sorts " (2) " Harlequin and the Three Wishes : or Puck and the Black Pudding " (3) " Disputes in China : or Harlequin and the Kong Merchants." This pantomime of Grimaldi's day was practically a *ballet d'action*. It was performed in dumb show with the assistance, perhaps, of a chorus here and there. In the famous " Mother Goose," one of Grimaldi's most celebrated pantomimes, there was no dialogue at all. Everything was explained by a system of placards. If a landlord wanted his rent, he would hold up a card with the words, " I have come for the rent." The tenant would then hold up another saying " I have no money." Moreover, the performers in the opening changed their dress *coram populo* to appear as the characters in the Harlequinade.

Next to Grimaldi, Tom Matthews was, perhaps, the most celebrated clown. He was at Drury Lane in the part for thirty years, and his speciality was the singing of " Hot Codlins," always demanded and redemanded by the gallery. This was considered a very broad not to say shocking song, but it was only a very vulgar duet between the singer and the big drum which would come in at the end of a line with a bang to supply the place of what was thought to be a "naughty" word! I append the words for the information of those curious in such matters; we are not so easily shocked now!

HOT CODLINS

A little old woman her living she got
By selling codlins hot, hot, hot;
And this little old woman who codlins sold,
Tho' her codlins were hot, she felt herself cold;
So to keep herself warm, she thought it no sin
To fetch for herself a quartern of . . . . (Oh, for shame !)
   Ri tol iddy, iddy, iddy, iddy,
   Ri tol iddy, iddy, ri tol lay.

This little old woman set off in a trot,
To fetch her a quartern of hot, hot, hot!
She swallowed one glass and it was so nice,
She tipped off another in a trice;
The glass she filled till the bottle shrunk,
And this little old woman they say got . . . .
   Ri tol, etc., etc.

This little old woman while muzzy she got,
Some boys stole her codlins, hot, hot, hot!
Powder under her pan put and in it round stones :
Says this little old woman, "These apples have bones !"
The powder the pan in her face did send,
Which sent the old woman on her latter . . . .
   Ri tol, etc., etc.

The little old woman then up she got,
All in a fury, hot, hot, hot!
Says she, "Such boys sure never were known;
They never will let an old woman alone."
Now here is a moral, round let it buz . . . .
If you mean to sell codlins, never get . . . .
   Ri tol, etc., etc.

Some clowns took to the profession by accident, so to speak. Flexmore, for example, who was a dancer by profession, having been on one or two occasions cast for clown, stuck to the rôle. Harry Payne was playing the bear in a pantomime in which Flexmore was clown, and was told to "stand by," as Flexmore was ill and probably could not get through the piece. But Payne was marked by destiny for a clown's career. His father, W. J. Payne, was a celebrated clown trained under Grimaldi and Bologna and his son followed for many years in his father's steps ; I remember him well in many Christmas shows.

Clowns and pantomimists in general ran in families. The Bolognas, the Bolenos, the Leclercqs, the Lauris, the Paynes, the Rowellas, the Lupinos are examples out of many, though I do not know if there was ever any other Flexmore besides the original one, or a second Hildyard, Croueste, or Delavanti. Harry Boleno, who took Grimaldi for a pattern, began his career at the Old White Conduit House, a Variety Show and Tea Gardens in the Islington district. He died an old man in 1875—his last days as landlord of a public-house most appropriately called "The Clown." He used to enter into the spirit of the "rally" very keenly and occasionally was too rough with the supers of the street who complained that they were hurt by him. Forrest was a good tumbler and played the violin and other instruments. Croueste was the Cremorne clown at one time, and when weather permitted would reach the gardens at Chelsea via the Thames in a boat or tub or some such conveyance drawn by swimming geese. Other clowns also advertised themselves in the same queer way like Barry of Astley's and Usher of the Old Vic, who drove down to the theatre in a barrow drawn by geese harnessed tandem, and Boswell, who drove eight cats.

There was once a female clown, though such a phenomenon seems almost absurd ; it was doubtless due to the endeavour to prove that whatever a man can do a woman can do as well ! This was Miss Cuthbert who did "Joey" in a pantomime at the old Strand Theatre, in the fifties of last century. It was called "The Magic Mistletoe : or Harlequin Humbug" ; but she was an incomplete clown, being quite incapable of doing any kind of tumbling or knock-about business, and had to employ a youth to do that work for her. That same youth acquired some degree of fame in after years as the "Heathen Chinee" in "Bluebeard" and in a successful farce by a woman called "Our Flat." His name was Willie Edouin. According to Thoms, the antiquarian, the present day clown is descended from Punch, but he comes rather from Stenterello, the Florentine Maschera who is a near relation of Punch, but who is accustomed to play the same tricks on innocent people in a play as the clown does.

As mentioned before, the characters in the old-fashioned

pantomime Opening always bore some relation to the characters in the Harlequinade, and the good fairy in the transformation scene used deliberately to change one lot into the other.   The clown was the comic character of the Opening, the Pantaloon the doddering old father, the Harlequin and Columbine the pair of lovers.   As each of these different characters of the first part went down one trap, its corresponding character in the Harlequinade came up another. It is even related that at the old Adelphi Theatre Toole used regularly every night to go down one trap, while Wattie Hildyard (a very celebrated clown of later nineteenth century) came up another, and that these two actors never met each other in life !

In the Circus, Barry, Holloway, Footitt and Wallett were well-known clowns.   The two last-named generally dressed the part in the costume of a Royal Jester with cap and bells, and Wallett styled himself the " Queen's Jester " on account of the many times he had appeared before Queen Victoria who, it is well known, liked to " command " circuses, menageries and other travelling shows. Little Sandy was another famous circus clown, and Whimsical Walker, happily still with us and who has given a most amusing account of the life of a wearer of the motley.   A pantomime clown of a much older date than I can remember myself was Carlo Antonio Delpini, who was considered the best clown of the days prior to Grimaldi. He was an ingenious mechanician and devised many clever tricks and transformations for pantomimes.   Such was his fame that he was specially employed by the Prince of Wales (afterwards George IV) to arrange a Masquerade at the Pantheon in 1783.   He was an Italian, born in the parish of St. Martin in Rome, and he died in the parish of St. Martin, London.   He always had a curious idea that the number " 8 " would be associated, in some way, with his death. As a matter of fact, he died in the year 1828, aged 88.

Our modern clowns are a poor lot, as compared with those of forty years or more ago, that is, the clowns who appear in panto-mimes.   There are still a few in the Halls and the name of Grock will occur to all as perhaps the last embodiment of a really good clown.

Harlequin in the old shows was, as we have seen, the lover in the Opening.   Until the nineteenth century he did not appear in the spangled dress familiar to us, but continued in the Harlequinade dressed as the hero of the piece.   A famous Harlequin was Ellar, whose story is a romantic and sad one.   Blanchard gives a most interesting account of him from which I have taken the following. In 1815 he was at Covent Garden in a Ballet-pantomime of " Robin-son Crusoe," produced in July of that year.   The evening programme consisted of General Burgoyne's opera " The Lord of the Manor,"

Pocock's melodrama of " The Miller and His Men " (dear to the possessors of troupes of penny-plain, twopence coloured) and the Ballet-pantomime. In this show, Ellar was advertised to appear on the stage in a highly unconventional manner :

" Mr. Ellar will positively for this night only, fly from the back of the gallery to the extremity of the stage, a descent of upwards two hundred feet, in a most surprising manner never before attempted by any person."

Two years before that, he had been engaged at Covent Garden in a double company of pantomimists, the other Harlequin being young Bologna, Grimaldi one of the Clowns and Barnes one of the Pantaloons.

In the Opening, Ellar would always show a little bit of the spangles below the costume of the Prince or Lover to indicate his mysterious character to come. His face was blue from the effects of a dose of nitrate of silver given him by a jealous woman, or so the story runs. In his latter days, he suffered from great poverty. He had lost his skill in his profession and all energy, and had to earn a precarious livelihood by playing the guitar after nightfall in fashionable squares, or dancing for small coins in East End music-halls. In spite of all he had earned in his better days, he died a pauper. He was Grimaldi's contemporary, and for some time they used to act together at Sadler's Wells and Drury Lane the same night, and, when necessary, change their costumes in the cab between the two theatres.

The Young Bologna referred to above (his father was a clown) was a well-known Harlequin in the latter years of the eighteenth and the early years of the nineteenth century. He lived to be a very old man, dying in the sixties—in harness to the last. His final appearance was disguised as a black man and acting assistant to Anderson, " The Wizard of the North," whom I remember myself quite well as the popular conjuror at the Egyptian Hall in Piccadilly (the site of which is, I think, now occupied by an arcade leading to Jermyn Street) assisted by two daughters who were celebrated for the neat way they did the " butterfly trick " with bits of tissue paper.

Apropos of Harlequins, how I should have enjoyed that particular pantomime at the old Adelphi when Marie Wilton was the Harlequin to the Columbine of Mary Keeley, daughter of *the* Mrs. Keeley, and wife of Albert Smith. What a delightful Harlequin the Lady Bancroft of the future must have been !

Many actors who rose to the front rank in their profession began their stage careers as Harlequins. Such a one was Robert Pateman, the melodramatic actor of the Olympic ; Vance, the " Lion Comique" was also a Harlequin in his early days ; Milano, the ballet master and teacher of society dancing at private houses, was a Harlequin, and so was Charles Fenton, afterwards "principal boy" in some pantomimes and in later life in the burlesques at the old Strand with the Swanboroughs. And there were many others in those days, for one had to act where and what one could.

Columbines often appeared in the Opening as dancers in the ballets, or even in the principal female parts. A columbine, as such, had no special thing to do which could not be done by anyone with the necessary lightness of foot and knowledge of dancing. They had not to talk and be funny like the Clown or Pantaloon or jump through traps like the Harlequin. So we find at some of the older houses good dancers like Tessy Gunniss and Caroline Parkes coming to the front in the Harlequinade as the sweetheart of Harlequin—or charming actresses like Jessie Vokes and her sister Rosina. Miss Cushnie, a great dancer of the Italian school (Mme. Milano) was a celebrated Columbine ! Owners of the now out-of-date toy theatres will remember that on the sheets of characters relating to pantomimes there were always one or two "Sprites." These were an invariable feature of the Harlequinade in the early and mid-years of the nineteenth century, but gradually disappeared from the bill as the Harlequinade lost in importance. The Deulin family were a famous lot of sprites and some of the forefathers of the present-day Lupinos. Yet another feature of the cast which has quite dropped out was the "Harlequina," a sort of hybrid Harlequin always played by a woman and generally styled "à la Watteau." She was probably at first introduced to find a part for some lady who would otherwise have been left out of the comic scenes.

A most important personage of the Harlequinade was the Policeman. In the Italian Maschera he was called "Il Sbirro," and had all the power and majesty of the Law on his side, so that when Stenterello or Brighella stole, or assaulted innocent people, or otherwise misbehaved themselves, retribution was at hand in the person of the Sbirro. Thus, in the eighteenth-century pantomimes he was the agent through whom the eloping lovers (Harlequin and Columbine) were tracked and brought to book, and he was likewise the terror of the thieving Clown.

But when, in the thirties, Sir Robert Peel instituted his new Police Force the members of it became the target of all sorts of jokes and ridicule. The pantomime writers took up the popular idea and the Policeman of the Harlequinade instead of being a terror to evil-doers became the butt of Clown, Pantaloon and Harlequin alike.

In one of Grimaldi's old trick scenes, he used to steal various objects—such as a coat, a pair of boots, a hat and a milliner's dress-stand, and construct a dummy out of them. Harlequin, in passing, touches the dummy with his wand ; it changes into a Policeman who arrests Clown for his thefts. The trick was repeated in later years and is one of the few cases in which the Policeman of the theatre comes into his own. A butt had to be provided for the Clown, and it was amusing for the occupants of the pit and gallery to see the dread officer of the Law successfully defied and treated with scorn.

Towards the middle and close of the nineteenth century, when Pantomime had developed its Opening at the expense of the Harlequinade, and Harlequin and Columbine were no longer recognized as being intimately connected with the sweethearts of the story, further attractions had to be found, extraneous additions, so to speak, and it may be added excrescences, to add to the interest of the whole. Donato, the one-legged dancer, was one of these extras in 1864, and later came the eccentric dances of the Girards, Kiralfys, Majiltons and others.

In 1878 at the Gaiety there appeared a charming " aerial " dancer, Mlle. Ænea, the first of the flying fairies that were afterwards brought to such perfection by Madame Grigolati's Troupe at Drury Lane. It seems rather curious that this trick of the invisible wire support has gone so entirely out of fashion, though I believe it was employed in the gorgeous production of " A Midsummer Night's Dream " at Drury Lane at Christmas, 1924, which, to our eternal disgrace, was stopped in the height of success to make room for an American musical comedy.

For many years the Vokes Family bore the chief burden of the Drury Lane Annual. Old Vokes was a theatrical costumier, and the little ones took to the stage one by one as they grew up like ducklings to their natural element. They began by playing such parts as the Little Princes in " Richard III," Mamilius in " The Winter's Tale " (you will remember that this was the rôle in which Ellen Terry made her debut with the Charles Keans), Henri in " Belphegor," Prince Arthur in " King John " and the like. Fred Vokes (the " man with the elastic leg ") spent his earlier days as assistant to the Wizard of the North, Professor Anderson, to be discovered in portmanteaux or vanished under cones. His father wanted to make a tailor of him, but his legs were not destined to be crossed on a board but whirled over the heads of his sisters. Jessie Vokes, the eldest, who acted as mother to the rest, was on the stage as young as four years old with Creswick and Shepherd at the old Surrey. There she fell in with Tessy Gunniss, the ballet dancer, pupil of Mrs. Conquest, and Flexmore the Clown, who taught her dancing. Blanchard says that Victoria Vokes made her debut at two years old, and that Rosina was made use of as a baby in long clothes !

For a very long while Drury Lane pantomime was not complete without the Vokes Family.   Then one fine day Cecil Clay married Rosina and took her away from the footlights.   Jessie died soon afterwards, and Victoria took to playing the heroine of Drury Lane drama.   They all died young and their places in Christmas pantomimes have never been adequately filled.   I ought to have mentioned that their first appearance in London pantomime was not at Drury Lane, but in 1866 at the Lyceum under E. T. Smith, in a piece written by W. S. Gilbert, perhaps his first production on the London stage, though a burlesque of his called " Dulcamara," founded on " L'Elisire d'Amore," was brought out at the St. James's in the same year.   In this Lyceum pantomime there was a charming French dancer, one Mlle. Finette, who was probably one of the first, if not the actual first, to dance the cancan in London.   She was well known on the Continent, having been in Germany and elsewhere with a troupe run by Raphael Felix, brother of the great Rachel.   Her end was similar to that of another great dancer, Pitteri of the Alhambra in the seventies, for she died a pauper and forgotten in a hospital in Constantinople as Pitteri died lonely and penniless in a mean lodging in Marseilles.

In 1880, a different kind of pantomime was brought out at the Gaiety when the Hanlon-Lees Troupe produced a real miming piece called " Le Voyage en Chine."   This was almost a reversion to the older type of pantomime when there was no dialogue, and the interest depended principally on the transformations and tricks. The tricks of the Hanlon-Lees were most ingenious.   Omnibuses turned over on the stage, spilling their passengers in all directions ; Pullman cars blew up ; footmen fell through the ceiling on to a dinner table.   It was all very clever fooling, but as an entire evening's entertainment was certainly wanting in backbone.

Meanwhile, the music-hall element had crept into the pantomime, especially at Drury Lane.   Herbert Campbell, Dan Leno, James Fawn and others vulgarized the show more and more every year, though it is more than probable if Leno had been allowed to work out his parts in his own way, without so much of the music-hall business, he would have taken a different line.   He was incomparably the best " Dame " ever seen (not excepting even Danvers the Dame Hatley of " Black Eyed Susan " at the Royalty), and I shall not easily forget one year in particular when he played the Queen in the pantomime seriously as a *grande dame* with the most decorous and regal manners.   The effect was side-splitting.

Various couples or trios of stage ladies billed as " sisters " were a feature of that time—Sisters Mario, Sisters Leamar, Sisters Bilton and many others.   The relationship went out of fashion on the stage

for a time, but we have recently had the " Trix Sisters " and the
" Dolly Sisters "—the name being now placed first.

Perhaps, when the years have gone the full circle again, there
may be a revival of the old-fashioned pantomime with a good Opening
and some sort of a Harlequinade ; and, apropos of the old-fashioned
annual, why has the Grand Transformation Scene become so entirely
a thing of the past ? Some of these at Drury Lane and Covent
Garden were miracles of ingenuity and splendour. Opening with
a scene of dim outlines, suggestive of demons and evil things, very
gradually the beauties of Fairyland would be unfolded. The dim
outlines would, bit by bit, dissolve into something of unearthly beauty.
Lovely beings would appear from leaves, from flowers, from the air,
from nowhere ! when, finally the entire length of a long stage was
disclosed, showers of gold and silver rain would drop slowly from the
skies and radiant lights from coloured flames illuminate the wings.
There was one at Drury Lane called, I think, " The Birth of the
Rose " which I especially remember. At that same theatre, the effect
of the scene was immensely heightened by the graceful flights of
the Grigolati Troupe, who on invisible wires really seemed to fly
up and remain suspended in mid-air.

At outlying theatres, like the Grecian and the Surrey, the Transformation Scene was always expected to take a long time to unfold.
Whatever the ultimate result, a great deal of actual " transforming "
was imperatively demanded by the clientele of these houses. At
the Marylebone in Chapel Street, Edgware Road, the stage was of
enormous depth, claimed to be the deepest in London, and advantage
was taken of this to secure a special effect in the Transformation
Scene by the unfolding of apparently unlimited vistas of Fairyland.

It should not be forgotten that in the days of which I am now
speaking there was nothing like the present-day knowledge of lighting
effects.   Electric light was not in use, and I commend the idea to
Mr. Basil Dean of giving us one Christmas a non-vulgar pantomime, up to date as regards the fairy scenes and with the best singers
and dancers.   It could be produced with schemes of colour and light
never seen before in similar productions.

It seems more than likely, however, that there will be no more
pantomimes at Drury Lane. They will be confined to the suburban
theatres and the provincial managements which are not, as a rule,
able to spend so lavishly as the Harrises and Collinses of old. The
pantomime, indeed, anywhere has for some time degenerated into a
sort of rather vulgar Revue with none of the Fairy element or real fun
of former years.   I cannot help thinking that there is a future for a
really charming Fairy piece, simply told with fine scenery, good
music, but " tuny " (not " Tannhäuser " and the Pathetic Symphony)

bright songs, pretty women, a good chorus, a grand Transformation Scene, and a Harlequinade done by actors who understand their business, and endowed with all the tricks and magical changes possible.

There are plenty of Fairy Tales in Perrault and D'Aulnoy to form the plot of the Opening, without having recourse to the hackneyed " Cinderella " or " Robinson Crusoe," and even if these are all considered to be played out it is surely not beyond the wit of some of our writers to invent a new plot.   Years and years ago there was a charming book for children on the adventures of one Tuflongbo. It was, I think, written by Holme Lee and I know it is a long time ago because I had it as a small boy.   There were two separate volumes of it and a most perfect pantomime could be evolved.   At any rate, it would be a change from the variety show of the present day into which the music-hall artists have each to drag their special bit of business without any reference to the story, just as Nicholas Nickleby had to produce a play for the Crummles' family in which he had to introduce, at all costs, the Infant Phenomenon, a " Combat for Two," and the Tub and the Pump.

CHAPTER III

THE CITY OF LONDON THEATRE, NORTON FOLGATE

WHO now remembers the City of London Theatre in Norton Folgate? It was near Bishopsgate Station and, like so many of its class, specialized in melodrama for the greater part of the year, but always had a pantomime at Christmas. It was a theatre of the City in name only, being just outside the limits. The Corporation have tolerated one or two singing-rooms within the City, but from the days of Shakespeare, and before, they have never permitted a theatre to be opened within the boundary.

It was built by the architect of the old Lyceum, and opened by Cockerton in 1835. In 1837, Mrs. Honey was the manageress, and then Cockerton had it again in partnership with that Richard Shepherd who afterwards ran the old Surrey so long with Creswick.

In 1844, Mrs. Walter Lacy, the directress, aspired to elevate the taste of its audiences, and produced "The School for Scandal" followed by a burlesque, and the same tactics were pursued by the Honners, who succeeded her in 1846. Robert Honner was the son of a solicitor and the schoolfellow and friend of Grimaldi. He took to the stage on his father's death and was apprenticed to Leclercq (father of the celebrated family of dancers and pantomimists), and thereafter had a very varied experience in the profession. He was at the old Sans Pareil Theatre (afterwards the Adelphi), with Ducrow at Astley's, at the Coburg, at Sadler's Wells under Grimaldi, at the Surrey under Elliston, stage manager for Davidge at the Surrey, lessee of Sadler's Wells, then of the City of London and finally stage manager for John Douglass at the old Standard Theatre, Shoreditch, where he remained till he died in 1853. His wife was an actress, Miss McCarthy by name, and co-operated with him at the City of London Theatre. They put on several of Shakespeare's plays and also followed the general craze for bringing out adaptations of Dickens's books. This was a very widespread notion in those days, especially at the outlying theatres the managements of which generally kept a writer on the premises for the purpose of adapting any story that was much in the public mind at the moment. In "The Battle of Life" (one of Dickens's Christmas Stories) Mrs. Honner was considered especially good as Clemency. She had had almost as varied an experience of the profession as her husband, having made her first appearance in London at the Pavilion as long ago as 1831. She frequently played Susan in Douglas Jerrold's piece. She survived her husband seventeen years.

One of the most popular and successful managers of the City of London Theatre was Nelson Lee, who ran it for over eighteen years. Lee was a well-born man, son of a Colonel Lee who was on duty at Nelson's funeral the day his son was born. The boy was naturally christened " Nelson " and obviously intended for the Royal Navy, but the bent of his mind was wholly towards things theatrical and Bohemian. He wanted badly, at first, to be a conjuror, having been fascinated by the tricks of a celebrated Indian conjuror of the day, who had performed at the Old Vic what time it was known as the Coburg. Nelson succeeded in learning enough of the conjuror's profession to get an engagement at Vauxhall Gardens, but it is to be presumed he did not find it a paying line, for shortly afterwards he is heard of at the Surrey Theatre as Harlequin and " general utility." That was in 1828. He was one of the company in the original Richardson's Show, and then, after spending a little more time in London in such parts as he could get (chiefly Harlequin and the like), he became joint proprietor with a Mr. Johnson in 1837 of " Richardson's Travelling Theatre," the legitimate successor of the old Show. Every year he improved his position. In the forties, he was lessee of various theatres—the New Standard, the Marylebone, the Pavilion and others, and finally settled down at the City of London, where he remained till his death, in 1865.

After Lee, the theatre fell to a low level, and closed altogether in 1868. The frontage of the old house is still, I believe, standing *in situ.* It was undoubtedly one of the most important of the East London Playhouses. After the abolition of the privileges of the Patent Theatres in the forties, many West End tragedians starred there at one time or another. Among them I may mention Mrs. Henry Vining (*née* Quantrill) who had succeeded Mrs. Warner in the direction of the Liverpool Theatre and was also with Davidge at the Surrey. She was the mother of Mrs. John Wood.

THE GARRICK THEATRE, LEMAN STREET, WHITECHAPEL

Much farther east than the City of London Theatre was the Garrick in Leman Street, Whitechapel. This was built on the site of an earlier house run by one Thomas Odell in 1729, where David Garrick made his first appearance on the stage as a Harlequin in substitution for Yates, suddenly taken ill. The new house, opened in 1830, was called the Garrick to commemorate that event.

Like all the East End Theatres, it was a house for the crudest dramatic fare—blood-curdling melodrama or romantic spectacles. It was burned down in 1846 after a performance of " The Battle of Waterloo " and when rebuilt was for a time under the direction of Benjamin Oliver Conquest, father of the elder George Conquest (who was born at the Garrick) and was ruler at the Grecian and the Surrey for so many years.

In 1859, it was a Music Hall, but does not appear to have been a success as such. The standard of the house at that time was a low one, even for the East End. In 1874, it was under the direction of J. B. Howe, so long a favourite at the Britannia, Hoxton, who renamed it the Royal Albert and tried to raise the level of the performances and improve the taste of the audience. But in spite of his efforts the latter remained the same. The man who pays the piper has a right to call the tune, and the fare offered to them by Howe was not what they liked or thought it should be.

At one time the house fell to the level of the merest " Gaff," giving several shows each night almost in the old style of Richardson's Show.

In 1879, another effort was made to provide a better kind of entertainment under the management of a Miss Bulmer (Mrs. Sturgeon), a rather clever actress who had recently appeared in an adaptation of " Les Tentations "—called " Led Astray "—at the Olympic with Helen Barry. Miss Bulmer produced an English version of " Le Voyage en Chine " and spared no expense to make it a success. The cast was a good one and a notable first appearance as a professional actor was that of Beerbohm Tree, who got quite a good notice for his whimsical make-up and acting as an eccentric old lawyer.

I do not think this theatre was noted specially for any other production and it is a remarkable case of failure to make good. The traditions of former theatres on the same site were excellent, though the long fight between the managers of the Patent Theatres and the Minor Theatres was then at its height. " The Winter's Tale," for instance, had been revived at the old Leman Street (or Goodman's Fields) house for the first time for one hundred years and notable names on the bills at various periods were Yates (the original Sir Oliver Surface), Walker (the original Macheath in " The Beggars' Opera "), Mrs. Giffard and others.

THE CITY THEATRE, CRIPPLEGATE

In Milton Street, Cripplegate, the " Grub Street " of needy authors, a little theatre was opened in 1831 by John Kemble Chapman (at one time a lessee of the Tottenham Street Theatre), whose wife was Ann Tree, sister of Mrs. Charles Kean and of Mrs. Bradshaw.

This house tried to combine instruction with amusement much after the fashion of the Polytechnic and Panopticon of later years. An announcement was set forth something in the following style :

The City Pantheon or School of practical Instruction for Elocution, Music and the Drama
late the City Chapel, Chapel Street, Fore Street, Cripplegate.
" Delectando pariterque monendo "
" Learning's Triumph o'er our barbarous foes
First reared the stage ! " (Dr. Johnson).

The Second period and Exemplification will take place on Monday, the 3rd August, 1829
When the Tragedy of " Douglas "
with new dioramic illustrations by Mr. Bedford, and other appropriate accomplishments, will be recited by the Professors, Subscribers, and Students, &c., &c.
The City Pantheon is intended to comprise a systematic course of Tuition in Elocution, Action, Dramatic Reading, Vocal Music, Dancing, Fencing, &c. ; and to afford students and amateurs frequent opportunities of respectable practice ; and foster and develop talents which without such advantages, might be entirely lost to their possessors and the public.

It will be seen that this out-of-the-way little theatre aspired to be a sort of dramatic Academy for beginners. It is also probable that the Directors imagined by thus putting instruction in the forefront they might be able to " drive a coach and horses " through that particular Act of Parliament which forbade any dramatic shows except at the Patent Theatres.

Chapman came here after he had been deprived of the use of the little house in Tottenham Street for encroaching on the privileges of the Patentees. At the Milton Street Theatre he continued to be sorely harassed by them, but he fought stubbornly for a long time and succeeded in giving to the public many productions with good all-round companies. Edmund Kean played here in " The Merchant of Venice," " Lear," " Richard III " and probably other rôles, and there were in the company Ellen Tree (Mrs. Charles Kean), James Vining and others well known afterwards in the West End.

Here was produced an early version of Gerald Griffin's novel, *The Collegians*, under the title of " Eily O'Connor : or the Foster Brothers." A later version was Boucicault's " Colleen Bawn."

Isaac Bickerstaffe's burletta, " Love in a Village," was given by Buckstone, Mrs. Chapman and the elder Blanchard—father of the writer of pantomimes. " Black Eyed Susan " was given with Vining and Mrs. Chapman. Another favourite was Miss Apjohn, better known in later life as Mrs. Frank Matthews. It has been asserted that Mrs. Stirling made her debut here, but her grandson, and biographer, denies it.

After a time, Chapman got tired of fighting the Patent Theatres and gave up the direction of the City Theatre to Davidge of the Coburg across the water, who made it a double of that house in the most ingenious manner. Coaches were employed to take the company from one house to the other, fitted up as dressing-rooms to save time.

Though many good actors appeared at the City house, it was always a doubtful financial venture, and the payment of salaries never a certainty. One day, a stranger called, offering a guinea for an old monumental tablet that had been in the chapel out of which the theatre was constructed, and which the company had used for grinding their paints on. His offer was joyfully accepted and spent on a meal !

One of the company was a Miss Harriet Smithson, an Irishwoman of extraordinary beauty, but the possessor of such a pronounced brogue that London audiences would hardly stand her performance. She was born in 1800 in County Clare, her father being a touring theatrical manager in Ireland. She seems to have made her first appearance in England at Birmingham under Elliston, but as early as 1818 made her debut at Drury Lane, then under Stephen Kemble. She was afterwards at the Coburg and again at Drury Lane in 1823-24 under Elliston. I do not think it is true that she made a hit at the City Theatre as an actress, because the public there would not put up with her accent, but on account of her good looks a part was always found for her in which she did not have much to say. Perhaps it was on account of her beauty that Abbott, the Director of the English Theatre in Paris at the time of the Restoration of the Bourbons, engaged her in his company, which included Macready the elder. There were many English residents in the French capital when Charles X was on the throne, and the English theatre had a vogue for years. The chief item in Abbott's programme was generally a play of Shakespeare's, and Miss Smithson, having by accident been entrusted with a more or less leading part, made such a huge success by her beauty and created such a furore by her acting that she was promptly cast for Juliet, Desdemona, Ophelia, etc. She came to be known as " La belle Irlandaise," drew all Paris, and her appalling brogue mattered not a bit, for the majority of the audience understood nothing of what she said and only went to see her beauty and her acting.   On her benefit night, King Charles sent her a handsome present, and the Duchesse de Berri a set of Sèvres.   She afterwards travelled in the French provinces and on her return to Paris married Hector Berlioz, the composer.   The marriage was a very unhappy one.   They separated, and her lot fell on evil days.   Her attraction for a Parisian audience was at an end and she was never really accepted in England.

With all her brogue, she must have been a fine actress.   When Rachel heard of her death, she said : "Voilà une pauvre femme à qui je dois beaucoup."

After Abbott's company had returned to England, Miss Smithson remained in Paris, confident that she could, after her great success, carry on by herself.   But she broke her leg and her vogue was over for the time ; she became very poor and at last accepted the offer of marriage made her by Hector Berlioz, who had been infatuated with her for a long time.   They were both dreadfully poor and "when poverty comes in at the door love flies out of the window."   He tired of her and left her much alone.   When she died, she was buried at Montmartre, but her poor remains were not allowed to rest there for long.   Berlioz had married again and ten years after his first wife died he lost his second, and conceived the horrible idea of exhuming the body of his first wife so that it might be reinterred with that of his second.   Disgusting details are extant of the scene at the Montmartre grave—how the body of poor Harriet Smithson was in a very advanced state of decomposition, how the head fell off and other gruesome happenings too horrible for cold print.   After her death, Liszt wrote his condolences to Berlioz.   It was very characteristic of the Abbé whose outlook on women had been so selfish all his life. He said to the widower : "Elle t'inspira : tu l'as aimée : tu l'as chantée : sa tâche était accomplie."   There was one son of the marriage, who served in the Crimean War as a naval officer with the French fleet.   Apropos of her Irish accent, it is well known than an average English audience has always resented a bad pronunciation of English on the stage, and this is perhaps the reason why two of the greatest of America's actresses, Clara Morris and Maude Adams, have never liked to come to England, their twang being so pronounced.   It was also one reason why Boucicault failed so egregiously when he attempted to play Ruy Blas, a Spanish grandee, with a strong Dublin accent.

After 1831, the record of the City Theatre was an uneventful one.   Many a good performer undoubtedly played there on their way " down West," but the salaries were always uncertain, so that they got away as soon as they could.

In 1832, Benjamin Webster the elder, and Mrs. Waylett (known at the Royalty Wellclose Square and other houses of an early date), ran the place. In 1833, it was sold " lock, stock, and barrel " for three hundred and ten guineas, and given up to the production of Vaudeville and light entertainments. In 1834, the bill once more consisted of five-act plays, but still the pay-day was approached with misgiving ! In 1835, unlicensed, and therefore liable to be shut up at any moment, Oxberry and Mrs. H. P. Grattan were there. In the following year, came the end : it was pulled down and warehouses built on the site.

In passing, it may be of interest to note that besides Mrs. Chapman and Mrs. Charles Kean, there was a third sister, Maria Tree, who was the original Clari in a very popular singing piece—" The Maid of Milan " for which Howard wrote " Home Sweet Home," though the rest of the music was by Henry Bishop. She appeared at Covent Garden as Rosina in an English version of Rossini's " Barbiere di Siviglia " in 1819, but was also equally successful as an actress in such parts as Viola and Rosalind. She married a Mr. Bradshaw, and her stage career was brief.

THE ROYALTY THEATRE, WELLS STREET, WELL-CLOSE SQUARE, E.

In Goodman's Fields, there was once a theatre run by Giffard, the man destined to become the cause of the pernicious Patent Act that held up dramatic art in London for so long. After the disappearance of that house in about 1750 and of the little theatre in Ayliffe Street, the East End of London had no place of theatrical entertainment until 1787 when the Royalty Theatre in Wells Street, Wellclose Square (so called from an ancient well which once existed in Goodman's Fields) was opened to the public.

It created quite a sensation at the time. No theatre had ever been allowed to be built within the limits of the City itself, and the rule still holds good, but there were one or two sprang up in later years just outside the boundary of which the City of London Theatre in Norton Folgate was perhaps the nearest to the Gates. One of the journals of the eighteenth century, said :

" I know no reason why the ' quality ' at both ends of the Town should not have the same diversions. This will be a great ease to the Ladies of Rag Fair who are now forced to trudge as far as Lincoln's Inn Fields to mix themselves with quality, The Mumpers of Knockvargis will now have the Playhouse come to them who were not able to stump it to the other end of the Town on their wooden legs."

" Mumpers " seems to have signified " Gipsies " or " Beggars."
I have not traced the meaning of Knockvargis.

In an old London Handbook the theatre is minutely described.
It was evidently an event in the theatrical world, this opening of a
playhouse so far East, and a good deal of fuss was made over it :

" The auditorium is of a parabolic form.   The proscenium,
which is 28 feet wide, has its arch decorated with the Royal Arms
and scarlet drapery.   There are stage doors with boxes above.   The
pit, which is the best elevated of any theatre, and contains thirteen
seats (*Note* : *I suppose this means* " 13 *rows* ") is 26 feet deep and
35 feet in width.   The full tier of boxes contains 3 private boxes
on each side with chairs, and eight central open boxes enclosing four
private or family boxes at the back.   Above, on each side, are the
slips or side boxes with a private box at each extremity.   The gallery
occupying the centre is very spacious.   Above it is another gallery
going round the interior ; that was formerly opened at 6d., but finally
closed.   The light is dispersed from ten cut-glass lustres, suspended
round the boxes."

This description is interesting, as it probably gives a good idea of
most of the theatres of the period which sprang up so quickly in the
early years of the nineteenth century and which were generally
forced to close down by the action of the Patentees.

Several conventional features are to be noticed which have quite
disappeared from the theatres of to-day.   One was the little door
on each side of the Proscenium which was painted to represent the
doors of a house with knocker and all complete and were called
the " stage doors."   These doors were generally surmounted by the
representation of windows with muslin curtains and flower pots,
etc.   The idea was that they should be something quite distinct from
the stage itself, and in order that the illusion should not be destroyed
actors, when taking their calls, always came out of one of these little
houses, walked across the stage and entered the other little house.
On the stage they were the characters of the play.   They appeared
before the curtain *in their own characters* to receive the applause.
This appears to me to be a much better notion than the present-day
one of drawing up the curtain to see all the characters of the play
standing in a stiff row and not even taking the trouble to bow or
acknowledge the applause of the audience.   The effect of these
little house doors can be seen from the illustration of the Proscenium
of this theatre shown on the opposite page.

Another convention was the green carpet (generally of baize)
which was always laid on the stage when there was to be a tragedy

THE OLD ROYALTY THEATRE: WELLCLOSE SQUARE, E.   INTERIOR, SHOWING THE STAGE DOORS
FOR "CALLS"

From a coloured print in the British Museum

enacted or some terrible scene to move the spectators. It was supposed to be a good thing to prepare the audience for a thrill, and so when they saw the green drugget they knew for certain that their feelings were going to be harrowed.

This theatre, the first to appear in the East End for nearly fifty years, was the object of attack by others besides the Patentees. The narrow-minded bigots who still rear their unpleasant heads and air their prurient ideas from time to time were not wanting so long ago as 1803. In that year, the Rev. T. Thirlwell, a Member of the Society for the Suppression of Vice, put forth a pamphlet bearing the portentous title of : " A Solemn Protest against the Revival of Scenic Exhibitions and Interludes at the Royalty ; containing remarks on Pizarro, The Stranger, and John Bull."

If the dull plays mentioned in that Title were feared by this Reverend gentleman's Society, what would he have said to some of the productions of recent times, " Damaged Goods " for instance ?

The Royalty was built by John Palmer the actor, who opened in 1787 with " As You Like It," and a musical after-piece in which Braham, the tenor, made his first stage appearance as Cupid. Its annals are of the slightest interest, but it may be noted that in 1788 it was reopened (probably after a closure by the Patentees), by Macready the elder, father of the great actor, when the programme was as follows :

" Collin's Brush "—a sort of variety entertainment.

" The Contrast "—a serio-comic spectacle with dance and song.

" Amurath IV : or The Turkish Harem "—a musical sketch.

Feats of Strength and Agility by Mr. Moritz, who had the honour of exhibiting before their Majesties, the Royal Family, and several of the Nobility.

" The Festival of Hope : or Harlequin in a Bottle "—a pantomime.

The company included the elder Wallacks, the Hollands, Mrs. Wybrow, Mr. Rayner, and Delpini, the celebrated Clown. Macready had a licence for burlettas and pantomimes only, and he appears to have very soon tired of what must have been a thankless task.

After the fire at Astley's in 1794, the burned-out company were taken to the Royalty to fill in a vacant date, but their stay would naturally be of a short duration. Fifteen years later, it was called " The East London Theatre " and later still it was bought by a stage-struck Member of Parliament, one Peter Moore. It was destroyed by fire in 1826.

Rebuilt, the name again was changed and it was called " The Brunswick " perhaps out of compliment to the reigning House, and opened in 1828 with a version of Scott's novel *The Bride of Lammermoor* called " The Mermaiden's Well : or the Fatal Prophecy," which was preceded and followed by a Farce and Ballet. This programme ran but three days and it was arranged to produce a play on " Guy Mannering." During the rehearsal of this piece a dreadful catastrophe occurred. In order to render the new theatre more fireproof, it had been fitted with an iron roof, and though the owners had been repeatedly warned that the flimsy brick walls would not stand the weight they persisted in their design. The roof fell in and buried all in the ruins. Fifteen were killed and many injured.

The " unco' guid " of the day, a particularly bigoted and fanatical lot, seized the opportunity to declare that it was the sinfulness of theatres and the play-actors—a wicked unregenerate lot—who acted in them, which was the cause of the disaster and that in this manner the Almighty had shown His severe displeasure with all who took any part in such ungodly amusements. It is a fact that a sermon was actually preached against theatres in general in the smoking ruins, *before all the sufferers had been removed.*

No attempt was made to rebuild the unlucky house, the site being afterwards occupied by a " Sailors' Home." Its name was not allowed to be lost altogether, for Miss Fanny Kelly adopted it for the little bandbox of a playhouse which was built for her in Dean Street, Soho, and which has had such a long and distinguished career. This Miss Kelly lived to be the doyenne of her profession dying in her ninety-third year. It is not generally known, I think, that she was the only woman to whom Charles Lamb (" Elia ") made a proposal of marriage. He is said to have been very much attached to her.

SHAKESPEARE THEATRE, CURTAIN ROAD, SHOREDITCH

The records of this old house are scanty in the extreme. It is known that Grimaldi once played there, but it was a very small place. At first, it was devoted to horsemanship, but later on opened with a musical play and a drama founded on the murder of an Italian boy by Thurtell and Weare. There has always been a rumour that the youth who represented the boy became a famous actor in his after years. As a matter of fact he grew up to be Mr. Marchant, a much appreciated member of the companies at the Britannia, Hoxton, Marylebone and other theatres famous for the production of melodramas.

The Standard Theatre (or rather theatres, for there were at least three of that name) run by John Douglass, a manager of the Crummles type with dramas of the most realistic kind, afterwards occupied the site of the little Curtain Road Theatre, but the last of the quite historic " Standard Theatres " is now, alas, merely a palace of the empty Movies.

EAST LONDON THEATRE, WHITECHAPEL

This building was originally opened about 1844, being then known as the " Effingham Saloon." It was rebuilt in 1867 and renamed " The East London Theatre." The exact situation was in the Whitechapel Road nearly opposite a place of entertainment called " The Paragon Music Hall," which had previously been " The Eagle Tea Gardens and Saloon," and is now, of course, a Cinema.

As a Saloon attached to a tavern, and also as a theatre, it was a favourite resort of sailors, when on shore leave, and their following, probably including all that was low among the female population of the neighbourhood. If ever Pleasant Riderhood, who you will remember kept a " Lending Shop " in this vicinity, induced one of her sailor-men to take her to a theatre, it would have been to the Effingham Saloon, for the same mob of drunken seafaring men and frowzy women who frequented the Dancing Taverns of Ratcliff Highway (such as " The Rose and Crown " and others of equally infamous memory) formed the major part of the Effingham audiences and later of those of the East London Theatre. The prices of admission were very low—Boxes 1s. 6d., Pit 6d., Gallery 4d. and 3d.— Wapping and the Docks were largely represented, the dramatic fare provided having to be strong accordingly to suit their tastes. The heroes were all of the working-class order and if anyone in the play appeared in a black coat he was at once recognized as the villain and soundly hissed before he had attempted to open his mouth !

The theatre could never have really paid its way, though the manager at one time was Morris Abrahams, who also ran the Pavilion Theatre in the Mile End Road and the Albion (or Oriental) at Poplar and was an " old theatrical hand." The bill consisted generally of lurid melodrama and occasionally of any kind of Variety.

One production was noteworthy perhaps, for here was first given a version of Charles Reade's novel *It's Never Too Late to Mend* that had such a run at the Princess's and was revived more than once. I feel sure that the savagery of the prison scene was given in all its crudity to satisfy an " Effingham " audience.

The East London was destroyed by fire in 1870 and not rebuilt as a complete theatre but as a sort of temporary place where plays were produced in Yiddish for the amusement of the hordes of Russian and Polish Jews abounding in the neighbourhood. In these productions, the hero was always a Jew and the villain always

a Gentile.   I suppose that in this way the Hebrews fancied they
were getting a little of their own back !

Eventually the place degenerated into a hall for Boxing Contests,
run chiefly for and by Jews and not bearing a too savoury reputation.
It was then known as " Wonderland."   It was again burned down,
but I believe there is something of the same kind now carried on
at or near the site of the old Effingham.

THE ORIENTAL THEATRE, POPLAR, E.

A Music Hall in Poplar was turned into a theatre in 1867, and
christened " The Oriental," and later, the " Albion."   It afforded
the usual melodramatic fare beloved by the neighbourhood, but
lasted a few years only.   It is now the Queen's Palace of Varieties,
Poplar.

ROYAL BOROUGH THEATRE, TOOLEY STREET, S.E.

Between 1834 and 1836, there was a theatre in Tooley Street,
Borough, which was pulled down to make room for the buildings
of the South-Eastern Railway.   The records are very scant and the
place could have had a local importance only.

So much has been said in this chapter (and there will be more to
note later in connection with other theatres) about the effect of that
particularly unjust law conferring special privileges on the Patent
Theatres, that it may be as well to give some brief account of the
situation in the London theatrical world before 1843, in which year
the privileges were abolished and all theatres placed on the same
footing.

In these days when all theatrical managers are allowed, within
certain bounds of decency, to produce what plays they like, it is very
hard to realize the situation in which they were placed by the
Licensing Act of 1737.

This tyrannical " Dora-like " Act limited the number of theatres
where legitimate drama could be performed to two, established a
close censorship over what was produced and hindered dramatic
development in England for just over a hundred years.

The original cause of the Act was a play by an unknown author
called " The Golden Rump " which was intended to hold up the
King and his Ministers to ridicule, and pour abuse on the connec-
tions of the Court.

The anonymous writer of this piece sent the MS. to an actor
named Giffard who was also Stage Manager of the little theatre in
Goodman's Fields, where Garrick made his debut in later years,

and whose site was afterwards covered by the more modern Garrick Theatre, Leman Street, Whitechapel.

Giffard was terrified at this audacious, abusive composition. He took the MS. to the autocratic Walpole who, furious at the abuse levelled at himself and colleagues, brought in forthwith an Act establishing a strict censorship over all plays produced in London.

By this Act, the only two theatres permitted to perform the legitimate drama (signifying chiefly Shakespeare) were Covent Garden and Drury Lane. These houses were known as the "Patent Houses," and were opened in the winter months when the London season was at its height. After a time, a sort of half-licence was granted to the "Little house in the Haymarket" to take the place of the two Patent Houses during the summer months, but only during the summer months, and this occasional "summer licence" was in process of time grudgingly granted to various other houses, such as the "Sans Pareil" (afterwards called the "Adelphi"), Sadler's Wells, the Royal Amphitheatre of Arts (*i.e.*, Astley's), the Surrey, etc.

In the early years of the nineteenth century, dramatic art in England was at a very low ebb. Good actors were scarce, the public stayed away, and the two Patent Houses resorted to all kinds of entertainments to fill their coffers. Circuses, Performing Animals, Freaks like the "Man-fly who walked on the ceiling" and any curiosity likely to draw, were put on by the managements of the only two theatres where Shakespeare could be legally performed, and if any of the so-called Minor Houses attempted to provide their patrons with legitimate drama the Patentees immediately invoked the Law of 1737 in all its force and stopped the performances. It was a case of dog in the manger with a vengeance. The scandal was very great, and many were the subterfuges resorted to by the unlicensed houses to evade the law and do what the Patent Houses did not.

A hard and fast rule laid down for the guidance of the Lord Chamberlain who was then, as now, in control, was that every piece given at any theatre except the two Patent Houses should contain a certain number of songs with a piano or some other instrument making itself heard from time to time. This was intended to exclude Tragedy and High Comedy, which were, in no sense, musical entertainments, and the production of which was to remain the exclusive privilege of the two Patent Houses.

Not being allowed to give either Tragedy or Comedy, and not wishing to be always doing Pantomime, the managers of the Minor Theatres evolved the word "burletta" to signify an entertainment that came within the meaning of the Act. But as the Italian proverb says " Fatta la legge, trova la malizia "—which means that Laws beget craft or, as we should say in English " You may drive a coach and four through any Act of Parliament—" a way was soon found of stretching the meaning of a " burletta " (*i.e.*, a piece with a song or two and a musical instrument), to include all sorts of plays serious and comic : farce, pantomime, melodrama, burlesque or even, at a pinch, Shakespeare—with incidental music.   The Patentees fought hard, for they were in a bad way.   Their more wealthy patrons were leaving them for the Italian Opera, or concerts, or miscellaneous shows.   Their poorer and less-educated clientèle who wanted, so to speak, something for their money, were no longer content with the Man-fly and wild animals, and did not appreciate Shakespeare or the high-brow Restoration Comedy.   So they took to crowding the Minor Houses where they could feast on exciting melodrama and bloody horrors of all sorts.   Plays like " The Miller and His Men " and " Raymond and Agnes : or the Bleeding Nun " were among the earliest of the dramas presented for the delight of the more uncultivated playgoers who then, as now and ever shall be, formed the majority of the audiences.

Legally, these unlicensed playhouses were not allowed to take money at the doors, but ingenuity was not wanting to evade this part of the Law also.   At the Strand Theatre, the management opened a sweet-stuff shop next door where you could buy an ounce of peppermints at an exorbitant price, and have a ticket for the pit thrown in ; or a better kind of sweet at a still more expensive rate and get a seat in the boxes.   Other theatres followed with similar devices.   Such a state of affairs could not, of course, continue.   The law was being openly set at defiance, but at the same time the sufferers from its injustice were doing their best to get it altered.   Agitations, petitions and outspoken remonstrances grew in number daily.   Success was confidently anticipated, as the Rules were scandalously unfair and freely broken.   In the thirties, a number of small theatres sprang up all over the town in the hope that the Law would be speedily repealed. This will account for the numerous mushroom playhouses of no importance whatever which kept appearing and disappearing after a life of anything from three or four months to three or four years and some of which I have noticed in the chapter dealing with Minor Playhouses.   There were doubtless many others whose records are entirely lost.

Bulwer Lytton took a prominent part in the fight, pleading earnestly for freedom for all alike.   In 1843, the battle was won, the advocates for the continuation of the Patent Monopoly being defeated. In that year, a Bill was introduced into Parliament by Sir James Graham and became Law.   The Patent privileges were abolished and all theatres were placed equally under the jurisdiction of the Lord Chamberlain.

It is probably true that the managements of the Minor Theatres who thus obtained their liberty had looked forward to making large sums by the production of the works of Shakespeare and other standard dramatists. But they reckoned without their hosts, or rather without their patrons.

The new type of audience, which took to playgoing as a duck takes to water, did not much care about Shakespeare. They wanted something they could understand. So the newly licensed houses soon abandoned the " Legitimate " in favour of " The Murder in the Red Barn " and " The Bandit of the Blind Mine." Sadler's Wells was, perhaps, the only playhouse (with the possible exception of the Marylebone) of the newly-emancipated that could always command an audience for the higher kind of drama.

The Licensing Act of 1743 had the effect of legalizing as many theatres as places of dramatic entertainment as the Lord Chamberlain pleased, and the fact still holds good that any company of actors playing without his authority or without the temporary licence of a Magistrate falls under the statute " 30 Eliz Cap. 4.2." It was a Law for the suppression of " Rogues, Vagabonds and Sturdy Beggars " and all unlicensed players were declared to come, legally, under this heading. I do not know that it has ever been repealed.

CHAPTER IV

ABOUT the year 1770, there existed a passage across St. George's Fields, Southwark, facing Somerset House on the other side of the river, which was known as " Curtis's Halfpenny Hatch." Hatches were gates at which halfpenny tolls were exacted, and they appear to have been quite common on the outskirts of London, giving access to short cuts from one part to another and leading through nursery grounds or other private lands.

E. T. Smith in that delightful collection of gossip, *A Book for a Rainy Day*, records that he visited the Halfpenny Hatch near St. George's Fields, and that it stood at the back of St. John's Church, Waterloo Road, in a sort of dell, by reason of the earth being raised for the pavements of the adjacent streets. This Hatch was built subsequent to 1771 by William Curtis, the famous botanist, for the accommodation of such of the public as chose to use it. The Curtis estate was afterwards sold to a wealthy lead-smelter of the name of Roupell, and the Hatch and its owner are now commemorated in the names of Hatch Row, Roupell Street, Lambeth. In Mr. Whitten's edition of *A Book for a Rainy Day* from which I have taken the above information, is a note that Palmer Street in the vicinity is still locally called " Up the Hatch," though of course no Hatch has existed within living memory.

The object of this somewhat discursive preamble to a Chapter on Astley's is that it enables us to fix almost exactly the site of the first Amphitheatre opened by Philip Astley which in after years developed into the Astley's known to many people still living.

Philip Astley was the son of a cabinet-maker at Newcastle-under-Lyme and was born in 1742. He seems to have been poorly educated and left home to enlist in a cavalry regiment. He stood over six feet, was strongly built, with a powerful voice, and attracted the attention of his officers by his behaviour in a battle on the Continent where he captured the colours of the enemy. While serving in Elliott's Horse, he learned several feats of horsemanship, and on his discharge was presented by General Elliott with his white charger, " Gibraltar," which performed every night in the Ring for a long time.

Inspired, perhaps, by the feats of one Johnson and others who exhibited similar feats at a Tavern in Islington, he resolved to exploit his expert knowledge of horses by starting an exhibition of his own, so

ASTLEY'S ADVERTISING CART

From an old print

EXTERIOR OF ASTLEY'S

From an old print

he bought another horse and with these two animals opened in a field near Westminster Bridge, on the Surrey side, between that bridge and where Waterloo Bridge was built later.   In that place, Astley formed his first Ring with some stakes driven into the ground and a rope, and collected tribute from such spectators as could be induced to attend at the end of each performance.

It is interesting to note that " Gibraltar," the white charger, was always well looked after till he died.   He was known to all the company as " The Spanish Horse " and when Davis succeeded Astley at the Amphitheatre the old animal had the same care as if his master had been alive.   He lived to be forty-two years old, and when, owing to the loss of teeth, could not chew corn, he was allowed two half quartern loaves a day.   In his public performances, he got through several amusing and clever tricks.   He would fetch the tea-things, take the kettle off the fire, ungirt his own saddle and wash his own feet in a pail of water.   On his death from natural decay, Davis had his hide tanned and made into a " Thunder drum " which always stood on the prompt side of the Amphitheatre.

An information was lodged against Philip Astley by some jealous impresario, for taking money for a show without a licence, but a lucky accident got him out of his trouble.   George III was one day crossing Westminster Bridge on a spirited horse which got out of control.   Astley, who was passing at the time, came to his assistance, and in return the King granted him a licence for his Show. He then invested £200 in a mortgage on a piece of waste ground nearer Westminster Bridge, not far from where the theatre was built later.   The mortgagor disappeared, leaving a lot of timber on the ground, and with this material Astley roofed over the best seats in his Ring leaving the cheaper ones still open to the weather.

The entrance to the Show was reached by steps from the road, and a green curtain covered the door where Mrs. Astley stood to take the money.   Pictorial representations of the performances were affixed to the outside wall, and round the top of the covered-in part were figures of horses with their riders.

This somewhat primitive circus must have had the appearance from the outside of those booths and shows which are still seen at country fairs where you get, outside, highly painted, garish pictures of what you may expect to see inside.   It was opened in 1770, among the attractions being a clown (Porter by name) and young " Master Astley " in " Billy Button's Ride to Brentford " an old Ring piece that may be still done in country Shows.   I have seen it several times. The only music was a solitary drum beaten by Mrs. Astley.

At this early stage of his venture, Astley used to parade West End streets with his horses and troupe in a manner similar to provincial circuses at the present day when visiting small towns.   He led the procession, dressed in uniform, and mounted on " Gibraltar," followed by two trumpeters and two riders in full costume of some kind, the rear being brought up by a coach in which sat the clown and a " Learned Pony " who distributed handbills.

Astley was a very shrewd business man and ever on the look out for bargains or some means by which he could increase the attractions of his Show.   In 1772, he bought cheap a lot of scaffolding that had been used at the funeral of Augusta, Princess Dowager of Wales (mother of the King) and he also cleverly obtained a quantity of hustings timbers (always considered the perquisite of the mob), by buying them off the mob for gallons of beer !   With this rough material, he roofed in all his Ring and constructed a ceiling painted to represent green boughs, for it was still a tradition that Circuses were open-air entertainments.   When finished, he christened it " The Royal Grove " and this was the first name of what was afterwards always known as " Astley's " or, in the vernacular, " Hashley's."   He had to endure the open or disguised opposition of the Patent Theatres, so usually shut up his place in the winter, and took his company to Paris or other continental centres.   In the days of the Terror in France, he went to Dublin instead.

In 1798, when England was at war with France, Astley accompanied the Duke of York to the front.   On this occasion, he gave all the men of his old regiment a complete outfit of needles, thread, buttons, etc., and, moreover, set the females of " The Royal Grove " to work to make a lot of flannel waistcoats in the corner of each of which was sewn one shilling, which went by the name of a " friend in need."   All this was duly chronicled in the news-sheets of the day and made an excellent advertisement for " The Royal Grove."

The ramshackle old Circus had been burned down in 1794, while Astley was in France.   He hastened home and rebuilt it as quickly as possible, giving it the name of " Astley's Amphitheatre of Arts " and opening it in 1795.   He went back to France, but seems to have been detained as a prisoner of war after the Peace of Amiens.   He escaped to the frontier disguised as a French officer, and got across to England only to find that his wife was dead and his theatre burned down for the second time (1803).   Once more he rebuilt it, opening in 1804 as " The Royal Amphitheatre." In the meantime, he also built a Circus in Paris which afterwards became the celebrated Cirque Franconi.   He must have been a very successful man in all his schemes to be able to carry on with so many new ventures in spite of the war and two fires !   For, in 1805, he started yet a new scheme.   He first leased a plot of ground from Lord Craven in a street called " Via de Aldwych " (afterwards Wych Street), near Drury Lane, and approximately the site of Craven House, where " The Queen of Hearts," Elizabeth of Bohemia, had spent the latter part of her days.   The account of this fresh venture of Astley's will be found in the chapter relating to the Olympic Theatre, the outcome of Astley's Circus.   Suffice it to say here that he did not make it a success and sold it all to Elliston, then lessee of Drury Lane.

Like all really great showmen, Astley was an adept at advertisement.   In addition to his parade through the town, he exhibited one of his " clown horses " at a Hall in Piccadilly, combined with some Conjuring, and what was universally known then as " Ombres Chinoises," a sort of Magic Lantern or Galanty Show—the Cinema in its infancy.   An early advertisement states :

" The entertainment will consist of horsemanship, by Mr. Taylor, Mr. Astley, Signor Markatchy, Miss Vangalla and other transcendent performers : a minuet by two horses in a most extraordinary manner : a comical musical interlude called ' The Awkward Recruit ' : and an amazing exhibition of dancing dogs from France and Italy and other genteel parts of the globe."

A more detailed advertisement of 1772 gives a good general idea of the Show in those days, and it may be noted here that Astley's was really the forerunner of all Circuses in every country. One specimen of such advertisements does for all :

" Horsemanship and new feats of activity. This, and every evening at six, Mr. and Mrs. Astley, Mrs. Griffiths, Costmethopila and a Young Gentleman will exhibit several extraordinary feats on one, two, three and four horses at the foot of Westminster Bridge. These feats in number are upwards of fifty : to which is added the new French Piece, the different characters by Mr. Astley, Griffiths, Costmethopila, &c.   Each will be dressed and mounted on droll horses. Between the acts of horsemanship, a Young Gentleman will exhibit several pleasing heavy balances, particularly this night with a Young Lady nine years old, in a manner quite different from all others.   Mrs. Astley will likewise perform with two horses in the same manner as she did before Their Majesties of England and France, being the only one of her sex that ever had that honour.   The doors to be opened at five and begin at six o'clock.   A commodious gallery, 120 feet long, is fitted up in an elegant manner.   Admittance there as usual.

" N.B.—Mr. Astley will display the broadsword, also ride on

a single horse, with one foot on the saddle the other on his head, and every other feat which can be exhibited by any other.   With an addition of twenty extraordinary feats—such as riding at full speed with his head on a common pint pot, at the rate of twelve miles an hour.   To specify the particulars of Mr. Astley's performance, would fill this side of the paper, therefore please to ask for a bill at the door, and see that the number of fifty feats are performed, Mr. Astley having placed them in acts as the performance is exhibited.   The amazing little Military Horse, which fires a pistol at the word of command, will this night exhibit upwards of twenty feats in a manner far superior to any other, and meets with the greatest applause."

In 1776, the personnel of the Show was greatly increased, and the advertisement announces : "   . comic tumbling, the learned little horse, the Roman Battle, Le Force d'Hercule, &c., &c.   Gallery 2s., Riding School 1s."

When the Amphitheatre was opened in 1780, there was still more to be seen : Tumbling, Clowns, Horsemanship, Slack-rope Vaulting, Tricks on Chairs and Ladders and the Egyptian Pyramids.

Every one, from the highest to the lowest, went to Astley's. Horace Walpole therefore was of course there, as he always did what the fashionable world did.   In his affected style, he writes to Lord Stafford :

" I could find nothing at all to do and so went to Astley's, which indeed was much beyond my expectations.   I do not wonder any longer that Darius was chosen King by the Instructions he gave to his horse : nor that Caligula made his, Consul ; Astley can make his dance minuets and hornpipes.   But I shall not have even Astley now ; Her Majesty the Queen of France, who has as much taste as Caligula, has sent for the whole of the Dramatis Personæ to Paris."

A good many years later, Astley's was still the fashion.   Lady Bessborough, sister of the great Georgiana Duchess of Devonshire, and *chère amie* of the first Earl Granville, writes to him as follows :

" Think of my going to Astley's last night.   There is a battle on the stage with real horses galloping full speed, and fighting to a beautiful white light like day dawn, that is quite beautiful, and like one of Bourgignon's pictures animated.   What followed is not so good.   A Harlequin Farce, no less than Calypso and a Polish nobleman rivals Telemachus with Eucharis.   Minerva, to save him from Calypso's anger, turns him into Harlequin, and Calypso into Columbine, the Pole into Pantaloon, and at the end, poor Ulysses and Penelope who never found themselves before in such company, are brought down from heaven to embrace their son Harlequin and ask Pantaloon for his daughter as his wife. You will not be much edified by this history, but the excessive extravagance of it amused me."

In this year, when Lady Bessborough wrote (1807), there was one Hengler, a rope-dancer, in the programme ; his son was the first of the famous family that afterwards had so many Circuses of their own.

But I have gone too far ahead. To hark back to 1788, there was on the bill in that year an item which reminds one of the Vincent Crummles's Show. This was—"A single combat with the broadsword between Young Astley as a British sailor, and Mr. J. Taylor as a Savage Chief"—only the Infant Phenomenon is wanting to make it complete ! The bill included a general engagement between British sailors and savages ; tumbling ; a new comic dance called "The German Chasseurs" ; a Grand Entry of Horses and a Minuet by Two Horses ; a new comic drama called "The Ethiopian Festival" ; including Pas de Deux by Monsieur Ferrer and Madame Fuzzi ; the whole concluding with the Magic World—probably another name for the old Ombres Chinioses. This Magic World seems always to have concluded the entertainment, the items of which were varied by " Ring Plays " such as " Gil Blas " ; or " The Jew Outwitted "—perhaps a Circus version of "The Merchant of Venice." One curious item was " A Real Gigantic Spanish Pig, measuring twelve feet from head to tail 12 hands high, and weighing twelve hundredweight."

Philip Astley died in Paris in 1814, aged 72. He was buried in Père La Chaise. His son John (the " Young Astley " of the bills) survived him only a few years. He died in 1821 in the same house and in the same bed and was buried in the same grave.

The management of the Circus now devolved upon Davis, who had worked with Astley. He was the first to introduce Hippo-dramatic spectacles with camels and elephants, but he was not a great Showman, and it was by a chance that the place came into the hands of perhaps the greatest Circus manager ever born, Andrew Ducrow. It happened in this way.

A magnificent spectacle, "The Cataract of the Ganges," was produced by Elliston at Drury Lane in 1823, with a great cast, including Wallack the elder, Harley, Younge, Benjamin, etc. It was written by Tom Moncrieff who had done " Tom and Jerry "

for the stage and also " Don Giovanni in London," and among
the performers was one Andrew Ducrow, whose father, Peter
Ducrow, had appeared at Astley's in 1793 (the year of Andrew's
birth) as " The Flemish Hercules." Andrew was a very good
actor of the Circus kind. He had been a member of the Cirque
in Paris, and Bunn, the then manager at Covent Garden, wanted
him for a spectacle called " Cortez." Davis wanted him also to
help with the management of Astley's. Whether it was on account
of his father's former connection with the place, or whether the
terms offered by Davis were better than those offered by Bunn,
I don't know, but Davis got him. The manager of Astley's had
not the Showman's instinct of Astley himself, and when the proprietors of the Amphitheatres wanted to raise the rent he funked
it, and allowed Ducrow to take over the whole Show in partnership
with a man called West.

Andrew Ducrow was the most successful manager that Astley's
ever saw. He was always thinking out new features and looking
for talent in every direction. He brought "Poses Plastiques
Equestriennes" from Paris to England for the first time. They
were afterwards done at a Circus at the Alhambra, among the
performers being Harry Boleno, in later days a famous Clown.

The fame of the "Poses Plastiques" at Astley's spread far and
wide—even to the Land of Cakes ! Christopher North in his
now forgotten *Noctes Ambrosianæ* makes the Shepherd say :

" Since, as Ducrow takes his attitude as steadfast on the steed
as on a stane, there ye behold, standin' before you, wi' helmet,
sword and buckler, the image of a warrior king . . . . these impersonations by Ducrow prove him to be a man of genius . . . .
thus to convert his frame into such forms, shapes, attitudes, postures,
as the Greek imagination moulded into perfect expression of the
highest state of the soul, that shows that Ducrow has a spirit kindred
to those who in marble made their mythology immortal."

But Ducrow was only a successful showman with a *flair* for the
good things of the Ring when he saw them in any other theatre.
He was an extremely illiterate man and had the deepest contempt
for the speaking parts of his equestrian dramas. " Cut the dialect,"
meaning dialogue, "and come to the 'osses ! " was a favourite expression of his, and one morning after listening to what seemed to
him an interminable conversation between two of the actors, who
were leading up to a fight, he broke in with :

" Hold hard, gentlemen. Here's a deal of cackle without any

good in it. I'll show you how to cut it : YOU say, 'Yield thee Englishman'—then YOU say 'Never.' Then YOU say, 'Obstinate Englishman, you die.' Then you both fights. There, that settles the matter. The audience will understand you a deal better, and the poor 'osses won't catch cold while you're jawing ! "

In 1832, Ducrow engaged a lion and tigress out of a menagerie, also some zebras, and arranged a bull-fight wherein he was the Matador and the bull was probably a disguised horse. He was a clever rope-dancer, an accomplishment he had perhaps learned from his father, Peter Ducrow. On one occasion, he was not satisfied with the performance of another dancer, and got on the rope himself in dressing-gown and slippers to show him how to do it.

His Ringmaster was Widdicomb, who had previously been Ring-master at a Circus in Vauxhall Gardens and had also appeared at the Coburg as the " lover " in the Harlequinade when Grimaldi was there. There was another Widdicomb (Henry) at Astley's with Ducrow. He became a successful actor in the Legitimate, travelled with Charles Dillon for some time and for twelve years was in Shepherd's company at the old Surrey. He is better known to a later generation of playgoers as acting with Fechter at the Lyceum in the sixties—Craigenfeldt in " The Master of Ravens-wood," Gravedigger in " Hamlet," Ramponneau in " The King's Butterfly " (a play written round the Pompadour), etc. He died in 1868. There was yet another Widdicomb (Fred) whose career I have not been able to trace.

Ducrow married, *en secondes noces*, a Miss Woolford, a member of the Circus troupe—another example of how the circus, like the more legitimate theatre, runs in families. It has been said that wherever there is a circus there is a Cook and a Woolford, and the same might be said of many another name.

In 1838, trained wild animals were the rage. Van Ambergh, the greatest wild beast trainer ever seen, was at Astley's. Carter, a lion tamer, drove a lion in harness in a drama specially written for him, but there must have been many " fakes," for when we read of a " Brazilian Tiger " we may be pretty sure that it is a leopard or some such beast from South America where real tigers are unknown.

Astley's was burned down for the third time in 1841, and it is said that Ducrow died from the shock. He passed away in 1842, and Batty, a very experienced Circus proprietor, hastened home to secure the right of rebuilding the house for himself ; he ran it for eight or nine years most successfully, dying worth half a million pounds. Under his direction, Ring Dramas and spectacles took on a more definite shape, " The Wandering Jew " was one of these with Van Ambergh as Monk, the wild beast tamer, with real wild beasts. Another was " The White Maiden of California " by Fitzball, in which there was a most effective scene of a cavern where the hero is lying asleep. The ghosts of the dead Indian Chiefs buried in the cavern arise from the ground mounted on cream-coloured horses, both riders and horses being trained to remain perfectly still as statues.

Clowns at this period were Wallett (known as the " Queen's Jester ") who dressed the part in a tunic heraldically designed and carried a fool's bauble, and Barry, who often drove down to the theatre in a tub on wheels drawn by a flock of geese. Grimaldi was here sometimes when his father lived in Stangate close by.

After Batty's death, Astley's was taken by William Cooke. Either he or a later director (E. T. Smith) was the inventor of matinées. There was a good deal of opposition to these at first, led by John Oxenford, who declared that morning performances would reduce all theatres to the level of Penny Gaffs. Though equestrian dramas of a sort had long been a feature of establishments like Astley's, Cooke was the first to give them the special prominence that so much increased their popularity. His great ambition was to do all the plays of Shakespeare in the form of equestrian dramas, and he certainly did good business with " Macbeth," " Richard III " and others.

The most remarkable points about these Ring Dramas were blood, thunder and noise in general. The humble British tar or soldier was set to fight with savage chiefs and tyrants of all sorts, to rescue British beauty in distress, to fight always against the most impossible odds and, needless to say, always to come out " top dog ! " " The Cataract of the Ganges " in which Ducrow had first attracted the attention of Davis the Astley's manager, was one of the spectacles produced at the Amphitheatre, and there must have been something really attractive in this farrago of adventure, for it was again brought to light at Drury Lane in 1873 with a cast including Edith Stuart, Charlotte Saunders, Rignold, J. C. Cowper and others.

Great Battles were produced on the stage at Astley's as soon as intelligence of their happening had reached the enterprising manager. The Battle of Waterloo was, perhaps inevitably, the favourite. In this an actor named Gomersal impersonated both Wellington and Napoleon. He was considered the very image of the French Emperor, a fact which you may remember was noted by Colonel Newcome when he took Clive to the theatre. On one occasion, when business had not been very good, only one horse was available for both Napoleon and Wellington. This did not really matter very much, as they never appeared in the Ring at the same time ; but in the second scene, when Wellington entered, mounted on the same horse which Napoleon had ridden in the first scene, a voice from the gallery called out " And where did you get that horse, please ? " Gomersal did not lose his head. In the third scene he entered on foot, to harangue his army and thank them for their valiant deeds. He made a great speech and wound up as follows :

" But what I am most proud of in ye is that, by the prowess of your glorious arms, ye have rescued from the hated thraldom of the bloodthirsty British soldiery my favourite charger, who has so many occasions carried me, and ye, to victory."

Then he produced the solitary horse amid thunders of applause, and, in the character of Napoleon, retained the animal for the rest of the evening. Gomersal, on the strength of his likeness to the Emperor, also took part in other " Battle Plays " dealing with the Napoleonic campaigns of which the favourite, perhaps, was " The Burning of Moscow," as it lent itself so much to spectacular efforts.

At the time of the Crimean War, these " Battle Plays " came once more to the front. One of these was " The Battle of the Alma." Princes Mentschikoff and Gortschakoff were the chief characters on the Russian side. They were represented as living in luxury and eating tallow. The Allied Army was, to all intents and purposes, commanded by a British sailor and a French *vivandière*, and there was a comic correspondent always in danger of being shot. The final scene of all was invariably arranged for the Ring itself. Russian Cossacks and English Dragoons exchanged a few sword cuts : then the Cossacks dropped from their horses dead, and the audience burst into loud cheering to the waving of Union Jacks, the singing of " Rule Britannia," the burning of plenty of red fire and groans for all the dead enemies.

The last of these military *pièces d'occasion* was probably one on the Abyssinian Campaign with Lord Napier of Magdala as the chief character. After military dramas dealing with British victories, the most popular kind of equestrian show in the Ring was that dealing with highwaymen of immortal memory. " Dick Turpin's Ride to York," " Claude Duval " and other Gentlemen of the Road formed admirable subjects for equestrian dramas. In the first production of " Dick Turpin " the Luke Rookwood was a Mr. Cartlich (afterwards the first Mazeppa) ; Widdicomb, Sir Ranulph Rookwood ; Mrs. Pope, Sybil ; while the part of Dolly

Gudgeon was taken by a Miss Goward, who might or might not have been that very Miss Goward who blossomed into Mrs. Keeley.

" Dick Turpin " is probably still to be met with in provincial Circuses (I came across it not so many years ago), but I fancy " Claude Duval " is a Ring Drama entirely of the past.   A still more popular show was " Mazeppa or the Wild Horse of Tartary," founded on Byron's poem published in 1819.   This was first given at Astley's in 1831, the title rôle being played by Cartlich, the *jeune premier* for all the Ring Dramas.   Cartlich had been with the original Richardson's Show and Richardson had left him a legacy in recognition of the bold way in which he shouted out the attractions from the platform outside.

He was therefore well qualified to mouth and rant and bring out the full force of the tragedy.   With him as the King of Tartary was Gomersal, who has had the distinction of being mentioned by name in the Bon Gaultier Ballads.   The Drolinski was Paul Herring, a recruit from the old Albert Saloon at Hoxton and afterwards a very famous pantomimist.   Other male Mazeppas were Yates, John Henderson, James Holloway, Thomas Moffatt, Henry Powell, Walter Roberts and Charles Mortimer.

The spectacle of " Mazeppa " was adapted from the poem by the stock author of the theatre, one H. H. Milner.   The poem itself had been based on a story (perhaps apocryphal) told by Voltaire in his History of Charles XII of Sweden.   A Press puff of the period says :

" Mazeppa has found his way to the stage with the accompaniment of appropriate scenery, alternately savage and splendidly gorgeous processions, dress, decorations, &c. : gallant knights and ladies fair : banquets, tournaments and real horses.   The story has been considerably varied and amplified to bring these powerful auxiliaries into play, and an imposing spectacle is the result."

For more than thirty years, male Mazeppas held the stage.   Then in the early sixties, when Astley's was under the management of E. T. Smith, the first female representative of the Tartar Prince appeared.   This was that extraordinary personality, Adah Isaacs Menken, as she was always called, though her in and out marriages (and consequent divorces) were so numerous and so uncertain, that one never could say exactly by what name she should be legally addressed at any given moment.

The story of Adah Isaacs Menken is one of the most romantic and one of the saddest in the world, and I am tempted to stray aside for a page or two from the account of Astley's as a theatre to note

ADAH ISAACS MENKEN AS "MAZEPPA"
From a photograph by C. Reutlinger, Paris

MAZEPPA BOUND TO THE WILD HORSE
From a coloured print in " Dramatic Tales and Romances

WYCH STREET:—DRURY LANE

From a print in the Crace Collection

some of the incidents that went to make up her chequered career. For some of the facts I am much indebted to a little brochure by Mr. Northcott, the present archivist of the Royal Italian Opera, who has collected most interesting information with regard to the life of this unhappy woman.   Other facts in this connection I have obtained from an old friend of mine who knew her personally and admired her exceedingly.

She has been the subject of much controversy, many people, like my old friend, maintaining that she was a pure-minded, highly gifted woman, who has been maligned by the whole world, and others that she was very much the reverse.   Highly gifted she certainly was, for to a large extent she was self-educated, but it is now generally conceded that she was a very inferior actress and that the attraction which drew such large audiences was chiefly due to her beauty and to the sensational plays or spectacles in which she freely displayed a magnificent figure.

Some time in the early thirties of the last century, there was in Newcastle Street, Strand (now swept away by the devastating Kingsway), a dealer in second-hand clothes who had an assistant in his shop of the name of James McCord, a man of Irish descent.   This McCord emigrated to the United States and settled as a " general merchant " (for which you may read " Old Clo " man) in the little town of Chartrain in Louisiana, now known as Milneburg. Here he married a Creole, and by her had two daughters and a son, the last named dying an infant.   The elder of the girls, born in 1835, was christened Dolores Adios.   She was the Adah Isaacs Menken of the future.   Mrs. McCord, left a widow, married a Dr. Campbell of the American Army, who interested himself in the education of the two girls.   Dolores must have been a sort of Infant Phenomenon, for she is said to have translated the Iliad into French when only twelve years old, and knew English and Spanish as well, though French was her native tongue, as is generally the case with the people of Louisiana.

The two sisters made their first appearance on the stage in a ballet in New Orleans, where Dolores called herself Bertha Theodore.   She then was engaged as *prima ballerina* at a theatre in Havana.   Leaving the stage for a time, she is heard of as a teacher of Spanish and English in a young ladies' school, but one cannot imagine her a success in such a rôle, and, in fact, she gave it up soon afterwards and joined a travelling circus under the renowned Victor Franconi.

In 1853, as yet only 18 years of age, she was *première danseuse* at the Opera House, Mexico City, and appeared in " Giselle," a famous ballet that Théophile Gautier and Adolphe Adam wrote between them for Carlotta Grisi, sister of the great prima donna, Giulia Grisi. We next find this extraordinary young woman taking a holiday and hunting wild buffalo in Texas. Here she had adventures indeed, for she was captured by Indians and narrowly escaped becoming the squaw of the Chief. She managed to get away and was taken care of by General Harvey at Austin (Texas). He, by the way, was grandfather of Minnie Palmer of " My Sweetheart " fame.

Dolores McCord then settled for a time in New Orleans and tried a career in journalism and literature. Here she met the man who was to be her first husband—she had four or five altogether. He was a Jew by the name of Menken, who had given her music lessons. I think there is no doubt it was purely a love match, and they were married at Galveston. She went so far as to become a Jewess, in which religion she remained faithful to her death, and moreover, though she changed her husband more often than most women do, she retained the name of Menken throughout her life, using as a first name Adah—a corruption of Adios—perhaps a Jewish form of it.

But, of all women, she was not one to be governed. Her very exotic and highly strung temperament prevented her from knuckling under to anyone. Menken reproved her for smoking cigarettes and she left him—loving him deeply all the time.

After this, she took to the legitimate business, and at the New Orleans theatre appeared as Bianca in that most doleful of all tragedies, the " Fazio " of Milman. It was an enormous success, but Menken could not continue in the same groove for any length of time, so she took up male parts for a change—Robert Macaire, Rob Roy, Jack Sheppard and the like. Then she turned once again to serious tragedy and played Lady Macbeth to the Macbeth of James Murdoch. But this was a dismal failure, so she switched off at once to a new career, becoming a model for a sculptor at Columbus (Ohio). In September, 1858, Menken, her husband, got a divorce for " incompatibility of temper and desertion " and she promptly took another spouse in the person of one John Carmel Heenan, the prize-fighter known as " The Benicia Boy," the same who fought the historic fight with Sayers. They seem to have been married at an inn, but there was not enough money between them to live upon, so she went back to the stage, appearing as Juliana in " The Honeymoon " in New York, followed by an essay as Lady Teazle, in which she failed badly.

In 1861, her chance came at last. Some impresario conceived the brilliant idea of exploiting her magnificent figure as Mazeppa in that version of Byron's poem by one Milner, but boiled down and altered to suit an American audience.   This had first seen the light, as noted above, in London at Astley's in 1831, with Cartlich a male Mazeppa, and it had also been given in New York in 1833, but always with a man in the title rôle.

Menken came out at Albany (New York) and she was undoubtedly the first female Mazeppa, though she was followed by innumerable ladies who were possessed of the requisite figure.

Ill-treated by Heenan, she got a divorce from him in the State of Indiana, though she had somewhat anticipated this by marrying in the State of New York her third husband, the humorist, Robert Newell, who wrote under the pseudonym of Orpheus C. Kerr. This matrimonial venture turned out no better than the others, and on her return to the States, after her first visit to England, he easily obtained a divorce.

Orpheus C. Kerr and his writings are now forgotten, though at one time the popularity of the *Orpheus C. Kerr Papers* in England warranted an issue of a cheap yellow back edition.   He was a Satirist of the time of the Civil War (1860—1865) a Northerner and used to laugh at the War much as one American statesman of the time did, who declared at a Public Meeting (when the War was barely half through) that it had been so far " a gigantic frolic for the North."   The *Orpheus C. Kerr Papers*, the work by which he is best known, was a series of satirical letters to imaginary people.   He did, though perhaps unintentionally, achieve a certain success in unmasking the frightful venality, corruption and incapacity of practically every public Department.   He accused the United States Administration of the Army of being a scheme of systematic peculation and the officers of habitual drunkenness.   A single specimen of his " wit " may suffice.   He describes a lady of the Confederate side in lurid colours with no veneer of politeness or regard for her sex :

" Madam, if sandwiches are not plenty where you come from, it is not from want of tongue."   The wife of the Southern Confederacy swept from the room.   She frowned at every Federal she passed, except one picket.   She had detected him in the act of admiring her ankles as she picked her way through the mud. " Woman, my dear boy, has really many sweet qualities, and if her head is sometimes in the wrong, she has always a reserve of feminine goodness in the neighbourhood of her gaiters."

Rather poor stuff, I think ! and I searched in vain for something better.   What could Menken have possibly seen in this man to marry him ?   Her personal sympathies should have been, one would think, with the South, but, somehow, she could not help taking a husband when one offered himself for the post, though it was rather unfortunate for her that she did not always take the trouble to ascertain if her previous husband was still alive !

In 1862, she was at the Bowery Theatre in New York in various male parts such as Tom in "Tom and Jerry," Richmond in a hash-up of " Richard III " etc. After performing for a time in Sam Francisco, she sailed for England in 1864. It must have been a very strenuous life, for there were no facilities for transport as there are in these days, and it meant long weeks of travelling from one point of the vast Continent to another. It probably suited her temperament, restless individual that she was—never happy in one place for long.

In London, she was taken over by E. T. Smith, who, among his other accomplishments, was an adept at advertisement. When he realized that he had a little gold mine in Menken, he boomed his venture for all it was worth, placarding the town with huge posters showing a representation of an apparently naked woman bound to the back of a wild horse tearing its way among stark precipices and over gloomy mountains. He managed to excite the curiosity of all London, who flocked to Astley's to see what it was really like. Menken, though she appeared to be quite nude, was in reality clothed from head to foot in close-fitting, flesh-coloured tights. She was, however, meant to represent a nude figure, and the illusion was so complete, and her figure so perfect, even behind the scenes, that James Fernandez, acting with her once, pinched her leg to see if it was real or " made up," for which impertinence he received a sharp cut from her whip. By all accounts, she was a very beautiful woman, but not in the least like a man in her figure and could never have passed for one, however dressed. As an actress, she was of no account. Her performances were never discussed from the point of view of good or bad acting, but always with reference to her appearance, and to the amount of clothes she actually wore on the stage. It may be said that, in England at any rate, she was never given a chance to show what she could really do in the way of acting. She appeared in various characters, generally male ones, such as William in " Black Eyed Susan," Léon in "The Child of the Sun," and others, but had always to return to Mazeppa, and it is as Mazeppa she will ever be remembered. Other ladies in the rôle, including the American productions as well, were Addie Anderson, Charlotte Crampton (said to be also a very good Hamlet), Kate Fisher, Maude Forrester (" with her celebrated horse Lightning "), Len Hudson (killed by her horse slipping), Oceana Judah, Kate Raymond, Amy Sheridan,

Kate Vance, Lisa Weber, Fanny Burgoyne (at the Olympic ; she also fell from her horse on one occasion), Josephine Fiddes, Lisa Crook, and Florence Temple.   The last-named in America once rode a rather docile, coal-black steed.   This animal was most unfortunately at once recognized by a member of the audience, who brutally called out :   " Where's the hearse ? "

Menken had many understudies of the part at Astley's.   One was Ada Murray, selected on account of her resemblance to the original.   Miss Murray made a more personal name for herself as Virginie in " Drink " produced by Walter Gooch for Charles Warner at the Princess's.   When Josephine Fiddes (Mrs. Dominick Murray) appeared as Mazeppa at Astley's in 1878, the theatre was under the management of Miss Virginia Blackwood, a showy actress in her way and a very experienced manageress who well knew the value of bold advertisement.   She issued a printed appeal to the audience, beseeching them to restrain their very natural excitement when the horse dashed up the " Mountains," lest too loud applause should excite the animal, and endanger the life of the rider :   for the horse was said to be a wild black steed " imported direct from the Ukraine " for the purpose   This was realism with a vengeance, for it will be remembered that the scene of the original poem is laid in the Ukraine.   The story compares well with that of the conscientious actor who blacked himself all over to play Othello.

Contrariwise, as Tweedledum might say, a rumour got about that one of Mazeppa's horses was an ex-bus-horse, who was so accustomed to the ways of his old driver that it nightly refused to start on its wild career till it had heard the familiar " gee-up " and the knock of a heel on the footboard !   But this tale may be one of the *ben trovato* kind.

When Menken made her first appearance as Mazeppa, she had in her company Sam Emery (father of the late Mrs. Cyril Maude) as Abder Khan, and Edward Atkins, a very funny actor who was popular in the annual pantomimes.   Milano arranged the ballets and the musical director was the ubiquitous James Tully, once of the Bower Saloon and other Minor Theatres and later of Drury Lane.   It has been asserted that the late Miss Kate Santley was also in the cast, but that little lady always declared that she was not old enough to remember it !   James Fernandez was certainly in the bill, about his last appearance prior to his triumphant debut at the West End.

Added to her other drawbacks, Menken spoke English with a foreign accent, and was without the talent of a Celeste or a Béatrice to compensate for it.   Her temper was a very violent one.   She never hesitated to give way to it, if provoked by anger or jealousy, and jealousy was perhaps her besetting fault. On one occasion she recognized in a private box a man against whom she harboured a grudge, and, not being wanted for a short interval on the stage, made her way to the front of the house with a dagger intending to do him some mortal injury. E. T. Smith only appeared just in time to prevent a catastrophe and send her back to the coulisses.

At intervals, when not acting at Astley's, she travelled the provinces with Ginnett's Circus, doing Mazeppa and other horsy plays, and she also did her great part at the Pavilion (the Drury Lane of the East End) at Sadler's Wells and at Liverpool. It was at Sadler's Wells she made her final stage appearance in London in May, 1868.

Soon after her successful introduction to London playgoers, Menken went for a holiday to Paris and there made great friends with Dumas the elder and with Théophile Gautier. In England she gained the friendship, if nothing more, of a number of prominent men of the day. Dickens, Swinburne, Thackeray, Robert Reece, John Oxenford and the pseudo-parson, Bellew, were among those who delighted to fête her, and when not acting she was a notable figure at first nights and other dramatic and social gatherings. She was seen at that never-to-be-forgotten first performance of Reade's " It's Never too Late to Mend," when the audience rose in violent protest against the brutalities of the prison scene.

Charles Reade, author of the play, knew her well, and records in his Diary that she was " a clever woman with beautiful eyes ; bad actress ; made hit playing Mazeppa in tights ; goodish heart."

In 1866, she returned to New York to do Mazeppa again there. On this visit, she married James Paul Barclay, a Wall Street broker, and settled down for a time in a house of her own, which she named " Bleak House " in compliment to Charles Dickens. Barclay, who is said to have spent thirty thousand pounds on her, left her after two or three months, and was found dead—and penniless—in Philadelphia.

Back in Europe again, she came out in Paris at the Châtelet Theatre in an exciting melodrama called " Les Pirates de la Savanne," in which she had a good opportunity of showing off her figure as a male character in a picturesque Mexican get-up. It ran for a hundred nights, and she also did other parts at the same theatre ; but Mazeppa was her *cheval de bataille*, to which she reverted, sooner or later, in every engagement. Her story seems to have always possessed a mysterious fascination for students of femininity, but there does not appear to have been much mystery about her.

She was a woman of great charm, but also of an extraordinary temperament, always craving for some kind of excitement and restless for change. She was an inveterate smoker at a time when hardly any woman smoked at all, and had to be followed about at Astley's by an attendant with a tray for the discarded cigarette ends. She drank heavily of champagne and brandy, and perhaps for this reason appeared on the stage as Mazeppa less often than was supposed, as she had an understudy always available.

After her death, a small volume of poems of very unequal merit called *Infelicia* appeared, and it will always be a matter of keen controversy whether she wrote them or not. The book was dedicated to Charles Dickens, who sent her the following note :

DEAR MISS MENKEN,

I shall have great pleasure in accepting your dedication, and I thank you for your portrait as a highly remarkable specimen of photography. I also thank you for the verses enclosed in your note. Many such enclosures come to me, but few so pathetically written, and fewer still so modestly sent.

Faithfully yours,

CHARLES DICKENS.

A characteristic note from one of the vainest of men who was never without a supreme consciousness of his own worth, and of the condescension it behoved him to show to lesser lights.

Swinburne was credited with the authorship of some or all of the poems in *Infelicia*, but he strenuously denied he was responsible for any. It was said of them, that some were good enough to be by him, and some were bad enough to be by anybody ! Thomson, Swinburne's private secretary, edited the book for publication. He was Dramatic Critic of *The Weekly Dispatch* and wrote of her : " I worshipped the very ground she trod on, for she was the noblest as well as the most gifted woman I have ever known."

Swinburne called her his Dolores, described her as " The World's Delight," and wrote in her album :

> Combien de temps, dis, la belle,
> Dis, veux-tu m'être fidèle ?
> Pour une nuit—pour un jour
> Mon Amour.
> L'Amour nous flatte et nous touche
> Du doigt, de l'œil, de la bouche—
> Pour un jour, pour une nuit—
> Et s'enfuit.

George Moore translated the lines as follows :

" How long canst thou be
Faithful ? " she said to me
" For one night and a day
Mistress I may."
Love flatters us with sighs,
And kisses on mouth and eyes
For a day and a night
Before his flight.

The Saturday Review called the book " an amusing little book by a distinguished woman," but another paper said it was a pathetic little volume.

The late Clement Scott, the critic, waxes enthusiastic about Menken. He calls her " an extraordinary woman with a soul, and really of great refinement of nature," and goes on to say, " I have seen some of her love letters and they were very beautiful." And then he prints a copy of one which he thinks is worth preserving as descriptive of this curious artistic nature. It runs as follows :

Cataldi's, 42, Dover Street,
Friday, a.m.

To-day, Roberto, I should like to see you if you are good-tempered and think you could be bored with me and my ghosts. They will be harmless to you, these ghosts of mine : they are sad, soft-footed things that wear my brain, and live on my heart—that is, the fragment I have left to be called heart. Apropos of that, I hear you are married—I am glad of that : I believe all good men should be married. Yet I don't believe in women being married. Somehow, they all sink into nonentities after this epoch in their existence. That is the fault of female education. They are taught from their cradles to look upon marriage as the one event of their lives. That accomplished, nothing remains. However, Byron might have been right after all : " Man's love is of his life a thing apart : 'tis woman's whole existence." If this is true, we do not wonder to find so many stupid wives—they are simply doing the " whole existence " kind of thing. Good women are rarely clever, and clever women are rarely good. I am digressing into mere twaddle from what I started out to say to you. Come when you can get time, and tell me of our friends, the gentle souls of air : mine fly from me only, to fill my being with the painful remembrance of their ost love for me—even me ! once the blest and chosen. Now a royal tigress waits in her lonely jungle, the coming of the king of forests. Brown gaiters not excluded.

Yours, through all stages of local degradation,

INFELIX MENKEN.

"Fancy," says Scott, "a woman who played Mazeppa in pink silk fleshings, and married a prize fighter, writing like this to relieve her 'soul '—and she had one ! "

> Where is the promise of my years
>   Once written on my brow !
> Ere errors, agonies and fears
> Brought with them all that speaks in tears,
> Ere I had sunk beneath my peers,
>   Where sleeps that promise now ?

> Myself ! Alas, for theme so poor.
>   A theme but rich in Fear,
> I stand a wreck on Error's shore,
> A spectre not within the door,
> A homeless shadow evermore,
>   An exile lingering here.

"Here we have the cry of the heart of a wounded woman." Thus Clement Scott, with perhaps a little exaggeration, from which he was often not free. Many will agree with him, but the facts of Menken's life are at hand for any to read and each will form his own opinion on them. I would sooner leave the judgment in the hands of the men than of the women. No woman would have any mercy on such as Adah Isaacs Menken.

In 1868, she must have felt that the end was not far off, and, like the wild animal she really was, hid herself in a corner of Paris to die. She knew that she was in the last stage of consumption and suffered in addition from a malignant abscess in her side.

Forgotten, and almost in want, she lingered on in a shabby lodging in the Rue Caumartin near the stage door of the Théatre Porte St. Martin, and there she died on August 1st, 1868, being only thirty-three years of age. As her end approached, she refused all food, and lived on iced water. Her last moments were peaceful, and she died in the religion she had adopted—that Jewish Faith which was also the Faith of her first husband, the only one of the number she had really loved. She was buried at Père-la-Chaise, but afterwards removed to Mont Parnasse. On her funeral stone, two words only : " Thou knowest."

Dumas is said to have been much affected by her death, saying, " Poor girl, why was she not her own friend ? " a silly remark which might be made of any one of us.

But I must get back to Astley's. I have gone too far ahead in order to get together all the facts about the old play, and in so doing was tempted to linger over the career of the greatest of all Mazeppas whether male or female.

In 1862, a year or two before Menken drew all London across the water, and made the old sawdust house quite a resort *à la mode*, Dion Boucicault had tried, and failed, to do something of the same kind. He changed the name of the famous old House to the " New Westminster Theatre Royal " (forgetting, perhaps, that it was not in Westminster at all) almost entirely rebuilt it, added a row of comfortable stalls, placed a garden and fountain in front of the orchestra and projected an open-air café on the roof. This latter part of the plan did not, however, materialize. There was a great flourish of trumpets, as was always the case with everything this hot-headed Irishman did, or tried to do. He was going to reform London theatres from floor to ceiling : the seats were to be all comfortable ; the refreshments were to be of the best ; everything was to be modelled on the American style. Somehow or other, it did not come off, though it cannot be denied that Boucicault was instrumental in bringing about, in the course of time, many much needed reforms.

The opening night was Boxing Day 1862, and the piece was a dreadfully dreary pantomime called " Ladybird : or Harlequin Lord Dundreary." How anyone so well versed in theatrical ways could imagine for a moment that Dundreary was the fitting subject for a pantomime is beyond comprehension. There was plenty of talent in the cast. Edith Stuart (afterwards an excellent dramatic artist) ; Miss Cushnie, a first-rate dancer, as Columbine ; and Huline, a member of a family of pantomimists (whose name is still to be met with on the Variety Stage) as Clown. But it failed, as it deserved, and in January 1863 Boucicault put on a version of Scott's " Heart of Mid-Lothian," which he called " The Trial of Effie Deans." In the cast of this play there were many well-known names. Two Vandenhoffs, Tom Swinbourne (afterwards the King to Irving's Hamlet), Dewar (the Captain Crosstree of the Royalty " Black Eyed Susan "), Rose Leclercq as Madge Wildfire and Boucicault as the Counsel for the Defence. It was no good, so Boucicault gave up in despair the self-imposed, and totally unnecessary task of trying to convert old Astley's into a fashionable West End theatre.

Shortly afterwards the theatre resumed its original name of " Hashley's " and came under the dominion of E. T. Smith— perhaps the most wonderful and indefatigable impresario of all time, not even excepting Barnum himself. He was the son of an Admiral Smith, was born in 1804, and was originally intended for the Royal Navy, being actually appointed midshipman on Lord Cochrane's ship. A fond mother, however, could not let him go, and managed to fetch him back just before the vessel sailed.

He was early in life a policeman, then an auctioneer, and then turned his attention to speculation of all kinds. It is absolutely incredible to think over all the things that he did, the theatres he took, the Shows he managed, the businesses he set on foot.

He turned Crockford's gaming saloons into a fashionable restaurant, which he called the " Wellington "—it is now the Devonshire Club. He had an interest in Vauxhall Gardens. He ran the Marylebone Theatre for a time and, subsequently, Drury Lane (in 1853), which he opened with " Uncle Tom's Cabin " and a pantomime on the subject of Hudibras ! G. V. Brooke, Charles Mathews, the Keans and other celebrated artistes appeared under his management, and he shares with Cooke the tradition of having invented matinées. He was the real founder of the Alhambra, the building of which had previously been opened with a sort of pseudo-scientific entertainment (something like the Polytechnic) and brought over Leotard and other foreign performers, though he bought it ostensibly to open it as a Sunday show with sermons and sacred music ! He leased Her Majesty's (the old Opera House) and organized Italian Opera with such singers as Titiens, Giuglini and Piccolomini. He managed Cremorne from 1861 to 1869 and tried to get up a Tournament in imitation of the Eglinton fiasco. He ran the Lyceum for two years about the same time. From 1863 or 1864 he was at Astley's. Later, he had the Surrey and the rather disreputable Highbury Barn Gardens with the accompanying Alexandra Theatre, and also the Regent Music Hall in Westminster. He opened the Cremorne Supper Rooms in Leicester Square, and the Radnor at the corner of Chancery Lane and High Holborn, and a dining hall in the basement of the Royal Exchange, for which he engaged as barmaid the beautiful Alice Rhodes, who was condemned to death for the Penge murder, though afterwards she was pardoned.

It may be said that Edward Tyrrell Smith was a showman who never refused to consider any kind of show that promised to have money in it. All was fish that came to his net. He mixed up his artistes in the oddest way. He got hold of comedians like Charles Mathews, tragedians like Brooke, leading ladies like Miss Glyn,

Chinese Conjurors, or the " Man-fly " that crawled on the ceiling, and would put them all into the same programme if he could.   It has been said that he was capable of alternating Rachel with a circus clown.   He did actually try to introduce Sayers and Heenan, the sensational prize-fighters, to the audience at Her Majesty's, between the acts of the Opera, but was dissuaded and brought them on the Alhambra stage instead.   But he was clever enough and his *flair* for good advertisement was extraordinary.   He had Sala in the chair at a dinner when he started the Alhambra as a going concern, and always did the right thing and engaged the right people when initiating a new scheme.   He might have been more successful from a financial point of view if he had not attempted so much at once ; but as was truly said : " No human being is capable of running three or four theatres, an Opera, a Circus, a Tavern or two, and various other business propositions at one and the same time, without making a failure of some or all of them."   To that list might be added Cremorne Gardens, an undertaking in itself.

He was essentially a great caterer for all classes of *noceurs*, whether of the class that loved to make late nights at Cremorne and have supper at the Leicester Square Supper Rooms afterwards, or those who patronized the humbler but equally disreputable Highbury Barn.   He died in 1877, an old man, forgotten and almost in poverty, an easy prey for the self-sufficient preachers of the day, who moralized at length on the inevitable end of one who had so largely administered to the requirements of the ungodly !   These pious people, perhaps, did not know, or more likely chose to forget that he had befriended and restarted in life hundreds of persons who, without him, would have been lost indeed.   Yet of the crowd he had so helped barely half a dozen went to his funeral.

I have been tempted to digress rather at length on the career of this, the greatest impresario London has ever known, whose life must have been so full of interest, but who has been so completely forgotten.   This was the man who was running Astley's when Menken made her first sensational appearance.

But Astley's was not always given over to sensations.   In 1870, Phelps was there in " Othello " supported by Hermann Vezin as Iago, and that fine actress Mrs. Hermann Vezin (previously known as Mrs. Charles Young) as Desdemona.   Before that, in 1868, a Miss Agnes Cameron had put on the stage a version of Disraeli's novel *Alarcos*, which seems to have been a dismal failure.   The hopes and instructions of the author were that it was to be magnificently mounted.   The scene representing the interior of Burgos Cathedral was to be lit up brilliantly, Mass was to be going on at several side chapels and confessionals in full working order. The scene of an interior of a *posada*, or wine-shop, was to be full of life, bravoes gambling and gipsies dancing. Instead of which, the interior of the Cathedral was represented by a back-cloth showing a street scene and confessionals stuck out into the street. Charles Verner, a known actor of the day, played Alarcos. The directress of the theatre, Miss Agnes Cameron, was an American of some note in her own country, but it was the poorest production ever seen, and it must indeed have been a most bitter disappointment to poor Disraeli whose ideas were so grandiose.

Two years previous to the production of " Alarcos," there was a play founded on Miss Braddon's famous novel, *Lady Audley's Secret*, called " The Mysteries of Audley Court," and in 1867 there was one on Dickens's *Hard Times*, bearing the sensational title of " Under the Earth : or the Sons of Toil."

Sometimes more money was spent on the *décor* and general mounting. In 1868, when the last of the great battle plays was produced— " The Conquest of Magdala : and the Fall of Theodore "—there were real Grenadier Guards engaged for the soldiers, and the Naval Brigade was represented by a charming *corps de ballet* of ladies, who danced a hornpipe. On the other hand, the costumes used on this occasion were some left over from a production of Boucicault's " Colleen Bawn," which must have fitted rather oddly with the Abyssinian play. Once in 1874, Miss Ellen Terry acted at Astley's. This was when Charles Reade took his company from the Queen's, Long Acre, to play " The Wandering Heir." In this Miss Terry played her old part of Philippa Chester : she also played Susan Merton, the heroine of another of Reade's plays, " It's Never Too Late to Mend." Three years prior to that, however, Astley's *revenait à ses premiers amours*, Sanger having opened it once more as a Circus and playhouse combined. It was actually under their direction till the end, though not always used as a Circus. The interior was remodelled and improved, and " Mazeppa " was revived in 1872 with Marie Henderson as the Cossack chief.

The Sangers ran Astley's chiefly in the winter, touring the country with their circus in the summer. As in most other theatres of the day, at Christmas there was always a pantomime, generally preceded by " Scenes in the Ring," but the Ring was also available for spectacles that partook of the nature of plays supplemented by horsemanship and arena effects. It was, in short, run something on the old lines followed by Batty and Cooke. For example, in 1878, a great spectacle was produced called " Fair Rosamond : or the Days of the Plantagenets," which was advertised as follows :

SANGERS' GRAND NATIONAL AMPHITHEATRE
(LATE ASTLEY'S)

The proprietors do publicly challenge the entire profession to equal the exciting and effective scenes of the Battle of Bridgenorth ! !

Sounds almost like the flamboyant posters of Astley and Ducrow. The above was produced as the piece immediately before the pantomime, but the " Scenes in the Ring " came first of all in the evening's bill.

It was announced in the papers as Sangers' (late Astley's), and " Sangers " was written up in letters of flaming gas over the door, but it remained " Astley's " to the end in the hearts of all theatrical folk and playgoers. The early cachet of the place was lost, however ; other and smarter circuses had arisen nearer to the West End. It had had its day and the end came (in 1895), when it was the turn of the Westminster Bridge Road to be " improved."

CHAPTER V

IN the reign of Queen Elizabeth, Drury Lane was called "Via de Aldwych," and it got its new name from Drury House, built just before the accession of James I for Sir William Drury, a naval officer.

A trace of the old name survived in Wych Street, one of the narrowest, dirtiest and most disreputable thoroughfares the West End has ever known. This slum began in Drury Lane near the spot where Nell Gwynne would stand, half dressed, to watch the sights of the streets, and it ended in Newcastle Street, a lane nearly as bad, where "Old Clo" shops abounded.

It was altogether a vile neighbourhood with the vilest associations. In a grimy little court, turning out of Wych Street, Jack Sheppard served his apprenticeship to Mr. Wood, the carpenter, and a hundred years later the father of the lovely Adah Isaacs Menken was an assistant in one of the many evil-smelling, disease-propagating dens, where old rags and cast-off finery were sold, which predominated among the shops of the district.

It was full of gabled houses of Tudor days, with richly carved porticoes and mullioned windows—reminders of cleaner and more prosperous times—but it was inhabited by the dregs of the town, the thieves, the informers, the harlots, the go-betweens and the hangers-on of every kind of vice.

In the midst of the stench and filth of this most unsavoury district, the old Olympic raised its head, a very oasis in a desert of foulness, almost hidden in the purlieus of Drury Lane, close to the burial-ground from the gates of which Jo would chase the scurrying rats, and near the spot where Lady Dedlock found her rest at last.

What can be told of this wonderful theatre which, alas, exists no longer? A complete history of it and of the hundred names with which it will ever be associated, would require a whole volume to itself, extending over more than a century of time. By turns, circus, gaff, concert hall, theatre, it saw the triumphs of Philip Astley, of Madame Vestris and her husband, Charles Mathews, of Robson, the great tragi-comic, of the Alfred Wigans, of G. V. Brooke and Helen Faucit and Mrs. Stirling, of Henry Neville in "The Ticket of Leave Man" and other plays, of Nelly Farren's early days, and of scores of actors and actresses in more modern times ; till it was finally swept away to make room for that apotheosis of staring ugliness—Kingsway !

Philip Astley, who had already made a name for himself in the Westminster Bridge Road, built the house early in the nineteenth century and opened it as the Olympic Saloon for horsemanship and kindred shows. In an old Guide, called *The Picture of London*, for 1813, it is included among the "Winter Spectacles," and is called "Astley's Theatre in Newcastle Street," but at the time of the publication of the Guide it had not been completed and the advertisement runs as follows :

"Mr. Astley has lately obtained a licence, through the medium of the Duke of York, to erect a theatre within the city and liberty of Westminster, and has chosen his spot in Wych Street near the Strand, and within a short distance of the two winter theatres, where he has built a house for the exhibition of the same kind of diversions which characterizes the Amphitheatre of Arts."

Astley was, as usual, very clever in obtaining material and labour as cheaply as possible. The framework of the new building (which could have had no pretension to any architectural beauty, being indeed only a sort of gaff) came from the timbers of an old French Seventy-Four called the "Ville de Paris" (generally spoken of as "The Wheel de Parry"). Astley collected workmen from the neighbouring public-houses, made the uprights of the building out of the yards and bowsprit of the ship, the stage of the deck, and the outer walls of sheet iron covered with coarse canvas. He procured a licence through the intervention of the Queen (or the Duke of York) in return for a pair of small ponies which he had trained and presented to the Royal children.

Near the actual site of the Saloon was a disreputable tavern bearing the sign of "The Queen of Bohemia," part of it having been a portion of Craven House, the residence of Elizabeth, Queen of Bohemia, daughter of Charles I, surnamed "The Queen of Hearts." Craven House was, in its turn, built on the site of Drury House (whose owner had been killed in a duel) by Lord Craven soon after the Restoration of Charles II.

I must make a short digression in favour of this Lord Craven, though he has nothing to do with the subject matter of this book. In 1624, he was sixteen years of age and a great favourite with Charles I. He was especially attached to Elizabeth, the daughter of the King, and fought for her rights on the Continent. He did not return to England during the Civil War, being still detained in Germany or Bohemia looking after the Queen's interests. His well-known devotion to the Stuart cause brought about the confiscation of his estates by the Parliament, and among them was his Town residence, Craven House, then situated in the city, near Leadenhall Street. On the restoration of Charles II, he recovered all his property, but sold the City house to the East India Company, whose Headquarters it remained for a long time. Then it was that he bought Drury House and took up his abode in the West End of the Town. He was one of the bravest men that ever lived. During all the time of the Great Plague he never left London, remaining to look after the interests of the soldier guards for whose benefit he built a row of pest-houses in Tothill Street, Westminster. It is said he could never resist going to a fire (in which he resembled Horace Walpole) and his horse was popularly believed to be able to "smell" one at a great distance. In 1670 he was given the command of the Coldstream Guards, and when the Dutch troops at the Revolution advanced to take St. James's Palace he mustered his guards and wished to oppose them by force. He never married, remaining devoted to the Queen of Hearts all his life (there is a tradition that he married her at last, but there is no proof of this) and died in 1697, having lived through five reigns and one of the most troubled periods of English history. I am indebted for these particulars of Lord Craven to a charming account of "The East India Company" by Mr. Foster.

To return to the story of the Olympic. For all his royal patronage, Astley did not make a success of the new Saloon or "Pavilion" as it was sometimes called. Nothing that he could provide in the way of special attractions—horsemanship, burlettas, or prize-fights—would make the public go to the new house. He dropped ten thousand pounds over his venture and then sold it to Elliston, a popular and successful manager at the Surrey and other places. It went for less than three thousand pounds and Elliston opened it as "Little Drury Lane," but the monopoly of the managers of the Patent Theatres was still in force, and their opposition was quickly aroused, for they could not afford to disregard the rivalry of such a popular and well-known manager. Though the Lord Chamberlain closed the theatre, Elliston was not to be beaten. Through friends at Court, he got a fresh licence, and reverted to the name of the Olympic Pavilion as a concession to the pride of the Patentees.

Everything he produced, melodrama, farce, operetta or burlesque, was called a "burletta" (see Chapter III on the East End Theatres), but he sometimes ventured on forbidden ground, as for example in 1818 when he produced Milman's "Fazio"; a dreary tragedy in which many years later Charlotte Cushman made a success.

He was a believer in his own " luck " and confident of overcoming all obstacles.

In 1818, he rebuilt the theatre, engaged a good company for comedy and melodrama, and for the earlier extravaganzas of Planché, and with the profits thus made aspired to still higher things, becoming in 1819 lessee of Drury Lane. Under the terms of his lease, he could not have anything to do with any other theatre, and therefore tried to sell the Olympic Pavilion, but was only able to let it to a company including such well-known names as Dowton, Wrench, Oxberry and Mrs. Chatterley. This was in 1820. Two years later, Oxberry undertook the sole management, but, though he produced " Tom and Jerry " and other popular pieces, no money came in and he closed down rather abruptly. A stage-struck publican of the adjoining public-house, " The Craven Arms," then tried his hand and also failed after great losses.

In the meanwhile, Elliston, having had a most disastrous time at Drury Lane, was sold up, and the Olympic went in the general debacle of his property. It fetched nearly five thousand pounds, the purchaser being Scott, who had built the Sans Pareil Theatre— afterwards the Adelphi. Scott ran melodrama for some time— " The Idiot of the Mountain " and similar pieces—with more or less success. He only opened in the winter months, and one may suppose had some interest at his back which prevented him from being persecuted by the managers of the Patent Theatres. I presume it was run on popular lines, for Pantomime at Christmas was a regular feature and the prices of admission were very low : Boxes 4s. ; Pit 2s. ; Gallery 1s.—with half-price at nine o'clock. Under this management, the theatre was entirely lit with gas for the first time.

Soon after this, in 1830 to be exact, Madame Vestris took the Olympic, and inaugurated the first successful season it had ever had. She could not get any other house, and being fully deter- mined to have a theatre of her own resolved to make a slum-centre the most fashionable rendezvous in the Town.

Lucy Eliza Vestris was the granddaughter of the famous engraver Bartolozzi, and was born in the parish of Marylebone in January, 1797. She was clever from her youth up and was a highly trained musician with a lovely voice, able to sing in English, French and Italian. In 1813, when only sixteen years old, she married Armand Vestris, an opera dancer, the third of the name and grandson of that most conceited dancer of all time, who styled himself " Le Dieu de la Danse."

Armand Vestris was one of the most depraved and dissipated of men. He was twenty-four at the date of the marriage and

THE QUEEN OF BOHEMIA'S PALACE OR CRAVEN HOUSE, IN DRURY LANE; AS IT APPEARED IN THE YEAR 1800.

View of Part of Craven House in Wych Street, The Site of the Olympic Theatre

CRAVEN HOUSE IN 1800
REMAINS OF CRAVEN HOUSE ABOUT 1806
SITE OF THE OLYMPIC THEATRE
From an old print in the British Museum

EXTERIOR OF THE SECOND OLYMPIC THEATRE
From a coloured print in the British Museum

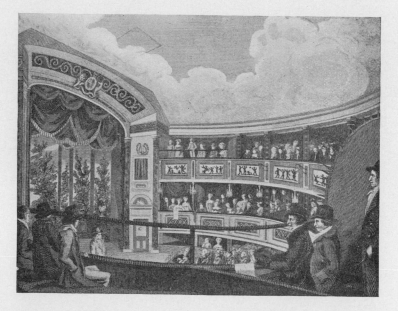

INTERIOR OF THE SECOND OLYMPIC THEATRE
From a coloured print in the British Museum

probably entered into it with the direct idea of profiting by his wife's talent and capacity for earning money as a singer. On her side, there was no pretence of affection, and she perhaps found it more convenient to be a married woman, as her own *affaires de cœur*, beginning at the top with the Prince Regent himself, soon began to make a noise in the world of Fashion.

Through his own position as one of the chief male dancers at the Opera House (or King's Theatre as it was then called) Vestris obtained an engagement for his wife and she appeared with the greatest success in Winter's opera, "Il Ratto di Proserpina."

The earnings of an operatic artiste, however good, were quite unable to keep pace with the extravagance and financial troubles of this choice young blackguard, and he deserted his wife, fleeing to Italy to avoid his creditors and taking with him as travelling companion one of his dancing partners of the opera. His wife was in Paris at that time, and was by no means inconsolable. She at once returned to London with a " protector " in the person of Windham Anstruther, who promised her marriage as soon as she could be divorced from Vestris. He was, however, very short of cash, and found himself unable to keep his word, so Lucy Eliza had to go on the stage again. It was about this time that she appeared as Macheath in " The Beggars' Opera," one of her finest impersonations. Her répertoire was a very large one, for she excelled not only in comedy parts in opera (such as Macheath, Susanna in " Le Nozze di Figaro," and Pippo in " La Gazza Ladra ") but also in the comedies of Shakespeare (Mrs. Ford in " The Merry Wives of Windsor," Rosalind in " As You Like It," Luciana in " The Comedy of Errors "), and in other parts like Lady Teazle, Diana Vernon, Letitia Hardy in " The Belle's Stratagem " ; and even in " The Jealous Wife." She was, perhaps, greatest in what were called " breeches parts," now called " principal boys." She sang the title-rôle in " Fra Diavolo," which is usually given to a baritone or tenor, at the Tottenham Street Theatre (afterwards Prince of Wales's), and in a hotch-potch called " Don Giovanni in London," produced at Drury Lane with enormous success the first night but withdrawn in less than a week. She had her strong likes and dislikes ; among the latter being Velluti, a male soprano for whom Meyerbeer wrote " Il Crociato in Egitto," and she refused to sing in that opera with him. Probably, he bore too strong a likeness in his ways to Armand Vestris, and she knew the breed !

One of her fancies, in which she was not singular, for Braham did the same thing, was to interpolate any song in which she thought herself likely to make a hit in any work no matter what the incongruity.   The most popular of these was " Buy a Broom " and, as the Buy a Broom girl, dressed as a Bavarian peasant, Vestris was painted and modelled and sold everywhere.   The first verse and refrain of the song ran as follows :

" From Deutschland I come with my light wares all laden,
    To dear happy England in summer's gay bloom ;
  Then listen, fair lady, and young pretty maiden,
    O buy of the wandering Bavarian a broom.
      Buy a Broom ! Buy a Broom (spoken).   Buy a broom !
    O buy of the wandering Bavarian a broom.

The popularity of " Buy a Broom " lasted for many years, and I have heard that it was this song with which Nellie Power (principal boy at the Surrey and Vaudeville Theatres for many years) made her debut in 1866 when she sang as a little girl of about twelve years old.

There are many old enough to remember the " Buy a Broom " girls who used to sell brooms in the streets of London with " One for the Lady and one for the Baby," and the sellers were generally dressed up in some peasant-like costume.   " Cherry Ripe " was written for Vestris specially by Charles Horn, and another favourite song of hers was " I'm a-roaming."

There was much excuse for the fast and loose way in which this very charming lady passed her days and nights.   Her mother appears to have been a profligate and unscrupulous woman and Lucy Eliza and her sister (who was as beautiful as herself) were both brought up without the least regard for the moral decencies of life.   Her marriage with the vicious Armand gave her a further excuse for throwing her cap over the windmill and she indulged herself without any restraint.   She was admired by all and commanded as much money and influence as any woman could want ; but when a lady's tastes run to having fresh violets on her table all the year round and roses in her rooms throughout the winter, a very heavy balance at the bankers is a necessity.   She could earn any salary all the year round, and when properly managed as to her business affairs (as seems to have been the case when she was run by a certain Captain Best soon after her husband's flight) all went well ; but she would occasionally take matters into her own hands and the results were most dire.   At one time she practically maintained a young nobleman with whom she was (or thought she was) in love ; and he, being a person of no resources and very little honour, took advantage of her infatuation.   She was blackmailed and had to have recourse to money-lenders and other sources to obtain funds for the payments demanded.

I have already related how she made a success of the dirty old Olympic, attracting the most fashionable audiences in London and making large sums of money which she spent in advance on the extravagant mounting of her pieces. She was not only extravagant in the way she mounted her pieces, but she tried at the same time to have everything on the stage as accurate in all details as could be managed. This accuracy, however, did not extend to her own dresses, for such was her love of jewels and personal adornment that she was often seen in the part of a chambermaid or soubrette in white satin with many diamonds, while her mistress in the play would appear in soiled book muslin.

Accuracy in make-up and costume was not general on the English stage until the advent of the Charles Keans. Macready always dressed the part of Othello in a negro-like wig and a long sort of gown. Fredericks, an actor who was very jealous of his success, when asked for an opinion of Macready's acting as Othello said, " I have nothing to say about his acting, but he *looked* like an elderly negress, of evil repute, going to a fancy ball."

When it is considered that Vestris's husband, Charles Mathews, was equally extravagant, it is easily understood that bankruptcy was the inevitable end. Even her wonderful successes at the Lyceum in the pieces of Planché were not enough to set the improvident couple on their feet—so great was their extravagance. It was indeed unbounded. It is related that she cut up an Indian shawl valued at three hundred guineas because she fancied the pattern of it for a turban in Weber's " Oberon."

Mathews was much younger than his wife, but it is generally agreed that their marriage proved a happy one. When she was lying on her death-bed, he was in prison, and was released to see her for the last time. She was sixty years of age when she died in 1856, but appears to have kept much of her beauty and power of fascination. She was a great authority on dramatic production and was the very first to make real improvements in the manner in which plays of all kinds were put on the stage. It is said that she was a very kind-hearted and charitable woman, giving much away in private charity. An obituary notice of her in *The Era* of the day concludes as follows :

" Of the good she did, of the refined influences that were shed over dramatic art at her instigation, and of the benefit the public and profession have derived in consequence, too little, unfortunately, will be remembered."

A detailed account of her life, with some mention of her numerous amours (including Prince Florizel) will be found in a delightful book written by Mr. Charles Pearce, a skilled biographer of more than one lady, fair and frail, and I can only give a very brief account of the career of this extraordinary woman, who was certainly the first Actress-Manageress, and, moreover, the first to go in for gorgeous mounting and accurate details of stage-furnishing. Whether at the Olympic or later at the Lyceum her productions were always of the highest class. My concern here, however, is only for her doings at the Olympic as the manageress of that theatre.

Her great taste was unquestionable, both as regards arrangements in front of the house and on the stage. The old theatre was re-decorated by Crace in a most gorgeous manner. The painted ceiling represented a silk curtain drawn tight by garlands of flowers held by flying Cupids ; a crystal chandelier hung from the centre ; the proscenium was decorated with wreaths of flowers ; proscenium boxes were introduced in place of the stage doors ; the panels of the dress-circle were adorned with copies of Bartolozzi's works. Such was the elegant theatre that had arisen on the site of Astley's old Pavilion in the Wych Street purlieus. The stage doors alluded to as being formerly in the proscenium were two painted doors like any ordinary street doors with knockers and handles complete, and in my account of the theatre in Wells Street, E. (see Chapter III), I have given some account of their *raison d'être*.

The opening programme of Madame Vestris was what we may call a " Quadruple Bill," as it consisted of four pieces. In those times, the first piece was a farce or a slight musical *lever de rideau*, and the last piece always a farce. No actor or actress of any position would ever consent to " play the audience out " in the farce, so a more or less dull piece was given at the end of the evening, and it did not matter whether you missed it or not.

One of the principal plays at the beginning of Vestris's management was on the subject of " Mary Queen of Scots." This was put on for the appearance of Miss Foote, who appears to have been a partner with Vestris in her Olympic venture. It was well mounted in every way. Real furniture, *i.e.* solid carved oak furniture, carpets, realistic stained glass windows were seen on the stage for the first time, and all stamped with the Royal Stuart Arms. Play-goers have an idea that the earliest sumptuous productions date from the Kean days at the old Princess's and that previous to Kean's management there had been an entire absence of anything like reality in stage appointments. This is by no means the case. At the Olympic and at the Lyceum under Vestris, and to a lesser degree

EXTERIOR OF THE THIRD OLYMPIC THEATRE

From an old Print

AS JACOB EARWIG IN "BOOTS AT THE
SWAN"

AS DADDY HARDAERE

THE "GREAT LITTLE" ROBSON

From photographs by Adolphe Beau

at the Grecian under Rouse, the mounting of plays had been very beautiful as compared with what preceded and what immediately followed them. Vestris spent very large sums on her productions and her taste and Planché's were responsible for spectacles which can only be compared with those of much later days. After her last failure in management, there was a relapse into the carelessness of former times ; the producing of plays of any kind went from bad to worse, till it was once again brought to something more worthy of the profession under Kean, Fechter and the Wigans. Even Webster at the Haymarket, Chatterton at Drury Lane, and Phelps at Sadler's Wells, were content with second-rate scenery and dresses, and paid very little regard to accuracy in details. When the Bancrofts arrived at the Prince of Wales's the reform was completed by them, and the interval of slipshod productions was at an end, but it must not be forgotten that, considering the means at their command, Vestris and her husband, Charles Mathews, were quite as artistic and thorough in their productions as the foremost managers of the latter years of the century.

The other principal piece of Vestris's first programme was one of those mythological or fairy extravaganzas by Planché with which her name is so closely associated. It was called " Olympic Revels " and the subject enabled all the gods and goddesses of Olympus to appear in person. They were drawn up to and down from the clouds by machinery, and, though the effect would be looked upon as childish in these days of mechanical devices, it was new then and excited great applause. Vestris as Apollo, in a short tunic and showing, I should imagine, a good deal of leg, had the chief singing part, and her lovely voice was one of the attractions of the piece. Music was a prominent feature in all these Planché pieces. Some of the titles were " Olympic Devils : or Orpheus and Eurydice," " The Paphian Bower : or Venus and Adonis," " Deep Deep Sea : or Perseus and Andromeda," " Telemachus: or the Island of Calypso." These were in the earlier days when everything mythological was in high favour. Afterwards came extravaganzas founded on well-known fairy tales like " Riquet with the Tuft," " Bluebeard," " Puss in Boots," etc. The music was generally written specially for the piece. Blewitt, Tully and John Barnett (composer of " The Mountain Sylph ") wrote for several of them. One very remarkable piece was " The Court Beauties " of the time of Charles II in which all the principal Lely portraits were reproduced—thus anticipating, to some extent, modern " Living Pictures." The scene was laid in Pall Mall and Birdcage Walk with cages live singing birds hanging there as they used to be in Charles II's time. Some real tapestry which had actually been worked by the ladies of Charles's Court was bought by Vestris at the Carlton House sale and used in this piece, and also a dozen thorough-bred King Charles Spaniels which must have considerably added to the cost of the production.   A passage nearly a hundred feet long leading from the back of the stage through an alley to Craven Buildings was utilized to add depth, and the wall in the scenery was painted in perspective, so that an immense stretch of Birdcage Walk was seen.

During the run of this programme, " Mary Queen of Scots " and " Olympic Revels," the former piece was for some reason taken off the bill, and the entertainment finished consequently at 11.0 instead of at midnight.   This was so much appreciated by the audience that, on the suggestion of Planché, Vestris decided to end at that hour every evening.   She may be thus said to have been a precursor of the " Early-closing Movement," and the first to have a programme of reasonable length.

In 1835, Charles Mathews, son of an actor of repute and himself destined to be a leader in his profession, joined her company and in 1838, though he was much her junior, they were married and continued in management together.   It was, however, a disastrous partnership from first to last.   They avoided bankruptcy once or twice, but it came at last after Mathews had been more than once in a debtor's prison.   Unbridled extravagance on the stage and off was at the bottom of their failure.   The large sums they realized during the successful seasons at the Olympic and afterwards at the Lyceum ought to have enabled them to retire early and with a fortune.   But a lady who has been accustomed to have Parma violets in her rooms all the year round and masses of roses in the depth of an English winter, and who will pay the most exorbitant sums to obtain real King Charles Spaniels for one piece, is not likely to save much money.   Her husband seems to have had much the same lavish ideas and from a business point of view was worse than Madame herself.   Vestris and Mathews did not always rely on Planché for their programme.   Liston and Bland (the latter a very clever comedian) were members of her regular company and Frank Matthews (no relation to her husband) and Mrs. Keeley, then known as Miss Annie Goward.   Liston is, of course, well known to us through innumerable engravings and memoirs.   He it was who introduced Charles Mathews to the public in 1835 and so became sponsor for him, but he retired soon afterwards and his place was taken by William Farren (the second of the name), who had already been before the public for some time.   Mr. and Mrs. Charles Mathews gave up the Olympic in 1839, and the management was assumed by Samuel Butler, a tragedian whose appearances were in no way notable.   He ran the theatre for a few months only, the chief note of his season being the first appearance on the Olympic stage of Fanny Stirling, who was in after years to score so many successes on the same boards.   Butler was succeeded by George Wild, who reigned from 1841 to 1844.

Wild, whose real name was Brodie, was the son of a Mrs. Brodie who kept a pastrycook's shop in Great Titchfield Street.   He was a very clever comedian, besides an enterprising manager, ran the Marylebone Theatre in 1851 or thereabouts, and in his later years was acting at Drury Lane.   At the Olympic he reduced the prices of admission to 2s. 6d., 1s. and 6d., and though some of his productions were quite good in their way the character of the audiences must have degenerated a great deal since the Vestris days.   *Punch* once said (during Wild's regime) that the Olympic was to the Adelphi what a tap is to a tavern, that the pieces produced " smack of the spittoon " but are pictures of real life " when a live horse and real cab is introduced from the St. Clement's stand."   In these realistic touches Wild anticipated by many years the London dramas at Drury Lane, Princess's and Standard in Shoreditch.   He was very angry at the criticism of *Punch* and immediately published a long list of authors who had written for his theatre (including such well-known names as Moncrieff, Sterling, Fitzball, Mark Lemon, Albert Smith, Leman Rede), and headed it " List of Dramatists whose pieces smack of the Spittoon."   Wild always put on a pantomime at Christmas as long as he had the Olympic, the clown being frequently Tom Matthews, one of the best of his day.   His reign at the Wych Street house closed ingloriously and suddenly.   In July 1844, a performance of Henry IV (Part I) was announced.   The night arrived in due course, but no Falstaff with it !   In the third act, an amateur took up the part and led the show to disaster.   That was the last night of Wild at the Olympic.   He afterwards acted at various other theatres, and died in 1856.

In January, 1846, the Olympic was under the direction of a Miss Kate Howard (daughter of a Madame Caplin), whose programme consisted of a pantomime with Jefferini as Clown, and a burlesque on " The Cricket on the Hearth."   This latter was a failure as it deserved to be.   Dramatizations of Dickens's novels are without number, but there are very few instances of a burlesque on any of them.   Miss Howard did not have the theatre long, and it came into the hands of George Bolton, who put on a very poor drama of London life called " Life."   Though the company was a fairly good one, including Mr. and Mrs. Walter Lacy and Leigh Murray, the piece failed to attract.

In 1847, Davidson took the Olympic and scored an immediate

success with Gustavus V. Brooke as Othello, supported by Miss Glyn. This lady was a popular actress in Shakespearean parts, her best being Lady Macbeth. She had made a first appearance at Sadler's Wells under Phelps as Volumnia, and played a round of similar parts there. In 1854, she was at the St. James's in an historical play written by Tom Taylor and Charles Reade called "The King's Rival." The theatre was under the management of a Mrs. Seymour, who cast herself for Nell Gwynne. Miss Glyn was Frances Stewart, Vandenhoff the King, and Mead, Duke of Richmond. Toole made his London debut in this piece as Pepys, and Lydia Thompson was also in the cast. In the following year Miss Glyn was in an Egyptian play ("Nitocris") by Fitzball at Drury Lane. Barry Sullivan, Mrs. Selby and George Wild, one-time manager of the Olympic, were also in this piece, which was mounted with great lavishness at an enormous cost. At the Princess's in 1867, when Miss Glyn was no longer young, she played Cleopatra in a revival of Shakespeare's tragedy with Henry Loraine (the elder) as Antony, Walter Joyce as Lepidus and Henry Forrester as Cæsar. In her later life Miss Glyn gave many series of Readings at St. James's Hall and elsewhere, which by all accounts must have been rather dreary entertainments. She married Mr. Dallas of *The Times*.

This was not Gustavus Brooke's first appearance in London, for he had previously acted at the Vic. He was an Irishman with a good deal of practical experience in the provinces and Ireland, but had seen many ups and downs, having on one occasion to fit up a theatre under a railway arch, and live there as well. Brooke was well before my time. Opinions as to the merit of his acting were very diverse. Some hailed him as a great tragedian, the greatest since Macready, whose style he followed. Others, among whom appears to have been Blanchard, thought but poorly of his powers. He is described as a very fine man, tall, and of good appearance generally, and with a magnificent voice. All seem to agree that his acting was natural and largely free from artificialities, though he aimed at producing the same kind of effect as Macready. He undoubtedly created a furore in London, America and elsewhere and for a time was the manager of the Melbourne Theatre. His great part was Othello, but he also acted rôles like Sir Giles Overreach and in plays now forgotten, such as Sheridan's "Pizarro" and Home's "Douglas."

Professor Henry Morley said of Brooke when he appeared at Drury Lane :

"Drury Lane has reopened, and Mr. G. V. Brooke is for the

present its chief attraction.   It is a pity that he should prefer to
act Shakespeare—for which he is as little qualified as the company
engaged to support him—rather than a good ranting, roaring melodrama which he would play admirably.   This would be infinitely
better than making a melodrama of ' Othello.' "

Morley was always a disgruntled sort of critic and adopted the
professorial tone of condemnation, perhaps, more often than was
justified.   He was often apparently unjust if we are to place any
reliance on other critics of his time.   He had downright opinions
of his own and would not stand anyone differing from him.   But
he evidently thought he owed some *amende* to the memory of Brooke
when he heard of his death in the foundering of the *London,*
which, outward bound for Australia, went down in the Channel
with a loss of over two hundred lives.   Brooke set a great example
to the other passengers on board, trying to save lives, and working
hard at the pumps till the end.   Morley wrote : " Though he
could not act Shakespeare, he must have been a noble fellow."

Mrs. Gustavus Brooke, *née* Miss Avonia Jones, was an American
actress of some considerable power.   She had a great reputation
in Australia, and made her debut in London in 1861 as Medea at
Drury Lane.

She also appeared at the Adelphi and the Surrey Theatres, and
anticipated Sarah Bernhardt in the rôle of " Theodora," Empress
and courtesan.   Perhaps her most popular success in London was
in " East Lynne."   She was, if not the first, one of the earliest
of the innumerable Lady Isabels.   She died in 1867, having never
recovered from the death of her husband.

In March, 1849, the old Olympic met the usual fate of theatres
and was burned down, but was rebuilt very quickly and opened
on Boxing Night of the same year with " Two Gentlemen of
Verona."

The new manager was one Watts, who spent his money lavishly
in all directions, paying enormous salaries and mounting plays
gorgeously at great expense.   Nobody seemed to know much about
him.   He ran the Marylebone Theatre at the same time and appeared
to be responsible more or less for an American actress, Cora Mowatt.
The Olympic was costing him £400 a week, a very large sum for
those days, but the ready money was always forthcoming.   During
his management, Gustavus Brooke appeared with Cora Mowatt,
and other members of the company were such well-known people
as Mrs. Ternan, Mrs. Fitzwilliam, Mrs. Henry Marston, Mrs.
Wynstanley and Julia St. George.   The last-named was principal
boy in " The Yellow Dwarf " at the Olympic with Robson in

1854, and I remember her as a singing fairy at a Covent Garden pantomime in the seventies or eighties. In March, 1850, the crash came and with it the explanation of where the money came from. Watts had been embezzling funds from the Globe Insurance Company for years. He was sentenced to ten years' transportation, but cheated the law by hanging himself in his cell.

The elder Farren then took over the theatre and tried to revive the old tradition of the house with light comedy and burlesque, but, although he engaged Mrs. Stirling, Compton, Leigh Murray and other leading actors, the venture was not successful and he reverted to tragedy with Helen Faucit and Gustavus Brooke as the stars.

One or two uneventful years followed with little worthy of note save, perhaps, the appearance of Laura Keene as Pauline to the Claude Melnotte of one Henry Farmer. She was an American and never the success in England that she was in her own country. I think her chief claim to remembrance is that she once put on "Our American Cousin" (Dundreary) as a stop-gap, giving Jefferson (the great Rip Van Winkle) the star part of Asa Trenchard and permitting Sothern, who was also a member of her stock company, to do what he liked with the Dundreary part as long as he acted it. Every one knows how in the subsequent run of the play Trenchard has to take a back seat and Lord Dundreary becomes the main personage in the play. Miss Keene made a small fortune over it and Buckstone at the Haymarket (who also put it on under protest) thirty thousand pounds. The year 1853 was a notable one in the history of the Olympic, for it was the year when Robson made his first appearance in the West End, his previous engagements having been at the Grecian and other outlying houses. He was not a Londoner born, though he became by environment and profession a cockney of cockneys, and his life from a very early period had been connected with acting in some form or other.

Somewhere behind the Coliseum, to the east of St. Martin's Lane, or on the site of the building itself, there used to be a little district that went by the name of Bedfordbury.

It was an odd little cluster of courts, alleys, holes and corners, of which, perhaps, the only vestige remaining is the narrow street full of shops of all sorts that leads from St. Martin's Lane to Garrick and Bedford Streets. In the centre of this cluster of narrow thoroughfares, where you could buy everything second-hand and cheap from old furniture to odd keys and farthing literature, was a little square where, in 1836, one Thomas Robson Brownhill, a boy of fifteen years of age, from Margate, was apprenticed to a Mr. Smellie, the copperplate engraver and printer of Cruikshank's plates.

Tom's father had not known quite what to do with him. The boy was crazy for the stage and would hear of nothing else, but finally consented to go in for engraving, thinking, no doubt, that he might be brought into touch with the theatrical world more easily in London than in Margate.

He was a born mimic and actor ; it was in him, and had to come out. He would amuse the other workmen at the engraver's with imitations of well-known performers, and haunted the minor theatres of the neighbourhood, especially the Catherine Street house, where amateurs would from time to time get a chance to see what they could do. The Catherine Street little theatre is responsible for the early start of many a dramatic aspirant who afterwards attained the highest rank in his profession (see Chapter XV).

" Little Bobbie," as he was called—for he was very short— was apprenticed for seven years, but only finished four of them. He lived with his parents near Vauxhall when they moved up to town and, when his master gave up his shop, the boy ventured to open in Bryde Street, Covent Garden, as an engraver on his own. The pull of the profession was, however, much too strong. He shut up his shop and accepted an offer from a country manager to do " second utility " which meant practically anything you were called upon to do. He took his second Christian name for a stage name, and made a start in a sort of barn at Whitstable—what would be now called a " fit-up." He appears to have got on from the first, for we hear of him at Uxbridge, then at the City of London Theatre, and finally at the old Grecian, where he stayed for six years and where he first made his name by the singing of " Villikins and his Dinah," singing it in the theatre and then again on the platform in the open-air. It was intended for a very serious, even tragic, song, but in Robson's hands became a comic affair of the most screaming kind. I fancy it is to this beginning that may be traced that extraordinary mixture of comedy and tragedy with which his name will always be associated.

Robson left the Grecian in 1850, the year before it came into the hands of the Conquests, and was in Dublin and Belfast for three years. Then his time came at last. Farren, who was running the Olympic, cast him for the title rôle in Talfourd's travesty of Macbeth. When Farren failed and the dirty little house was taken over by the Wigans, Mrs. Wigan persuaded her husband to retain Robson in the company, for she was convinced of his genius. It was for them a lucky decision. Once more the Olympic became the fashionable theatre that it had been in the days of Eliza Vestris. The audiences were again of the West End and aristocratic type, and Burlesques written especially for Robson by Talfourd and

Brough followed each other in quick succession.   In " The Yellow Dwarf" particularly his acting was said to be sublime in its savage intensity, and life-like and human in its commonplace features. It was called " Tragedy Off Stilts "—something between tragedy and comedy.

Some critics thought he had the makings of a great tragic actor ; others that he was merely a clever interpreter of farce.   But the real tragedy of his career lies in the fact that he never realized his enormous success.   He never felt quite sure that he had really satisfied his audiences.   He used to suffer horribly from nervousness on first nights and got into the habit of taking stimulants to counteract this, and dull the constant pain from which he suffered.

Many contemporaries have described him in detail.   One says :

" . . . little stunted creature, with hoarse voice, nervous gestures and grotesque delivery, his snarls, his leers, his hunchings of the shoulders, his contortion of the limbs, his gleamings of the eyes and his grindings of the teeth was a genius."

Another contemporary describes him in one of his famous burlesque parts :

" .   . capering about the stage, a quaint buffoon, suddenly he would change to grim earnest—eyes which had been winking with a knowing vulgarity suddenly looked you full in the face.   A passionate cry, a wail of misery, bright tears, and then, before they were dry, was again prancing about, a comic mountebank."

After the Olympic was burned down (the third burning, I think) a wealthy cheesemonger found the money for the rebuilding, and it was again under the Alfred Wigans, who kept on Robson in his extraordinary series of burlesques.   He was already in middle age when he made his great successes at the Olympic and had been vegetating previously for years in obscure places of entertainment drawing only 25s. or 30s. a week, out of which he had a wife and family to support, and earning it dancing and tumbling and singing comic songs at places like the Grecian Saloon.   His success came to him too late.   He was ill, and kept up his strength by the frequent use of stimulants.   His last appearance on the stage, still at the Olympic, was in 1862, and he died in 1864.

I make no excuse for entering, with some detail, into the career of this remarkable man whom Oxenford declared to have been the greatest actor since Edmund Kean.   He is quite forgotten now, but there has never been anyone to fill his place completely.   At the outset, he had not much chance of showing what he could do, though he made some impression as Shylock in Frank Talfourd's burlesque of " The Merchant of Venice." His time was yet to come, and it came in 1858 when the Alfred Wigans succeeded Farren in the direction of the theatre, and a new era of success set in for the little house.

Alfred Wigan was descended from an old Lancashire family who really spelt their name Wogan. One of his ancestors had signed the Death-Warrant of King Charles I and, though they were afterwards devoted to the Stuart cause, considered it advisable to alter their name slightly. Wigan was born in 1818. His family were well off, and could have given him a start in any profession, or even allowed him sufficient to enable him to live without working. Later on, however, circumstances compelled him to choose a profession, and he chose the stage. His first professional appearance is generally stated to have been in " The Village Coquettes," a burletta or musical play by Charles Dickens with music by John Hullah. Blanchard, however, who had a decided talent for fishing out the minutest details with regard to theatrical information of all kinds, recounts how he once acted at a very curious minor theatre (if indeed it could be called a theatre at all) which had a short and very precarious existence at the Old Manor House in the King's Road, Chelsea. As Blanchard was in that scratch company at the same time, the story is probably true. (See Chapter XV on the Bower and other Minor Theatres.) Wigan, with his wife (*née* Pincott, a niece of James Wallack), was with Madame Vestris at Covent Garden. He and his wife always acted together whenever possible, and they were the Trip and Maria in a revival of " The School for Scandal " in 1845 by Macready, who played Joseph Surface. Wigan was at the Strand in its early days, under Haywood, and in 1844 with the Keeleys at the Lyceum. They were both at the Princess's in the heyday of the Charles Keans' management, and occasionally at other houses, such as the Haymarket and the Surrey, but it was at the Olympic that they had their chief successes when Mrs. Stirling was the leading lady and Robson at the zenith of his career.

Their opening programme included a very powerful drama by Tom Taylor called " Plot and Passion " founded on episodes of the French Directory when Fouché was in power. In this, Robson created the part of Desmarets, the police spy, and, great as he was in burlesque, he was far greater in melodrama and tragedy. Of his performance of Desmarets, Morley wrote :

" The success of the night was undoubtedly the assumption of

a serious part by the burlesque actor Robson.   That there should
be other and higher things to report of a performer, who, while
other people were burlesquing in reality, could put such a startling
reality into burlesque, was not to be doubted.   But one hardly
expected it so soon.   The part he plays in 'Plot and Passion'
(a drama of which the central figure is Fouché, its characters being
the agents or objects of his villainy and its catastrophe his disgrace)
is that of a mean, double-faced, fawning, cunning, treacherous tool,
in whom the sordid passions have not wholly extinguished others
that place him finally at the mercy of his victims.   Here the actor's
opportunity is that of a constant and quick transition within the
limited range of the emotions expressed ;   and from meanness to
malice, from cringing humility to the most malignant hate, from a
cat-like watchfulness to occasional bursts of passion that seemed
to defy control, Mr. Robson passed with a keen power and ready
self-possession that never missed the effect intended to be produced."

When he combined his marvellous powers of tragedy and burlesque
in one part, as in "The Yellow Dwarf" and other extravaganzas,
he was terrible in the effect he made, and unlike anything ever
seen on the British stage.   In his character of the Yellow Dwarf,
"he was positively astounding" (says Monsieur Adolphe Beau,
the well-known theatrical photographer of the sixties), "painted,
of course, yellow all over, with very large ears and such a gait ;
one might have thought of a sudden apparition of some supernatural
being ;   he was so dis-humanized, if one may be allowed to coin
such a word."

George Augustus Sala gives a very striking description of his
tragedy in burlesque.   He says :

"In 'The Yellow Dwarf' he was the jaundiced embodiment
of a spirit of Oriental evil ;   crafty, malevolent, greedy, insatiate—
full of mockery, mimicry, lubricity and spite—an Afrit, a Djin,
a Ghoul, a spawn of Sheitan.   How that monstrous orange-tawny
head grinned and wagged !   How those flaps of ears were projected
forwards, like unto those of a dog !   How balefully those atra-
bilious eyes glistened !   You laughed and yet you shuddered.   He
spoke in mere doggerel and slang.   He sang trumpery songs to
negro melodies.   He danced the Lancashire clog hornpipe.   He
rattled out puns and conundrums ;   yet did he contrive to infuse
into all this mummery and buffoonery, into this salmagundi of the
incongruous and the outré, an unmistakable tragic element—
an element of depth and strength and passion, and almost of sublimity.
. . You were awestricken by the intensity, the vehemence he threw

into the mean balderdash of the burlesque monger. These qualities were even more apparent in his subsequent impersonation of Medea in Robert Brough's parody of the Franco-Italian tragedy. The love, the hate, the scorn of the abandoned wife of Jason, the diabolic loathing in which she holds Creusa, the tigerish affection with which she regards the children whom she is afterwards to slay— all these were portrayed by Robson, through the medium, be it always remembered, of doggerel and slang, with astonishing force and vigour."

I have quoted at length from such different authorities as Morley and Sala to give some idea of the effect that Robson produced on his contemporaries. In truth there must have been something very wonderful about his acting. It is sixty years since he died. There must be very few who can recall him distinctly and none who could give a mature opinion of his powers.

With the attractions of good plays, and exceptionally good actors to play in them, the old Olympic once more became the fashionable theatre of the town. Queen Victoria and Prince Albert were there in 1856 to see a gloomy play written under an assumed name by G. R. Lewes, the author of the best English life of Goethe. In the same year, Ristori, the great Italian tragedienne, was present to see Robson in a burlesque of "Medea," the tragedy which she had made peculiarly her own. All she could say was "Che uomo straordinario." During his run of management Alfred Wigan produced several interesting plays, among them, "Still Waters Run Deep" in 1855 with himself, George Vining, Sam Emery, and Danvers in the cast. Mrs. Mildmay was played by a Miss Maskell who had been in the fairy pieces of Planché with Robson. Mrs. Sternhold was originally played by a Mrs. Melfort, who was by no means a success ; so the part was taken up very soon by Mrs. Alfred Wigan herself.

She was a very clever actress. There is a story that she used as a child to perform on stilts in the London Squares and at race courses, and that fashionable people taking their tea in smart London houses would be sometimes startled by the apparition of a small figure clad in tawdry muslin and spangles looking in at the window and tendering a scallop shell for alms. Considering that her mother, Elizabeth Pincott, had been a daughter of old William Wallack and a sister of the highly successful actor James Wallack, the story looks a doubtful one ; but you can never tell how true these old traditions may be.

In 1856, Mrs. Stirling created one of her most famous parts in "A Sheep in Wolf's Clothing" by Tom Taylor, and Miss

Herbert ("the lovely Miss Herbert"), was also in the company ;
her first appearance in London.

I do not think Miss Herbert was ever a really great actress, but
she must have been a most attractive one. In " The Porter's
Knot " at the Olympic, she was the heroine, with Mrs. Leigh
Murray as the old mother, and Robson in his incomparable impersonation of Sampson Burr. She was there for about four years
acting with Mrs. Stirling, Miss Swanborough (the eldest one,
afterwards Mrs. Lyons), Walter Gordon and others. She then
went to the St. James's, first under the management of Horace
Wigan and subsequently directing the theatre herself. Irving
was in her company for several seasons, and she produced a series
of plays on the novels of Miss Braddon—" Lady Audley's Secret,"
" Eleanor's Victory," " Only a Clod," etc. " Idalia," founded
on Ouida's novel followed, and " Hunted Down," in which Irving
made, perhaps, his first great London success as Rawdon Scudamore,
the " villain of the piece." There was a fine revival of " The
School for Scandal," in which Miss Herbert was an excellent Lady
Teazle to the Sir Peter of Frank Matthews, the Mrs. Candour
of Mrs. Frank, and the Charles of Walter Lacy. After her reign
at the St. James's Miss Herbert was at the Adelphi and at the
Royalty with that queer creature, Nation, and was also Helena to
the Bottom of Phelps at the Gaiety. I believe she was with Mrs.
Bernard Beere when the latter played Fedora, but retired definitely
soon afterwards and led a retired life at Brighton for many years.
Playgoers of the sixties all have a soft corner in their hearts for this
charming lady whose acting, if not great, was so gracious and
pleasing and against whom not even the most censorious tongues ever
dared to say a word.

Hack writers of plays were always on the look out for novels
with stirring plots which they could adapt for the stage.
Dickens had been a quarry yielding much material, though
the author in no case reaped any reward from the play.
At the Britannia, Hoxton, Edwin Drood was given as adapted
by " The Great Macdermott " (the " we don't want to fight "
man) who played Datchery, with Reeve (father of Ada Reeve) as
Edwin Drood, John Parry as Grewgious, and Jane, the clever sister
of Harriet Coveney, as " Opium Sal." Perhaps the best of these
early versions of Dickens was one of " Martin Chuzzlewit " at
the Lyceum in which Robert Keeley was Mrs. Gamp ; his wife,
Bailey the " Tiger " ; Alfred Wigan, Montagu Twigg ; Frank
Matthews, Pecksniff ; Emery, Jonas Chuzzlewit ; and Mrs.
Alfred Mellon, Charity Pecksniff. " Oliver Twist " had been
done over and over again (see the Chapter on the Queen's Theatre)

once at the Surrey with Edward Terry as " The Artful Dodger " and Shepherd as Sikes. " The Tale of Two Cities " was given at the Lyceum under the Fechter regime ; " No Thoroughfare " at the Adelphi with Fechter, Carlotta Leclercq, Webster and Mrs. Alfred Mellon. There was one version of " Dombey and Son " in which Irving played Mr. Dombey.

Most of these adaptations, especially the earlier ones, were done by the so-called " Stock-Authors " who were kept at many theatres to produce plays to order, with sometimes only a day or two to complete their work so that they might forestall a rival house.

Boucicault was stock-author at the Princess's and also (in the forties) one Reynolds who had been the original representative of Pickwick when the first version was brought out at the Strand. MacDermott wrote for the Grecian ; Fitzball for the Surrey ; Hazlewood for the Britannia ; Planché for Madame Vestris at the Olympic and later at the Lyceum ; Gilbert à Beckett for the St. James's ; William Brough (uncle of Fanny Brough) for the Lyceum ; Savile Faucit for the Vic ; Henry Milner for Astley's, etc. Such authors must not be confounded with writers like Merritt (Adelphi and Grecian), or Cecil Raleigh (Drury Lane) and the like, who were often employed to do the plays for the same theatre for years running, but were not, so to speak, " kept on tap " on the premises.

About 1857, adaptors of plays from novels seem to have discovered for the first time the great suitability of Wilkie Collins's tales for the stage. The Wigans had retired from management in that year, leaving the theatre in the hands of Robson and Emden who put on " The Lighthouse " by Collins, followed by " The Red Vial," afterwards published as a novel called *Jezebel's Daughter*. In this, Mrs. Stirling gave a very powerful rendering of the Widow Bergmann and Robson added to his reputation in the part of an idiot who brings about the final catastrophe of the play.

In 1861 Henry Neville made his first appearance at the Olympic in a play translated or adapted from the French piece " Le Ramoneur " ; but his greatest triumph came in 1863 when " The Ticket of Leave Man " was produced.

For anything that the London playgoers knew to the contrary, this was a new and original English melodrama, but it was all the same an adaptation of two French pieces—or perhaps of only one—sometimes called " Léonard " and sometimes " Le Retour de Mélun." Tom Taylor, who prepared this play for the English stage, was quite clever enough to give it such a completely English atmosphere that no one not in the secret could say it bore any resemblance to

a French piece.   He was as clever as Boucicault had been in turning
" Les Pauvres de Paris " into " The Streets of London " and
" Les Oiseaux de Proie " into " After Dark."   George Conquest,
who had a library of unused French and other plays stored at the
Grecian, spotted the origin at once.   Clement Scott says that Taylor
got only £150 for his work, and was probably glad to get that and
sell it outright.   In these days the royalties on a success such as this
turned out to be would have run into thousands.   Neville had
already made his mark at the Olympic and elsewhere.   In November,
1862, a play by Watts Phillips was produced called " Camilla's
Husband " in which he had played the hero with Kate Saville (a
niece of Helen Faucit) as the heroine, supported by Horace Wigan
and Robson.   It was Robson's last appearance on the stage ; he
died the following year—1864.

" The Ticket of Leave Man " ran for over 400 nights, a very
long run in those days ; and, though the cast was an excellent one
in every particular, it was Neville's performance that made the
play at the start.

Henry Neville was the son of an actor-manager known as " Handsome Jack Neville," who had intended his boy for the army but
was prevented from carrying out his intentions by financial em-
barrassments.   The actor son was as handsome as his father and
had a charm of manner which endeared him to all his associates.
His success as the *jeune premier* in drama never deserted him even
long after he had ceased to have the right to be called "*jeune*."
No one knew how old he was, and he used to say with a smile that
when he was shut up in his coffin they would know from the inscription on the outside, and not before !   At the Olympic under
the managements of Horace Wigan and Miss Ada Cavendish, and
later under his own direction, he showed the London playgoing
public the best types of romantic drama such as hitherto had only
been properly done by Fechter.   Lewis Waller succeeded to the
tradition, but since Waller's death it is dead.   There is no actor
of the present day, unless it be Mr. Leon Quartermaine or Mr.
Robert Loraine, who could fill a romantic " lead."

Neville is said to have played Bob Brierly, the hero of " The
Ticket of Leave Man " over two thousand times, and still continued
to do so in his old age.   Perhaps his best performances, after that
of Bob Brierly, were Claude Melnotte to the Pauline of Kate Saville,
and Lord Clancarty in Tom Taylor's romantic drama of the period
of William of Orange.   He was also a fairly good Romeo, but
perhaps too robust for the part.

Kate Saville was the leading lady of the Olympic when Neville
first went there.   She came of a great theatrical family.   Her

HENRY NEVILLE AS BOB BRIERLY IN "THE TICKET OF
LEAVE MAN"

From a photograph by Adolphe Beau

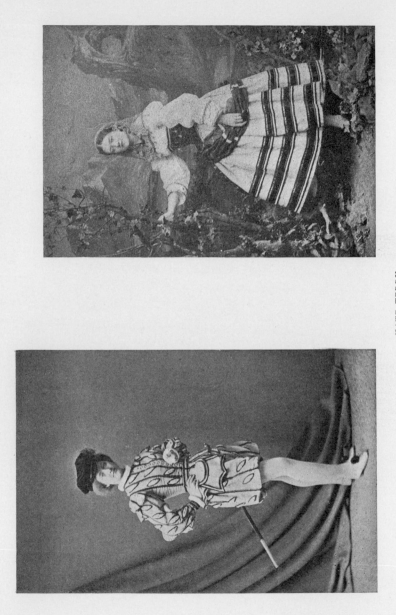

AS VIOLA IN "TWELFTH NIGHT"
From photograph by Stereoscopic Co., Ltd.

KATE TERRY

AS BLANCHE DE NEVERS IN "THE DUKE'S
MOTTO"
From photograph by Southwell Bros.

mother was Mrs. E. Faucit Saville, sister-in-law of Helen Faucit, and wife of that Saville who, in the character of Bill Sikes, used to drag Nancy round the stage of the Old Vic to the frightful swear-words of the gallery, and smear her face with red ochre by way of a bloody realism.

Miss Saville was the original May Edwards of the new drama. She had had some experience of the stage, having been the heroine of " Ivy Hall," that disastrous version of " Le Roman d'un Jeune Homme Pauvre " in which Irving made his debut at the Princess's. She retired from the stage to marry a wealthy native of Nottingham and lived for many years afterwards. Early in the run of the piece, Kate Saville was replaced in the rôle of May Edwards by Lydia Foote, niece of Mrs. Keeley, who remained for some time at the Olympic. Horace Wigan (brother of Alfred Wigan) was the first Hawkshaw, the detective. He supplies one of the surprises and catch-words of the play. Being asked " Who are you ? " he tears off a false beard and other disguises and exclaims, " *I* am Hawkshaw, the detective." A sort of Sherlock Holmes of mid-nineteenth century.

In the play was also a garrulous old woman of the Dickens type —Mrs. Willoughby—with an unceasing flow of gossip and con-versational back-chat. This part was most amusingly done by Mrs. Stephens, known affectionately for years as Granny Stephens, and incomparable in her particular line. She was not a young woman then (1863) but I find her sixteen years later (1879) in the cast of " Betsy " at the Criterion. When " Betsy " was revived in 1882, the old woman's part was played by Eleanor Bufton (Mrs. Swanborough), who had been Regan to the Lear of Charles Kean in the fifties.

Granny Stephens went on from year to year apparently immortal. She created the Showman's wife (Mrs. Jarvis) in " The Lights o' London " in 1881 and the old lady's part in " The Private Secretary " in 1884. She lived to be 93 years of age.

Sam Willoughby the " tiger," her son in the play, was first done by a very charming and good-looking young lady, Miss Raynham, who afterwards went to play " Principal Boy " in the Strand burlesques. She might have mounted much higher in the pro-fession but died of consumption before she was thirty. Nellie Farren took up the part of Sam when the drama was revived in 1875 at the Olympic with a slightly different cast. When Neville and J. R. Taylor opened the Opera House in the Haymarket as a speculation at cheap prices, the old play was put on again. Charles Vandenhoff played Neville's old part ; Arthur Stirling was Hawk-shaw ; Edward Righton appeared as Melter Moss (written for Robson but never played by him) ; Clara Jecks (daughter of clever

Harriet Coveney) was Sam Willoughby; Amy Roselle, May Edwards; and that delightful comedian, Miss M. A. Victor (once of the regular company at the old Grecian) was Mrs. Willoughby. It has been revived again and again at different London houses and, like "East Lynne," is still one of the safe productions to fall back on in a provincial tour.

I have lingered perhaps unduly on this astonishing play, but it was in truth a representative English drama (though adapted from the French) and is so still. The Lancashire lad, Bob Brierly (acted by Neville, a real Lancashire lad with the true touch of the vernacular), the young English heroine, the old woman and her cockney son were one and all thoroughly English. Not till Barrett gave us "The Lights o' London" and "The Silver King" was there a play which struck such sympathetic chords in the hearts of an English audience.

In 1864, after "The Ticket of Leave Man" had finished its phenomenal run of over four hundred nights, it was a wonderful company that assembled under the direction of Horace Wigan at the theatre in the slums. Henry Neville, Kate Terry, Lydia Foote, Louisa Moore and Nelly Farren—the last-named already showing promise of what she would become in the future.

On this occasion the programme consisted of a long melodrama called "The Hidden Hand" adapted from the French of "L'Aïeule," with a farce to precede and a farce to follow. Nelly Farren appeared in, and was successful in, all three pieces. No sinecure there! Kate Terry remained as leading lady at the Olympic for some time, and in 1866 there was a notable performance of "The Hunchback" in which she was cast for Julia; her sister was Helen; Neville, Master Walter; and Horace Wigan, Modus.

This eldest of the gifted Terry sisters is thought by some to have been the most brilliant actress of them all. When she retired from the stage at the early age of twenty-three on her marriage to Mr. Lewis (of Lewis and Allenby) she had not probably attained her full powers—although she had started her professional career with the Charles Keans at the Princess's, playing fairies in the pantomimes, and Shakespearean parts like the Boy in "Henry V," and Prince Arthur in "King John." At the astonishingly early age of fourteen, she was a charming Cordelia to Kean's Lear, one of a remarkable cast, including Miss Heath (Mrs. Wilson Barrett) as Goneril, Eleanor Bufton (Mrs. Edward Swanborough) as Regan, Ryder as Edgar, Walter Lacy as Edmund and a Miss Poole (who had made her debut as long ago as 1831) as the Fool—perhaps making it a singing part, for there was much music composed for the occasion by Hatton, and Miss Poole had been a notable singer.

In 1862, Kate Terry joined Alfred Wigan's company at the St. James's with Mrs. Alfred Wigan, Miss Herbert, Nelly Moore, Fred Dewar (the Captain Crosstree of the Royalty " Black Eyed Susan ") and Sam Emery. She created the part in Boucicault's " Hunted Down " (afterwards played by Miss Herbert) when the piece was first given at Manchester ; she was a charming Viola in " Twelfth Night," doubling the part with that of Sebastian ; and an excellent Beatrice in " Much Ado About Nothing," though old playgoers who saw both her and her sister Ellen in the part are unanimous in preferring the latter.

In 1863—64, she was in " The Duke's Motto " at the Lyceum with Fechter, as Blanche de Nevers to his Henri de Lagardère. This is the finest specimen of a *cappa e spada* drama and is always welcomed whenever reproduced, in spite of its rather old-fashioned air and improbable situations. But, to do it justice, it requires a Fechter or, at least, a Lewis Waller and a fine emotional actress and a company who can all act in clothes unlike those they wear day by day ! Waller did it almost as well as Fechter, but there is no one can do it now—as I think I have said before. Kate Terry was also with Fechter in " Bel Demonio : a Love Story," adapted from " L'Abbaye de Castro," which had already been played at the Olympic under another name. George Jordan, an actor better known in the States than in England, was also in the cast and the stately and useful Miss Elsworthy. After playing Ophelia (one of her best parts) to Fechter's Hamlet, Kate Terry resigned her position as leading lady at the Lyceum to Carlotta Leclercq. When she joined the Olympic company in 1864, she played almost continuously with Henry Neville, migrating with him to the Adelphi in 1866, where she made her adieux the following year.

On her last performance she appeared as Juliet, and at the close of the performance there ensued a scene which has seldom been equalled on the English stage. The usual farce, which always wound up a programme, however distinguished, in those days had begun, the stalls and boxes were half cleared and still the pit and gallery shouted and called and would not allow the unfortunate comedians to proceed. At last, in response to an inquiry by one of the actors what they wanted, there was a loud shout from all in the House—" Kate Terry," and she had to appear in front again, dressed to go away, and make her little speech of thanks. The account of this evening as given in *The Daily Telegraph* makes quite unforgettable reading for those interested in the work of the stage. Kate Terry had only been fifteen years on the stage, having begun when she was but eight years of age, and her extraordinary hold on the London playgoer had not commenced more than five years before she finished her dramatic career, but it was a hold that nothing could shake. What the secret of her power over an audience was is not easy to determine at this distance of time. All accounts agree that she had a very definite charm and much emotional force, but there must have been something more than this or she could not have made the successes she did in such a variety of parts. Her Ophelia is said to have been the best seen up to that time and, if in Juliet she was not equal to Stella Colas or Adelaide Neilson, the explanation may be that there was, as with her sister Ellen, more pathos and charm in her acting than great power. The sisters were both absolutely perfect as Ophelia and Beatrice, but both stopped just short of perfection in the more exacting rôle of Juliet.

Nelly Farren, who was in all three pieces at the opening of the 1864 season, remained at the Olympic in drama and mythological burlesque in 1868, and two or three years later drew all London to see her in " Giselle," a burlesque by Byron on Loder's old opera, " The Night Dancers." I miss her name from the cast of " The Woman in White," by Wilkie Collins, in which Ada Dyas doubled the parts of Ann Catherick and Lady Glyde and Vining was Count Fosco ; Billington, Sir Percival Glyde ; Mrs. Charles Viner, Marian Halcombe ; and Marie Henderson (a famous Mazeppa), Mrs. Catterick.

Many of Wilkie Collins's novels have found their way to the stage. I have already noted " The Lighthouse " and " Jezebel's Daughter " produced at the Olympic under Robson's management. At the same theatre was also given " The Frozen Deep " in 1866, with Neville, Montagu, Horace Wigan, Dominick Murray and Lydia Foote in the cast ; it had been previously done at Dickens's London residence, Tavistock House (where he had a perfectly fitted theatre) by amateurs including Mark Lemon (editor of *Punch*), and Dickens himself. " No Thoroughfare " was at the Adelphi in 1867 with Fechter, Webster, Billington, Belmore, George Neville, Mrs. Alfred Mellon and Carlotta Leclercq, a stupendously fine cast for a really dramatic work. This is one of the earliest plays that I can remember well as a youngster, and I have never forgotten the thrill of the " Clock scene " and the last scene of all on the high Alps. " Black and White " at the Adelphi had Fechter and Miss Leclercq ; " Man and Wife " at the Prince of Wales's in 1873 was acted by Hare, Coghlan, Willie Herbert, Mrs. Leigh Murray, Lydia Foote, and Dewar, who made a hit with the character part of Bishopriggs, the Scotch waiter. " Rank and Riches " was at the Adelphi in 1883 with George Alexander and

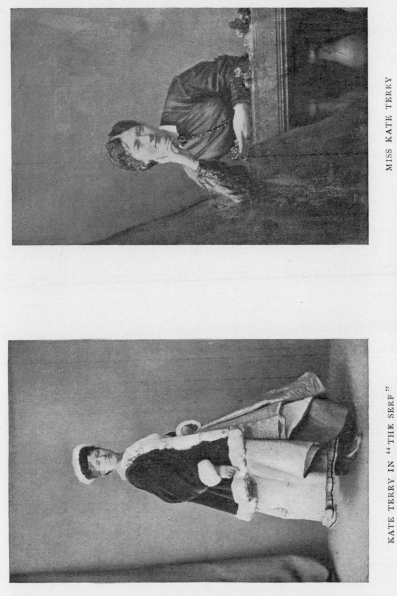

KATE TERRY IN "THE SERF"   MISS KATE TERRY

From photographs by Stereoscopic Co., Ltd.

EXTERIOR OF PRINCESS'S THEATRE, OXFORD STREET

From a print dated 1851

Alice Lingard : "The New Magdalen" at the Novelty in 1884 with Ada Cavendish, Louise Willes and Archer ; "The Dead Secret" at the Lyceum in 1877 under the Bateman management, and " Armadale " was dramatized under the title of " Miss Gwilt " with Ada Cavendish in the title rôle. Some of these should be worth reviving, especially the last-named, if an actress could be found to take the chief part—which is more than very doubtful !

But to return to the chronicle of the Olympic. The theatre gradually came to be regarded as one where you could see an exciting drama well acted without the crude and melodramatic incidents met with in the drama of the Adelphi, and it even became the fashion to distinguish between the two kinds of melodrama by calling one the "Adelphi drama" and the other the "Olympic drama." This was turning the tables with a vengeance, when one remembers that *Punch* had once said : "The Olympic is to the Adelphi what a tap is to a tavern."

One or two dramas of no importance, a revival of "The Ticket of Leave Man," a production of "Twelfth Night," with Kate Terry doubling the parts of Viola and Sebastian and Lydia Foote as Olivia, and a play written round "Henry Dunbar," were the chief events of 1865 ; nothing appeared to run for any time. Meanwhile Kate Terry was captured by Fechter and, of the original company Horace Wigan had got together, Lydia Foote, Henry Neville and Nelly Farren were the only ones left. In December, 1866, Horace Wigan was still manager, but Webster had become the lessee. "London Assurance" was put on with rather a good cast, including Charles Mathews as Dazzle ; Mrs. Charles Mathews (the second wife), Lady Gay Spanker ; Milly Palmer, Grace Harkaway ; Neville, Charles Courtly ; Nelly Farren, Pert ; Dominick Murray, Dolly Spanker. I think this was the first appearance of Mr. and Mrs. Charles Mathews together at a London theatre. She was Miss Lizzie Weston, whose first husband was A. H. Davenport—commonly called "Dolly Davenport." The story is an old one and not worth raking up. Suffice it that there was a fracas at the stage door between Mathews and Davenport, a vast amount of gossip and a divorce, and Charles Mathews brought home to England his second wife, née Weston, late Davenport, who at once established herself in the affections of London playgoers. She was a clever actress, and at home a charming hostess in her little house in Pelham Crescent near the Keeley's, and within a stone's throw of the Swanboroughs in Michael's Grove, the Farrens, the Yateses, the Vinings, Buckstone in Brompton Square, Planché in Brompton Crescent, the Mansells in Thurloe Square, Palgrave Simpson in Alfred Place West, the Alfred Wigans in Hans Place, and a host of other gay Bohemians who lived within that musical and theatrical circle that had its centre about the famous Bell and Horns public-house (now, alas, vanished to make room for a garage), where the roads divided at a point opposite the shabby brick building which was the first Oratory at Brompton. It was a "gay" road that led to Walham Green (where lived Grisi and Mario at "Percy Cross"), to Putney for the river and the Boat Race, and to Richmond for the "Star and Garter" where so many naughty parties would assemble for Sunday outings and suppers, and whither Richard Feverel used to drive Mrs. Mount. We are not a whit more virtuous than we were then, but I cannot help thinking we enjoy ourselves and our little escapades far less. The fruit, being no longer forbidden, has lost its savour. The escapades are no longer "naughty" and have ceased to be "nice."

At the end of 1867, Charles Mathews, Nelly Farren and Henry Neville were still at the Olympic, with the addition of Mrs. Stirling; but the theatre had lost its vogue, and the plays produced about that time are not of much account. Various adaptations from the French succeeded each other with a suspicious rapidity as if they were obliged to get through a certain number at all hazards. A version of Yates's novel *Black Sheep* showed Mrs. Charles Mathews as an unexpectedly strong melodramatic actress, and her husband as an uncommonly bad one. At the close of 1868, the management, then in the hands of old Ben Webster, fell back once more on "The Ticket of Leave Man." The difficulty in those days as it has been ever since, and perhaps ever shall be, was the difficulty of finding a good play. Shakespeare was regarded as a bad investment. The actors were there, but the material was bad; it was always a case of asking good workmen to make bricks without straw. There were Robertson and Reade and Byron and Boucicault producing origi..al work from time to time, but I know of no other.

In 1869, Liston held the reins and fell back upon hackneyed but popular stuff. "Masks and Faces," with Webster in his original part of Triplet, Miss Furtado as Mabel Vane, Neville as Pomander, and Mrs. Alfred Mellon as Peg Woffington, was followed by a variety of pieces. Gilbert's "Princess," a sort of extravaganza founded on Tennyson's poem, which was afterwards used for the basis of his opera, "Princess Ida," had a moderate success, early in 1870, with an undistinguished cast, and Miss Bateman appeared in "Mary Warner" with Belmore, W. H. Vernon and one of her sisters in May. A version of La Motte Fouqué's *Undine* was put on in July with Charles Warner, Belmore, Fisher, Mattie Reinhardt, and Lizzie Russell; in August a play by Tom Taylor with Warner and

Compton and Miss Reinhardt. There was also "Perfect Love" a play on the subject of Oberon, Huon and Titania in which Warner was Sir Huon; Mrs. Liston, Oberon; and Mrs. Joseph Irving (mother of Ethel Irving) Titania. In the same year (1870) there was seen at the Olympic a version of Dickens's *Old Curiosity Shop* by Andrew Halliday, in which George Belmore played the Grandfather, John Clarke was an eerie Quilp and Little Nell was that youngest of the Terry sisters, Florence Terry, who promised to develop into such a charming actress, but left the stage early, dying in 1896. In May, 1871, a certain amount of success was scored with a drama by Byron called "Daisy Farm" with Charles Warner, Belmore and others, but perhaps the chief success of that year was the burlesque, "Giselle," which I have already referred to when speaking of Nelly Farren. It was in that piece and a preceding skit on a mythological subject in which she played Alectryon that Miss Farren showed what a wonderful little person she was in burlesque. It is not too much to say that her performance in "Giselle" alone was enough to bring back to the Olympic a great deal of the popularity it had lost by a series of inept productions.

The latter part of the year 1871 was taken up by "The Woman in White"—with Ada Dyas, Mrs. Charles Vyner, Wybert Reeve and George Vining. Nothing of any interest seems to have happened in 1872; in 1873, a very gloomy drama by Westland Marston "Put to the Test," was produced founded on an Italian piece "La Malaria." It dealt with the tragedy of Pia Tolomei, born in Siena, and done to death in the fetid air of the Maremma. She was beautiful, unhappy and died young. Maurice Hewlett has very vividly condensed the sad tale of her fate in his wonderful *Road in Tuscany* :

" Here, in these swamps, amid standing pools and tangled brakes, she, than whom Siena had made nothing more fair, grew hollow-cheeked and filmy-eyed, and very ready for Death when he had pity upon her."

It is hardly a tale for the stage : Dante put it all into one line :

Siena me fè, disfecemi Maremma.

More elaboration is unnecessary : it is even impertinent.

Ada Cavendish was excellent in the thankless part of Pia (one of Ristori's great parts), but she could not save the play.

In October of the same year, Henry Neville took over the management. For his first leading lady, he had Emily Fowler, a graceful actress, who had begun in burlesque but made her name later in several dramas. Edward Righton, G. W. Anson, both good comedians, and Mrs. Stephens were also in the company. His opening piece was by Byron, but in a few weeks he put on a version of " Le Mariage de Figaro " of Beaumarchais, made by Mortimer and called " The School for Intrigue." In this, he was the Almaviva ; Righton, Figaro ; Emily Fowler, Suzanne ; and Marion Terry made a notable success as the Countess.

In 1874, he adventured into Shakespeare, giving a really fine production of " Much Ado About Nothing," in which he was, as might have been expected, a dashing and altogether satisfactory Benedick. Emily Fowler was Beatrice ; Marion Terry, Hero ; Vernon, Don Pedro ; and Righton and Anson, Dogberry and Verges. This is often overlooked as a fine production when giving accounts of the play. Of course it has been overshadowed by the Lyceum presentation, which has probably never been equalled, and certainly never surpassed.

About this time, Ada Cavendish appeared in a version of Wilkie Collins's *New Magdalen* and scored an immediate success. It has been revived more than once since then, notably at the Novelty Theatre in the eighties when Frank Archer (perhaps better known as a dramatic critic) was the Julian Gray.

Drama, sensational or domestic, was the proper fare at the Olympic. When the management aspired to give Shakespeare, it was generally a failure.

An outstanding success was achieved by a version of a French Porte St. Martin play which was produced under the title of " The Two Orphans," also by a romantic drama of the period of William of Orange called " Lady Clancarty," in which latter piece Ada Cavendish was very good indeed and Neville found one of the best parts of his career. It was well written, with a good, even an exciting plot, and has been frequently revived.

" The Two Orphans " was of a different class : a melodrama, with horrific incidents and blood-curdling happenings, especially the scene with La Frochard, a villainous hag, admirably played by Mrs. Huntley. Incidentally one may note that Rutland Barrington made his first professional appearance in " The Two Orphans." He afterwards toured with the Howard Pauls for three years, but in 1877 settled down with the Gilbert and Sullivan operas at the Opera Comique.

Ada Cavendish left the Olympic in 1875, after having done so much to restore its reputation as a theatre always worth a visit.

She was a very handsome person who had made her London debut some ten years earlier as a very scantily dressed Venus in a burlesque of " Ixion " at the Royalty in Dean Street. By her performances at the Olympic, she established herself as an emotional actress of the first rank, her best part being, perhaps, Mercy Merrick in " The New Magdalen," which she must have played many hundred times. But she always suffered from extremely bad health and died in 1895 at the comparatively early age of forty-nine. She was the second wife of Frank Marshall, the playwright.

Once more, in 1875, was " The Ticket of Leave Man " revived with Neville in his original part and Mrs. Stephens again as Mrs. Willoughby. Nelly Farren was the Sam, and a most delightful Sam she must have made. Emily Fowler was a charming heroine, the rôle created by Kate Saville, and Charles Harcourt was the detective. An historical play called " Buckingham," by Wills, dealing with the period of the Roundheads and introducing Cromwell and Lord Fairfax, wound up the year rather badly.

During the following three years (1876—1878) over a dozen entirely new plays were produced at the Olympic, besides revivals of old successes. None of the new pieces achieved any great success, though among them were plays by such experienced authors as Charles Reade, Joseph Hatton, Tom Taylor, Paul Merritt, Farjeon, Wilkie Collins and W. S. Gilbert. Most ran for only a month or even less. Neville was still acting and Mrs. Stephens, and a new leading lady in the person of Fanny Josephs.

Among the revivals was " Henry Dunbar," with Neville in his old part, Forbes Robertson in a minor rôle and still another new leading lady in Bella Pateman. Robert Pateman was in this revival, and he remained at the theatre for some time. He was a very forcible actor of grotesque and semi-tragic parts, something in the style of Robson but far behind him in power and genius. He was equally good in melodrama or pantomime, and one of the last of his appearances was as Cassim Baba in a Drury Lane " Forty Thieves." He played the Artful Dodger in a version of " Oliver Twist " with great success and was first-rate as the informers and mean villains in Boucicault's Irish dramas, such as Michael Feeny in " Arrah-Na-Pogue " and Harvey Duff in " The Shaughraun," though these were not given at the Olympic but at the Princess's and the Adelphi. Some of his parts in the Drury Lane autumn dramas were always certain to provoke hisses and other complimentary sounds from the pit and gallery. As Desmarets in " Plot and Passion," another Robson part, he was very good. His

particular line, in short, may be said to have been the impersonation of "grovelling villainy."

In 1877 was seen another of Wilkie Collins's novels—*The
Moonstone*—with Neville, Bella Pateman, Swinbourne (as the
detective), and Hill as an excellent doddering old Betteredge ; but
it was not the success that had been anticipated.

One of the Reade dramas during these years was "Jealousy,"
an adaptation from the French, with Sophie Young and Miss
Gerard in the cast. After the departure of Ada Cavendish, Neville
seems to have changed his leading lady with nearly every production.
"The Two Orphans" had one of its periodical revivals in 1878,
with Marion Terry replacing Emily Fowler as the blind girl and
Helen Barry a new-comer in the cast. The remainder as
before.

After Neville left the Olympic to join the company at the Adelphi,
the old theatre in Wych Street passed through many different hands
with varying fortune. A version of "Oliver Twist" by a Mr.
Searle introduced an American actress—Miss Rose Eytinge—as
Nancy, and the author as Bill Sikes, with Anson a very indifferent
Fagin and Pateman as the Artful Dodger.

In 1879 there was a most interesting production. This was a
version of Goethe's "Faust" (but original in many ways) entitled
"Gretchen" by W. S. Gilbert, with Marion Terry as the sinning
heroine. Mr. Pemberton, who has written so much and so charmingly on the subject of dramatic art in England, says :

"It was a most interesting production and no doubt much of
its charm was due to the gentle and maidenly style and quiet earnest-
ness of Marion Terry. . . . it was not only original but brilliant,
and if the piece failed to draw the multitude, it was through no
fault of its author."

Miss Fortescue, formerly of the Savoy Opera, toured with it in
the provinces. In the original production at the Olympic, Conway
was Faust, Archer was Mephisto and the Lisa was Mrs. Bernard
Beere.

The other manager who tried his luck here in 1879 was Frank
Harvey, later the manager of the Beatrice Comedy-Drama Company
for so long. His pieces were successful at suburban theatres,
whose audiences are not so critical about the acting as long as they
got a good sentimental play with plenty of heroics and a sensational
scene or two thrown in. In 1879, there was also "East Lynne"
to be seen and wept over, with Miss Heath (Mrs. Wilson Barrett) as
Lady Isabel, and in the following year (1880) quite a memorable

production of a version of " David Copperfield " by the Gaiety Company, with Edward Terry as Micawber and Royce as Uriah Heep. " Little Doctor Faust " with the celebrated Gaiety quartet was in the same programme and other burlesques of the Theatre of The Sacred Lamp were given during the time that the company were out of their own house.

A version of " L'Assommoir " quite distinct from that produced by Warner at the Princess's had an inferior cast on the whole, but including such favourites as Fanny Josephs and Righton and a fine actress in Louise Moodie. About this time also Charles Wyndham came with his company in " Brighton," founded on the American piece " Saratoga," which had such a successful run at the Criterion, and John Hollingshead tried his luck with a play by Besant and Rice called " Such a Good Man," including also in the same programme a slight operetta of Offenbach's adapted by Farnie. Nelly Bromley was in the company ; she was the original Plaintiff in Gilbert and Sullivan's " Trial by Jury " at the Royalty, and retired from the stage on her marriage with one whom *The Family Herald* would have dubbed " a scion of the nobility."

1880 also saw the production of " Mabel," a drama in which Arthur Dacre made his appearance, with Vernon, Anson, Carlotta Addison and a still more famous Carlotta—Carlotta Leclercq— who nearly thirty years before had been with the Keans at the Princess's and afterwards was the heroine in Fechter's romantic dramas. In spite of this strong cast, the piece failed, and the management fell back on a revival of " The Two Orphans," with Neville and Mrs. Huntley in their original parts and Marion Terry a most pathetic representative of the blind girl.

Towards the end of the same year, " Still Waters Run Deep " was staged with a company including the Kendals, Terriss, Hare and Cissy Grahame.

Next year, there was a very curious play by Buchanan and Harriet Jay called " The Mormons : or St. Abe and His Seven Wives." The cast was composed of a lot of nobodies except the veteran McIntyre (who had played Mogg, the convict, in " The Great City " at Drury Lane in 1865 and had been known at the Surrey and other transpontine houses before that), and Stanislaus Calhaem, also somewhat of a veteran whose Australian aborigine in " It's Never Too Late to Mend " was long remembered. These dramas by Buchanan and Jay (of which there were several) hardly ever succeeded, in London at any rate, and in 1881 the Olympic took a new line and went in for comic opera, though I believe it was not actually the first time that light opera had been done there for, in 1869, " L'Oeil Crevé " in an English version by Burnand was given under the title of " Hit and Miss : or All My Eye and Betty Martin." This time it was " Claude Duval," a light opera by Edward Solomon, one of the husbands of the beauteous and much married Lilian Russell. Celli, George Power, Arthur Williams, Marion Hood were in it, and Harriet Coveney, whose earliest appearances had been at the Grecian Saloon and Olympic Temple Eagle Tavern City Road, as the Grecian Theatre was called, forty years before, in 1841. She was still acting at the Gaiety in 1888. Possibly the chief production of 1882 (the theatre being then under the direction of John Coleman) was " The Shadow of the Sword " by Robert Buchanan, but the ill-luck of the place pursued it and this strong drama had to be soon withdrawn. At the end of the year Miss Marie de Grey (a very handsome and far from incapable actress) put on " Adrienne Lecouvreur " adapted by Herman the author of the *Silver King*. The cast included Macklin as Maurice de Saxe and Fred Terry as the Abbé. The run was a very short one.

1883 opened a little better. There was a fine melodrama adapted from the French of " La Voleuse d'Enfants " by Grundy and called " Rachel," and later in the year that great actress, Genevieve Ward, appeared in her best part of La Marquise de Mohrivart in " Forget-Me-Not," a very free version of " L'Aventurière," one of the finest dramatic pieces ever seen on the English stage. She also created the rôle of Sarah Duchess of Markborough in " The Queen's Favourite," Grundy's version of Scribe's " Verre d'Eau," and played Nance Oldfield and other parts she had made her own.

Genevieve Ward was undoubtedly one of the greatest actresses that ever trod the London stage. She was an American (aggressively so, and would flap her wings and give the Eagle's screech on the slightest opportunity !) and was never intended in the first place for the stage. She married a rich Russian nobleman, who afterwards tried to repudiate the marriage. Miss Ward went with her mother to St. Petersburg and through the intervention in the first place of the American Minister and afterwards of Prince Dolgourouki, the Chamberlain of the Czar, Count de Guerbel was forced to marry her. She relates the whole circumstances most dramatically in her memoirs, how she went to the ceremony dressed in the deepest black and left her husband at the close of it. She then adopted the operatic stage as a career and was considered very fine as Norma, and in similar tragic rôles. Her operatic stage name was Guerrabella. In New York, she lost her voice and studied for the theatre under Charlotte Cushman and again in Paris under Regnier, one of the finest actors of the French school.

Her range of characters was sufficiently wide but tragedy was her forte. Lady Macbeth, Medea, Queen Katharine, Constance, Meg Merrilees, Emilia (in " Othello," a much finer part than Desdemona) and Queen Margaret in " Richard III," which she played to Irving's Richard. Other parts she acted at the Lyceum in its great days were Queen Eleanor in Tennyson's " Becket," and Volumnia in " Coriolanus." Very late in life she was in a play founded on the French Revolution at the St. James's playing to perfection the part of an old aristocrat awaiting death in the prison of the Conciergerie. No one who saw her in that scene will forget her last game of piquet with another *condamné* and her first shrinking and subsequent proud exit when she had to face the mob at the gate of the prison. But it was in " Forget-Me-Not " that she will be best remembered by London playgoers and the abject terror of her final escape from the Corsican who is seeking her life dwells in my memory still. Though she was very American in many ways, she was yet, curiously enough, *très grande dame*. I had almost forgotten to mention an earlier appearance of hers in a very old-fashioned drama at the Adelphi in the early seventies. This was then known as " The Prayer in the Storm : or the Thirst for Gold," but had been previously acted under the name of " The Sea of Ice " and earlier still (in 1854) as " The Struggle for Gold : and the Orphan of the Frozen Sea." The various titles alone will give the character of the piece. The great sensation scene was a floating block of ice on a raging sea with a maiden kneeling on it and praying earnestly for help. This never failed to bring down the house. Of course it was an adaptation from the French—the original being called " La Prière des Naufragés." In the first production the child on the broken ice is said to have been Madge Robertson (Mrs. Kendal), but I don't like to be sure about it ; it was so very long ago, and I have not been able to verify the original cast. Celeste played in it more than once.

In 1884 and 1885 there was reversion to very ordinary melodrama and farce, that is farce of the kind of " The Great Pink Pearl," which had already been done at the Criterion, and " Twins "— the humour of which turned on the close resemblance of two brothers, one of whom was a professor and the other a waiter. One of the melodramas was " Alone in London " with Leonard Boyne, Herbert Standing and Amy Roselle—one of those perennial pieces like " East Lynne " and " A Royal Divorce," which can always be counted on reviving the fading fortunes of a bad season, and which are still running somewhere in the provinces. The other melodrama was " Passion Flower," adapted from the Spanish by

Clement Scott.   Of these two " Alone in London " was by far
the best.   It was a sturdy kind of a play by Robert Buchanan and
Harriet Jay, and afterwards was revived with great success during
the latter days of the Princess's.

Edward Terry was at the Olympic in 1886 with one of his earlier
plays after he had left the field of burlesque.   This was an adaptation
from the German called " The Churchwarden," and it was followed
by two of his successes—" The Rocket " and " In Chancery."
Soon, however, the theatre drifted back to its more usual form
of entertainment, viz., melodrama, and Cecil Raleigh, who wrote
so many of the big Drury Lane autumn dramas produced a play
called " The Pointsman."   The theatre was under the management of the lovely Agnes Hewitt, a very clever actress of *ingénue*
parts, who was Blanche Lundi in the revival of " Man and Wife "
at the Haymarket.   Willard and Maud Milton were also in
Raleigh's play.

In 1888, Miss Hewitt gave up the reins of management to Yorke
Stephens, who stuck to melodrama and put on " Held by the Enemy"
with Willard, R. S. Boleyn, Julian Cross and the golden-haired
Caroline Hill, who about ten years before had drawn crowds to
see her in " New Babylon " and about whom I shall have something
more to say in the chapter on the Holborn Theatres.

The year 1888 was the most unlucky year for the various manage-
ments of the Olympic.   Play after play was produced only to fail.
In February " His Romance " (from the German) with Bassett
Roe, Brandon Thomas, S. Calhaem, and pretty Rose Norreys.
In March a version of the popular novel, *Mr. Barnes of New
York*, called " To the Death," was staged with a really fine cast,
including Allan Aynesworth, Rosina Brandram, Jessie Bond,
Rutland Barrington (three Savoyards just released by the unfortunate
break-up of the Gilbert and Sullivan partnership), Florence West
(afterwards Mrs. Lewis Waller), Gillie Farquhar and Frank Rodney.
Young Rodney, who was the son of a wealthy brewer in Hampshire
and whose real name was Perkins, was a young actor of whom
great things were always expected, but who somehow failed to
rise to really great heights.   Perhaps he did not have the opportunity, for he was seldom seen in London.   Trained with the
Bensons at the same time as Otho Stuart, whom he often under-
studied, he was a most engaging *jeune premier* and accompanied
the Kendals in their tours on more than one occasion.   I knew
him well and admired him as an actor and as a good fellow.   He
died of cancer—much regretted by many friends.

In June another play had to be put on.   This was a version of
Nathaniel Hawthorne's story, *The Scarlet Letter*, with Janet

Achurch as Hester Prynne ; her husband, Charles Charrington, Fernandez, Frederick Harrison, Ben Webster, Junr., Dolores Drummond and Gertrude Kingston being also in the cast.

Miss Achurch was one of the most powerful actresses of her time. She was very fond of acting in Ibsen's plays and was therefore not so well known as she might have been to the general public, who do not as a rule care for the Scandinavian gloom. I saw her once (at the Court Theatre, I think) in a very weird piece by Masefield called " The Witch," and was held spellbound by the eerie force of her acting in a most wonderful play.

One of the matinées of 1888 at the Olympic (of which there were always many to introduce debutantes) was to bring out a lady called on the programmes " Madame du Barry," and who was described in the Press as having a " French name and a German accent." She attempted (it was a sorry attempt) the great part of Medea. Frank Rodney was Orpheus and Macklin was Jason. The latter was a " sound " actor who could always be relied upon in a certain type of part. He had made his debut at the Queen's under Miss Litton in a production of " King John," and went with her when she took the Court Theatre. He was in the " Green Bushes " with Celeste when she returned to the stage in 1873 and he was the Romeo to the Juliet of Ada Cavendish in Manchester in 1874.

In September of this most unlucky year—all new ventures having failed—the management fell back upon " The Ticket of Leave Man," a sure draw at its old home. Neville was there in his original part of Bob Brierly, but the others were new. One interesting experiment was Jennie Lee as Sam Willoughby. She of course was perfect in the part, but the audience were so accustomed to weep over her as Jo in " Bleak House " that she did not obtain the recognition she deserved. Old Mrs. Stephens's rôle of Mrs. Willoughby was taken up by Mrs. Huntley ; Agnes Hewitt was May Edwards ; and a small part was allotted to Robert Courtneidge, the manager of to-day.

Even " The Ticket of Leave Man " could only last out a month, and in October they tried their luck with a revival of " The Two Orphans" with Neville, Sugden and Mrs. Huntley in their original parts, Agnes Hewitt as the blind girl and " Marie " (is this the same as Miriam ?) Lewes as her sister.

In 1889, the house was opened by John Coleman with popular prices—a sure sign that all was not well with its affairs. He put on the evergreen " East Lynne," with a Miss Rose Meller about whom I have been unable to get any information. At the end of the run " A Silent Witness " was staged, still for Miss Rose Meller, who was supported by Frank Cooper, a member of that talented family which included Cooper Cliffe and others of the same name.

The Coleman venture was not a success and the last days of the old house had now arrived.

The Olympic Theatre was pulled down and entirely rebuilt in 1890. It was much enlarged, the new house being capable of seating three thousand persons. Some authorities have stated that this made it second in size only to Drury Lane and the two Opera Houses, but I suspect this means " in the West End," for Mrs. Lane's theatre in Pitfield Street, Hoxton, was quite as large, if not larger. Is it not always known as " The Britannia, the Great Theatre, Hoxton ? " And there was also the Standard Theatre at Shoreditch—a very large house—and the Pavilion at Whitechapel.

Wilson Barrett, anxious to retrieve his failures at the Princess's and recoup himself for extravagances incurred in imitating other successful managers, took the New Olympic, not being able to get to his old home in Oxford Street. He put on some of his former successes and likewise some of his failures (*e.g.* " Hamlet " in which he fancied himself tremendously). He also produced a new play —" The People's Idol "—which had but a qualified success in spite of the really good company he had got together, including Winifred Emery, Maud Jeffries, Lily Hanbury, Alice Cooke, Ambrose Manning and Franklin McLeay (who had made a name at the Princess's). Some of these were destined to achieve front rank in the profession in later years and were not so well known at the time, but it was an excellent company all round.

For many years Barrett had been anxious to appear in " Belphegor," that English version of " Paillasse " which had been the outstanding success of Charles Dillon. He thought the opportunity had now come to show that he could play the part as well as Dillon, or as Webster who had preceded him, or Fechter who came after. Previous productions of this well-known drama may be roughly outlined as follows :

Adelphi, 1851, Benjamin Webster the elder, Celeste, Woolgar, and O. Smith.

Surrey, 1851, Creswick and Harriet and Jane Coveney.

Old Vic, 185? " Belphegor the Buffoon : or the Assassin of the Revolution." The title rôle was played at the Vic by one J. T. Johnson, a great favourite of the time in the provinces, who was of the old style, mouthing and ranting. I remember as a boy seeing him act in the old theatre on the Green at Richmond. I made his acquaintance and he showed me with pride a looking-glass in his dressing-room which had been used by Edmund Kean.

Sadler's Wells, 1856. Mr. and Mrs. Charles Dillon. Rose Edouin as Henri, the small son of Belphegor.

Lyceum, Charles Dillon with Toole, and Marie Wilton as Henri.

Lyceum, 1865, Fechter with his son Paul as the child, Mlle. Beatrice as Madeleine, Carlotta Leclercq, Sam Emery, John Ryder, Widdicomb.

The names of the characters, as also the name of the various versions of this old French play, were frequently changed, and the adaptation put on at the Olympic by Barrett was called " The Acrobat." It will be remembered that the story deals with one Belphegor, an acrobat, his faithless wife and his forlorn, motherless child. Lemaitre, the great French character actor, first created the title rôle and it was always very popular in France, but even Charles Fechter with all his wonderful powers in romantic drama was not able to make it entirely acceptable in England, and he never came near Charles Dillon in the part. Nowadays such a play would not stand a chance with its old-fashioned " asides," its improbable situations and its sloppy sentimentalities. Westland Marston, a great dramatic critic in his day, said of Dillon that he was an actor of great emotional gifts but deficient in intellectual ones.

" The Acrobat " must be pronounced one of Barrett's decided failures and it did not hold the stage long. The production was in April, 1891, the cast including Winifred Emery as Madeleine, Lily Hanbury, Cooper Cliffe and George Barrett. Earlier in the same year, " The Silver King " and " The Lights o' London " had each been put on for short runs with Winifred Emery in the place of Miss Eastlake and Cooper Cliffe in the Willard parts, and a curious experiment had been made in the revival of Kotzebue's dismal play of " The Stranger " at a series of matinées. It can only be presumed that Barrett wished to show himself in a part which had been played by Macready and all the great tragedians of the forties and fifties, for he could not have imagined that such an impossible play would ever again command the success of former days. Miss Emery was the Mrs. Haller. How she must have hated the part !

" Ben-my-Chree," originally seen at the Princess's, was another revival. In the reproduction of " Hamlet " Cooper Cliffe was the Laertes ; Louise Moodie, Gertrude ; and Miss Emery, Ophelia.

May, 1891, saw another revival of "The Silver King," with Lily Hanbury in Miss Eastlake's part ; and soon after that Barrett gave up the theatre and it was taken by an American actress, Miss Grace Hawthorne, who brought over "Theodora" in which she had previously been seen at the Princess's. Murray Carson and Fuller Mellish (Rose Leclercq's son) were with her, but her venture did not promise success and the programme was changed to "Oliver Twist," or rather a mangled American version of Dickens's book in which she appeared as Nancy, Bassett Roe as Bill Sikes, Henry de Solla (whom I seem to remember as a derelict swell in "The Lights o' London") as Fagin, and James Welch as the Artful Dodger. There were possibilities about the Dodger, but the whole production must have been singularly modern (*i.e.*, American), and as unlike Dickens as even an American could make it.

In 1892, Signor Lago, who had had some experience as a con- ductor of Italian Opera at the Adelphi and elsewhere, tried a season at the Wych Street house. He produced novelties by Tschaikowsky and others in addition to the usual round of Verdi, etc., but the venture was disastrous and the theatre closed very abruptly. That delicate exotic, Italian Opera, had no chance in those days when the average theatre audience was not really a cultured one, and it has not a much better chance even now.

An excellent pantomime was put on at Christmas, 1892. There has nearly always been a pantomime at the old Olympic, but the custom had fallen into some disfavour. "Dick Whittington" was the subject. Edith Bruce, a very handsome "principal boy," was the Dick, Fred Emney the Alderman and Victor Stevens (one of the best "dames" in theatrical history) was the Cook. The Cat was Charles Lauri.

It was evident that the rebuilding of the Olympic on an ambitious scale had brought no change of luck. New and comfortable theatres had been opened in neighbourhoods far more convenient and less objectionable than the slums of Drury Lane. The exclusiveness of the Strand as the locality for all the chief theatres had been broken down. Shaftesbury Avenue had come into its own. The Olympic never had a real success after Barrett left in 1891, though many and most curious were the ventures put forth to allure the public.

In 1895, Miss Grace Hawthorne once more tried her managerial hand and staged a very odd version of Bunyan's immortal *Pilgrim's Progress*. This is said to have been a very funny affair, and I always regret that absence from London prevented my seeing it, for it appears to have been more like a pantomime than a version of the well-known allegory. Miss Hawthorne herself played Christian as a sort of " principal boy "—in tights complete ! There were one or two " trick scenes " of a sort, and other pantomime effects and even a Ballet ! It was a very sad kind of show and was soon withdrawn. No audience (that is, no British audience) could be found to swallow such a travesty.

The last years of the Olympic were "ragged ones," so to speak. There was a circus entertainment at one time, the house thus reverting to its very earliest traditions, and the last scene of all was a troupe of Midgets performing to almost empty benches at very cheap charges of admission and unlimited "paper." In 1899, the theatre was finally closed to make way for Kingsway and Australia House, not to mention the Gladstone statue ! A corner of the proscenium could for a long time be seen standing like a mournful remnant of former greatness in the middle of rank weeds, tin cans and other component parts of the rubbish of a waste tract.

In writing an account of a theatre like the Olympic, which perhaps more than any other of the lost London theatres had its ups and downs and frequent changes of management, it would have proved very dull to set down in regular order all the different failures and successes. I have merely endeavoured to bring out as clearly as may be the more interesting events in its chronicles and rescue from the oblivion of old newspapers and Memoirs some notable productions and appearances which may have been forgotten.

After the retirement of Henry Neville in 1879 and for the twenty years of existence still remaining, the Olympic gradually ceased to be a fashionable, or even leading London theatre, and with the exception of the seasons of Genevieve Ward and Wilson Barrett, and one or two attempts to resuscitate light opera, there is little or nothing to record.

But it was a theatre that had had its great days. It had been the scene of many notable premieres. Among the great " first nights " were " The Porter's Knot," " Still Waters Run Deep," " Plot and Passion," " The Sheep in Wolf's Clothing," " The Ticket of Leave Man," " The New Magdalen," " Lady Clancarty," " The Two Orphans," and many others. In this house Vestris first showed what an energetic manageress could do for the comfort and amusement of her audience ; Robson's great " creations " were all seen there for the first time : many actors and actresses made their reputations within its dirty walls—Gustavus Brooke,

Alfred Wigan, and his clever wife, Mrs. Stirling, Robson, Kate Terry, Kate Savile, Henry Neville, Ada Dyas, Ada Cavendish, Emily Fowler—to name only a few.

It hardly ever paid its way. Manager after manager left with heavy losses or with accounts scarcely balanced. Even the most successful seasons, those of Vestris, Robson and Neville, finished up with loss. Perhaps it was an unlucky theatre. Every actor and manager and playgoer knows that houses are lucky or they are not. Situation, good or otherwise, does not seem to affect the question. For years, to take one example, the St. James's Theatre was the unluckiest theatre in London, and it was really the actor-manager who saved it at the last.

It is a fact that the only times the Olympic had any semblance of success was when it was directed by an actor-manager or actress-manageress. Vestris, the Wigans, Neville made the best of their sojourns there, though the first-named (like Irving in his great days) would have made more and avoided bankruptcy if she had not been the most extravagant woman the stage world has ever known. When the next actor-manager comes along, if he be capable, business-like, artistic and, above all, an autocrat, he will make a fortune.

A feature of the old Olympic as it was, also of the Adelphi, the Princess's, and other theatres of that day, was that the pit extended all the way down to the orchestra. There were no stalls. The "quality" went to the Dress Circle or to the Boxes of which there were two kinds—the dress boxes in front and a range of inferior and cheaper ones behind them, known as "The Basket." Private Boxes came later. Prices of admission were very low. Pit, 3s. and 2s. ; Boxes 5s. ; Gallery 1s., perhaps the same as the modern Upper Boxes, and Upper Gallery 6d. A second price (generally one-half) to all parts at nine o'clock was a concession of which advantage was often taken, for you could still arrive in time for the greater part of the chief piece and the final farce or burlesque, or both. Alfred Wigan was, I think, the one to introduce stalls at the Olympic ; in his most successful seasons the price of these never rose above five shillings.

I have heard it said that the old Olympic was the last house in London to use the green curtain. At one time the final curtain was always green and generally of baize, but the one at the old Olympic in 1849 was of green velvet, parting in the middle, and was the cause of the fire that destroyed the theatre in that year. It is possible, though hardly probable, that a green curtain may still survive in some out-of-the-way provincial theatre, but I have not seen or heard of one for many years.

While on the subject of drop-curtains, how interesting it would be if one or two of the more celebrated theatres among those which really have a history, preserved their act-drops before which so many clever actors and charming actresses must have bowed their acknowledgments. One at least is so preserved and perhaps the most interesting of all to the present generation of playgoers. At the King's Theatre, Hammersmith, is still used (or was a short time ago) the act-drop that served as the background so long for Irving's graceful bows and Ellen Terry's sunny smiles of thanks. At the Haymarket, again, there was not long ago, and may be still, the drop curtain specially painted for the Bancrofts when they migrated there from Tottenham Street. On it is depicted a scene from " The School for Scandal " where the principal characters are dancing a Minuet. It is to be hoped that this will never be destroyed, for the figures are all actual portraits of the company, one of the best companies that ever acted in any theatre. Perhaps, however, the sentiment attaching to these old act-drops has vanished entirely in these days when no artiste ever thinks of smiling or even acknowledging the applause of the audience save by standing in a stiff, emotionless row to be gazed at again and again as often as the curtain is raised for the purpose. It is a very sorry substitute for old proscenium stage doors or the calls before the curtain which existed in my day. As a place of entertainment, the Olympic (at any rate the older building) would not be endured for a day by the present generation of playgoers, and the august County Council would have very rightly condemned it as an insanitary and dangerous building. It remains, however, one of the memories of my early days as a Londoner, and I always enjoyed its shows, sometimes taking advantage of the half-price myself.

Moreover, in spite of its horrible position in the back ways of Drury Lane and Wych Street, I always felt there was no danger in case of a fire, for I remember there were numerous exits on all sides by which you could easily and quickly escape into the surrounding courts and alleys.

Much history was made in those same slums and alleys. It will be a long day before Kingsway has any history worth recording— if ever. The old slums were full of Life, which, if dirty and disreputable, was at any rate warm with colour and quick with movement. The new area is like a presentment of Death—clean and respectable, cold, grey and still. As " The Londoner " (delightful person !) says :

" Change and decay in all around I see, as a melancholy hymn puts it. But no. There is change everywhere : not decay. A horrid trimness ; raw novelty."

I thank " The Londoner " for those words—" horrid trimness ; raw novelty." That is Kingsway in a nutshell.

CHAPTER VI

THE ROYAL PRINCESS'S THEATRE
(1) FROM THE EARLIEST TIMES TO THE END OF THE MANAGEMENT
OF CHARLES KEAN

THE Royal Princess's Theatre in Oxford Street is not, in reality, a lost London theatre. It is still standing, though it has been shut up and derelict for nearly a quarter of a century. It will probably never be used again as a theatre, and its ghost-haunted precincts may be levelled to form a foundation for hotel, flats or the ubiquitous cinema.

But the Princess's Theatre could not be omitted from such a book as this. Its place in the history of the London Stage is inferior in importance only to the two Opera Houses, Drury Lane and the " Little House in the Haymarket." It was here that the stage in England was first roused from the coma of the early Victorian era, which had such a deadly effect on all matters connected with Art and the Drama. Here first appeared the modern spirit of acting, to scatter once and for all memories of the stilted formalities of the Old School. Forrest, Macready, Charles Kean, Fechter, Boucicault, Wilson Barrett have trod the boards of the Princess's— an illustration of development in dramatic art which no other single theatre can show. Let me, then, trace back the history of the Princess's Theatre from its earliest days, though it may be still above ground.

In 1828, there was opened on the north side of Oxford Street a building with the somewhat grandiose title of " Royal Bazaar, British Diorama, and Exhibition of Works of Art." It was under the special patronage of George IV, and was a sort of Soho Bazaar, combined with other attractions.

This affair was the speculation of a certain Mr. Hamlet, a jeweller of Cranbourne Alley (the original of Thackeray's " Mr. Polonius "). The Diorama was composed of four large pictures of various continental views, by Clarkson Stansfield and David Roberts. These were all destroyed by fire in 1829, but the place was rebuilt and reopened in 1830 by Reinagle, R.A., who, ten years before, had started a similar panoramic show at a little hall in the Strand, which afterwards became the Strand Theatre.

In 1834, it was renamed the " Queen's " in compliment to Queen Adelaide, but it never paid as a Bazaar under any name— it was too near the Soho Bazaar and the Pantheon—and in 1836 it was finally made into a regular theatre at a cost of £47,000. It was first named the " Court " Theatre and afterwards—in 1840— the " Princess's " by which name it has ever since been known.

Hamlet opened it with Concerts under the direction of a Mr. Willy, but, having advanced large sums to the Prince Regent, the Duke of York and others on the security of bonds which they calmly repudiated, the unfortunate jeweller was compelled to go through the Bankruptcy Court and the property in Oxford Street was sold to a Mr. Montagu for only £15,000.

There was still some idea of making the theatre a centre for high-class musical performances, and on Boxing Day, 1842, it began a new career with Bellini's " Sonnambula," in which Eugenia Garcia sang Amina and Weiss (who later on attained a very high position as a bass singer) was the Rodolfo. The bill also included a burlesque on " The Yellow Dwarf " with a good cast, including Oxberry and Madame Sala, mother of George Augustus of that ilk.

There appears to have been, as usual, a good deal of rivalry among the prima donnas of the Princess's; for Madame Sala on one occasion expected to be allotted the chief rôle and it was given to Madame Fearon, the mother of Augustus Harris the elder, father of " Drurio-lanus " ; and on another occasion it was Eugenia Garcia who made a fuss about her proper position. This is only a repetition of what used to go on constantly in the greater companies of the big Opera Houses where the ladies would often have clauses inserted in their contracts to protect themselves from any possible mis-understanding with rival singers in the future.

There is a very good anecdote related of Madame Lablahe, when singing the part of Donna Anna in " Don Giovanni " with a tenor called Brignoli, who had a disagreeable habit of spitting constantly on the stage to clear his throat. Madame Lablache knew this and on this occasion, as she was wearing a very costly velvet dress, she whispered to him entreatingly : " Voyons, mon ami, ne pourriez-vous pas, une fois par hasard, cracher sur la robe de Donna Elvira ? " But history does not relate whether this was to save her dress or do an ill turn to a rival singer !

In 1843, the theatre was still paying its way well, and the company for the inevitable burlesque comprised Paul Bedford and Wright (afterwards the comedians of the Adelphi), Wieland, the panto-mimist, Oxberry and a very remarkable woman, one Emma Stanley, one of the very earliest and most successful of single entertainers after the style adopted by Woodin, Maccabe, John Parry, Albert Smith, George Grossmith, Corney Grain, and Barclay Gammon, but with the addition of costume.

Blanchard wrote for her " The Seven Ages of Woman," an

entertainment which she took all over England and to the Colonies and America as well. She used to give it at the St. Martin's Hall in Long Acre, where Dickens gave his Readings, and which became the Queen's Theatre. In spite of her successes, Emma Stanley died in 1881 a poor woman. At the Hanover Square Rooms (a notable Hall for concerts of the better kind, which was afterwards turned into the Club that Anthony Trollope caricatured as the "Bear-Garden" in his novel, *The Way We Live Now*) she gave the same Show, her final appearance being at the Old Egyptian Hall in Piccadilly in 1860. In this entertainment, she introduced thirty-seven distinct changes of character and costume, played on six different instruments and sang in English, French, German, Italian, Spanish, Russian and Greek.

In 1843, the Princess's started a Season in English Opera (or rather "Opera in English"), and Braham appeared in "Fra Diavolo." "Geraldine," a light opera by Balfe, was put on for Eugenia Garcia, the Ballet "Giselle" for a Mr. and Mrs. Gilbert and "The Don Pasquale" of Donizetti for Paul Bedford, Burdini and Eugenia Garcia. By the way, Paul Bedford is not the only opera singer who took up acting as distinct from singing. Madame Guerrabella, a dramatic singer of eminence, became Genevieve Ward, and Fred Younge and George Honey were both singers in Grand Opera at Covent Garden or Her Majesty's before they were members of the Bancroft Company at the Prince of Wales's.

Paul Bedford, indeed, had been in great operas with great singers. When Schroeder-Devrient created the title rôle in Beethoven's only Opera "Fidelio," he was in the cast ; but it was as a low comedian that he principally made his name. He played with Celeste in such pieces as "The Flowers of the Forest" and "The Green Bushes," in which latter piece he had a catch phrase, "I believe you, my boy," which he had picked up in a transpontine theatre and which was heard all over London. He died in 1871, but I saw him play his old part in "The Green Bushes" for Celeste's benefit some time in the sixties, when he must have been a regular Methuselah, for "Fidelio" was first produced in 1791.

These Operas at the Princess's appear to have been always followed by a variety turn of some sort. Tom Thumb, the midget, followed "Don Pasquale" in the same bill, or Henry Russell sang his own "Cheer, Boys, Cheer" or a pleasant change from Donizetti or Auber would be "Timour the Tartar," one of the most popular dramas done by Skelt for the Theatres of Toyland.

The Keeleys were at the Princess's in 1843. This was by no means Mrs. Keeley's first appearance on the London stage. As Miss Annie Goward, she had made her debut at the Royal English

Opera (the old Lyceum Theatre which was on the south side of the Strand near the corner of that bit of Wellington Street which leads directly to Waterloo Bridge) as Rosina and the Little Pickle in " The Spoiled Child." The programme on this occasion began with the overture to Cherubini's " Anacreon," followed by " The Beggars' Opera," in which Miss Stephens and Miss Fanny Kelly were Polly and Lucy respectively. Her next venture was in Grand Opera. Weber, who conducted his opera of " Oberon " just before his death, selected Mary Anne Goward from many candidates to sing " The Mermaid's Song " and understudy Mme. Vestris, who was cast for the rôle of Fatima. She also sang in the same composer's " Der Freischütz " with Miss Paton and Madame Fearon, and with Miss Kelly as Zerlina in Auber's " Fra Diavolo." In 1825, she married Robert Keeley. Her great successes were in farce and comedy, though Dickens declared that she was the ideal 'Smike' in "Nicholas Nickleby." Adaptations of Dickens's novels were then the rage : Mrs. Keeley was Dot in " The Cricket on the Hearth," and, more popular still, Bailey, the tiger in top-boots in " Martin Chuzzlewit." She played Macheath in " The Beggars' Opera " when it was brought out at Drury Lane in 1839 in opposition to Mme. Vestris in the same character at Covent Garden, but she and her husband, after a visit to America, joined Vestris for some three years at Covent Garden and then Keeley took the Lyceum on his own account and produced a series of burlesques and many adaptations from Dickens. She sang much with Madame Fearon at various times—Polly to the Mrs. Peachum of that lady, and Paul to her Virginia. Her range of characters was enormous. She was equally at home in farce or as an impudent Bailey Junior, in pathetic rôles like Smike or Nydia the blind girl in a dramatization of Bulwer's " Last Days of Pompeii." Jack Sheppard was, perhaps, her greatest part and she always declare that her work in that, which was so strenuous, destroyed her singing voice altogether. As a buttons, a servant girl (Betsy Baker), a Tiger (Bailey Junior), a Pompeian girl (Nydia), an Italian peasant, or a housebreaker (Jack) : in petticoats, in doublet and hose, in top-boots, in highlows, or in the rags of a beggar, she was equally good, equally amusing. Her professional work must have been very wearing and it must be remembered that the material advantages in those days were very different to what they are now. Incessant work, incessant change of programme involving incessant rehearsals and all for a pound or two, or less, per week. There was no minimum salary then, regardless as to whether you had to learn a part or only walk on the stage. *Tempora mutantur* indeed !

The Keeleys were greatly respected in every class of Society from the Queen (who sent for her to Buckingham Palace after she was ninety years of age) to the humblest galleryite. Their cheery house in Pelham Crescent, in the midst of a neighbourhood which swarmed with theatrical folk, was the rendezvous of all that was best in the profession. There were two daughters, both on the stage, who both died before their mother. One married Albert Smith, the novelist and entertainer ; and the other, Montagu Williams, the Q.C. Mrs. Keeley's niece, daughter of her brother Fred, married a Mr. William Faucit and appeared at the Strand in " Our Flat " under the name of Miss Annie Goward, which had been her aunt's first stage name.

In writing of these times in theatrical history, one should always remember that long runs were the exception rather than the rule, and runs of a year or more seldom if ever happened. One hundred nights was a fabulously long run at a stretch for a production of any kind. Whether audiences were more fickle or productions less costly, the bill was very frequently changed. Perhaps one reason was that the playgoing public was a much more restricted one : not nearly so many persons went often to a play and many never went at all ; it therefore took a much shorter time to come to the end of audiences for any particular piece.

Thus, in 1844 at the Princess's there was a constant change of piece and performers throughout the year. At Easter, Albert Smith's burlesque of " Cherry and Fairstar " with Bedford, Wright and Mrs. Grattan. The last-named, whose descendants still adorn the stage, wore in this burlesque a costume of spun glass costing three guineas a yard, which her dressers objected to repair because it cut their fingers !

In May of the same year, Auber's " Crown Diamonds," with Madame Anna Thillon ; in July, a burlesque of Aladdin ; in October " Don Cæsar de Bazan " with James Wallack, an American actor of repute, as the Don ; in the same month, an opera of Balfe's now entirely forgotten called " The Four Sons of Aymon " ; at Christmas a burlesque on the old play of " The Miller and His Men " with Compton and Oxberry. Other operas were done about this time, among them " Anna Bolena," " Lucia di Lammermoor," " Otello " (Rossini), " Puritani " and " Lucrezia Borgia," in the last named of which Anna Thillon or Eugenia Garcia sang the title rôle and the useful Mrs. Grattan was the Maffio Orsini. An English Opera by Loder, once very popular but now forgotten, saw the footlights for the first time ; this was " The Night Dancers," founded on the story of the ballet of " Giselle," in which appeared a very good singer, Madame Albertazzi.

After Hamlet, the jeweller, was sold up, the proprietor was a

Mr. Maddox, a Jew, whose real name was Medec. His brother owned a tobacconist's shop nearly opposite the theatre. Maddox was very desirous of making his new venture the chief place for the introduction of great artistes from other countries or the presentation of those who had made their names elsewhere.

Thus, it was he who engaged Wallack to appear in the great rôles of Lemaitre. This was an enormous success. Wallack was a very picturesque actor of the Fechter and Waller order, but with the more pronounced action and diction of that day. He made a furore in a play founded on the career of the brigand, Massaroni, in which he sang " Gentle Zitella," in such a manner as to make it the popular song of the day. I remember it as one of the tunes in all the Pianoforte Instruction books I ever saw.

This Wallack came of a fine old theatrical stock. The first one of any account was William Wallack, who married Elizabeth Field Granger, at one time a member of Garrick's company, by whom he had four children—Henry, James William, Mary and Elizabeth—all on the stage. I have seen it stated that William Wallack's wife was Miss Mary Johannot, a well-known actress at the London minor theatres, but in Lester Wallack's *Memories of Fifty Years* published in America in 1889, which is the best authority on the subject, it is said his wife was Mrs. Elizabeth Granger (*née* Field), though this may, of course, have been a second wife. Of these four children, Henry was the father of James William Wallack, Junior, and of two daughters, Fanny and Julia. " Young Jim Wallack," as he was always called, acted much in England such parts as Fagin in " Oliver Twist " and Mathias in " The Bells," and died in 1873. Fanny became Mrs. Charles Moorehouse and was very popular on the Edinburgh stage. Julia married William Hoskin and sang on the lyric stage in London as Miss Julia Harland. James William Wallack, the second son of the original Henry, was the one who appeared at the Princess's and was the best known of all of them in this country, though his father had been a member of the old company at Astley's and other minor houses before settling in America. Mary, the eldest daughter, was an actress in the States. Elizabeth, the other, never came to England. She married Mr. Pincott and was the mother of Mrs. Alfred Wigan. The J. W. Wallack of the Princess's was born in London in 1795, and appeared as a child in the spectacle of " Bluebeard " at the Royal Circus, afterwards the Surrey Theatre. When he settled in America, he turned " Brougham's Lyceum " in Broadway into the first theatre bearing the name of " Wallack's," of which there were three altogether. A curious sidelight is thrown on the mentality of the Americans of the day whose Puritanical

CHARLOTTE CUSHMAN

LAURA KEENE

GEORGE JORDAN

J. W. WALLACK JUNR.

SOME AMERICAN PLAYERS

From old American Prints

feelings did not allow them to call any building a theatre, and for many years such places of entertainment were known as Museums and had to have some sort of collection of Museum objects to which a dramatic show was added as an extra ! It sounds very much like the quintessence of hypocrisy. Wallack's earliest appearance in London seems to have been as Laertes to the Hamlet of Elliston at Drury Lane in 1815, when he could have been only seventeen years of age. I have gone into the story of the Wallack family because they originated in England, though afterwards they were the leading lights of the New York stage.

In 1845, two American actors were in the company at the Princess's Theatre, and Maddox was very anxious that they should appear together in the same play. These were Edwin Forrest and Charlotte Cushman.

Charlotte Cushman was descended from Plymouth pilgrims on both sides, Robert Cushman, her ancestor, having been one of the original schemers of the emigration. She was born at Boston in 1815. Her mother, left a widow in poor circumstances, kept a boarding-house to make both ends meet. Charlotte had a fine contralto voice, almost the voice of a man, and was being trained for the concert stage ; her ambition was, however, to succeed as an actress and she braved the displeasure of her whole family, who, as Presbyterians and descendants of a leader of the Puritans, set their face resolutely against it. She had her way and, as she puts it, " lost the respect of my family."

Her first appearance as Lady Macbeth in New York was not a success, for the American audience of those days had their popular favourites always and looked askance at new-comers, however good. So she had to enter a stock company at a minor theatre, playing in melodrama, comedy and farce. Here she was joined by her sister, Susan, who had been deserted by an infamous husband leaving her and her baby to starve. They came to England in 1845. Charlotte Cushman was certainly not qualified by any personal charms for the dramatic profession, and this is perhaps why she deliberately adopted male instead of female rôles ; but, in selecting Romeo as her best part, her unfitness for the stage was made more apparent still.

The authoress of *Gossip of the Century*, who was a Mrs. Byrne, wife of the editor of the *Morning Post*, and knew every one of any consequence in the profession, writes of Cushman thus :

" She was less fitted for Romeo than any other : her features were most singular : the depression of the nose gave to her countenance the appearance of having been sat upon : her face was, in fact, absolutely deformed, and it was impossible to forget it, for there was nothing in her acting either to compensate for absence of beauty, or to excuse her for placing herself in so prominent a position."

It should not be forgotten that this is one woman speaking of another : it seems almost hopeless to expect a fair or just criticism when it is one woman writing of another.   On the other hand, and as if to prove that there is no rule without an exception, Genevieve Ward, a countrywoman of her own, writes most enthusiastically about her :

" She was a great woman in every way : a fine, intellectual, big-hearted creature, a great tragic actress and America may be well proud of her.   She had not much regular teaching, her genius was innate.   She was generous to her fellow-actresses, and to me especially : in fact, she told a very dear friend of mine that her mantle had fallen on my shoulders."

There is a suspicion of the shriek of the American Eagle in that, coupled with the delightfully naïve assertion that the mantle of a great tragic actress had fallen on her own shoulders !   She herself was of course greater than Cushman could ever have been.   In private life this mannish lady appears to have been a most amiable person, liked by most people and helpful to many.   She had just mistaken her profession.   Personally, I have an idea that what made her go on the stage was a great desire to " wear the breeches " ; she was always known to the members of the profession as " Captain Charlotte."   One of her best parts was Meg Merrilees, in which an absolutely terrifying gaunt ugliness is rather an advantage than otherwise.   Her liking for male parts caused her to undertake, besides Romeo, such rôles as Hamlet, Claude Melnotte and once, even, Cardinal Wolsey !

Douglas Jerrold, who waged a constant warfare against Charles Kean and lost no opportunity of using his paper (*Lloyds*) to run him down, took advantage of Cushman's appearance at the Haymarket in 1855 as Romeo to publish the following :

" Miss Romeo, or rather Miss Cushman as Romeo, has appeared this week at the Haymarket.   The curiosity is not a novelty : we have before seen Miss Cushman as Miss Romeo : and though the lady lover is full of flame, it is the flame of phosphor—it shines but it does not burn.   We could as soon warm our hands at a painted fire, as feel the impetuous passion of an ungowned Romeo. The part of Juliet has been played by a young lady brand new from that nursery of the drama, Liverpool. However, Miss Swanborough, we must take another opportunity to see. Certainly there was never greater room for a young and passionate actress. By the way, as a lady acts Verona's youth, why should not a gentleman play Verona's maiden ? How would the subjoined, for a novelty, look in the Haymarket playbill ?—

Romeo..................Miss Charlotte Cushman.
Juliet.....................Mr. Charles Kean.

There would be attraction in this at least for one night. Nor have we the least doubt that the representative of Juliet would have at hand certain sagacious critics who would discover in his portraiture of the virgin of Verona, graces and delicacies and profundities hitherto unknown or unacknowledged. Miss O'Neill's Juliet was too feeble, Miss Fanny Kemble's Juliet too forcible : whereas Mr. Charles Kean's Juliet united the spirituality of the angelic nature with all the ardour of purely human passion. Mr. Paul Bedford has played Polly Peachum. Why should not Mr. Charles Kean play Juliet ? "

The Miss Swanborough referred to above was the eldest of the family and later became Mrs. Lyons. She was playing all the leading *ingénues* at the Haymarket. At the Princess's Charlotte Cushman played Bianca in Milman's " Fazio " and also Lady Macbeth with Edwin Forrest. Julia was another of her characters : but she was not fitted for female parts except such as Meg Merrilees, half masculine in kind. Her sister played Juliet to her Romeo, but was a very inferior actress. It may be interesting to note *en passant*, that Miss Cushman was not the only lady smitten with the idea of " playing the man," and the stage lover at that. Another female Romeo was Mrs. Charles Kean (I should like to have seen that, though I doubt if I should have behaved myself with due decorum !). Another was the American, Mrs. Conway, who with her sister, Mrs. Bowers, came to London in 1861 and had more than a mere *succès d'estime* ; Felicita Vestvali, a German woman who had been an opera singer, played Romeo to the Juliet of Milly Palmer (Mrs. Bandmann) at the Lyceum in 1867, with Ryder as Friar Laurence and Walter Lacy as Mercutio ; Mrs. St. Claire (*née* Mary Marshall), an ambitious, but notably bad, actress was another ; so was Miss Marriott, who ran Sadler's Wells successfully for quite a long time and also appeared as Macbeth, Richard III and Hamlet. In the last-named character she was said to be very good. Still another, in more modern days, is Miss

Esmé Beringer, whom Clement Scott declared to have been the best Romeo he ever saw.

Forrest, who was leading tragedian at the Princess's for a time, was a ranting, rather uncouth actor of the old-fashioned sort who played Othello and Lear much in the way you might have expected from a barnstormer of the country-side. His first appearance in London had been at Drury Lane in the rôle of Spartacus the gladiator. He was born in Philadelphia, U.S.A., son of a Scottish emigrant and a German lady, and he attained to great popularity in America, but what was liked in the States would not go down at all in London, and Forrest was by no means a success. When he appeared as Othello, Mrs. Stirling was the Desdemona and Miss Cushman Emilia, a much better part than Othello's wife. He failed disastrously, a failure no doubt due to his ranting style and coarse diction. In his rage, he accused Macready of organizing a body of opposition. There was probably no truth whatever in this accusation, but when Macready went to America in after years, it was the cause of what were known as the " Forrest Riots " during which twenty people were killed and Macready escaped by a miracle. It is true that the English tragedian was very touchy when a new star arose who promised to interfere with his position as sole head of the British dramatic profession. He had the same jealousy of Charles Kean as Forrest had of himself and would never meet him or go to see him act, which was foolish on his part, as he was a decidedly better actor than the manager of the great Shakespearean revivals at the Princess's.

In 1845, Mr. and Mrs. Charles Mathews (Madame Vestris) were acting at the Oxford Street house, but the details of the chief work of this charming actress belong rather to the story of the Olympic.

In the same year a young and inexperienced actress played juvenile lead at the Princess's. This was Mary Anne Hehl, who had made her debut on the stage in the early thirties of the nineteenth century as Miss Fanny Clifton, but is better known to us all as Mrs. Stirling.

In her Life written by her grandson, it is hinted that she may have appeared first of all at the old City Theatre, Cripplegate, where Edmund Kean and the Sisters Tree and others shone for a time, but it is more likely that her first try was at the Pavilion, White-chapel, in a medley of drama and ballet called " The Devil and the Widow," in which Madame Celeste, actress and dancer, was also making her debut. It is unnecessary to go into any details of this lady's career, as it has been so well and thoroughly done by her grandson, Mr. Allen ; I will therefore simply note that she played Desdemona to the Othello of Edwin Forrest, and was also with

Macready, and achieved a moderate success in Shakespearean rôles such as Rosalind, Catherine, Portia, Hermia and Cordelia. She played at the Princess's with Macready in Shakespeare, in inferior dramas like "The King of the Commons," a play in blank verse by Rev. James White, and in "The Chevalier de St. George," adapted from the French, in which Wallack played the lead.

Maddox, the Jew manager of the Princess's, seems to have tried a little of everything at the theatre by turns and stuck to nothing long. He produced heavy plays by Kotzebue (author of that awful piece "The Stranger") and translations of immoral pieces from Paris; he occasionally reverted to English Opera: early in 1847 Miss Romer was the principal attraction, while a still finer singer—Louisa Pyne—made her debut here, in 1850, singing with the tenor Harrison (father of the well-known reciter Clifford Harrison) in Balfe's "Gustavus," Macfarren's "King Charles II" and Halévy's "Val D'Andorre." Alfred Wigan was here in 1849 beginning to make his mark, and Mrs. Warner, whom we shall hear of again at the Marylebone, made various appearances with Macready, Creswick and others. There was always a pantomime at Christmas as usual at that time founded on anything but a fairy tale! "The King of the Kingdom : or the Enchanted Beauties of the Golden Castle" was the entirely attractive title of the first Princess's pantomime and others were "Harlequin King Jamie" and "Bluff King Hal." Blanchard wrote many pantomimes for the Princess's, especially in the days of the Keans, and that extraordinarily gifted pantomimist, Flexmore, was generally Clown, with his wife, Madame Auriol, as Columbine. In earlier days, the Leclercq family (children of a clever Mme. Leclercq well versed in pantomime traditions), Carlotta, Louise, Charles Arthur, etc., did the Harlequinade, Kate Terry was a Fairy, and Milano, Harlequin. The Harlequinade in those days was an important part of the whole, and I am tempted to quote from the programme of one of these pantomimes which were always eagerly looked forward to at the Oxford Street house. It was in 1852 and was billed as :

"A Grand Operatico, Tragico, Serio-pastoralic, Nautico, Demoniaco, Cabalistico Original Christmas Pantomine entitled
"Harlequin Billy Taylor : or the Flying Dutchman and the King of Raritongo."

A feature of the pantomimes of those days was the prominence given to the Harlequinade. In "Billy Taylor" there were no less than six set scenes of Harlequinade, viz., Exterior of the *Punch*

Office and Picture Maker's Shop ; A Model Farm Yard ; Brahma's Lock Manufactory and General Outfitter's Warehouse ; Exterior of the comfortable Catch-em and Keep-em Hotel (with a Pas de Parapluie by Mr. Flexmore. I think umbrellas were a novelty about that time) ; Bird's Eye View of London by Moonlight with the Cats' Serenade ; Interior of a Confectioner's Shop.

The prices of admission are instructive as compared with those of modern days. Dress Circle 5s., Boxes 4s., Pit 2s., Stalls 6s. (which may be retained all the evening). The doors opened at 6.30, and the performance commenced at 7.0. There was half price as near nine o'clock as was consistent with the non-interruption of the performance. And the bill ended up :

VIVAT REGINA ET PRINCEPS.

(No wonder the Keans were *personæ gratæ* with the good and great Victoria ; but the grammar was faulty if the inclusion of the Prince was gratifying !) Under the Maddox regime at the Princess's was the brother of G. A. Sala, who acted under the name of Wynn. Curious stories are related by G. A. S. in his Life, concerning the relations of his brother, Charles, and Macready. It appears that the latter could not endure the sight of young Sala and always addressed him as " Beast," but used to insist on his telling him how he looked and what was said of him in front. On one occasion when Macready was to play Othello and Charles Sala was not in the cast he said to him :

" Beast, I want you to go in front to-night, and give me after-wards a full and candid opinion as to the merits of my acting. Omit nothing ; tell me how I played and how I looked. I have an idea that I shall surpass myself this evening." . . . . My brother (it is G. A. S. telling the tale) duly occupied a place in the front row of the dress-circle—I scarcely think that there were any stalls at the Princess's in those days—and narrowly watched the per-formance from beginning to end. Then he went behind the scenes and repaired to Macready's dressing-room. The great artist was being disrobed by his dresser and was panting with excitement in an arm-chair. " Well, Beast, what was it like ? " My brother told him that he had derived the highest gratification from the performance, and he had never seen him play Othello more superbly. He was magnificent in his speech to the Venetian Senate ; the jealousy scenes with Iago were splendid ; the murder of Desdemona was superb and he died inimitably. Macready's face lighted up more and more as my brother answered seriatim his many queries.

" 'Tis well, Beast," he observed at last, " 'tis well, very well ; and now, what was my appearance—how did I look, Beast ? " My brother cogitated for a moment and then with perfect candour replied : " Like a bloody sweep ! "

Maddox's rule at the Princess's came to an end in 1850. At the very beginning, he had been puzzled how to find the money to finance his undertaking. It is said that the Duke of Brunswick, who was then an exile from his own country and living a most disreputable life in London, had provided some of the necessary cash ; he was at any rate seen behind the scenes most nights, padded and rouged and generally drunk : and perhaps Maddox had met His Royal Highness somewhere in his roving life, for he had been stage-manager, acting manager and general agent for years before he settled at the Princess's. Whatever was the source of his capital in the first place, it was apparently not an inexhaustible one and he was very glad to hand over the theatre in 1850 to Charles Kean, who started in joint management with Keeley.

It had always been Charles Kean's ambition to follow closely in his father's footsteps and gain renown as a producer of Shakespeare, and though he never approached his father as an actor of the highest rank, the stage owes him an unforgettable debt for what he and his wife did during the fifties at the Princess's Theatre. The joint management gathered round them a splendid company. Mr. and Mrs. Charles Kean were, of course, a host in themselves as tragedians and leading actors in Shakespeare and serious drama. Mr. and Mrs. Keeley were unequalled as comedians in any sort of humorous part. To support these were Harley and Bartley, both good low comedians, the latter one of the best Falstaffs ever seen ; Alfred Wigan, a man of good birth who could be always trusted to appear as a " Gentleman " and was indeed said to be the only gentleman in the profession at that time ; Drinkwater Meadows for old men parts ; John Ryder, a rough actor who had been trained under Macready and had all the traditional stage business of the legitimate drama at his fingers' ends ; David Fisher, J. F. Cathcart, and old Addison, father of Fanny and Carlotta Addison—and for panto-mime business Flexmore, who had been a clown and dancing master since the days of Grimaldi.

Besides the wives of the managers, there was Mrs. Winstanley, an experienced actress, who had done good work in America and was, in addition, something of a literary character, for she was the sole editor of *Bow Bells*. And there was Mrs. Alfred Wigan, *née* Leonora Pincott, said (with no probability) to have begun life as a little girl at country fairs and racecourses. Then there was

Carlotta Leclercq, a lovely girl, also with much experience in stage work, gained at the Grecian and elsewhere, belonging to a large theatrical family and with great talent as an emotional actress. There was Agnes Robertson, a ward of the Keans who married Dion Boucicault, and there was Miss Heath of the glorious golden hair discovered as a lovely girl of fourteen at the little theatre in Dean Street acting with amateurs ; there were Miss Murray who became Mrs. Brandram, Fanny Ternan, Eleanor Bufton, Kate and Ellen Terry, and others all beautiful and clever. No wonder that other managers, not without a spice of scorn, spoke of " the Keans' bevy of beauty " as if they were not talented as well.

With such a company, augmented from time to time as necessity arose, the prospects of the new venture were very bright. But they had also chosen their time well. The first Shakespearean season coincided with the opening of the Great Exhibition of 1851, the first Exhibition ever held, which attracted big crowds to London. The financial success, in short, was such that Keeley soon found himself able to retire from his share of the management and leave it in the hands of Kean and his wife.

The first programme of the joint management consisted of " Twelfth Night," preceded by a Farce and followed by a Ballet arranged by Flexmore. Kean himself does not appear to have had a part in the play. Mrs. Kean was cast for Viola (she must have been awful in the part !) ; Mrs. Keeley was Maria ; Meadows, Malvolio ; Addison, Sir Toby ; John Ryder, Antonio ; and James Vining, Fabian.

Probably, if Charles Kean had been born of any other father, he would never have attained the position he did. He was not a great actor in the sense that Phelps or Macready were great actors. But he was a well-educated man (his father had kept his promise and sent him to Eton when the tide of fortune turned) and this classical education assisted him in becoming the great producer of Shakespeare for which he will be chiefly remembered. He was not content with the slipshod way in which stage management had been carried on up to that time, even under Macready and Phelps, who had relied on their powers as actors and appeared often with the dingiest backgrounds and no pretence to any accuracy of scenery or costume. Kean aspired to put the plays of Shakespeare on with the closest regard to the periods of the respective plays, and searched authorities at the British Museum and elsewhere almost as eagerly as Irving did afterwards to ensure the correctness of costume, scenery and properties. He spent large sums on his great revivals, but made good profits. In the Great Exhibition year of '51 he produced twenty-seven pieces of which twelve were quite new and his profits for that year alone were stated to have been seven thousand pounds.

He seems to have had a great talent for general management of a theatre : his diction is always recognized as having been superb ; and he was versed in all the traditions of the past ; but he lacked the imagination and genius which made the productions of Irving and Fechter unforgettable by those who were privileged to see them. Mrs. Kean's genius was on the same plane as her husband's. She had had a long experience of the stage, appearing many years before at the old City Theatre in Cripplegate and other forgotten houses where rant still held sway and the old style was what went down best with the audiences. She was an excellent wife for him, and appears to have had quite as much to say in the management as he had. But she was a tragedy queen in everything she did and never forgot to " act " off as well as on the stage. Miss Ellen Terry, who as quite a little girl was much with the Keans at the Princess's, speaks of them both, and especially of Mrs. Kean, with love and gratitude, but in her book she lets us have a glimpse of the good lady which is illuminating to say the least of it. She says :

" No matter the character that Mrs. Kean was assuming, she always used to wear her hair drawn flat over her forehead, and twisted right round her ears in a kind of circular sweep—such as the old writing masters used to make when they attempted an extra grand flourish. And then, the amount of petticoats she wore ! Even as Hermione she was always bunched out by layer upon layer of petticoats in defiance of the fact that classical parts should not be dressed in a superfluity of raiment."

I have reproduced a picture of Mrs. Kean from an old print in which she looks like an early Victorian matron posing with her hand on a pedestal, as was the fashion of photographs of that day and " Period 1850 " written largely all over what was meant to be a representation of a lovely Greek statue. Many contemporaries and old playgoers have testified to her powers as an actress, but she must have been distinctly of the old school, the " mouthing, stiff, unbending school, whose movements were all by rote and according to tradition,"—the school of transition between the style of Kemble and that of Fechter. Her name has to be included among " Male Impersonators "—for she once played Romeo to Fanny Kemble's Juliet. A funny combination ! Mrs. Charles Kean inherited to the full the traditions of the great Sarah Siddons, and several good stories are related of her tragic manner in private life. One such is too good to be omitted.

A young actor had discovered that his black tights for the part of Horatio had not arrived, and he was obliged to put on red ones. After the show, he called to see Mr. Kean to explain matters. The door was opened by Mrs. Kean. " What do you want, sir ? " " To see Mr. Charles Kean." Mrs. Kean makes a stately and dramatic exit. She returns imploring silence with dramatic gestures. " What might your business be ? " she solemnly asks. Horatio explains that he wishes to apologize for his red tights. " Would Mr. Kean forgive him ? " Mrs. Kean exits again solemnly and returns with a more seraphic countenance. " Mr. Kean will pardon you ; but (pointing ecstatically to heaven), will you be forgiven *there ?* " It is also said of her that in the part of Queen Katherine she was especially terrifying in her gestures, and that the denunciatory finger held up to Cardinal Wolsey was more suggestive of " No pudding for you to-day, my boy," than anything else.

A rapid survey of the plays produced by the Keans in their nine years of management will be sufficient to show how much the British stage is indebted to them.

In November, 1851, " The Merry Wives of Windsor." Kean, Ford ; Mrs. Kean, Mrs. Ford ; Mrs. Keeley, Mrs. Page ; Mary Keeley, Anne Page ; Bartley, Falstaff ; Keeley, Sir Hugh Evans ; Wigan, Caius. January, '52 : " King John," the first of the famous elaborate Shakespearean productions. Kean, King John ; Mrs. Kean, Constance ; Kate Terry, Arthur ; Ryder, Hubert

Then followed " The Corsican Brothers," in which Alfred Wigan (and afterwards Walter Lacy) were such excellent Chateau Renauds. The revivals were put on three times a week, as a rule, and the other days taken up with various melodramas mostly adapted from the French and with productions like " Sardanapalus " which was brought out with the greatest magnificence in 1853, the burning of the Palace being said to have been equal to anything produced in modern times. " Louis XI," " Pizarro," " The Prima Donna " (a play by Boucicault in which Miss Heath made her debut), and " Pauline," also from the French, alternated with Shakespeare during these years. The last named was a drama almost of the transpontine kind with the most exciting plot, and it is said that Queen Victoria became so excited over one of the scenes that she grasped the curtains of the Royal Box tightly till the scene was over.

A version of " Faust " was put on with Kean as Mephistopheles ; and the small part of Karl, a little boy, was given to Ellen Terry.

Perhaps the most gorgeous of the Shakespearean productions

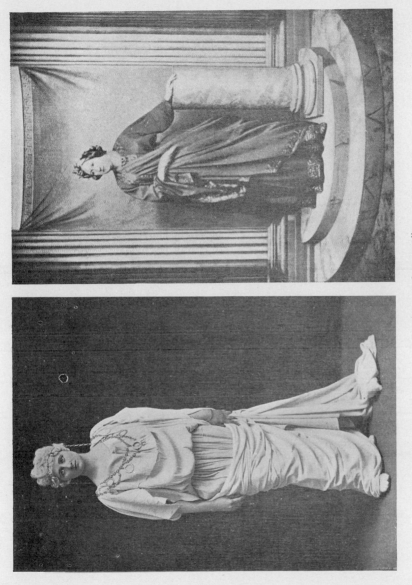

MARY ANDERSON
From photograph by W. D. Downey

"A WINTER'S TALE"
TWO HERMIONES

MRS. CHARLES KEAN
From an old print

was " Richard II," and in this Kean was at his best, because in his long speeches he had scope for that wonderful diction that was his chief merit. A scene was introduced which is not in Shakespeare, but only alluded to in a conversation between York and his Duchess —viz., the entry of Bolingbroke in triumph and the disgrace of Richard. In this scene, which was most gorgeously staged, Kate Terry played a small boy of the crowd who threw dirt at Richard as he passed.

Another magnificent production was " The Winter's Tale." In this Kean was Leontes ; Mrs. Kean, Hermione ; Miss Heath, Florizel ; Carlotta Leclercq, Perdita. It ran for 102 nights.

In " A Midsummer Night's Dream " a Miss Ternan played Oberon, Carlotta Leclercq, Titania, and Ellen Terry (then nine years old) Puck. In " The Tempest " Kean was Prospero ; Kate Terry, Ariel ; Carlotta Leclercq, Miranda ; Ryder, Caliban ; Frank Matthews, Stephano ; and Miss Eleanor Bufton (Mrs. Swanborough) Ferdinand. It seems to have been the practice often in those days to cast a female for the leading juvenile, or lover's, part. We have seen Miss Heath was Florizel in " The Winter's Tale," and in " King Lear " Miss Poole was " The Fool." Kate Terry, though a mere girl (not fifteen) played Cordelia and the two sisters were Eleanor Bufton and Miss Heath. Truly in those days a young actress had to be prepared to do anything.

" Much Ado About Nothing " was put on with the Keans as Benedick and Beatrice, and one wonders whether Mrs. Kean wore her usual early Victorian look and did her hair in the old-fashioned bandeaux as Beatrice. At the age she must have been then (1859) I cannot help thinking it must have been a distressing performance. Other Shakespearean plays put on were a very elaborate " Macbeth," " Richard III" and " The Merchant of Venice."

But with all his shortcomings as regards the acting of himself and of Mrs. Kean, Kean had good reason to boast of what he had accomplished when he finally surrendered the management of the theatre in the summer of 1859. He said :

" In this little theatre, where £200 is considered a large receipt and £250 an extraordinary one, I expended in one season alone little short of £50,000. I have given employment, i.e., weekly payment, to nearly 550 persons, and £10,000 has been expended on improvements and enlargements."

In the following review of Charles Kean's acting, while making every allowance for the fact that it was written or inspired by Douglas Jerrold who never ceased to pursue him with a very virulent hatred, there is much that may be admitted to be based on truth. Like Macready before him and other " star " actors who have succeeded him, he was probably led away by the conviction that he alone represented English dramatic art at its best and that those who were not with him were against him. In the dramatic profession perhaps more than in any other, an egotism is developed in successful artistes which produces jealousy to the nth power.

" The little importance which Mr. Kean attaches to good acting needs no further proof than the fact of his generally taking the principal character himself. An extremely insignificant figure, a voice without compass, depth or richness, and a delivery in the highest degree monotonous and ineffective are his principal characteristics. It is not enough to say he is not an actor. He has not the single attribute of an actor. And this is the man whose theatre, according to *The Times*, holds an exclusive rank for the performance of the tragic drama. In the exhibition of theatrical spectacles every one will allow that Mr. Kean is unrivalled ; but Sadler's Wells is as much before the Princess's in point of acting, as the Princess's is in front of Sadler's Wells in point of scenery. We claim a higher rank for Mr. Phelps's management than for Mr. Kean's. We do this on the same principle that we should pronounce Shakespeare in a plain sheep's skin a better book than Kotzebue in gilded morocco. . . . Mr. Kean and his imitators are investing with a meretricious splendour the remains of the drama whose vitality they have helped to destroy. If ever there be, as we yet hope there may be, a general revival of dramatic taste, and a true reverence for the works of our greatest dramatist, we may safely prophesy that Mr. Kean will come to be regarded as a master showman and the Princess's as a kindred establishment with Madame Tussaud's."

Kean occupied a middle position between the old school and the new. Those who admired the acting of Charles Dillon or Gustavus Brooke, or Barry Sullivan, would never allow the full meed of praise to Irving or Tree. Then, as now, there was a tremendous jealousy between the old " stars " and the new. Both Jerrold and Macready were envious of the rapid success of the younger Kean, the former perhaps from some personal motive, the latter because he recognized that the younger man had made his mark in a different way to his own method. He always spoke of Kean as " That young man who goes about the country," and they never met socially in private life. Jerrold, when he mentioned Kean in conversation, referred to him as " The son of his father." He was also a remnant of the older school—as seen in such of his plays as have survived. The stilted style has entirely disappeared from the British stage, and indeed nowadays we seem to be going too far in the other direction. The most admired style of to-day is that of the so-called " natural " school which may, in time, come to mean the school of those who don't attempt to " act " at all, but are clever at speaking the words of characters which one meets with in everyday life. If that be so, there is no longer any hope for Shakespeare or the costume drama, the personages in which did certainly not speak or act as we moderns do.

Kean was the means of opening the dramatic career to many who afterwards became famous in the profession. In addition to the names already cited, it is interesting to recall that Edward Righton was call-boy at this theatre and that Lionel Brough and David Belasco—whose stage name was David James—were both supers in the great procession scene of " Richard II ".

Perhaps one of the reasons that Charles Kean did not develop into a really great actor was that he had not had to go through the drudgery without which no actor can become really great. He was, as we have seen, educated at Eton and the way was made smooth for him as the son of his father. It had been the same with Macready. He had also been the son of a theatrical manager, though his father was not by any means of the same distinction as Edmund Kean. Richardson the Showman was once asked if he had ever seen Macready. " No, Master," was the reply, " I know nothing about him : he must be some wagabone as no one knows : one of them chaps as ain't 'ad any eddication for one thing. He never was with me as Edmund Kean and them Riglars was."

Phelps was by far the finer actor of the two, but his successes at that time were chiefly made at Sadler's Wells, then regarded as a sort of Minor Theatre, though many playgoers journeyed to Islington to see the great Shakespearean revivals.

But Charles Kean was the finest producer of Shakespeare that the London stage had seen up to that time. He was greater as a producer than as an actor. He used to ransack the British Museum for authority for the smallest detail, and was much chaffed for introducing a bear into " The Winter's Tale."

Charles Kean made one or two desultory appearances in London and elsewhere after the close of his great seasons at the Princess's. He filled a short engagement at Drury Lane, but his final appearance in London was at the Princess's in 1866. His wife survived him for twelve years, dying in 1880 at the age of seventy-five years She was one of four sisters, three of whom were on the stage. Her sister, Maria Tree, was the original Clari in " The Maid of Milan," and was thus the very first person to sing " Home, Sweet Home," which was written for that musical piece. Another sister was Ann Tree, who married Chapman, lessee and manager of the City Theatre, Cripplegate, and also of the Tottenham Street Theatre, which blossomed into the famous Prince of Wales's.

It is stated that Ellen Tree had been in love with Charles Kean for many years. There was a story to the effect that he once aspired to marry Miss Angela Burdett Coutts (afterwards the Baroness), who refused him, of course. He was a very conceited man and had not expected a refusal. Arriving at the theatre at Dublin one night, he said to Ellen Tree : " Ellen, if you wish to marry me, to-morrow or never ! " And " to-morrow " it was, for they were married the very next day and played together the same night in Tobin's " Honeymoon."

It may not be uninteresting to give a list of the principal productions of Charles Kean during his seasons 1851—1859 :

First Season, 1851—52. November. " The Merry Wives of Windsor," twenty-five nights. Played for the first time for many years as a Comedy and not as a semi-opera. Falstaff, Bartley ; Ford, Kean ; Page, J. Vining ; Fenton, Cathcart ; Shallow, Meadows ; Slender, Harley ; Hugh Evans, Keeley ; Dr. Caius, Alfred Wigan ; Host, Addison ; Pistol, Ryder ; Mrs. Ford, Mrs. Kean ; Mrs. Page, Mrs. Keeley ; Anne Page, Mary Keeley ; Mrs. Quickly, Mrs. Winstanley.

At Christmas. " Harlequin Billy Taylor," by George Augustus Sala.

Second. 1852. Feb. 9th, 1852. " King John." Constance, Mrs. Kean ; Hubert, Ryder ; Prince Arthur, Kate Terry.

Feb. 24. " The Corsican Brothers," adapted by Boucicault. Fabian and Louis dei Franchi, Kean.

June 7th. " Trial of Love," by Lovell for Mr. and Mrs. Kean. Followed by " The Vampire : a Phantasm related in three Dreams," by Boucicault, the author appearing as a Vampire (with an Irish brogue !)

Third. 1852—53. Sept. 18th, 1852. " Prima Donna," from the French by Boucicault. Walter Lacy (succeeding Alfred Wigan); Miss Heath made her debut. Ran thirty-four nights. Followed by a melodrama " Mont St. Michel : or the Fairy of the Sands," from the French by Bayle Bernard. Wright from the Adelphi made debut at this theatre.

Oct. 28th. " Anne Blake," domestic drama by Westland Marston. Mr. and Mrs. Kean. Ran forty-two nights.

Dec. 18th. Benefit of Bartley and retirement from the stage. Pantomime, " Cherry and Fairstar." Ran ten weeks.

Jan. 22nd. " St. Cupid : or Dorothy's Fortune," by Douglas

Jerrold. Ran thirty-seven nights. Mrs. Kean, Mr. and Mrs. Walter Lacy, J. Vining, Wright, Harley and Ryder.

Feb. 14th. "Macbeth." Ran twenty weeks at the rate of three performances a week. Mr. and Mrs. Kean. Rachel was present and went round to Kean's dressing-room to kiss him !

At Easter, a melodrama by Palgrave Simpson adapted from the opera by Scribe and Auber called " Marco Spada."

June 13th. Production of "Sardanapalus," by Lord Byron for the Keans' benefit. Mounted with great splendour and after much historical research. Ran sixty-one nights. Mrs. Kean, Myrrha ; Ryder in the cast.

Fourth. 1853—54. Oct. 10th. Resumption of run of " Sardanapalus," thirty-two nights. " The Rivals " and " Lancers : or The Gentleman's Son," from " Le Fils du Famille," ran forty-nine nights. Same as " Queen's Shilling " of the Kendals.

Pantomime, " Miller and His Men," with new tricks from Paris.

" Black Eyed Susan," just before Christmas, with T. P. Cooke.

Feb. 20th, 1854. " Richard III," Colley Cibber's version. Ran only nineteen nights.

March 28th. Serious drama, " Married Unmarried," adapted from the French by Morris Barnett. Ryder, Walter Lacy ; Miss Heath, Miss Murray. Ran fifty-eight nights.

April 19th. " Faust and Marguerite." Lydia Thompson as Karl.

June 5th. " From Village to Court," by Morton.

June 26th. For Keans' benefit. Production of " The Courier of Lyons." (Same as " The Lyons Mail.")

Fifth. 1854—55. Season delayed by illness of Kean and spread of cholera in London. 9th October. " Heart of Gold," by Douglas Jerrold. Ran only eleven nights. A failure.

Nov. 6th. " Schamyl," adapted from the French by Palgrave Simpson. Scene laid in Circassia and Russia. Ran twenty-three nights. A failure. Withdrawn for pantomime of " Bluebeard." Occasional performances of previous productions, such as " Hamlet," " Stranger," " The Courier of Lyons," etc.

Jan. 13th, 1855. Production of " Louis the Eleventh," adapted from Casimir Delavigne's play by Boucicault. Ran sixty-two nights.

May 16th. " Henry VIII ". Reappearance of Mrs. Kean after absence of eighteen months through illness. Played Queen Katharine. Kean as Wolsey ; Walter Lacy, Henry VIII ; Miss Heath, Anne Boleyn ; Ryder, Duke of Buckingham ; Cooper, Griffith.

Sixth. 1855—56. Oct. 22nd. "Henry VIII" revived. Fifty more nights. Other plays interlarded from time to time. "The Critic," "The Rivals," "The Heir at Law," etc. Frank Matthews added to the company.

Pantomime at Christmas on "The Maid and the Magpie."

March 3rd. "The First Printer," by Charles Reade and Tom Taylor. Charles Kean as Costar, the Dutch printer. Failure. Nine nights.

April 28th. "The Winter's Tale." Magnificently put on the stage. After the first part, classical allegory representing the flight of Time. Dionysian orgies staged with three hundred persons on at one time. Kean, Leontes ; Mrs. Kean, Hermione ; Miss Heath, Florizel ; Carlotta Leclercq, Perdita.

Seventh. 1856—57. Sept. 1st. Sheridan's adaptation of Kotzebue's "Pizarro." Kean, Rollo ; Mrs. Kean, Elvira ; Ryder, Pizarro ; Miss Heath, Cora.

Oct. 15th. "A Midsummer Night's Dream." Ran 150 nights. Miss Murray, Hippolyta ; Ryder, Theseus ; Miss Heath, Helena ; Miss Bufton, Hermia ; Miss Ternan, Oberon ; Carlotta Leclercq, Titania ; Ellen Terry, Puck ; Kate Terry, Fairy ; Clowns by Harley, Frank Matthews, Saker, Meadows and F. Cooke.

Mar. 12th, 1857. "Richard II". Kean, Richard II ; Mrs. Kean, Queen ; Ryder, Bolingbroke ; Walter Lacy, Lancaster ; Cooper, York. Ran eighty-five nights. Withdrawn for a time to make room for "The Tempest." Kean, Prospero ; Kate Terry, Ariel ; Carlotta Leclercq, Miranda ; Eleanor Bufton, Ferdinand ; Ryder, Caliban ; Harley and Frank Matthews as Trinculo and Stephano.

Eighth. 1857—58. Oct. 12th. "The Tempest" revived. Eighty-seven nights. "Richard II" revived.

Pantomime at Christmas. "Harlequin and the White Cat ; or the Princess Blancheflower and her Three Godmothers."

Revivals of other pieces. "Hamlet" and "Faust and Marguerite."

Apr. 17th. "King Lear." Kean, Lear ; Ryder, Edgar ; Walter Lacy, Edmund ; Miss Poole, Fool ; Cooper, Kent ; Kate Terry, Cordelia ; Goneril, Miss Heath ; Regan, Miss Bufton. Thirty-two nights.

June 12th. "The Merchant of Venice." Kean, Shylock ; Mrs. Kean, Portia ; Miss Chapman, niece of Mrs. Kean, was Jessica. Season closed Sept. 3rd

Ninth. 1858—59. Oct. 2nd. "The Merchant of Venice" revived. Followed by "King John." Kean, King ; Mrs. Kean,

Constance ; Ellen Terry, Prince Arthur ; Walter Lacy, Falcon-bridge ; Ryder, Hubert. Followed by " Macbeth."

Nov. 19th. " Much Ado About Nothing." Kean, Benedick ; Mrs. Kean, Beatrice ; Frank Matthews, Dogberry ; Meadows, Verges.

Pantomime at Christmas, " King of the Castle : or Harlequin Prince Diamond and the Princess Brighteye."

Revival of " Jealous Wife " (Mrs. Kean as Mrs. Oakley), " The Corsican Brothers," " Hamlet," " A Midsummer Night's Dream," etc.

Mar. 28th. For Keans' benefit. " Henry V ". Kean, Henry V ; Mrs. Kean, Chorus. Ran eighty-four nights.

CHAPTER VII

(2) FROM 1860 TO THE FINAL CLOSING OF THE THEATRE

IN September, 1859, the Princess's came under the management of Augustus Harris the elder (father of " Druriolanus ") whose mother was Madame Fearon, the well-known opera singer and wife of Glossop, the cheesemonger, who owned the Old Vic. He had had a stage training from his earliest years, and was well qualified by experience to take control of a theatre of his own.

He entirely redecorated the old house and renovated it so that it became one of the handsomest theatres in London. His first programme consisted of two pieces—" Ivy Hall," an adaptation of Octave Feuillet's " Roman d'un jeune homme pauvre " and " Love and Fortune," a sort of Watteau piece by Planché. " Ivy Hall " is only worth remembering as being the first piece in which Henry Irving made his bow to a London audience. He was a dire failure and at once returned to the provinces whence he had come. Other characters were by Frank Matthews, Kate Saville and Mrs. Charles Young—the last-named better known to us as Mrs. Hermann Vezin.

In Planché's piece, there was a string of well-known names, including Carlotta Leclercq and Louise Keeley. A lurid melodrama by Edmund Falconer, who was to have so much to do with the theatre in its later days, followed in November, but was replaced the very next month by another adaptation from the French called " Home Truths." Another failure. The company, including Mrs. Young, Ryder, Miss Leclercq and others, was a good one, but there seemed to be the usual difficulty in finding good plays for them to act. Pantomime was put on at Christmas : Espinosa, the famous dancer, appeared about this time, and I notice Rose Leclercq as a fairy and Louise Keeley as juvenile lead ; but the fortunes of the theatre seemed to languish with every piece produced till November, 1860, rather more than a year after he had started, when Harris suddenly "struck oil" with the first appearance of Fechter in England in a stirring version of " Ruy Blas."

At Easter, 1860, Phelps was engaged for a short time and in September of that year there was a production of " Macbeth," with

James Anderson and Miss Elsworthy in the chief parts. Anderson was already very well known on the London stage at Drury Lane and at outlying houses like the Standard and Britannia. He was a very handsome man with a fine delivery, leaning rather to the old style. He was the original Ingomar in the rather heavy tragedy which his namesake, Miss Mary Anderson, afterwards chose for her first appearance before an English audience. At the Britannia he once played Melnotte to the Pauline of Miss Elsworthy, and received £20 a performance. He died in 1895.

Miss Elsworthy was a "sound" actress, apparently ready to undertake any part at a moment's notice. She was a very handsome, stately-looking woman, who married one Andrew Archideckne, a member of the Garrick Club, the same whom Thackeray drew as Foker in *Pendennis*. Thackeray was very fond, by the way, of putting theatrical people into his novels. It is said that the original of "The Fotheringay" was Mrs. Nisbett, whom he caricatured because she did not return his admiration. Be that as it may, it is tolerably certain that the father of Mrs. Nisbett, Captain Macnamara, was the model for Captain Costigan. Miss Elsworthy was the Gertrude to Fechter's Hamlet, and she also played the *grande dame* parts with him in his romantic plays at the Lyceum.

When Harris "discovered" Charles Fechter in Paris, he was unknowingly the means of hastening the disappearance of the old-time actor of the Kemble school. Kemble and his predecessors, and Mrs. Siddons, great as they were, had always played their parts with a strict adherence to tradition ; and, though they had discarded the wig and powder which Mrs. Pritchard and her contemporaries wore at an earlier date, their action, gestures and elocution must have been "of the stage, stagy," that is, according to present-day notions. It was John Kemble who headed the revolt against the classic manner of those who came before him, but Edmund Kean went much further and, rather to the disgust of the old actors of *his* day, introduced a still more natural style. His son, Charles Kean, went further still, giving to his productions some resemblance to the periods of the various plays, and acting in them himself with greater regard to the natural manners of man.

He was still what we may call a "starched" actor, still followed much on the lines of his father's art, and of the art of that type of actor to which Macready, Ryder, and, to a much less extent, Phelps belonged.

His productions at the old Princess's Theatre were the marvel of the day, but, as for his acting, it is now generally admitted that he was "not in the same street" with Phelps. His wife, brought up in the old school at the Royalty Theatre, Wellclose Square, and no longer young when she first appeared at the West End, was still more stilted and affected and, like Siddons, could hardly ask for the salt at dinner without putting on the airs of a tragedy queen. Macready, though considered by his contemporaries a great actor, appears to have been also something of a barnstormer—though undoubtedly fine in Shakespeare and some old-fashioned plays.

But Charles Fechter was a revelation. With him came the first actor of the modern style. I have said he was "discovered" by Harris. So he was, in so far as London is concerned ; but he was a well-known actor of romantic rôles in Paris before he came to London. He was the original Armand in " La Dame aux Camélias " to the Marguerite Gauthier of Madame Doche, and also the original Fabien and Louis Dei Franchi in "The Corsican Brothers" when first produced in Paris, besides having made a reputation at the old Vaudeville (later the " Théâtre des Italiens ") in such pieces as Paul Féval's " Couteaux d'Or " and others of the same sort.

Though brought up in France, with French as his native language, Fechter was actually a cockney, born in London, in Hanway Yard, that queer backwater of Oxford Street which still runs behind the Oxford Music Hall—so called after Jonas Hanway, the great philanthropist and inventor of umbrellas. This little twisted thoroughfare was part of the foreign colony of London and Fechter's father was foreign (German or Flemish), though his mother was English. He always repudiated any connection with the Germans, and pronounced the " ch " in his name soft.

His master in the profession of acting was Frederic Lemaitre, one of the very greatest romantic actors seen in any country, and thus he came to London with a reputation already established. It was a daring experiment for Harris to make, but it succeeded beyond his wildest hopes.

The first play put on at the Princess's for the new "star" was an adaptation of " Ruy Blas " made by Edmund Falconer, author of the popular " Peep o' Day," an Irish piece second only in demand to Boucicault's " Colleen Bawn "—in which latter piece, by the way, Falconer was the original Danny Mann.

" Ruy Blas " was an excellent play for the debut of the new romantic actor. It showed off all his good points : his love-making, which gained for him the suffrages of crowds of women playgoers, for nothing at all like it had ever been seen on the English stage ; his scenes of passion in the more melodramatic parts ; his wonderful fencing ; the élan of the whole. Here was at last something quite

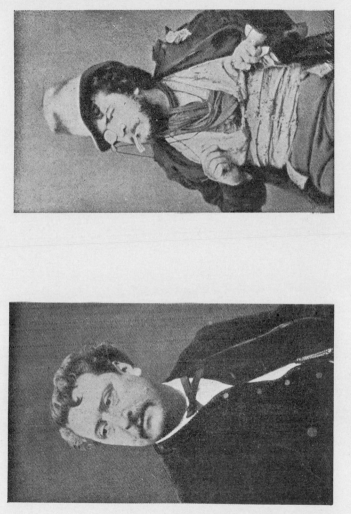

CHARLES FECHTER   FECHTER AS " ROBERT MACAIRE "

From Photographs by Adolphe Beau

different from the mouthing periods and stilted action of his predecessors, something that was like life, and glowing, ardent life at that. No wonder the women sobbed audibly and the whole audience thrilled at his art.

Harris determined to follow up his success with a bold stroke. He mounted "Hamlet" for the new-comer. Then the storm of opposition broke out and raged long and fiercely. Macready, Kean, Phelps and Ryder openly scoffed at the idea of a foreigner appearing in the chief creation of Shakespeare. They did all they could to pour ridicule on the attempt, and freely prophesied the break-up of the School of British Acting with all its great traditions if the interloper from Paris were permitted to play Hamlet. They prophesied better than they knew. The Frenchman did break up the old-fashioned School once and for all. His Hamlet was a revelation to playgoers and the tragedy was looked upon for the first time as a play to be enjoyed as a play, and not sat through as a lesson in literature.

Hamlet, the man, had hitherto been personified as a gloomy, misanthropic, dull person with raven-coloured hair and a sombre outlook on all and sundry. Fechter dressed him in a fair wig, giving him the appearance that a Dane might be expected to have, and made of him a courteous gentleman, human in his likes and dislikes and in the way he trod the stage—in short, an entirely credible individual.

As had been foreseen, his weak point was the foreign accent, but he got over this much more quickly than had been anticipated, and his romantic appearance and wonderful love-making tipped the balance in his favour.

The general prejudice against foreigners which still lingered in those mid-Victorian days, was by degrees disappearing, and Fechter did much to get rid of it altogether so far as the Stage was concerned. Only three years after his debut, London welcomed in the person of Stella Colas, a French girl, almost the best Juliet it had ever seen or ever would see, and a later generation acclaimed in the same part Modjeska, a Polish lady with a very pronounced foreign accent which stuck to her to the last. This unreasoning and most insular prejudice was sometimes the means of depriving England of the opportunity of seeing several great artistes. Maude Adams, one of America's foremost actresses, would never, it is said, come to England on account of her Yankee twang, and in earlier times Miss Smithson, a very fine actress, afterwards the wife of Hector Berlioz, an Irishwoman, was looked upon as very un-English on account of her strong Irish brogue, though her great beauty procured her engagements from time to time. Rachel openly declared she had learned much from her when she acted in Paris. Brogue is a fatal possession in anything but Irish plays. Boucicault once attempted the rôle of Ruy Blas, but a romantic hero of the Renaissance period with a strong Dublin accent was more than the audience could stand, and he was laughed off the stage.

Many prominent people in literary and artistic circles, besides Harris, hailed the advent of a new star on the theatrical horizon. Oxenford, Blanchard, Yates and Palgrave Simpson, among the critics, and Charles Dickens and Wilkie Collins in the literary world championed the new-comer. Dickens, indeed, became his firm friend and backer and lent him several thousand pounds in the course of his career, all of which was faithfully repaid.

Fechter's forte was essentially the leading rôles in romantic drama, and during his seasons in England he produced most of the better known specimens. As I have already noted, " The Corsican Brothers " was not new to him, for he had created the character in the original production. At the Princess's in this play he was supported by Rose Leclercq, then a handsome young girl, and by Harris himself as Chateau Renaud—the part played by Terriss in the Irving production at the Lyceum.

It is not, I think, generally known that the story of *Les Frères Corses* is, to a certain extent, founded on fact. The brothers in real life were Louis and Charles Blanc. Charles was a distinguished Art critic, French Academician and historian who died in 1882. Louis Blanc was known as " The Tribune of the People," or some such highfalutin name. On the mother's side, they were Corsican, and related to that Signor Pozzo del Borgo who, it is said, never forgave Napoleon for appropriating on one occasion all the gravy of a leg of mutton. In 1830, Charles went to visit a friend, a doctor, who lived about 150 leagues from Paris. One evening after dinner, he was chatting with the party in the garden when he started up in agony crying out that he had been struck, and at the same moment said that he was sure something had happened to his brother Louis. The next day, a letter came announcing that his brother had been struck down in the street by a blow across his forehead. This story was afterwards told by Charles Blanc to Dumas and was by him adopted as the base of his novel, *Les Frères Corses*, from which the play is derived.

When Fechter played Hamlet for the first time in London, Miss Heath (afterwards Mrs. Wilson Barrett) was the Ophelia; Miss Elsworthy, Queen Gertrude ; Shore, Laertes ; Sefton, Horatio ; Widdicomb (whose father had been ringmaster at Astley's in Ducrow's time) First Gravedigger. These continued to act with him for some time. He then attempted Othello—his one great failure.

He was physically unsuited to the part, and when he changed with Ryder and took Iago instead, one realized that he had his limitations. It is a failing of many actors and actresses that they do not realize there are rôles outside their capabilities. One has only to recall Irving, when he tried to play the lover Romeo, and Claude Melnotte, and Boucicault, when he made Ruy Blas sentimentalize in the accents of Dublin. Carlotta Leclercq was the Desdemona, and she was his leading lady in many of his productions at the Lyceum and Adelphi.

In 1863, Fechter with the help of Dickens and other friends went into management on his own account and opened the Lyceum with "The Duke's Motto," a very stirring adaptation of one of Paul Féval's novels. This was the first of the successful *cappa e spada* series of plays which filled the Lyceum with the rank and fashion of London for several seasons. The theatre had been done up and beautifully decorated, and his seasons can only be compared with those of later years, under the Irving regime which made theatrical history in the latter part of the nineteenth century. Curiously enough, the leading lady for some time in both cases was a Miss Terry, for Kate Terry, the eldest sister, was with Fechter in some of his greatest successes.

"Bel Dominio : A Love Story," an adaptation of "L'Abbaye de Castro," followed "The Duke's Motto." An inferior version of the same French original had been done at the Olympic some ten years before, under the title of "Sixtus V.," but was not a success. The company with Fechter, besides Kate Terry, included George Jordan (an American *jeune premier*, good-looking and capable but better known on the other side of the Atlantic), Sam Emery and Miss Elsworthy. "Hamlet" followed with a slight change in the cast, Emery playing the King ; George Neville, Laertes ; and Kate Terry, Ophelia—an Ophelia which only Lady Tree and Miss Gerard have surpassed.

"The King's Butterfly," a version of "Fanfan la Tulipe," of the same type as "The Duke's Motto," was Fechter's next venture. I have heard this described as a fine specimen of that kind of play. I saw it myself, but was too young to appreciate it. We were taken to everything Fechter played in as children, for he was a personal friend of my father's who admired his acting immensely. This was a story of the days of La Pompadour, a part played by Carlotta Leclercq, by this time quite established as Fechter's leading lady. Ryder, who had been won over to his methods, was also in the cast. A previous but different version had been done at the Princess's with Hermann Vezin and Amy Sedgwick.

After a revival of "Ruy Blas" Fechter put on a translation of

"Robert Macaire" and called it "The Roadside Inn." This was one of his greatest triumphs as a piece of acting, and a change from his usual line of ardent lover. He acted it according to the traditions of his old master, Frederic Lemaitre, with whom it had been a favourite rôle, and was admirably supported by Widdicomb as Jacques Strop. Comedy he made of it, but comedy of a very grim, fantastic kind. It is said that Charles Dickens was the originator of the intensely dramatic conclusion adopted by Fechter, according to which Macaire, when shot, falls backwards down a staircase into the arms of his son. In spite of the excellence of the performance, it did not have a long run. English playgoers are the most conservative in the world. They expected to see Fechter make love and fence, and get into innumerable difficulties and get out of them again, and would not put up with the grisly fantasy of Robert Macaire.

After this lapse, *il revenait à ses premiers amours.* There followed one after the other, in rapid succession, "Don Cæsar de Bazan," "Belphegor" and "The Watch Cry." "Belphegor" was well known to the older generation of British playgoers. Charles Dillon had made it famous at the Lyceum before, with Marie Wilton (Lady Bancroft) as the little son, and, as Madeleine, Mlle. Beatrice, a charming Frenchwoman who eventually joined the Frank Harvey Co. and toured the provinces with melodramas of the crudest kind. Fechter's own son, Paul, acted with his father. "The Watch Cry" was an adaptation of "Lazare le Patre" done years ago at the Grecian. After that, came what was perhaps the finest of all these costume dramas, a play founded on Walter Scott's *Bride of Lammermoor*, by Palgrave Simpson, and called "The Master of Ravenswood." The acting was fine, the mounting was perfect, and the last scene of all, "The Kelpie's Flow by Moonlight," where Edgar and Lucy (contrary to the ending of the novel) are swallowed up in the quicksands, would not have disgraced a management of to-day. Carlotta Leclercq was Lucy, Widdicomb was Craigenfeldt, and Emery made a wonderful part of Caleb Balderstone, the faithful old steward. This was in January, 1866 Runs were not so long in those days, and in May of the same year "The Corsican Brothers" was again revived. Claude Melnotte was his next essay, a part which gave him full scope for his genius in love-making ; Miss Leclercq was Pauline ; Miss Elsworthy, Widow Melnotte, and that essentially "sound" old actress, Mrs. Henry Marston, was Madame Deschapelles. Mrs. Marston had been a very popular actress for nearly forty years. She was a Miss Noel, born as long ago as 1810, a regular member for some years of Phelps's company at Sadler's Wells, and excellent in all old women's

"HAMLET"

"BELPHEGOR"

"OTHELLO"

"IAGO"

CHARLES FECHTER

From photographs by Adolphe Beau

parts. Her sister married Hodson of the Bower Saloon, so that she was an aunt of Henrietta Hodson—Mrs. Labouchere.

In November, 1867, Fechter was acting in Hamlet at his own theatre (Lyceum) when he was taken ill after the second act and had to give up his part to Ryder, who was playing the Ghost.

His illness does not seem to have been very serious, for in the following month he made his first bow to an Adelphi audience in Wilkie Collins's play of " No Thoroughfare." This is one of his performances that I remember the best. It was a most effective and thrilling melodrama founded on a tale of the same name which had appeared in *All the Year Round*. The cast was a particularly fine one, including Benjamin Webster the elder, Belmore, Billington, Henry Neville, Carlotta Leclercq and Mrs. Alfred Mellon. With such a good plot, sensational but not extravagantly so, I have always wondered why it has not been revived. There had been a French version played in Paris with the lovely Léonide Leblanc as the heroine, and Berton scored heavily in Fechter's part.

" Black and White," another play by Wilkie Collins, was produced by the Adelphi management for Fechter in March, 1868, after which he went for a prolonged tour in America ; not being seen again in London, I think, till 1872, when " Ruy Blas," one of the best of his revivals, was put on at the Adelphi, with Rose Leclercq and Fernandez in the cast. This season must also have seen the production of " Monte Cristo " with such disastrous results, as I have described in the chapter on Audiences.

Fechter ended his days in the States, much alone and almost in obscurity. He had had his cycle of success in the world of the stage ; in private life, he was not so fortunate. His wife was a Mlle. Rabut, a clever actress who had often acted in the same pieces with the great Rachel. But she was not content to play second fiddle even to such an artiste as Rachel Felix, so she left Paris and settled in Brussels as the leading tragedienne for years. There was one son and one daughter by her marriage with Fechter, but they did not get on together and agreed to live apart. It is said that, when in America, he married a Miss Price according to the American law, though his wife was still alive. That is also what Boucicault did, and there was no possible excuse in either case. Madame Fechter (*née* Rabut) survived till the year 1896. The children generally lived with their mother, and the son who had inherited his father's love for, and skill in, fencing, was unfortunately killed while fencing with a young friend.

Dickens said of Fechter : " He has the brain of a man combined with that strange power of arriving, without knowing how or why, at the truth, which one usually finds only in a woman."

Lewes, the critic, declared that his Hamlet was the best and his Othello the worst he had ever seen.

Another well-known critic, writing of his last appearance as Hamlet, said that "prosperity turned his brain after his first season at the Lyceum ; he had feminine proclivities, and was hysterical as a woman, collapsed at the end of the second act, and Ryder had to finish the show."

Apropos of his Hamlet, there was one innovation introduced by him which I do not think has ever been adopted by any other actor. In the last Act, the stage was arranged with a sort of gallery at the back approached by a staircase on each side. All the entrances and exits of the scene were by means of this staircase. At the end, the King tried to escape up one of the flights of stairs. Fechter rushes up the other, meets him at the top, and kills him there.

A commentator on the Stage of the period writes : " Fechter's power lay in that glowing passion, that wonderful picturesqueness which carried away the imagination of the audience. . . . His charm of manner, his pathos, his passion and, above all, his marvellous love-making, carried the audience with him. . . ." And this, remember, in spite of the foreign accent which was always very pronounced. He must have been a fascinating personality on the stage. I did not see him myself in his very earliest days, though I have had many personal accounts from those who did, but there will always remain with me the memory of what I did see and of the gracious ladies who acted with him. Who can make love on the stage as he did now that Lewis Waller is no longer with us ? No one (though I think Leon Quartermaine might if he chose). Who has the dash and élan to carry him through such a part as Don Cæsar or Ruy Blas ? No one ; with possibly the same exception, for I cannot forget his fine Mercutio in Miss Keene's production of " Romeo and Juliet."

And it was not only in the acting that Fechter so revolutionized the English stage ; with his regime a new era in every detail connected with the production of plays was begun. I cannot finish these notes better than by quoting from *The London Stage* by Mr. Barton Baker a passage where he clearly sets forth the astonishing changes brought about by the genius of the French actor. Mr. Baker says :

" He brought in a new order of things, sweeping away worn-out traditions, and was the pioneer of all those elaborate spectacles of which we are getting a little too much at the present day (1889). He began by revolutionizing the stage itself, and thereby rendered possible such mechanical effects as we never before dreamed of. The ancient grooves, trap-doors and sticky flats were done away with, the flooring was so constructed that it could be taken to pieces like a child's puzzle, and scenery could be raised or sunk in any part, while all the shifting was done on the mezzanine beneath ; ceilings were no longer represented by hanging cloths, or the walls of a room by open wings, but were solidly built ; the old glaring ' floats ' which used to make such hideous lights and shadows upon the faces of the performers, were sunk and subdued, and set scene succeeded set scene with a rapidity which in those days, when never more than one set was attempted in each act, was regarded as marvellous. There was also an attention to details of costume and general effect that had never been given except in the Shakespearean revivals of Macready and Charles Kean."

It has been an interesting and pleasant task to look back on the career of an actor who had such an outstanding influence on the theatrical history of this country—who abolished stilted attitudes and mouthing rant, substituting natural gesture and natural tone, paving the way for that brilliant succession of actor-managers who were the shining lights of the Stage during the closing years of the nineteenth century.

Apropos of the support to Fechter when playing in England, I do not think it is generally known that when acting Hamlet at the Prince of Wales's Theatre, Birmingham, the Laertes was Henry Irving, of whom a local critic wrote that " he was as bad as could be "—probably because he differed from the usual reading of the character as known to provincial audiences. Another note on casts of Hamlet is that Miss Priscilla Horton (Mrs. German Reed) was once Ophelia to the Hamlet of Macready.

Early in 1862, there was a lapse at the Princess's Theatre for a short time of the Fechter nights, and a melodrama of the crinoline period called " The Angel of Midnight : or the Duel in the Snow," was put on with Miss Marriott, a fine actress who afterwards ran Sadler's Wells for a time with great success, and whom I saw when she was a very old woman playing " The Vengeance " in the Convention scene in " Robespierre " at the Lyceum. A great piece of lurid acting it was too.

In 1863, Harris relinquished the management of the Princess's to James Vining, who started with " Othello," with Walter Montgomery in the title rôle, and then made a great hit by the discovery of what some said was one of the few perfect Juliets that have ever attempted the character.

This was Stella Colas, who literally came, saw and conquered the English playgoing public in spite of her nationality and her foreign accent.   She was a pupil of John Ryder, who was known in the profession as the " Juliet Maker."   He was indeed responsible for a great number of debutantes and mostly in the character of Juliet.   He had always been a stickler for the old style, the formal, not to say ranting style of the Kembles, Macready and the Keans. But he had nevertheless been one of the first to recognize the genius of Fechter in spite of the fact that he was a Frenchman, and when his instinct told him what magnificent material he had in the young Frenchwoman, Stella Colas, he could not resist the temptation of undertaking the responsibility of introducing her to the English stage.

The fact that Vining, the then manager of the Princess's, was getting desperately hard up and in want of a new sensation also induced him to take the risk of bringing out another foreigner in a play of Shakespeare.   The result was a far greater success than he could have ever anticipated.   Clement Scott says :

" She had youth, spontaneity, vivacity, girlish beauty and a fierce hidden passion on the eve of development—all essential for the ballroom and balcony scenes : and she had absolute tragic force at command for the 'potion scene.'   In the balcony scene, this fair-haired girl with the lovely figure, was a perfect picture : and her foreign origin enabled her to delight us with those tricks, fantastic changes, coquettings, poutings and petulance which comes with such difficulty from the Anglo-Saxon temperament.   Adelaide Neilson was half a gipsy ; Stella Colas was the most exhilarating of French or Italian girls—what does it matter ?—the temperament is almost the same—speaking love which she felt mysteriously but did not understand.   It was innocence on the verge of a tempest, nature rushing into a storm . . . . the Juliet of Stella Colas was the embodied fact that the love that lasts is measured and reasonable, and not a mere impulse of feeling.   But Stella Colas possessed far more than the fire of love that burns itself out.   She understood the agony of fear.   Critics talk vaguely of a girl Juliet and that she should be in her teens and 'sweet seventeen' no more. But the 'sweet seventeen' of England cannot play Juliet try as she will.   We want an early matured and developed Juliet. The potion scene, to be effective, must be tragedy, and 'sweet seventeen' only by a miracle can play tragedy.   This scene as played by Stella Colas I can never forget.   She conjured up the dreaded horrors of the lonely charnel house. We could see it as if we were on the stage . . . . the terror of the picture was so impressively conveyed by the actress, that she, who in the balcony scene had been an ideal of beauty and comeliness, now turned positively green with fear, and became prematurely old, ugly and haggard. There never was such a transformation. And what a piercing, unearthly shriek, exactly the right note, rang round the astonished house, when, working up the speech, forte forte and crescendo crescendo, she gave superbly the lines :

> ' And in this rage, with some great kinsman's bones,
>   As with a club, dash out my desperate brains ? '

The scream on that word ' dash ' I have never forgotten to this hour. It rings in my ears yet."

Clement Scott was a fine and experienced critic. When he published the above words in 1899, he had seen many a Juliet, including all the best that London had seen for forty years or more : Adelaide Neilson, Helen Faucit, Miss Bateman, Kate Terry, Milly Palmer, Miss Carlisle, Miss Wallis, Ellen Terry, Mary Anderson and a host of others more easily forgotten, and the impression he leaves on one's mind in the above criticism is that he had never known one to equal Stella Colas for a combination of all the varied qualifications required for the part.

She was well supported by Walter Montgomery as Romeo, George Vining as Mercutio, and a comparatively new-comer, Charles Warner, as Benvolio. George Rose (Arthur Sketchley), Charles Warner and others of the younger school agreed enthusiastically with Scott on the subject of the acting of Stella Colas. But the older, and rather disgruntled, school of critics would have none of her. Henry Lewes said :

" With all her vehemence, she is destitute of passion : she splits the ears of the groundlings, but moves no human soul."

Scott quotes this opinion, but adds " she certainly moved me ! " Other critics nickname her, not too wittily, " steel-collars " meaning, I suppose, that she was hard as steel. Henry Lewes, in another article on the lady, said her success was a proof of the lamentable condition of the English stage. He had to account for her real success somehow.

Blanchard in his Diary notes " A decided success."

The truth probably was that the elder men, having been brought up to revere Mrs. Warner, Helen Faucit and Mrs. Charles Kean, could not bring themselves to realize the beauty of acting that was not done according to tradition. Stella Colas also appeared in a melodrama called " The Monastery of St. Just," adapted from the French of Casimir Delavigne (who also wrote " Louis XI ") by John Oxenford. She doubled the parts of Donna Florinda and a boy novice. George Vining, John Nelson (husband of Carlotta Leclercq and afterwards Romeo to Miss Colas in the East End), and Mr. and Mrs. Henry Marston were in this play. It had been first produced in Paris in 1835 as " Don Juan D'Autriche " and again at Covent Garden in 1836 as " Don Juan of Austria " with Helen Faucit.

Stella Colas did not stay very long in London. She appeared at one of the East End theatres (the Pavilion, I think) and other places, but retired from the stage early in life, became Madame Stella de Corvin and was alive and well as late as 1895.

She was a pupil of John Ryder, as I have said, and was probably the cause of his reconsidering his old-fashioned ideas on the subject of foreign actors and the traditions of the old school. Fechter completed the cure. Walter Montgomery, the first Romeo to the Juliet of Stella Colas, was a very handsome and clever actor in romantic parts. He was an American, his real name being Richard Tomlinson. He married, at St. George's, Hanover Square, on August 30th, a Miss Laleah Bigelow, but had two days only of married life. On September 2nd he blew out his brains !

The success of Stella Colas was the turning point of George Vining's management. In the following year (1864) he began a round of successes with the plays of Dion Boucicault.

I am told that it has never been known who Boucicault really was, and it is a matter which certainly concerns no one to find out. He made his way from the bottom of his profession to the top, entirely by his own talents and exertions. The name was originally spelt Bourcicault and his two first names were Dion Lardner. He was born in Dublin in 1822, rumour said of a French refugee and an Irish mother, and his education was of the very best that Dublin could afford. His brogue was quite unmistakable, so the Irish part of his parentage was not to be doubted for a moment. His wife was the lovely Agnes Robertson, ward and adopted daughter of Charles Kean. He eloped with Miss Robertson and undoubtedly married her. I say " undoubtedly " for, in after years, for some reason of his own, Boucicault chose to try and repudiate this marriage, in order, probably, to marry a Miss Thorndyke. For this baseness he was most deservedly cut by all his former friends, that host of friends whom he had made during his London life, when he had a

MR. AND MRS. CHARLES KEAN

MR. AND MRS. DION BOUCICAULT
From old American print

charming house at Earls Court, afterwards, I believe, the residence of the Tattersalls, and then, going the way of all decent private dwellings, turned into a block of flats. A well-known American writer, Fiske, said of him that he had had yet another wife before he married Agnes Robertson. He was celebrated for his hospitality both in London and in New York, and though sometimes desperately hard up, always seemed to be able to find the money to pay for his entertainments.

As a dramatic author Dion Boucicault was one of the most hard-working ever known. In his teens he wrote " London Assurance," a comedy which still holds the stage, and it was produced at Covent Garden by Mr. and Mrs. Charles Mathews (Vestris). He was what was known as a " stock author," that is an author kept on the premises of the leading theatres to provide plays whenever required to do so. The outlying theatres like the Grecian, Britannia, Surrey and Marylebone all had their stock authors and some of the West End houses, such as the Adelphi and Olympic as well.

After " London Assurance " his first great success was " The Colleen Bawn," produced in 1860 with a cast including himself and his wife, Mr. and Mrs. Billington, Mrs. Alfred Mellon, David Fisher and Edmund Falconer (author himself of many Irish plays). It was seen again and again by playgoers on account of the cave scene where the Colleen Bawn is rescued from drowning. This was something quite new in sensational effects and was the fore-runner of many sensation scenes of subsequent dramas. Mrs. Dion Boucicault in her red cloak (given her by Mrs. E. M. Ward, the artist), became the darling of the London playgoing public at once : I knew her well as a boy and can never forget her charming manner : she must have been a most versatile as well as a popular actress, for she played in the after piece called " She would be an Actress," in which she had many characters to portray.

After his success with his plays at the Princess's Dion Boucicault took Astley's with a flourish of trumpets such as only an Irishman can blow, and lost a small fortune in the attempt to make it pay. He squandered over ten thousand pounds of a noble Earl's money on the production of a Fairy Spectacle (Babil and Bijou) at Covent Garden, and fled to America before the curtain had risen on the first scene. Fiske, who knew him well, wrote a good deal in praise of him as an actor and had also much to say about his doings off the stage. But the private life of one who lived so much in the lime-light, as did Boucicault, is, or should be, no concern of the general public. Whatever may have been his faults, he had all the good points and most of the bad points of a typical Irishman—charming and hospitable to his friends, witty and brilliant in his conversation, and popular in all circles, Bohemian or otherwise. His career has been described as a " meteoric one which burned up many in its progress."

As an actor, he was best in the portrayal of the Irishmen in his own plays, though he did not limit his appearances to those parts. He was in his drama of the " Octoroon " in which Mrs. Boucicault was Zoe, the slave sold by auction. This was a play which, though still sometimes given by stock companies in the remote provinces, was never a favourite with the London public, who did not like to see their favourite actress die (she ought to have been rescued somehow like Eily in " The Colleen Bawn ! "), and, moreover, did not quite understand that an octoroon is not really a nigger. It is a curious fact that in many cases an octoroon is not recognizable as such and it is often only with increasing age that the appearance of African descent is noticeable. A well-known English composer, who was an octoroon is said to have met with many unpleasantnesses in the United States on this account.

Boucicault wrote " The Vampire " and appeared in it himself with a white face not made up in any way. His brogue must have lent a touch of comicality to the Vampire as such, but his appearance as the monster who fascinates his victims before sucking their blood must have been ghastly enough, for it is related that the frequenters of the pit would often go into hysterics or faint. Many will remember a horrible story called " Dracula " by Irving's right-hand man, Bram Stoker, which deals with the doings of a Vampire. Boucicault also once attempted Louis XI. With his Dublin brogue, that must have been indeed funny !

At the Princess's in 1864 " The Streets of London," as adapted from the French by Boucicault, was brought out with some measure of success and it has even stood the test of a revival now and again. The original was a French piece called " Les Pauvres de Paris," first seen in 1856 at the Ambigu Comique Theatre. It had been done by various adaptors : at the Surrey under the title of " Fraud and its Victims " ; at the old Strand as " Pride and Poverty " ; and in America as " The Poor of New York." There were two sensations—a house on fire with real fire-engines and horses galloping on to the stage, and a scene where the heroine and her brother are just saved from being suffocated by charcoal fumes. The heroine was charmingly played on its first production by Miss Fanny Gwynne, who was afterwards at the Haymarket with Mrs. Kendal in Gilbert's fairy plays.

" Arrah-na-Pogue," an Irish play of the type of " The Colleen Bawn," followed in March, 1865, and scored an immediate success owing to the acting of Boucicault and his wife, Patty Oliver and Dominick Murray. It was revived more than once in after years, notably ten years after its first production. That was at the Adelphi when Boucicault's part was taken by an American actor, Williamson, and the hero, Beamish McCoul, was that ideal dramatic lover—Will Terriss. Shiel Barry (the miser of " Les Cloches de Corneville ") was the Michael Feeny in the Adelphi revival, a part that had been previously taken by Dominick Murray. There was one great scene in " Arrah-na-Pogue " which never failed to " bring down the house." This was the climbing of the outer prison wall by Shaun the Post by means of the ivy, and his hiding in the ivy when the soldiers looked out of the window with their lighted torches.

In 1865 came the production of " It's Never Too Late to Mend," by Charles Reade, the opening night of which I have spoken of in my chapter on " Audiences."

In 1866 Vining returned more to the legitimate and put on " The Huguenot Captain" with a fine cast, including Mrs. Stirling, Miss Neilson, Augusta Thompson, George Vining and George Honey. The last named will be best remembered as the original Eccles in Robertson's " Caste " ; he had previously been an opera singer.

This rather dull play of Watts Phillips was made a trifle livelier by the introduction of " The Parisian Grotesque Dancers," who were the first to introduce the cancan to the English stage. It does not seem to have created much alarm in the breast of Mrs. Grundy and her followers. The play only ran a short while, and in the November of the same year gave way to a version of " Barnaby Rudge," which was probably put on for the sake of Mrs. John Wood, a daughter of Mrs. Henry Vining, who was cast for the part of Miss Miggs. She played it with a great deal of spirit but not in the spirit of Dickens, for she made a regular Yankee girl of it, accent and all ! Katharine Rodgers (the " Formosa " of the Drury Lane sensational drama) was Barnaby and Augusta Thompson, Dolly Varden.

Mrs. John Wood became so well known to a later generation of players that they mercifully buried in oblivion her attempt to make a Yankee of the immortal Miggs. Her acting in " Poll and Her Partner Joe," in Pinero's farces at the Court (will she ever be forgotten dressed as a prima ballerina ?) and as the Drury Lane autumn dramas endeared her to a wide circle of playgoers of the latter years of the nineteenth century. They will remember her as Mrs. Page in " The Merry Wives of Windsor," as Lady Franklin in " Money," as Pocahontas in " La Belle Sauvage," as Mrs. Lovibond in " The Overland Route," as Philippa Chester in Reade's "Wandering Heir," as Lady Gay Spanker in "London Assurance," and scores of other parts during her tenure of the St. James's and her engagements at the Criterion and the Court Theatres. She was a dear woman, "Ma Wood" to all whom she loved and who loved her, including the writer of these lines to her memory.

The year 1867 at the Princess's was noted for the reappearance of Fechter in one or two of his characters, a spectacular production of "Antony and Cleopatra" for Miss Glyn, and the transfer of the Surrey drama "True to the Core," with Creswick in his original part of Martin Truegold.

The Shakespearean tragedy was well done. Henry Loraine was Antony; Henry Forrester was Cæsar and Walter Joyce was also in the cast. It must have been an "Old Style" production: Miss Glyn had been very successful as Cleopatra at Sadler's Wells with Phelps, but she was a stagy performer at the best, and the elder Loraine was quite one of the old school well known at the Marylebone and other outlying theatres.

"True to the Core" was one of the most successful nautical melodramas ever put on the stage. It was written by one Selous and had gained the prize offered by T. P. Cooke, the celebrated actor of Nautical drama. Cooke was an actor of the early nineteenth century. Born in 1786, son of a doctor, he was in the Royal Navy by the time he was ten years old, and was present in several of the great naval victories gained by Earl St. Vincent. He was only eighteen when he left the Navy (after the Peace of Amiens) and joined the dramatic profession, acting at the old Royalty (the house in Wellclose Square), Surrey, Drury Lane, Covent Garden and Adelphi; in short, wherever there was melodrama as the *pièce de résistance.* He was considered the best representative of the British sailor on the stage and played William in "Black Eyed Susan" as long ago as 1829. The Monster in "Frankenstein," the Vampire (which he also acted in French at the Porte St. Martin), the Red Rover, Vanderdecken and Aubrey in "The Dog of Montargis" (often put on in Toyland) were his chief parts. In 1860, at the good old age of 74, he played William for the Dramatic College performance, and died four years later.

"True to the Core" was revived again at the Adelphi in 1877 with Emery in Creswick's old part and Rachel Sanger (better known in burlesque) as the heroine.

The following year—Vining still in Management—saw the production at the Princess's of a melodrama adapted from the French play "Les Oiseaux de Proie," another version of which had already been seen in the East End under the title of "The Bohemians

MRS. JOHN WOOD

From a photograph given to the author by Mrs. Wood

of Paris." It was revived again at the Adelphi in 1877. This was called "After Dark," and was a very good specimen of a melodrama of London life. The cast was an excellent one for plays of that kind, including Rose Leclercq, as the heroine, with George Vining, Walter Lacy, Dominick Murray, J. G. Shore and handsome young Harry Montague. The sensation scene was on the Underground Railway (then somewhat of a novelty) where a man is laid on the rails, drugged, for the train to run over him. Another of the *dramatis personæ* is shut up in a neighbouring cellar and just manages to tear down the brickwork of the intervening wall before the train comes dashing by. The act was worked up to perfection, and few sensation scenes of a later date have produced the same amount of excitement.

In 1869, came the end of the Vining management—suddenly and with disaster, the house being closed in October without previous intimation. During this year, Fechter had made one or two appearances and Madame Celeste had been seen in "Presumptive Evidence," an unsuccessful play by Boucicault. Then another foreigner came along. This was Herr Formes, an ex-opera singer, who had sung as long ago as 1854 in "Der Freischütz" with Madame Caradori. At the Princess's he appeared as Shylock (in English) and made a thorough mess of the part. The Portia was an aspirant to dramatic honours in the person of a Miss Frances Bouverie. There was also a version of a French play called "Le Mangeur de Fer" in which Charles Mathews, an excellent comedian, tried to be a serious actor and failed lamentably. He was supported by his wife, Vining, a Miss Carlisle and William Rignold; but it was a really bad play anyhow, and was soon taken off.

Benjamin Webster took over the direction of the theatre after Vining's disappearance. He was an old hand at theatre management, having been lessee of the Haymarket for sixteen years and of the Adelphi for twenty, besides previous dramatic experience at the East End Royalty and City theatres in earlier days still. His apprenticeship to the profession had been a very hard one, for in his very early days he had lived in a second-floor back in Clare Market and danced at Drury Lane! His speciality was the production of melodramas, and he has the credit also of bringing Madame Celeste before a West End audience. But of course he was a good all-round actor, as all actors had to be in those days. I think his last appearance was in a little piece called "A Touch of Nature" in 1875, when close on eighty years of age. He died five years later. When he took over the Princess's, he maintained the same character in his programme, that is, melodrama with occasional lapses into tragedy when he could get a "Star" for the

leading rôle. He revived " After Dark," " The Streets of London "
and " Formosa," and produced a new play, also by Boucicault,
called " The Rapparree : or the Treaty of Limerick." The
company at the theatre at this time included William Rignold and
Hermann Vezin with, for leading lady, Katharine Rodgers.
Chatterton had now joined Webster in the management of the
Princess's and Edmund Falconer's " Peep o' Day " was revived
as well as Halliday's " Great City," one of the earliest melodramas
dealing with London life, in which Mrs. Kendal had made her
appearance in 1867, supported by a cast including names of
many in small parts who became famous actors in later years, such
as Charles Warner and Miss Le Thiere. In this piece there was
a great sensation scene where Mogg, the convict (played by McIntyre),
tore down the telegraph wires to aid in his escape and the final
tableau was a representation of Frith's picture of " The Railway
Station," where the villain is arrested as he gets into the train. In
this drama, also, a real hansom cab and horse was brought on to the
stage for the first time in dramatic annals, an incident repeated
in a drama at the Duke's Theatre, Holborn, and again in Hervé's
opera-bouffe " Le Petit Faust," in which the Devil himself drove
up in a hansom the driver of which was Charles Willmott, afterwards
manager of the Duke's, Holborn, the Grand, Islington, and the
never-to-be-forgotten Occidental Tavern in the Strand.

There was a French company from Paris at the Princess's in
1870 who put on " Frou-Frou," " L'Aventurière," etc., and there
were one or two new plays by Boucicault with Rose Leclercq,
George Belmore and other good actors.

In 1871, Phelps was acting here in a version of " Faust and
Mephistopheles " to the Marguerite of Rose Leclercq. What
a vast number of different parts did this talented lady play during her
career, from fairies and Columbines in pantomime to Olivia in
the Lyceum " Twelfth Night " and the elderly grandes dames
in the plays of Oscar Wilde. In this production of " Faust " the
part of the small boy, Karl, played by Ellen Terry under the Keans,
was given to Violet Cameron, daughter of one of the Sisters Brougham
of the old Canterbury Music Hall, afterwards to become a leading
light of Comic Opera.

Later in the year, a new drama by Edmund Falconer, author
of " Peep o' Day," was put on with Rose Leclercq still as leading
lady and the author himself in the cast. It was not a particularly
good piece, but ran for over a hundred nights, no inconsiderable
run in those days. Miss Furtado was seen towards the end of the
year in a poor play called " On the Jury," with Webster and Phelps,
and there was the usual Pantomime at Christmas.

Edmund Falconer was a fertile writer of Irish plays and an excellent comedian in parts like Barney O'Toole in "Peep o' Day," and Danny Mann in "The Colleen Bawn," which he created. But somehow he always failed as a manager sooner or later, whatever temporary success he might obtain with any special piece. In November, 1866, he took the opera house in the Haymarket to produce "Oonagh : or the Lovers of Lisnamona," founded on a novel of Miss Edgeworth. He played a miser, and Fanny Addison was the heroine. The drama went on for seven hours and was then not finished, though it was past 2.0 a.m. Finally, the stage carpenters took the law into their own hands, pulled the carpet from under the feet of the actors, then rang the curtain down and the unfortunate play was played no more. Record for a drama that was never finished—even once.

Nothing seemed destined for a decently long run at the rather unlucky Princess's. Everything was tried by turns in the hope o pleasing the public. Phelps and Creswick appeared together in Shakespearean productions, alternating parts like Othello and Iago (as Irving did with Booth in later years). Mr. and Mrs. Bandmann (from the Queen's, Long Acre), who may be said to have been the pioneers of travelling dramatic companies in India, played a short engagement, and the Rousbys appeared in Tom Raylor's "Twixt Axe and Crown," and in a play on Mary Queen of Scots written especially for the lovely Mrs. Rousby by Wills, with Rousby as John Knox and Forbes Robertson as Chastelard. She also created the title rôle in a new play by Miss Braddon called "Griselda," but it was a dull piece and soon taken off. A disastrous experiment was made in the reappearance of Charles Dillon, no longer the man who had made such a sensation in "Belphegor" at the Lyceum so many years before. Besides having lost all his powers as an actor (only the power to rant remaining) he chose for his reappearance Byron's tragedy of "Manfred," the gloomiest and most "unactable" play ever written. It was a failure and the management had to fall back upon old favourites like "Lost in London" and "The Lancashire Lass." Byron had a new play about this time called "Haunted Houses," with a most sensational scene of the fall of a block of tumbledown tenements, collapsing, I think, on the villain.

I have not adhered strictly to dates in this rapid account of the productions at the Princess's in the seventies, for, as a matter of fact, Mrs. Rousby as the Scottish Queen came later than Griselda, but dates are not of so much consequence when one is writing of such constant changes.

In 1875, melodrama was left alone for the time and London flocked to see a really fine spectacle—"Round the World in Eighty

Days," founded on Jules Verne's well-known story. In this Henry Sinclair, an actor who could be depended upon in almost any sort of part, played the travelling Englishman. He had been in the Drury Lane historical dramas of " Amy Robsart " and " Richard Cœur de Lion," and was later the original Corry Kinchela in Boucicault's " Shaughraun " and also in the revival of " True to the Core " at the Adelphi. A "sound " actor who would never let an author down ! The stately and beautiful Helen Barry, who had burst on the London public as Queen of the Amazons in " Babil and Bijou," was the Indian Princess. Miss Carlisle and the ever useful McIntyre were also in the cast. I remember a great scene of a cavern of snakes from which the Princess is rescued. The "property " snakes were wonderful and became the talk of the town.

Miss Heath was seen in " Jane Shore " by Wills, and, though it was a most lugubrious play, she always made a success in the scene where she is out in the snow, starving with cold and hunger, and recognizes her child. She was much caricatured for her rendering of this scene—her deep voice and rather old-fashioned delivery lending themselves to caricature. But she was a really fine actress and had played many leading parts with the Keans in their great Shakespearean revivals. She married Wilson Barrett, but was not personally associated with his greatest successes, though he acted with her in " Jane Shore," as did also James Fernandez and a small boy, called Bertie Coote as the Duke of York.

In the same year as Miss Heath's reappearance on the scene of so many triumphs, there was a notable season at the Princess's when Joseph Jefferson, the American actor, repeated his magnificent performance of Rip Van Winkle in the play by Boucicault founded on Washington Irving's tale. This had been previously seen at the Adelphi in the winter of 1865, when Mr. and Mrs. Billington and Paul Bedford were in the cast and O. Smith gave his noted performance of the Gnome of the Catskills in which he had no word to speak. At the Princess's revival Jefferson was supported by Mrs. Alfred Mellon in Mrs. Billington's old part.

Washington Irving had founded the tale in his *Sketch Book* on an old German legend of the Harz mountains, but the scene in the story and play was placed in the Catskills of the Eastern States. There had been many previous versions done for the stage, but till Jefferson thought out the whole matter no one had had the idea of keeping the gnomes and spirits of the mountains silent all through the piece, and thus a good deal of verisimilitude was lost because it was so difficult to imagine these mythical beings talking like ourselves. With a crew of silent ghosts of Henrik Hudson and his companions, it was far easier to convey the eerie nature of the play without trespassing too much on one's credulity. In fact, it resolved itself more into a dream or vision. It required, of course, a very capable actor to hold the attention of the audience by himself, surrounded by a crowd of uncanny beings with never a word to say, and certainly no actor has yet achieved the same measure of success in this piece as was attained by Jefferson. It remains his play and his alone. I think it will also be generally conceded that, of all the Americans who have appeared in London at various times, Jefferson is easily first in everything that goes to make a really great actor—not even excepting Booth. It may be likewise asserted without fear of serious contradiction that Joseph Jefferson was the first American actor to break down the prejudice that existed undoubtedly against the introduction of American actors to an English audience. We have got over that prejudice long ago, but there was a time, in the memory of living playgoers, when an American had a poor chance of a welcome on the English stage. We now very gladly accept all comers on their merits alone, and though an English public may have (and very often too) to put up with very second-rate acting which, nevertheless, has been judged first-class on the other side, yet it is all the more eager to acclaim the really great artistes no matter from what country they may come. The Forrest and Macready riots are now buried in oblivion, but the feeling that gave rise to them was very real indeed while it lasted.

Earlier in the same year that saw the renewal of Jefferson's English welcome at the Princess's was produced " Heartsease " a dreary version of " La Dame aux Camélias " with Helen Barry in the title rôle. This was by James Mortimer, the editor of *The London Figaro*, who was a very unpopular person with pit and gallery in those days : his appearance in the stalls was the signal for such a hubbub that only the straightforward and manly appeal of William Rignold saved the situation.

In the autumn, two or three months after that hullabaloo, the Carl Rosa Opera Company were at the Princess's. They opened with " The Marriage of Figaro " (Mozart) with Santley as Figaro and Rose Hersee as Susanna. If we could get such casting for opera in English in these days, there would not be so much to grumble at. In 1876 " The Corsican Brothers " returned to their former house where Fechter had scored such a success in the dual rôle. This time it was John Clayton, a very painstaking actor of good appearance (who married, by the way, Boucicault's eldest daughter and was the father of some clever actors of to-day), who was the representative of the two Dei Franchi. Barnes was the Chateau Renaud and Caroline Hill (whose name crops up in so many different chapters of this book) was the Emilie De L'Esparre.

In this year I must just mention a performance (a single performance only, I believe) of "The Lady of Lyons," in which Ellen Terry made her first appearance as Pauline to the Claude Melnotte of Charles Coghlan. Miss Terry records in her book that she played it better then than she did afterwards at the Lyceum to the Melnotte of Irving.

The days of the old Princess's Theatre were nearly numbered : it was to last only two or three years more. A series of revivals and productions of poor plays followed in rapid succession. "Abel Drake," founded on a well-known novel ; "Guinea Gold," by H. J. Byron ; "Number Twenty," by Hatton and Albery were three of the novelties ; but a finer production was that of a four-act Fairy Play by Ross Neil called "Elfinella." It was a play with music by Alfred Cellier and appears to have been quite a charming work, above the heads of the Princess's audiences of those days. Miss Heath was cast (or rather "mis-cast") for the title rôle. She was, to put it gently, no longer young. Maud Milton and Dolores Drummond, both of them actresses with a fine delivery, William Rignold and Charles Warner were also in the cast. Warner seems to have been in the Princess's company in many pieces, but it was in the year 1879—the last year of the old house—that he attained at one bound to the front rank of his profession by his performance of Coupeau in Charles Reade's revolting version of Zola's "L'Assommoir."

When Phelps was commanded to give a performance at Windsor Castle in January, 1861, the play given was "Richelieu." In the cast we find the names of Hermann Vezin, W. H. Vernon, Miss Heath and Miss Fanny Josephs, and the two pages were represented by the younger son of Phelps and a young man called Lickfold, who was making his very first appearance on any stage. Lickfold's father was a member of the company at Sadler's Wells under Phelps, and young Lickfold often got a seat in the orchestra seeing a great many of Shakespeare's plays, greedily absorbing details of the actor's art which was to stand him in such good stead when he blossomed into Charles Warner. There is no doubt (it is the unvarying testimony of all who saw the horrible play) that Warner's performance of Coupeau in "Drink" was the finest thing he ever did, not even excepting his Othello, which some consider only second to Salvini's. I am only concerned here with Warner at the Princess's, but he had had a vast experience prior to his success as Coupeau in "Drink." He began early, serving a very hard apprenticeship in the provinces in every conceivable kind of part for next to no pay. He was once laconically informed by the manager of the Hanley Theatre—"We change every night. The bill for next week is 'King Lear,' 'Romeo and Juliet,' 'Macbeth,' 'Measure for Measure,' 'The Gipsy King,' and 'Othello,'—with farces. You play in all." This was at the very beginning of his career. Under Nye Chart at the famous Brighton Theatre he found a better set of actors round him and had a higher salary— 35s. a week, to wit ! From there he soon reached London and obtained engagements at the best houses, such as Drury Lane under the Chatterton and Falconer Management, when he was in the bill with actors of the first class, like Phelps, James Anderson, Barry Sullivan, Helen Faucit, Mrs. Hermann Vezin, Amy Sedgwick and others. The répertoire was the entire round of Shakespeare's plays, besides many standard and new productions.

Phelps was always very fond of Warner, taking great trouble to bring him on and make a good actor of him. They were together at Sadler's Wells, the same old theatre in the orchestra of which he had first imbibed his passion for the profession. During his engagement there, he played the schoolmaster (Bradley Headstone) in a version of *Our Mutual Friend* called "The Golden Dustman." I have always thought this novel should make an excellent drama. Warner was at the Olympic in "Daisy Farm," by Henry J. Byron, in which the author and George Belmore also played. Then followed a Lyceum engagement with the Batemans and a season at the Vaudeville in Old Comedy in which he made a great success as Harry Dornton in "The Road to Ruin." He was also one of the original "Our Boys," with Miss Litton at the Imperial in Old Comedy, back to Sadler's Wells for a round of Shakespeare, and then in Adelphi and Drury Lane dramas as the hero. Some critics have said that he was the ideal hero of the Adelphi drama. I take leave to differ. No one in my opinion, and I am speaking from a very long and varied experience as a playgoer, has ever come within measurable distance of Will Terriss in such parts. He was much handsomer, much better at making love and far less stagy than Warner, who, at times, almost as if he were asking the approval of "the gods," would deliberately turn to the house with a note of interrogation in his look, as if to say, "How's that for high ? "

In "Drink," his finest part, there was very little or nothing of this. As the sober workman playing with his little child, or talking affectionately to his wife, there might have been some touch of self-consciousness as if he knew what a fine fellow he was, but the great final scene, when he is alone with the bottle and in all the horrors of delirium tremens, was a masterpiece of acting that the English stage has seldom, if ever, seen surpassed. It made men and women gasp and want to get away, such was the realistic character of the impersonation, and the effect on himself could be seen in the gasping, shaky figure that came before the curtain to take his call.

Warner spent much of his later life in Australia and the States and his end was very sad. Whether the continual repetition of Coupeau had had anything to do with it or not, I cannot tell. Details are unnecessary. It is a curious coincidence that the leading lady in " Drink " also came to a very sad end. I allude of course to Amy Roselle, whose husband, Arthur Dacre, shot her and killed himself immediately afterwards during an unsuccessful tour in Australia. Amy Roselle was a charming heroine of melodrama. She came of an acting family. Her brother was known as " Master Percy Roselle," and being almost a dwarf, was cast for parts like Number Nip, King Pippin, Pigwiggin, and Tom Thumb in the Drury Lane pantomimes, besides playing Prince Arthur in Shakespeare's " King John." She herself was an excellent May Edwards in " The Ticket of Leave Man," was with the Haymarket company in some of the Gilbert Fairy Plays, and was in the cast of " The Colonel," that skit on the æsthetes, when first produced at the Prince of Wales's.

Another member of the " Drink " cast was Philip Day, who had begun his stage career in burlesque and pantomime. He was a remarkably handsome young fellow and a clever actor as well, and we find him playing Horatio to the Hamlet of Walter Montgomery, and Steerforth in a version of " David Copperfield," in which Emery was so excellent as Dan Peggotty. In " Drink " he was the young betrayer, the heartless blackguard of the Boulevards, and did it very well. Fannie Leslie had an important part— Phœbe Sage—a character not in the novel but interpolated to add brightness to a heavy and sordid atmosphere. She was a brilliant artiste in many lines : principal boy of the Drury Lane pantomimes, and in Gaiety and Strand burlesques, and in later life an established favourite at the Music Halls. She married Walter Gooch, who rebuilt the Princess's. She was a bright actress, a charming singer and a clever dancer, and, I believe, after leaving the stage, set up a Dancing Academy of her own. One other member of the cast is worth noting, and that is Ada Murray, who had been one of Menken's innumerable understudies for Mazeppa. She played Virginie admirably. Philip Day was her companion in villainy and they made a very handsome pair of " bad lots."

After the run of " Drink " was over for the time, Gooch with the money he had made out of it rebuilt the theatre, the new house being about as dull and gloomy an interior as had ever been imagined, much less erected. It was not that it was actually ugly, and the acoustical properties were all right (I can speak at least as regards the pit to which I was a frequent visitor), but the decorations of the two circles were dreary and there was a general absence of brightness throughout. I fancy the scheme of decoration was supposed to be " Pompeian " ; whatever it was, it required good acting and an interested audience to counteract the effect.

It got neither the one nor the other at the opening performance. Edwin Booth, an American actor (son of the old English tragedian Junius Brutus Booth), who had been acting for the last thirty years at least, and therefore did not lack experience, and who had made such a name for himself in the States, was engaged with the idea of starting the new house with a " star " of some brilliancy in " Hamlet." It was not his first appearance before a London audience, as he had played in Shakespeare, " Richelieu," etc., at the Haymarket in 1861, about the same time that Fechter had made his sensational appearances in " Hamlet " at the Princess's. " The Fool's Revenge " (the story of Rigoletto) showed Booth at his best. Mrs. Hermann Vezin was the heroine—a part she had played at Sadler's Wells with Phelps.

Booth in Hamlet was very well supported. Swinbourne was the King—he afterwards played it with Irving—Ryder was the Ghost ; Farren, Polonius ; Edmund Leathes, Laertes ; Mrs. Hermann Vezin, the Queen—she had played Portia to Booth's Shylock nineteen years before—and the Ophelia was Miss Gerard, one of the best ever seen. Kate Terry is said to have been a fine Ophelia ; Lady Tree was a better one ; of those I have myself seen (not a few !) I shall always feel doubtful whether the best was Lady Tree or Miss Gerard. This last named was a very clever actress who had gained much experience in the provinces as leading lady in " Caste " and other of the Robertson comedies. She retired from the stage rather early in life and married Henry Abbey, the American impresario.

Booth, like many an American actor before and since, was much depressed by his failure to attract an English audience. The situation was saved by the kindly suggestion of Irving that he should join him at the Lyceum and that they should alternate the parts of Othello and Iago. This was duly carried out, and Booth in Othello was considered very fine, while the Iago of Irving was undoubtedly the better of the two. Booth finished his season at the Princess's in 1881, early in the year, and in May was put on a really fearful play. It is difficult to imagine what could have induced Gooch, not without theatrical experience, to sanction such a production. It was called "Branded" and was more of the type of the gory melodramas formerly found at the Coburg and the East London theatres than anything usually seen at a West End house. There was a very fine cast. Henry Neville, Archer, Caroline Hill, Maud Milton and Mrs. Huntley. Very briefly and baldly told, the story is something like the following : The hero (Neville) is a soldier convicted (wrongly of course) of murder and imprisoned at Toulon—I should say the scene of the play is in France. The heroine dies of shock and is laid out in a chapel —the coffin and funeral procession being all shown complete. The hero has meanwhile escaped and is hiding under the floor of the very chapel where they deposit his wife's body. After the funeral (having seen nothing of it) he emerges from his hiding-place. A faithful friend, corporal on guard at the chapel, tells him "Your wife is dead." "Then I have nothing left to live for," replies the escaped convict. "Yes, you have," says the faithful friend, "you have this !" producing the convict's child from under the flooring of the same chapel where the body lies and where the hero had also hidden himself. Meanwhile, the heroine, being, as you have already guessed, not really dead, had overheard a conversation between the caretaker of the chapel (Mrs. Huntley) a hag, with another accomplice, which proves the innocence of her husband. She dismounts from her bier and comes forward in her shroud. The chapel falls to pieces, an event which the district surveyor of the village had foretold might happen at any time and for which therefore we are prepared. In the final act the hero has become a rich banker, but his wife has gone mad. She, of course, recovers her reason and all ends happily. I tell the story from memory and the details may be not quite accurate all round, but the main facts are correct and the whole thing reminded me very much of a gruesome play I saw in my youth at the Grecian, which I have mentioned before, called "Catherine Howard," in which that hapless Queen is laid out in a vault hung with much black velvet and her lover comes to kiss "HER COLD PALE CORPSE," upon which she gets up in her shroud. The Grecian audience used to enjoy this grave scene hugely.

After this disastrous opening, Gooch leased the theatre to a fairly young and very ambitious actor of the name of Wilson Barrett, who was then playing at the Sloane Square Theatre with great success as Mercutio to the Juliet of Modjeska and the Romeo of Forbes Robertson.

His Mercutio has been declared by competent judges to be one of the best ever seen. It was a very fine performance, but in my humble opinion has been entirely eclipsed by that of Leon Quartermaine who, with Ellen Terry as an incomparable Nurse (even with her part "cut" to ribbons), saved the production of "Romeo and Juliet" by the American actress, Doris Keene, from the total oblivion it so richly deserved.

Barrett had had a truly varied experience, like so many of those who climbed by hard work to the top of the profession. In his early days he had been a harlequin, and before that, Mr. Chance Newton relates, in one of his pleasant chatty little notes on theatrical matters, he had appeared at the old Grecian Theatre, City Road, singing duets with his brother George ! He had been a member of that wonderful stock company at Nottingham responsible for the beginnings of Mrs. Kendal, the Savilles and many others, and had had to act as many as eight or nine different characters in the same week. He was at the Surrey with Miss Caroline Heath when he was about twenty-one years of age and had already been on the stage for four years. Miss Heath was playing Lady Isabel in the evergreen "East Lynne," and Barrett was suddenly called upon to play Archibald Carlyle. He married Miss Heath somewhere about this time, though she must have been nearly twenty years older than himself. In the late sixties he played with Phelps in Shakespearean productions at Drury Lane, and his wife was the leading lady. After this, he toured the provinces with his beautiful wife for some time and eventually took the Amphitheatre at Leeds, which he transformed into the "Grand Theatre, Leeds," one of the handsomest and best managed of all provincial houses.

The next great success was at the old Princess's, where he played in Wills's "Jane Shore." This was a great financial success, and it was with the money he made from it, chiefly in the provinces, that Barrett was afterwards enabled to venture on the management of the new Princess's Theatre and lay the foundations of his London fame.

It had been a dramatic mounting of the ladder of success. From the transpontine Surrey to the Grand Theatre, Leeds ; from Leeds to the Court Theatre, London ; from the Court to the Princess's ; from the Princess's a wanderer for many years, crippled with a huge debt (of which he eventually paid every farthing) back to London to the Olympic and elsewhere, his career reaching a high point of success (from a financial point of view) with that astounding farrago of cant and semi-religious sentiment, "The Sign of the Cross," and culminating at the Shaftesbury where his "Pete" in "The Manxman" was perhaps the finest thing he ever did. But I am digressing too much, and must hark back to the Princess's. The transfer of Barrett and his company from the Court to the Princess's was the beginning of his five years' tenancy of that house, during which many wonderful plays were produced, many good actors introduced to the London public, and his own reputation as an actor and manager, which before this (except for his Mercutio) had not really amounted to much, firmly established.

He put on " Frou-Frou " admittedly for the opportunity of showing Modjeska in a rôle which she considered one of her finest, but his first really great success was with " The Lights o' London," by George R. Sims, produced in the September of the first year of his lease of the Princess's. Sims had hawked his play round to one or two London Managers with no success. It was refused by the Gattis for the Adelphi ; it was refused by Harris for Drury Lane ; it was actually refused by Gooch himself for the Princess's. Barrett liked it, and took it on mutual terms from Sims. As is well known, it caught on at once (although one " disgruntled high-brow " dubbed it " Zola diluted at Aldgate Pump "), and one can imagine the feelings of the Gattis, Harris and Gooch when they saw the latest addition to the ranks of London managers coining money as fast as he could over a play which they had each and all refused ! It is not very difficult to account for the success of " The Lights o' London." In the first place, it was essentially an English play with English sentiment and in a language (as the Prayer Book says) understanded of the people. With but few exceptions, all previous melodramas had been adapted from the French, and the heroes and heroines had been almost always drawn from the ranks of the upper classes. But here was drama which could appeal to the rank and file of the audience—a " Pit Play " if ever there was one, and it is the pit which, in the end, decides the success or failure of a play. Another reason was the remarkable company which Barrett had gathered round him, many of them new to the town, and the principals, at any rate, new to this style of piece.

There was, as leading lady, Miss Eastlake, known indeed to London playgoers, but only in the risqué farces of the Criterion— " The Great Divorce Case," " Pink Dominoes," " Where's the Cat ? " etc. ; there was George Barrett, an excellent comedian, and E. S. Willard, altogether a new discovery, an actor of such power in the impersonation of refined villainy that he was at once acclaimed as one who would go far in years to come ; there was " Granny " Stephens, the original Mrs. Willoughby of " The Ticket of Leave Man " in 1863 ; and Walter Speakman with a reputation gained at less known theatres. The scenery and " extras " appealed to the Londoner—the street scenes, the Regent's Park Canal, where the hero rescues a man from drowning, the policeman, the park loafer (admirably played by young Neville Doone) ; they all worked together to make a popular success, and

Barrett became at one bound a London manager of the first rank.

On its first production (it was revived more than once) " The Lights o' London " ran for two hundred and twenty-six nights, and was followed in 1882 by " The Romany Rye." This was the second of the series of plays which a distinguished critic thought fit to stigmatize as the " gospel of rags." It was founded on Sims's novel, *Rogues and Vagabonds*, and ran for one hundred and thirty-eight nights, being afterwards taken all round the country, yet it was condemned by the critic of *The Times* as a " bad and mischievous play."

It was while this drama was being acted at the Exeter Theatre in September, 1887, five years after its first production, that the house was burned down with the loss of over a hundred lives.

There are upwards of forty characters in " The Romany Rye," and they are all, or nearly all, what may be described as " bad lots." A burglar disguised as a bird-fancier, a young boy thief, horrible waterside characters of the kind Dickens has put into his *Mutual Friend*, many vagabonds, gin-drinking hags, rascally attorneys, and money-lenders. There are subordinate plots of murder and revenge, and the seventeen scenes of which the play is composed abound in sensation and horrors. A shipwreck, a lifeboat, a waterside public-house (reminding one of the " Fellowship Porters "), the crowded quay of a seaport, common lodging-houses in the " Dials," Fanciers' shops (with real rabbits and birds complete), slums around Ratcliff Highway and underground cellars where all kinds of imaginable villainy is carried on. Well might it be called the " Exposition of the Gospel of Rags."

Barrett, Willard and Miss Eastlake were all in it : George Barrett played a thief afterwards repentant ; a charming young actress, Emmeline Ormsby, was the seductive (and seduced) gipsy girl, Laura Lee. One member of the cast was Robert Markby, a personal friend of my own who was exceedingly clever as a rascally money-lender. Markby was by no means a great actor—perhaps he never had the opportunity of showing what he really could do—but he was essentially "sound." He was the Trip when the Bancrofts first produced " The School for Scandal " at the Prince of Wales's, and Dazzle when " London Assurance " was given at the St. James's with Mrs. John Wood as Lady Gay Spanker. After he left *the* profession, he made a profession of teaching amateurs and producing their performances, for which his good manners and experience of society well fitted him.

But perhaps the greatest popular success of Barrett's management of the Princess's was " The Silver King " by Jones (the first drama he wrote) and Herman, produced in November, 1882. It has always been my own opinion that " Clito " was a greater play, but " The Silver King " made a wider appeal and, on its first production, ran for two hundred and eighty-nine nights.

Matthew Arnold, who had almost ceased to attend theatres, wrote a criticism of this play. He was surprised at the changes brought about on the stage and in the audience since he had seen Macready many years before at the same theatre. He said he remembered Macready as a powerful actor in great pieces, but ill supported by his company, that his circumstances were dingy and his audiences poor and uninteresting. He was surprised to find the theatre gay, well filled, the audience lively, intelligent and interested, and he was also surprised to find that, while Barrett's ability naturally distinguished him, his support was excellent. This bears out what I have pointed out in the opening of my chapter on the Two Theatres in Holborn, viz., that from the accession of Queen Victoria to the early fifties the Stage in England was in a bad way. It was con sidered hardly respectable to make a practice of going often to the play, and dramatic taste was at such a low ebb that, from 1841 to 1866, it had not been found necessary to add a single playhouse to those already open in the London area, though the population must have increased enormously during those twenty-five years.

It is worth while to quote part of Matthew Arnold's criticism of " The Silver King," remembering that he was a poet of the first rank and an Oxford scholar of the highest education. He said :

" It is not Shakespeare . . . . it is melodrama. The essential difference between melodrama and poetic drama is that one relies for its main effect upon an inner drama of thought and passion, the other upon an outer drama of (as the phrase is) sensational incidents, and, so far, is clearly melodrama . . . . in general, in drama of this kind, the diction and sentiments, like the incidents, are extravagant, impossible, transpontine ; here they are not. This is a very great merit, a very great advantage. In general, throughout the piece, diction and sentiments are natural. They have sobriety and propriety. They are literature. It is an excellent and hopeful sign."

After the great success of " The Silver King " playgoers were wondering what Barrett would do next. It had been whispered about for some time that his ambition was to do Hamlet at the same theatre where Macready, Charles Kean and Fechter had done it. But the time for that was not yet. Instead, in December, 1883, he put on a play dealing with classical times called " Claudian," by Herman and Wills. The dispute raged fiercely as to the respective shares of the two authors, but it was generally recognized that Herman was responsible for the story and Wills for the adaptation to the stage and the dialogue. There was nothing to be very proud of in either case, for it was a very poor play, as a play, but it met with more than the average measure of success by reason of a spectacular earthquake. Such a scene would have been likely to make the fortune of a much poorer piece, and all London flocked to see palaces crumble and solid marble columns break up.

In 1884, Barrett made his great effort and showed London his idea of Hamlet. It may be summed up in a general way by saying that it was different from any other actor's idea and had its own good, and even great, points.

As a boy in the sixpenny gallery of the old Princess's, Barrett had seen Charles Kean in one of his great revivals, and then and there had vowed that he would not only manage that very theatre, but himself play Hamlet on that very stage. At any rate, that is the story he himself told his audience on the first night of his Hamlet when he had been called before the curtain to receive the congratulations of a huge and appreciative crowd.

" Twenty-five years ago (he said) a poor and almost friendless lad stood outside the walls of the theatre that once stood here, and determined to devote his last sixpence to the enjoyment in the gallery of one of the celebrated revivals of Charles Kean. Coming out of the theatre, he swore to himself that not only would he become manager of that theatre, but that in the distant future he would play Hamlet on that very spot. Ambition is in this instance justified, for the little boy was myself, and I have played Hamlet to you this evening."

There is another story that relates how, after the fall of the curtain on that night (or it may possibly have been on the first night of the " Claudian " earthquake—my informant was not sure), he turned round with his back to the curtain and facing the crowd of his company on the stage called out to them, "Where's Irving now ? " This is probably exaggerated or altogether apocryphal. Yet it is a fact that he had more than a little jealousy of the great manager of the Lyceum, copying him in many little matters and trying to outdo him in any way he could. In his early days, Irving had his good fairy in Lady Burdett Coutts. Barrett, it is said, had something approaching an " Ange Gardien " in Lady Jeune. Irving had great suppers on the stage after first night performances. Barrett must do the same. In both cases, there was a great deal more money spent than was at all necessary. In both cases it led to financial disaster. The final upshot was more fortunate for Barrett than for Irving, for he was a much younger man and had time to recoup his losses. This he did by the aid of "The Sign of the Cross," a perfectly rotten play which Irving's sense of Art and, it may be added, of propriety, would have prevented him putting on the stage at all. When the great Lyceum manager died there was little or nothing to leave. When Barrett died, he left fifty-seven thousand pounds, and he had, in addition, paid all the debts heaped up by the unsuccessful seasons of the later years of his management at the Oxford Street House.

The Princess's stage had known many Hamlets. Here had been seen Macready, one of the last of the heavy funereal Hamlets with the sepulchral voice and the gloomy stalking to and fro. Here, also, had been seen Charles Kean, a shade less gloomy perhaps than his rival Macready (how they hated each other !), but still redolent of the old school. Here had come Fechter to upset old-fashioned ideas, wear a blonde wig, make love as only he knew how, and, generally, play the part as a human being instead of as something (like his father's ghost) not of this world ! Here had been seen other less important actors, among them Edwin Booth, an American Hamlet, with an American reading of the rôle quite unacceptable to an English audience.

Barrett also discarded the funereal hues of the traditional Hamlet and played it in a flaxen wig. Moreover, he introduced many startling and most effective alterations in the mounting of the play. We are generally accustomed to visualize the Play-Scene as shown in Maclise's picture—a vast, rather gloomy Hall, with the King and Queen posed on one side, Ophelia and Laertes on the other and Hamlet lying at her feet. Barrett would have none of this. He pitched the scene in a beautiful garden by moonlight, with a built up stage such as might have been used by any travelling Thespians of the day. Torches held by retainers in barbaric attire lit up the presentation of the "Mousetrap," and when, at the close of the play within a play, the King and Queen left hastily in dismay, Hamlet leaped on to the garden stage with his shout, "Why, let the stricken deer go weep, etc." Of course it was not according to the instructions in the text which describe the scene as "Hall in a Castle," and this, with some other modifications of the usual traditions, gave plenty of opportunity for cavillers and disgruntled persons to cavil and "disgruntle."

The effect of the whole was undeniably good, in parts great, and Barrett's Hamlet will always be remembered as a sincere effort that was justified in itself, though unfortunately from a financial point of view it was anything but a success. Miss Eastlake made a charming, if somewhat modern Ophelia : her mad scene was especially good. Willard was the King—forcible but refined like everything he did. Frank Cooper was Laertes—handsome and courtier-like, and the Queen was Margaret Leighton, not a great actress, but who had a beautiful voice and a perfect training for the delivery of blank verse. I remember her as a fine " Chorus " in a revival of " Henry V " at the Queen's, Long Acre.

In 1885, there was a revival of " The Silver King " and the production of two new plays. One was by Lord Lytton on the subject of " Junius," a finely written tragedy but not actable, which was withdrawn for yet another example of the " gospel of rags " called " Hoodman Blind " by Jones, author of " The Silver King." It was a drama of strong interest and the characters were distributed as usual among the members of the Princess's stock company. Wilson Barrett as the hero ; George Barrett as the comic relief ; Willard as the villain ; Miss Eastlake as the sorrowful maiden.

The chief interest of the piece lay in the impersonation by Miss Eastlake of two sisters, one good and the other bad ! They bore a startling resemblance to each other and the villain causes the good sister to lose the affection of her husband (the hero) by getting the bad one to impersonate her in shady circumstances. Miss Eastlake again showed what an extremely clever emotional actress she was. She seemed to do better in every new character she tried, culminating at last in the terrible, vivid and tragic portrayal of Clito, the Athenian harlot.

This was produced in May, 1886, and was said to be the work of Sydney Grundy and Wilson Barrett. It was a most original play, showing Athens at the height of its riches and prosperity and the debaucheries and follies resulting from the luxurious living of the wealthy classes.

Miss Eastlake made the play. She had an unsympathetic character in the courtesan, but her acting rose to the occasion, and I do not know if any actress of her day, or before it, could have done it so magnificently. Whether caressing the ignoble hero (surely the most ignoble hero that was ever seen on the stage ; this was the blot of the play) or giving herself away for the disgusting woman that she really was, she dominated the scene, and when, in the last act, pursued by relentless enemies, she grovelled on the ground, beating the floor in the agony of her terror, she touched the utmost limits of realistic acting. The horrible delirium tremens act in " Drink " as done by Charles Warner, is the only scene I can recall in my long experience as a playgoer, to equal it for sheer horror.

Clito, the hero, was that poor kind of creature who is fond of preaching to others about the paths of virtue, and the first to fall when exposed to the lure of the courtesan. I cannot help thinking that Barrett loved a part that had some " preaching " in it, especially if it were dressed in classical buskins. Claudian, Junius, Clito, and Marcus in " The Sign of the Cross," were all " pulpit " rôles. The last named, probably the most successful of all, enabled him to pay off his large accumulation of debts and start free with fresh capital. It was, as I have said, quite contemptible as a play, owing its marvellous popular success to the support received from clergymen of all denominations (especially Nonconformists) and from the terrifying shriek of Haidée Wright, as the boy to be thrown to the lions, which was eagerly anticipated every night. There is a story of one old lady, not able to get to the theatre for the earlier part of the performance, asking the check taker as she panted up the stairs, " Has she shrieked yet ? " But this was a Lyric Theatre production with which I am- not concerned here any more than with the later plays by Hall Caine in which Barrett showed such power as a sentimental actor at the Shaftesbury Theatre.

Prior to the presentation of " Clito," in May, 1866, there had been a short run of a new play by Henry Arthur Jones called " The Lord Harry," the first performance of which had been the occasion of a scene very similar to that which took place at the Haymarket Theatre when first taken over by the Bancrofts. The reason was the same. On the appearance of Barrett on the stage, he was received by shouts of " Where's the pit ? " accompanied by catcalls from the gallery. It appears that a few extra rows of stalls had been added, thereby reducing the accommodation in the pit, and rumours had also been spread about that some of these stalls had been given to friends of the management and not been paid for. After the curtain had fallen on the first act, Barrett came to the front and in a manly and thoroughly determined speech informed the audience that he would give in charge anyone who had got into the theatre without payment, but that he was resolved to rule the theatre as he liked considering that he had to risk his money for the privilege of doing so. The would-be rioters were subdued by his firm attitude, but the play had been ruined and never got a fair start.

After the finish of " Clito " the American actor, Gillette, had a play produced called " Held by the Enemy," but its life was a short one and it was followed in September (Hawtrey as manager) by " Harvest " by Henry Hamilton (better known as the author of many Drury Lane autumn dramas), with Amy Roselle as leading lady. This had no better fate, and in December " The Noble

Vagabond " was put on for the reappearance of Barrett. Though not a bad play, it had no great success.

Wilson Barrett's wife was a Miss Caroline Heath, who had been leading lady at the old Princess's with the Keans and Fechter and later on in Wills's dreary " Jane Shore." She was a good deal older than her husband had been, long famous for her elocution, and was a great favourite with Queen Victoria, being appointed by her to be her private reader. She had a fine contralto voice, and at one time had some idea of going on the operatic stage, but preferred the dramatic side of the profession and started as one of Charles Kean's bevy of beautiful English girls. She remained with the Keans throughout their long tenancy of the Princess's and supported Fechter as Gertrude to his Hamlet and Pauline to his Claude Melnotte. A season at Sadler's Wells brought her out as Juliet, and as Fiordelisa in " The Fool's Revenge " (Rigoletto). At the Surrey she was acclaimed as one of the best of Lady Isabels in " East Lynne " by that transpontine audience who probably knew every word and every tradition of the famous tear-compeller. I think it was before Barrett took over the Princess's that she suffered from mental depression which she never shook off during the last years of her life. She died in 1887, many years before her husband.

About the year 1887, the Princess's came under the direction of a Miss Grace Hawthorne, a tall, handsome American actress said to be descended from one of the Puritan pilgrims of the seventeenth century. She must have had abundant means of her own or else was backed by others who had, for she met failure after failure with a grim determination to go on at any cost. Her company was always a good one, with actors like Barnes, Abingdon, Bassett Roe, Fernandez, and actresses of the standing of Cicely Richards, Eva Sothern, Dolores Drummond, Mrs. Huntley, etc. Her usual programme was melodrama—and the first was put on in 1887 called " The Shadows of a Great City." This had a short run, but in the following year, 1888, the failures were many and came quickly one after the other.

Early in that year a play called " Siberia," in six acts, was closely followed in February by " Mirage," a version of *As in a Looking-Glass*, a novel which Mrs. Bernard Beere had made her own in another version. It failed and was succeeded by an adaptation of a popular shilling shocker of the day by Fergus Hume called " The Mystery of a Hansom Cab." This lasted a little longer, so a novelty was not wanted till April, when " Dorothy Gray," a melodrama in five acts, was produced, but at the end of that month Miss Hawthorne had had enough of it, for she made way in May

for the return of Wilson Barrett, who put on a piece by himself
and Hall Caine, " Ben-my-Chree," founded on " The Deemster,"
which had a certain amount of success and was toured in the provinces
later.

At the close of the summer season, Barrett left the house once
more to Miss Hawthorne, who reproduced " The Still Alarm,"
a very good specimen of melodrama which can still be seen sometimes in the provinces. In this, Mary Rorke was the heroine,
but gave up the part to Miss Hawthorne, who was persevering
in her attempts to gain the affections of the London playgoing public.
Fannie Leslie and Harry Nicholls were also in the cast. " Hands
Across the Sea," by that old experienced writer of plays, Henry
Petitt, was given in November, for which Neville joined the company.

In 1889, Wilson Barrett returned to the scene of his former
triumphs for what was destined to be his last appearances at the
Princess's Theatre. He opened with " Hamlet," but with the
exception of George Barrett as the First Gravedigger and Miss
Eastlake as Ophelia the cast was a different one from that of his
first production. Miss Eastlake was more modern than before,
and it was made clear that her forte did not lie in the direction of
the legitimate, while, in strong emotional parts such as the courtesan
in " Clito," she was almost without a rival. The revival had a
very short run and was followed by a new play by Hall Caine called
" Good Old Times," which only ran for a fortnight in spite of
a strong cast. Lewis Waller made what, I think, was his first
appearance with Barrett in this play. Another novelty followed
in " Nowadays," a drama of sporting plot, said to be the best of
its class which had been produced since " The Flying Scud " at
the Holborn nearly twenty years before. In this piece, Miss
Hawthorne returned to her stage, and Waller and the charming
Rose Norreys were also in the cast. Barrett's season wound up
with a revival of " Claudian " with the original cast and then in
June of the same year (1889) a really fine melodrama called " True
Heart " was put on with a magnificent cast, including Bassett Roe
as the villain, Yorke Stephens, Leonard Boyne, Seymour Hicks
as a bos'n and Grace Hawthorne. There was a tremendous
sensational scene of a ship drifting on to the rocks and the launch
of a most realistic lifeboat which worked the audience up to a high
pitch of enthusiasm, especially at the moment when the hero calls
for volunteers to man it. His " Who will come with me ? " addressed
nightly to the gallery, though meant for the crowd on the stage,
never failed to arouse loud cheers from the " gods." But there
must have been something about Miss Grace Hawthorne's management, or perhaps about her presence in the cast of a play, for that

play to be a failure no matter how good it might be. "True Heart" was a stirring melodrama with an exceptionally fine lot of actors and actresses in it, but it was withdrawn after it had barely a month's trial, and the fair manageress fell back on "The Still Alarm," with herself and Fannie Leslie in their old parts That ran for a month or thereabouts and was followed by the ancient Adelphi drama "Proof," in which Carlotta Leclercq found a part nearly forty years after she had been playing at the old Princess's under the Keans.

In November, again a new play, "The Gold Craze," was tried and failed, and then a better result was obtained with a good melodrama by Petitt and Sims called "Master and Man," in which were found Neville, Robert and Bella Pateman, Barnes, Fanny Brough and Mrs. Huntley. Miss Hawthorne took a back seat for a time. But she returned in May of 1890 with an expensive and ill-cast version of "Theodora" written by Buchanan, really a translation of the one used by Sarah Bernhardt. There had been another version of the same story at the Surrey many years before, in which Avonia Jones (Mrs. Gustavus V. Brooke) had achieved considerable success. Somewhere about this time, I think Miss Hawthorne put on "A Royal Divorce," an historical piece dealing with Napoleon and the Empress Josephine, and this never failed to attract an audience whenever produced. It is still running in the provinces, I feel convinced. Written by Wills, it was, like most of his pieces, deficient in historical accuracy, but one or two good situations managed to save it from absolute failure. Murray Carson, who bore a strange resemblance to the portraits of the great Emperor, must have played in this many hundreds of times.

The next courageous person who tried to make money at the Princess's Theatre was Mrs. Langtry. She gathered large audiences for the first week or two who were anxious to see what she would make of such a strenuous rôle as that of Cleopatra in Shakespeare's tragedy. Coghlan was the Antony. It is hardly necessary to say that the result was a failure. Coghlan had always been much better in modern pieces than in Shakespeare, and Mrs. Langtry possessed nothing but her beauty to qualify her for such a rôle. She was often excellent in comedy—had indeed made a more than passable Rosalind—but her acting from the very commencement of her career had been "taught" : there was nothing of the divine fire inherent in her.

Large sums were spent on the mounting of "Antony and Cleopatra" produced in November, 1890 ; in February, 1891 it had to be withdrawn and a very ill-judged, not to say stupid play called "Lady Barter," by Coghlan, was put on. In this most sordid piece, Mrs. Langtry had to play a character for whom no one could feel the slightest sympathy, and the acting of Lewis Waller and the author himself was not enough to save it from the condemnation it thoroughly deserved. "Linda Grey," by Sir Charles Young, with Mrs. Langtry, May Whitty, Laura Linden, Herbert Standing and some other well-known actors was the next venture of the fair manageress. It ran nine nights, and then she gave up the hopeless task of making the unlucky theatre pay.

From 1891 to the beginning of 1894 melodramas, some good, some very much the reverse, held the boards of the Princess's. Perhaps one of the most interesting items of this period was a revival of one or two of the old Boucicault dramas that had been so successful on the stage of the old Princess's. "Arrah-na-Pogue," in my opinion the best of all Boucicault's Irish plays, was put on with Neville, Wilfrid Shine (in Boucicault's old part), Arthur Dacre, Amy Roselle and, as "Arrah," a young lady described as Miss "Ella" Terriss. The same "Ella," or "Ellaline" as we know her, also appeared in Trissy Marston's part in a subsequent revival of "After Dark."

Another feature of this period (the house was under the direction of a Mr. Herbert Basing) was the reappearance, after many years, of the original Colleen Bawn, Mrs. Dion Boucicault herself. She played the part of an elderly woman in a piece called "The Life We Live." It was a pronounced failure, but the really great acting of Mrs. Boucicault in a most pathetic death scene helped to show to the younger generation of actresses what one of the older generation could do.

"Hoodman Blind" was revived, and Drury Lane dramas ("The World" and "The Derby Winner") that had been taken off in the middle of a successful career for the pantomime were carried lock, stock and barrel from the Lane to Oxford Street. Warner revived "Drink" and "It's Never Too Late to Mend," two plays which always attract a certain kind of audience, but few of the new pieces produced seemed to catch on.

In May, 1894, there was a brief season of French Plays, when London saw for the first time the story of "The Two Orphans" (an old success of the Olympic) done as a dumb show. It was not a success : London knew its Orphans well and would not put up with the absence of speech and curtailing of sensational incident.

In its latter years, the Princess's qualified more and more as the house for the "gospel of rags," a gibe which had been thrown at Barrett for his "Silver King," "Lights o' London," etc. Play succeeded play, all dealing with the low and sordid sides of London life. Many were freely adapted from the French, as "The Streets of London" and "After Dark" had been done before them, and the scenes and surroundings altered to suit a London audience.

George R. Sims and Arthur Shirley were responsible for some of these. "The Star of India," "How London Lives" (from "Le Camelot"), "Two Little Vagabonds" (from "Les Deux Gosses"), and "Alone in London," by Buchanan and Harriet Jay, previously seen at the Olympic, were among them. The last-named still holds its place in provincial touring companies, but the best of them all was "Two Little Vagabonds," in which the delightful Sidney Fairbrother was one of the *gosses* and Kate Tyndal the other.

Towards the end of its days a version of "Lorna Doone" was staged, and one of Guy Boothby's novels, *Dr. Nikola*, but nothing could change the ill-luck of the house. It would be profitless to enumerate the various productions. The last play acted on the boards of the Princess's appears to have been one called "The Fatal Wedding," which was given in 1902, the year in which the theatre opened and closed its doors for the last time.

About 1901, Benjamin Keith, pioneer of Music Halls in the United States, got the Princess's a bargain. Theatre managers were tired of a house which had, it was said, outlived its luck, for there is no one who so firmly believes in "luck," good or bad, as your theatrical manager.

Keith had begun life by selling peanuts in the enclosure of Barnum's Circus. He saved enough money from his sales to buy some sort of a "freak," started a show of his own and by degrees was enabled to open a Music-Hall Agency in New York, from which he amassed a huge fortune. He was an odd-looking man in appearance, and could be easily spotted for what he was.

Keith's idea seems to have been to turn the Princess's into a place of "Continuous Vaudeville"—vaudeville being, in the American language, an expression for any light entertainment of sorts. You were to pay one payment at the doors, entitling you to a twelve hours' continual amusement, a free Parcels Office for those who had been shopping, and where they could have their parcels sent, a free crèche for those who had babies to be looked after while they were amusing themselves. In fact, a sort of "Home from Home," with all the Vaudeville thrown in! Everything free for the one payment except, presumably, refreshments, out of which you may be quite sure Mr. Keith meant to make a handsome profit.

The scheme came to nothing, but, as far as I know, the place is still the property of Mr. Keith or his heirs, and is slowly going to rack and ruin with rats, vermin and decay. There was some project of erecting an hotel on the site, but that fell through, and it is said Keith utterly refused to make the alterations considered necessary by the L.C.C. The site itself should be valuable, but the building has probably seen its last days as a theatre.

CHAPTER VIII

THE TWO THEATRES IN HOLBORN AND THE PANTHEON THEATRE

THE ROYAL AMPHITHEATRE, HOLBORN

AT one time Holborn could boast of two theatres situated within a hundred yards of each other. One was, during its fourteen years of life, known by many different names—the Holborn, the Duke's, the Mirror, the Curtain and possibly other names. The other lost Holborn theatre, at first somewhat grandiloquently called the " New Royal Amphitheatre," was near the site of Kingsgate Street (now also lost !), where once lived Mrs. Sairey Gamp " over the bird-fancier's, and opposite the celebrated cats' meat warehouse."

It was opened in May, 1867, with a combined " horsemanship " and theatrical entertainment. At one time the building had served for the sales of horses—a sort of minor Tattersalls—and was of considerable size, almost circular in form as if actually built for a circus.

The opening programme in 1867 included a musical drama or rather a play with singing, and also introducing Professor Pepper's Show from the Polytechnic wherein he exhibited a Magical Cabinet from which all sorts of people came forth unexpectedly. After this there were clowns, acrobats, and jugglers to follow. Altogether, a very mixed show.

Some quite first-class circus turns appeared at this house in its early days. Alfred Bradbury, for a long time the " Champion Jockey of the Ring," the Hanlons, better known as the Hanlon-Voltas, Azella, who had the distinction of being the first female trapezist, Mlle. Pereira and Madame Senyah (*i.e.*, Mrs. Haynes) other mid-air artistes, and the Carré Troupe.

But it was badly managed from the first. The wrong people always seemed to get control. In 1872, for instance, it was acquired by a gutta-percha merchant with a mania for taking theatres for the production of equestrian entertainments. This gentleman was also the owner of the Palais Royal in Argyll Street, Regent Street, when Charles Hengler, fresh from Astley's, bought it and converted it into " Henglers' Cirque," one of the smartest and most charming shows of the kind ever seen in London. The same building was later made into the Palladium, a successful and most respectable music hall with Sunday Concerts and all complete.

Under another management, the Holborn Amphitheatre saw the debut of Lulu, a protégé of Farini, who had been with that enterprising showman previously at Cremorne as a small member of the " Farini Troupe," known as " El Nino Farini." He was for a long time believed to be a beautiful girl, but turned out to be a boy. The *clou* of his performance was being shot thirty feet into the air from a platform by means of a very powerful spring, and the turn was a very sensational one and absolutely novel at that day. This feat was varied and surpassed in later years by Zazel, shot from a cannon at the Aquarium, while another pupil of Farini called Zæo, who also appeared at the "Westminster Cremorne," created a sensation by falling backwards from a high trapeze into a net. Many living playgoers will doubtless remember the posters showing Zæo's bare back, which so aroused the indignation of the Rev. Mr. McDougall and others of his ilk, that they had to be modified or withdrawn. It was the beginning of the end of the Aquarium. I wonder what the same Mr. McDougall would say to the bare backs of the ladies of Society in the stalls of the theatres nowadays, whole rows of whom appear to the occupants of the pit as if they were entirely undressed !

Farini was a gymnastic professor who in early life had been educated as a doctor in Canada. He boasted of having crossed the Niagara Falls on stilts in the early sixties. He was an incomparable showman with any amount of bluff and swank !

Another Showman (in the literal sense of the word, for he was by no means a literary or even a well-educated person) was Frederick Strange, who took the Amphitheatre in 1873. Arthur A. Beckett, in an amusing volume of Reminiscences, relates how he took a scenario of a dramatic spectacle to the Alhambra when Strange was director of that house, which had just been turned into a theatre. The scene of the spectacle was the reign of King Alfred when the Danes were invading England. After listening to the exposition of what great effects could be obtained from the period of the Norse Kings, Mr. Strange asked quite casually : " Do you think you could get in a Chinese Ballet ? " It was a bit of a staggerer, but he was informed by the aspiring authors that they would arrange for some of the old Norse Rovers to have returned from the Chinese Seas and brought back with them a number of Chinese captives who could form the members of a Chinese Ballet troupe. " Excellent," replied Mr. Strange, " I really believe I see my way. There's only one other thing, but that won't be difficult if you manage it properly. We must have a Minuet danced by shepherds and shepherdesses dressed *à la* Watteau in silk stockings, patches and powder." It only remains to be added that Mr. Strange never produced the spectacle involving such abnormal leaps and bounds in the domain of history.

But Mr. Strange's proposals were nothing to what Braham, the singer, used to do in the way of dragging in incongruous items to suit his own particular talents. At the Surrey in 1829, he was playing Henry Bertram in "Guy Mannering." In the second act, Bertram is on a lonely heath in a wild part of Scotland, a storm of rain and lightning in progress and he very much depressed at having lost his way. Turning to the wings, he sees a piano and a music stool ! He exclaims " Ha ! what do I see on this lonely heath ? A Piano ? Who could be lonely with that ? The moon will shortly rise and light me from this unhallowed place : so to console myself, I will sing one of Julia's favourite melodies." Sitting down to the piano, in the middle of the thunderstorm, he proceeds to sing, " Is there a heart that never loved ? "

He seems to have always insisted on a piano being handy no matter what the play or the situation. When doing young Meadows in " Love in a Village," he finds a piano and a stool placed near a fountain. " How careless of Rosetta," he says, " to leave her piano in this damp place, although I am not sorry she has done so, as it will help me to pass the time till she returns," and sings a song. Once when playing the Seraskier in the opera of " The Siege of Belgrade," he says suddenly : " I never see these Turkish banners but I am reminded of bonnie Scotland "—that being the cue for his song, " Draw the sword, Scotland." After these examples of incongruity, which are perfectly genuine, Mr. Strange may be forgiven for wanting a Watteau Ballet in a spectacle dealing with the times of King Alfred.

Strange was always great on Opera Bouffe ; he had been smitten with the same enthusiasm for that form of entertainment first brought to England by the Brothers Mansell, which apparently seized so many London managers in the seventies, and his first production at the Holborn Amphitheatre was a version of Offenbach's " Orphée aux Enfers," which he called " Eurydice." In this spectacle the Sisters Vaughan (Kate and Susie and another who was not a sister at all) appeared in a Ballet of the Furies in a scene meant to represent Hell itself. They were very clever dancers who had been trained by Mrs. Conquest at the Grecian, and they created no small sensation by appearing in black skirts and black tights spangled with gold, a most daring innovation which drew crowds to the theatre.

Some account of the earlier days of Kate Vaughan has been given in the part dealing with the Grecian Theatre : her later history is well known. After years of starring at the Gaiety as a member of the famous Gaiety Quartet, she tried the legitimate drama with more or less success, and, incidentally, was one of the best Lady Teazles I ever saw. Her last illness was a lingering and painful one, and she lies buried in South Africa, far away from the scenes of all her successes. Her sister, Susie Vaughan, was not only a good dancer, but an excellent comedy actress. She eventually took to the Halls for a time, doing double turns with H. B. Fair, the original singer of "Tommy make room for your uncle."

In this Furies' Ballet, the Sisters Vaughan introduced, probably for the first time, that style of dancing afterwards made so popular by Kate at the Gaiety, and which formed a marked contrast to the stereotyped Italian school. They entirely discarded the stiffened, outstanding skirt (professionally known as the "Tu-Tu") and adopted a longer and more clinging garment. In so doing they merely reverted to the fashion of the skirts worn by the older school of danseuses—Taglioni, Cerito, Carlotta Grisi, etc.

In 1874, this curious theatre was the scene of another experiment. John Hollingshead of the Gaiety produced an adaptation of Rossini's old comic opera, "La Cenerentola," calling it "Cinderella" tout court. The company was a very good one, including Charles Lyall, Rose Lee, Kate Munroe, Constance Loseby, Ludwig and others, many of whom have made their mark in serious opera and in the better kinds of Opera Bouffe.

In 1874, also, a spectacle called "Melusine," with music by Hervé, was put on, but met with only a moderate amount of success.

After these failures and by way of making up for his losses, "Honest John," as he was always called, actually tried heavy tragedy, bringing out that most lugubrious piece—"The Maid's Tragedy," by Beaumont and Fletcher. But tragedy was not in the line of the inventor of the Sacred Lamp of Burlesque, and so he gave up the Amphitheatre in disgust.

In 1886, George Rignold, a robust actor somewhat in the style of a modern and modified Charles Dillon, produced a version of "Adam Bede," which the public would not have at any price. He was more successful with "Amos Clarke," in which he was supported by Caroline Hill, who could thus say she had been leading lady at both the Holborn theatres. Rignold might have succeeded better with a better play, for in spite of some mannerisms of the old-fashioned kind he was a good actor. In the seventies, he had been a prominent member of the company at the Queen's Theatre, Long Acre, acting with Henrietta Hodson, Miss Wallis, the Bandmanns and others in Shakespeare and old pieces like "Virginius." His best part was, perhaps, Caliban in "The Tempest," though, after a long stay in Australia, he made a notable reappearance at Drury Lane in "Henry V"—a fine revival in which I should like to have seen Odell's rendering of Pistol. His interests, however, were probably always at the Antipodes and he made Australia his home.

The Amphitheatre, Holborn, did not have a very long life as a theatre, and the notable productions were very few. Like all similar failures, it changed its name several times. At different periods it was known as the Royal Amphitheatre, the National Theatre, the Alcazar, the Connaught, and the New Royal Holborn Theatre.

In a later phase, the building was turned into a Stadium for Boxing Contests, which, during the War, was handed over to the Y.M.C.A. and converted into a huge caravanserai for the accommodation of soldiers home on leave from the Front. It is now once more a Stadium, much in request by Amateur Boxing Societies.

THE HOLBORN THEATRE

This theatre occupied a plot of ground at the corner of Brownlow Street and Holborn, afterwards filled by the First Avenue Hotel. It was opened in 1866, the first new theatre to be built in London since the Princess's in Oxford Street, which had been finished in 1841.

It is an emphatic comment on the low ebb to which dramatic art had been reduced at the beginning of the second half of the nineteenth century that there should have been no demand for a new theatre for twenty-five years.

It is stated to have been essentially a "proper" Age, though there are not wanting those who say that its propriety was merely veiled impropriety. The repeated veto of the Lord Chamberlain on all entertainments which he thought savoured in the least degree of either "impiety" or "impropriety" had been carried to a ridiculous excess. The expression "O God!" was invariably altered to "O Heaven!" up to about the year 1860, and in earlier days, that is in the first years of Queen Victoria's reign, such expressions as "Oh la!" or "Oh lud!" were deemed profane. "La Dame aux Camélias" was forbidden as a play (under that title at any rate) for many years, though it was licensed as "Camille" and again as "Heartsease" and was always allowed on the operatic stage as "La Traviata." Perhaps the licenser knew well that no one knew or cared for the meaning of what the operatic singers sang as long as they sang it well. In short, all entertainments which might be said to have been in the least risqué were taboo. It was an Age when England qualified for her degree of First Hypocrite of Europe ! when all scandal was hidden away, shoved into corners to flourish, as such things will, better in the darkness than in the light. I can remember when it was the height of impropriety to mention " Legs " at all, and I knew one house in Weston-super-Mare where the " Legs " of the piano were concealed in chintz pants ! I have heard that they are still so clothed in some of the smaller towns in the United States. We have certainly progressed since those days. Nowadays, subjects are openly discussed and limbs openly displayed that would have been carefully avoided and covered up in the days of our grandmothers.

The Holborn Theatre always varied much in the style of its entertainments and in the degree of success with which it was managed. The very first production was also one of its two greatest successes. This was a drama by the prolific Boucicault called " The Flying Scud," and the cast was a very strong one. In it we find George Belmore (a first-rate actor, now quite forgotten) as Nat Gosling, one kind of jockey, and fat little Charlotte Saunders as Bob Buckskin, another kind, who is ever bewailing his inability to " get down to the weight." Vollaire, better known later at the Olympic, played a typical stage Jew, Fanny Josephs the usual swell lordling, and George Neville, the hero. In the cast was also that very clever actress Miss Josephine Fiddes (Mrs. Dominick Murray) who had been Menken's understudy in " Mazeppa " at Astley's.

But the best acting of a play in which all were good, was the acting of George Belmore, one of the cleverest actors that the London stage had seen since the death of Robson and of much the same style. His real name was George Garstin, and one of his earliest, if not actually his first appearance, was at the Marylebone under Sam Emery in 1856, in a drama called " The Creole : or Love's Fetters." He was excellent as a half-witted character in a version of Miss Braddon's " Aurora Floyd," and as Jacob Vance in Burnand's play of " The Deal Boatman." When Fechter was at the Adelphi Theatre, Belmore was in the cast of " No Thoroughfare" with him, and also in Wilkie Collins's " Black and White " ; he was in the company at the Princess's for some time and was in " Mary Warner " at the Olympic with Miss Bateman (Mrs. Crowe). He eventually joined Irving at the Lyceum, playing Sam Weller in the version of " Pickwick," in which Irving was Jingle, Odell, Job Trotter and old Addison, Pickwick. His most important part during his Lyceum engagement was Cromwell to the Charles of Irving in Wills's travesty of history. When John S. Clarke convulsed London playgoers with his impersonation of Dr. Pangloss in "The Heir at Law," at the old Strand Theatre, Belmore was the Zedkiel Homespun. After that he was actually in pantomime at the Princess's with Kate Vaughan and pretty Alma Murray, who in more recent times was the Beatrice Cenci when Shelley's forbidden play was produced at Islington. When Byron's fine melodrama, "The Lancashire Lass," was revived in 1878 with Will Terriss, Lydia Foote, Mrs. Alfred Mellon, Sam Emery and Alma Murray, Belmore was cast for the character part of "Spotty." He married Alice Cooke, daughter of William Cooke of Astley's fame. I think his last appearance in London was as Newman Noggs in a version of "Nicholas Nickleby." He died in America in poor circumstances. He was a great character actor whose equal would be very hard to find on the stage of to-day.

"The Flying Scud" ran for two hundred nights, a long time for those days, and was succeeded by a drama by Tom Taylor dealing with the gold diggings and racing, called "The Antipodes : or Ups and Downs of Life," in which Miss Ellen Terry played the heroine, with Sam Emery (father of Mrs. Cyril Maude), Charlotte Saunders and Mrs. Raymond in the cast, the last-named being better known as a member of the Swanborough company at the old Strand, though she had also made a name as Miss Smith in Conquest's company at the Grecian.

In its early days the Holborn was sometimes taken by amateurs to show off their talent on a larger stage than was afforded by the Bijou or Royalty, the usual houses for amateurs. On one such occasion, a burlesque of that good old crusted melodrama "The Miller and His Men," which now only survives in the répertoire of the theatres of Toyland, was put on by a most aristocratic company, including the Marquis Townshend, Sir Randal Roberts (afterwards a professional actor), Lord Arthur Pelham-Clinton, Sir John Sebright and a Mr. Maitland (father of the Brothers Mansell, who were responsible for so many operas bouffes). The ladies appear to have been recruited from the Strand company, as we find the names of Ada Swanborough, Eleanor Bufton and Mrs. Leigh Murray.

In 1868, the theatre was under the management of pretty Miss Fanny Josephs, who put on one of Craven's domestic dramas and "The White Fawn," a well-mounted fairy extravaganza founded on the old French tale of *La Biche au Bois*. This Miss Josephs, besides being a very pretty woman, was a most versatile and accomplished actress. One of her earliest appearances was at Sadler's Wells under the management of Phelps in 1860, when she played Celia to the Jacques of Phelps, the Orlando of Hermann Vezin and the Rosalind of Mrs. Charles Young (afterwards Mrs.

Hermann Vezin). Miss Josephs was also in the company taken "By command" to Windsor Castle in 1861. She had, moreover, her experience of pantomime at the Wells, for members of the stock company there had to play anything and everything for which they might be cast ; Shakespeare one night, and perhaps pantomime the next. Such a system, though it entailed incessant hard work on the part of the artistes, had one decided advantage ; they could never get into a groove as do many of our best actors and actresses nowadays.

From pantomime it is but a short step to burlesque, and Miss Josephs was with the Swanboroughs at the Strand what time Marie Wilton was still "principal boy." She had an engagement in comedy with the Charles Mathews at the St. James's for a time, but in 1865 was once again with Marie Wilton, this time at the Prince of Wales's Theatre in Tottenham Street, playing in both the burlesque and the comedy which always preceded it.

After essaying management on her own at the Holborn and other theatres, she gradually relinquished burlesque for serious work, playing Lady Sneerwell in "The School for Scandal" when first given by the Bancrofts at their old house. She was once in the cast of a version of "L'Assommoir" (not "Drink"), leased the Olympic for a time and acted in some of the earlier Drury Lane autumn dramas.

After Fanny Joseph's season, the Holborn was taken by that old-fashioned actor, Barry Sullivan, perhaps the last of the mouthing, ranting school of former days. He had inherited all the traditions of the Kemble, Kean and Macready school and was distinctly out of date, for that style of acting had come to an end with the retirement of Fanny Kemble. Besides, he was not nearly such a good actor as his great predecessors and there was nothing in his art to compensate for his mannerisms and rant. In the provinces he was often accepted by the elder playgoers who had, perhaps, never seen anything better, but the London public would have none of his "Legitimate" impersonations—neither his Romeo (that must have been pretty bad !) nor his Claude Melnotte, nor his Hamlet. A public which had crowded to see and applaud Fechter would not be likely to swallow Barry Sullivan even with the compensation of seeing that fine actress, Mrs. Hermann Vezin, in the leading lady's part. His season at the Holborn, during which he produced such old-fashioned pieces as "The Gamester," was short, and in January, 1871, his venture came to an abrupt end.

In that same year, the Brothers Mansell (who had recently astonished the weak minds of Victorian playgoers with their production of "Chilperic" at the Lyceum) tried their hand at the

Holborn and produced a translation from the French on the subject of " Edmund Kean," with Thomas Swinbourne in the title rôle ; the results were very poor and the following year saw them back to their first love—opera bouffe—with a version of Offenbach's " Vie Parisienne " with Fred Mervin (an excellent actor and singer who in after years was seen at the Alhambra in " La Fille du Tambour Major " and other pieces of Offenbach), and Lionel Brough as comedian. Among the ladies of the cast we note the names of Lottie Venne (*est-il-possible ?*), the evergreen Harriet Coveney and a certain Miss Fanny Whitehead, who was destined to reach the highest point of success as an actress under the name of Mrs. Bernard Beere.

The Mansells came of a talented Irish family whose real name was Maitland. Their father, not an actor by profession, was a very clever amateur and usually took the lead in the getting up and stage managing of the amateur performances for the Royal Benevolent Society and other charities which were among the social features of the Season in the sixties. His two eldest sons were adept at stage management, and principally went in for French Opera Bouffe. They ran the St. James's for a time with " Les Brigands," " Vert-Vert," etc. ; they were at the Globe with other specimens of Offenbach's work and the younger one took the Coronet one year and tried to make a new success of " La Fille de Madame Angot." But they were always getting into trouble with the Lord Chamberlain, and when that official commented on the scanty attire of the ladies in " Vert-Vert," they lengthened the dresses and advertised the costumes as designed by the Lord Chamberlain. For this piece of impudence they were never allowed to succeed again. The elder of the two ran a flower shop at South Kensington for a little time near to where their old home had been in Thurloe Square. His son is Mr. Lauderdale Maitland, a well-known and clever actor in robust, melodramatic parts.

In 1872, the programme at the Holborn was once more drama with a company comprising Henry Marston, a veteran actor of great experience, Mrs. Hermann Vezin, Lin Rayne (a clever if rather affected actor who was the best Sir Benjamin Backbite I ever saw) and Marie Henderson, a lady with a magnificent figure which she had frequently exhibited in the dress (or undress) of Mazeppa. In 1874, the house came under the management of Walter Joyce, perhaps better known to the theatrical world as the genial proprietor of the " Bun Shop " in the Strand, a hostelry much frequented by the profession. He produced a play with J. S. Clarke, but the ill-luck of the theatre held fast for the time and once more it changed hands.

Horace Wigan took it in 1875 and renamed it the " Mirror "—a sure sign that all was not well with the place. Houses are unlucky which have to change their names like those unfortunate individuals of the human species who also find it well to do so now and then ! Wigan still relied on melodrama and put on " The Hidden Hand," a gloomy play that had been seen at the Olympic ten years before, with a great cast including Henry Neville, Kate Terry, Lydia Foote, Louisa Moore and Nelly Farren. At the Mirror, the most noteworthy member of the cast was Rose Leclercq.

About this period of the existence of the Mirror, John Clayton brought out his version of " A Tale of Two Cities " called " All for Her," with Rose Coghlan, Caroline Hill and Horace Wigan in the cast. John Clayton, whose real name was Calthrop, was a good actor of sentimental parts such as D'Alroy in " Caste," Joseph Surface in " The School for Scandal " (Vaudeville) and Hugh Trevor in " All for Her." But he was also seen in light comedy in most of the Pinero plays produced at the Court. His earliest appearances were as long ago as the St. James's under the regime of Miss Herbert. He married the eldest daughter of Dion Boucicault, sister of the first Peter Pan.

There was once a season at the Mirror directed by a Mr. Tom Charles whose experience in management had chiefly been in the provinces. On this occasion, Byron's " Sardanapalus " was given for the debut of a Miss Gainsborough as Myrrha. She was a very beautiful woman, one of the innumerable pupils of John Ryder, and made several successful appearances in the better class of theatre, one being as Rowena in a version of " Ivanhoe " at Drury Lane in which Genevieve Ward was Rebecca ; Terriss, Ivanhoe ; Fernandez, Isaac of York ; and Arthur Matthison (a clever singer and writer also of good plays), King Richard. But " Sardanapalus " was not the sort of play to be given successfully at a small, unimportant theatre like the Mirror, and though the stage version had been cleverly arranged by Charles Calvert, facilities for scenic display were wanting, and the company was not at all a strong one. The title rôle was assumed by an actor of the name of Darnley from the provinces. Many who saw it must have recalled the magnificent production by the Charles Keans at the old Princess's some twenty years previously when the effects of the burning palace could hardly have been surpassed by Irving or Tree in their best days.

By far the most successful season of all at the Holborn Theatre was when it had been rechristened once again, this time as the Duke's. It was then under the direction of Charles Willmot and Clarence Holt and the drama that drew all the town was " The New Babylon " by Paul Merritt of Adelphi and Grecian fame.

In this play, Caroline Hill, of the beautiful golden hair, played a modern Phryne, and attracted West End audiences in crowds for months, for the piece ran from February, 1879, to June, 1880— nearly a year and a half, and would have run longer still but for the destruction of the theatre by fire. There had been dramas dealing with London life with sensation scenes before this, forerunners of plays that were afterwards brought out at Drury Lane in the autumn. The Princess's had given us "The Streets of London" with a real fire engine, and "After Dark" with an underground railway scene. Drury Lane itself had seen the production of the "Great City" with a real hansom cab and a picturesque representation of a London railway terminus, and "Formosa" with a cast including Henry Irving, Mrs. Billington and Katharine Rodgers, which had also been revived at another theatre but was never a great success, for the morality of the piece was called in question, it being early days for the theatre to be dealing with courtesans. "The Flying Scud," as we have seen, was another piece of the same kind, and there was also a short-lived drama at the Holborn called "The Odds" the run of which was terminated by a curious incident. The chief scene was a representation of a steeplechase. In the distance, some figures of mounted persons were seen to leap a brook. On the first night, by some mishap to the machinery, after the pasteboard riders had jumped the brook, they were seen to pop back again tails foremost! That little accident killed the play!

But "The New Babylon" approached much nearer to the autumn melodrama of Harris's days at Drury Lane, than any of the others mentioned. London playgoers were more advanced in their views, and more ready to sit out the story of a "woman of the town" than in the days of the production of "Formosa." The original advertisement gives one a very good idea of what the play was like. It certainly was a specimen of the "puff direct" :

New Babylon by Paul Merritt is the Talk of London !
Stalls filled nightly by the Elite of London !
The Theatre filled in every Part !
The most attractive Drama ever written !
Suits all Classes !
The Collision on the Atlantic !
Tattersalls with its Sale of Horses !
Cremorne, with its Dancing Platform, and Ten Thousand Lights !
Goodwood on the Grand Race Day !
The Thames Embankment—with its Electric Witness—and
The Seven Dials by Night—are Pictures that must attract !

It really reads like a poster of the great Druriolanus. Would it pay in these days ? It might, but I doubt it. Playgoers are more blasé, or is it that they are less intelligent ? It might almost seem as if the latter were the explanation when inferior Revues with futile jokes and " legs " draw better than a good story, exciting and well acted.

Caroline Hill, the chief attraction of this wonderful show, was a clever and experienced actress. From 1864 to 1871, she had been a regular member of the Haymarket Company, appearing in burlesque, in old comedy (with Charles Mathews), and in Shakespeare—" As You Like It "—Sylvius to the Rosalind of Mrs. Scott Siddons and Celia when Mrs. Kendal was in the cast. She was in most of Sothern's productions, with Miss Kate Bateman in a dreary play called " Mary Warner," and in " New Men and Old Acres," with the Kendals with whom also she played in the Fairy Comedies of W. S. Gilbert (Cynisca in " Pygmalion and Galatea " and others). She was in " The Corsican Brothers " with John Clayton and took light comedy parts in the Drury Lane dramas—" Youth," " Pluck," etc. She supported Miss Olga Nethersole in that most unpleasant play, " The Dean's Daughter," and, in short, it would take a whole chapter to give an adequate description of her stage career. I believe she is still very much alive and to be seen in most first-night audiences.

Charles Willmot, who, with Clarence Holt, ran the Duke's at the time of " The New Babylon," was a most popular man in the profession. He was an Australian, and at one time directed the fortunes of the Occidental Tavern in the Strand (built on the site of the Old Coal Hole, where low songs were the rule), when it became the rendezvous of all that was gay and witty (and it must be added impecunious) in theatre-land. It was a real bit of Bohemia of which he was a most generous host. Actors have changed their haunts since those days and have left Bohemia for Belgravia—or as near to it as they can get.

Willmot rebuilt the Philharmonic at Islington, renaming it the Grand. He had one fad, amounting to an obsession. He never would insure his theatres, and, as it happened, both the Duke's and the Grand were burned down to his heavy loss. After the second casualty he did insure, and spent many premiums for nothing —a clear case of locking the stable door after the steed had been stolen. He was a most liberal man in all matters connected with his company and staff, and paid them all a full week's salary when the Islington house was destroyed. He died in 1896.

Clarence Holt, his partner, a rough and ready actor of the ranting school, had the unenviable reputation of being the most foul-mouthed member of his profession. In his first production of "Black Eyed Susan," he would exhort the Susan in his arms to show more pathos —and his *sotto voce* exhortations were accompanied by the most horrible oaths. All his life, he was the victim of grievances, real or imaginary. In his own line, generally "heavy lead," he was considered a good actor. Willmot and he both played in the dramas at the Duke's, the former usually taking the part of the typical Jew without whom no melodrama was complete.

A clever actress in "The New Babylon" was Ada Murray, who had had a wide experience of the stage. She had been in the Ballets at Cremorne, was one of Menken's numerous understudies in the sixties, was in "Babil and Bijou" at Covent Garden, and was the Susan to the William of Clarence Holt at the Duke's. She was specially selected by Charles Reade for the part of the spiteful Virginie in his drama of "Drink" with Charles Warner, and in later years was with the Kendals in "The Squire" at the St. James's and with Minnie Palmer in "My Sweetheart." Perhaps her last appearance on the stage was in some "mime" parts in the later Alhambra Ballets. Truly, a varied and hard-working stage career.

The Holborn was, as we have seen, chiefly a theatre for melodrama, but the various managers who presided over its fortunes were, as a rule, most unlucky in their choice of pieces, with the exception of "The Flying Scud" and "The New Babylon."

At one time the house was under the management of a Mr. Burleigh, who seems to have been an actor of some experience, for he had been with Miss Herbert at the St. James's and was also known at the Old Vic. He put on a play called "Behind the Curtain" intended to be a story of the lives of members of the profession. In spite of a sensation scene showing a theatre on fire during a performance, the piece failed, on account of the false picture it gave of the manner in which actors and actresses lived.

W. G. Wills had an early play of his acted here. This was "Forced from Home," in which Fanny Brough was the persecuted heroine—an unusual kind of rôle for her. One of the scenes was Waterloo Bridge with an attempted suicide ; there was a "real" hansom cab with a "live" horse—always, apparently, a draw.

Another production was "Miss Multon," the American version of "East Lynne," which crusted old hardy annual is never played in the States under its own name, having, I suppose, been pirated in the first instance. There was also an adaptation of "Le Pendu" called "Jezebel : or the Dead Reckoning," and in 1871 a version of the story of *Salammbo : Queen of Carthage.* There were other entirely unimportant productions, none of which attained to the dignity of a " run " or will be ever heard of again—except " East Lynne," which is always being played somewhere in the provinces if not in town.

The Holborn Theatre of so many names had but a short existence —1866 to 1880—but if only for " The New Babylon " and " The Flying Scud " it may be said to have been not wholly a fruitless one.

After the building of this theatre which, as I have said, was the first new London theatre for twenty-five years, a furious mania for theatre construction set in, and in the following quarter of a century over five and twenty theatres were put up in central London, without reckoning outlying houses at Kennington, Camberwell, Hammersmith, Notting Hill Gate and other suburban districts, which sprang up as fast as they could be built. The Queen's (Long Acre) was opened in 1867 ; the Globe and Gaiety in 1868 ; the Charing Cross in 1869 ; the Vaudeville, Court, Opera Comique and Philharmonic in 1870 ; the Criterion in 1874 ; the Aquarium in 1876 ; the Comedy in 1881 ; the Avenue and Novelty in 1882 ; the Prince of Wales's in Coventry Street and the Empire in 1884 ; Terry's in 1887 ; the Shaftesbury and Lyric in 1888 ; the Apollo and Garrick in 1889 ; followed by the Prince's, the new Globe, new Queen's, Ambassadors and St. Martin's. The increase was perhaps nearly balanced by the number of playhouses which disappeared or were turned into Cinema Shows.

THE PANTHEON OPERA HOUSE, OXFORD STREET

Passing the wine stores of Gilbey and Sons, nearly opposite Peter Robinson's in Oxford Street, few people realize that the portico at the entrance is identically the same one that led into the foyer of an actual Grand Opera House, where for a year or two crowds flocked to listen to the Venetian Georgi, said to have been the laziest prima donna ever gifted with a marvellous voice.

The building of the Pantheon was first opened in 1772 for concerts, masquerades, etc., in opposition to Carlisle House in Soho Square, which had gained rather an unenviable notoriety under that mistress of intrigue—Teresa Cornelys.

In 1776, Lorenza Agujari was engaged to sing at the Pantheon concerts at a fee of £100 a night—an enormous payment in those days. She failed to draw sufficiently to pay expenses, and after two separate engagements retired to make way for " La Georgi," daughter of a gondolier, and a " Piazza artiste " at Venice whose fame had reached London via Paris.

Georgi, after leaving her native Venice, had sung her way to Lyons, where she used to perform in the various cafés, doubtless

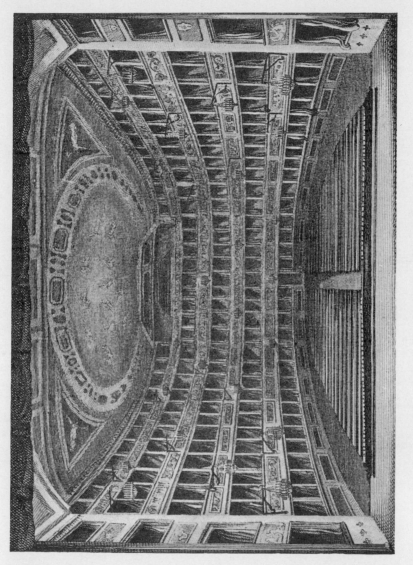

THE PANTHEON OPERA HOUSE, OXFORD ST.

From an old print in the British Museum

taking round the plate for what she could get. Eventually she reached Paris, singing there with great success. The directors of the Pantheon heard so much of this new Venetian uneducated beauty, that they engaged her for their concerts, on condition that £100 per annum should be deducted from her earnings to pay a *maestro* to cultivate her voice.

Sacchini was the first to take her in hand, but found her so lazy and obstinate that he gave her up as unteachable. Piozzi then undertook her, but also gave her up in despair before he had succeeded in making her a finished singer. When she returned to Italy, her engagement at such a well-known house as the Pantheon stood her in good stead, and she was able to obtain several good engagements at the opera. Training goes for much, but there is also a good deal of truth in the Italian saying which, roughly translated, says "There are a hundred requisites necessary to make a good singer, of which whoever is gifted with a fine voice has ninety-nine."

In 1788, the regular Opera House in London was burned down, and Mr. O'Reilly, its proprietor, took the Pantheon as an Opera House for four years ; but its career as such was very short, for it also was burned down in 1792.

Rebuilt once more, it was opened as a concert hall only, but there were many ambitious spirits who wished to make a regular Opera House of it, so once again it was rebuilt, this time on the model of La Scala, the great theatre of Milan, containing 175 private boxes and a spacious pit, 60 feet wide by 60 feet deep. It had, however, to encounter the opposition of the Haymarket Opera House ; which was too strong for it, so efforts were made to obtain a licence to run it as an English Opera House. Here, however, it had been forestalled by Arnold at the Lyceum. Then the directors went one step lower and started it as the Pantheon Theatre for Italian burlettas and ballets. Spagnoletti was the leader, and Miss Stephens, afterwards Countess of Essex, sang here several times.

All its efforts to prove a successful rival either to the Haymarket house or the Lyceum were unsuccessful, and it fell on evil days. Three years rent were owing, amounting to three thousand pounds, and it was sold by auction, every bit of the interior being pulled to pieces, even the boards of the pit being carted away and the nails torn out of the walls. The sale barely realized a third of what was required. Cundy, a wine merchant, who had lost much money in the concern, tried to get a licence to run it as an ordinary theatre for the performance of drama, etc., but nothing came of it.

In 1815, Elliston, the manager of the Olympic, and later of

Drury Lane, was in treaty for the Pantheon, but that affair was not concluded either.

It was a very large house if, as stated, it was the size of La Scala. It was much too large for an Opera House in London, at any rate, where really good Operas have never been, and never will be appreciated by the crowd, who do not seem able to rise above the Gilbert and Sullivan style of musical work. So the attempt to run it as even a theatre was given up, and the building was adapted for the purposes of a bazaar like so many others all in the immediate neighbourhood—the London Crystal Palace (now part of Peter Robinson's premises), the Soho Square Bazaar, and the Queen's Bazaar which afterwards became the Princess's Theatre.

But it remained a poor kind of show, I remember, even as a respectable Victorian Bazaar, and dull as all of them were.

Finally, it came into the possession of Gilbey and Co., who have it still. Only the old portico remains with its little classical frieze and its rather severe outline. I hope no " Improver " will improve that away altogether.

The accompanying illustration of the interior shows what a magnificent Opera House it must have been, for a year or two at least.

CHAPTER IX

THE QUEEN'S THEATRE, LONG ACRE

THERE may be a few old playgoers still going strong who can remember the Queen's Theatre in Long Acre, opened in 1867 on the site of the St. Martin's Hall. This is a lost London theatre which, though it did not have a long life (it lasted only eleven years), could boast of having been the scene of many important events.

St. Martin's Hall was erected in 1850 by John Hullah in furtherance of his efforts to encourage choral singing, for which the only place available in London, outside the theatres, was Exeter Hall. Charles Dickens used it for his Readings in the early sixties, and the German Reeds were here before they settled at the Gallery of Illustration and St. George's Hall.

It is on record that an American once recited here the whole of the twelve books of *Paradise Lost* without a single mistake, and without an interval ! It was also utilized for Promenade Concerts under that energetic impresario, Frederic Strange of the Alhambra, whom I have mentioned in connection with the Royal Amphitheatre, Holborn.

The theatre, larger than any in London except the two operahouses and Drury Lane, was most artistically designed and decorated by Albert Moore, the artist, and Telbin, the scene-painter. It was built as a speculation by Mr. Lionel Lawson of *The Daily Telegraph* and leased to Henry Labouchere (of *Truth*), though the nominal lessee was Alfred Wigan, who had risen to fame at the Olympic and Princess's.

The real director, Labouchere, afterwards bought the theatre and ran it for the pleasure and experience of his wife, the lovely Henrietta Hodson (see Chapter XV dealing with the Bower Saloon, Lambeth, for some account of the origin of the Hodson family).

Shakespeare and melodrama, varied now and then by the inevitable burlesque, formed the staple dramatic fare at the Queen's. It opened in October, 1867, with an adaptation by Charles Reade of his novel *White Lies*, which he called " A Double Marriage," and the cast was a galaxy of actors and actresses who were destined to become famous in later years. Among them were Ellen Terry, Fanny Addison, Alfred Wigan, Charles Wyndham, Lionel Brough (his London debut) and a Mrs. E. F. Savile of the Nottingham Theatre, wife, I think, of that E. F. Savile who used to draw down the curses of the Old Vic gallery when, as Bill Sikes, he dragged Nancy about the stage by the hair of her head, and smeared her face with blood—or red ochre. Mrs. Savile was therefore a sister-in-law of Helen Faucit.

Reade's play was not a success and was succeeded by "Still Waters Run Deep," originally produced at the Olympic in 1855. Mrs. Alfred Wigan was the Mrs. Sternhold (a part she had also played at the Olympic after it had been relinquished by a "Mrs. Melfort"). Ellen Terry was Mrs. Mildmay, Charles Wyndham, Captain Hawkesley, and W. H. Stephens was also in the cast.

Two months or so saw the end of that revival and then, early in 1868, the new theatre had its first success in "Dearer than Life" by Henry J. Byron, which was that kind of piece so often described as "A Domestic Drama" or as "A Play with strong Domestic Interest." It was acted by Irving, Toole, Brough, Wyndham, John Clayton, Henrietta Hodson and Mrs. Dyas, and was followed by the usual burlesque without which no programme in the sixties was complete. This latter was an early effort of W. S. Gilbert founded on Donizetti's "Figlia del Reggimento" and called "La Vivandière : or True to the Corps"—a pun on the title of Selous's popular play in which T. P. Cooke made his name. Brough, Toole, Miss Hodson and the lovely Pauline Markham were in the cast and the music was arranged by Wallerstein, a teacher of music who once strongly recommended my father to have me taught the violin on account of the length of my fingers ! Alas ; I never got further than a simple "Air with Variations," and always loathed the hours of practice it involved.

Irving remained at the Queen's for some time, chiefly in melodrama like "The Lancashire Lass," a fine play of its kind, revived more than once. He was in the cast of "The Rivals" for the benefit of Mrs. Alfred Wigan, and one critic damned him with faint praise as a "respectable Falkland." He also had his first association with Ellen Terry at the Queen's in Garrick's much mangled version of "The Taming of the Shrew," which gives only the scenes between Katharine and Petruchio and thus is probably more mangled even than that hash-up of the same play which is associated with Ada Rehan and the Daly Company. It would not be worth mentioning but for the fact that it was the first occasion on which these great artistes acted together in Shakespeare. It was after this engagement that Ellen Terry made her second retirement from the profession.

Another rôle of Irving's before he left the Queen's was Bill Sikes in a version of "Oliver Twist," which, curiously enough, only ran a month in spite of its wonderful cast. Henrietta Hodson was Oliver ; Nelly Moore, Nancy ; Toole, the Artful Dodger ; Ryder, Fagin ; Lionel Brough, Bumble ; and John Clayton, Monks. I can picture to myself to this day the horrible scene of Fagin in his den and the last act where Sikes tries to escape over the roofs. Miss Hodson also played Smike in a version of " Nicholas Nickleby " with great success.

Miss Nelly Moore was one of the best young emotional actresses of the time. As far back as 1859, when only sixteen years of age, she was playing good parts. She was with Miss Herbert and Kate Terry at the St. James's in 1860, was the original Ada Ingot to the David Garrick of Sothern, and remained at the Haymarket for many years, playing in Shakespeare, old comedy, melodrama or burlesque according to what was required of her, as was the custom in those hard-working days. She died at the early age of twenty-four, within a year of her success as Nancy and before she had had time to put forth her full powers.

Another drama produced at the Queen's with more or less success was " The Turn of the Tide " founded on Mrs. Edwardes' novel, *The Morals of Mayfair.* Irving was not in this, but the original company was strengthened by the addition of Mr. and Mrs. Frank Matthews, Hermann Vezin, George Rignold and that really fine actress, Sophie Larkin.

During the Labouchere management of the Queen's, in the early seventies, there was rather a successful revival of several of Shakespeare's plays. These included a magnificent production of " A Midsummer Night's Dream " with Phelps as Bottom ; and a very fair one of " The Tempest " with the music of Arne and Purcell. In this Henrietta Hodson was Ariel ; Ryder, Prospero ; George Rignold (who remained some time at the Queen's), Caliban ; H. C. Sidney, Ferdinand and a poor actress, Miss Rhodes, Miranda. " The Tempest " was followed by " Cymbeline " with Miss Hodson as Imogen, Ryder as Iachimo, and Lewis Ball and Henry Marston also in the cast. That extremely turgid play, " Virginius," was put on for the same leading lady to appear as Virginia and then a new actress was introduced in the person of Miss Wallis, a pupil of Ryder who was seen with him in " Amos Clarke," by Watts Phillips, and in a play dealing with the Cavaliers and Roundheads called " Cromwell," with Rignold and a Miss Marlborough. This was produced, I believe, as an antidote to the " Charles I " of Wills, but it was not nearly so effective a play. Miss Wallis was quite a debutante, having made her first appearance earlier in the same year (1872) at the Standard Theatre, Shoreditch, as Pauline to the Claude Melnotte of Creswick, rather a heavy lover, I think ! After these various excursions into " the Legitimate " the Queen's relapsed into mere melodrama, one of the latest productions of the Labouchere management being an adaptation of " Les Chevaliers du Brouillard," that turned out to be a Jack Sheppard play with all the names of the characters altered to meet the " morality " requirements of the Censor.   In its English dress the play was called " Old London."   Jack Sheppard was translated into Dick Wastrell (Henrietta Hodson) ;   Jonathan Wild became Velvet Crawl (John Nelson) ;   Blueskin became Old Nollekins (W. Belford) ; and Mr. Wood, Mr. Smiles (Vollaire).   The same French original had been previously done in English under the title of " The Knights of the Fog."   It was not, I think, till the Gaiety produced a burlesque called " Jack Sheppard " that the old nomenclature was revived.

On the whole, under the skilful management of Labouchere and with the charming personality of his wife as leading actress, the new theatre did well ; but it had its failures as well as its successes. It is hard to understand why the version of " Oliver Twist " with its really magnificent cast should have failed so decidedly as to be withdrawn after one month's run.   Perhaps one of the reasons was that the playgoing public were beginning to tire of the numerous adaptations of Dickens's novels with which the London stage had been inundated for years.   It was a case of *toujours perdrix* and the public wanted a change.   A more decided failure still was " The Last Days of Pompeii " brought out by Ryder at enormous expense, with great expectations based on an eruption of Vesuvius, an earth-quake, an amphitheatre scene, and a realistic representation of a Roman banquet, naughty ladies and all !   But nothing went right. The earth would not quake properly ;   the eruption would not erupt ;   and there was nothing at all realistic about the representation of the banquet or the amphitheatre.   Even an acrobat engaged from a music-hall to amuse the guests at the banquet could not manage to keep on the rope.   But let Mr. Labouchere speak for himself.   In *Truth* for August 16th, 1877, he thus amusingly describes the disasters of that production :

" The piece on which I lost most was an adaptation of ' The Last Days of Pompeii.'   Everything went wrong in this piece. I wanted to have—after the manner of the ancients—acrobats dancing on the tight rope over the heads of the guests at the feast. The guests, however, absolutely declined to be danced over.   Only one acrobat made his appearance.   A rope was stretched for him behind the revellers, and I trusted to stage illusion for the rest. The acrobat was a stout negro.   Instead of lightly tripping it upon his rope, he moved about like an elephant and finally fell off his rope like a stricken buffalo.   In the second act, the head of a statue

HENRIETTA HODSON (MRS. LABOUCHERE)

From an old photograph by H. N. King

was to fall off and to crush Mr. Ryder who was a magician. There was a man inside the statue whose mission was to push over the head. With folded arms and stern air Mr. Ryder gazed at the statue awaiting the portentous event that was to crush him to the earth, notwithstanding the mystic power that he wielded. The head remained firm on its neck. The man inside had solaced himself with so much beer that he was drunk and incapable, and Mr. Ryder had, much to the amazement of the audience, to knock down the head that was to crush him. In the third act, the stage represented a Roman amphitheatre. In the midst of the gorgeously dressed crowd, sat Mr. Ryder. ' Bring forth the lion,' he said. The audience thrilled at the idea of a real lion being marched on to the stage. Now I had no lion, and I had discarded the idea of putting a lion's skin on a donkey. An attendant therefore walked in and said, ' Sir, the lion will not come.' Those of the audience who were not hissing roared with laughter. The last act was to represent the eruption of Vesuvius and the destruction of Pompeii. The mountain had only been painted in time for the first night. I had never seen it. What was my horror when the curtain rose upon a temple with a sort of large sugar loaf behind it. At first I could not imagine what was the meaning of this sugar loaf. But when it proceeded to emit crackers, I found that it was Vesuvius."

Henrietta Hodson made a most charming Nydia, the blind girl, showing what she could do in pathetic parts as well as in the rôle of "principal boy" in burlesque or any other kind of " breeches " part.

The truth was that Ryder, entrusted with the production of the elaborate piece, was a first-class experienced actor of the old school, well able to look after the acting part of the show, but with no idea of modern sensational productions. A very different result was seen when Barrett, with his genius for stage management, brought out " Claudian " with its earthquake, " Clito " with its banquet of fair hetæræ, and " The Sign of the Cross " with its Roman scenes—a worthless play but a popular success.

John Ryder was born as long ago as 1814. He made his London debut at Drury Lane as the Banished Duke in " As You Like It." The cast is worthy of note. Macready was Jacques ; James Anderson, Orlando ; Phelps, Adam ; Keeley, Touchstone ; Henry Compton, William ; Priscilla Horton (Mrs. German Reed), one of the pages ; Sims Reeves, one of the foresters ; Mrs. Nisbett, Rosalind ; Mrs. Stirling, Celia ; Miss Phillips, Phœbe ; and Mrs. Keeley, Audrey. I do not think it possible that this cast has ever been equalled except, of course, on the occasion of benefits and special occasions when prominent members of the profession offer to take small parts to do honour to the *bénéficiaire*. All the members of it were leaders in their various lines in after years.

By the year 1843, Ryder had become a permanent member of Macready's company. In that year he played the part of Cardinal Pandulph in "King John" to the King of Macready, the Hubert of Phelps, the Bastard of James Anderson, and the Constance of Helen Faucit. Ryder remained with Macready for some years, going with him to America and on his return playing in all the great productions of the Princess's from 1845 to 1847. He joined the Kean and Keeley management of the same house in 1850 and was a regular member of the company at the time of the Kean Shakespearean productions. Later on, he appeared with Fechter at the Lyceum and the Adelphi, and at some time or other was seen at most of the London principal theatres. Ryder was a solid, "sound," rather heavy actor of the old school, converted to more modern views by the splendour of Fechter's acting. Perhaps he gained greater repute as a teacher of young aspirants to dramatic fame than as an actor. Especially was he known as a "bringer-out of Juliets," being responsible for a number of these during his long stage career—some of them very good and some very bad. He has the distinction of having trained and given to the London Stage Adelaide Neilson and Stella Colas—perhaps the two finest Juliets it has ever seen.

During the Labouchere regime of the Queen's there had been the usual number of burlesques, chiefly with Henrietta Hodson, Toole and Brough to keep up the fun. "The Stranger, Stranger than Ever," "Fowl Play," "Tomkins the Troubadour," and others, were put on and disappeared after short runs. There was also a season or two of old comedy to relieve the constant succession of melodramas. After Labouchere got tired of running a big theatre solely for the gratification of his wife (it must have cost him a pretty penny from first to last) the Queen's underwent various vicissitudes and changes. John Ryder continued to be a sort of standing dish whenever he had a new debutante to bring out. At the time that Miss Litton was managing the house, he brought forward a Miss Olive as Constance in "King John" supported by himself and Rignold ; later on, he showed us Miss Leighton (a much better actress) in "The Hunchback," and in 1875, on the occasion of his benefit, he produced "Macbeth" with a Lady Macbeth who was billed as "Zuleika the Princess," but whom I have been unable to identify.

Other managers of less importance ran the Queen's from time to time. In 1869 and 1870 it was for a short period the scene of the appearances of a lady always known as "the beautiful Mrs.

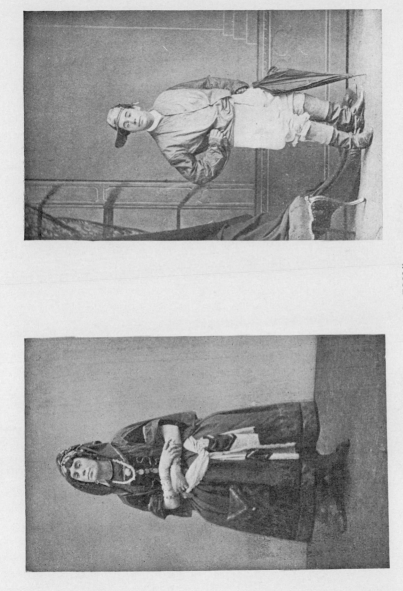

IN BURLESQUE OF "IL TROVATORE"
From photograph by Bauch and Bensley

J. L. TOOLE

IN "THE STEEPLECHASE"
From photograph by Marcus Ward and Co.

Rousby," for whom Tom Taylor had a mania for writing historical plays. She had been a Miss Dowse, daughter of an army officer whom Rousby, lessee and manager of the Jersey theatre, had met there and married when she was but sixteen. Beautiful she certainly was, if not a great actress, and scored a very popular success in a play called "Twixt Axe and Crown" dealing with episodes in the life of the Princess Elizabeth before she became Queen. It was the usual type of historical play setting all history at naught. In one scene of this, as the Princess Elizabeth, she is discovered in a dungeon of the Tower awaiting execution by order of her sister, so elegantly called in our English history books—"Bloody Mary." The scene is very dark ; Mrs. Rousby with her beautiful hair hanging down her back is shivering with dread ; we hear the hammering of the scaffold as it is erected outside ; she delivers a long speech on the iniquity of her sister and her own situation and then, uttering a blood-curdling shriek, falls fainting to the ground. Playgoers would go again and again on purpose to hear this shriek, as they did many years later to hear Haidée Wright shriek in "The Sign of the Cross." Such were the means by which Mrs. Rousby made her name as an actress—great beauty and a loud shriek, and she was doubtless much helped by the confirmed belief of Tom Taylor that his mission in life was to write historical plays for her to act in.

Mrs. Rousby was very picturesque in an adaptation of Victor Hugo's "Le Roi S'Amuse" (better known as the story of the opera "Rigoletto") in which play her husband scored a real success. She was also Cordelia to his Lear and Rosalind to his Orlando. Her career was meteoric: she died at the early age of twenty-seven and her end was a very sad one.

In the early seventies, the Queen's was occupied by a German actor called Bandmann, who had made some reputation in America. His wife, née Milly Palmer, was a clever actress with much experience on the London Stage at the Strand Theatre and also at the Olympic with the Wigans. She had also played Juliet to the Romeo of Felicia Vestvali, who shares with Charlotte Cushman and Esmé Beringer the honour of having been a fairly good representative of the lover of Verona. The Bandmanns acted much in the Colonies and in India.

Charles Reade had a good deal to do with this theatre at various dates. Many pieces by him were produced there for the first time, as, for example, a really charming play called "The Wandering Heir," in which Mrs. John Wood was the original representative of Philippa Chester, a picturesque heroine of a "costume period." When Mrs. Wood was obliged to surrender the part it was, at the earnest solicitation of Reade, taken up by Ellen Terry. This was really a notable event, and it is quite possible that, had Mrs. John Wood been able to continue in the rôle, one of the most charming actresses of modern times might have been altogether lost to the stage. For, twice in her life, Miss Terry had definitely decided to give up the profession and for a few years had not trod the boards, only coming once out of her retirement to play Helen in " The Hunchback " for the benefit of her sister, Kate. She came back to please Reade, and so rendered the future seasons of the Lyceum a possibility. It is sometimes very wonderful to reflect what great events hinge upon very accidental happenings. An old cliché, but how true !

One ought not to omit to notice certain Shakespearean productions at the Queen's when it was under the direction of that rather curious personality, John Coleman. He was a great friend and admirer of Phelps and put on " Henry V " to allow of the old actor (then fast approaching his end) appearing as Henry IV. This was in 1876. Incidentally, it also afforded Coleman himself the opportunity of showing how bad he could be in the title rôle, a part for which he was wholly unsuited. Mead (a good actor, Ghost to Irving's Hamlet) was Pistol ; Ryder (without whom no Queen's cast would seem complete) was Williams ; Emily Fowler, Princess Katharine ; and Margaret Leighton was enabled to exhibit her fine elocution as Chorus. Two interesting names in the cast were Kate Phillips (Mrs. H. B. Conway) as the Hostess's Boy and Clifford Harrison (son of the great tenor and afterwards a Society Reciter) as Charles, Duke of Orleans.

Perhaps the only other event of note was the appearance of Salvini as Othello, which he had previously played at Drury Lane. I should not, however, omit the mention of a season of Promenade Concerts in 1877 under Riviere and Alfred Cellier.

The Queen's was a very fine theatre, in advance of the times in many ways. It had a most comfortable auditorium and an up-to-date system of stage machinery. But it lacked a guiding spirit. An actor-manager of the type of Irving or Tree would have made it the leading theatre of London, but Irving had already started to make the Lyceum that. Tree's star had not yet arisen, and Phelps's day was over. He gave one or two fine Shakespearean performances at the Queen's as we have seen, but his actor-manager's days had been in the past at Sadler's Wells—which he had raised from the rank of an outlying unconsidered temple of melodrama to be one of the leading theatres of the town. Labouchere was simply the slave of his wife and cared for nothing that did not bring her to the front, and he had not, moreover, the energy to work as Irving and Tree and Alexander worked in after years. There was Alfred Wigan, it is true, who held the reins at the Queen's in its first years. But Wigan, clever actor as he was, had not the genius of the successful manager, and when at the Olympic and at other houses had made a mess of it more than once. He and his clever wife were among the leading performers of their day, but lacked entirely the business capacity necessary for the conduct of a great theatre. His first appearance in London had probably been at that odd little theatre in King's Road, Chelsea, known as the Manor House, of which I have given some account in my chapter on Minor theatres. He acted with the Keans at the Princess's and with Fechter, but the chief years of his life as an actor are associated with the Olympic and a more detailed account of him and his talented wife properly belongs to the chapter dealing with the old house in Wych Street.

Of Phelps, a whole volume could be written ; indeed, his devoted admirer, John Coleman, has given a volume of Phelps's Reminiscences to the world, and Mr. Chance Newton (" Carados " of the *Referee*), almost as enthusiastic an admirer, has done the same, in addition to the Life by Robertson. Few words are necessary therefore here, and all the details of his magnificent enterprise at Sadler's Wells should be sought in a history of that theatre or in Robertson's Life. Samuel Phelps was distinctly an actor of the old School, by which I do not mean to say that he mouthed and ranted like the Kembles, or that he gave himself the airs and graces which appear to have gone so far to detract from the general effect of Macready's acting. But there is little doubt that he often acted on certain well-defined lines, according to rules laid down by tradition, and it was his innate genius which enabled him to break through these hard and fast traditions on occasions and show what a really great actor he was ; as, for example, in his terrific impersonation of Sir Giles Overreach and, in a different manner, in his Falstaff. Some actors are " born " and some are only " trained." From the various accounts that have come down to us (for I am not old enough to have seen Kean, and I only saw Phelps in his latter days), I am inclined to think that Phelps was a " born " actor and Charles Kean only a " trained " one. They were the second and third actor-managers of modern times, if you reckon Macready as the first. The distinction of being " born " and " trained " is more clearly seen if you realize that, while they both had a measure of success as actor and manager too, Kean was the most successful manager and Phelps undoubtedly the better actor. Without all the paraphernalia of scenery and costume, it may be agreed that Kean's productions at the Princess's must have fallen rather flat. On the other hand, Phelps drew crowded audiences to the old-fashioned house by the New River just to see his acting, for the mounting was never better than any average playhouse might have managed. Phelps gave up his own theatre after a time and allowed others to manage him. But his acting was always a magnet to draw large audiences even when the mounting was poor and the support inferior.

In his day, and long after, he was considered the best Sir Peter Teazle and the best Falstaff, for his genius came out strongest in comedy. His Hamlet, Lear, Othello and other rôles in Shakespearean tragedy were probably just those parts wherein the traditional heavy manner prevented him from showing himself at his best ; but on the other hand he excelled in Richelieu and Bertuccio (" The Fool's Revenge "), which were dramatic rôles with no traditions behind them. As Bottom, in what the profession affectionately calls " The Dream," he was superb : it is in this part I remember him best. But in truth his range of characters was very great and his eighteen years as sole manager and " star " of Sadler's Wells, where he produced nearly all the plays of Shakespeare, form a magnificent testimony to his worth as an actor and as an upholder of all that is great on the English stage.

Phelps is now almost forgotten—or lives only in the memory of the oldest of old fogies—but there are still enough of such fogies living to bear witness to the genius of an actor equally good in tragedy and comedy, in Shakespeare or in modern drama.

The Queen's Theatre was in existence for eleven years only, but the name of Phelps is alone enough to ensure its immortality in the History of the Stage.

CHAPTER X

THE Strand Theatre in the East Strand, destined to be the Home of Burlesque for so long, originated, like many others, in a Panorama.

It was first advertised in 1820 as " Reinagle's and Barker's New Panorama near the new Church in the Strand." Reinagle afterwards a member of the Royal Academy (he was a sort of journeyman to Allan Ramsay the Court painter, and used to finish off the portraits after Ramsay had painted the features) painted the Panorama and View of Naples with the eruption of Vesuvius, which proved a most popular Show. One Burford took it over from Reinagle and ran it till 1828.

The old Show in the Strand became a chapel for a short time. Then came the moment when the monopoly of the Patent Theatres began to be so hotly disputed that there appeared a certainty of victory for those who claimed free trade for all houses of the Drama. A Mr. B. L. Rayner was put forward among others to plead for the Minor Houses, the little place was reconstructed as a regular theatre, and started in 1830 as " Rayner's New Subscription Theatre in the Strand," the opening programme consisting of two burlettas, one of which was a very palpable satire on the quarrel with the Patent Theatres. It was from the start, and continued to be to the end of its life, a very small house. There was no gallery ; the prices were Boxes 4s., Upper Boxes 3s., and Pit 2s. The fight went on. Fresh theatres were being built all over the town in rash anticipation of an eventual victory over the Lord Chamberlain. For a long time, the little Strand Theatre fought as tenaciously as the larger houses, but it could not command an audience however good the company. Salaries were always in arrears ; frequently the members of the orchestra put on their hats in the middle of a piece and walked out, leaving the vocalists to sing to the accompaniment of one violin only. Various managers tried their luck with various kinds of entertainment. Miss Kelly, a charming actress who eventually ruled at the Soho Royalty Theatre and lived to be over ninety years of age, opened in February, 1833, with a programme in which she was advertised to assume twenty different characters, but she, who had succeeded in other places, failed here. In October, 1833, Wrench and Russell tried their hand ; but the theatre was shut by order of the Lord Chamberlain within a week, after which Russell tried by himself with an entertainment written for him by Dibdin.   All sorts of artful dodges were resorted to in order to evade the strict letter of the Law.   It had been declared illegal " to take money at the *doors* "—so the money was taken at a *window !*   An adjoining sweetstuff shop was added to the premises ; you paid 4s. an ounce for rose lozenges, and a ticket of admission for the boxes, or you paid rather less for peppermints and got into the pit.   An arrangement was once made with Cheesemonger Glossop of the Coburg (Old Vic) the husband of Madame Fearon and father of Augustus Harris the elder, by which those who bought seats for the Vic had also the right of admission to the Strand.

In 1834, it was opened by Mrs. Waylett, a singer of repute, who appeared in comedy, farce or the inevitable burletta.   She was by this time the wife of Alexander Lee, a man who had been lessee of Drury Lane and was the composer of many popular ballads. His passion for her was said to be a " veritable madness."   She was a drunkard, had a very bad temper and led him a most terrible life ; yet he was inconsolable at her death and was found, a corpse, doubled up on a chair beside the bed on which she lay dead.   In his time he had been wealthy, but after Mrs. Waylett's death in 1851, he sank lower and lower, finally finishing up as the piano player in the " Poses Plastiques " of the infamous " Baron " Nicholson in Bow Street.   He was " Tiger " to a brother of that Lord Barrymore who, with his brother and sister, were respectively styled " Hellgate, Cripplegate and Billingsgate."   One of the duties of a Tiger in those days appears to have been to jump down from the cabriolet or gig at a sign from his master and accost any pretty woman who might be passing at the time, get her name and address and generally act the part of a common pimp.   Mr. C. E. Pearce, from whom I have gathered these particulars, adds that Lee was a weak-minded creature who probably did his part quite satisfactorily.

In the company at this odd little theatre at this time were Chippendale, Henry Forrester, Miss Priscilla Horton and Mrs. Nisbett.   With such " stars " the house managed to keep its head above water until 1836, when the ban was partly removed and the theatre placed on the same footing as the Olympic and the Adelphi.

In the previous year, the first burlesque had been produced in what afterwards became the principal home for such entertainments. It was on the subject of " Manfred " and Miss Horton was the Astarte.   This production was taken to be a very heinous offence against the Patent Theatres and the Lord Chamberlain showed his displeasure by closing the place, only to reopen it the following year by the grant of a partial licence.

Douglas Jerrold and his brother-in-law took the theatre when it had been thus partly regulated and put on a tragic play called " The Painter of Ghent." During their short management, the famous drama by Jerrold, " The Rent Day," was also played. Burlesque made its reappearance, in " Othello " according to Act of Parliament, in which the Lord Chamberlain's proceedings were most mercilessly satirized. Hammond, who appears to have been a really comic actor, was cast for " Othello, an independent nigger from the Republic of Hayti," and Harry Hall, a still more popular comedian of the day was the Iago. The theatre had been somewhat enlarged, a gallery added and the prices reduced.

At that time, the novels of Charles Dickens were appearing in monthly parts, and as soon as each one was completed it was invariably pirated and turned into a drama for production, sometimes at more than one theatre at a time. At the Strand there were versions of " Pickwick," " Nickleby " and " Martin Chuzzlewit," but always with the inevitable burlesque or extravaganza to follow. Shakespeare was tried, and in 1841 the Keeleys were here and Mrs. Stirling, and also somewhere about this time Madame Celeste, whose career in London is, however, chiefly associated with the Adelphi and the Lyceum.

Madame Celeste was one of those foreign actresses who adopted England as their country more or less, and always preferred to act either here or in the United States. She was born in the year 1814, of very poor and humble parents ; some give the date of her birth as 1811, but the actual year is of scant importance. In Paris she appeared with the great Talma as the boy in " Le Vieux Celibataire," and she was also one of the children with Pasta in " Medea." Her first engagement out of her own country appears to have been at the Bowery Theatre in New York, where she arrived when only fifteen years of age and where she married a year or two later a Mr. Elliott, who left her a widow not long afterwards. For some years she spoke not a word of English and when playing in English-speaking countries always took the part of a dumb character, as, for instance, Fenella, the dumb girl, in " Masaniello." She was very good in what were known as " Breeches " parts. Her London debut was at the theatre in Tottenham Street, then known as the " Queen's," in a *ballet d'action*. In later years she starred most of the minor theatres in London, such as the Vic and other East End houses and played at the Strand, Surrey, Adelphi, Lyceum, Drury Lane and Princess's. It was at the old Surrey, some time in the forties of the nineteenth century, that she first spoke on the stage. The house was then under the direction of Osbaldistone, who never announced new pieces weeks beforehand, as is the custom nowadays, lest a rival manager should forestall him. His novelties were always given out on a Saturday and, with the Sunday intervening, he was fairly safe. On one of these Saturdays he announced that Celeste would appear on the Monday in a speaking part for the first time. The house was crowded as he had expected. The moment came when in a pathetic scene she exclaimed, " My shee-ild ! My shee-ild ! " That was all she had to say. When she was more advanced in the language, Planché wrote a piece called " The Child of the Wreck " especially for her. It was always recognized that her forte lay in the direction of a part affording her opportunies for singing, dancing and action. Her range was very wide. One year she was principal boy and harlequin in a pantomime. She played Vanderdecken in a drama written round the adventures of " The Flying Dutchman " ; another evening she would appear as Mephistopheles in a stage version of " Faust," but as she improved in her knowledge of English, her chief successes were made in melodramas like " Flowers of the Forest," " Green Bushes " and a version of Dickens's " Tale of Two Cities," in which she made a great impression as the vengeful Madame Defarge. She ran the Adelphi in company with old Benjamin Webster for many years and then took on the Lyceum on her own, where she was supported by the Keeleys. They had previously been running the " unlucky " house in Wellington Street, where no one seemed able to make money, though many, like the Keeleys themselves, Charles Mathews and his wife (Vestris), scored artistic successes. In this connection, the " Martin Chuzzlewit " of the Keeleys will always be quoted as a brilliant specimen of a wonderful cast. Emery as Jonas Chuzzlewit ; Frank Matthews, Pecksniff ; Alfred Wigan, Montagu Tigg ; Keeley, Sairey Gamp ; Mrs. Keeley, Bailey ; Miss Woolgar (Mrs. Alfred Mellon), Charity Pecksniff ; and Mrs. Alfred Wigan, Mercy Pecksniff, etc.

Miami was Celeste's great part and one which she played many hundred times. I saw the play (" Green Bushes ") with her in this part when she appeared for the last time in 1874 at the Adelphi. She was then at least sixty years of age, if not more, but her acting was wonderful as the deserted Indian maiden ; as was also that of Mrs. Billington, who was the Geraldine. I shall ever be proud of having been at that performance. Celeste, like many another actress, had got into the habit of advertising her " Very last appearance," and then a few years later taking another engagement and having another " very last." Few old actresses have stood so many reappearances so well.

MADAME CELESTE

AS CYNTHIA IN "FLOWERS OF THE FOREST"
From photograph by Adolphe Bean

Perhaps the most notable thing about Celeste is that she began her career on the English-speaking stage without being able to say a word in the language. For many years she was a dancer and nothing else, and she seems to have been recognized as a very capable one. I have seen a programme (one of those long shaped black printed affairs) of the Broadway Theatre in New York— dated 1847—in which "The School for Scandal" is given with three Wallacks (Henry, Fanny and Lester), Mrs. Winstanley, a favourite "old woman" in London as Mrs. Candour, and a Miss Rose Telbin (yet another stage name) as Lady Teazle. The programme announced that, prior to the Comedy, there would be an Overture by the Orchestra and a *pas seul* by "Miss Celeste."

To return to the chronicle of the old Strand. After the management of Harry Hall the theatre went through many vicissitudes and changes of directors. At one time it sank so low as to be the scene of a sort of Variety Entertainment and Tom Thumb was advertised as an attraction. It went one degree lower still with an Exhibition of dirty natives from South Africa, but at last, in 1849, its luck took a turn for the better. Farren took the house, got together an excellent company and brought out standard works like "The Road to Ruin," "The Love Chase," etc. Among his supporters were Mrs. Glover, Mrs. Stirling, Compton, Mr. and Mrs. Leigh Murray and others. He produced a version of "The Vicar of Wakefield," with himself as Dr. Primrose, Mrs. Glover (then fast approaching the end of her career) as Mrs. Primrose, Mrs. Stirling as Olivia. This was not the first acting version of Goldsmith's tale. One, by Dibdin, had been seen at the old Surrey Theatre as long ago as 1819, and in 1823 it was done as a sort of opera at the Haymarket with Daniel Terry (no relation to the famous more modern family, but a great friend of Sir Walter Scott), as Dr. Primrose, Mrs. Garrick as Sophia, Liston as Moses, Mrs. Orger as Wilhelmina Skeggs, and Miss Chester as Olivia. It was also done at the Haymarket Theatre almost simultaneously with the production at the Strand, with Webster as the Vicar, Mrs. Keeley as Mrs. Primrose, Mrs. Fitzwilliam as Skeggs and a Miss Reynolds as Olivia. In 1871 it was done at the Standard, Shoreditch, with Emery as the Vicar, Mrs. Leigh Murray as his wife, Emily Pitt as Olivia, Amy Steinberg as Skeggs, McIntyre as Jenkinson and Tyars as Burchell. In 1878 Wills's version was produced at the Court with Hermann Vezin as the Vicar, Ellen Terry as Olivia, Norman Forbes, Moses ; Frank Archer, Burchell ; Terriss, Thornhill ; Mrs. Gaston Murray, Mrs. Primrose ; and Kate Aubrey, Sophia. The finest production of all was, of course, that of the Lyceum by Irving, who used Wills's version and had the luck to have Ellen Terry and Terriss still in the cast, while his acting of the Vicar will never be forgotten even by those who have not professed to be among his whole-hearted admirers.

All these years the Strand had held fast by burlesque when the programme was not degraded to variety. Playgoers may talk of the "Sacred Lamp of Burlesque" at the Gaiety (generally with their tongues in their cheek), but the real home of burlesque has always been the little old Strand.

In 1851, William Copeland, brother of the famous actress, Mrs. Fitzwilliam, scenting the profit which might be made out of the Great International Exhibition, took the little house and changed its name. He called it, most ineptly, "Punch's Playhouse," apparently without any special reason, and stuck to the original programmes of drama (or comedy) and burlesque. At first he met with a good measure of success. The Keeleys starred there for a short engagement, and other members of his company were Walter Lacy (a good Shakespearean actor, an excellent stage lover and, in after life, long years after, a first-class producer and general adviser), Mr. and Mrs. Selby, Edward Stirling, Tom Robertson, the dramatist (brother of Mrs. Kendal), and the "Great little Charlotte Saunders" inimitable in burlesque.

Charlotte Saunders was, perhaps, one of the best burlesque actresses in its best days. She was generally cast for a "breeches" part. In the first burlesque of "Kenilworth" in 1858 she was Tressilian ; then Claude Melnotte to Patty Oliver's Pauline ; Romeo to Marie Wilton's Juliet ; then William Tell, followed by Dandini in "Cinderella," and Ivanhoe to the Rowena of Miss Swanborough. She was equally good in serious drama : as the fat jockey in "The Flying Scud" and in the gold-diggings drama at the same theatre with Ellen Terry as the heroine. When Patty Oliver opened the Royalty Theatre in Dean Street, Soho, with short domestic drama followed by burlesque, she captured Charlotte Saunders and kept her for two or three years. The Olympic had her for drama for a short time, and she appeared in that almost prehistoric drama "The Cataract of the Ganges." She was a frequent panto-mime hero, and well I remember her at the old Holborn Theatre as Valentine in "Valentine and Orson." Perhaps she was specially fitted by nature for certain low comedy or burlesque parts, for she was very short and very fat, but she was a good actress all round and, in the latter years of her life, an excellent exponent of old women's parts. One performance of hers I should much like to have seen, viz., that of Audrey in a production of "As You Like It" at the Pavilion in Whitechapel. The Rosalind was Mrs.

Charles Young (Mrs. Hermann Vezin). That ought to have been an "As You Like It" worth seeing.

The manager of Punch's Playhouse did not seem able to change the luck with the name. He soon gave it up and was followed by several different managers with very diverse programmes. Barry Sullivan, a popular specimen of an actor of the disappearing noisy school, appeared there in Shakespeare, but, as may be gathered from the recognized character of the little house, did not achieve any great success—though he was made very welcome in many other theatres. Of course the theatre was also "out of luck." A long series of failures had accustomed people to expect nothing much from the Strand productions. But the tide was on the turn. After some disastrous experiments in grand opera financed by a Bond Street box-office keeper and run by Rebecca Isaacs, and the general apathy of Barry Sullivan's season, the theatre sank very low indeed. Miss Isaacs put on "The Beggars' Opera," with herself as Polly Peachum and a Miss Isabella Featherstone (destined to become famous as Mrs. Howard Paul) as Lucy Lockit, and she also adventured "Der Freischütz," but it was not a Grand Opera house, and her experiments in that direction must have resembled those of these latter days when "Opera in English" is puffed and praised presumably only because it is in English and not because of any intrinsic merit as performances of Grand Opera. There were some burlesques in this sad interval (the little house could not get away from burlesque at any time) there was a pantomime generally at Christmas—one in 1856 on the curious subject of "Black Eyed Susan"; one of the burlesques was on "Belphegor," which Charles Dillon had lately made a famous play. In this, there were H. J. Turner, and J. Clarke, who remained at the Strand for many burlesques to come and the title rôle was taken by a Miss Cuthbert, one of the few female clowns I have been able to trace. There was also a small boy, "Master Edouin"—the Heathen Chinee of the future—whose assistance was presumably indispensable to Miss Cuthbert, for when she was Clown in a Strand pantomime, not being able to do the tumbling herself, she engaged Master Edouin to do it for her! An adaptation of "Little Dorrit" in 1856, a pantomime in 1857, and we can skip the rest till the dawn of the Strand's golden years in 1858, coinciding with the coming of the Swanboroughs. It was really a prosperous time that was now approaching for the despised little house. From being the outcast, the "Cinderella" of the London playhouses which no one thought it worth while to visit, it became the Mecca of burlesque lovers and the objective of every one who wanted to hear pretty music, see pretty girls, and have a hearty laugh.

Previous extravaganzas and burlesques of the Vestris type had relied more on pleasing the eye than on appealing to the ear or the intelligence. A new generation of playgoers and seekers of merry evenings had arisen since those days which wanted something more ; something they " could bite into " as it was once rather coarsely said. In the same way that lovers of drama had forsaken the heavy " legitimate " for the blood-curdling horrors of " Oliver Twist " as done at the Vic and " Susan Hopley " or " Sweeney Todd " as done almost everywhere, so those who wanted a merry evening asked for something really funny, lines that would make them laugh, songs they could catch hold of, dances rather of the cellar-flap order. In short, the refinements of the Vestris School were above the heads of the rather vulgar class who now formed such a large proportion of the audiences, and the new entertainment at the Strand suited them to a nicety. It was also found to meet the tastes of the more educated and refined stalls and boxes.

The playgoers of the day, especially the pit and gallery, knew " The Miller and His Men " and " The Red Rover " by heart ; so they could appreciate to the full skits on those redoubtable melo-dramas. The public in general had devoured eagerly all the novels of Walter Scott as fast as they had come out ; the stalls and boxes knew all about the plots of the Italian operas, many of them supremely ridiculous and crying out to be burlesqued. Byron—H. J. of that ilk—recognized the possibilities of the situation and for years concocted parodies bristling with puns, crowded with bright songs and gay dances, and the fortune of the hitherto unlucky little house was changed as by magic from the year 1858.

The company was the very best for the purpose and much new talent was continually being discovered. The Swanboroughs were a talented family with ramifications of married sons and daughters-in-law. The old lady did not act herself except in private life where she had the reputation of being a continual Mrs. Malaprop, and, if half the funny things she is supposed to have said were really uttered, they ought to have been written down and published for the merriment of the world at large. Her eldest daughter, Miss Swanborough, had been a favourite actress at the Haymarket for some years and must not be confused with Ada Swanborough, who came out later.

Under Vestris at the Lyceum and the Olympic fairy plays had been given called " extravaganzas," but with very little extravagance about them beyond the fancifulness of the fairy story itself. " The Yellow Dwarf," " The King of the Peacocks," " The Island of Jewels," and many others, had delighted the elegant audiences who had flocked to see and admire the charming manageress and the fantastic *décor*. But, as I have already said, the moment had arrived for something more suited to the stronger palates of a new generation of playgoers which had sprung up with the abolition of the Patent Monopoly.

Byron took serious operas like " La Gazza Ladra," " Fra Diavolo," " l'Africaine," and turgid old melodramas, and turned them into ridicule. He did the same with Scott's novels, with the stories of Roman and Greek mythology and the legends of German mediævalism. He crammed his pieces with excruciating puns which made the audiences laugh in spite of themselves, and the result of it all was a long series of successes engineered by him, by the brothers Brough, by Burnand and by Reece, extending over a dozen years, until they were eclipsed by the lighting of the " Sacred Lamp " of John Hollingshead at the Gaiety and the rise of the famous Gaiety Quartet.

Auguste Filon, a Frenchman, who wrote a most illuminating Review of the English Stage of his day, said of H. J. Byron that he wrote a million nonsensical things but not a single indecent thing, but this same critic goes on to note that the coming of " Burlesque " to the English Stage threw it open to scores of actresses of a new type, who posed, but did not perform, and were called upon to fill not rôles, but tights ! This was severe and perhaps *mal à propos* from a Frenchman, but there was more than a grain of truth in it. Many ladies of the burlesque stage remained all their lives in burlesque or pantomime if they did not retire with a competence— from elsewhere ! But, on the other hand, how many of our finest actresses of to-day began in burlesque either at the Strand or under the glare of the Sacred Lamp ? We have only to mention Marie Wilton—the Lady Bancroft of so many splendid years, and Ada Cavendish, Mrs. Stirling, Mrs. Leigh Murray of the older ranks, Ethel Irving, Gladys Cooper, Violet Vanbrugh, all three of whom, I believe, performed to the light of that same holy lamp. Actors, too, have shone in burlesque and attained to the foremost ranks afterwards, Tree certainly, and Irving, who, I believe, once appeared as a " Dame " in his earliest days, and did not Charles Wyndham dance in a breakdown at the Royalty dressed in the petticoat of a Deal smuggler ?

The flappers and their young men of the present day have never seen a burlesque. They have their Revues with a Beauty Chorus and popular music-hall artistes doing turns therein, and they have their musical comedies with a chorus of gentlemen in morning coats or evening clothes, and silk hats, identical paces and vacuous faces —but burlesques they do not know. For this they are much to be pitied, in that they have never laughed at the joyous follies of

the Strand, Royalty or Gaiety or seen a " Break-down by the Strength
of the Company," or been present at such an occasion as the reappearance of Nelly Farren, when the gallery boys let down a
huge banner inscribed " The Boys welcome their Nelly." There
are, alas, no Nellys on the stage, nor Patty Olivers, nor Marie
Wiltons, nor Angelina Claudes—and this brings me to my next point,
the personnel of the Strand burlesques. Here graduated Marie
Wilton, and Patty Oliver, and David James and Thomas Thorne,
and Amy Sheridan and Ada Swanborough, and Edward Terry,
and Angelina Claude and Lottie Venne and Harry Cox and a score
of others who dispersed to keep the sacred lamp alight at the Prince
of Wales's, the Royalty, the Vaudeville and the Gaiety. The last-
named is now given over to the less boisterous (but hardly less vulgar)
delights of musical comedy, the Vaudeville is sacrificed to the inanities
of Revue, the Royalty (one of the merriest of all London houses
from the sixties to the eighties of last century) has adopted the more
decorous modern comedy, and the Prince of Wales's—the old
Dusthole of many joyous memories—has been transmogrified into
the high-brow and rather dull Scala with a tendency to cleave to
the Movies, though, as I write, I hear that it is to be taken over
entirely by ambitious amateur companies who certainly will not
be troubled by any ghosts of the Past, being quite persuaded that
they themselves surpass anything that has gone before ! The old
Strand itself has been " improved " out of existence ; though another
theatre, not at all in the Strand, has, rather impudently, stolen its
name.

Marie Wilton, the Lady Bancroft of most living playgoers, was
the first under the Swanboroughs to start the Strand on its giddy
round of successful burlesques. She had been as a child at the
Lyceum with Charles Dillon, as the boy attendant on the clown
Fanfarronade (played by Toole) and she had danced in burlesque
there ; I fancy she was in a pantomime at the Adelphi as Harlequin
(how much I should like to have seen that Harlequin !). When
the old Adelphi was in process of being rebuilt, the Strand was
lucky enough to secure her for its " principal boy," and as principal
boy she remained there until in 1865 she went into management
on her own account at the Tottenham Street Theatre. I can't
help quoting here a passage from a letter of Charles Dickens to his
friend and biographer, John Foster, in which he writes :

" I really wish you would go between this and next Thursday
to see ' The Maid and the Magpie ' burlesque. There is the
strangest thing in it that ever I have seen on the stage—the boy
Pippo, by Miss Wilton. While it is astonishingly impudent, must

be or wouldn't be done at all, it is so stupendously like a boy and unlike a woman that it is perfectly free from offence. I have never seen such a thing. She does an imitation of the dancing of the Christy Minstrels wonderfully clever which, in the audacity of its thorough-going, is surprising. A thing that you cannot imagine a woman doing at all ; and yet the manner, the appearance, the levity, impulse and spirit of it are so exactly like a boy, that you cannot think of anything like her sex in connection with it. It begins at eight and is over by a quarter past nine. I have never seen such a curious thing and the girl's talent is unchallengeable. I call her the cleverest girl I have ever seen on the stage in my time, and the most singularly original."

James Rogers, James Bland and " Johnny " Clarke were in the piece, which was a most uproarious success, and it was revived about twenty years afterwards with Nelly Bouverie as Pippo and Marius, Harry Cox, Penley and Lottie Venne in other characters.

I always regret that I am not old enough to have seen Marie Wilton in the Strand burlesques. The first piece of the kind I saw there was " Paris : or Vive Lempriere," which I think was the earliest of the mythological burlesques produced at this house. My recollections of this are very hazy now. I can recall most of the succeeding Strand burlesques, especially the second version of " Kenilworth "—the first had been done in 1858—with Ada Swanborough as Amy Robsart, Miss Raynham as a most picturesque Earl of Leicester and Thomas Thorne as a " Dame," in this case Queen Elizabeth. As children, whenever we had a choice, my sister and myself generally chose the Strand. It was so exhilarating that though we sometimes, I suppose, missed the full force of the humour, we could always appreciate the dancing and the singing. I fell in love with one Elise Holt, who played subordinate " boys' " parts, but to my very youthful eyes looked most enchanting in doublet and hose. I wonder if she is alive now !

The " Home of Burlesque " was a very small theatre indeed, quite the smallest in London at that time, with the possible exception of the Royalty in Dean Street and the little houses let to amateurs. It was generally packed to " capacity " for each successive production, until the sad day arrived, in 1882, when Mrs. Swanborough was forced by the authorities to rebuild it. The cost was heavy, the loss great, and the genial old lady had to go through the Bankruptcy Court in 1885. She died in 1889, aged 86 years.

Before the coming of the Swanboroughs, the Strand had earned a name for good burlesque. There had been entertainments of a similar kind written by Talfourd chiefly on mythological subjects. In one of these, Mrs. Stirling had appeared as Minerva, Mrs. Leigh Murray as Apollo and Rebecca Isaacs as Venus. But this was as long ago as 1850 when the theatre had been under Miss Isaacs's direction and the principal part of the bill was serious opera. In 1858, the house settled down to its long period of success with the first burlesque on "Kenilworth," the cast of which included Miss Swanborough (the eldest daughter), Marie Wilton, Patty Oliver, Charlotte Saunders, Mrs. Selby, John Clarke (not John S. Clarke), and H. J. Turner.

All these were noted in burlesque and continued to be so after they had dispersed to different theatres. They carried on at the Strand together for some time. "Romeo and Juliet" was done with Charlotte Saunders as Romeo and Marie Wilton as Juliet. "Fra Diavolo" was another, and "The Miller and His Men" was another. The stilted form of grand opera or the highfalutin diction of old-fashioned melodrama were equally good objects for burlesque. They were always short entertainments, generally playing about an hour or a little more, and were preceded by a domestic drama or comedy in two or three acts and followed by a farce to wind up the evening's show. H. T. Craven, himself a clever actor of the Robsonian School, wrote many of these first pieces, innocuous enough, such as "Milky White" and "Meg's Diversion" both for the Strand and afterwards for the Royalty when taken over by Patty Oliver, and sometimes acted in them himself. Patty Oliver, indeed, would play the emotional heroine in the drama and the singing and dancing "principal girl" in the burlesque the same night.

Miss Martha Oliver was one of the most refined and accomplished actress of her day in many lines. She was equally good in emotional drama as in burlesque. She could make you cry one minute and laugh the next. Her first appearance on any stage was probably at a little theatre in Salisbury when she was about six or seven years old, but her talents soon brought her to London and she appeared with Mrs. Warner in 1847 at the old Marylebone Theatre in Chapel Street, Edgware Road, in a round of Shakespearean productions. From there, she went to the Lyceum, then under the management of Mr. and Mrs. Charles Mathews (Vestris), with whom she stayed for six years (1849—1856). Her next engagement was at Drury Lane where her success as Helen in "The Hunchback" was so widely recognized that Buckstone secured her for the Haymarket, where she remained three years, though she occasionally reappeared at the Lane. In 1858, she joined the Swanboroughs and played various characters in comedy and burlesque for three or four years. In 1863, she started her successful seasons at the Royalty, which had fallen into some disrepute as a playhouse where nothing good was seen, and she raised its fortunes to the highest point, the little place being crammed every night to applaud the pretty manageress in comedy and burlesque. Miss Oliver was the means of introducing Andrew Halliday prominently to the public as a reliable dramatist, and one or two artistes who mounted high in their profession in after years owe their success to her encouragement; notable among whom was Charles Wyndham, who had a small part in the great burlesque "Black Eyed Susan" that ran for years.

This was perhaps her high-water mark of success in that form of piece and it is said that she had sung during her career, "Pretty See-usan, don't say No" nearly two thousand times, so numerous were the encores demanded nightly, till the artistes were actually out of breath and could do no more. In the chorus of that same song were Dewar, as Captain Crosstree, a very clever actor who afterwards was in the Prince of Wales's company with the Bancrofts, Charles Wyndham as "Hatchett, a smuggler," Rosina Ranoe as William (in later life the second wife of Burnand, who wrote the burlesque, his first having been her sister Cecilia Ranoe), Nellie Bromley as Dolly Mayflower, and the intensely comic Danvers (from the Highbury Barn Theatre) as Dame Hatley. Other successful burlesques produced by Miss Oliver at the Dean Street house were "The Lady of the Lake," "Claude Duval," with fat little Charlotte Saunders as the highwayman, "Ulf the Minstrel," with Lydia Maitland as Ulf, "The Merry Zingara," in the cast of which I find a Miss Fowler (playing a "breeches" part), who afterwards became well known as a good actress in emotional drama, and ran the Charing Cross Theatre for some time. In 1863 Miss Oliver was at the Princess's in a fairy piece; and from that time she does not seem to have settled down at any particular theatre. When the Opera Comique was opened by Hingston in 1871 she was in the company, and in 1875 was still there. She died a painful death from cancer on the last day of 1880, very much respected by all who had known her for her unblemished life and her many acts of kindness and charity.

At the Strand in 1861 came the first appearance of Ada Swanborough, a younger sister of Mrs. Lyons, who, for some unexplained reason, had been brought up as a boy till she was sixteen and passed in the world as such. She took the place of Patty Oliver in the Strand burlesques and also in the opening pieces, but was by no means so good an actress.

After Miss Oliver's departure and when Marie Wilton had also set up a theatre of her own, the company at the Strand was somewhat reorganized. Among the actors we find the names of David James, Thomas Thorne, J. D. Stoyle, Charles Fenton and H. J. Turner, and the ladies include Fanny Hughes and Eleanor Bufton (both connected with the Swanborough family), and Miss Raynham, a charming actress of boys' parts, who died young of consumption. She had been the original Sam Willoughby in " The Ticket of Leave Man " at the Olympic.

Thomas Thorne and David James were burlesque actors who played up to each other in much the same way that Paul Bedford and Wright had done at the Adelphi in years gone by. Thorne was genuinely funny in himself and had something of a jerky, cracked voice like Edward Terry which made his words sound funnier still. He was one of a large family of actors and actresses : Sarah Thorne ran the stock company at Margate for years and gave many excellent artistes to the stage ; Fred Thorne was a relation and Emily Thorne an excellent portrayer of old women's parts at the Folly and other houses. Thorne had worked his way up from the lowest rung of the theatrical ladder. He had been at Sadler's Wells in the days of Phelps's great seasons, at the Standard in Shoreditch, and at the Surrey with Anderson and Shepherd in thrilling melodramas like " Afloat and Ashore " (of the style of " True to the Core "). That was in 1864, the year before he came to the Strand, at which house he promptly became a general favourite, generally cast for " Dames' " parts in the burlesques, such as Selika in a ridiculous parody of Meyerbeer's " Africaine," " Joan of Arc," and the Dame in " Der Freischütz."

Apropos of this latter piece—which came out on October 9th, 1866, at the Strand—the Prince of Wales's Theatre, which was in a sense a rival of the other house for this style of piece, promptly produced on the 10th October a different burlesque on the same subject with Lydia Thompson, Lydia Maitland, Younge and Clarke and I believe there was also one done at the Standard, Shoreditch, at the same time ! It was the last piece produced there before the theatre was destroyed by one of its periodical burnings.

Thorne and James deserted the Strand in 1870 and opened (together with " Handsome Harry Montagu ") the new Vaudeville Theatre. They aimed at producing high-class comedy, both ancient and modern, but for a long time, at the beginning of their reign, they always had a burlesque as well. " Don Carlos " was the first, but one I remember more distinctly was " The Orange Tree and the Humble Bee : or the Little Princess who was lost at Sea." They introduced Nelly Power to the West End among others. Thorne played Silky in the old-fashioned " Road to Ruin," in which Charles Warner was such a good Dornton ; " The School

for Scandal" was played to what must have been a record run
for that comedy, with charming Amy Fawsitt as Lady Teazle,
Farren as Sir Peter and a wonderful cast all round. But prior
to that, Thorne gave Irving his first real chance when he produced
"The Two Roses"—that phenomenal success that was afterwards revived by Irving at the Lyceum. Another of Thorne's
parts was Caleb Deecie, the blind man in "Our Boys"—the play
that was voted "rubbish" when it was read to the company who
declared it would not run a week. It ran for over a thousand
performances. It is still running somewhere I feel sure. The
amateurs, anyhow, will never give it up. Other characters in which
Thorne made a name were Tom Pinch in rather a poor version
of "Martin Chuzzlewit," Partridge in an adaptation of "Tom
Jones," and the Methodist minister in "Saints and Sinners," a play
of Henry Jones. Mrs. Thomas Thorne was Adelaide Newton,
who appeared with Tree at the Whitechapel Garrick when "Le
Voyage en Chine" was put on. It appears to have been a very
unhappy marriage, though she was a charming actress, and had
been one of the original two Roses, and previously with the Strand
burlesque company, where she had met Thorne. I understand
that he died out of his mind, and was in poor circumstances as well.
In this he differed from his partner, David James, who left several
thousand pounds at his death. James was a Jew, Belasco being
his real name. His first appearance on the London stage seems
to have been as a super in 1857 in the company of Charles Kean
at the Princess's, where he went on in the processions and shouted
with the crowd. In 1863, he was in Burnand's burlesque of
"Ixion" at the Royalty in Soho, in which Ada Cavendish startled
the world by appearing on the stage as a very scantily attired Venus,
and Rogers was a funny Minerva made up as a sort of Cornelia
Blimber, spectacles and all. David James was at the Strand a short
time before Thorne, and I think he acted there rather longer, for
he was certainly in the cast of "The Heir at Law," in which John
S. Clarke made such a capital Dr. Pangloss. This was in 1870,
the year of the opening of the Vaudeville, and thereafter for a few
years his career runs on parallel lines with that of Thomas Thorne.
Later on, he joined the Haymarket and was seen in "The Overland
Route" as Lovibond—with Mrs. John Wood, an inimitable Mrs.
Lovibond—and as Stout in the revival of Lytton's "Money."
Another revival at the same house (that of "Caste" in 1883)
brought him out as Eccles which had been originally created by
George Honey. One of his latest appearances was in the Gaiety
"Jack Sheppard," where he played Blueskin. I did not see this,
but understand that it was an indescribably funny performance.

J. D. Stoyle was a very funny little actor, short and stout like Charlotte Saunders, and with a curiously comic way of his own. His first appearance at the Strand was as Nelusko to the Selika of Thomas Thorne. I personally remember him only in a very funny performance of Prince Paul in the "Grand Duchess" with Julia Matthews as Her Serene Highness of Gerolstein.

What was the secret of the extraordinary success of these burlesques at the Strand? It was wonderful "team-work," of course. They all played up to each other, not each one trying to get into the limelight for himself—or herself—as in modern Revues. But it was more than this. Burton Baker in his book on *The London Stage* suggests a possible explanation. It chiefly lay in the evident enjoyment of the performers themselves and the zest with which they danced and sang through their parts. Something of the same kind was seen later in the burlesques with Nelly Farren, Terry and Royce at the Gaiety. The enjoyment was catching and came direct over the footlights to the audience, who gave it back in their laughing and applause. Mr. Baker says :

"There certainly was a 'go,' an excitement about burlesque at the Strand in those days that was never approached by any other house. The enjoyment of the performers was really, or seemingly, so intense, that the wild, ecstatic breakdown into which they broke at the end of every scene seemed perfectly spontaneous ; it was a frantic outburst of irrepressible animal spirits, and they seemed to have no more control over their legs than the audience had over their applause. You might call it rubbish, buffoonery, vulgarity, anything you liked, but your temperament must have been abnormally phlegmatic if you could resist the influence of that riotous mirth, and not be carried away by it."

The "Squash Hollow Hornpipe" introduced here in "The Maid and the Magpie" was probably the first of the cellar-flap breakdowns so popular in all the burlesques of the old kind.

The irrepressible animal spirits alluded to by Mr. Baker in the above extract seem to have quite gone out of date, and perhaps did not survive the early period of burlesques, though, in certain of the Gaiety productions, there were not wanting evidences that, given any encouragement, they would break out again. Burlesque became more refined (thereby losing a great deal of its character) ; and, as the ladies of the ensemble grew to imitate more and more "ladies" off the stage, and the men of the ensemble sighed after frock-coats and shiny hats in private life, the animal spirits

disappeared altogether, and musical comedy was the result, with bands
of most correctly behaved young women and troops of young men in
the latest fashions of the day. Most of these young men and women
would feel singularly awkward if they had to put on tights and
trunk hose. It is a parallel case to the disappearance of the *cappa
e spada* drama. Few actors or actresses would feel at home in
costume plays. They must be in their everyday clothes or they
can't attempt to act. The result is that they don't succeed in
" acting " at all.

The Strand burlesque that lives longest in the memories of old
playgoers is probably " The Field of the Cloth of Gold." It ran
for many months, was revived more than once, and was a most
exhilarating affair. Written by Brough, it was, as usual, crammed
full of puns, one of which may be quoted as the neatest of its kind.
Katharine of Aragon, landing in France after having suffered
badly from *mal de mer*, says :

> Yesterday all was fair, a glorious Sunday,
> But this *sick transit* spoils the *glory o' Monday*.

It is quite possible that the average pittite of to-day would altogether miss the point of *sic transit gloria mundi*, but the roars of
laughter at the time it was said, proved that it was appreciated
then. It is nowadays considered bad taste, I believe, to make any
Latin or Greek allusion in speech or conversation, even in " The
House." Our new masters shriek out, " Why can't you speak
English ? " and show their own intimate acquaintance with the inner
intricacies of their mother tongue by the use of expletives and
expressions which may be Greek indeed to many of their
hearers.

The part of Katharine of Aragon was played, if I remember
rightly, by Mr. H. J. Turner, an actor of experience with a very
comic delivery. Lydia Thompson was " principal boy " and others
in the cast were Thomas Thorne, David James, Fanny Hughes,
Amy Sheridan, Elise Holt, Charles Fenton and Ada Swanborough.
Another play on words in the same burlesque was :

> Wandering the forest long, I *long for rest*.

But it was the fashion of the day. Every burlesque was full
of the same sort of word-twisting, some good and some awful !
As I have said, the matter burlesqued was of all kinds : mythological,
operatic, historical, legendary, but all with lively songs and breakdowns. Dresses and scenery were pretty and smart enough, but

no manager would think of spending the vast sums which are in these days laid out on a New Gaiety or Daly's production.

After the flitting of James and Thorne to the Vaudeville, the traditions of the theatre were still carried on. Some of the original Swanborough circle remained and were joined by Edward Terry, Harry Paulton and Kate Santley, and a new author was found in H. B. Farnie, who, clever though he was in many ways, never produced anything so witty as his predecessors, Byron, Brough and Burnand.

Kate Santley was an especially valuable acquisition. She could sing better than most ; her dancing was light and clever ; she had more than an average share of good looks and a very long experience of stage work of all sorts. Her family was of German origin and had emigrated to the United States when Kate was a child, but at the outbreak of the Civil War in 1860 they once more returned to England and she tried to earn a living by teaching music. This appears to have been a failure and we hear of her in the company of the Charles Keans in Edinburgh in 1862, where she performed under the name of Miss Eva Stella and was the Fairy Queen in the pantomime there in 1864. Irving was in the same company at the time, and when he played Robert Macaire Miss "Stella" was cast for one of the minor parts. In 1867 she came to London and, calling herself Miss Kate Santley, was engaged at the Marylebone and other Music Halls of the day, including the Oxford, where she performed at the same time as Emily Soldene. She became so popular for her singing of " The Bells go a Ringing for Sarah " and other songs that theatrical managers spotted her as a promising recruit for burlesque and fairy pieces. At the Queen's Theatre, under the management of Labouchere, she achieved instant success in " The Stranger stranger than Ever," " The Gnome King," and other light pieces, with Toole and Henrietta Hodson as associates. In 1869 she was at Drury Lane in the pantomime with the Vokes family and from that time never looked back. Ten years later she was firmly installed at the Alhambra, playing in such pieces as " Le Roi Carotte," " The Black Crook," " La belle Hélène," " La Jolie Parfumeuse," and " Dick Whittington," which Offenbach wrote especially for the Alhambra. Her Strand engagements (in " The Idle Apprentice " and other burlesques of Farnie) had been previous to this, and she was a well-established favourite with London audiences. The stage " Rows " during the run of " Don Juan " are well known to all old playgoers. Rose Bell and Kate Santley were at daggers drawn for some reason never made quite clear, and injudicious friends in front of both parties (whether paid or not does not matter) would applaud and hiss accordingly. During these manifestations the performances were brought to an absolute standstill, and Harry Paulton would curl himself up on the stage at the corner of the proscenium and pretend to go to sleep till all was over. The case went into court, but an arrangement was reached, and peace restored. The "immortal" Lottie Venne was also in that production. Kate was manageress of the little Royalty for years. Indeed, she was the actual proprietress. It was said that it had been a birthday present from a wealthy admirer! Be that as it may, she kept her hold on it, assuring herself an income for life that enabled her to end her days in comfort at Brighton in 1923, when she must have been over eighty years of age. What her age was, no one ever knew. Once, when asked if it was not true that she had appeared with Menken in " Mazeppa " at Astley's in 1864, she replied she was not old enough to remember that production. But we know she was with the Keans in Edinburgh in 1862 ! It does not matter. Her loss to the stage (and especially to Opera Bouffe) was enormous. There are no Kate Santleys left.

Harry Paulton who was with Kate Santley at the Strand in " The Idle Prentice " and other pieces, was also with her, as we have seen, at the Alhambra. He was a comedian of a fruity sort with a rich vein of humour. One of his great successes at the Alhāmbra was in " Le Cheval de Bronze " of Auber, where there is an air which was immediately recognized by the delighted audience as the tune to which the circus lady rides round the Ring on a large pad mounted on a staidly ambling steed, who could probably not go to any other tune so well. Paulton was in " Niobe " with the beauteous Beatrice Lamb at the Strand in later years.

With Kate Santley at the Strand were Marius (who had made his first appearance in " Chilperic " in 1870), Lottie Venne and Angelina Claude—a most charming actress. Penley and J. G. Taylor were added when a comic opera called " Princess Toto," by W. S. Gilbert and Frederic Clay, was produced, but it was not a very great success. That was in 1875, and in 1878 a bigger hit was made with " Diplunacy," a skit on " Diplomacy " which had just been brought out at the Prince of Wales's. This was one of the cleverest parodies ever seen on the English stage. Marius, Mitchell and Harry Cox burlesqued the three men, Penley was Baron Stein, Rachel Sanger—the same who had begun her career at the disreputable Highbury Barn—mimicked Madge Robertson as Dora, and Lottie Venne made the hit of the evening in a caricature of Lady Bancroft as the Countess Zicka, a part, by the way, which clever Marie Wilton ought never to have attempted and which she abandoned on the revival of the play at the Haymarket in favour of that of Lady Henry Fairfax. Another skit was brought out the same year, for the management had found out what a clever company of mimics were got together. This was on the old melodrama "The Red Rover," beloved of all transpontine audiences, and the Strand piece was a delightful parody of the "Penny-plain Twopence-colour" type of play, the company faithfully reproducing the attitudes of the various types of characters as shown on the sheets of Skelt, Redington, Webb and other artists of the Theatres of Toyland. Such theatres are much out of fashion nowadays, more's the pity, and it may be of interest to some to know that there is still a merchant at 76, Hoxton Street, Shoreditch, who will sell you anything for the Toyland Theatres from a proscenium, wings, footlights and orchestra up to a melodrama or pantcmime complete.

Edward Terry joined Nellie Farren to "light the sacred lamp of burlesque" at the Gaiety and good burlesque at the Strand languished and finally died out after a final flicker under Edouin. The theatre came under the direction of Alexander Henderson, husband of Lydia Thompson, who began a series of English versions of French light opera with the best results, creating altogether a new atmosphere at the little theatre and attracting another kind of audience. Florence St. John ("Jack" St. John to all her friends) will long be remembered as the Madame Favart of Offenbach and the Olivette of Audran. She had sung many years before under the name of Florence Leslie at the Oxford Music Hall what time Soldene was also there. Her real name was Margaret Greig. She came of Devonshire stock and at the age of fifteen ran away with a young naval officer, one Harford St. John, whose name she retained to the end of her life. He died of consumption. Later, when singing at a concert for a Catholic charity, she met Lithgow James, an opera singer, and married him, travelling with the Rose Hersee and Blanche Cole opera companies. After a while, again a widow, she married Marius (his real name was Charles Duplany) and when divorced from him took a fourth husband in the person of Arthur Cohen.

Jack St. John came to a very miserable end. Seriously ill, dying in fact, she refused all help from outside, living on what she could make by the sale of her jewellery and clothes and being obliged, at times, to stay in bed to keep warm. An old friend heard of her condition and raised a sum of money for her, but she would not accept it and died independent to the last, leaving a gap which has never been quite adequately filled. It is said that, of all her husbands, she only cared for Marius, and it may have been true. He was very handsome and had a charming manner in his younger days. He, too, came to an untimely end. He died in 1896, barely forty-six years of age, on the way home from South Africa, and was buried at sea.

Other light operas with other "stars" followed. Dolaro made her last appearance in London in "Naval Cadets" with Violet Cameron, who had also been with St. John in "Madame Favart" and "Olivette." After the rebuilding of the theatre in 1882, luck seems to have been gradually leaving this house of so many pleasant memories. In 1882, a piece called "Frolique" was put on. This was by Byron and Farnie, but made no great impression. In 1883, there was a season of Shakespeare and old plays under John S. Clarke, and in this year Minnie Palmer, the evergreen "My Sweetheart," was here at the same time as her compatriot Lotta was over the way at the Opera Comique.

Later, there was a revival of "Our Boys" and the production of a very funny play by Anstey written round his own "Vice Versa."

Daly's Company from the United States, who had made their first appearance in England at the Folly Theatre, paid a second visit in 1886 and chose the Strand Theatre, producing worthless farcical comedies like "A Night Off," "Nancy and Co." and "Casting the Boomerang," in spite of the fact that in the persons of John Drew, Mr. and Mrs. Gilbert and Ada Rehan they had material for the best comedies that had ever been written.

In 1887, a curious adaptation, or mixture, of "Nana" and "La Dame aux Camélias" was produced, presumably for the sake of allowing a Mrs. Kennion to appear in the title rôle. It was a ghastly piece of stupidity and is only worth a passing notice from the fact that Fred Terry appears to have made his first London appearance in it. In September of the same year a very charming original light opera, called "The Sultan of Mocha," was put on by Lydia Thompson who was then running the theatre. In this I notice the name of one of the Sisters Levey in a small part.

The year that followed—1888—was as disastrous for the management of the Strand as it was for the Olympic and other London houses. New pieces were produced in rapid succession and nothing seemed to catch on, though the companies were good and some of the plays charming. Such was "Babette," a light opera with music by Michals. Lydia Thompson was still the principal "boy" supported by Henry Bracy, Fred Mervin, Camille D'Arville and Susie Vaughan. It lasted barely a month, and in February the Edouins first took charge of the theatre, staging a farcical comedy called "Katti the Family Help." In this appeared Alice Atherton (Mrs. Edouin), Albert Chevalier and Susie Vaughan.

In April the programme was supplemented by a burlesque skit on Mrs. Bernard Beere's performance of "Ariane" which at that time was drawing good houses at the Opera Comique opposite. It was called (rather feebly) "Airey Annie." Edouin and Chevalier were principally concerned. Later in the year came "The Treasure," another farce. Frank Rodney, Gillie Farquhar, Kate Lawler, C. W. Somerset and Miss Compton (Mrs. Carton) had joined the company, and I notice also the name of Eleanor Bufton (Mrs. Swanborough) who thus renewed her connection with the theatre in which she had achieved all her earlier successes in burlesque. She did not long survive this engagement, dying early in the nineties, as did also another very old stager, Miss Harriet Coveney, who, with her sister Jane, had been in the Grecian company as long ago as the forties and had starred in every conceivable kind of part.

The Strand had become a sort of clearing house for experiments in new plays and new performers, and was frequently let to budding playwrights or aspiring debutantes—for afternoon scratch perform-ances. One such matinée was given in 1888 for the airing of a play by Pierre Leclercq, a member of the well-known family of pantomimists and actresses. The Charringtons (Janet Achurch and her husband) were in this, Carlotta Leclercq and her nephew, Fuller Mellish. It was called "A Love Story"; but I cannot trace any second performance.

Still in the unlucky 1888—in June, the Edouins put on a new Farce called "Run Wild," having added Harry Eversfield and Grace Huntley (a clever "principal boy" in Drury Lane panto-mimes) to their regular company. It failed. After this there was a faint flicker of success. The management invoked the old spirit of Strand burlesque—such burlesque as had been such a gold mine in the sixties and seventies. The new experiment was called "Aladdin : or the Wonderful Scamp" and was a real old-fashioned piece with breakdowns and good comic business. Edouin was the "Dame"—the immortal Widow Twankay ; his wife, Alice Ather-ton, was Aladdin ; Grace Huntley was the Princess Badralbadour ; Susie Vaughan, a dashing Sultan and Albert Chevalier, Abanazar the Magician. It went with great "go" and when its attractions were exhausted another of the same kind was tried called "Atalanta" with a new company including Marie Linden and the beautiful and talented Alma Stanley, one of those actresses who always seem to me to have missed their chance or, perhaps, never got one. This was in November, 1888, and wound up the disastrous year with hope for the future.

The hope was not realized. In May, 1889, a stupid farcical

comedy, "The Scarecrow," failed, though Fanny Brough and Willie Herbert were in the cast ; and in the same month a new piece of like description was put on called " Æsop's Fables." This had a certain amount of success, with Penley, George Giddens, Rose Saker, Ellaline Terriss and Alma Stanley in the cast—especially good was Miss Stanley as Paquita, a romantic and explosive Spaniard always setting all the men at loggerheads about her.

In June, 1889, a special matinée is worth notice for two reasons. It brought forward Alma Stanley in a serious emotional part showing to what heights she could have risen given the chance ; and the name of " Irene Vanbrugh " first came before the playgoing public.

In this year I note a production at the Avenue Theatre which recalled memories of the old Strand. This was a revival of Brough's burlesque " The Field of the Cloth of Gold." Not the first revival since the old Strand days and decidedly not the best. Chevalier was good as Francis I, and Marie Linden in Ada Swanborough's old part. But Queen Katharine, which had been made so funny in the hands of H. J. Turner, was lost when given to a woman—even one so clever as Miss Maria Davis—and the rest of the cast was negligible.

A matinée at the Strand in July, 1890, saw the revival of Milman's gloomy tragedy of " Fazio," once a standing dish at the theatres where the " Legitimate " was played but laid on the shelf long ago. In this Waller was the Fazio, and a Miss Claire Ivanowa (for whom the matinée was probably given) the Bianca. The Aldabella was a Mrs. Bennett whom I remember as the much persecuted heroine in a score of melodramas at the Surrey. The style that suited the Surrey was, however, hardly one for a play like " Fazio."

In 1891 the Edouins were still in command. Between January and August five new farcical comedies were rapidly produced one after the other and all were too poor to last. Miss May Whitty seems to have become a regular member of the company and Miss Florence West (Mrs. Lewis Waller) appears on the programme once ; as also Fanny Brough, Eva Moore and Marie Illington. Another name of note was that of Miss Annie Goward, who was a relation of Mrs. Keeley and thus made her debut under the same name.

Next year, 1892, " The New Wing," a farcical comedy after the style of " Our Flat," had a measure of success, the cast including Beatrice Lamb and Nina Boucicault, youngest daughter of the great Dion, and the first Peter Pan.

In April of this year they " struck oil " once more with " Niobe ; All Smiles," a semi-farcical comedy, a sort of burlesque of " Pygmalion and Galatea," and having some connection with Anstey's " Tinted

Venus." The success was partly due to the really great comic powers of Harry Paulton and partly to the absolute fitness of Miss Beatrice Lamb for the part of the statue which comes to life. It had quite a long run. The next good "draw" was the revival of "Our Flat," originally produced at the Opera Comique by the Edouins and to be given again and again by them when other pieces failed to attract. This was in 1894, and, thereafter, various changes were rung on farces which had been previously given with some success, and new ones, with Fanny Brough, Alma Stanley and J. L. Shine occasionally in the cast, and once a relapse into burlesque with " Jaunty Jane Shore "—by no means a success.

In 1895, James Welch appears to have been a regular member of the Strand company under Edouin and in November of that year I note a piece called " The Lord Mayor " in the cast of which occurs the name of Laurence Irving.

In 1897, there was a short season of Ibsen at the Strand. Genevieve Ward played in " John Gabriel Borkman," and also in " Pillars of Society." But it was by no means a suitable house for Ibsen and, in spite of the personality of the actress, the attempt was abandoned.

Perhaps the greatest success of the latter days of the Strand was made by the curious mixture called " The Chinese Honeymoon " which so hit the public taste of the moment that it ran for over a thousand nights and brought to the front an odd little actress, called Louie Freear. She must have sung " Sister Mary Jane's Top Note" hundreds of times. She was rather a queer little personality, and always raised shrieks of laughter when she began the chorus of her song with words something like these :

Sit back, hold tight, Mary's going to sing.

I don't know if she was really successful in any other piece except " The Lady Slavey," which I never saw. Tree thought he saw in her the ideal Puck for his production of " A Midsummer Night's Dream," but she failed woefully in the part. She seems to have been meant for " slavey " parts and nothing else.

It is interesting to note that Marie Dainton and Lily Elsie were also in the cast of " The Chinese Honeymoon."

The other farce that drew, in these days, audiences to the Strand was " Our Flat," already mentioned. It was written by a Mrs. Musgrave, who, it is said, sold all the rights for fifty pounds. In all, it must have realized many thousands, for it was played all over the world. She wrote another piece called " Cerise and Co.," which was a failure. The last time I saw " Our Flat " was in Cape Town, though I cannot remember a single member of the cast. Willie

Edouin had considerable scope for his whimsicalities and comic talents, and it was a most easy piece to put on, requiring little scenery or properties. It has become, consequently, a favourite piece for amateurs.

The last days of the Strand were but feeble reflections of its former triumphs, but there remains one actor of note to be considered a little more at length in connection with this theatre.

This was the American, John Sleeper Clarke, not to be confounded with the Clarke who had been a colleague in burlesque with Marie Wilton and married the beautiful Miss Furtado of the Adelphi Theatre.

John S. Clarke, as he was always called, made his first appearance at the Strand so long ago as 1868, as Major Wellington de Boots in "The Widow Hunt," with the inimitable Mrs. Raymond *née* Miss Smith (a clever actress from the Grecian Theatre), as Mrs. Wellington de Boots.

This most amusing of comedies had been done in 1859 at the Haymarket under the title of "Everybody's Friend," with Mr. and Mrs. Charles Mathews, Compton and Buckstone. It was given again at the Olympic in 1865 with some American actors and again at the St. James's in 1867 with a most interesting cast, including Irving and Ada Cavendish in the Mathews' parts, Eleanor Bufton as Mrs. Swansdown and Sophie Larkin as Mrs. Wellington de Boots. In 1875, Clarke made his first appearance in the character with Emily Thorne (a sister of Thomas Thorne) as Mrs. de Boots, Miss Bufton again as Mrs. Swansdown and Harry Crouch and a charming actress, Linda Dietz, in the cast. Clarke revived it again and again—in 1879 and 1883—and I saw it at the Strand when it was repeated in 1885. How many times this amusing piece has been revived in all does not matter ; it is sufficient to note that it has always paid well for its revival. Clarke was a first-class humorous actor and received a warm welcome whenever he appeared. After Major de Boots, his chief character was Dr. Pangloss in "The Heir at Law," but he was equally good in certain Shakespearean parts, as, for example, Dromio in "The Comedy of Errors" or in Sheridan (Bob Acres in "The Rivals") or in adaptations of Dickens of which perhaps the best was Newman Noggs in a version of episodes from "Nicholas Nickleby." He was excellent as Graves in Lytton's "Money," and could make good in emotional parts such as Tyke in Morton's old play "The School for Reform."

Taken altogether, Clarke was a most remarkable actor, perhaps the best that has ever come from America. Yet, good as he was, he was not good enough to revive the fallen fortunes of the Strand. Perhaps the fare he offered was too good for the Strand audience.

His revival of " The Comedy of Errors " was put on in a most lavish manner, but failed to attract.

I think the lost spirit of the old Strand burlesques must have been hovering about the place, resenting the frequent changes in the style of the programme.   Certain it is that the only real successes after the light opera seasons had come to an end were provided by the two farcical comedies " Our Flat " and " Niobe," and that musical mixture " The Chinese Honeymoon."

Strand audiences expected to laugh, and laugh boisterously at rather silly things.   Humour more subtle was lost on them.   Other theatres have their paramount " spirits " in the same way.   Serious plays at the Gaiety go to pieces, and I don't think burlesque or farcical comedy would succeed at either the Princess's or the Lyceum, or melodrama at the Empire or the Alhambra.

And so the day at last arrived when the " Little old Strand " had to be cleared away for widening schemes and the approaches to Kingsway. It had fulfilled its destiny and was ready to go, having faithfully for many years contributed liberally to the gaiety of London play-goers.   Its name, as I have before remarked, has been stolen by a theatre in Aldwych which, not being in the Strand, has no right to it at all.

With no irreverence, I say R.I.P. to the spirit of the little house, for indeed I think it had a soul of its own.

CHAPTER XI

" THE RICKETY TWINS " : THE GLOBE AND THE OPERA COMIQUE THEATRES

THE Globe and the Opera Comique theatres were two uncomfortable, ramshackle houses back to back in that part of East Strand and Newcastle Street which lay between the churches of St. Mary le Strand and St. Clement Danes. The area in the immediate surroundings of these two lost theatres was once covered by Holywell Street, Newcastle Street and part of Wych Street, together with the adjacent courts and alleys—all pulled down for the making of Aldwych, and the widening of the Strand.

There does not seem to be much doubt that the projectors of these two houses knew of the coming demolition and deliberately ran up the theatres as cheaply as possible with a view to making large profits when the time should come for an order for their destruction. Whether this be the fact or not, both these theatres were constructed in the loosest manner and with the greatest disregard for the comfort, or even the safety, of the public. The County Council of the present day, to which, whatever may be their grandmotherly faults, we owe a big debt of gratitude for safeguarding us from faulty and dangerous buildings, would not have passed the plans for either house. The exits were few and narrow—especially in the case of the Opera Comique—the safeguards against fire were inadequate and the general accommodation for playgoers miserable in the extreme. By a curious fatality, however, these were two of the very few theatres that were never destroyed by fire—a fate which overtakes the majority of theatres at least once in their existence.

THE GLOBE THEATRE, NEWCASTLE STREET

This house was built on the actual site of Lyon's Inn which dated back to the time of Henry VIII, and was at one time the abode of Weare, so barbarously murdered by Thurtell in the early days of the nineteenth century. It was the second speculation in theatre-building of Sefton Parry (the first was the Holborn) and was opened in November, 1868, the same year that saw the birth of the Gaiety, one year after the Queen's and the year before the Folly (then called the Charing Cross) was first opened. This was a period of heavy speculation in the erection of theatres and places of entertainment ;

the careers of and not a few of the lost London theatres began about that time.

The Holborn, the Queen's, the Amphitheatre, Holborn, the Globe, the Gaiety, the Charing Cross, the Philharmonic and the Opera Comique were all opened for the first time within four years— 1866-1870—and they have all gone !

The first production at the Globe was a decided success. This was a comedy-drama of modern life called " Cyril's Success " from the prolific pen of Henry J. Byron. The piece was a very good one and might, one thinks, with but slight alteration be revived to-day, that is, if an equally good company could be got together to act it. The names on the bill of the play include those of W. H. Vernon, David Fisher, John Clarke, Miss Henrade (a clever actress who had worked her way up from pantomime fairies to play such parts with Fechter as Madeleine in " The Corsican Brothers " and the Player Queen in " Hamlet "), Maggie Brennan and " Granny " Stephens. In the following year, the author of this play, Henry J. Byron, the witty creator of many Strand burlesques, the perpetrator of puns innumerable, and writer of many a charming comedy, made his first appearance in London as an actor in a play of his own called " Not such a Fool as he Looks," and proved himself to be as capable an actor as he was witty a writer.

Early in 1870 the management tried romantic drama with a piece called " Philomel," by H. T. Craven, the author of several pleasing and harmless plays like " Milky White," " Meg's Diversion," etc., but though the cast included such names as Henry Neville, Lydia Foote, Mrs. Stephens, John Clarke and the beautiful and unhappy Amy Fawsitt—afterwards at the Vaudeville one of the best Lady Teazles I ever saw—it was not a success.

The epidemic of opera bouffe (from the French), started at the Philharmonic and encouraged by those inveterate lovers of it, the Brothers Mansell, reached the Globe ; and " Falsacappa," a version of Offenbach's " Brigands," was put on in 1871, followed in 1872 by Hervé's " L'Œil Crevé " in French.

I think that Blanche D'Antigny appeared in this season ; she was a notorious importation from the Parisian Opera Bouffe stage, not beautiful by any means, but most successful in her own particular line—which appears to have been the captivation of wealthy adorers. Her voice was a mere nothing, but her figure was said to be perfect and her jewels were undoubted. As Fredegonde, the shepherdess, in the first act of Hervé's " Chilpéric " she is said to have worn less clothing than any previous actress who had appeared on the London stage. Like the majority of these " ladies " she had a miserable end, though in her case it was not her own fault. She caught the smallpox in Paris, was turned out of her hotel and died soon afterwards. She was the original of Zola's Nana—smothered in diamonds in her life and dead of a terrible disease.

Other Bouffes followed " Falsacappa," the company including Cornelie D'Anka, a very beautiful woman with rather a lurid career who " looked " all her parts better than she sang them, Marguerite Debreux (the Mephisto of the Lyceum " Petit Faust,") and Harriet Coveney. There was a production of " Madame Angot " with D'Anka a splendid *looking* Lange and Constance Loseby, a charming Clairette, who could at least sing the music.

Early in the seventies Harry Montague (" Handsome Harry ") tried to be a successful manager on his own, having left the trium-virate at the Vaudeville, because he thought he did not get his fair chance with those inveterate lovers of burlesque, Thorne and James. Montague was one of the earliest examples of what are now known as " Matinée Idols," that is, extremely good-looking young men adored in public or in secret by the young women of the day, who buy their photographs—" for home consumption "—and not infrequently send them flowers and *billets-doux* and other tokens of admiration. I do not think this mania was carried to the same extent in Montague's day as it has been in the early decades of the twentieth century, when, as I know in one case, the lucky man finds nightly, on reaching his dressing-room, a stack of flowers and a score or so of letters from strangers—some begging for an appointment, others merely for a smile of recognition for a particular unit in the stalls, and others couched in extravagant terms of admiration. In this particular instance, I am told, the recipient hands all the letters, etc., to his wife to amuse her during his absence

Montague had collected a fine company—David Fisher, Compton, Carlotta Addison, Fanny Josephs and Sophie Larkin, who appeared in one or two comedies by Byron with success, and he might have continued for many years to run the theatre with advantage to himself and the public, if he had not, in a mistaken idea of what he could do himself, produced a fairy comedy by Albery called " Oriana " with music by Fred Clay, in which he cast himself for a part entirely out of his line. In this character he had to sing, and though he possessed a very pretty voice it was also a very small one, and an unkind rumour spread about the theatre that ear trumpets were to be had on hire as well as opera glasses ! Rose Massey was his leading lady. She acted much in the States afterwards.

Montague was originally " discovered " by Boucicault who engaged him for " Jeannie Deans " when he opened old Astley's with a flourish of trumpets as the New Westminster Theatre. Afterwards he was taken up by the Charles Mathews, and he was in the cast of "The Frozen Deep"—Wilkie Collins's play at the Olympic.

A little later, he drifted to America, where he was as popular as in England ; but his brilliant career came to rather a miserable end, and he never saw his native country again. There is a story that he was in love with, and loved by a young English girl of high birth, whose parents would not hear of her marrying an actor. She accidentally heard of his death in the States while at a dinner party, and gave the secret away by fainting on the spot. Whether this tale be true or not, it seems certain that there was some romance in his life.

Montague was one of those *jeunes premiers* whom one cannot imagine making a success in a costume part, though he must have had to wear one many a time in his stage career. He was notoriously incommoded by a strange dress and was essentially at his best dressed in the fashion of his day, and making love to what Quex called a "creamy English girl."

It is indeed quite curious how some actors are quite thrown away on costume plays, while others are never at their best in lounge suits and modern dress clothes. Waller and Kyrle Bellew were examples of the latter, more at ease as D'Artagnan, or Lagadère, or Beaucaire, or Charles Surface, than they would have been as heroes of a modern comedy. Montague was the exact opposite, and examples of both kinds of actors could be multiplied many times. On the other hand, Terriss and Kendal were equally at home in a rôle of any period. Actresses are the same. It requires the supreme genius of a Mrs. Kendal or a Miss Terry to wear past and present day costumes with equal charm. Lady Bancroft, though inimitable as " principal boy " in burlesque, was at her finest when playing in the dress of the nineteenth century.

It is perhaps one of the reasons why plays are so frequently miscast in these days. Authors and managers do not realize always that many artistes, while quite good in the kind of clothes they are accustomed to wear every day, are woefully " out of it " when they try to get into the skin of folk of a past century.

" Blue Beard," Farnie's burlesque on the old fairy tale, was an enormous success when transferred to the Globe from the Charing Cross Theatre, and I have given some account of this really witty production in another chapter. It ran for a long time with the original cast.

In 1876, a version of " Armadale " was produced under the title of " Miss Gwilt." Ada Cavendish played Lydia Gwilt, the heroine-adventuress, Leonard Boyne was Midwinter, and Arthur Cecil gave a wonderful sketch of the villainous Dr. Downward.

In 1877, under the direction of Edgar Bruce, Jennie Lee appeared as Jo, an adaptation of the Dedlock and Tulkinghorn episodes in "Bleak House." Like most plays founded on the novels of Dickens, this was hardly a success. So much of the interest of the great novelist's stories lies in the development of character rather than incident : the plot is vague as a rule and "spread out" if I may use the expression, and a really good play can seldom be made from them. This specially applies to his earlier novels, but, though *Bleak House* is one of his later ones, it forms no exception to the rule. Jennie Lee was most successful in bringing out the sentimental spots in the story often reducing the audience to tears by her portrayal of the woes of the persecuted crossing-sweeper, but that clever actress, Louise Willes, could make nothing of the Lady Dedlock, nor Dolores Drummond of the wicked maid, Hortense.

Jennie Lee was another example of an emotional actress developing from a chorus girl in burlesque or opera bouffe. In Florimond Hervé's "Chilpéric," put on at the Lyceum by the Mansells in 1870, she was the king's page, and at the first production put up her foot on the side of the throne to tie her shoe string. This unrehearsed bit of business brought such roars of laughter that it had to be repeated every night. In "Petit Faust," the second production of the Mansells, she was the crossing-sweeper in silken rags with a golden broom, clamouring for a copper from the Devil when he drove up in a real hansom cab from the Lower Regions.

"Jo" must be included with those phenomenal emotional successes which appeal to the unsophisticated and are always "running" somewhere in the provinces, like "East Lyne," "The Royal Divorce" and "The Ticket of Leave Man."

Edward Righton succeeded Edgar Bruce in the direction of the Globe and put on "Money," "She Stoops to Conquer," and other old-fashioned comedies. He had a first-class company, including Henry Neville, Ryder, Farren, Mrs. John Wood and Mrs. Chippendale, and he alternated his old comedies with melodrama by Paul Merritt and a revival of Plowman's burlesque of "Ivanhoe" that had been such a success at the Court Theatre. In this he resumed his old part of Isaac of York and was supported by Constance Loseby, Rachel Sanger and Charles Collette, a very good cast for a small burlesque.

"Poll and Partner Joe," one of the rare successes of the earlier St. James's, was produced by Righton in 1878, with Mrs. John Wood in her original part—as lively and effective as ever. Toole also appeared this year, but there was nothing really of note till the transfer of "Les Cloches de Corneville" from the Folly Theatre with Shiel Barry still as the Miser. An account of this marvellous success which brought a fortune to London Managers but only a few pounds to the original composer, belongs properly to the account of the Folly Theatre. It is sufficient to say here that, like the " Blue Beard " burlesque transferred from the same little theatre, it ran for hundreds of nights.

In 1880 and 1881 there was a recrudescence of opera bouffe. " Naval Cadets," music by Génée, with Violet Cameron, Dolly Dolaro, Lizzie St. Quentin, Paulton, Loredan and Willie Gregory ; " Les Mousquetaires du Couvent," adapted by Farnie, with Celli, Bracy, Paulton and Alice May ; " La Boulangère a des Écus," music by Offenbach, with Paulton, Celli, Tilly Wafman and Madame Amadi; and then in 1882 a number of successes and failures which made that year quite a notable one in the annals of the ramshackle theatre.

One of the productions was a single matinée performance of Hamilton's adaptation of Ouida's *Moths* remarkable for its splendid cast, including the author himself, Kyrle Bellew, Herbert Standing, Louise Willes, Carlotta Addison and Marie Litton.

In January of this "comet" year, Hermann Vezin produced a new play called " The Cynic," by Herman Merivale, which was simply the story of Faust and Marguerite translated into modern times and modern dress, the devil being a gentlemanly person, in correct evening dress most of the time. It was cleverly written and well acted by Hermann Vezin, Arthur Dacre, Marie Litton and Louise Willes, but was failure No. 1 of this year of failures.

In March, melodrama of the most lurid description took possession. This was represented by " Mankind " a hotch-potch of horrors which might possibly be revived with success in these days when bloody murders and foul crime of all sorts are reported verbatim in the Press and pictures of the " scene of the tragedy " with asterisks and fearsome details fill the pictorial papers. It would be certain to find its public ever ready to sup greedily on horrors. The story turns on the passionate love of a strange being, half man, half monkey, rejoicing in the name of Zacky Pastrana, for a young English maiden. There is a ghastly murder which Zacky takes on himself to shield the girl's lover (needless to say, innocent !) on condition that when he comes out of prison, she will marry him—the man-monkey. Of course it all ends happily, as a proper melodrama should end, but the horrors with which the play abounds, and which take nearly four hours to unfold, are enough to satisfy the most earnest students of the London Sunday Press. This medley was put together by George Conquest and Paul Merritt, two past masters in the art of making your flesh creep. Conquest himself played Zacky Pastrana, adding yet one more to his queer representations of animals and semi-humans. Kyrle Bellew and Marie Litton were the lovers.

It is interesting to note that a wave of melodrama was passing over the West End of London at this time. At the Princess's, Sims's first great London success, " The Lights o' London " had just been produced by Barrett, and " Taken from Life," another of Merritt's sensations, was running at the Adelphi.

In May, 1882, the theatrical and playing worlds of London were much exercised by a pretty quarrel between two dramatists and two managers over two plays closely resembling each other. These were " The Squire," produced by the Kendals at the St. James's, and " Far from the Madding Crowd," brought out by Mrs. Bernard Beere at the Globe. The title of the latter was also the title of a novel by Thomas Hardy, and the play at the Globe was avowedly founded on that novel, being written by Comyns Carr in collaboration with the novelist himself. On the other hand, " The Squire" was by Pinero, who asserted it was an original play of his own.

At this distance of time, no useful purpose is served by going fully into the details of the controversy. One point, however, stands out clearly. While " The Squire " was an excellent piece and attracted large audiences every night, the play at the Globe could not be saved from disaster even by the superlative acting of Mrs. Bernard Beere, who attained the position of a great emotional actress at one stride— a position she never lost. It is easy to forget the past. New generations arise knowing not those who are remembered by us old fogies with regret, for they have their own favourites of the present and cannot really know that the best now is far below the best of former years. " Bernie," as she was known to all her friends, is forgotten, but with the exception of Mrs. Kendal and Ellen Terry there was no English actress of her day who came within measurable distance of her, and now there are none at all.

She was what is generally described as an " emotional actress," and was very high up in that category, giving the idea at times that she had in her the makings of a great tragic actress. But her temperament stood in the way. Tragic rôles require great declamatory powers and also a power of restraint and repose at moments. There was little restraint and no repose about Bernie, and I don't think she could have declaimed blank verse of the more stately kind. In the higher walk of purely emotional acting, she was superb—in certain rôles supreme. During the time she was before the public, there was no one could play Fedora or Floria Tosca as she did. Few would have even looked the parts, and none could have approached her in her passionate interpretation of them.

She was Fanny Whitehead, daughter of a well-known Norfolk artist, member of the Bohemian Club that met at the " Wrekin " where so many Bohemians forgathered. This was a Tavern in

Broad Court, near Drury Lane, now occupied by model lodging-houses, whose landlord at one time was Warner, husband of the tragedienne, Mary Huddart. Miss Whitehead was born somewhere about 1856 in Norfolk. I don't think her family counted for much, but they must have been respectable at any rate, for her godfather was Thackeray, the novelist, who appears to have recognized her talent as a child for he always spoke of her as " the little actress." An uncle of hers was Mr. G. Wingrove Cooke, a barrister on the staff of *The Times*.

Her first appearance in public in London was as a barmaid in the Promenade of the Alhambra. She must have been then a mere girl in years, for in 1877, when only about twenty-one years of age, she had been already some little time on the stage and was playing at the old Opera Comique. In November of that year, she had her first good comedy part—that of Lady Sneerwell in " The School for Scandal " to the Lady Teazle of Ada Cavendish. Next year she was Emilia to the Othello of Henry Forrester, and in 1880 Miami in " The Green Bushes," an old-fashioned melodrama which Celeste had made her own at the Adelphi years before. In 1881, she was still at the Adelphi in Byron's version of " Michael Strogoff," Jules Verne's tale of adventure, one of a cast that included the author, Charles Warner, James Fernandez, F. W. Irish, Miss Gerard and that veteran, Mrs. Hermann Vezin. In the same year she played Lisa in the " Gretchen " of W. S. Gilbert. Thereafter, she alternated between serious emotional drama and high comedy and perhaps attained the zenith of her career at the Haymarket in 1883 as Fedora to the Loris Ipanoff of Coghlan, the Bancrofts being also in the same cast.

As Fedora she was universally pronounced to be second only to Bernhardt, some critics going further still and maintaining that her acting was every bit as good, and that, moreover, she looked the part more thoroughly than the French actress.

In the following year, still at the Haymarket, she scored another remarkable success as Countess Zicka in " Diplomacy," a part woefully miscast in the former production by the Bancrofts at the Prince of Wales's.

From that time, she never once looked back—with two notable exceptions—to which I will refer later. A complete list of all her impersonations would show an extraordinary wide range of characters, though, knowing well her own limitations, I don't think she ever essayed the higher tragic rôles. One cannot imagine her, for instance, as Lady Macbeth or Phedre.

In her later years, her most notable appearances were as Mrs. Sternhold in " Still Waters Run Deep," with Charles Wyndham ;

in " A Woman of No Importance," with Tree ; as Floria Tosca at the Garrick under John Hare ; to the Scarpia of Forbes-Robertson, the Cavarodossi of Waller and the Queen of Rose Leclercq. Many playgoers and critics consider her best part to have been Lena Despard in " As in A Looking Glass "—with its terribly realistic death-scene. Sarah Bernhardt was one who thought it a magnificent performance. She could be hardly brought to believe that any Englishwoman could act so well, but was too conscious of her own superiority not to perceive the greatness of the other, and had the grace to acknowledge it in the most thorough way possible. It is said that her verdict was " Elle est superbe, et je veux créer ça à Paris "—which she eventually did, if only to show that there was no rôle in which anyone else excelled that she could not also make her own.

But even in such a short sketch as this one should not omit to mention her two failures—in " The Promise of May " and in " Far from the Madding Crowd." At the first performance of the former, everything was up against her. She had to contend with a very bad play by the Poet Laureate ; with the presence, in a private box, of Mr. Gladstone whom the pit and gallery chose to regard with loud outspoken disfavour ; with a most unfortunate *lapsus calami* on the part of Tennyson who had innocently allotted to the character played by Hermann Vezin a couple of lines with a double entendre that set the whole house (already inclined to " guy " the piece) rocking with laughter. Moreover, the second night, that egregious person, the Marquis of Queensberry, stood up in the stalls and openly denounced certain lines also spoken by the unfortunate Vezin. In short, the whole production " got the bird " as no show had for many a day.

The other piece that failed was the adaptation of Hardy's novel to which I have already referred.

No discredit attaches to Mrs. Beere for either of these mischances. In each case, she had to contend with a really bad play, and an awful first night. No wonder she succumbed.

As an emotional actress, indeed, she had more than one high qualification : a magnificent stage appearance, a great emotional power and —what is hardly ever found among modern actresses—a wonderful diction. All her lines were beautifully said, not a letter slurred, not a syllable inaudible. On that ground she meets the divine Sarah on equal terms.

In her private life, she was, in truth, not a little odd. At Church Cottage, a sort of tiny residential *bonbonnière* rather hard to find, hidden under the shadow of that hideous Anglican temple St. Marylebone, which tried to cast about the place an aura of classical respectability, " Bernie " used to give the most delightful supper parties, generally on a Sunday night—not at all classical and which many might consider not at all respectable—to all sorts and conditions of men and women.   At these gatherings, Oscar Wilde, then at the zenith of his fame, would scintillate with epigrams more or less brilliant, and Corney Grain would often be found " at the piano."   It was the caprice of the hostess herself to appear at table dressed as a man, in correct evening get-up, which was quite in keeping with the *bizarrerie* of her surroundings, the character of her intimates and the whimsicality of her own disposition.

Mrs. Beere was married three times : firstly, to Captain Dering, son of Sir Edward Dering ; secondly, to Mr. Bernard Beere ; and, thirdly, when no longer young, to H. C. Olivier.

Her last days were far from happy.   She was in very bad health, and her domestic surroundings were not calculated to afford her any consolation for the decline of her powers as an actress.   She died in a nursing home in Maida Vale from heart failure following on peritonitis.   A sad ending to a brilliant career, but, perhaps, partly her own fault.   She had lived every moment of her life at high pressure and had to pay the bill at last.   Some say it was the tremendous strain of her acting as Floria Tosca that hastened her end.   Others declared that she had indeed lived " not wisely but too well."

At the height of her success she had many friends—friends of both sexes and of all sorts, a decidedly mixed crowd.   At the close of her life, there were not so many *en évidence*.   It was the old story. It was the way of the world.   The friends of success are not the friends of failure.   They fall away when the object of their one-time friendship becomes poor or is ill, or " out of the swim," or no longer amusing in any way.   With a return to prosperity, they would flock round once more—for what they could get !

Yet I may hope that " Bernie " kept some of her friends to the last, in spite of all that told against her—and indeed I do know of one woman who was a very timely help at an opportune moment.   All honour to her.   It is hard to believe that this was the only one who went near her in her agony, and I do not think it was so.   However that may have been, there must be still some alive who recall her acting with the greatest pleasure.

No woman has since appeared competent to fill the place left vacant when she passed to the other side.

In September, 1882, there was a reaction at the Globe Theatre to comic opera, a poor specimen of the English kind being put on by Sydney Grundy and Edward Solomon called " The Vicar of Bray." In spite of Penley, a really humorous actor, and some clever ladies in the cast, it barely lasted two months, and was replaced by a new play written for Mrs. Beere by Tennyson and called " The Promise of May." It was one of the historic failures of the London stage. The stars in their courses fought against it. I don't think it ran a week. The real story of that evening has not, I think, yet been printed. Perhaps it is unprintable.

Another attempt of Mrs. Beere's at the Globe was in a dramatization of Charlotte Bronte's " Jane Eyre." I shall always regret that I did not happen to see this impersonation of hers which, according to the best contemporary critics, was of astounding force. The version was by Wills, and Mrs. Beere's success was, perhaps, greater than it really appeared. She was badly supported, Kelly being especially stated to have been a failure in the chief male character.

I may note that a version of " Jane Eyre " had been brought out two years previously at the insignificant Park Theatre in Camden Town with a clever actress, Stella Brereton, as the heroine, but Mrs. Beere left her, of course, a long way behind. At the Globe the cast included Kate Bishop (mother of Marie Löhr) as Blanche Ingram and Carlotta Leclercq (forty years before a Columbine in pantomime) as Lady Ingram.

In 1883, Sydney Grundy's polished comedy of modern manners, " A Glass of Fashion," commanded a certain amount of success. It was well written and well acted by Miss Lingard, Carlotta Leclercq, Lottie Venne and Beerbohm Tree, but the ventures of that year were not of much account. " Lady Clare," an English version of Ohnet's " Maître de Forges "—not nearly so well written or so well put on as the Kendals' play founded on the same romance and known as " The Ironmaster "—had but a short run. To tell the truth, it was the case of " The Squire " and " Far from the Madding Crowd " all over again. It was quite useless to compete in a new version of a play if Madge Robertson had already created the chief part in the same story. She just overshadowed her contemporaries in her own particular line and they had to accept the situation as it was.

When the Globe came under the management of Hollingshead and J. L. Shine, they relied chiefly on the personality of the Dion Boucicaults, father and mother of the present actor of that name, and the attraction of Irish plays of the nature of " The Shaughraun," etc., so that once more the Newcastle Street Theatre changed the style of its programme.

In 1884, the second of the outstanding successes of the Globe materialized in " The Private Secretary," an adaptation of a German play, " Der Bibliotheker," that had been first seen at the Prince's Theatre with R. C. Carton and Beerbohm Tree in the chief parts. Tree was not the first representative of the part that Hawtrey made famous. The original was Arthur Helmore—still, I believe, going strong in this world of woe. When it was transferred to the Globe by Hawtrey, he took Carton's part and Penley replaced Tree. Hawtrey had taken the theatre as a very doubtful speculation, having to collect the money from money-lenders and where he could get it to pay the current salaries ; it turned out a little gold mine and still produces a good income for its fortunate owners, as does also " Charley's Aunt," the third phenomenal success of an otherwise unlucky house. It is curious to note that the three productions (" Les Cloches de Corneville," " Private Secretary " and " Charley's Aunt ") which made the fortunes of the Globe Management of the day—not to mention also " Blue Beard "—were all first produced and failed at other theatres, two of the four having been first tried at the Folly.

After some years of " The Private Secretary " and a successor to it called " The Arabian Nights," in which Hawtrey once more excelled as a liar, Wilson Barrett made his *rentrée* in London, after his American visit, at the Globe with a play by Sims and himself called " The Golden Ladder." His company included Miss Eastlake and Mrs. Henry Leigh ; Cooper Cliffe ; his brother, George Barrett ; and a clever child, Phœbe Carlo, who was the first Alice in Wonderland. This was almost a great melodrama, but the audience took upon itself to object to the realities of a prison scene and the sufferings of Miss Eastlake as the heroine were declared to be too poignantly real. The same " sloppy " sentimentality had been shown years before on the first night of " It's Never too Late to Mend," at the Princess's.

" The Golden Ladder " did not run for more than a few weeks and was followed by " The Lady of Lyons " with Miss Eastlake in the title rôle and Barrett as Melnotte. This was a failure, because Miss Eastlake, however good she might be in the drama of rags and tatters or as an emotional Greek courtesan, lacked the distinction necessary for the part of a *grande dame*. The cast was excellent in all other respects, Mrs. Henry Leigh, as Madame Deschapelles, being exceptionally good.

After the withdrawal of Lytton's play, the programme was constantly being changed, for the year 1888 was no luckier for the Globe than for other theatres. " Bootle's Baby " was dramatized, and Minnie Terry made what was, perhaps, her first appearance on the stage as the Baby ! Then in October came a weird play called " The Monk's Room " with Willard, Hermann Vezin and Miss Alma Murray.

But it was not till December of that year that any remarkable novelty was seen at the Globe. This was the visit of Richard Mansfield, an American, with a great name in his own country and from whom great things were expected. He made his debut in "Prince Karl" and falling ill (or failing to attract) retired for a time, Kate Vaughan taking over the theatre for a revival of Old Comedy. She chose "She Stoops to Conquer" with quite a good cast, Lionel Brough playing Tony Lumpkin; May Whitty, Miss Neville; Willie Herbert, Marlow; and Carlotta Leclercq, Mrs. Hardcastle.

Mansfield returned in 1889 to appear in "Richard III," which Americans considered his best part. He had good support with Carlotta Leclercq as the Duchess of York, Mary Rorke as Elizabeth Woodville, and Isa Bowman and Bessie Hatton as the young Princes. But he failed to draw, and gave up his season in disgust with the bad taste of English audiences.

I never saw him personally, but have always heard it said that he was greatly chagrined at the comparative failure of his visit, for he himself was fully persuaded that he was the equal, or maybe superior of Irving, then at the zenith of his fame.

In 1890, E. F. Benson, the Sir Frank Benson of to-day, had his first London season at the Globe, producing "A Midsummer Night's Dream" with all the completeness and taste which have ever since been the keynotes of his management. The achievements of Sir Frank Benson as a producer and as a trainer of young people for the dramatic profession are too well known to require many words from me. He has been instrumental in giving some of our best actors and actresses to the stage : his company has been a real school for the advancement of dramatic art, and he, with his clever and sympathetic wife, have done more for the English stage than any other combination of modern times. When there are more companies like the Bensons', affording experience of all kinds for the aspirant to dramatic fame, there will be a genuine revival of English dramatic excellence —and not till then.

In Shakespeare's fairy play, Benson and Herbert Ross were the lovers, their ladies being Ada Ferrar and Kate Rorke. Weir was Bottom, one of the best I know. Stephen Phillips, the poet, author of "Nero," "Paolo and Francesca" and "Herod" was Quince; Otho Stuart was Oberon; Mrs. Benson, Titania; Grace Geraldine, Puck; and Jessie Bateman, Cobweb the fairy.

For the next two years the fortunes of the Globe languished again. There was a light opera called "The Black Rover," founded on the story of The Flying Dutchman with John Le Hay, Ludwig and Collette, and then Norman Forbes took the house for a time, with disastrous results I am afraid, producing a doleful play (from America) called "All the Comforts of Home"—the title of which alone should suffice to da n it. This was followed by, inter alia, a piece called "The Scapegoat" in which Lewis Waller and his clever wife (acting as Florence West) appeared with Annie Hughes and the evergreen Carlotta Leclercq.

Without adhering strictly to dates, one may recall one or two productions about this time in which the Wallers appeared—such as " Gloriana " by James Mortimer (editor of *The London Figaro*) at the end of 1891, " A Bohemian " in 1892, and a play founded on incidents in the life of Shakespeare with young Thalberg (a very handsome *jeune premier* but not much of an actor) as Shakespeare, Beatrice Selwyn as Queen Elizabeth, Mary Keegan, a bright young actress from the provinces as Elizabeth Throgmorton. It was a poor play and ran for a week only, and would be hardly worth mentioning but that Mrs. Dion Boucicault (the original Colleen Bawn) was also in the cast.

At the end of the year there was a return to light opera in the production of " Ma Mie Rosette " by Ivan Caryll, among the artistes being Laurence D'Orsay, Frank Wyatt, Jessie Bond and Juliette Nesville—the original " Miss Helyett " which had had the distinction of being the first musical comedy.

Then came the third long run—that of " Charley's Aunt " with Penley as the old lady from Brazil " where the nuts come from." This ran for four years and Penley made a fortune. Hearing that the new Kingsway was likely to absorb the Novelty Theatre in Great Queen Street he bought that unlucky little house for a sum usually set down as £150,000. But the Kingsway in its cold austerity passed it by and Penley was saddled with a theatre that had a name for being the unluckiest in London and which he could not let at all. Poor little Penley, who gave such pleasure to countless thousands of playgoers, eventually went out of his mind. Too much success was not good for a man of his rather feeble character.

Charley's Aunt brought, as usual, imitators in her train. George Grossmith, who had made his name in Savoy Opera, thought he could do as well as Penley in a similar part, and produced " Miss Francis of Yale "—a dismal failure as it deserved to be.

In 1898, once more the theatre returned to melodrama, but melodrama of the romantic kind with Lewis Waller and his clever wife, Miss Florence West, as the chief characters in a stirring version of Dumas' masterpiece *The Three Musketeers*. This book had been dramatized more than once already, notably for Charles Dillon whose forte was *cappa e spada* rôles. In such parts, however, Waller was distinctly his superior for he had none of the mannerisms that disfigured all acting of the Dillon School and, indeed, he seemed to be a personality of the period represented rather than of the more prosaic times of the nineteenth century. He was absolutely at home in the dress of romantic lovers of a swashbuckling sort, like Lagardere and D'Artagnan ; he made them seem real and possible in these matter-of-fact times. And his handsome wife was the finest support that any actor could desire.

The play was an extraordinary success while it lasted, but it had been produced under some difficulties and the affair is not quite clear on many points. It appears that Waller had engaged Henry Hamilton the clever play-wright, to prepare a version of " The Three Musketeers " for him and his wife. A few days after Hamilton had nearly completed his version Beerbohm Tree announced that he was about to produce " His Majesty's Musketeers," founded on the novel of Dumas by Sydney Grundy. Waller got his play out first in spite of the fact that Fredericks, the manager of the Stratford Borough Theatre, threatened to get an injunction to prevent him cancelling an engagement with him. Fredericks failed to get the injunction and the play, after a preliminary run at the Metropole, Camberwell, was put on at the Globe. Then Tree (who, it is asserted, did not wish Waller to blossom into a great actor manager) sent for him and offered him such big terms that he felt he could not refuse and he bound himself to Tree for three years. The run of the " Musketeers " at the Globe ended suddenly, although it was undoubtedly a far finer play than that prepared by Grundy, and Waller was an ideal D'Artagnan, which Tree was not. I have had another and more intimate version of the affair told me by Mrs. Lewis Waller when we forgathered in South Africa—but it is ill work stirring up mud of any kind and the actors concerned have passed beyond the veil.

Playgoers flocked to the Globe to see the new D'Artagnan, and old stagers congratulated themselves that at last the great days of the romantic drama had returned, while the younger generation were all delighted with something the like of which they had never seen before, for Irving's limitations made it impossible to compare him with Waller, and the best days of Henry Neville were away back in the sixties and seventies.

The élan of the whole performance carried the audience away with enthusiasm. There was no waiting, no disastrous pauses— that is, pauses that would have been disastrous in a play dealing with the adventures of the Gascon. The long speech describing his search for the Duke of Buckingham, his grim scene with Miladi when he uncovers the felon's mark on her shoulder and the general " Swagger " of the whole conception are quite unforgettable for all who saw it.

Mrs. Waller's " Miladi " was a fine performance ; her rage and fury when D'Artagnan had unmasked her, and her impotent beating at the doors of the locked room with the dagger that had failed to reach his heart, were evidences of how great an emotional actress she really was. Many years afterwards when she was acting in South Africa, and I saw a good deal of her in Maritzburg and Durban, we talked over this performance. She always declared it was the finest thing Waller ever did, not even excepting his Hotspur to the Lady Percy of Lady Tree ; and she said her own performance as Miladi was nearly the best thing she had done, though I think she fancied herself most in a rather disgusting play called " Zaza," which Réjane had created in Paris.

Hamilton's version of the Dumas Romance should have run for a year, but it lasted barely three months.

Early in 1899, Hare took the Globe for a revival of some of Robertson's comedies that had been so successful at the old Prince of Wales's Theatre. He began his season with "Ours," but it was merely a preamble to the production of a new play by Pinero called " The Gay Lord Quex." This was wonderfully well written, well cast and extraordinarily well acted. The company included Hare himself, Dawson Milward, then doing lovers' parts, Irene Vanbrugh, Miss Fortescue (at one time a fairy in " Iolanthe " at the Savoy) and Fanny Coleman. Each part was well filled, being cast with a proper regard to the capabilities of the individual actor or actress. Great acting was necessary for the scene between Quex and the ill-bred manicurist, and great acting it was. Years afterwards this fine play was revived at a theatre much too big for it, with a musical comedy star as Quex and a revue artiste as the manicurist. The force of miscasting could go no further and it was withdrawn.

The career of the Globe Theatre was fast approaching to a close. In 1900, Wilson Barrett had it for a short season and in 1901 the chief attraction was that most charming of all actresses in costume parts—Julia Neilson.

She produced a play on the subject of Nell Gwynne called " Sweet Nell of Old Drury," and though it was a trifle crude, in parts savouring too strongly perhaps of melodrama, the success was never in doubt, owing to the fine acting of Julia Neilson as Nell, and of her husband, Fred Terry, as Charles II.

What a wonderful family are those Terrys ! Time seems to have no effect upon them as it does on mere ordinary mortals. Fred Terry, as I write, is still playing the young man on the stage as if the flight of time had verily stopped for him alone. He may be a grandfather, but he is younger than ever.

In 1902 the old theatre was shut up for good and all. The long threatened house-breaker came along. Holywell Street was shifted to Charing Cross Road as regards its book shops, and its old clothes shops probably went to Monmouth Street and the Dials generally. It was a dirty and insanitary place enough and Newcastle Street, the actual situation of the Globe Theatre, was the same ; but I have spent many most delightful days rummaging among the printed treasures of its dusky recesses. Charing Cross Road does not afford the same thrill of expectation, nor is it so fertile in what it yields of value. Mr. Josephs, who was in Holywell Street so long (as his father before him I believe), is now in Charing Cross Road ; but for him also, I fancy, the regret is for the older, if less sanitary, thoroughfare. Mine is, I confess.

THE OPERA COMIQUE THEATRE, EAST STRAND

This back to back twin of the Globe, familiarly known as the " Op. Com." and derisively as the " Theatre Royal Tunnels," was entered from the narrow part of the Strand nearly opposite the door of the Strand Theatre. It was a queerly planned house ; like the Globe, jerry-built in the hope of big profits when the street should be widened, and it was approached by long underground passages and stairs where, in the event of a fire, hundreds of persons would certainly have lost their lives. Like its twin, however, it was never burned down.

A theatre so recklessly planned would not now be permitted. It was opened in 1871, three years after, and finally shut in 1899, three years before the Globe. It could therefore only boast of eighteen years of existence.

It is hard to see why this theatre was called the Opera Comique, and the name was always a handicap. Perhaps because it was built at the height of that rage for opera bouffe which began in 1870 and continued to nearly the end of the eighties.

At first it justified its name, starting with an operetta founded on a comedy of Molière's, with music composed by that same D'Oyley Carte who afterwards managed the Savoy Operas with such success. He was probably a better manager and organizer than composer, for I have not traced any other musical plays by him. His first wife was a Miss Keith Prowse and thus were the foundations of a great theatrical business house well and truly laid.

D'Oyley Carte's operetta was called " The Doctor in spite of himself," and seems to have been a poor show. In the cast were several well-known names. E. Atkins, a very useful and experienced actor who had done a bit of everything in his career. He was in the original cast of " The Ticket of Leave Man," with Neville, and acted with Fechter in some of his productions. He was also a great pantomimist and I have a dim personal recollection of him as the Queen of Spades in a pantomime long, long ago—where and when I have forgotten. With him were Lin Rayne, Lizzie Russell and the Capt. Crosstree and Black Eyed Susan from the Dean Street Royalty—Fred Dewar and Patty Oliver. There was a Ballet included in the programme, but the necessity for a change was soon apparent and a change indeed it was, for the Comédie Française company from Paris in their entirety came over and opened at the new theatre amid a flourish of trumpets and after a public welcome at the Crystal Palace, on which occasion Lord Granville, Lord Dufferin, Lord Houghton, and others assisted the critics and chief London Managers to welcome the great French artistes. The company included Got, Delaunay, Bressant and Maubant, Madame Favart and Mlle. Reichemberg. It was an odd coincidence that the failure of an English adaptation of a Molière comedy should be redeemed by the appearance of the whole company from the House of Molière itself. For many years, there had been a steady hostility against the introduction of foreign artistes on to the English stage. Mitchell, the Bond Street librarian, had practically the monopoly of introducing French players to London, and the St. James's Theatre was usually the only house at which you could see them. Then first one and then another broke down the monopoly. Old John Ryder, the most determined opponent of anything foreign, had succumbed to the success of Fechter and of his own pupil, Stella Colas, who is said to have "set the critics' teeth on edge but have delighted the general public"—not a bad way of saying that she was a fine actress, for the critics of those days were in general a disgruntled lot who placed English actors first and any foreigner a bad second.

It is true that Rachel and Dejazet and Desclée and others had been seen at the St. James's and the Princess's and also the Grand Duchess of Gerolstein herself, Hortense Schneider. But their visits did not pay the impresario who brought them over, and it was left to the Comédie Française to break through the rule and acclimatize, so to speak, foreign players in England.

After the Comédie Française came French Opera Bouffe adapted into English words : Hervé's " L'Œil Crevé," Offenbach's " Bohemians," Jonas' " Wonderful Duck " (" Canard à Trois Becs ") followed by a piece by Burnand called " Little Tom Tug." This brings the story of the theatre down to the end of 1873. In the following year a French company came from Brussels and made quite a success with opera bouffe in French—" Angot," " Giroflé-Girofla," " La Petite Mariée " and others less well known to English playgoers. These were under the regular managements of the theatre which varied from time to time. But I should have noted in 1873 some appearances of the great Italian tragedienne Ristori who was seen in some of her most famous impersonations, including

MR. AND MRS. KENDAL

AS ORLANDO AND ROSALIND IN "AS YOU LIKE IT"

From a photograph kindly lent by Mrs. Kendal

Elizabeth, Queen of England, Marie Stuart and (in English) the sleep-walking scene from " Macbeth."

For the time nothing seemed to succeed at this theatre ; nothing lasted very long and it was certainly not a popular place of amusement. There was no pit, its place being taken by a ground-floor dress circle, probably better for seeing, but which did not seem to the conservative British playgoer quite the same thing. Management succeeded management without much success. Burnand seems to have had a good deal to do with it in the seventies and in the autumn of 1875 was actually the manager, his company including Mrs. Leigh Murray (a veteran), Willie Herbert, W. J. Hill, Patty Oliver Flockton and Markby. In this year, under Hollingshead, Mr. and Mrs. Kendal appeared in a round of serious plays, including " The Lady of Lyons," " She Stoops to Conquer " and " As You Like It." For some unexplained reason, their season was not a success though in my opinion Mrs. Kendal's Rosalind has only been equalled by that of Miss Litton, and never surpassed.

In 1876, the Gaiety Company are here and one of their best burlesques—" The Bohemian G'yurl " is seen for the first time with the Gaiety quartet—Terry, Royce, Nelly Farren and Kate Vaughan all complete—preceded by comedies by Byron in which the author himself took part.

In 1877, Charles Mathews, then about seventy years of age, reappeared on the stage in some of his best known parts like " My Awful Dad," etc. I saw him at this time and it was certainly rather a melancholy performance, an instance of how to linger too long before the public. Just before this sad resuscitation from the Past, Soldene had given a season with Offenbach " Madame L'Archiduc " which she declared to me was the part she did best, but which was certainly the least popular of all her rôles. And there had been also previously to Mathews (I am not keeping strictly to dates) under the direction of Hare, some further performances of standard plays like " The Lady of Lyons," " She Stoops to Conquer " and " As You Like It," with the Kendals, Arthur Cecil (Touchstone), Ryder, Mrs. Buckingham White, Hermann Vezin (Jacques) ; but these were, so to speak, scratch performances, or very short seasons.

In 1877, Rose Leclercq appeared in Matthison's version of Mrs. Hodgson Burnett's tale *That Lass o' Lowrie's* and created quite a sensation as Liz, the mill hand ; but it ran only a couple of months or so and after another failure came the first real success of the Opera Comique—the first of that brilliant series of Gilbert and Sullivan Operas which enabled their fortunate proprietor to build a new house specially for them in the Savoy and give rise to the expression " Savoy Opera."

" The Sorcerer " was the first of the regular series, though it was the second or third of the collaboration that went on for years. Some time before, a short musical piece, " Trial by Jury," had been given at the Royalty as a first piece before " La Perichole," but this has now been incorporated in the regular series and there are many unaware that it was not produced in sequence with the others. There had also been a musical absurdity called " Thespis " at the Gaiety.

The first of the series at the Opera Comique was well cast, for among the artistes we find Rutland Barrington, Temple, George Grossmith, George Power, and Mrs. Howard Paul, who had been before the public for many years and was a really great artiste in her own line. She was born Isabella Featherstone and had played many famous parts. She was excellent as Macheath at the old Strand in " The Beggars' Opera " and had previously played (in 1853) Lucy Lockit in the same. She was Her Highness of Gerolstein at Covent Garden in 1867—one of the best of the English ones—and sang in " Babil and Bijou " in 1872 when Lord Londesborough dropped some ten thousand pounds over that production. Mrs. Howard Paul once appeared with great success at Drury Lane as Lady Macbeth to the Macbeth of Phelps and, what is more, doubled the part of Hecate in the same production. A great artiste. She died in 1879.

" H.M.S. Pinafore " followed in 1878 ; " The Pirates of Penzance " in 1880 ; and " Patience" in 1881. This was transferred to the new Savoy Theatre and the " Op. Com." knew Gilbert and Sullivan no more. It is unnecessary for me to give any details of these wonderful light operas. They are *sui generis* and their tale has been told, and charmingly told, by Mr. Walbrook in his book on the subject, a book which every lover of the theatre should have among his works of reference.

" The Spectre Knight " with charming music by Alfred Cellier, book by Albery, had preceded " The Sorcerer," and was suspended for the production of the Gilbert and Sullivan Opera. I do not know that it was ever revived. Cellier was the first conductor of the Savoy operas which were in the beginning produced by a company styled " The Comedy-Opera Company Limited." This was before anyone connected with the scheme had imagined that the success would be so great. It was a venture to make money and several companies were formed for the provinces, among the personnel of which it is interesting to note names of some who were seen at the Savoy later—notably Rosina Brandram. Harriet Coveney's name also crops up and she was no doubt as cheery and gay as she had been forty years before at the old Grecian Saloon.

After the departure of the " Savoyards," the theatre then being under the management of John Hollingshead and Barker, the programme was " Princess Toto," a rather pretty light opera by Gilbert with music by Clay. This had been originally produced at the old Strand Theatre in 1876 with Kate Munro, Emma Chambers and Harry Paulton. At the Opera Comique the characters were taken by Richard and George Temple, Robert Brough, Loredan, Alfred Bishop and Annette Albu. In 1882, there was a burlesque (" Vulcan ") with Brough, Temple and Annie Rose (Mrs. Horace Nevill) ; this was followed for a short run by a farce of George R. Sims called " The Mother-in-Law " and then a curious experiment was made of providing the whole evening's entertainment without the assistance of a single man—though I strongly suspect that the scene shifters and all those who had to do the really "hard chores" would have been found to belong to the despised sex. The company was Miss Lilla Clay's, all ladies ; the members of the orchestra were all ladies ; the piece was written by a lady ; it was called " An Adamless Eden " and contained no male part. The effect was curious but not unpleasing for a little while. After a time it became monotonous, and the scheme of " doing without us " fizzled out.

Lotta, the much appreciated (in America) American actress, made her first appearance in 1883, and, oddly enough, another American favourite, Minnie Palmer, was acting at the same time at the old Strand Theatre exactly opposite. Lotta, whose real name was Charlotte Crabtree, was an enormous favourite in her own country, and I was adjured by American acquaintances not to fail to go and see her—so I went.

I am glad it was not the first night when a curious play called " Musette " was put on with Arthur Dacre in the cast. The piece seems to have been of the type one would expect to meet at the outlying transpontine theatres or even at a Richardson's Show, with wicked noblemen pursuing innocent maidens of the poorer class, a sort of *London Journal* or *Family Herald* story. It was received with hisses and cat-calls. Every player was hissed indiscriminately, no matter what he or she said or did, and there was an organized riot of the most determined kind. It was said that the playgoers resented the preliminary puffing which had heralded the coming of the American actress ; it was also said that the riot was arranged by a rival actress ; it was likewise urged that the real cause was the unpopularity of Arthur Dacre with the virtuous audience because he had recently been the chief figure in a divorce case. I do not think the true reason was ever discovered. Whatever it was, it killed the stupid play and nearly sent the actress home by the next boat. She was a plucky little thing (one of the very smallest actresses I have ever seen) and had a good following among the American colony in London.

In fact, one was pestered with her praises before ever she appeared.
The obnoxious piece was withdrawn and the obnoxious actor with
it, and Lotta tried her luck again with a version of scenes from "The
Old Curiosity Shop " in which she doubled the parts of Little Nell and
the Marchioness as had often been done before by Virginia Blackwood
and other English actresses.   Her success was immediate and complete ; but I do not fancy she paid a second visit to this country.
She was sufficiently appreciated in her own, and after keeping a
boarding-house for many years died worth a million dollars.

Miss Elizabeth Marbury in her book of Reminiscences says that
the majority of American great dramatic successes are home-brewed.
Miss Marbury is a successful play agent and placer of plays from all
sources, and may be presumed to know what she is talking about.
But because these great home-brewed plays are successes in the States,
it does not follow that they will be successful over here.   There is
no reason why we should expect them to be so.   Two nations so
absolutely diverse as the American and the English, especially in
their ideas as to what constitutes good taste, are sure to have different
views as to the value of dramatic work.   I do not think Lady Bancroft ever went to America and I am not sure that they would have
appreciated her if she had gone.   Dan Leno—a really humorous
actor—was a frost in the States, and Dixey, whom my American
acquaintances assured me was a really great actor, and who was
certainly very popular in the States, failed utterly here, nor was his
failure as an actor the least bit redeemed by his lack of good taste.
I am sometimes told that the best American actors and actresses do
not come here, but it is surprising if they do not, for they all sigh
after the approval of a great London audience.   Perhaps the best
plan would be for each nation to maintain its excellence in its own
country, and be content with that.

Mrs. Bernard Beere, after her astounding successes at the Globe,
appeared at the Opera Comique in a piece called " As In a Looking
Glass," founded on the novel of the same name by F. C. Phillips.
This writer, author of several smart stories of a rather decadent kind,
was better known in the dramatic world as Francis Fairlie, adaptor
of the texts of many French Opera Bouffes for the brothers Mansell.
Another play on his disagreeable novel *The Dean and His Daughter*,
was put on at the St. James's in 1888 for Olga Nethersole.

Lena Despard, the besmirched heroine of "As In a Looking Glass,"
was by no means an easy part, but Mrs. Beere played it to perfection.
The grim death scene was a triumph of realism and I have been
assured that even Bernhardt, great actress as she was, could not equal,
much less surpass, Mrs. Beere as Lena Despard.

In February, 1888, another success was scored by Mrs. Beere in an adaptation by Mrs. Campbell Praed of her book *The Bond of Wedlock* which was produced under the title of " Ariane." Mrs. Bernard Beere made as much as she could of the play, but it was evident that, skilful story-teller as was Mrs. Praed, she had not the knack of writing a successful play, and the run was short. In the cast were old favourites like Marius, Neville, Boyne, Laura Linden and clever Fanny Coleman who made such a hit as the old peeress in " The Gay Lord Quex."

In July of the same year, Mrs. Beere played in " Masks and Faces " and after that her connection with the theatre finished. In August Bandmann put on a version of " Mr. Jekyll and Mr. Hyde " in competition with Mansfield, the American actor, who had produced another version of the same story at the Lyceum two days before. It was sharp practice and foolish for an actor like Bandmann to try and beat the American in what was considered his best part, and he failed to attract paying audiences.

The next show at the Opera Comique has a sentimental touch about it. It was a light opera written by the veteran, Blanchard— then fast approaching his end—and called " Carina " after that beloved wife whom he had lost in early years when she married another and emigrated to New Zealand, and then found in the autumn of his life to be a comfort to him in his last days. This tale of Blanchard's sweetheart whom he thought he had lost for ever is one of the most romantic I have ever known and has the distinct advantage of being absolutely true and ending as all tales should with " they lived happily to the end." Durward Lely (late of Savoy Opera), Camille D'Arville, Collette and Snazelle were in the cast.

1889 saw the production of a very curious piece called " The Panel Picture," in which Lady Monckton and Henry Esmond acted. It was, according to all accounts, an impossible piece with an incomprehensible story, and ran only eight nights. One of the characters has to say " What's going on in the house ? " and as this was just what the audience wanted to know the remark was received with roars of laughter and killed the play—dead.

A series of revivals followed. " Little Lord Fauntleroy," with Marion Terry as Mrs. Errol, and " Forget Me Not," for a series of matinées.

Towards the end of the year Willie Edouin put on a piece of absolute nonsense called " Our Flat," which he bought for about fifty pounds and which must have put hundreds if not thousands in his pocket. Revived again and again, and beloved of amateurs for the ease with which it can be staged, I have already made some mention of it in the chapter on the Strand Theatre. I note also in the same year (1889) a romantic opera called " The Castle of

Como," with a plot founded on "The Lady of Lyons," and early the following year a revival of "Juana," that gloomy play which Barrett had originally produced at the Court Theatre, in 1881, wherein the heroine stabs herself and goes raving mad. Not a cheerful entertainment, but well played by Frances Ivor and Leonard Outram.

In 1891 the programme was entirely changed and once more success appeared to be in view for the Op. Com. A burlesque of a good old-fashioned kind called "Joan of Arc" was put on with Arthur Roberts, J. L. Shine, Emma Chambers, Katie Seymour, a dainty dancer of the Kate Vaughan type, and Alma Stanley, looking gloriously handsome in a "Breeches" part. It ran for quite a respectable time and was succeeded by an adaptation by Henry James of his novel *The American*. This was played by a really good company, including Kate Bateman (Mrs. Crowe), Louise Moodie, Elizabeth Robins, Adrienne Dairolles—a bright actress in a light rôle—and Edward Compton. In spite of it all, it failed and the Compton Comedy Company, who were running the theatre at the time, fell back on Old Comedy and put on Holcroft's "Road to Ruin." Compton was so ill-advised as to try a new play founded on Longfellow's *Courtship of Miles Standish*, in which Miss Fortescue essayed the part of Priscilla. It was a failure and he had better have stuck to old comedy.

The year 1892 was a bad year for the little house, and failure succeeded failure : a play from the German, with Jessie Millward as the heroine ; a season of Variety, with Frank Lindo as a mimic —perhaps the most noteworthy of the artistes ; and a Musical Comedy by Edouin and his clever wife, with Fred Mervin and Harry Eversfield thrown in.

In 1893, George Moore had a play called "The Strike at Arlingford," with Mrs. Lewis Waller and Elsie Chester in the cast, but it barely ran a month, and was succeeded by a season of Arthur Dacre and his wife, Amy Roselle, in a drama of David Belasco's. Neville, Standing, Fulton, Sam Sothern, Oscar Asche, Lena Ashwell and Eva Moore were in the cast, but it made no impression. During these years of the decline of the Op. Com. there had been a burlesque on the story of "Trilby," with Nellie Farren, but, alas, not the Nellie that the boys had loved at the Gaiety, and she had to give up very soon. There were some French plays, and Kate Vaughan in some old comedy revivals. The theatre was often taken for the productions of the Independent Theatre—Ibsen and the like—and Mrs. Langtry made a fitful appearance in a piece by Robert Buchanan called "A Society Butterfly." It was a rôle that suited her, for it was practically a slice of her own life and did not require much acting, so to speak ; but it was not a success. Robert Buchanan as a playwright is not a name to conjure with except in such pieces as " Alone in London " and plays of a similar kind which have their special audiences.

In 1898 " Alice in Wonderland "—now a hardy annual—saw the light for the first time at the Opera Comique, and I think one of the last, if not the very last novelty produced here was in 1899— a piece by George R. Sims called " A Good Time : or Skipped by the Light of the Moon," the nature of which may be gathered from the title.

Previously to that I should have noticed a season by the company of the Deutsches Theater from Berlin who did some plays in German ; the audiences appear to have been limited in number, as might have been expected. One of the plays produced was " Der Bibliotheker," the original of " The Private Secretary."

In 1899 the theatre was closed for good and all. It was quite an artistic little house in appearance, but, as I have already noted, much handicapped by its foreign name and still more by the death-traps through which one had to pass to get in or out of it. It was a boast of the management of the Comedy-Opera Company (Gilbert and Sullivan Operas) that there was a separate exit for the stalls into Wych Street, and the fact was boldly printed on the programmes to calm the fears of fire or panic. But nothing was said about the facilities for occupants of other parts of the house. They had to be contented with a struggle through the tunnels into the Strand. It was the house that gave us the Savoy Operas. For that we may be grateful. We may be also grateful that it is no more.

CHAPTER XII

IN the year 1870, there was at the beginning of Upper Street, Islington, just opposite " The Angel " (now, alas, turned into a Lyons' Tea-shop) a rather grubby Hall known as the Philharmonic, but often referred to by its habitués as " The Spittoon " from its lack of the virtue which ranks next to godliness. Charles Head, a betting man, but not inexperienced in managerial affairs, had the notion of taking it and producing a better class of entertainment than its supporters had been generally accustomed to—in fact, a sort of Variety Show. Very astutely, he appointed Charles Morton to be his manager. Thirty years before this, Morton had been a sort of potman at a public-house in Belgrave Road, where sweepstakes on sporting events were drawn, and he apparently prospered, for in 1848 he was able to take " The Canterbury Arms " in the Westminster Bridge Road. This place he enlarged, and added a picture gallery, one of his pictures being the gigantic painting by Haydon of Quintus Curtius leaping into the gulf, that afterwards hung for so long at Gatti's in Villiers Street and may be there still.

Sala christened the Canterbury " The Royal Academy over the Water," but in spite of many jeers and gibes it flourished exceedingly and became one of the best frequented Halls in the town. Many remarkable people sang there for the first time, among them one Louie Crouch, daughter of the composer of "Kathleen Mavourneen." This astonishing person blossomed out years later into the notorious Cora Pearl, who used to receive her intimate friends dressed in diamonds and nothing else !

Morton was the very man to undertake the revivifying of a Hall like the Philharmonic. Besides being a very dirty place, it was a most awkward shape for a theatre, being an oblong, so that there were several points in the auditorium from which a clear view of the stage would have been difficult if not impossible.

It had had its better days in the past, for now and again, in the early sixties, an English Opera Company had achieved a considerable success with versions of " Norma," " Puritani " and other works of Bellini, etc. Its usual programme, however, consisted of a very mixed Variety Show ; and, as it was not licensed by the Lord Chamberlain, no play, or anything in the nature of a play with plot and dialogue, could be produced.

Morton cleaned it out and furbished it up as much as possible ; some cunning little private boxes adorned with blue silk curtains were introduced into the auditorium, and a long buffet formed, stretching the whole length of the corridor, at which there was no restriction as to the kind of drinks you could buy, and which was presided over by a specially selected bevy of beauty. The entertainment was a fixed one, and partly faked, for, as there was no dramatic licence, plays of any kind, whether musical or not, had to be boiled down to the dimensions of a sketch. In this way, Hervé's " Chilpéric " was put on to last only thirty-five minutes, and Soldene, fresh from her triumphs at the Lyceum in the same part, was engaged to sing the title rôle. As this part of the programme did not begin till after ten o'clock, Soldene was at liberty to accept engagements elsewhere for the early part of the evening. She thus appeared at the East London Theatre (then under the management of Morris Abrahams) as a Prince in a pantomime.

One item of this varied bill was a turn by the Clodoche Troupe from Paris in as close an imitation of the cancan as the authorities would permit. One of the Clodoche Troupe was a M. Alias, who married Miss Price, the *costumière* of the Philharmonic, and settled down in London as the famous firm of theatrical *costumiers* —Monsieur et Madame Alias.

In 1871 the management of the Philharmonic got their licence and produced, in fear and trembling, " Geneviève de Brabant," not thinking for a moment that they were starting on a prosperous run of over a year and a half. London went crazy over this rather insignificant opera bouffe by Offenbach. It is quite impossible to say, at this interval of time, what was the particular charm that drew all fashionable London to such an out-of-the-way theatre. The singing of Soldene in a part that fitted her like a glove may have had something to do with it, or the personality of " Dolly " Dolaro as Genevieve, or the humour of Marshall and Felix Bury in their topical Gendarmes duet—or perhaps it was the bevy of beauty presiding over the long bar ! The music is pretty with the lilt peculiar to Offenbach's work, but it is by no means one of his best. It became the fashion, whatever the reason, to toil up the long Pentonville Hill, and when, in 1872, the Prince of Wales (Edward VII) saw a portrait of Soldene, as Drogan the pastrycook, hanging over the prize ox at the Islington Cattle Show, and booked a box to see the original, its continued success was assured. Another feature of this show was that the " Golden Youth " who so admired the Philharmonic ladies was accustomed to provide them with real champagne and truffled patés for the picnic scene.

Half-way through the run of the opera, the " Parisian " Colonna

Dancers, whose outrageous antics at the Alhambra had brought down the wrath of the Lord Chamberlain and shut up the theatre, were engaged for the Philharmonic and their cancan introduced into the Opera. In the troupe was a little Miss Sarah Wright, daughter of one of Morton's old waiters at the Canterbury. She was billed as " Mlle. Sara," nicknamed " Wiry Sal " and high-kicked herself into fame. Another member of this troupe was a Miss Gerrish, who became the first wife of Marius.

The cancan, about which so much fuss was made when it was danced at the Alhambra, but which had been previously seen at the Princess's when Mlle. Finette did it, is supposed to be a near relation of the mad, unbridled dance of the drunken " petroleuses " of the French Revolution which went by the name of the " Carmagnole." Carlyle, who describes it in his *French Revolution*, evidently put it down for a licentious exhibition of the drunken and bloodthirsty women and men who danced round the unfortunate victims of the guillotine, but I strongly suspect the origin of the dance must be sought much farther back than the eighteenth century in France and is more likely to be a modern version of the Bacchanalian orgies of the Ancient World imported into Rome via Greece, from Oriental countries.

We have had the cancan with us for a long time now, but it has never been quite the same thing in London as it is in Paris and Marseilles. Finette, a French dancer, danced it at the Princess's in 1866, in the Lyceum pantomime in 1867, and at the Alhambra in 1868. When the Colonna Troupe at the Alhambra was the cause of the theatre losing its licence, Payne was dancing with them. Several dancing families have done a mild version of the cancan in various pantomimes. The Girards, the Majiltons, the Wises, the Kiralfys (Imre, Bolossy and Anita originally tumblers at the old Oxford Music Hall and afterwards controlling the White City), Fred Storey and Fred Vokes were all famous for their high kicking ; but the innuendo of the cancan can only be shown by the French themselves.

In " Geneviève de Brabant " there was an old " super " who had seen better days or perhaps it may be more truthfully said had once obtained some sort of renown. This was G. H. Ross, the singer at the Coal Cellars in Maiden Lane of the disgusting " Sam Hall " ballad which, it will be remembered, so excited the wrath of Colonel Newcome. In private life Ross was inoffensive enough, with a passion, it is said, for the cultivation of dahlias.

In 1875 a version of " La Cour du Roi Petaud " by Delibes was put on at the Philharmonic under the title of " Fleur de Lys " —with Soldene and Dolaro in the cast. In the same year was seen

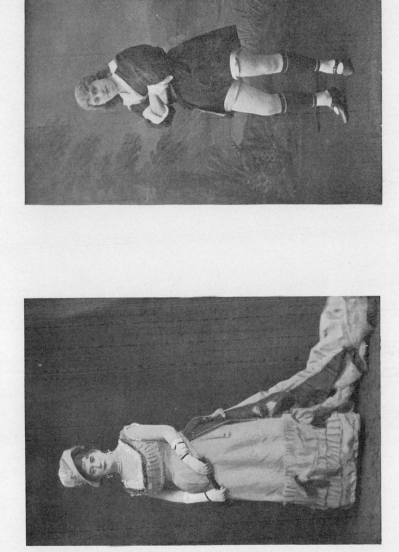

MISS EMILY SOLDENE
From photograph by Stereoscopic Co., Ltd.

EMILY SOLDENE
AS DROGAN IN "GENEVIEVE DE BRABANT"
From photograph by W. D. Downey

"Les Georgiennes" by Offenbach, with Richard Temple, Rose Bell and Carlotta Zerbini and also the first English performances of "La Fille de Madame Angot," with Julia Matthews as Lange and Dolaro as Clairette, but none of the operas bouffes produced at the Philharmonic had the success of "Geneviève de Brabant." The novelty of going to the extreme outskirts for one's evening's amusement soon died down ; perhaps the absence of Soldene herself, who does not seem to have been engaged during the latter years of the theatre, tended not a little to discount the former popularity of the place.

In 1882, the programme included a drama called "London Pride " and a burlesque, " Little Amy Robsart " ; and I note the name of Marie Linden in the company. But I suspect in these latter years the audiences were purely local ones. There was no Soldene magnet to draw West End audiences up the Pentonville Hill. In that same year it met the usual fate of a theatre : it was burned down. Rebuilt on a more convenient plan and reopened in 1883, it was again destroyed by fire in 1887. Again rebuilt and enlarged, it became in 1888 "The Grand Theatre, Islington." Presently it became a Music Hall or Variety House, then a suburban theatre for the reception of travelling companies, and is now—what all theatres are, I suppose destined to be—a Movie House. But the history of the Philharmonic, as such, begins and ends with its seasons of opera bouffe, and Soldene was the sun round which all the lesser lights revolved, for without her, it would never have been "discovered" by the smart set of the day, or filled with a West End audience.

Miss Emily Soldene began her professional stage life about the year 1865 at the Oxford Music Hall, as a singer of excerpts from the more popular operas of the day, calling herself Miss Fitzhenry there, but appearing also at the same time at the Canterbury under her own name.

At the Oxford in those days, there was an unusual display of music-hall talent : Jolly John Nash, Arthur Lloyd, Harry Randall, Harry Rickards, Stead the Perfect Cure, Vance, Leybourne, Louie Sherrington, Mr. and Mrs. Brian (later of the "Swallow" and "Rule's "), Kate Santley (with "The Bells go a ringing for Sarah "), the D'Aubans and Wardes, the Hanlons, the Kiralfys, Alice Dunning (afterwards Alice Lingard), a ballet with the sisters Gunniss and Herr Jonghmanns as conductor. Soldene, it may be noted, had higher aspirations at one time than merely singing at a music-hall. Her voice was a powerful and well-trained organ, and in 1864 she sang at the old St. James's Hall in Piccadilly (presumably for a charity) with Sims Reeves, Patti, Albani, Guerrabella (in later life Genevieve Ward), and, of all people in the world, Giulia Grisi. The last-named was an old woman at the time and was, it is said, hissed by some ill-conditioned members of the audience who presumably had never heard of her or of her former position in the world of song. I was at this concert, a very small boy, and I suppose I was taken just to be able to say that I had once heard Giulia Grisi, but I remember very little about it, except that I saw an old woman in a blue silk dress with black lace (I wonder why I remember that dress !) who sang, rather appropriately, " The Last Rose of Summer."

Soldene's first great success was when she replaced Florimond Hervé himself in the title rôle of his opera " Chilpéric " at the Lyceum in 1870. The Mansells had induced him to come to London to sing the part, but he did not remain very long. In the cast of that opera bouffe were names which became famous in the profession in later years in very different lines. Charles Coghlan played a court physician (a small part) ; Marius was the shepherd, Landry ; Emily Muir (a cousin of Mrs. Dion Boucicault) was the Fredegonde ; one of the pages in the chorus was Jennie Lee, the famous " Jo " of after years ; Odell had a small part ; Dolaro made her first appearance on the London stage (her father was playing in the orchestra) as Galsuinda, the Spanish princess. The music is charming of its kind, and the irrepressible gaiety of the whole most infectious, but it did not have a long run and was followed by another of Hervé's works—" Le Petit Faust "—in which Tom Maclagan, who had sung with Soldene at the Oxford, was the Faust ; Soldene, Marguerite, Odell, Martha ; a very chic little importation from Paris, one Marguerite Debreux, Mephisto ; and Lennox Grey, a beautiful woman, daughter of old Mrs. Caulfield of the Haymarket, Wagner. In the chorus was Camille Dubois, who afterwards married the Hon. Wyndham Stanhope and was well known in many another opera-comique. Mephisto was driven on to the stage in a real hansom cab, the driver of which was Charles Willmott, in later years the proprietor of the Occidental Tavern in the Strand, and part proprietor of the Holborn Theatre during the run of " The New Babylon " and of the Grand, Islington, when it was burned down for the last time. The little street arab in silken rags with a golden broom was Jennie Lee.

Soldene had a long career in opera bouffe and opera-comique. One of her great successes was as Lange in " Madame Angot," but she always declared it was the rôle she liked the least. Her favourite rôle, after Drogan, was Madame L'Archiduc, which was a failure as far as London was concerned. It is not often remembered that when this work was given it was followed in the same programme by Gilbert and Sullivan's "Trial by Jury," in which Clara Vesey, Soldene's pretty sister, was the Plaintiff.

When she appeared in "Geneviève" at the Alhambra in 1878, Constance Loseby was in Dolaro's part of the Duchess ; Aynsley Cook was in that cast and also Dallas, a member of the Gaiety burlesque company. In the Alhambra production, a grand ballet was introduced in which the prima ballerina assoluta was charming Madame Pertoldi, wife of Tito Mattei, the composer and the mime was Théodore de Gellert.

Little Dolaro, " Dolly Dolaro " as she was affectionately called, fell on evil days at the end. She was of humble origin, her father being in the orchestra of the Lyceum in the "Chilpéric" days. Her aspirations soared higher than the position of an opera bouffe soprano and she left the company after a little while to live a more "protected" life. She was an excellent Carmen, and sang that rôle with the Carl Rosa Company at Her Majesty's in the Haymarket in 1880, in the same year also appearing as Frederic in Thomas's "Mignon." Previously to that she had done "La Périchole" at the Royalty in 1875 on the same bill as the first production of "Trial by Jury."

In 1881, I find her returning from a visit to the States and giving an entertainment at the Dilettante Club in Argyll Street assisted by an opera bouffe tenor, Willie Gregory, and others. But she returned to the States almost immediately afterwards and was ill and rather down in the world when Soldene was travelling there in the height of her successes. They had had a row of some kind over this side (it is said that they used to quarrel regularly in earnest in the famous quarrel duet in "Angot "), but Soldene was a very large-hearted woman who never bore malice. She went to see Dolaro in New York ; found her the proprietress of a "Millnery Parlour" (anglice, "Bonnet Shop ") and in the last stage of consumption. A benefit was arranged for her to defray the expenses of a stay in Florida, but Dolaro said "Better to die in New York than live in Florida," and die she did, soon afterwards.

I knew Soldene personally when she was living near Twickenham with her two little boys. She had run away with the son of a Mr. Powell, first sub-editor of The Daily News when Charles Dickens was editor. The Powells lived in York Road, Lambeth, next door to George Hogarth, dramatic and art critic and writer, and Dickens, dining with them one day, met Catherine Hogarth, his future wife. One of Soldene's latest appearances in London was at Drury Lane in "Frivoli," an opera specially composed for her by Hervé. This was in 1886 and in the cast with her were Rose Hersee (a singer in English "Grand " opera), Marie Tempest,

Kate Munroe and Harry Nicholls. I do not think it was a great success, for Hervé had written himself out, and though Florence St. John helped in a revival of opera bouffe, some few years later, it was already on the wane.

Much of Soldene's career was passed in America and Australia, but she always seems to have considered England her home and, in the end, came back here to die.

Nearly forty years after her debut in " Chilpéric " at the Lyceum, a complimentary benefit was arranged for her at the Palace Theatre through the exertions of Mr. Richard Northcott. Over a thousand pounds was realized. She must have been on the wrong side of sixty then, but appeared in the white knickers and pastrycook's cap of Drogan, and sang the famous Serenade—" Lady look down "— as well as she had sung it hundreds of times at the Islington "Spittoon." Her reception was most enthusiastic, and she parted from her affectionate public on the best of terms.

I have said she was a large-hearted woman. There must have been a great deal of charm about her personally ; she had so many friends who loved her, and she was the best company in the world. That world was the duller for her departure. *Requiescat in pace.* Perhaps I have dwelt too much upon a personality gone from ken so long ago and living only in the memories of the old fogies like myself who knew her. The stories about her are endless and all amusing, and many of them are to be found at length in her own Reminiscences, from which I have taken a few of my facts and dates. No account of opera bouffe in England would have been complete without a lengthened account of Emily Soldene.

What is opera bouffe really ? It is said to be a French expression for Comic Opera, but this is a mistake. Opera-comique and opera bouffe are both forms of French musical art, but quite distinct in themselves. Opera-comique is not confined to France alone, but can be found among the works of composers of all nations. Opera bouffe is essentially French, and French only. I would narrow it down still further—for I hold that real opera bouffe is confined to the works of a few composers of whom Offenbach and Hervé are the chief. Offenbach was certainly the inventor of this delightful form of entertainment, and Hervé followed close in his footsteps.

I shall be asked what about Lecocq, Planquette, Audran, Messager, Jonas and a dozen other French composers ; Strauss, Suppé, Mullocker, Fall, Léhar and other Germans and Austrians ; why leave out some of the old Italians such as " Cenerentola " and " Matrimonio Segreto," for example ; and the Spanish operettas of the " Gran Via " type ?

SELINA ("DOLLY") DOLARO

I would reply that, with the possible exception of one or two by Lecocq and Emil Jonas, the " Fledermaus " of Strauss, the " Donna Juanita " and " Boccaccio " of Suppé, and the great " Gran Via," the works of these composers are operas-comiques and not operas bouffes.

All genuine opera bouffe is imbued with the spirit of burlesque, serious matter being rigorously excluded, and it must be laced (or perhaps " unlaced ") with more than a touch of indelicacy, possibly even indecency. Again, the opera bouffe has no really coherent tale to tell ; an opera-comique has. " La Fille de Madame Angot," the most delightful of Lecocq's many works, is a tale of the French Directory with a quite reasonable plot. " Véronique " is a sort of pastoral and a very charming pastoral too. " Les Cloches de Corneville " is a legend of Normandy adapted for the stage, with serious and sentimental moments.

But what is the plot of " La Belle Hèléne " or of " Chilpéric " ? It is all a travesty of a mythological legend, or a bit of history, or a caricature of some current absurdity. In opera bouffe, not even the love-making is real. No tender sentimental duets for youths and maidens with a seemly marriage looming in the middle distance, a " live-happily-ever-afterwards " sort of affair. Mistress, not sweetheart and wife, is the central feminine interest of opera bouffe —and generally a temporary mistress at that ! This explains what I have called the " strain of indelicacy " and also why, at its first coming to London, there were so many who did not think it " Quite proper, you know " to be seen among the audience at an opera bouffe. The new kind of show was to them something similar to an unbowdlerized, yellow-backed French novel.

Some of the German composers tried their hands at a genuine opera bouffe, but German music, like German everything else, is rather heavy-handed. It may be occasionally bright and even cheery and quite well written, but it always lacks the froth and sparkle of Hervé and Offenbach. The difference is as the difference between still Rhine wines (very good in their way) and the champagne of France ; between the heavy Teutonic dress of a German Frau and the elegant attire of a Parisienne. There is nothing dégagée or relaxed about German music. It is cabined, cribbed and confined like the figure of a German Frau, in the heavy " stays " of German rules and regulations. It often tries to imitate the French and sound a bit " naughty "—like Berlin apeing Paris— and only succeeds (like Berlin) in being vulgar and commonplace.

Austrian light opera is a little better, has a little more of the genuine spirit of opera bouffe—in the same way that Vienna was, and is still, much more really gay than Berlin. Perhaps we might include Strauss's "Fledermaus," and Suppé's "Boccaccio," or "Donna Juanita," as two very fair imitations of the real thing but one detects at once the difference between these charming specimens of opera-comique and "Orphée" or "Chilpéric." The "Gran Via," a short piece produced in Madrid and sung many thousand times all over Spain, Spanish America and even in Italy, is a sort of short opera bouffe, but the story is only concerned with the building of new streets in Madrid a long time ago, essentially a *pièce d'occasion*, and the interest being so purely temporary and local has prevented it obtaining a hold on non-Spanish countries. The music, which is charming with a most catching lilt, was, I believe, once taken bodily for one act to a musical piece brought out at the Royalty. The only other two works neither by Offenbach nor Hervé, which occur to me at the moment are " Le Canard à Trois Becs " of Emil Jonas and " Les Cent Vierges " of Lecocq. These are, possibly, operas bouffes.

The "Cenerentola" of Rossini, the "Matrimonio Segreto" of Cimarosa, and "Crispino e la Comare" of Ricci, are comic operas of a kind with lively music and amusing plots. They are given in Italy as opera buffa—but the effervescing sparkle is rather flat and the audacity absent.

Yet Jacques Offenbach himself was a German Jew. His family's real name was Eberscht, but he was in Paris before he was fifteen, and finally became the most Parisian of Parisians. He was born in a mean street in Cologne in 1819, and his father, Juda Eberscht, took the name of Offenbach from his birthplace at the time he was appointed Cantor of a Synagogue in Cologne in 1818. Young Jacob learned to play the violin at a very early age, and in 1833 was studying at the Paris Conservatoire under Cherubini. About this time, he is said to have "devilled" for Flotow, and it is even asserted that parts of "Martha" and "Stradella" are by him.

So far as can be ascertained, his first undoubted composition was the incidental music to a piece called "Pascal at Chambord"; but, at this early stage of his career, he relied more upon what he earned by playing the violoncello at private concerts. There is no doubt that he was a more than ordinary good 'cello player.

In 1844 he was in London, and performed at a concert given by the famous Fanny Puzzi in the concert-room of Her Majesty's Opera House, at which most of the leading operatic artistes of the day sang—among them being Grisi, Mario, Persiani, Madame Dorus-Gras and the two Lablaches. Costa and Benedict conducted and *The Musical World* stated : " Herr Offenbach, a violoncellist, made a highly favourable sensation."

In the same year a concert was given by Madame Louise Dulcken (the sister of Ferdinand David, a most accomplished artiste and pianiste in ordinary to Queen Victoria), and later Benedict gave a concert at which the vocalist was Anna Thillon, and the principal instrumentalists Dulcken, Mendelssohn and " Master " Joachim. At all these important musical réunions, Offenbach played with much success.

Shortly afterwards he returned to Paris, became a Catholic, and married an old sweetheart, a Spanish lady named Herminie de Alcain. This was entirely a love match and they appear to have lived very happily all their lives.

In 1848, the year of the Revolution, the Offenbachs left Paris and stayed a short while at Cologne, but in 1849 he returned to France to be conductor of the orchestra at the Comédie Française. About this time, he wrote two one-act operettas—" Marietta," which was developed into " Madame L'Archiduc," and " Pepito," which he elaborated into " Le Postillon en Gage."

In 1858, he started on his own, taking a very tiny theatre called " Les Bouffes Parisiens "—and nicknamed " La Bonbonnière "— where he brought out two short pieces in one act each, which were always reckoned among his most successful efforts. These were " Les Deux Aveugles " and " Une Nuit Blanche."

The number of one-act operettas which he wrote was very large, and may be accounted for partly by the fact that the " Bouffes Parisiens," like many other small theatres, was only licensed for pieces of four characters, and partly because a *lever de rideau* was always expected before the chief piece of the evening.

Next he took a small theatre in the Rue Choiseul, gave it the same name as the other and conducted it with much success. This engagement was signalled by the first appearance in Paris of Hortense Schneider to whom Offenbach assigned the principal part in " Tromb-Al-Cazar." Schneider had been discovered by him singing in a small theatre in Brussels where she was only paid about six pounds a week. It was not long before she could demand and obtain at least 2000 francs, or something like £80 a week.

" Orphée aux Enfers," " Geneviève de Brabant " and " Daphnis et Chloe " (elaborated into " Les Bergers ") followed closely on each other's heels, and in 1861 he took a step which, as much as anything, led him on to the position he kept for so many years as the musical idol of the Parisians. He became a naturalized Frenchman.

Between 1861 and 1867, he added to his successes with " La Chanson de Fortunio," " Le Pont des Soupirs," " La Belle Hèléne," " Barbe-Bleue " and " La Vie Parisienne ; " and in 1867 outshone

them all with " La Grande-Duchesse." This was the year of the
First Great Exhibition in Paris, and Hortense Schneider was one
of the sensations of the season.

There was a side entrance to the Exhibition reserved for Royalties.
Schneider drove up in state, and demanded that the gates should
be opened for her to enter the Exhibition. She was informed that
the entrance was reserved for Royalties. " Justement," she replied.
" Je suis la grande-duchesse de Gerolstein." She was at once
admitted without further demur, but, whether through ignorance
or in sheer admiration of her unbounded impudence, history does
not relate.

" The Grand-Duchess " has been seen in London time after
time with many representatives of the title rôle. Schneider herself
was in it at the St. James's and also in " Orphée aux Enfers," " Barbe-
Bleue " and " La Belle Hélène." Notable English " Grand-
Duchesses " were Julia Matthews, Mrs. Howard Paul, Cornelie
D'Anka, Florence St. John and Soldene.

After his *chef d'œuvre* setting forth the adventures of Her
Highness of Gerolstein, Offenbach produced in rapid succession
a number of operas bouffes. Sometimes they were brought out
at the Gaité, sometimes at the Variétés, or the Opéra-Comique,
or the Renaissance : for all Paris went Offenbach mad and his
operas were given simultaneously at many theatres. The list
includes " Robinson Crusoe," " L'Ile de Tulipatan," " La Périchole," " Vert-Vert," " La Diva," " La Princesse de Trébizonde,"
" Les Brigands," " La Boule de Neige," " Le Roi Carotte," " Les
Braconniers," " La Jolie Parfumeuse," " Madame L'Archiduc,"
" La Boulangère a des Ecus," " Le Voyage dans la Lune," " La
Créole," " Le Docteur Ox," " Madame Favart," " La Marocaine "
and " La Fille du Tambour-Major." That was his last opera
bouffe. He had, however, always aspired to write a more serious
work, perhaps because Rossini had said he was the Mozart of the
Champs-Élysées ! So he set to work to put his best talents into
" Conte d'Hoffmann " and finished it just before his death, but did
not live to see the first night.

Offenbach was one of the most prolific writers of musical scores
that the world has ever known. In twenty years he produced
over a hundred operas of various kinds, some only of one act, but
the majority an entire evening's entertainment.

His works are the champagne of the operetta world. No other
composer has succeeded to quite the same extent in putting into
whatever he wrote the *joie de vivre*. His life in Paris coincided with
the gayest, giddiest and maddest years of that gay, giddy and mad
capital. It is astonishing to remember that he was a German

by race, not a half and half Alsatian as some have asserted, but a full-blooded Teuton. In Strauss (Johann the elder) we have another German who had the knack of writing music with a joyous lilt, but even in the " Fledermaus "—the gayest thing that Strauss wrote—we do not find that bubbling over of the joy of life, those effervescing strains which are the characteristics of Offenbach, and, in a lesser degree, of that other French opera bouffe composer, Florimond Hervé.

No one with any knowledge of operetta music could mistake " Die Fledermaus," gay and charming as it is, for French, or " Orphée " or " La Grande Duchesse " for German music. We are grateful for what Germany and Austria have given us, but I think we could have done without all the Strauss, Suppé, Léhar and Fall sooner than lose our heritage from the converted, naturalized German Jew of Cologne. He has given us many happy hours. At any rate, an old fogy like myself can feel that he owes him a deep debt of gratitude. I am indebted to a little pamphlet by Mr. Northcott for some of the personal details of Offenbach's life.

A really British opera bouffe is outside the bounds of possibility. The British character forbids it It would be the Beer, not the Champagne, of music and strong beer at that. Sullivan, Solomon, Cellier and others have all written light scores wedded to humorous stories, and worthy to be ranked with the work of Auber, Boeildieu, Strauss and Lecocq. Not one of them could have set a *risqué* plot to music, not one could have conceived the " Dites-lui " of the immortal Grand Duchess or the " Je suis un peu grise " of la Périchole. Both those charming ladies are quite outside the ken of the average Briton, as are also the Jupiter of " Orphée " and Chilpéric. It is, therefore, not to be wondered at that when Opera Bouffe, the naked article, burst upon an astonished London some time in the sixties of last century, London was not prepared for it. Playgoers were shocked, highly amused, or brazenly appreciative according to the nature of the individual. Some declared they could never go to see such shows—or, well—they could not take their womenfolk. Others (who perhaps understood French) said that the words should have been kept in that language so as not to corrupt the " man in the street " by disgraceful " doubles entendres." Others said that it did not in the least matter what language was employed seeing that the actors, and above all the actresses, took good care there should be no mistake as to the meaning. It was specially pointed out that an Englishwoman like Kate Vaughan should not have been allowed to make an exhibition of herself and her troupe of dancers by appearing in black tights spangled with gold and executing a cancan in a scene frankly meant to represent Hell itself !

It was soon manifest, however, that this new and shocking style of entertainment had come to stay. For a period of about twenty-five years Opera Bouffe ousted all other kinds of light shows from the theatres, even rivalling the old burlesques at the Strand under the Swanboroughs, which indeed they replaced in their own home.

I think " La Belle Hélène " was the first opera bouffe given in London, though it may possibly have been preceded by a version of " Orphée." In 1866, the " Face that launched a thousand ships " was seen at the Adelphi in the person of Miss Furtado, a very pretty actress, who afterwards made a great hit as various heroines of melodrama. This was a very free version of the original, called " Helen or taken from the Greek." Mrs. Alfred Mellon was the Paris, Toole the Menelaus and Paul Bedford Calchas. Riviere conducted the orchestra and the chorus master was a Signor Lago, who many years later conducted a season of Italian opera at the Lyceum.

" Barbe-Bleue " (Offenbach) was done in the same year with Nelly Farren and Amy Sheridan in the cast, but this appears to have been also a very free version, and the music is stated to have been " arranged " by James Tully, that same Tully who is always cropping up as a musical director, whether at an insignificant out-lying house like the Bower Saloon, a short-lived place like the Colosseum Theatre in Albany Street or at Drury Lane itself.

Five years later, another English version of " Barbe-Bleue " was seen at the Gaiety with Julia Matthews, Stoyle, Annie Tremaine, etc. Blanchard, who has a note on most productions, has not much to say about this revival—just one word " Indecorous " ! But then Blanchard was not fond of opera bouffe. I fancy he did not understand the genre : he was too English. When the Mansells produced " Chilpéric " at the Lyceum in 1870, all he said about it was " Most abominable rubbish." Yet that production was very well done with good singers and plenty of fun—of rather a " French " kind, it is true. Florimond Hervé himself was cast for the title rôle when it first came to London, and made a most gallant appearance entering on a white horse which Soldene, to her dismay, had to mount when she took up the part. " How am I to do it ? " she asked of Mrs. Maitland, the mother of the Mansells. " My dear Soldene," replied that lively Irishwoman who had often done it herself, " just throw your leg over, and there you are ! " Dolaro, who was one of the best representatives of

Carmen ever seen, had a good part, and Emily Muir and Miss Fitzinnan (afterwards Mrs. Frank Marshall) were well-known actresses. It was certainly not abominable rubbish for most playgoers.

When " Chilpéric " was put on for the opening of the Empire as a regular theatre, the cast included Herbert Standing in the title rôle, Paulus, Wardroper (one of two brothers who used to do a sort of drawing-room entertainment), Paulton, Camille D'Arville, Sallie Turner and Sismondi, a dancer from the Alhambra. Hayden Coffin made his debut as a member of the chorus. He did not have a leading part till the production of "The Lady of the Locket."

Meanwhile, the real and original " Belle Hélène " had arrived from Paris and was showing herself at the unlucky St. James's Theatre in "Barbe-Bleue " and at the Princess's in " La Périchole." Hortense Schneider's success was a foregone conclusion for those who cared for French productions and could understand the language. Her audacities must have been a revelation to more than one stolid British mind. We have progressed much since that time. Schneider's appearances were not the only time we had the original French companies in London in opera bouffe. A French " Grande Duchesse " was over here in the eighties and Granier, one of the most charming of all French artistes, did " La Belle Lurette " and other opera bouffe heroines.

After 1866, and all through the seventies, London was overwhelmed by a torrent of opera bouffe. In 1867, Her Highness of Gerolstein was impersonated by Julia Matthews (one of the cleverest if rather coarse representatives of the amorous ruler), supported by Aynsley Cook as General Boum, Stoyle as Prince Paul, Frank Matthews, Odell, and Augusta Thomson as Wanda. In 1868, she was at the Olympic in the person of the incomparable Mrs. Howard Paul, and in the same year transferred from Covent Garden to the Standard, Shoreditch, with Julia Matthews and, later, Soldene. In 1870, she was at Astley's. In 1875 and again in 1878 she visited the Alhambra—Cornelie D'Anka, a magnificently handsome person, being in the rôle on each occasion. In 1897, I trace her to the Savoy with unforgettable Florence St. John, the best English Grand Duchess of them all, with the possible exception of Mrs. Howard Paul. " Orphée " was at the St. James's and Princess's with Schneider in 1869 and 1870, at the Surrey Gardens and the Amphitheatre, Holborn, simultaneously in 1873, at the Royalty with Kate Santley in 1876, and at the Alhambra with another Kate (charming Kitty Munroe) in 1876. Finally, at His Majesty's in 1911 was produced an amazing up-to-date hotch-potch founded on Offenbach's opera which was only remarkable for the singing of Courtice Pounds and the whimsicalities of Lottie Venne as Public Opinion transmogrified into a Mrs. Grundy in a crinoline. This has always appeared to me to have been an unpardonable attempt of Tree's. The original was entirely spoilt. But it was not his line. In the realms of opera bouffe he was quite *dépaysé.*

These were the early representations of Offenbach's three chief operas bouffes in London. It is unnecessary, and would be tedious, to go through in detail the long list of similar productions during the sixties and seventies. In eleven years—1870 to 1881—upwards of two dozen operas bouffes, all by Offenbach, were given in London (many of them more than once with different casts) and three of Hervé's, without counting the light operas of Lecocq, Planquette, Audran, Messager, etc. There were seasons at the Gaiety with "The Princess of Trebizonde" (Toole and Nelly Farren in the part created by Chaumont) and "Trombal-cazar" and others; seasons at the Comedy ("Erminie," "Boccaccio," "Falka," "Rip van Winkle," "Mascotte," "Cigale," etc.); seasons at the Strand with Florence St. John ("Favart" and "Olivette"); seasons at the Avenue ("Les Manteaux Noirs," "Lurette," "La Vie Parisienne," etc.); seasons at the Globe ("Les Cloches de Corneville," "Les Brigands," etc.); seasons at the St. James's ("Les Mousquetaires du Couvent," "Les Dragons de Villars," "Les Brigands," "Vert-Vert," etc.); and for many years at the Alhambra, where the list of operas-comiques and operas bouffes is far too long to quote in full, but included a round dozen of Offenbach's, and others by Suppé, Lecocq, Hervé, Strauss and even "Le Cheval de Bronze" of Auber. Many of these works, when they did achieve representation before an English audience, had to be bowdlerized to suit the requirements of the Censor, acting on behalf of the British Mrs. Grundy. Such was undoubtedly the fate of "La Femme à Papa" by Hervé, produced at the Criterion in 1882 under the innocuous title of "Little Miss Muffet," in which Miss Mary Moore (Lady Wyndham) made her first appearance on the regular stage. The French original by Hennequin was not possible in a literal English translation. The Censor, as I have already noted, also laid a heavy hand on "Vert-Vert," when given by the brothers Mansell at the St. James's.

It will be seen that I have included in the above rather hasty and incomplete list of light operas given in London many that I would not set down as real operas bouffes. This was merely to indicate what a rage for that kind of entertainment, or something like it, occurred in the sixties and seventies of last century. Some of these pieces ran for an enormously long time. "Les Cloches de Corneville" registered a run of 705 performances ; "Favart" 502 ; "Olivette" 466 ; "La Cigale" (with a delightful American singer, the Chevalier Scovel) 423. The casts were naturally constantly changing. In the "Cloches" (as it came to be almost affectionately called) Violet Cameron was the original Germaine— a part afterwards taken up by Florence St. John—Kate Munro the original Serpolette, Loredan Grénicheux and Howson the Marquis. The Gaspards (the great miser character) were innumerable and included Shiel Barry (who made his great success the first night because of, not in spite of, a cold in his head), Howson, Odell, Younge, Eldred, James Fernandez, Royce and others. Tree made one of his earliest successes in "Madame Favart" on tour. Violet Cameron, daughter of a "Sister Brougham" of the old Canterbury Music Hall, played an enormous number of parts in opera bouffe, though not so many probably as Soldene. The list could be extended beyond the bounds of this chapter. But the opera bouffe was not destined to flower permanently in British soil. With the advent of Arthur Roberts, musical comedy took its place but has, in turn, been ousted by Revue. It is extremely doubtful if any of the old works of Offenbach or Hervé or Lecocq would pay to produce in these days. They require good singers, and these are scarce indeed. I should find it very difficult to name off-hand anyone of the present day who could sing the parts once filled by Julia Matthews, Soldene, Mrs. Howard Paul, Kate Santley, Kate Munro or Florence St. John, unless Miss Marie Tempest stepped into the breach (what an incomparable Grand Duchess she would make !). The ladies of the modern musical stage are as good-looking as ever, but they can neither act nor sing, and opera bouffe requires that they should do both.

Some little time ago, Sir Thomas Beecham tried to bring out opera bouffe on the scale of Grand Opera. He selected "La Fille de Madame Angot" for the experiment and Drury Lane Theatre for the locale. Miss Gladys Ancrum was cast for Mlle. Lange and Desirée Ellinger for Clairette. Both were competent operatic artistes who had sung with distinction in Mozart and Wagner. The result was possibly not what Sir Thomas expected, but it was certainly not surprising to connoisseurs of opera bouffe. The quarrel scene was the sedatest thing in quarrels you ever saw ; the whole fun of the piece was submerged in a grand setting and missed by a serious cast of performers. It made one laugh—but on the wrong side of the mouth, so to speak. A good deal of money must have been wasted in this foolish attempt to make Angot respectable.

CHAPTER XIII

THE MARYLEBONE THEATRE AND THE TWO ALEXANDRA THEATRES

THE MARYLEBONE THEATRE

IN 1831, there was opened in Church Street, Edgware Road, a theatre called the New Royal Sussex Theatre. There are traces of a house of dramatic entertainment on the same site which had been known as the Portman Theatre perhaps from its promixity to the Portman Market, but I have been unable to ascertain whether it was so called prior or subsequent to being christened the Royal Sussex. In any case, it was originally nothing better than what was generally called a " Penny Show "—that is, a playhouse where the crudest form of melodrama was the regular fare, and the cheapest prices prevailed. The name of the house was altered very soon to " Royal Pavilion Theatre, West " and in 1837 to " Royal Marylebone Theatre "—the " Royal " being in each case, a somewhat arbitrary assumption.

Many of the old theatres can boast of a long line of different managers, but I think the Marylebone must have the longest of all. No management, with the exception of that of J. A. Cave, and perhaps of Lee and Johnson, seemed to be able to make it pay. There might have been a touch of ill-luck about the house, or else the different directors of its fortunes tried to fly too high. The immediate neighbourhood is not an aristocratic one, to put it very mildly, and the regular frequenters of the theatre preferred stronger fare than managers of the type of Mrs. Warner, Stirling, Emery and other earnest members of the profession cared to provide.

They demanded something with many corpses and plenty of blood in it—like the " Oliver Twist " of the Old Vic, or " Maria Martin " or "Sweeney Todd." The scrupulously correct, not to say classical, methods of Mrs. Warner did not attract them ; they only wished to be amused, not instructed as well ; they preferred the jam without the powder.

Tedious to any reader would be a long and accurate list of the various people who tried to make at least a living, if not a fortune, out of the Marylebone Theatre. It would include several well-known names in the profession. Among them would be Nelson Lee (of whom later) ; John Douglass, one time of the little Tothill Fields Theatre and afterwards of the Standard, Shoreditch ; Mrs. Warner, the " Suburban Siddons " of Sadler's Wells and eke of

Drury Lane and Covent Garden ; Walter Watts, the bankrupt suicide of the Olympic, who found the money to start the Warner season ; E. T. Smith, the would-be manager of a dozen London theatres and opera houses at one time, of whom I have written more fully in the Chapter on Astley's ; James W. Wallack, the semi-American, and uncle of Mrs. Alfred Wigan, who had the privilege of introducing Madge Robertson to the London stage ; Emery, the colleague of Robson at the Olympic and Fechter at the Lyceum ; Clarence Holt, the coarse-mouthed barnstorming manager of the Duke's and the Islington Grand ; Giovanelli, the ex-clown and one time director of the Highbury Barn Theatre ; Charles Harcourt, a refined West End actor ; Miss Henrade, in early life a pantomime fairy and afterwards in drama with Fechter and in comedy with H. J. Byron. There were many others whose names mean less than nothing to the playgoer of the present day : Hyde, Cooper, Stammers, Edgar Bolton, Meadows, Seaman, Bigwood (I think I remember this name at the Britannia the Great Theatre), Elliston, Augusta Thomson, Bodenham, Montgomery, C. Lacy, Worboys, Sydney, etc. This list of names, for which I am in part indebted to Mr. Clement Scott's book, is not complete ; but it is long enough to show how unlucky most of them were and how profitless it would be to go through the events of their managements in detail.

Lee and Johnson were among the earliest managers of the Marylebone Theatre. Some particulars of Nelson Lee (ex-harlequin and general utility performer) will be found in Chapter II in the section referring to the City of London Theatre. When Richardson, the owner of the celebrated Richardson's Show, died or had given up the Show, it was carried on, by Nelson Lee and Johnson in partnership, as "Richardson's Travelling Theatre." They made such a success of their venture that they were enabled to take the Marylebone for a short time, where the pieces given did not probably differ very much in their style and structure from those of the old booth, though doubtless they took longer to play.

This seems to have been one of the few successful managements of the Marylebone, for Lee with his share of the profits was able to go on to the Pavilion, Whitechapel, from there to the Standard, Shoreditch, and thence to the City of London in Norton Folgate, where he was still manager at his death. He left a considerable fortune.

Of the other managers, Mrs. Warner claims priority, for she had been leading lady with Macready at Covent Garden and Drury Lane and with Phelps at Sadler's Wells before taking up management on her own.

Her maiden name was Mary Amelia Huddart, and she was the daughter of an actor, well known in his day, who had been a chemist in Dublin. Her theatrical life began on the Plymouth, Exeter and Bristol circuit when she was about fifteen years of age, her first manager being Brunton ; but she appears to have reached London fairly soon.

In her early London career, she played at many of the Minor Theatres in a round of important characters such as Constance (" King John "), Alicia (" Jane Shore "), Emma (" William Tell "), and the Queen in " Alfred the Great." In 1830, when just over twenty-four years of age, she was starring with Macready at Drury Lane as Belvidera in " Venice Preserved." In 1836, she was still at Drury Lane, then under the management of Bunn and acting with Forrest, the American rival of Macready, in " Macbeth," " Othello " (Emilia), etc. In the following year she was at the Haymarket as Evadne in " The Bride's Tragedy " and similar parts, and it was in that year that she married Warner, landlord of the " Wrekin," a celebrated theatrical tavern in Broad Court, Drury Lane.

After four or five years with Macready at the two chief London theatres, she joined Phelps in his management of Sadler's Wells, remaining there for nearly four years and playing the leading tragedy rôles in the plays of Shakespeare and other writers of " the Legitimate."

In 1847, smitten with the idea of running a theatre herself according to her own ideas, she took over the Marylebone under Watts who found the money for the start and of whom I have spoken more fully in the chapter on the Olympic Theatre. Her intention appears to have been to make it the rendezvous of all playgoers interested in the higher forms of dramatic art, but, as I have already pointed out, the audiences of Lisson Grove and the regions round about wanted to be amused in their own way. The result was very disastrous for Mrs. Warner when the defalcations of Watts put an end to his career and she had to fend for herself, though she struggled on bravely for a time.

Her first production was " The Winter's Tale " with herself cast for Hermione, and she followed this up by playing Julia (" The Hunchback "), Lady Teazle, Mrs. Oakley (" The Jealous Wife "), Lady Townley, etc. She also put on Beaumont and Fletcher's " Scornful Lady " with such a lavish mounting that the Athenæum, usually most disgruntled in all its dramatic criticisms, burst out to a pæan of praise almost lyrical in its enthusiasm :

" . . . . a truly magnificent scene, representing the Lady's parlour, with its chimney piece from Italy of Carrara marble, articles of vertu then in use among the rich and tasteful, such as early Chinese vases, clocks and the then novel luxury of small carpets—all made to harmonize with the architectural style of the apartments."

Her tenancy of the theatre lasted for barely a year, and she must have had to pay out a good deal of money after the death of Watts, so was well content to return to the Haymarket for a season to try and recoup her losses. She afterwards made a trip to the States, where her rather early Victorian style doubtless pleased the Americans of that day. Her last appearance in London was as Mrs. Oakley in " The Jealous Wife."

I suppose Mrs. Warner was not what would now be considered a great actress. She probably went through her parts with a good deal of power, adhering very strictly to the traditions established by long usage in each case. Otherwise she would not have been accepted in those days by that large circle of playgoers and critics, who formed the majority, and who expected certain parts to be played in a certain manner, and lay in wait for all the " points " sanctioned by years of tradition. Not till the arrival of Fechter and the Modern School were these traditions broken up.

The Athenæum says of her acting as Lady Macbeth that she played the part " with great care and force," which was rather " damning her with faint praise," for many of her contemporaries could probably have done as much. She had not the fire of Siddons, nor even of Charlotte Cushman, nor the intelligence and grace of Fanny Kemble and Helen Faucit and her acting must have resembled in many ways that of the worthy and " steady " Shakespearean performer, Mrs. Charles Kean. I can picture her with the same " British-Matronly " appearance and perhaps the same early Victorian way of doing her hair in loops down over her ears no matter what the character or period she had to represent. A large cameo or portrait brooch pinned in front of her buxom, stiffly-corseted breast—whether her costume was ancient, mediæval or modern—completes the picture I have formed of her or Mrs. Kean in my mind's eye. The illustrations, side by side, of Mrs. Charles Kean and Miss Mary Anderson each as Hermione in " The Winter's Tale " facing page 135 will explain what I mean.

Her elocution is always highly praised by her contemporaries, and she was often called upon to deliver inauguration or farewell addresses. Thus, when Phelps started his Shakespearean seasons at Sadler's Wells, lines were specially written by Thomas Serle for Mrs. Warner to deliver. Serle, by the way, was a very prolific dramatist of the period who had been an actor with Edmund Kean,

Charles Kemble and Charles Young. He married one of a remarkable trio of sisters, daughters of Vincent Novello, the composer. The other two were Clara Novello (Countess Gigliucci) and Mrs. Cowden Clarke, compiler of the Concordance to Shakespeare.

The last days of Mrs. Warner were not very happy. From no fault of her own, she had to go through the Bankruptcy Court, and she suffered from a very painful internal disease of which she eventually died. Queen Victoria had a great respect for her (as she also had for Mrs. Charles Kean and Helen Faucit, all three eminently respectable ladies), and in her last illness made frequent inquiries for her, placing a Royal carriage at her disposal whenever she was able to go out. Her son was John Lawrence Warner. He tried to be an actor and failed.

I have mentioned the "Wrekin," the old theatrical tavern near Drury Lane of which Warner was landlord. Blanchard gives many interesting particulars of this haunt of the dramatic and journalistic professions. He describes it as standing in the very centre of Broad Court, exactly half-way between Bow Street, on the one hand, and Drury Lane, on the other, and he speaks of it as the "Favourite resort of authors, actors, poets, painters and penny-a-liners." Tradition said it had been, in the seventeenth century, the scene of many an adventure between Charles II and Nell Gwynne. In the following century, its proprietor hailed from Shropshire and renamed it the "Wrekin" in honour of the famous hill of his county. Tewkesbury ale and Shrewsbury cakes were the standard luncheon during the tenancy of the Salopian Boniface, and after his death it passed into the hands of one Harrold, an uncle of Blanchard's, who enlarged the premises and obtained a licence for the sale of wines and spirits—it having been previously a mere "Cake and Ale House." It was always a place of reunion for literary and dramatic clubs, who in those days, having no buildings of their own, met in taverns.

One such club was the "Catamarans" to which belonged Theodore Hook, Tom Sheridan (son of Richard Brinsley Sheridan), Charles Mathews, both the Kembles, Munden, George Coleman, Morton, the dramatist, Reynolds, the newspaper man (editor of a disgracefully coarse series of penny novels, but also churchwarden at St. Andrew's, Wells Street), Monk Lewis and many others well known in dramatic and journalistic circles.

Harrold had the "Wrekin" for five and twenty years. It then passed through various hands till it reached those of the husband of Mrs. Warner, who after a period of "co-management with a blithesome widow" courted Mary Huddart and settled down to a respectable life as a married man.

Other clubs meeting at this famous old tavern (what a delightful word that is, so much preferable to public-house) were the "Mulberries" (chiefly literary) and the "Rationals" (chiefly dramatic). The site of this old house is now covered by model lodging-houses and I suppose it was one of the earliest to disappear of those cosy places of reunion where one might enjoy a social glass in the company of wit and humour. There can't be many left. The spirit of the Age is against them, and what social enjoyment could one have in a place where there is a mechanical piano ever on the go? This is a bad digression brought about by the marriage of Mary Amelia Huddart, the tragedienne, to Warner, the publican.

The usual programme at the Marylebone was Drama—Legitimate or otherwise, though once, at least, there were Promenade Concerts under Jullien—but at Christmas there was always a pantomime, and these shows, like those at the Grecian and Britannia and other outlying houses, were not, as a rule, based on a nursery tale but made up "new and original" every year. One such was "Harlequin XXX Sir John Barleycorn or the Fairies of the Hop and the Vine."

The stage was celebrated for its great depth, said to be the deepest in all London, and so wonderful Transformation Scenes could be arranged, opening up vista after vista to an apparently illimitable distance. The Harlequinade was also of the best with clowns like Tom Matthews, who had learned from the great Grimaldi himself.

E. T. Smith had the Marylebone from 1850 to 1852 and only relinquished it to take on Drury Lane and a few other places of amusement! In 1853, it came under James W. Wallack, who opened with a comedy and burlesque, succeeded at Christmas by the usual uncommon pantomime ("King Ugly Mug and My Lady Lee of London Bridge") and followed in February, 1854, by Edward Stirling's romantic drama adapted from "La Prière des Naufragés," called "The Struggle for Gold and the Orphan of the Frozen Sea." Another version of the same play was "The Sea of Ice" and yet another was given at the Adelphi (which I remember with great delight) and which was called "The Prayer in the Storm or the Thirst for Gold"—played *inter alios* by Fernandez, Genevieve Ward and Cicely Nott (Mrs. Sam Adams). At the Marylebone in 1854, the principal characters were taken by Wallack and his wife, and E. F. Edgar than a leading *jeune premier*, while the child, Marie, who is left floating on the block of ice and says her prayers in the midst of the storm, was Miss Madge Robertson—our Mrs. Kendal. I think this must have been her first appearance on the London stage; at least, I have been unable to trace an earlier one.

Wallack did not disdain the gentle art of advertisement.   His poster referring to this production is set forth as follows :

> : : : the Frozen Sea—
> Stupendous effect of the breaking-up of the ice—
> The child of the Lascours saved by the timely assistance of a Danish vessel, which appears in full sail !
> > N.B.   This Scene will occupy the entire Stage, and will constitute the Most Magnificent Mechanical Effect ever witnessed.

Miss Robertson was also billed to appear as the blind child in an adaptation of Dickens's *Seven Poor Travellers* and a couple of years afterwards was a tiny elf in a pantomime.   Her father and mother and brother were also in the Wallacks' company. She once played the pathetic child in " The Stranger " but rather spoilt the pathos when, catching sight of her nurse in the audience, she suddenly called out " Oh, Nursey, look at my new shoes ! "

The Wallacks went in for Shakespeare as well as mere melodrama, and gave creditable representations of " As You Like It " and other plays, chiefly, perhaps, for the exhibition of Mr. and Mrs. Wallack in the leading parts.   The principal interest for me, however, in their management lies, not in their own doings, but in the fact that I have traced the early appearance of a young lady whose equal as an emotional and dramatic actress on the English stage I have never seen, though I am an " old fogy " and have been a constant playgoer for nearly sixty years.

In 1857, Emery took over the theatre in Church Street producing a very good melodrama (" Ruth Oakley ") in which one is interested to find the name of another child actress in the small person of Miss Ranoe afterwards (in the sixties) William to the Black Eyed Susan of Patty Oliver, and eventually the second wife of Sir Francis Burnand.

Emery was a very fine character actor.   He was at the Olympic for some years, creating several new parts during that time, notably Fouché in Tom Taylor's " Plot and Passion " and many rôles in plays founded on the novels of Dickens such as Peggotty in " Little Em'ly " (*David Copperfield*) Captain Cuttle in " Heart's Delight " (*Dombey and Son*), Jonas Chuzzlewit, and John Peerybingle in a version of *The Cricket on the Hearth*.   He must have been forty when he took the Marylebone and over sixty when he played Captain Cuttle.   He was with Fechter in some of his productions, notably as Caleb Balderstone in " The Master of Ravenswood."   The name is more familiar to present-day playgoers in the person of Miss Winifred Emery (Mrs. Cyril Maude) whose loss the stage has recently had to deplore.

In 1858 came the first tenancy of Joseph Arnold Cave, perhaps the only really successful manager of the Marylebone, with the possible exception of Nelson Lee. He produced many exciting melodramas of the kind to suit the neighbourhood, and his avoidance of anything tending to the more high-brow sort of play may have ensured his comparative success. The pantomime always remained the chief event of the year, and Cave knew exactly, from experience, what would please his audience in this line. They were gorgeous enough to satisfy those who liked Grand Transformation Scenes and glittering Fairy Dells and entrancing Princes and Princesses and their trains, funny enough for such as looked chiefly to the comic scenes, while the Harlequinade was always made a special feature. Though other theatres have also claimed to have the "Longest stage in London," there was no doubt whatever about the extended length of the Marylebone stage. I remember I always went to a Pantomime there whenever possible on purpose to see this huge extent of stage. Now that the old house has been degraded to the level of a mere Cinema, I presume the proprietors have been able to make money by letting or selling this length of ground ; for the Movies only require a flat background and may be shown up against a mere wall quite as well as on a stage.

Perhaps some playgoers will remember Cave better as the manager of the Old Vic, which he had in the sixties and the early seventies and again in the eighties when it had been rebuilt. One of his productions there during his first tenancy was a version of Pierce Egan's *Tom and Jerry* put on under the title of "Life in London Fifty Years ago." The part of Jerry was taken by James Fawn, in later life a singer at the old-fashioned music-halls and often seen in the pantomime at Drury Lane. Cave was recalled to be the first manager after the building of the Vic and it was about then that he made popular a song with the refrain "I'm ninety-five ! I'm ninety five ! "

The Marylebone and the Vic were not the only places of amusement run by this busiest of men. He managed the Alhambra for a time and the Aquarium (or Imperial) theatre and that rather modern transpontine house the "Elephant and Castle," and I believe he had something to do with a queer little place, half theatre and half music-hall, somewhere in Bayswater called the "Cosmotheca." This out-of-the-way hall is said to have been the scene of the first public appearance of Dan Leno on a stage. Cave in his boyhood was employed in a warehouse in the City where Flexmore, the future clown and dancer, was also working, and Cave being himself an expert step dancer (a sort of *dieudonné* art which cannot be acquired if it is not "in you") taught the steps to Flexmore who afterwards became very famous as a dancer and clown at the Grecian and elsewhere.

Before blossoming into a regular actor, and long before he was a manager, Cave sang as a Christy Minstrel—as blackened minstrels were always called till they took the name of Moore and Burgess Minstrels—singing sentimental ballads and comic songs with odd refrains such as "Wheel about and Turn about and Jump Jim Crow."

When he was established as a manager his companies included at various times many names of great note in the dramatic profession, for he had under him Ben Webster the elder, Paul Bedford, Phelps, James Anderson, Walter Montgomery, Ryder, Warner, Hermann Vezin, Marie Litton, Madame Celeste and Mrs. Stirling. He seems to have always retained an affection for any place with which he had been once associated, for I find him going back to the Marylebone after having left it for some years and again taking over the "New" Old Vic which he had managed so well years before.

Cave lived to a good old age. In his last days, chiefly through the help of the *Referee* and other friends he was admitted a Brother at the Charterhouse as Odell and Morton, the dramatist, had been before. He died there two years before the Great War, being nearly ninety years of age.

The Marylebone was entirely rebuilt and enlarged in 1864 and the new management tried to cater for a definite kind of audience, for it was called "The Western Home of East End Melodrama" thereby letting the public know that they need not go so far afield for a real blood-curdler, but could get one not far from Marble Arch.

In 1868, the director was a Mr. H. R. Lacey, who flew at higher game, for he obtained permission to rename the theatre the "Royal Alfred" after the second son of Queen Victoria, and actually induced that Royal Highness to be present on the opening night. The play produced on this auspicious occasion was called "Pindee Singh" written round the Indian Mutiny. Amy Sedgwick, an actress of more than ordinary ability, was cast for the title rôle, an Indian Princess who falls in love with a Major of the British Army. This was played by George Melville, a *jeune premier* better known at Sadler's Wells and who had been in the original cast of "It's Never Too Late to Mend" at the Princess's.

Amy Sedgwick was a very popular actress in London in the late fifties and sixties of the nineteenth century. In 1857 she made her first appearance as Pauline in "The Lady of Lyons" and in the same year created the rôle of Hester Grazebrook in "An Unequal Match," a comedy which has always been very popular with budding actresses.

She was at the old Princess's for a time, but the greater part of her career was passed at the Haymarket, which theatre she herself managed for a season. She retired from the stage, I think, when she became Mrs. Pemberton and before the public had had time to get tired of her, and took to training young dramatic aspirants. I suppose Miss Sedgwick, though a famous comedy actress in her day, is now quite forgotten.

In spite of the fillip given to it by Royal patronage, the " Royal Alfred " continued to be a dismal failure as a theatre and Mr. Lacy gave up after a short trial of three or four months.

Miss Henrade, who had acted successfully with Fechter and others, next tried to make the Marylebone a success ; her venture also failed ; she herself was probably too refined an actress for the neighbour-hood.

It then came to be more or less like the suburban theatres of the present day, where prominent actors from the West End took their companies now and then for a short season. Miss Henrietta Hodson, for example, was here once for a little, with her company from the Queen's, Long Acre.

After struggling along as the " Royal Alfred " for some years, and vainly trying to live up to its august name, the theatre once more, in 1873, was known as the Royal Marylebone Theatre.

As I have said, Cave had it again, but its *dégringolade* had begun ; it was sliding down the hill. Playgoers would not go to Church Street, Edgware Road, with all its unpleasant surroundings when so many new theatres had been built nearer West End haunts and in more pleasant neighbourhoods. It gradually fell to the rank of a third-rate house for cheap melodrama, though some may have made the journey at Christmas to see the pantomime, especially after Cave had taken it under his wing for the second time.

One curious event I ought not to omit. That is the production of a version of *Le Juif Polonais* at the Royal Alfred two nights before Irving electrified London with his totally distinct version of the same story at the Lyceum under the title of " The Bells."

The true inwardness of this more than odd coincidence is, and perhaps always will be, " wropt in mystery." As a mere playgoer and not in any of the secrets of the craft I can't explain it—but the facts are these.

On November 25th, 1871, the Bateman management produced as a stop-gap (for no one, except perhaps Irving himself, anticipated the enormous success it became) a play founded on MM. Erckmann-Chatrian's weird tale, *Le Juif Polonais*. It was made by Leopold Lewis, a solicitor, who, I don't think, ever produced a successful play before or since. Every one knows the electrifying reception of that piece, how it brought much gold to the depleted treasury of the Lyceum and the pockets of the Batemans, and how it was revived again and again. A few nights *previous to this*, a rather freer version of the same story, called "Paul Zegers," made by Burnand, had been put on at the Royal Alfred, then under the direction of Charles Harcourt. It differed slightly from the Lyceum version in that the actual murder of the Polish Jew was seen on the stage. It failed as completely as the other version succeeded. It may have been only a curious coincidence, but curious it certainly was. It does not seem likely that Irving knew of this intended production or its failure in time to postpone his version, or he would have hesitated another risk of failure after the bad times that the Bateman management had been experiencing. The original Matthias in the French play was Talien, who played it as a common peasant. Coquelin afterwards did the same.

I do not think many more high-class experiments were made at the house in Church Street. Its frequenters would tolerate nothing but the good old melodrama that they understood and appreciated. "Jack Long of Texas or The Shot in the Eye" was a specimen containing, I believe, a good representation of a prize fight.

In the same year, 1871, there appeared at the Marylebone (still called the Royal Alfred), an actor who had passed a most adventurous life before adopting the stage as a profession. This was William Pennington, who, son of a North London schoolmaster, had begun life as a teacher, then emigrated to Australia, then tried teaching again, and finally enlisted in the famous "Cherry Pickers," *i.e.*, the 11th Hussars. He was twenty-two years old at the time and soon afterwards was sent out to the Crimea, where he took part in the Battle of the Alma, and in the famous charge of the Light Brigade at Balaclava under Lord Cardigan. He acted at Drury Lane with Phelps and at the Haymarket with a company of his own, including James Anderson, John Ryder, Ada Cavendish and Henry Marston, but he chiefly appeared at the outlying theatres like Sadler's Wells, where he appeared in the time of Miss Marriott, and at the Marylebone. His recital of "The Charge of the Light Brigade" was always enthusiastically received, probably largely owing to the fact that he had taken part in that charge himself. He was a great favourite of Mr. Gladstone's and came to be known as "Mr. Gladstone's own tragedian," and the Premier took Mrs. Gladstone to see him when acting at the Royal Alfred. After this engagement, he appears to have supported Miss Genevieve Ward in her first appearance on the English stage at Manchester in 1873—and he played again at Drury Lane two or three years later in an adaptation of *Peveril of the Peak*.   In his later life, he became a public reciter and reader and posed as the model for the central Hussar in Lady Butler's great picture of " Balaclava."

A Mr. Charles Sinnett was a standing dish at the Marylebone for many years.   He was Conn in a production of Boucicault's " Shaughraun " in 1885, and thirty-one years before had played the hero in " The Struggle for Gold," when Mrs. Kendal had made her first appearance.   His acting was, of course, of the most robust order suited to the theatre and its neighbourhood, or he would not have been there so long.

A type of drama much favoured at the old Marylebone was the gruesome type like " Susan Hopley " or " Katharine Howard " with corpses and coffins, bloody murders and bleeding victims.   Only one thing never changed.   As long as it was a theatre, there was a pantomime at Christmas.   Perhaps there is a pantomime at Christmas still.   One ought to be able to make a very good sort of pantomime out of a Movie Show, and it is to that sad state that the famous old home of melodrama has been reduced at last.

THE ALEXANDRA THEATRE, HIGHBURY BARN

The Alexandra Theatre at Highbury Barn, at one time known as Willoughby's Tea Rooms, was an outlying house attached, like so many of its kind, to a tavern.

The site of this old place of amusement was one of more than ordinary interest.   There was, long ago, a sort of castle called Highbury House, forming the country seat of the Priors of St. John's, Clerkenwell.

Later, the ground on which this has been built was partly covered by a street called Highbury Place which, in mid-eighteenth century, consisted of about forty houses inhabited by respectable, middle-class folk.   In No. 38, for instance, lived Abraham Newland, chief cashier of the Bank of England, who gave his name to bank-notes early in the nineteenth century much in the same way that the modern Treasury notes used to be called " Bradburys."   It was, in short, a thoroughly respectable neighbourhood.

Adjoining the tavern referred to above, was an old farm-house, said to have formed part of the original manor-house, and a large barn attached to this farm-house eventually gave its name to the place of entertainment.

It may be noted that the Barn had at one time been a cook-house and eating-place for those who like to dine now and then away from home and in a more or less "picnicky" style. It was frequented by Oliver Goldsmith in his day, and it is on record that his dinner used to cost only 10d., including two courses, pastry and a penny for the waiter.

Later on, the owner, one Willoughby, laid out a bowling-green and tea-gardens and started to cater for public dinners, clubs, etc. On one occasion, in 1808, eight hundred persons sat down to hot dinners ; upwards of seventy geese being roasted for the occasion at the same fire.

In 1818, the property was purchased by the proprietor of the Grove House, Camberwell, and from his hands passed into the possession of John Hinton, ex-landlord of the " Eyre Arms," St. John's Wood, who, finding a falling-off in the number of beanfeasts and dinners, tried to resuscitate the fortunes of the place by organizing concerts with the Band of the Grenadier Guards.

In course of time, the place was considerably enlarged and embellished, becoming a large tavern with a ballroom in which there were several fine pictures that had belonged to the Duke of Northumberland at Sion House.

In 1860, the then manager, Archibald Hinton, son of the previous owner, gave up possession to take over a similar undertaking at Norwood called the Anerley Gardens, and the Highbury Barn began its most successful period under Edward Giovanelli, an ex-clown of the fifties and uncle of the famous Leopold family, who built a commodious theatre in the grounds and christened the whole place " The Alexandra Theatre and Highbury Barn." He enlarged the ballroom for use in wet weather, though on fine days there was always dancing alfresco on a huge platform in the grounds, said to be 4000 feet square.

A burlesque on the subject of " Ernani " was one of the first pieces to be given in the new theatre, the cast of which included the inimitable Danvers (afterwards famous as Dame Hatley in the New Royalty " Black Eyed Susan ") and Rachel Sanger, member of a well-known theatrical family, who in later years was Fatima to the Blue Beard of Lionel Brough, the Selim of Lydia Thompson, and the Heathen Chinee of Willie Edouin, in a burlesque that ran for years.

Many artistes who made their way to the top of the profession are to be found among those who appeared from time to time under Giovanelli or the ubiquitous E. T. Smith who succeeded him (see the Chapter on Astley's). Many singers, actors, actresses and variety artistes were engaged in the endeavour to make the Alexandra Theatre pay. Rebecca Isaacs and Vernon Rigby in 1862 ; Blondin in 1868 ; Natator the Man-Frog and the Siamese Twins in 1869—are some

THE GARDENS AT HIGHBURY BARN

From an old print of 1851

of the names I have come across showing the variety of the entertainment provided. Blondin, of course, may be said to have had a reputation world-wide. He was the most famous tight-rope walker of all time, his real name being Jean François Gravelet. He was born at St. Omer in 1829, educated at a public school at Lyons, but soon took to the calling he followed to his death. In 1888, I saw him at the Aquarium when he was over sixty-four years of age. Perhaps he owed his great celebrity and fortune to the idea of crossing Niagara Falls on a rope. He succeeded in doing this many times, blindfolded in a sack, trundling a wheelbarrow, on stilts, carrying a man on his back, and finally sitting down midway while he made and ate an omelette. He created a great sensation in London once by turning somersaults on stilts on a rope 170 feet from the ground. It is a fact that he once seriously offered to wheel Queen Victoria across Niagara Falls in a barrow. He retired at the age of 72 and lived at Ealing in a house he had christened " Niagara House," where he had a high rope fixed up in his back garden to practise every day till the day of his death which occurred at the age of 73 years, twelve months after his final performance in public. It is well known that he never felt so safe when there was a net spread under him according to the regulations ; he said it made him nervous. The pole he carried was of an enormous weight enabling him to keep his balance under all circumstances. It is said he first began to practise rope walking when only four years old.

During all the earlier years of its existence Highbury Barn had been a most respectable place where citizens might take their wives and daughters with perfect confidence, but this did not continue, and in 1870 the dancing licence was refused in consequence of repeated complaints about the noise and rioting. When E. T. Smith took it over in 1871, he engaged Leotard, from the Alhambra, and other celebrities in trying to make it pay, but the place had acquired a bad name from the character of its frequenters—women of " the oldest profession in the world " and a low type of men expensively got up in women's clothes. The theatre itself only lasted six years, and was finally closed down in 1871.

THE ALEXANDRA (OR PARK) THEATRE, CAMDEN TOWN

This small and rather pretty house in Camden Town—not far from the two famous public-houses, the " Britannia " and the ' Mother Redcap "—opened on May 31st, 1874. Its first manager was Thorpe Pede, a musician of some repute, who had previously been known for his setting of a version of " Oberon " at the Olympic two or three years before.

It cost £20,000 to build, and may be considered to have been the forerunner of those suburban houses where the management makes a speciality of importing whole companies from various sources to play in popular successes, and thereby save the local inhabitants the trouble and expense of a journey to West End theatres. The first programme, however, included two original pieces, an operetta called " Marguerite " by the manager himself, and a drama by Reece called " Friendship : or Golding's Debt." In the operetta, one finds the names of J. W. Turner and Gertrude Ashton, both artistes who made their names in " Opera in English " and in the drama (a poor piece) were Tom Swinbourne, Henry Forrester and Miss Carlisle.

Thomas Swinbourne was what is generally known as a " sound " actor, that is, one who could be fairly trusted to get through certain parts, if not with distinction, at any rate without disaster. Ten years before the opening of the Camden Town Theatre, he had appeared at Drury Lane as Othello to the Iago of John Ryder and the Desdemona of Fanny Clifford, and previously to that had been a favourite in the provinces. He was in the version of " The Heart of Midlothian," with which Boucicault had opened the " New Westminster " (Astley's) with such a flourish of trumpets, and at Drury Lane as Hubert to the King John of Phelps and the Prince Arthur of Percy Roselle (the dwarf brother of Amy Roselle), and also as Joseph Surface to the Sir Peter of Phelps. He was thus a very experienced actor and became a member of the Bateman company at the Lyceum when managed by Irving, playing Jason to the Medea of Miss Bateman (Mrs. Crowe), Macduff to Irving's Macbeth, Buckingham in " Richard III," King in " Hamlet," etc. He was said to be always a most popular member of the profession.

In 1875 Walter Bentley and a Miss Clayton appeared as Claude Melnotte and Pauline. The lady does not seem to have been of much account, but Bentley was another of those reliable actors who could be trusted not to let the show down ! He was a very good looking man and excellent in parts like Claude Melnotte, Rob Roy (at Sadler's Wells with Mrs. Bateman who played Helen Macgregor) Romeo and juvenile lead generally.

The fare at the Alexandra did not vary much. As might be expected from the character of the neighbourhood, it was principally strong meat that was set out for local consumption. Melodramas or plays with a strong sentimental interest paid best. In 1877 a very old piece by Leman Rede was put on called " The Rake's Progress." This had been done as long ago as 1833 at the old City Theatre in Cripplegate where the fare was always of the strongest. The author, a well-known journalist, had written several plays of sorts, but " The

Rake's Progress" appears to have been the most successful. He was a cousin of the celebrated Mrs. Waylett (see the Chapter on East End Theatres). In the production at the Alexandra was Lin Rayne who afterwards was in the Bancrofts' company at the Prince of Wales's and was one of the best Sir Benjamin Backbites ever seen.

In the same year, the theatre was taken over by a Madame St. Claire who put on "Romeo and Juliet" for the purpose of showing herself as Romeo and her daughter as Juliet. Kyrle Bellew made an early appearance as Paris and a very experienced actor, H. P. Grattan, was the Mercutio. But Madame St. Claire seems to have been more of a spiritualistic medium than an actress. As Mary Marshall she had taken part in many séances. Perhaps the spirits had advised her to try her luck on the stage. If so, it was bad advice.

Many adaptations from the French were produced at the Alexandra Theatre, which, by the way, had become the Park Theatre (perhaps from its vicinity to Regent's Park) by 1879. The Douglasses from the Standard Theatre, Shoreditch, were by that time interested in its fortunes and the company was largely made up of artistes who had made their name at the big theatre in the East End. Among these were Stella Brereton and Amy Steinberg, two very clever actresses, the latter of whom had played at Sadler's Wells and Drury Lane with Phelps and Barry Sullivan, Edward Price and others. The companies also included West End favourites like McIntyre, Fanny Addison, Odell and Ada Murray. The adaptor of these plays was the "stock-author" of the Standard, James Willing ; at least, he may be regarded as such considering the number of plays he wrote or adapted for the Shoreditch house.

He wrote, for instance, a version of Charlotte Brontë's "Jane Eyre" that was given at Camden Town late in 1879. In this, Stella Brereton did well as the heroine and Odell gave a realistic picture of the clergyman.

The following year Miss Brereton appeared in a version of "Edwin Drood" as the heroine Rosa Budd, and later on in the same year the indefatigable Willing was ready with a play founded on Ouida's novel *Held in Bondage*, which had quite a good run and was well put on and well acted.

Soldene brought a company in "Geneviève de Brabant" and other bouffe successes, and English Opera companies—or rather companies for the performance of operas in English were frequently there. It was during a visit from one of these that the theatre was finally destroyed by fire in September after a performance of "La Sonnambula" by a troupe styling itself "The National Grand Opera Company."

This house only lasted eight years from the time it was first built to the night it was burned down, and no attempt was made to rebuild it. It was quite a pleasant little house which I remember very well, but must be considered as one of the least notable of all London theatres.

CHAPTER XIV

THE IMPERIAL THEATRE
(With some prefatory Notes on the Aquarium itself)

WITH a perfectly laudable, but generally futile, endeavour to combine instruction with amusement, to sweeten the bitter taste of a lesson, to hide, in short, the powder in a pleasant jam, many worthy people of this land of England have started at various times Institutions or Exhibitions, or Shows, with the object of imparting scientific knowledge to the graceless ignoramuses of an idle world.

Thus, the Great and Good Victoria, egged on by her very German and rather *guindé* spouse, conceived the idea of the First Great International Exhibition, not only as a gathering place for representatives of all Nations of the Earth, and a prelude to Universal Peace, but also as a means of affording instruction for the masses.

The building itself, embodying this Great Idea, was designed by the genius of Sir Joseph Paxton.

> " As though 'twere by a wizard's rod
> A blazing arch of lucid glass
> Leapt, like a fountain, from the grass
> To meet the sun ! "

It survives in the Crystal Palace, now chiefly noted for firework nights, football matches and for the fact that it is the most difficult place for a Londoner to get to, though only a mile or two away. Nothing remains in Hyde Park to mark the spot, or remind one of the Exhibition of 1851, save an elm tree, which, by special order of Queen Victoria, was included under the glass roof—and a public-house near bearing the sign of " The Paxton's Head."

But the ultimate development of this gracious idea was a series of Annual Exhibitions which each year became less and less of an Exhibition and more and more of an Amusement Park, culminating at last in the Earls Court and White City Shows, frankly run for the gaiety of the men and women of all worlds including the half one !

Nor were the so-called Exhibitions the only places opened for the combination of instruction with amusement. In Leicester Square, in the centre of the district where all the foreign naughtinesses of our

capital are said to abound, a building was raised in 1854, called the
" Royal Panopticon of Science and Art." It was incorporated by
Royal Charter, opened, I believe, with due formality—*and* with
prayer !—and it failed—failed disastrously. All the scientific
toys and exhibits were ignominiously sold up and the undertaking
put into Bankruptcy. There was, evidently, too much powder
and too little jam. The building was then purchased, lock, stock
and barrel, by that well-known impresario, Mr. E. T. Smith (who
doubtless got it very cheap) and opened (oh, Mr. Smith !) on Sundays
for sermons and sacred concerts.

But this astute showman must have had other plans in his mind
when he bought the place beyond the mere providing of a Sabbath
day resort. In the prospectus of the defunct Panopticon an awe-
struck public had been informed that :

" While the eye is gratified with an exhibition of every startling
novelty, which Science and the Fine Arts can produce, and the ear
is enchanted with soul-stirring music, the mind shall have food of
the most invigorating character."

When Smith came into power, he must have said to himself
" We want a thorough change," so Sunday sermons having failed to
draw, he executed a bold *volteface* and turned the place into a Circus
with Clowns, Ladies through Hoops, Haute Ecole and all complete,
including, later on, Léotard—the most wonderful trapezist London
had ever seen.

From a Circus, with its cosy little tables where one could sit and
drink while one looked at the horses, to the Alhambra Music Hall
as known to the *viveurs* and *noceurs* of the mid-nineteenth century
was but a step. Long before the naughty Promenade at the Empire
aroused the indignation of Mrs. Ormiston Chant there was a naughty
Promenade at the Alhambra.

And yet another Institution for Instruction and Amusement
arose in January, 1876, near the site of old Tothill Fields, where
Pest houses of the Great Plague had stood and on the very spot
where Vincent Crummles and the Infant Phenomenon (Davenport
and his daughter in real life) had perhaps enacted the " Indian Savage
and the Maiden." It was called, somewhat grandiloquently, " The
Royal Aquarium and Winter Garden, Westminster."

Instruction was said to be obtainable—perhaps of a fishy kind—
but you could also lunch and tea and dine in the galleries and elsewhere and there was a theatre attached, though in a separate building.
Concerts and Variety Shows were organized and the space was filled
in round the sides with Flowers, Perfumery, and Glove Stalls and

Side Shows, with Freaks and, of course, Fish. The fish, though few in number, were on view for some time ; in fact, I think that one or two lingered on to the very end twenty-seven years later, in 1903— but I have always wondered whether anyone went to look at them and if the water was ever changed !

The Royal Aquarium, in short, was intended to be a sort of Crystal Palace in London within easy reach of Charing Cross, a covered-in promenade for the wet weather, with the glass cases of live fish thrown in. In truth, the attractions of the place soon began to be very "fishy" indeed. Ladies promenaded there up and down o'nights without the escort of any gentleman friend (till, maybe, they found one) and the appeal of the management to sensation-lovers was very wide indeed. Bare-backed ladies dived from the roof or were shot out of a cannon, or sat in a cage covered with hair and calling themselves "Missing Links." Zulus, Gorillas, Fasting Humans, Boxing Humans and Boxing Kangaroos, succeeded one another in rapid changes, and failed in time to attract. After less than thirty years of life, the sect of the Wesleyan Methodists bought up the place and reared on the site that very unecclesiastical-looking dome which squats like a huge broody hen within a few yards of the Abbey. So did the Salvationists turn the dear old Grecian into a Hall of Hallelujah lads and lasses. So did Mr. Spurgeon hold the Surrey when his Tabernacle was burned ; but the Surrey survived that adventure : the others succumbed.

The Albert Palace in Battersea Park and the Alexandra Palace on Muswell Hill were embodiments of similar efforts to "raise the masses." The last-named is still in existence to give solace to northern Londoners and, incidentally, to provide one of the most curiously-shaped and most rowdy race-courses in the kingdom ; but the Albert Palace after lasting but a few years has been all destroyed with the exception of a very magnificent organ which cost a vast sum and was sold cheap to the Fathers of a Dominican Church.

Which ends my prefatory notes and brings me at last to the real subject of this chapter—the Imperial Theatre once called the Aquarium and once the Afternoon Theatre.

I think the original idea was to make it a real afternoon theatre but that did not pay its way, as was to be expected, and so it became an afternoon and evening theatre both.

Labouchere, who was never happy unless he had a finger in some theatrical pie, and had an actress wife to satisfy as well, seems to have been the first director of its fortunes ; but it changed hands so many times and was such an unlucky house altogether, even after it had been gorgeously rebuilt by Mrs. Langtry, that no complete chronicle of it year by year could be made interesting to the general reader. I shall therefore glance at the principal events in its life of thirty-one years, for it outlived its parent, the Aquarium proper, by three years.

Perhaps the most successful of all the Seasons at this theatre was that in which Marie Litton, supported by an excellent company, including Farren, Edgar, Ryder, Lionel Brough, Kyrle Bellew, Denny, Carlotta Addison and Mrs. Stirling, appeared in a round of Old Comedy Revivals such as "The Liar," "The Beaux Stratagem," "She Stoops to Conquer," etc. These were at first only done in the afternoon and another entertainment was provided for the evening audiences. But afterwards owing to their success they were continued as a regular evening show. At Christmas, whatever the company may have been playing during the year, there was always a pantomime, and one of these was produced under the management of J. A. Cave, the successful director of the Old Vic and the only manager who made the Marylebone pay.

In this pantomime it is related that the famous Jenny Hill—then a small child—made her first appearance as "the legs of one of the animals" and by some mischance was left behind on the stage with her own clothes on her head, placed there for safety or for the protection of herself from the other part of the animal's frame. The pantomimes at the Aquarium were no great productions, probably about on a level with those produced by Manager Cave at the Vic or the Marylebone, but it was a tradition of those days for most houses to have a Christmas Show of some kind. I myself can remember regular pantomimes at the Adelphi, Princess's, Covent Garden, besides at Drury Lane and all the outlying houses ; and no East End Theatre was ever without its pantomime at Christmas. Sometimes they ran till nearly Easter and sometimes only a few weeks. As far as I remember the pantomime at Mrs. Sara Lane's Great Theatre at Hoxton used to run longer than any other.

Towards the end of 1877, Phelps, the last great actor of the fifties and sixties, the last of the great contemporaries of Charles Kean, played for a short time under Miss Litton's management at the Aquarium Theatre. He appeared in many of his best impersonations and was engaged to continue his performances in 1878. In the February of that year he reappeared in Richelieu and other parts and on March 1st made his last appearance on the stage. He was playing Wolsey in "Henry VIII" and was supported by young Norman Forbes-Robertson in the part of Cromwell.

In his great speech beginning "Farewell, a long farewell to all my greatness," he seems to have acted with all his old force and vigour, but before he had reached the end of it he fainted on to the shoulder of Norman Forbes and was practically carried off the stage. The audience was loud and vehement in their applause and recalls, but

Phelps had made his very last appearance on the stage and was no more seen. It is curious, as stated in his biography, that the part of Wolsey was the one he had always expressed a wish to take his farewell in—and it is yet another example out of many where the farewell words of an actor have most marvellously coincided with the circumstances.

The pantomime of 1879 was on the subject of " Aladdin," but in the afternoons of the same season the Vokes Family, who had usually been seen in pantomime at Drury Lane only, turned up at the Aquarium Theatre in " Fun in A Fog," a rough sort of " tumble and trip " entertainment, something like what is called a Revue in England, which was supplemented by Buckstone's old piece " A Rough Diamond," in which Victoria Vokes was a capital Nan.

In 1880 the character of the entertainment at this theatre underwent many changes. It was a year of change. Some of the plays were produced at the afternoon performances only, but even allowing for that the record of the year was a record of " failures."

There was a very charming production of " As You Like It " by the company in which Miss Marie Litton was leading lady, and which I think was run by the Laboucheres. The cast was an exceptionally good one. Hermann Vezin was Jaques, Kyrle Bellew, Orlando ; Farren, Adam ; Lionel Brough, Touchstone ; Miss Litton, Rosalind ; Helen Creswell, Celia ; and Sylvia Hodson (a sister of Mrs. Labouchere) Audrey. Miss Litton (afterwards Mrs. Wybrow Robertson) was the most charming Rosalind possible, very nearly the best I have ever seen, though I have always considered Mrs. Kendal actually the first for excellence. I have seen Mrs. Potter, Ada Rehan (an American version of the character and quite good in its way but not an English type), Mrs. Langtry and one or two minor ones, but I prefer Mrs. Kendal to them all. Ellen Terry never played the part, I believe ; she would have surpassed any possible Rosalind of the past, present or future. One has only to remember her Beatrice to feel that. Miss Litton in everything she undertook was most thorough. She had previous successful seasons at the Court Theatre and very few English actresses have had the same charming presence coupled with real dramatic talent.

The same year brought a Dutch company from Rotterdam to play in " Anne Mie " a piece of domestic interest, but which was so favourably received at the Imperial that an English translation was made for the Prince of Wales's and the leading part entrusted to Genevieve Ward, who was supported by Fernandez, Flockton, Forbes-Robertson and Cissy Grahame. Madame Beersmann, the leading lady of the Dutch company, also appeared in a Dutch version of Giacometti's play of " Marie Antoinette " which, I think, was one of Ristori's great parts. Mr. and Mrs. Florence, American comedians of repute in their own country who were acting at the Gaiety, appeared in this same year at the Imperial in the afternoon in a play called " The Mighty Dollar." They were supported by an English company, including J. L. Shine, Myra Holme (Mrs. Pinero), Connie Gilchrist and Kate Vaughan.

Earlier in the year there had been a failure in an English version of Goethe's *Wilhelm Meister*, which was christened " The Lord of the Manor," in spite of some clever acting by Kyrle Bellew, Edgar and Lydia Cowell.

1880 also saw a trial of Comic Opera at this unlucky theatre. Edward Solomon, who had early in his professional career, as accompanist on the piano at the old Mogul Music Hall in Drury Lane, got a chance with his light opera of " Billee Taylor." This had a *succès d'estime* and it was capitally cast, for the cast included such old stagers as Stoyle, Harriet Coveney and Emma Chambers and two very creditable singers in Fleming Norton and Frederic Rivers. But it had not enough in it for a run and was soon withdrawn. Arthur Williams, the comedian, who made such a deserved success in " The Messenger from Mars " at a later date was also in the cast. The book was a poor one, and if the public wanted genuine light opera in English there were the Gilbert and Sullivan pieces holding the field against all comers.

At Christmas that year the pantomime was " Little Red Riding Hood," but in the afternoon the Hanlon-Lees were giving their fine show which, I think, was called " Fun on a Liner." This was a real pantomime—a whole piece gone through in dumb show with great effect.

The theatre was used for afternoon performances of plays from other theatres ; one such, in 1880, being a farcical comedy from the Folly called " Impudence," a very amusing piece of its kind (the " Pink Dominoes " kind) extremely well acted by the author, Carton, his wife (Miss Compton), Leonard Boyne, Righton, Laura Linden, Emily Miller and others.

During Labouchere's management (or ownership) of the theatre he brought out a version of the Dedlock episodes in " Bleak House " called " Jo," of which I have already given some notice in my account of the Globe Theatre. Miss Jenny Lee was again the Jo and Dolores Drummond the Hortense ; I don't think the remainder of the cast calls for any comment. It was repeated at the Strand some years after with undiminished success.

In 1881, there were some performances of " Led Astray," a play adapted by Boucicault from " La Tentation." Helen Barry resumed her original character of Armande, which she had created some years previously. She is remembered for her debut as the Queen of the Amazons in " Babil and Bijou " at Covent Garden in 1872, for which she was chosen on account of her fine figure and height. On the first night of that stupendous production, it is said that she had attached a long tail of magnificent hair to the inside of her helmet to add to the effect of her own. Her helmet fell off in the procession and picking it up too hastily she put it on wrong side foremost with the result that her lovely hair was not " hanging down her back " but over her face. This may be a " story of the stage " and I tell it as a piece of gossip ; I was there myself as a boy home for the holidays but did not notice the incident.

In 1882, Mrs. Langtry was at the Imperial in " An Unequal Match," in the part created by Amy Sedgwick. She appears to have satisfied the critics, though I do not think she was ever reckoned a really great actress. Her beauty, which fascinated all who saw her, men and women alike, was a great asset, as was also the fact that she could bring on to the stage the manners of a lady accustomed to live with ladies and gentlemen. It has always seemed an astonishing thing to me that we should expect artistes to assume on the stage the carriage and manners of a class to which they have always been strangers in their private life. When they can do so, they are actors indeed and in truth. The opposite of this was exemplified by Mrs. Langtry's acting in the earlier scenes of " An Unequal Match " where she could not help looking and talking like a lady though she was not meant to represent one.

Kate Hodson, another clever sister of Mrs. Labouchere, gave a most delightful performance of the Yorkshire barmaid who is translated to the upper classes—as they are sometimes called. Sala in one of his longest criticisms says her performance was " full of vigour, decision, intelligence and ' go ' ; she was equally at home as the Yorkshire barmaid with a broad dialogue and as the suddenly civilized soubrette." She played Audrey when Mrs. Langtry essayed the part of Rosalind later in the season. But it was not astonishing when one remembers what stock she came of : her father, George Hodson, an actor of much experience ; her mother, Miss Noel, sister of Mrs. Henry Marston, another famous actress, and her sister, Henrietta, born at the old Bower itself in the very atmosphere of the oranges and the sawdust. It would have been very surprising if the sisters Sylvia and Kate Hodson had not also acted well. Mr. Sala in the same criticism in which he eulogizes Miss Kate Hodson says of Mrs. Langtry's performance of Hester Grazebrook :

" If Mrs. Langtry—and she is clever enough for almost any artistic achievement—would learn a little of the Yorkshire dialect,

and be a little more rustic and awkward in the First Act, her impersonation of Hester Grazebrook would be altogether unexceptionable.
But in this first act, as the ostensibly uncultured daughter of the
village innkeeper, she has the *allures* of a duchess. Her garb is
commendably simple ; but, as she moves and speaks in it, one is
reminded of one of the maids of honour who, in the *Memoirs of
De Grammont*, are described as masquerading on Tower Hill as
Milk-maids and orange wenches."

This confirms what I said above. Mrs. Langtry was not sufficiently good an *actress* to disguise the fact that she was really a lady.
Other actresses are not good at disguising the fact that they never
were ladies.

Miss Calhoun, a very beautiful American, and perhaps one may
say a very American beauty, took up Mrs. Langtry's part in " An
Unequal Match " and also succeeded her as Rosalind at the Imperial.
This young lady had the same advantages as Mrs. Langtry. She
was very beautiful and moved and spoke like a lady, but her stage
performances were not remarkable for very much power. The only
part I saw her in was as Dora in the Haymarket revival of " Diplomacy " in 1885. I did not think her an actress of the front rank ;
perhaps I was not an unprejudiced judge, for I had seen Mrs. Kendal
twenty times in the same part. Miss Calhoun retired early from the
stage, married a Roumanian prince and I hope, as the fairy story
books say, lived happily ever afterwards. The Langtry season may
be subjected to one deserved criticism. The fair manageress did
not take enough trouble to bring together a good enough company
to support her own efforts, especially when it was a question of doing
Shakespeare's plays. In " As you Like It," for example, Touchstone was quite good played by J. G. Taylor, an actor with a humorous
countenance and a humorous delivery ; Miss Hodson, as I have
already said, was an excellent Audrey. As for the rest, it was as if
Mrs. Langtry had copied Catalani and said " Moi, et quelques
poupées." A scratch pack not worthy of the lady who led it.

In 1883, the management of the Imperial put on " Camille "
which is the name by which the American version of " La Dame
aux Camélias " is known. It is the same old " Traviata," the same
old story founded on the pathetic story of Marie Duplessis which
Dumas made money of and which was banned by the righteous
authorities of English-speaking countries for so long. That is, it
was banned under its own name, but had been permitted under the
title of " Heartsease" for Modjeska, and was now licensed under the
title of " Camille " for a most charming actress, Miss Lingard.
The theatre was under the direction of Edgar Bruce for a time

and when he took over the Princes Theatre in Coventry Street he took Miss Lingard with him. She appeared there in " The Palace of Truth " and also in a version of Ibsen's *Dolls House*. Perhaps her greatest success was made in an adaptation of Conway's story *Called Back*, in which Tree made such a sensational appearance as Paolo Macari.

For some years the Imperial dragged on an uneventful existence. Sometimes a theatrical " Star " would take it for a short period but generally with disastrous results. But usually it was occupied by companies from other theatres or rash adventurers with plays of their own or more money than dramatic talent. It was never a success as a theatre and from that account could be had cheap for all such ventures.

In April, 1903, this unlucky house was taken by Ellen Terry in order to produce in conjunction with her son, Gordon Craig, a translation of Ibsen's *Vikings*. Mr. Craig is well known as an enthusiast on the subject of the production of plays, and has his own ideas with regard to lighting and scenery in general. This is not the place to enter into an exposition of Mr. Gordon Craig's views. He has done that himself in more than one clever publication on the subject. Apparently the theatre as constituted nowadays does not lend itself to his ideas.

" The Vikings " as seen at the Imperial was a most notable production. Miss Terry herself played Hiordis and nothing that she appears in could ever be wholly a failure. But the season was a very short one and from a financial point of view most disastrous. Miss Terry in " The Story of My Life " is quaintly informative on her son's projects and the difficulties encountered in their realization. She says :

" I think there is a great deal to be said for the views that he has expressed in his pamphlet on *The Art of the Theatre*, and when I worked with him I found him far from unpractical. It was the modern theatre that was unpractical when he was in it ! It was wrongly designed, wrongly built. We had to disembowel the Imperial behind scenes before he could even start and then the great height of the proscenium made his lighting lose all its value. He always considered the pictorial side of the scene before its dramatic significance, arguing that this significance lay in the picture and in movement—the drama having originated not with the poet but with the dancer. When his idea of dramatic significance clashed with Ibsen's, strange things would happen. . ."

Miss Terry revived " Much Ado About Nothing " at the Imperial during her short stay there, and her experiment in management might have been more successful if she had been left to carry it out by herself. It was an opportunity of making the Imperial one of the leading theatres in London, entirely thrown away. The house had been magnificently rebuilt by Mrs. Langtry and from having been one of the most uncomfortable, grubby theatres in town with, *inter alia*, the most extortionate staff of attendants ever known, had been transformed into a vision of beauty with everything done for the comfort of the audience.

In the November of the same year that saw Miss Terry's unlucky excursion into management Mr. Lewis Waller took over the theatre, opening with "Monsieur Beaucaire" that had already been played over four hundred times elsewhere. He held the place till 1906, producing many interesting and even good plays. Among these, was a version of "Ruy Blas," founded on Victor Hugo's work, which ought to have been a success and was a failure. It was made by John Davidson and may be cited as another example of how a poet can fail as a dramatist. It was declared to be tedious, and this despite the fact that the hero was Waller (who has surely never before been called "tedious") and the leading lady Mrs. Patrick Campbell. The fact is it was more a fine piece of literature than an actable stage play. I regret not to have seen it, but during these early years of the century I was far away from London and can only report from hearsay or from contemporary documents. Mrs. Campbell in her book about her life says that Waller spoke the blank verse to the audience and that she said her lines to him! Perhaps it is not to be wondered that the piece only ran for fourteen days, acted under such conditions.

Other plays put on by Waller during his tenure of three years of the Imperial were "Miss Elizabeth's Prisoner," "Hawthorne U.S.A.," "The Perfect Lover," "The Harlequin King," "Brigadier Gerard," "Henry V" and "Romeo and Juliet." Of these perhaps the most successful was "Brigadier Gerard." The novel was well known to the public in general and the hero an ideal part for Waller. Although Mrs. Langtry must have spent many thousands in her lavish rebuilding, she probably more than reimbursed herself when she sold the place in its entirety to the Wesleyan Methodists who had bought the Aquarium. I am not aware of the full details of that transaction but it seems likely that the astute finance committee of the Methodists made a good deal, for the theatre was sold to the company owning the Royal Albert Music Hall, Canning Town, who took it down carefully, numbering all the pieces, and re-erected it as the Music Hall of Dockland.

It was a curious ending for a theatre that had had such a chequered career and that at one time looked as if it might have maintained a high position among the theatres of the West End. But some theatres are born lucky, some unlucky, and some have good luck or bad luck "thrust upon them." The Imperial was essentially one of the unlucky ones.

TOOLE'S THEATRE
(Late Charing Cross or Folly Theatre)

As long ago as 1855, there was in King William Street, leading from Chandos Street to the Strand, a little place which was known as the Polygraphic Hall. It was used for entertainments by single performers, such as conjurors, lecturers and entertainers of the type of Albert Smith and Emma Stanley.

In 1855, it was the scene of a show by W. S. Woodin, and continued to be so with infrequent intervals down to as late as 1861.

Woodin was the son of a Bond Street dealer in works of Art and had been intended for the Church, but he was determined to be an actor of some kind and eventually got Blanchard to write several amusing trifles which he elaborated as time went on. "Woodin's Carpet Bag," and "Odds and Oddities" were two of these entertainments which he carried through without any assistance whatever, enacting several different characters in the course of the evening.

Such shows were very popular in the fifties and sixties when there were so many good mid-Victorian people who did not approve of the theatre but had to find some amusement somewhere. Mrs. German Reed's was another and Maskelyne and Cooke to this day attracts folk whom nothing could induce to enter the doors of a wicked playhouse.

In 1869 this Hall was transformed into the Charing Cross Theatre and opened with a triple bill. It has been said, by the way, by many authorities, and has come to be widely believed, that the site of the Charing Cross Theatre was formerly the site of the Roman Catholic Chapel of the Oratorian Fathers of St. Philip Neri, who are now settled at Brompton. This is incorrect. The Oratorians had their building on the piece of ground now occupied by the Adelaide Gallery Restaurant of Messrs. Gatti, which, however, had also been a little Hall for concerts and single entertainers.

The triple bill with which the little theatre (it was hardly bigger than the old Strand) opened was made up of an operetta, "Coming of Age"; a three-act drama "Edendale"; and a burlesque by Gilbert on the opera of Norma called "The Pretty Druidess : or the Mother, the Maid, and the Mistletoe Bough." Miss Madge Robertson delivered an inaugurative address in the course of the evening and the new house started under very favourable auspices.

The company included several good actors : J. G. Shore, G. R. Temple, Kathleen Irwin, Cicely Nott, Miss Ernstone (afterwards the original of one of the Two Orphans) and others. The same style of programme was adhered to for some time and the names of Miss Emily Fowler, and of Messrs. Philip Day and Flockton appear in the bills.

In 1870, a comedy by Wybert Reeve was put on, with Emily Fowler still as the leading lady, and there was a revival of an old "Ixion" burlesque, and the production of a new one by Gilbert with special music by Frederic Clay, called "The Gentleman in Black." Danvers (the original Dame Hatley in the Royalty "Black Eyed Susan") and young Robson had joined the company, and the general scheme seemed to have settled down to one serious item and a burlesque—very like what the programme of the Swanboroughs at the Strand and Patty Oliver at the Royalty had always been.

By 1872, Miss Fowler seems to have got tired of theatre management, and the house got into the hands of John S. Clarke, the celebrated American actor, who was so often in London and, moreover, managing London houses, that playgoers were apt to forget he was not an Englishman.

Clarke got a good company together for the presentation of old English Comedy, including Mrs. Stirling who played Mrs. Malaprop in "The Rivals" to the manager's Bob Acres. He also put on "The Widow Hunt" which he has played at so many different London houses and with so many different casts.

In May, 1873, the theatre was let by Clarke to a Mr. Richard Younge who brought his own company to appear in a new comedy by Byron called "Time's Triumph" which calls for no comment.

In 1875, the theatre was still under the lesseeship of Clarke, who appeared there from time to time but seems to have sublet the place now and again to aspiring young actors and actresses who thirsted for the laurels of the stage. A Miss Edith Lynd produced a drama on the latter years of the life of the notorious Comtesse Dubarry, introducing Marat and other Revolutionary folk.

It was followed by a new light opera by Clay called "Cattarina" only remarkable for the appearance in the title rôle of charming Kate Santley and of Henry Walsham who afterwards sang a good deal in "Opera in English" and in such works as "Les Cloches de Corneville."

In the same year, in November, a Miss Annie Lafontaine, a pupil of Amy Sedgwick, undertook the management of the Charing Cross and opened with "An Unequal Match," playing Hester Grazebrook which Miss Sedgwick had created at the Haymarket in the fifties. She was supported by Kate Phillips as the barmaid,

Lytton Sothern (son of the original Lord Dundreary) and John Nelson, the husband of Carlotta Leclercq. The dramatic world did not hear much of this young lady after this attempt, so perhaps she retired early from the profession—probably when she became Mrs. Henry Graves.

In 1872, also, the Gaiety Theatre company paid one of its occasional visits to another theatre and appeared in comedy and in the comic opera of " Rip Van Winkle " in which Fred Leslie was such a success. Nelly Farren was with them at the time. Soon after this, in fact in the very next year, the theatre entered on its first period of real success. It was taken over by Alexander Henderson, who had married the charming Lydia Thompson, and at once a big hit was made with a revival of Farnie's absurdity " Blue Beard " which had had such a run at the Globe. In the first cast Rachel Sanger had been the Fatima. She was the pretty dark-haired and dark-eyed girl that had made a great success at the Alexandra Theatre, Highbury, in the sixties. But when " Blue Beard " was revived at the Folly, she had gone one step higher to play the heroine in T. P. Cooke's nautical drama " True to the Core " revived at the Adelphi. Violet Cameron was the new Fatima, but Lydia Thompson (Selim), Lionel Brough (Blue Beard), and Willie Edouin (Heathen Chinee) were all in the original cast. There was also, I remember, a very diminutive little lady, Miss Ella Chapman, an American I think, who played a minor part but was an excellent banjo performer and had a solo all to herself. The Chinee was a strange character not in the old fairy story, and he was named Corporal Zoug-Zoug It was played by Willie Edouin in a spirit of burlesque that did much to secure the long run of the piece. Edouin had begun at the Strand in the fifties as a small boy in a pantomime (how strange it seems to hear of a pantomime at the Strand !). In later years he was better known as the producer of " Our Flat " in which both his clever daughters—May and Rose—appeared at different times.

It was in 1876 that Blue Beard drew laughter loving playgoers to the little theatre in King William Street, and it is instructive for the young actresses of the present day (who think to capture the prizes of the profession after a year or two) to note that at that time Miss Thompson had already been twenty-four years on the stage. Her first appearance seems to have been as a ballet dancer at Her Majesty's in 1852, but she soon relinquished the opera ballet for the regular stage.

In 1854, she was in the cast of " The King's Rival," by Tom Taylor and Charles Reade, at the St. James's Theatre, and it is worthy of note that this was also the play in which Toole made his first London appearance. In the same year she was in an extravaganza at the Haymarket as Little Silver-hair and in the following year as Little Bo-peep. 1859 saw her at the St. James's in " Cupid's Ladder," but by 1861 she had arrived at playing an important part in a drama of Edmund Falconer's called " Woman : or Love against the World." Then she went to the Prince of Wales's in the early seasons of the Bancrofts playing the principal boys' parts in burlesque, notably in " Der Freischütz " in the year when three or four London houses each had a burlesque of Weber's opera. As " principal boy " in burlesque Lydia Thompson could stand comparison with Marie Wilton or Miss Raynham of the Strand, or even with Nelly Farren.

She was charming to look at, a good singer, a really clever dancer, and the life and soul of the scene while on the stage. She was born in 1836, so was only sixteen years of age when she danced at Her Majesty's Opera House. One of her trips to America was full of sensational incident. She took with her a troupe of very lovely girls (among them the strikingly beautiful Pauline Markham) who were known as " Lydia's Blondes." They made a startling effect on the American youth, and one paper *The Chicago Times* presumed to make some uncalled for remarks concerning them. Miss Thompson, accompanied by Pauline Markham, proceeded to the office of the editor and said she was going to horsewhip him. He produced a revolver in the American fashion, but Pauline Markham held on to him and prevented him shooting while Lydia laid on lustily with a raw hide whip. She was fined by the magistrate two cents, or one penny, but the editor appealed and the fine was increased to 2200 dollars (about £450) which the " Blondes " always considered very cheap for the satisfaction they had got out of the affair, and it was very likely paid for them, as the sympathy was all on their side.

Lydia Thompson was twice married—first to a Mr. Tilbury, a coachmaker, who invented a particular kind of carriage to which he gave his name. Their daughter, Zeffie Tilbury, became well known and most popular on the London stage. Her second husband was an Australian, Alexander Henderson, at one time a veterinary surgeon, but who developed into an impresario of light opera and, in partnership with Farnie, produced many an amusing piece for singers like Florence St. John and Kate Monroe. Mrs. Henderson died in 1908 aged 72 years.

One of the few successes at the Folly (which was now the name of the former Charing Cross Theatre) was " Les Cloches de Corneville," in 1878. Farnie got it very cheap from Paris and Planquette, the composer, is said to have made less than £50 out of it altogether, though it must have realized many thousands in its career and is still being done by light opera companies.

No one believed in it at first and, when the first night arrived and it was found that Shiel Barry, to whom had been entrusted the part of the miser, Gaspard, had such a fearful cold he could hardly speak, every one said the piece was doomed. But that cold made the opera. Shiel Barry had never possessed a singing voice to begin with, but the croak with which he half said, half sang his part was so suited to the character that it was acclaimed a wonderful impersonation. After he had quite got rid of his cold he had to invent a croak and played it always in the same way for hundreds of nights—the longest run being after it had been transferred to the Globe. Shiel Barry had been recognized as a clever impersonator of informers and spies in Irish plays by Falconer and Boucicault, but no one ever thought he would make the success of his life in a French light opera. Violet Cameron was the first Germaine (the leading lady) in " Les Cloches " and she was succeeded by Florence St. John. But there were many different casts. At the Globe in 1879 Wilford Morgan (a fine tenor) was the Marquis ; a Miss Clement, Germaine, and a Miss Clara Thompson, Serpolette. At the reproduction in 1880 Celli, Henry Bracy, Harry Paulton, Mlle. Silva and Mlle. D'Algua were in the cast ; but the Miser seems always to have been Shiel Barry.

About this time Lydia Thompson produced a merry little piece called " Tantalus : or Many a Slip twixt Cup and Lip," by Arthur Matthison and Charles Wyndham. I note the name of Rose Cullen in the cast. She afterwards made a great success in emotional drama and comedy in America. W. J. Hill was also in this piece. He was better known in farcical comedies like " Charley's Aunt " and some of the Criterion's naughty pieces. Dolaro had the theatre for a short time for French light opera—producing Maillart's " Dragon de Villars," but in 1879 the little theatre came under the direction of Toole, though it was still called the Folly, and appeared in one of his favourite characters—Paul Pry—one of Liston's great parts.

During Toole's lesseeship of the Folly (he did not christen it Toole's till 1882) he frequently sublet the house while he was on his provincial tours or if he took an engagement at another theatre. On one of these occasions it was occupied by the celebrated Fanny Davenport, an American actress, who had a great reputation in her own country but did not succeed in making much impression on an English audience.

I remember her appearance perfectly in a very gloomy play called " Diane de Lys " by James Mortimer, the editor of the *London Figaro*, who had had some experience as a playwright and introduced " La Dame aux Camélias " to the British stage, camouflaged as " Heartsease." Miss Davenport's company included Mr. Hermann

Vezin, Philip Day (an early matinée idol!), Sophie Eyre and Eleanor Bufton, so she did not want for good support. But she was a very tall, not to say commanding, woman—something like what I have always pictured "The Fotheringay" to have been—and the Folly Theatre was one of the very smallest in London. Her height, and I may add breadth, made the house look smaller still, and when one remembers that Hermann Vezin was as remarkably short as she was remarkably tall, it will be understood that everything was out of proportion. Miss Davenport had talent, undoubtedly, but she was certainly not the huge success that all my American friends said she would be. I should not omit to say that there was not the faintest trace of American accent in Miss Davenport's speech, which was decidedly refreshing after the mangled English we get so often from the actors from the other side. Of course this lady was English born, though all her career on the stage had been in America. She was related to a very well-known English theatrical family, though I am unaware if she was any relation of that Davenport who was the model for the immortal Vincent Crummles. I do not think she made many appearances in London. In the same year Toole put on a quadruple bill at his theatre which was one of the best entertainments I ever sat through at a theatre.

The four pieces making up this programme were "Deaf as a Post,"—an old farce adapted from the French of "Le Sourd ou L'Auberge Pleine"—followed by a domestic drama dealing with the fortunes of a French émigré (admirably played by Farren), called "After Darkness, Dawn." The third item was a delightful bit of absurdity by Henry J. Byron, entitled The Villainous Squire and the Village Rose, described on the bill as a "Bucolic Pastoral." It was a skit, of course, on the old-fashioned rustic Melodrama, and included many a sly hit at the two dramas then playing at the St. James's and the Globe which were ostensibly, or not, founded on Hardy's Far from the Madding Crowd. I remember one Miss Bella Wallis as an artless country damsel. This is some time ago—1882 to be exact—and Miss Wallis's two charming daughters are now making rapid reputation for themselves. I saw one of them as the adventuress in "At Mrs. Beam's" at the Royalty Theatre and the other (Miss Hilda Moss) will take the lead in her profession in either light or serious rôles. When she is a famous actress, I shall remind her what she did for my Hospital Party during the War and how she turned up every Saturday no matter what the weather or how severe the Raid of the moment.

The fourth piece of the quadruple bill was "Robert Macaire": Toole as Jacques Strop, a part he often played with Irving.

In 1883, Toole made a very interesting and successful experi-

ment.   He revived at his little theatre one or two pieces in which he
had been successful many years before in the early days of the Queen's
Theatre in Long Acre.   One of these was Byron's *Dearer than
Life* given at the Queen's in 1868 with a cast including Toole,
Irving, Charles Wyndham, John Clayton, Henrietta Hodson and
Lionel Brough.   Another early success revived was " Uncle Dick's
Darling," said to be founded on Dickens's *Doctor Marigold*
which had been produced at the Gaiety in 1868 with Toole, Irving,
John Clayton, Miss Neilson, Miss Litton and Miss Elsworthy.
Yet another was " Artful Cards," by Burnand, which Toole loved
to revive on every possible occasion.

The year 1884 saw one of the most important events in the short
life of this theatre.   Daly's Company of American artistes made
their first appearance in England.   So much has been written and
said about this celebrated ensemble that it is not worth while to devote
much space to it.   It was essentially an ensemble ; they all acted
together most perfectly ; individually they were also excellent artistes.
If I had any fault to find with them it was on account of the liberties
they took with Shakespeare, who ought to be out of the reach of
American alterations, and on account of the worthless pieces on which,
outside Shakespeare, they wasted their excellent performances.

The play with which they opened their first season in England
was called " Casting the Boomerang " and was a conglomeration of
rubbish adapted from the German.   Other versions were put on in
London at various times ; one was called " The Hurly-Burly."
Any company less individually excellent and less accustomed to play
together than Daly's would not be able to make much of such a poor
piece.   But each member of the American company seemed to fit
into the whole in his or her proper place and this was doubtless due
to the many years they had acted together.   When they paid their
second visit to London they opened at the Strand Theatre
with another utterly unworthy piece called " A Night
Off."

Ada Rehan was the leading lady and much ink has been used in
broadcasting her praises.   But in my personal opinion the finest
actress was Mrs. Gilbert, probably the best " old woman " that
was ever seen on any stage.   John Drew, the leading man, was also
excellent and the smaller parts were all well looked after.

But Ada Rehan, charming as she was, always remained Ada
Rehan ; whether posing in the dress of Rosalind, or Viola, or
Katharine the Shrew, she was never anything but herself.   A very
charming self, I grant you, but certainly not a great actress.   Nancy
Brasher, one of her modern parts, was Ada Rehan in person, but when
she put on a costume of another age, it was still only Ada Rehan

dressed up and not the character she was representing. Even Mr. Shaw—who claimed her as his countrywoman, and therefore would not have refrained from praising her had she not been the charming lady she was—says in that curious style of his : " The critic in me is bound to insist that Ada Rehan has as yet created nothing but Ada Rehan," and later on in the same article " Nobody in England as yet knows whether Ada Rehan is a creative artist or a mere virtuoso." In the Shakespearean plays given by the Daly "Company of Comedians " not one was presented as Shakespeare wrote it. They were all altered and pulled about by Mr. Daly to suit the supposed requirements of his Company. This was reverting to what Garrick and other eighteenth-century managers did with the great English plays ; and Dryden before him, who, not content with " Antony and Cleopatra," one of the sublimest tragedies ever written, must needs produce a play founded on it called " Lost for Love." Miss Rehan really was not given a chance in the modern plays in which she appeared. As one critic put it " We owe Mr. Daly a debt of gratitude for introducing to us so often his excellent ' Company of Comedians,' but his frittering away of Miss Rehan's genius is nothing less than a crime."

In 1885 Toole returned to his own theatre. *The Upper Crust* by Byron had a trial again after being on the shelf for a year or two, and then he revived, or rather made a new version of an old play called " Dominique the Deserter " which had been seen in London fifty years previously. It was now called " Old Harry," but was not by any means a success.

Miss Eweretta Lawrence, previously seen in Adelphi melodrama, took over the theatre this year in one of Toole's periodical absences, and produced a play called " On Change " adapted from the German of the same author as wrote *Der Bibliotheker* from which " The Private Secretary " was taken.

Farren was in it and Rosina Filippi ; it did not attract much notice.

During the last years of the theatre bearing his name, Toole appeared in many different parts with intervals of letting the theatre for unimportant ventures and sometimes shutting it altogether. Among the plays produced during his tenancy were " Walker London ; " " Auntie ; " " The Upper Crust ; " " Girls and Boys," a three-act comedy by Pinero which is entirely forgotten, but which gave Toole a most amusing part and incidentally provided Miss Myra Holme (Mrs. Pinero) with some opportunities to show she could act ; and old favourites like " Paul Pry," " Robert Macaire," and the Queen's revivals I have already noticed.

In 1895 the theatre closed its doors for good and all and was absorbed into the extension wing of the Charing Cross Hospital. Toole had made it a home of his own, but, barring his productions, it was chiefly noted for the start of " Les Cloches de Corneville," the revival of " Blue Beard " and the first visit of the Daly Company to England. Twenty-six years is not a very long life for a theatre, but new ones were being built with improvements in the way of greater comfort for the audience and increased facilities for development of machinery and lighting on the stage. The old houses which had sufficed in years less sophisticated—like the Strand, the Olympic, the Globe and the Opera Comique—had to give way to more modern ideas. They were all " lost " within a few years of each other. Toole's in 1895 ; the Olympic and Opera Comique in 1899 ; the Strand about the same time ; and the Globe in 1902.

CHAPTER XV

THE BOWER SALOON AND OTHER MINOR THEATRES

IN Stangate Street, Lambeth, near the ancient site of the Stangate Ferry, by which, in the fourteenth century, the Bishop of Winchester crossed to his Palace at Westminster, once stood the Bower Saloon, a common little place of amusement which was at a later date called the "Royal Stangate Theatre," and was referred to in Robertson's "Caste" as "the little house in Stangate."

There is still some dispute as to the actual site, but wherever it stood it was in the midst of a neighbourhood much given over to the home life of actors and their families, especially those who were not earning first-class salaries. Lodgings to suit the purses of the poorer kind of "pro" abounded. Astley's, with its traditions of Ducrow and Batty and Cooke, was within a few yards. The Surrey was not far off, and one or two minor gaffs were dotted about Lambeth and Kennington. Barnard's Tavern opposite Astley's, and the "Pheasant" in the rear of it somewhere near the Bower itself, were public-houses at which actors of the lower and "barnstormer" class met to discuss the bad times or see whom they could "touch for a sub."

The Bower Saloon was built in 1837 by one Phil Phillips, scenic artist at the Surrey, Adelphi, Lyceum and other theatres, and was originally just a Saloon attached to the "Duke's Tavern" in Stangate Street, somewhere at the back of Astley's Amphitheatre, not far from where St. Thomas's Hospital now stands.

Phil Phillips, the builder, was rather a notable man in a small way. He was a contemporary of Clarkson Stansfield and had studied to be an artist. He painted Dioramas for the old Surrey Theatre, and when he bought and enlarged the Bower Saloon, in 1838, he intended it for the production of musical shows illustrated by Panoramas and Views ; but the scheme failed. He was, however, a good scenic artist, and at one time, under the patronage of Queen Victoria, he opened a Gallery near Hyde Park Corner (somewhere about the present position of the Alexandra Hotel Tap) which he called the "Chinese Gallery," where he exhibited a Panorama illustrating the visit of the Queen to Ireland in 1849. His wife was daughter of Rouse, the eccentric proprietor of the old Eagle Saloon from which the Grecian Theatre took its origin.

As a place of entertainment, the Bower had its ups and downs of success and failure. In the end, after a life of about forty years, it fell to the level of a noisy and rather disreputable gaff.

It could hardly, however, be described as such and was certainly a paying concern when run by George Hodson, who at one time had been the manager of "The Yorkshire Stingo," near Lisson Grove, that old hostelry and tea gardens from which the first London omnibus started. He was an Irish comedian famous enough in his day as the typical stage Irishman of the Halls, with green swallow-tailed coat, red waistcoat, cord breeches, worsted stockings, brogues and a caubeen, and carrying a shillelagh and a bundle. The type may be met even now in some of the provincial Halls.

Hodson was the founder of a large theatrical family, the best known of which are his son, who ran the Bower after his death, and his grand-daughters, Kate, Sylvia and Henrietta. Other members of the same family and their husbands made names for themselves in later days, among whom was Musgrove who controlled the Shaftesbury Theatre, and brought the "Belle of New York" to London.

But the best known of all was undoubtedly Henrietta Hodson, whose connection with the Bower began at a very early date, for she was born on the premises, rumour asserted on an improvised bed in the pit after an evening performance.

Miss Henrietta in later life was the wife of Henry Labouchere (of *Truth*), but her first husband was a Mr. Pigeon. She ran away with Labouchere who married her as soon as it was made possible either through the death of Mr. Pigeon or a divorce. In the last part of her life, she was one of the most popular hostesses of London Society in rather a Bohemian set, her card and roulette parties on Sunday nights being crowded with all sorts of interesting people, if not always quite of *la haute volée*. Towards the end of her life, she tended to be rather *dévote*, and joined the Roman Catholic Church before her death in 1910. Her daughter—the grand-daughter of the old couple who ran the gaff in Lambeth—married well : first, the Marchese Di Rudini, at one time Prime Minister of Italy, and, secondly, Prince Odescalchi. I have had occasion to refer many times to Henrietta Hodson in the pages relating to the old Queen's Theatre in Long Acre, which was leased and run for some time by Mr. Labouchere for the appearances of his charming wife.

Mrs. Labouchere's mother was *née* Noel, sister of Mrs. Henry Marston, a very popular actress, and she was by no means the only dramatic celebrity who was connected with the Bower Saloon. This rather dirty and disreputable little theatre became a veritable nursery for great actors and actresses. Let me glance at a few of the names of those who graduated at the Stangate Saloon and had their hours of triumph afterwards on the stages of first-class West End Houses.

J. B. Howe, one of the props of Mrs. Sara Lane's Company at the Britannia, Hoxton, was there, and the " Great Little Robson," whom we met before in the chapter dealing with the Olympic, and who was one of the greatest actors the world has ever seen. Then there was James Fernandez whom many living playgoers will remember at the Adelphi and Drury Lane and at the Lyceum with Irving. He made his first bow to a West End audience in 1865 as Laertes to the Hamlet of Walter Montgomery, but he was the hero of many a play at the Bower, and he was also with Menken in " Mazeppa " at Astley's before he reached the Strand. It is interesting to note that the Ophelia to his Laertes was a young lady making her first appearance before a London audience—one Madge Robertson, from Nottingham, whom we have all learned to know and love as Mrs. Kendal. She must have been truly an ideal Ophelia in years, looks and performance.

Augustus Harris, the elder—father of Sir Augustus Harris Druriolanus—was at the Bower in 1841, and had to play anything that came to hand—clown, harlequin, pantaloon or light comedian. He is now practically forgotten as an actor, but made a very creditable Chateau Renaud at the Princess's in Oxford Street in " The Corsican Brothers " with Fechter. His very first stage appearance had, however, been in America with his mother, Madame Fearon, as a child coachman in an opera founded on the story of Cinderella (perhaps *La Cenerentola* of Rossini). Madame Fearon was a distinguished operatic artist who had been Prima Donna at La Scala in Milan. She was most popular in London and always ready to sing for the benefit of her fellow-artistes, as, for instance, when she appeared for Grimaldi's benefit at the close of his career. Her husband was a Mr. Glossop, a prosperous tallow-chandler, with a mania for the theatre, who managed the Old Vic after Davidge's day.

Augustus Harris, the elder, was more successful as an impresario than as an actor. In his time, he ran several of the more important theatres in London, and was managing the Princess's in 1859 when Irving made his first, and most disastrous, appearance on the London stage in an adaptation of Octave Feuillet's *Roman d'un Jeune Homme pauvre* called " Ivy Hall." Very clever at adapting plays for the English stage, and at unearthing talent in foreign countries, Harris has the credit of having introduced Fechter to a London audience, and also was the means of bringing out Espinosa, a supremely clever dancer whose family continues to this day in the same tradition. Harris was only forty-seven when he died.

Of the managers of the Bower, the most successful after Hodson seems to have been Biddle, from the neighbouring Astley's, whose daughter, Adelaide, blossomed into Mrs. Charles Calvert—one of the best actresses of her time.

The musical director of the Bower orchestra at one time was a Mr. Tully who had been chorus master for Madame Vestris at the Olympic and Covent Garden, and in a similar position with Bunn at Drury Lane. He also led the orchestra at the production of " Mazeppa " at Astley's with Menken. Several little operettas by him, " The Swiss Village " and others, were put on at the Bower Theatre.

Anything, in short, was given at this queer little place from " Maria Martin or the Murder in the Red Barn " to " Mabel's Curse," by Mrs. S. C. Hall, and even " Macbeth." Pantomimes were the regular thing each Christmas, though it has always been a puzzle to me how these very tiny theatres could do a pantomime at all ! " Mother Goose " in 1875 was the last Bower pantomime. After that date the little house was somewhat reconstructed, and renamed the " New Stangate Theatre," but it fell lower and lower in the scale, and was finally closed down altogether about 1878 or 1879. Long before that date it had lost all pretension to be any more than the very lowest kind of gaff. Like so many places of entertainment which began as a saloon attached to a public-house, it was outclassed by the regular theatres, but it has the distinction of having been the training-ground of many distinguished members of the profession.

THE KING'S CROSS THEATRE, ARGYLL STREET, W.C.

This is, or was, a very tiny house near the Great Northern Terminus, which has been known by many different names. It was opened in 1832, by Buckstone and Mrs. Fitzwilliam, and as long as William IV was alive was known as the " Clarence " out of compliment to him. But its very first name was the " Panharmonium " (inevitably corrupted into " Pandemonium ") having been so christened by an Italian teacher of music who used it as a singing-hall for his pupils.

In its early days it was under the management of a Miss Lawrence when Edmund Kean, who appears to have acted at all sorts of out-of-the-way places, played there in " Richard III ". In 1838, it became the " New Lyceum " and one of the plays put on was " Pizarro." Later names have been the " Regent," the " Argyll " and the " Cabinet."

This wee house of many aliases has always been a favourite place in which ambitious amateurs or budding professionals might attempt

big parts.   For instance, any young man could try his luck there in
" Hamlet " on payment of a fixed tariff according to the importance
of the rôle.   Rosencrantz cost 2s. 6d., but Horatio was 5s., and if
he wished to aspire to the title rôle he had to produce a whole sovereign.

In the late thirties of the nineteenth century, about 1836 to
1839—that is, in the years before the Patent Act was repealed—
all the minor theatres of London constituted the centre of a little
stage-struck neighbourhood.

Charles Dickens, who made a study of everything theatrical
during the whole of his life, points this out and adds that each of
them has an audience exclusively its own.   The orchestra usually
consisted of two fiddles and a flute who had to get through any
number of overtures till the performers were ready.   The theatre
was usually lit up by half a dozen little oil lamps set round the only
tier of boxes.   In the same article he gives the list of charges for
performers in Shakespeare's " Richard III ".   Richard III commanded as much as £2 ; Earl of Richmond £1 ; Duke of Buckingham 15s. ; Catesby 12s. ; Tressel 10s. 6d. ; Lord Stanley 5s. ; and
the Lord Mayor of London 2s. 6d.   The lady performers had
nothing to pay for their parts.

That amusing comedian, Arthur Williams, made his debut at
the King's Cross, and two others far more amusing than he—Toole
and Robson—also trod its boards at one time.

It was once the scene of the debut of a very clever pantomimist
who afterwards obtained some renown as a clown.   This was Jeffries,
who made his first appearance at the King's Cross as Desperetta,
a comic rôle in " The Dumb Maid of Genoa," in 1837.   Jeffries
was a Clerkenwell tobacconist by trade, but did comic turns, chiefly
clown, at the Olympic, Sadler's Wells, City of London or Vic, or
even at such unimportant places in outlying districts as the Mont-
pelier Garden Theatre, Walworth.   He called himself Jefferini and
his portrait survived for some years in the sign-board of the Old Clown
Tavern, Clerkenwell.   Tom Matthews, a pupil of Grimaldi, had
trained him for the profession and he was said to be a good clown.
He does not seem to have confined his energies to pantomime and
still less to his legitimate business of tobacconist, for he made a good
deal of money out of a gaming-room established over the shop.

In 1859, the King's Cross Theatre was taken by a certain Harry
Montagu, at one time with Ginnett's Circus.   He had recognized,
in the person of an itinerant conjuror performing outside a public-
house, an old colleague of his circus days, and exploited him as a
Wizard under the name of Monsieur Philippi.   They had some
measure of success in the provinces ; but, coming to London to this
ill-fated little place, the good luck attending them on tour deserted

them and once more the unlucky midget of a theatre had to close its doors.

Blanchard gives in an old publication an amusing account of his one visit to the King's Cross Theatre. He says that, standing under the portico for shelter from the rain, he was accosted by the money taker who said to him " Come in, sir : just a goin' to begin." He paid a shilling and entered, to find an audience of not more than thirty persons, mostly in their shirt-sleeves. The overture was " Home, Sweet Home " played by an orchestra of one solitary fiddler, who was hooted away for playing out of tune. The piece was " Clari," a well-known music drama of the day, but the strength of the company consisted of but three men and two women, who doubled all the characters, going off as one and returning as another, with but a slight alteration of costume, which was yet not exactly costume, as it was merely the everyday dress of the actor, with perhaps the coat sleeves turned inside out or a collar removed or added ! He did not wait to see the end of the piece.

In 1867, the little theatre, then called the " Cabinet," seems to have had a season of better luck, and we find a programme consisting of a play called " Myra " founded perhaps on the story of *Don Juan*, followed by Morton's adaptation from the French—the well-known " Box and Cox." The cast of these pieces does not appear to have contained any striking names. In both, there appeared a young man called Polini who was making his stage debut. He was, I think, the father of Mrs. Owen Nares.

THE WESTMINSTER THEATRE, TOTHILL STREET, S.W.

The character of the performances at this curious little house may be best imagined if you realize that T. D. Davenport, who opened it in 1832, has always been supposed to have been the original from whom Dickens drew his immortal Vincent Crummles. He must not be confounded with the H. L. Davenport, an American actor of some repute who acted at Drury Lane, Sadler's Wells, etc. T. D. Davenport had succeeded Edmund Kean as the manager of the old Richmond Theatre on the Green—a house I remember perfectly well, with open boxes over the partitions of which you could converse with the people in the next box. His daughter, who may be considered as the " Infant Phenomenon," and is actually alluded to as such in theatrical memoirs and diaries, became an actress of note in the United States. She married an American, a Mr. Lander, who was killed during the American Civil War. After her husband's death, Mrs. Lander made her appearance at the Lyceum (in 1869) as Elizabeth Queen of England, in a translation of the drama by Giacometti which was written for Ristori and in which that great actress was considered to be very fine. Mrs. Lander was supported, among others, by Allerton, Charles Harcourt and Charles Coghlan.

In 1833, John Douglass, afterwards manager of the Standard Theatre, Shoreditch, and other outlying houses, ran the Westminster, and in his company were such good actors as Joseph Raynor, Munyard and Davidge—the last connected with the Old Vic, the Surrey and the City Theatre, Cripplegate. This little house only lasted three years and its actual site is still a matter of dispute. It probably stood somewhere near the spot where the stage-door of the Imperial Theatre was in after years, not far from the existing Caxton House.

THE ROYAL KENT THEATRE, KENSINGTON HIGH STREET

The Royal Kent was opened on Easter Monday, 1834, under the patronage of the Duke of Kent, father of Queen Victoria. There was a separate entrance down a mews for Royalty. The only notable name that I can trace in connection with this playhouse is that of Denvil, the original Manfred in Byron's tragedy of that name. He also played Shylock at Drury Lane, and his descendants are still to be found under the same name in modern programmes. Another actor here was the brother of George Augustus Sala, whose professional name was Wynne. The house was finally closed in 1840.

THE ROYAL PANTHEON THEATRE, CATHERINE STREET, STRAND

This playhouse stood at the corner of Catherine Street, Strand, and other names it bore were " Jessop's Hall " and the " Little Catherine Street Theatre." It was chiefly used by amateurs, and, as at the King's Cross Theatre, anybody could play more or less important parts if they were ready to pay for the privilege of doing so. At both these little theatres, there were societies which were virtually clubs for aspiring amateurs, many of whom became successful members of the profession in after life. It was not a bad training school for the stage, and I have heard that Henry Neville was one of those who took advantage of it in early days. A well-known actress of the nineteenth century—Mrs. Sumbel Wells—used to give imitations of Mrs. Siddons and other leading actresses here. The site was afterwards occupied by the offices of the *Echo*—somewhere near where the new Gaiety Theatre now stands.

THE ALBION THEATRE (*alias* NEW QUEEN'S), WINDMILL STREET, W.

This unimportant playhouse is only worth mentioning as having been the scene of the debut of the great Sally Booth as Juliana in " The Honeymoon." It was opened in 1832 as the " Albion," but in 1833 was rechristened the " New Queen's." It lasted but four years, being finally pulled down in 1836. The site was afterwards occupied by the notorious Argyll Rooms, and in more recent times by the Trocadero Music Hall which was turned into the Trocadero Restaurant. Miss Booth, known as " the lively Sally Booth," was a very favourite actress of the first half of the nineteenth century. She was born in 1793 and died in 1841. Her range of parts was extensive. She played Cordelia, Juliet, etc., but appears to have been more successful in lighter rôles. She was at the Surrey under Elliston, and at Covent Garden, the Marylebone and other houses. She was the original Claudine in " The Miller and His Men," a lurid melodrama which has not been acted for years except by the companies of the " Penny-plain, Twopence-coloured " sort.

THE ARGYLL THEATRE, ARGYLL STREET, REGENT STREET

This was a small private theatre lasting from 1819 to 1823, where French plays were given by subscription. The performance began at nine and ended at midnight, after which the audience gave themselves up to dancing. Only subscribers were admitted. The Argyll medicated Baths were built on or near the site of this little playhouse. They were conducted by a Doctor who was father of Sir Charles Wyndham, and who is also said to have had something to do with Dr. Kahn's Museum, which was next door to the old Pavilion Music Hall.

THE GLOBE THEATRE, BLACKFRIARS ROAD, S.E.

Sir Ashton Lever, a Lancashire worthy, who had made a very curious collection of all sorts of birds, beasts and other curios, brought together from all parts of the world, bought Leicester House in 1771 as a place to put them in and called it the " Holuphusicon." This collection was eventually disposed of by means of a lottery—8000 tickets at a guinea each. A Mr. Parkinson won it and built the Rotunda in Albion Place on the south side of Blackfriars Bridge, for the display of what he called the " Museum Leverianum." The scheme failed and the odd collection was sold by auction in 7879 lots, the sale lasting 65 days and the catalogue filling 410 octavo pages. This was in 1806, and the building afterwards became a penny wax-work show at first, but in 1833 was opened as a theatre.

It never prospered as a playhouse even of the most primitive description, and in 1838 was transformed into a concert hall with John Blewitt as the director. Blewitt was a most prolific composer of all kinds of songs, chiefly comic ones. He wrote " Barney Brallaghan " and also the tune for " The Perfect Cure," which Stead was wont to sing with a jumping refrain.   For many years, he provided the music for the pantomimes at Covent Garden, Drury Lane and the Olympic, and at one time was musical director at Vauxhall Gardens.   He died in 1853, an old man and very poor.

After the wind-up of Blewitt's concerts, the Globe degenerated more and more and finally got to be a low haunt for inferior prizefighters.   It was never opened as a theatre again.

The site of this short-lived place of entertainment is now occupied by a large ironmongery store which has adopted the name of the "Rotunda" for its own business, and displays it proudly on an illuminated pane.

THE ORANGE STREET THEATRE, CHELSEA, S.W.

This was a little theatre near the spot where the Church of St. Barnabas, Pimlico, now is, in the King's Road, Chelsea.   The open space in front of the church is still sometimes called Orange Square, and the "Orange" public-house at the corner perhaps identifies the site still more closely.   It was just one of those little theatres which grew up in a mushroom-like crop soon after 1830 when there were great hopes that the privileges of the Patent Theatres were coming to an end.

Near the spot, in the eighteenth century, was a fashionable restaurant or eating-house and tea-gardens where modish folk of the day would come to eat turtle.   George Selwyn, Lady Townshend (mother of the first Marquis), Lady Caroline Petersham, and the Marquis of Granby—whose portrait adorned the outside of the elder Weller's public-house at Dorking !—would forgather there to talk scandal and gossip about their neighbours.   Close by, were the "Star and Garter" and "Jenny Whim's"—two other tea-gardens, but not, I think, any dramatic shows at either place.

On the site of the Orange Theatre had previously existed "Strombolo House" also a place of indoor and outdoor amusement.

The little Orange Theatre was, more or less, a private playhouse, chiefly used by amateurs.

THE PECKHAM THEATRE, HIGH STREET, PECKHAM

In High Street, Peckham, there was formerly a theatre which was in existence in 1828, and was then under the direction of one Penley. But its foundation, according to tradition, was more than one hundred and fifty years before that.   Peckham Fair was instituted, it is said, by Charles II at the earnest request of Nell Gwynne in remembrance of the fact that she had once herself acted at a small booth or theatre close to the "Kentish Drovers," a well-known public-house at

Peckham. Hanover Chapel, a dissenting tabernacle of some kind, was erected on the site of the little theatre. Nell Gwynne is said to have acted in almost as many places as the Virgin Queen is said to have slept in, but the traditions of the theatre—even to the name of the manager, who may have been one Flockton—have been handed down and there seems no reason to doubt that some sort of a theatrical booth existed here for many years before it became a conventicle.

Flockton probably ran it for some time. He was one of the great showmen of Bartholomew Fair, and was the chief among Puppet proprietors. His dolls were called the " Italian Fantoccini " and were something similar to those seen at the Teatro dei Piccoli at Rome, which are now generally called Marionettes. He seems to have had a fancy for a " foreign touch." When on tour with his show, his assistants were always attired in some sort of Turkish costume ; he had also at one time a fine Newfoundland dog, which he had taught to fight and overcome the Devil in an Interlude. He died at Camberwell in 1794, having made a fortune of over five thousand pounds. His Company consisted chiefly of his own family and the greater part of his money was divided among them.

At Peckham, there was also a conjuror billed as " Mr. Lane, first performer to the King with his snip-snap, rip-rap, crick-crack thunder tricks that the grown babies stared at like worried cats." This extraordinary genius was advertised to drive about forty tenpennynails into any gentleman's breech, place him in a loadstone chair, and draw them out without any pain. There is very scanty information about the little playhouse at Peckham, which, however, did appear to exist at one time and probably only really disappeared about the time that the Fair, which had degenerated into a nuisance, was abolished in 1827.

THE COLOSSEUM THEATRE, ALBANY STREET, REGENT'S PARK, N.W.

Behind the old Colosseum in Regent's Park, where crowds went to see the celebrated dioramas " London by Night " and the " Earthquake at Lisbon," there was opened, in 1841, a playhouse constructed to hold 800 persons. Farces and Ballets formed the programme. The musical director was James Tully, who had filled or was to fill, a like position at the Bower Saloon, Drury Lane, etc. The place was run on a sort of co-operative principle akin to that attempted by the British National Opera Company. Pay day, however, was always a date to look forward to with doubt, and the actors deserted gradually one by one, as better engagements were offered. The house was closed down finally after a life of only three months— perhaps the shortest-lived playhouse on record.

THE SANS SOUCI THEATRE, LEICESTER PLACE, LEICESTER SQUARE

Built by Dibdin, the song-writer, at the latter end of the eighteenth century. Reopened in 1833 for the performance of vaudeville by subscription. A very tiny house. In 1834, a French company performed here, but without success. It is said that Edmund Kean appeared here as an acrobat in his boyhood. "Baron" Nicholson, ex-pawnbroker's assistant, and afterwards manager of the infamous "Judge and Jury" Show, calls it in his memoirs an "elegant little theatre"; but it lasted a very short time and never prospered under any management. After it ceased to exist as a theatre, it was converted into an hotel—the "Hotel de Versailles" —but that has now also disappeared.

THE BIJOU THEATRE : ATTACHED TO HER MAJESTY'S OPERA HOUSE

This was a little playhouse, attached to, and forming part of the building of Her Majesty's Opera House in the Haymarket. It was once used for light comedy and drawing-room entertainments of the German Reed sort. Charles Mathews and his second wife (formerly Mrs. Lizzie Davenport), produced here their sketch which he called an "At Home"—in which they both played a number of different characters. He was here with it in 1862, the year of the second Great Exhibition.

The Bijou was also very largely used by what were known in the sixties as "Amateurs of Rank and Fashion" who had generally played at Campden House, Kensington, till it was burned down. The Amphitheatre, Holborn, and the St. James's were likewise the scenes of their achievements. They were frequently stage-managed by a Mr. W. H. Maitland, himself a good amateur actor and the father of those persistent producers of opera bouffe—the Brothers Mansell. Among other amateur efforts at the Bijou were some Shakespearean performances got up by Palgrave Simpson, a worthy dramatist of the sixties—but no actor! He played Macbeth in a moustache and imperial like the third Napoleon. A Miss Aylmer Blake (Mrs. Aylmer Gowing), a lady with histrionic aspirations but small capability, was the Lady Macbeth. Clement Scott, the critic, was the Fleance and Arthur à Beckett, son of a well-known dramatist and himself a critic of the drama, was the Doctor in the sleep-walking scene. "King John" was also put on at this miniature theatre. One can only wonder at the temerity of budding Thespians who could dream of producing two such tragedies in a stage hardly big enough to hold a dozen players with comfort.

There was another very curious performance at this little play-house. This was a production of a farce dealing with Scenes at a Dentist. It was written for the students of the English Catholic College at Rome, and was given a trial performance at the Bijou in the presence of no less a personage than a Prince of the Church— Cardinal Wiseman to wit, the predecessor of Manning as Head of the Catholic Church in England.

THE MANOR HOUSE THEATRE, KING'S ROAD, CHELSEA

In 1837, there was, in King's Road, Chelsea, a dilapidated old house, shut in a garden of fruit trees and plots of waste ground called "The Old Manor House." An enterprising Mr. Richard Smith took possession, and opened it as "The New Vauxhall and Royal Bath Gardens." Hot and cold baths were established, and concerts given, but the project in that form did not pay, so he built a small theatre on the site and turned the empty tank of the tepid swimming-bath into a green-room. Blanchard, whose description of the place forms the basis of this short notice, as a young man, helped to run the show for a time, and among the actors who appeared there and afterwards made a name for themselves were Mr. A. Sydney who became Alfred Wigan, Richard Flexmore, the celebrated clown and pantomimist, and Nye Chart, afterwards the lessee of the Brighton Theatre. It was, of course, the merest caricature of a playhouse, but such names are in themselves enough to preserve it from entire oblivion.

The first transformation of the dilapidated old house into a place of entertainment took place in 1837, and the money devoted to the purchase of the place and the building of the theatre is supposed to have been accumulated by Smith in a previous official post at Crock-ford's Gaming Rooms. The costumes for the plays were hired from Whitechapel and taken away every night. The bill was made up of oddments, farces, musical pieces, dances and pantomimical burlettas. Earnest and hopeful amateur authors and actors tried to get their works produced or obtain a first appearance in one of Shakespeare's plays, and there was a retired prize-fighter who wished to play either Hamlet or Richard III (he didn't mind which) as long as he would be allowed to introduce a scene representing Tom Cribb's parlour and a gathering of " the Fancy." The place probably lasted about ten years.

In the end, Smith, finding it anything but a profitable speculation, built Rodney Street on the site of the grounds, with a public-house at the corner, and the theatre itself became absorbed in a building known as the " Commercial Rooms."

THE ALBERT SALOON, SHEPHERDESS WALK, HOXTON

Near the Grecian Theatre, in the same lane, was another place of entertainment known as the Albert Saloon. This was a garden theatre, or rather a theatre in a garden. It was not very substantially built, and the words of the play with the shrieks of the heroine and the curses of the villain could be distinctly heard through the wooden walls from the outside. But it had one remarkable feature enabling it to be used as a winter or summer place of entertainment, that is, as an outdoor or an indoor theatre. Outdoor theatres were very popular in the early days of the nineteenth century. Nearly all the tea-gardens had some sort of a stage attached to them, but the English climate would often put an end to the show. At the Albert Saloon there were two stages built at right angles to one another, the proscenium of one opening into the garden and the other into the actual saloon for wet weather. This arrangement may be still met with in many continental cities, but it does not seem to have ever been adopted in England at any other place than the Albert Saloon in Shepherdess Walk.

In spite of the rather ramshackle nature of the place, many well-known artistes and pantomimists graduated here, among whom may be mentioned Paul Herring, the famous pantaloon.

Paul Herring's real name was Bill Smith, and for many years he had travelled with Richardson's Show as a " general utility " man and later, as the best clown the Show had ever known. Nelson Lee, the East End impresario, who had in early life been a Harlequin, took over " Richardson's " in partnership with one Johnson. He discovered what real talent Bill Smith possessed and, having re-christened him " Paul Herring," procured him the openings which enabled him to become famous in pantomime at good houses. He lived to be seventy-eight years of age, and died in 1878. His first hit was made as the " Imp of the Devil's Gorge " at the Albert Saloon, and he was at the Old Vic and many of the West End houses as clown till he got too old for the part, when he took up that of pantaloon. One of his last appearances as pantaloon was probably in the Drury Lane pantomime of 1875 when he was about seventy-four years of age—one of the pantomimes in which the Vokes family appeared in the opening—but he was kept on to play the old woman in the Harlequinade ; Chatterton ordered that any super who should chance to hurt him in the " rally " should be fined.

Another actor here was Edward Edwards, one of the best melodramatic actors of the thirties and forties. He was renowned for his rendering of parts in plays like " La Tour de Nesle " and other pieces translated from the French (Porte St. Martin dramas). He was also one of the earliest to be cast for Triboulet in " Le Roi S'amuse" of Victor Hugo, when it was first done in English as " The King's Fool." Hugo's play was in after years produced by the Rousbys in a version put together by Tom Taylor called "The Fool's Revenge." It is, of course, still better known in its operatic form of " Rigoletto."

In the summer time the grounds of the Albert Saloon were more in request than the Saloon itself. There were balloon ascents by Mr. Green, the well-known aeronaut and others. The place was shut up in 1857. It seems to have been a very popular place in its day, though the records concerning it are scanty enough

THE JAMES STREET THEATRE, W.

In the eighteenth century, there stood in James Street, which leads from the Haymarket to Whitcomb Street, a little place of amusement called " The James Street Theatre." Its site was near a Royal Tennis Court that existed as late as 1863, but the position of which is, I think, now occupied by Simpkin, Marshall and Co. This little house and the China Hall of Rotherhithe perhaps should not find a place in an account of the Lost Theatres of the Nineteenth Century, but I have not been able to discover when they finally closed their doors.

The show given there was usually a very miscellaneous entertainment indeed, but it really was a theatre of a sort, for the prices of admission specify—Boxes 1s. 6d., Pit 1s.

In 1728, it was occupied by Fawkes, a conjuror, who exhibited several feats of legerdemain, including the " flower trick " of the Indian Jugglers afterwards done by Dr. Lynn at the Egyptian Hall.

There is an old playbill of the middle of the eighteenth century, headed " At the Old Theatrical Show-Shop, James Street, Haymarket " announcing a piece called " The Wife Well-managed : or a Cure for Cuckledom " by Mr. Punch and his queer company, probably nothing but a Punch and Judy Show on a larger scale. Many things were being brought from Italy at that time and this may well have been a version of one of the Maschere—perhaps Stenterello who, in appearance, is a sort of Punch.

On the same bill was announced—Master Lawrence on the tight rope, Mr. Lawrence on the slack wire, another Master Lawrence (aged seven) with a hornpipe playing the violin at the same time. Evidently a talented family the Lawrences—like the Crummleses. At the same time there was a pantomime called " Harlequin Everywhere " and a new drama called " True Blue : or the Pressgang." Prices of admission : 3., 4d., 6d. and 1s. At another time the

James Street Theatre was opened for an Exhibition of Mechanics and Engineering. I suspect it was an obscure little hall, sometimes used as a theatre and sometimes for anything it could be let for, and was probably just a specimen of that kind of gaff of which there were so many in London and the traces of which are entirely lost.

THE CHINA HALL THEATRE, ROTHERHITHE, S.E.

In the latter part of the eighteenth century there was a little theatre in the district of Rotherhithe which was known as China Hall. It was at the back of a public-house bearing the same name and which, I believe, still exists. There were gardens and tea-arbours and probably bowling-greens, and in the summer the theatre was also open for the performance of such pieces as "Love in a Village," "The Wonder," "The Comical Courtship," "The Lying Valet," etc. It was cheap enough : Boxes 3s., Pit 2s., Gallery 1s. It appears to have been on the same spot in the reign of Charles II, for Pepys mentions a theatre he visited called "China Hall" in that neighbourhood. It was burned down in the latter part of the eighteenth century, though, I believe, rebuilt and would be hardly worth mentioning at all but for the fact that the famous George Frederick Cooke, whom his contemporaries declared to be one of the finest actors ever seen, acted there in 1778. Cooke, according to Lamb, who wrote a long account of his acting in "Richard III" for *The Morning Post* was indeed something of a marvellous actor. Sir Walter Scott declared that he was finer than Kemble as Sir Giles Overreach and he was also a noted Sir Pertinax Macsycophant. But of course he was of the old school of ranters and would be hissed off the stage of to-day. He was a drunkard and would often appear on the stage hopelessly drunk and apologize to the audience for his "old complaint." He died in America in 1812. He had not captured fame when he appeared at the little summer theatre in Rotherhithe, but he gave it a cachet by his work in after years. He must, of course, not be confounded with T. P. Cooke the sailor actor of "True to the Core," "Black Eyed Susan," who was born in 1786 and died in 1864.

CHAPTER XVI

RICHARDSON'S SHOW AND OTHER THEATRICAL BOOTHS

"RICHARDSON'S SHOW" was only one of the many Theatrical Booths set up in fairs and similar gatherings all over England, during the years when theatres were few and far apart, and communications between larger towns that might be expected to boast of a theatre was necessarily difficult and slow. Nor was Richardson's the chief of such Booths, nor even the largest, but it is the one which has survived longest in accounts of old times, and, as far as I know, it is the only one which is ever called back to life by actors of to-day, professional or amateur, in the cause of charity.

In Morley's book on Bartholomew Fair some account is given of various theatrical booths which made their annual appearance there, or at Southwark Fair, and, though Richardson's also comes in for a short notice, it is quite evident that there were many of greater importance in their day.

Is it generally known that Fielding, one of England's greatest novelists, author of *Tom Jones*—in his earlier days, before he had begun to make a name in literature, and when he was often very much exercised as to where his dinner was coming from—was a proprietor of an important theatrical Show known as " Fielding's and Reynold's Booth," and afterwards as " Mr. Reynold's Great Theatrical Booth " ? Here were performed works of a higher class than are usually associated with Shows at a Fair, as for example, " The Beggars' Opera," given in 1728 by Fielding only eight months after its first production by Rich. This was at Southwark, not at Bartholomew Fair. Another very important Show was " Mrs. Mynn's Booth " for which Elkanah Settle, a poetaster of some repute in the late sixteenth and early seventeenth centuries, arranged an imposing spectacle called " The Siege of Troy." Settle was one of the best contrivers of theatrical machinery of his day, and in later years received an annual sum from the owner of " Mrs. Mynn's Booth " for providing entertainments exclusively for performance there, called " Drolls." He himself acted in some of his productions, on one occasion playing a dragon " in a green case of his own invention." Settle, like many a better man, died an inmate of the Charterhouse. The Booth he wrote for afterwards took upon itself the title of " Ben Jonson's Booth."

More than one of the proprietors of these Shows had been members of the companies at Drury Lane or the Haymarket, who, dissatisfied with their treatment by the managers, left them to shift for themselves. Such a one was Pinkethman who had been a Harlequin and other things at Drury Lane. He got friends to go into partnership with him and started a Show which was called " Pinkethman's, Mills's and Bullock's Booth." This was afterwards managed by Giffard, a prominent person in theatrical circles in the early years of the nineteenth century.

" Doggett's Booth " was set up by a comic actor of Drury Lane who had played leading parts with Betterton and Mrs. Bracegirdle. Like others, he opened at Bartholomew Fair when the great theatres were closed for the period of the Fair. One of his pieces is recorded as bearing the comprehensive title :

> The Distressed Virgin ; or the Unnatural Parents ; being a True History of the Fair Maid of the West ; or the Loving Sisters.

Harper was another one who had revolted from the tyranny of the Patentees and gone over to the Haymarket. His Show was known as " Lee and Harper's Booth."

Drury Lane Theatre, and also possibly the " little House in the Haymarket," always closed their doors during the days of Bartholomew Fair. It was not worth while to keep open when all their public had gone to amuse themselves and get drunk at Smithfield. One good result of this arrangement may be noted. In the same way as the actors went from the theatres to the booths, so the former often recruited good performers from the troupes of the gaffs for their own service. In this manner more than one good actor or actress found their way to the regular boards. Mrs. Pritchard, who acted with Garrick and became famous in her day, was originally a booth actress. Edmund Kean often played in a travelling Show, as also George Frederick Cooke, said to be the greatest Richard III ever seen.

These primitive " fit-ups " were taken from Fair to Fair, though, as far as London was concerned, Bartholomew and Southwark and perhaps Brook Green, Hammersmith, were the only ones of any importance. They were usually set up in or near an inn yard for obvious reasons of convenience for audience and performers alike.

" Richardson's Show "—officially called " Richardson's Theatre " —differed in many respects from the other great theatrical booths. It certainly catered for a class of audience who were content with dramatic fare and talent of a lower order, and only insisted that there should be a drama in which a ghost appeared at least twice, and a pantomime in which they could laugh at some of the more showy tricks. A poster of the "Richardson Show" of 1814-1815 will serve as an excellent example of the entertainment offered :

A Change of Programme each Day.

RICHARDSON'S THEATRE.

Mr. Richardson has the honour to inform the Public that, for the extraordinary patronage he has experienced, it has been his great object to contribute to the convenience and gratification of his audience. Mr. R. has a splendid collection of Scenery, unrivalled in any Theatre ; and as they are painted and designed by the First Artists in England, he hopes with such Decorations and a Change of Performance each day, the Public will continue him that Patronage it has been his greatest Pride to Deserve. The Entertainment to commence with a new Melodramatic Romance with New Scenery, Dresses, Decorations, &c., by the most eminent Artists, called :

"MONK AND MURDERER : OR THE SKELETON SPECTRE."

Baron Montaldi	Mr. H. Carey
Desperado (His Confidant)................	Mr. Reed
Nicolina (Steward of the Castle)..........	Mr. Wilmot
Edmund (Page to Edgar).................	Mr. Odey
St. Julian of France........................	Mr. Denney
Harold the Dane	Mr. Waters
Mohammed the Persian....................	Mr. Hunter
Edgar (An English Knight)................	Mr. Seymour
Romaldo (the mysterious Monk)..........	Mr. Brown
Emilina (daughter of the Baron)..........	Mrs. H. Carey
Lauretta (Her Confidante)................	Mrs. Wilmot

A short Sketch of the Scenery.
1. A Gothic Hall in Montaldi's Castle.
2. View of the Rocks of Calabria with Appearance of the Mysterious Monk.
3. Mysterious Forest.
4. A Rustic Bridge ; with distant View of the Castle ; grand Procession of Knights, &c.
5. Gothic Chamber.
6. Interior of the Castle ; decorated with Banners, Trophies, &c.
   and a Grand Combat with Shield and Battle-Axe.
The Piece will terminate with the Fall of the Murderers, the

Ascension of the Spectre Monk, and the predicted Union of the English Knight and Emilina.

The whole to conclude with an entire new Pantomime called :

"MIRTH AND MAGIC : OR A TRIP TO GIBRALTAR."

Harlequin......Mr. Riley.   Pantaloon......Mr. Green
Lover............Mr. Smith.
Sailor (with the Song of " The British Flag ") ...Mr. Raymond
Market-Woman...Mr. Wilmot.   Countryman...Mr. Waters
Landlord .... Mr. Sewell
Clown............Mr. Bageman.   Columbine...Mrs. Wilmot
The whole to conclude with the Grand Panoramic View of
The Rock of Gibraltar.
Painted by the First Artist.

The Booth would open early in the afternoon and the programme be repeated with intervals of only a quarter of an hour until the closing of the Fair.   During the intervals, the entire company (with, however, one exception) appeared on the front platform with Country Dances, Clowns with jokes, and other inducements to make people pay their money and come inside.   Admission was 2s., 1s. and 6d.   The payment of 1s. appears to have been enough to admit one anywhere, and it was considered the mark of a real " greenhorn " to pay more than that.   For 6d., one stood at the back of the booth, and as the floor was "raked " at a good angle, it was probably as advantageous a place from which to see and hear as any part of the interior.

Mr. John Richardson, usually spoken of as " Muster " Richardson, dressed in a blue frock coat with brass buttons and breeches of corduroy, was in evidence everywhere about the Front, now shouting, "Walk up, Ladies and Gentlemen, just a goun' to begin," and now and then giving a hasty glance inside to see how the house was filling.

The programme nearly always consisted of a melodrama as given in the poster quoted above, and a pantomime with perhaps a comic song interlarded between, sung generally by a comic rustic in a smock frock to enable the company to change their appearance for their new characters.

The serious drama was changed every day and selected from a fairly large répertoire.   " Virginius," " The Wandering Outlaw," " Wallace, the Hero of Scotland " for example, which enabled a complete change of costume for each day.   Or there might be something that was much on the tapis at the time, as for example " Der Freischütz " which created such a furore in the early part of the century. All the plays were quite unique and arranged for the special purposes of the Show by Richardson himself. One thing only was *de rigueur*. A Ghost must always appear exactly twice in each play. In " Virginius," it was a female ghost (Lucretia perhaps) ; in " The Wandering Outlaw " or in " Wallace " it was a male ghost, but, whether male or female, it was always precisely the same to look at. A figure dressed completely in a long robe of white, to represent a shroud, and with face chalked to match, the only spot of colour being a daub of red where the heart should be. The Ghost was considered the chief attraction of the Show and was therefore never allowed to be seen GRATIS with the rest of the Company on the outside platform. But all the others, even Zamiel the Spirit of Evil in " Der Freischütz," danced the country dances, *coram publico*, during each interval, to attract a new audience.

Though the Ghost might never appear except in a white shroud, the costume of the other performers fitted the period of the play— more or less. Virginius wore some kind of toga to represent an ancient Roman ; Wallace put on a kilt and tartan plaid ; the Outlaw had a plumed hat, a belt with a large buckle, and " Charles II " boots. By this change of dress, the outside platform presented a different appearance each day. If the Fair lasted more than three days, the répertoire was drawn upon still further.

The Pantomime was very short, nearly all Harlequinade, with two, or at the most three, set tricks. The outside stage was quite an extensive affair, having to accommodate a crowded country dance (between the two entrances, which served as ingress and egress for the audience), and the proprietor, or more often his wife, at the pay table ; besides the big drum which was beaten at intervals with much noise and persistence.

Richardson sometimes had the only theatrical booth in a Fair (except at very large gatherings like Bartholomew and Southwark). If he had a rival, it was often Scowton, and sometimes these two worked together as partners. As the various Fairs increased in row- diness and became a nuisance, they were gradually abolished, the Shows of those remaining decreased in importance and reduced their prices of admission, until in 1832 we find at Bartholomew Fair Richardson and Wombwell (the Menagerie) with only one price of 6d., and all the other Shows a penny each, including two other theatres, one of which was called " Ball's Theatre " and the other simply advertised " The Red Barn Tragedy "—which was, I suppose our old friend, Maria Martin.

Some other well-known Richardson Dramas were " The Castles of Athlin and Dunbaine : or the Spectre of the North," " Donalind and Rosaline : or the Spectre of the Rocks," " Agnes of Bavaria : or the Spectre of the Danube," " The Haunted Cavern : or the Mysterious Chest," " The Hall of Death : or Who's the Murderer ? "

Another description of Richardson's " Itinerant Theatre " at the Bartholomew Fair of 1838, taken from an old publication of the period, gives a more detailed description of the booth itself and the performances given there. According to this account, the outside of the booth was in height upwards of thirty feet and occupied one hundred feet in width. The platform on the outside was very elevated ; the back of it was lined with green baize, and festooned with deeply crimson curtains, except at two places where the money-takers sat, which were wide and roomy projections. There were fifteen hundred variegated illumination lamps, disposed over various parts of the platform, some of them depending from the top in the shape of chandeliers and lustres, and others in wreaths and festoons.

A band of ten performers in scarlet dresses, similar to those worn by beef-eaters, continually played on clarionets, violins, trombones and the long drum ; while the performers paraded in their gayest " properties " before the gazing multitude.

Audiences rapidly ascended on each performance being over, and paying their money to the receivers in their Gothic seats, had tickets in return ; which, being taken at the doors, admitted them to descend into the theatre. A bill of the play was obtainable at the doors on request. I have already quoted the particulars given on one such bill. Another one of a later date announced " An entire new Melo-drama called THE WANDERING OUTLAW : OR THE HOUR OF RETRIBUTION." This dealt with the doings of the Elector of Saxony and a Baron of Holstein, a " Wandering Outlaw " and an " Accusing Spirit " ; and among the supers were mentioned " Monks, Vassals, Hunters, Nuns and Ladies." The bill also announced that the piece ended with the death of the Baron of Holstein and the appearance of the " ACCUSING SPIRIT." On the same bill was the pantomime of " Harlequin Faustus : or the Devil will have his Own." This was a very celebrated panto-mime of the early days of the nineteenth century, and besides the principal *dramatis personæ* there were a quantity of supers described as " Attendant demons, sprites, fairies, ballad singers, flower girls, etc." The pantomime always finished with a " Splendid Pano-rama " and between it and the melodrama a young lady sang " He loves and he rides away."

The same description from which I have taken the above also

gives some particulars of the interior of the "theatre." This was about one hundred feet long and thirty wide, hung all round, like the outside, with green baize and crimson festoons. The attendants inside kept on their cry "Ginger-beer, apples, nuts and a bill of the play" for which you paid a penny if you had not one from the outside. The seats were simply rows of planks, the stage was elevated somewhat above their level and had a proscenium like a regular theatre and surmounted by the Royal Arms. The orchestra was lined with crimson cloth (there was a great deal of red about the place!) and the four or five musicians were in military costume. The writer of the article says that when he was present at the Show there were at least a thousand persons in the booth. This meant a twenty-five pounds house at sixpence a head and that repeated practically every hour throughout the day and the evening for four or five days meant as much as a thousand pounds for the duration of the Fair.

He also describes the other Booths, but Richardson's seems to have been the only one where theatrical representations were given. There were twenty Shows altogether, the chief of which, after "Mr. Richardson's" appear to have been "Clarke's from Astley's lighted with Real Gas Inside and Outside" which was a Circus entertainment with horses in the Ring, tight-rope dancers and clowns complete; and "Wombwell's Menagerie" which were both Six-penny Shows. All the other Booths charged only a penny for admission; some of these were minor Menageries with quite a small collection of animals, and some were minor circuses, for example, "Samwell's Company," which consisted only of children dancing on a tight rope and a dancing horse. I think the chief attraction of this Show must have been the lady outside who took the money and who is described as "a slender lady with three feathers in a jewelled turban and a dress of blue and white muslin and silver." Another kind of entertainment was usually called a Puppet Show and consisted of scenes rudely painted let down successively one after the other and representing any event of the present or past likely to interest the rustic crowd, as, for example, "The Murder of Mr. Weare and Probert's Cottage with the Execution of Probert," "The Greenland Whale Fisheries," "The Battle of Waterloo," and "The Coronation of George IV". Then there were the usual "Fat Ladies and Dwarfs" and there was "Ball's Theatre," a Penny Show, which consisted chiefly of Juggling and Conjuring and was a well-known Booth at all Fairs. Another Booth announced "The Black Wild Indian Woman, the White Indian Youth and the Welsh Dwarf." The uses of advertisement were well known in those days. As you left the Fair you were presented with printed slips headed "Serious Notice in perfect confidence," which gave particulars of the performances at Sadler's Wells not far off. The items of the "Wells" programmes were very similar to those of Richardson's, beginning with a "Romantic Tale of mysterious horror and broad Grin," never acted before, called "The Enchanted Girdles or Winki the Witch and the Ladies of Samarcand"—followed by a burletta "which sends people home perfectly exhausted from uninterrupted risibility called 'The Lawyer, the Jew and the Yorkshireman.' The whole to conclude (by request of 75 distinguished families and a party of 5) that never-to-be-sufficiently-praised pantomime called 'Magic in Two Colours or Fairy Blue and Fairy Red or Harlequin and the Marble Rock.'" The bill further informed the public that Sadler's Wells were the only Wells from which you might draw WINE at three shillings and sixpence for a full quart, and ended up by stating that there was a full moon during the week.

Mr. Arthur à Beckett, sometime editor of *The Sunday Times*, has left an amusing account of an Amateur Richardson's Show at a Fancy Fair and Fête held on the site of the Exhibition of 1862 at South Kensington, in which he was personally concerned. The Fair was for the benefit of the British Home for Incurables and the newly wedded Prince and Princess of Wales were there. Two separate Shows were devoted to the interests of the Drama. At one was given rather frequently, a magnificent military spectacle written by F. C. Burnand, and called "The Siege of Seringapatam." Mr. à Beckett himself, however, was concerned with the other Show, the opposition house, so to speak, presided over by Viscount Raynham (afterwards fifth Marquis Townshend) and his sister, Lady Anne Sherson.

F. C. Burnand, the author of the military spectacle, appeared in person, wearing breeches, top-boots, a short red collar and an enormous cocked hat and carried an immense staff like the Parish Beadle's. During the interval he paraded the grounds of the Fair accompanied by his troupe, thus going one better than the original Richardson whose company always stuck to the outside platform of their booth.

In Mr. à Beckett's booth, they played "The Port Admiral" by Thomas Gibson Bowles (afterwards M.P. and editor of *Vanity Fair*) and "Brigawyio the Brigand" by Frank Marshall, a well-known dramatist. Bowles, of course, was the gallant Jack Tar, and he was famous at dancing a hornpipe. All the ladies' parts were done by men. Marshall himself was a "Beauty in Distress," and à Beckett a maiden of sweet seventeen in a Dolly Varden gown and golden wig. Lady Anne Sherson sat by the big drum like a modern and aristocratic

Mrs. Grudden, taking the money and passing the people into the Show.

At the Fêtes held at the Crystal Palace every July for some years, in aid of that moribund institution, the Dramatic College for aged actors and actresses, there was always a Richardson's Show, and, as these were got up and performed by well-known members of the profession, they must have been a success. In fact, they were generally the chief entertainment of the day. But these Fêtes gradually degenerated by the intrusion of the " Ladies of the Half-World " and in time they became so disreputable that no respectable woman would have anything to do with them. It is recorded of some statesman (Disraeli, I believe) that at the Refreshment Stall, the fair Hetaira put her lips to the edge of the cup of tea she was handing to him and said : " *Now* it is a guinea." " Certainly," said the Statesman, handing her the money. " And, *now*, will you please give me a clean cup ? "

I had nearly omitted to mention the little subterfuge always employed at a Richardson's Show when the audience for the next performance was getting impatient outside. Richardson learned it, I believe, from John Audley, a famous Showman of a bygone day. When he judged that there was nearly enough waiting outside to make up a new Show, he would poke his head inside the booth and call out " Is John Audley there ? " This was a signal for the actors to hurry up a little and finish the Show.

The new audience was collected as soon as possible with the cry " All in to begin." Richardson's Show was at Greenwich Fair as late as 1836. I have not been able to trace its final appearances— that is, of the original show, for I believe imitations are annually reproduced at the " World's Fair " of the Islington Agricultural Hall : they are always called " Richardson's Show," however.

Cartlich, the first Mazeppa at Astley's in the thirties of the nine-teenth century, was on the staff of Richardson's Show and when the old showman died he left him a sum of money "in recognition of the bold way in which he was accustomed to shout for the people to come in." Cartlich was the first of the many male Mazeppas—there were no women in the part until at least thirty years later when Menken took it up in America, and, in 1865, created such a sensation at Astley's by her apparent " undress," though she was fully covered in very tightly fitting silk fleshings which looked like nudity from the audience.

After Richardson's death, Nelson Lee and Johnson took on the old Show in partnership, and ran it successfully for a time. But Lee was ambitious and his later career is connected with the City of

London Theatre in Norton Folgate (see Chapter II on " The Lost Playhouses of the East End ").

The original Mr. Richardson was buried, it is said by his own request, in the same grave as one of his performers, viz., " The spotted boy." This was a little negro whose skin was fair, but naturally mottled with black : a child of amiable manners, much attached to Richardson who was very kind to him. He was the last of the natural curiosities at Bartholomew Fair. His parents were natives of Africa and both black. He had been with Richardson since he was fifteen months old, and died when he was only four and a half years.

CHAPTER XVII

THE PRIVATE THEATRE AT CAMPDEN HOUSE, KENSINGTON

(With Notes on the Amateurs of Rank and Fashion of the mid-Nineteenth Century)

THOSE whom Blanchard liked to call the "Amateurs of Rank and Fashion" in the fifties and sixties of last century, assembled to show off their dramatic talent at various places most of which are now "lost." They did, it is true, sometimes take the St. James's or Royalty Theatres, but as a rule the locale was either the Bijou Theatre; a tiny house attached to Her Majesty's Opera House in the Haymarket, or a still smaller house which formed part of Campden House, Kensington. The Amphitheatre, Holborn, was another rendezvous of these "players at playing" and that is also gone.

Cromwell lived here once and there is reputed to be a subterranean passage passing to the river bank of which he availed himself when he wished to leave the house secretly. It was also an occasional residence for William and Mary and was altogether a perfect specimen of a palatial Royal Residence though it had never actually belonged to the Crown. It was the property of Baptiste Hickes, Viscount Campden, after whom it was called and who was the Founder of Hickes Hall in Clerkenwell, built early in that century and used as a Sessions House for Clerkenwell by Sir Baptiste Hickes, a silk mercer in Soper Lane in the reign of James I. The neighbourhood of the house was called Campden Hill after the owner and the Arms of Sir Baptiste Hickes (1612) and his sons-in-law, Lord Noel and Sir Charles Morrison, were to be seen in the windows and on the ceilings of this mansion.

The house was rented from the Noel family for five years for the use of Anne, Princess of Denmark, afterwards Queen Anne. She lived there with her son, the Duke of Gloucester, who died young, the only one of the Queen's children who survived infancy.

After the Queen's death, the house was sold to Nicholas Letchmere (afterwards Lord Letchmere) and later became a boarding school for ladies of a very high class. It subsequently was bought by one Mr. Wooley.

The building itself was a very handsome house of the Tudor style of architecture with large grounds attached, and stood on the top of Campden Hill overlooking the back of the Holland House estate. It was said to have been the birthplace of Queen Anne herself, but it is only certain she lived there at times.

Mrs. Byrne, in her amusing two volumes *Gossip of the Century* published in 1892, gives some interesting particulars of Campden House. She was the wife of the then editor of *The Morning Post* and her position as such gave her many opportunities to observe the fashionable and artistic worlds. Her receptions were famous in their day. All the great singers of the Opera and Concert world appeared at them and Society followed as a matter of course to parties where they got so much for nothing.

Mrs. Byrne says :

" Campden House was admirably adapted for such entertainments ; it was not only a model palace of Queen Anne's day, and extremely picturesque within and without, but the grounds were very tastefully laid out in the style of the period ; it contained a most perfect little theatre with all its appointments and properties and it was on this stage that the performers exhibited whether dramatically or simply vocally. The matinées given here, which generally occupied a long afternoon, were arranged in three parts, the intervals serving for a stroll in the grounds, where the visitors met ; and tea was also served in one of the quaint old rooms opening into the garden. There were interesting curiosities and relics, ancient portraits and tapestries, to be seen in the old lobbies and galleries, which were kept in their pristine style."

In the sixties this old house belonged to a very curious old person called Wooley about whom several odd tales were afloat, but who had plenty of money and was always ready to lend his house for charitable purposes.

I say " lend " his house, but many artistes declared that the hire of chairs and benches, and of the band that played in the gardens during the intervals, the providing of refreshments, etc., made it such an expensive affair that they spent far less by taking Willis's Rooms or the Rooms in Hanover Square. An arrangement was also always made with the proprietor by which all these expenses fell on the concert or theatrical giver, and there also existed an understanding by which a prescribed fee was paid to the servants of the house. Malicious gossip said that those unfortunate people never got any other wages—but gossip is often a liar.

There is no doubt, however, that there was a good deal of compensation for all this outlay. There was certainly something very smart about a Campden House entertainment. It was a nice drive when the weather was fine and ladies could show off their *toilettes* in the old gardens with their stone terraces and balustrades. There were romantic bypaths and alleys for young couples to flirt in, and it was easy to dodge one's chaperon in those days when, as you may remember, she was a veritable she-dragon, and without whom no young lady ever went to a party at all. Old Mr. Wooley was always visible for he, of course, had tickets for himself and friends, and frequently himself acted with the Amateurs, but he was not the master of the house for the time being. This fine old mansion was burned down and utterly destroyed, as was also Tunbridge Castle, another residence of the same owner. People remarked on the co-incidence, and there was a good deal of gossip, half of which may have been true, as to his private character and its connection with the double catastrophe.

Jules Lefort, the celebrated romantic singer in mid-nineteenth century, was also a very clever amateur actor and many French performances were got up at Campden House with his assistance.

Every year there was a performance at this little theatre for the benefit of the Royal Benevolent Society and these were generally under the direction, or, perhaps I should say, under the acting management of one Mr. W. H. Maitland, father of the three Brothers Mansell who were so much concerned with the popularizing of opera bouffe in England and who used to get regularly into hot water with the Lord Chamberlain over every new piece they produced.

I have before me as I write the programmes of two performances given by this particular band of Amateurs of Rank and Fashion in 1860 and 1861. The company consisted of nearly the same people each time.

The gentlemen were Viscount Raynham, M.P. (afterwards 5th Marquis Townshend), Captain Mackinnon, A.D.C., Lord Wallscourt, Hon. Evelyn Ashley, Mr. W. H. Maitland, Hon. Reginald O'Grady, Mr. Selwyn, Captain Sherson, Major W. Porter, R.E., Lord Kingsale, Mr. Thomas G. Bowles, Captain Perry, R.N., and the proprietor, Mr. W. F. Wooley.

The ladies were Lady Colthurst, Lady Anne Sherson, Miss Newton, Miss Barker, Hon. Mary Boyle, Hon. Mrs. Wrottesley and Mrs. Milner Gibson. The playlets produced (a triple bill each time) were "Our Wife or the Rose of Amiens," "The Omnibus," "Betsy Baker," "A School for Coquettes," "Urgent Private Affairs," and "You can't marry your grandmother."

The amateurs were, as can be seen, not ambitious. They had not the courage, perhaps, of the budding Keans and Siddons of to-day. Yet there were many really good artistes among them. Miss Mary Boyle acted whenever she had a chance. She was my mother's cousin, one of those ladies in the Society of the day who was said to know everybody, and, according to Tennyson, *did* know everybody. He made her the subject of a little poem. Miss Barker, generally spoken of as "Nancy" Barker, was a very clever miniature painter, and no theatricals at Hampton Court were complete without the assistance of Mrs. Wrottesley ; Mrs. Milner Gibson was another Society leader of the sixties. She was great on two subjects—the Italian Risorgimento in Italy and Spiritualism. She entertained Garibaldi and Mazzini when they came to England in 1864 and, though the wife of a Cabinet Minister, must have been at times a thorn in the side of a Government who desired to keep out of continental troubles. Her séances with Hume and other professors of the art spiritualistic were largely attended by the believers in the curious manifestations of the time. She and Mrs. S. C. Hall must have absorbed a lot of nonsense in a few years. But it is presumed that Mrs. Milner Gibson repented her of her credulity, for I believe she became a Roman Catholic before she died, and Holy Church does not countenance tambourines in the air, and floating bodies, and voices from nowhere in a darkened room.

The musical arrangements were sometimes under the direction of Dan Godfrey the elder, bandmaster of the Grenadiers' Band and sometimes under Mr. Musgrave, the conductor of the Strand Theatre orchestra, the same who was responsible for all the gay music of the celebrated Strand burlesques. Mr. Arthur à Beckett, in his *Green Room Recollections,* speaks of an amateur performance in the grounds, after Campden House had been burned down. His account is amusing enough to quote. He says :

"There was no dressing-room, and so we had to get into our costumes behind some bushes and play on a sort of terrace without any scenery. The bazaar itself was a dead failure. Half a guinea was charged for admission in aid (if my recollection is not at fault) of some Italian charity. Only about a dozen people turned up and they were severally accosted by a little girl in red, green and white, who asked them 'to buy a cigar for only five shillings.' Among the spectators were Mario and Grisi and I remember they roared at our performance. It must have been funny, for we were all in an extremely bad humour and played the piece, as the French would say '*sans plaisir.*' Even Thomas Gibson Bowles, the author, who appeared as a gallant British tar, was on that occasion comparatively feeble. As for myself, I was hopelessly bad. Well, it was a little trying, for it began to rain and we could not help envying our scanty audience their sheltering

MISS NANCY BARKER
IN "THE SCHOOL FOR COQUETTES"

HON. MRS. WROTTESLEY AND
MR. W. L. MAITLAND IN
"THE SCHOOL FOR COQUETTES"

LADY ANNE SHERSON
IN "THE SCHOOL FOR COQUETTES"

MR. T. G. BOWLES
IN "YOU CAN'T MARRY YOUR GRANDMOTHER"

AMATEUR THEATRICALS
CAMPDEN HOUSE: KENSINGTON: JUNE 5TH. 1861.

umbrellas. This, I imagine, must have been the first attempt at establishing 'Pastoral Plays.' It was not entirely successful."

The Thomas Gibson Bowles to whom reference is made in the above extract was the editor of *Vanity Fair*. He was a relation of Mr. Milner Gibson, *à la main gauche*, and was indeed most celebrated for the dashing way he danced a sailor hornpipe. When Richardson's Show was revived by amateurs at a bazaar at the Exhibition of 1862, under the direction of my mother, Lady Anne Sherson, he was the life and soul of the booth, playing always the gallant tar ever at hand to rescue the British maiden in distress. His career as a member of Parliament is fresh in the memory of many people.

But sometimes the Amateurs acting for the benefit of the Royal Benevolent Society aspired to a more public recognition of their talents than could be afforded by the limited number of aristocratic friends who could give a guinea for a seat. On these occasions they would take a regular theatre and I have a programme of one such entertainment given at the St. James's Theatre on July 10th, 1863, when the majority of the seats sold for half a guinea, but the general public were admitted to the Gallery on payment of half a crown. The programme was, as usual, a triple bill. "A Peal of Belles," "The White Horse of the Peppers," and "A Rough Diamond." On the bill I find, in addition to names I have already mentioned, those of Frank Marshall, a playwright of the period, whose second wife was the beautiful Ada Cavendish, and Arthur à Beckett, once, I think, the editor of *The Sunday Times*. One of the principal features seems to have been the dancing of my mother and Algernon Joy in the "Connaught Jig" and of my mother in the Lancashire Clog Dance interpolated into the part of Nan the Rough Diamond. I have been told that I was present at this performance, but must have been a very diminutive person in a kilt and may be excused for not remembering anything about it. Indeed, my earliest memories begin with the year previous in connection with the Great Exhibition of 1862 ; but it often happens that memory plays that trick of skipping a year or two in its records.

Lady Barrett-Lennard, wife of the Sheriff of Essex, had a company of her own who used to perform for charity at one or other of the little amateur houses. Her troupe included Charles Collette (afterwards a professional in the Bancroft Company at the Prince of Wales's), and a Mr. "Augustus Montagu" under which pseudonym was hidden a well-known personality at the Admiralty. Mrs. Milner Gibson often organized her own troupe, and

Palgrave Simpson, the dramatist, author or adaptor of hundreds of most successful pieces in the fifties and sixties, sometimes played with the amateurs besides writing plays like " The School for Coquettes," etc., which were acted by them. He was the adaptor of many plays for Fechter, including one of his chief successes— " The Master of Ravenswood."

At the Bijou Theatre in the Haymarket, there was in 1863 a very good amateur performance for the same Royal Benevolent Society that got an excellent notice in *The Era*. The pieces played were that old farce " The Loan of a Lover," " The White Horse of the Peppers " (quite an ambitious attempt for the amateurs of that day), and the farce, " Ticklish Times." The company were much the same as at Campden House in 1863, with the addition of Admiral Duckworth-King and Mr. Uniacke Lawler, an Irish portrait painter of the sixties with the most powerful brogue I ever heard.

The *clou* of the evening's performance seems to have been again the Connaught Jig danced in " The White Horse of the Peppers " by Mr. Algernon Joy and Lady Anne Sherson. *The Era* gets quite enthusiastic over this :

" The celebrated Connaught jig was quite admirably danced by her, and the trouble which her ladyship must have taken to acquire a mastery of those difficult steps, and the physical exertion which was necessary for their accomplishment, can scarcely be considered counterbalanced even by the enthusiastic applause which denoted the triumphant result. Both her ladyship and Mr. Algernon Joy, her partner on the occasion, infused such life and energy into it, and seemed so thoroughly to enjoy the whole affair that a hearty encore was the result and an avalanche of bouquets and exotics fell on the house, not reaching the stage, investing the occupants of the stalls with floral honours."

I wonder, by the way, when it ceased to be a custom to throw bouquets and other " floral honours " from the house on to the stage instead of having them handed up by the leader of the orchestra or brought on by attendants in livery, which always gives rise to the suspicion that they have been truly " provided by the management." I think the old custom was a very charming one provided that persons in the audience did not try to throw from too great a distance—though I may recall in this connection that I had a relation who declared he had thrown a bouquet from the back of the gallery on to the stage at Covent Garden. I always doubted the story, and if it were true the handle must have been loaded,

AMATEUR THEATRICALS IN 1863

"THE CONNAUGHT JIG"

Lady Anne Sherson and Mr. Algernon Joy in "The White Horse of the Peppers"
St. James's Theatre

which would have made it an appalling thing to alight on the head of a stallite.

But ladies threw their own bouquets from the boxes to their favourites on the stage, bouquets which in those days were an integral part of a lady's full toilette. Nowadays no one troubles to carry flowers to the theatre, nor do the men even sport a buttonhole, except His Majesty the King, who is never without one, and one or two others who form a pleasing exception.

But I have wandered far away from the subject of amateur theatricals, my only excuse being that when I recall all these pleasant days and nights of years ago I allow myself to indulge a little in the garrulity of age and to stray from the direct paths of my subject.

Charles Dickens was, as is well known, an enthusiastic amateur. At Tavistock House in Bloomsbury he had a miniature theatre complete in all detail and here he produced plays of his own and of Wilkie Collins and others. Augustus Egg, a forgotten artist of the Royal Academy, was a constant actor at Dickens's performances, and Wilkie Collins himself wrote more than one play for Tavistock House, in which he was a performer.

The staff of *Punch* had a company of their own, including Mark Lemon, Sir John Tenniel, Lord Churchill and Arthur Sketchley, the amusing author of *Mrs. Brown at the Play*.

The Duke and Duchess of Bedford were also very keen on amateur theatricals, and many really good programmes were got up at Woburn Abbey. But there was a rage for them at the time and the full history of the amateurs of the mid-nineteenth century has yet to be written. Perhaps this chapter is entirely unnecessary, but, on the other hand, there may be one or two " veterans " who remember the sixties and will like to recall some of the pleasant times of their youth.

CHAPTER XVIII

THE LOST THEATRES OF TOYLAND

IN discussing the pieces produced at the Grecian Theatre, I have chiefly dealt with Melodrama and Pantomime, the two forms of dramatic entertainment which were always the staple fare at that house.

In Toyland, where there are many traditions of "Lost Theatres," the chief items of the bill were also Melodrama and Pantomime, and it may not be uninteresting to say something about those lost dramatic performances which but for the praiseworthy labours of a worthy citizen of Hoxton would be altogether shows of the Past. Thanks, however, to that ingenious and sensible merchant, it is still possible to set up a Theatre Royal on the dining-room table and enact drama or pantomime by means of sheets of "Penny-plain" or "Twopence-coloured."

For in the theatres of Toyland, the reason of the staple entertainment being also drama alternated with pantomime is not far to seek. It is obviously much easier to employ the silent *dramatis personæ* of such places in dramas where strong situations count rather than words, or in pantomime where much of the piece is gone through in dumb show and the scenic effects are the things that matter.

Leaving the Theatre Royal Pollock at Hoxton out of the question, as not being a lost temple of the Toyland Drama, let me consider one or two other houses which have now completely vanished.

Perhaps the earliest of any importance in modern times was "West's Theatre." Mr. W. West lived in Wych Street in the early part of the nineteenth century, not far, you will see, from the great theatre of Old Drury, the Opera House, Covent Garden, the old Olympic and the Lyceum. His theatre was a much larger one than the other and later well-known places of Toyland, and the sheets of "Penny-plain," or "Twopence-coloured," were consequently also larger, and probably cost more than the traditional pence.

His characters were often designed from living originals, so that you could, if you so pleased, exhibit Mr. Edmund Kean or Mr. Kemble or perhaps, later, Mr. Macready in the plays in which they performed at the Patent theatres. Sarah Siddons, the "Tragic Muse," was doubtless to be found on a sheet of tragic characters, and her niece, and feeble imitator, Fanny Kemble. But it has not been my privilege to witness a performance at West's Theatre, and I can only repeat what has come down by tradition.

As at other theatres of the town, the favourite play of Toyland seems to have been " The Miller and His Men "—not the burlesque so profanely produced at a later date and much exploited by " Amateurs of Rank and Fashion," but the good old crusted melodrama as given at all the playhouses of the early and mid-nineteenth century—especially at " Queen Victoria's Own Theayter " in the New Cut or at Drury Lane and Sadler's Wells.

West's Theatre appears to have had two rivals in Toyland, viz., Marks's and Hodgson's, but I cannot trace how long their companies survived and they were probably disbanded many years ago.

Skelt's Theatre was the next, I think, in point of time and importance. It was situated in the Minories close to the old church where the dried head of Lady Jane Grey's father was exhibited, for gain, not long since, as I am able, personally, to testify.

The Skelt répertoire was a large one, embracing, of course " The Miller and His Men " (in which I remember the Claudine as a very fine figure of a woman with an astonishing leg development). It specialized in Eastern plays, there being a very numerous selection of them, such as " Timour The Tartar," " Forty Thieves," " Aladdin," and other dramatizations of Oriental legends.

Processions were prominent in the Skelt plays, and I cannot help thinking that the costumier and artist of the establishment had leanings towards gorgeous scenery and embroidery—say, of the " Chu Chin Chow " order—or else there was a large stock of tinsel and Oriental ornaments to work off !

One of the best productions of Skelt's Theatre was " Der Freischütz," founded on the same legend that Weber set to music. This was a very popular opera, at one period being sung at two Opera houses simultaneously with three burlesques on it running at the same time at other theatres. The great scene in " Der Freischütz " is the " Wolf's Glen " where Kaspar by the aid of Zamiel (our old friend Mephistopheles under another name) casts the magic bullets with many eerie spells. Such a scene would give much scope to the Theatres of Toyland in the way of scenic display and lurid effects.

It is worthy of remark that each Theatre of Toyland had its own idiosyncrasies strongly marked. Though " The Miller and His Men," for example, was produced by one and all, any experienced Toyland playgoer could tell at a glance, and without reading the name, at what theatre it was produced. Skelt differed from Park, Park from Redington and Redington from Webb.

After the Theatre in the Minories came Park and Redington, though I am not certain in what order these two should be placed.

Park was at Camden Town. I am not sure of Redington's address and it is many years since I saw one of his sheets. Park specialized in dramas of the " blood and thunder " type, such as the Old Vic loved to put on its boards. " Raymond and Agnes : or the Bleeding Nun," " The, Spectre Bride " (with fine ghost effects) and " The Red Rover." Redington went in more for short pieces like " Charles II " and " The Waterman "—presumably as a *lever de rideau* for the longer plays or pantomimes. Webb's Theatre, which was located in Old Street, St. Luke's (how often I have made the long journey thither from the far West End of Town !) went in extensively for plays of the patriotic type like " The Battle of the Alma " or " The Battle of Waterloo "—the kind given so often at Astley's in which Gomersal (famous for his extraordinary likeness to the Great Napoleon) used to double the parts of Napoleon and Wellington on the same night. But Webb's had also a very good selection of pantomimes. One in particular—" Jack and the Beanstalk "—with many tricks and much change of scene, was most elaborate, affording scope for " Marvellous and Wondrous Effects," as we were careful to announce on our programmes. Extra talent was requisite for the due production of this pantomime : for I remember that in the book of words it was distinctly laid down that the Clown was to sing either " Hot Codlins " or " Tippitywitchet," or both, a stage direction which must have frequently prevented the pantomime from being played in its entirety.

There was yet another Theatre in Toyland. This was presided over by one Green, and was to be found somewhere in a side street near Regent's Park. It was the last of the old ones to disappear. Green and Redington are said to have had the most extensive répertoires and Webb the smallest ; but Webb's were always very complete productions and cost more to put on the Stage.

Besides the actual scenery and the cast of characters, producers of plays in Toyland had to go to some expense for what may be called " Extras." Ready-made tricks for the Harlequinade, Combats (fours, sixes, twelves, sixteens even) for the patriotic pieces, extra fairies, houses, ships, foot pieces (land and water), rocks, odd trunks of trees and other bits and pieces, sky drops and interior drops, gauze for transformation scenes, tinsel, gold paper, coloured paper, red fire (when authorized by the authorities !), oil for the footlights, and, above all, slides. These last-named formed no inconsiderable item in the cost of mounting a play : for, consider, every time a character had to change its attitude, or perhaps close with another character in a deadly combat, he had to exit and re-enter on a fresh slide in a different attitude. It may therefore be realized that the importance of each character rose in proportion to the number of slides used for it in the play.

Trap-doors, always an effective stage device, were very awkward to manage, though I overcame the difficulty in my theatre by setting the stage over a gap in the dining-room table (made by removing a leaf !) so that I, or a confederate, could manipulate the trap with ease from underneath.

But the Toyland Theatre that I ran for so long was an unusually well-equipped one. In front, in the wings of the proscenium, solid ladies and gentlemen (albeit of a diminutive size) sat in private boxes to enjoy the performance. The members of the orchestra, though sounding not a note, were ensconced in a proper well, each player separate with his instrument, not, as in the lower class of Toyland Theatre, all merely painted along a slip ; the drop scenes were on canvas and rolled up from the bottom, as did also the regulation green baize final curtain. Finally, the footlights extended all along the front (not a mere paltry two or three) and, moreover, they could be really lit. It will therefore be seen that my Theatre bore the same relation to other Toyland theatres as Drury Lane, say, does to a minor house of the East End.

As an illustration of the difficulty experienced with the movement of slides, I may be permitted to quote some stage directions in a scene from " The Miller and His Men " :

Exeunt Karl and Riber L. Re-enter Karl stabbing Riber L. (Plate 10 penny, or Plate 9 smaller editions).

and again :

Exit Count Friberg asleep R. Re-enter Count Friberg with drawn sword R. (Plate 1 penny, or Plate 4 smaller edition).

When several manœuvres of this kind have to be executed at once or rapidly in succession, it will be easily seen that a good supply of slides and a fairly large staff behind the scenes are necessary. In the final scene of the same play, where a lady villain (I think Ravina was her name) sets fire to the mill, she is entered torch in hand, the mill burns up, she exits and re-enters without torch and in a dying attitude ; all the other persons on the stage are equally active, while some one must attend to the burning mill—to prevent ructions of another kind !

The plays still to be had from the Hoxton merchant comprise many of the old lot. All that are available can be had in the smaller size and some few still in the larger. I have heard it said that the industry is a dead one : that no new plays will be printed, and that we shall have to be contented with these old favourites of the past. It seems indeed a pity that no one will take the trouble to adapt " Chu Chin Chow " for the Toyland Houses : it would have an enormous run !

I once had a Galanty Show from the same source as my Toyland Theatre, viz., Cremer's " Toy Emporium " in Regent Street. It was not nearly so satisfying. Story was wanting ; the brilliant red, blue, green and yellow of the play's characters and scenes were wanting ; there were no wondrous changes possible, no tricks beyond making the figures jump over the lamp and so disappear in the air—which got very monotonous after a time.

It always seems to me now that the Galanty Show of those days bore the same relation to the regular Toyland theatres of Skelt, Redington and Webb as the Movies of the present do to the acting playhouses. Shadows only on the Galanty sheet and shadows only on the Movies Screen : and who cares to substitute the shadow for the substance ? Not I, for one.

Many years ago, I came across a theatre from German Toyland. I would not have it as a gift ! It was about the same size as the larger of the English Toyland Theatres, but the *dramatis personæ* were solid dolls whose heads nearly touched the flies. They stood on discs of wood and were manipulated from the top by thick bits of wire stuck in their poor heads. When two or three were gathered together on the stage, there was hardly room to move them about, and I can't imagine what would happen if one had to die in the course of the play ! There would have been no room for it to lie down in any position without showing its disc. Moreover, it was not possible to " exit Count Friberg asleep and re-enter Count Friberg with drawn sword " so that action was limited, or, rather, absent altogether. The scenery was well painted, but the whole affair was very heavy and solid. Yes, solid is the proper word. It was as solid and as heavy as the Germany whence it came. I should think that Byron's " Werner " or Kotzebue's " Stranger " would be the only plays one could produce on such a stage.

The ideal method for the Theatres Royal, Toyland, is undoubtedly that of the " Teatro dei Piccoli " of the Italians, but until we have learned to manipulate the strings as they do let us keep to slides with all their awkwardness and expense. Imagination can in most cases supply all deficiences. But no imagination will serve with a Toyland Theatre from Hunland—such as I saw and have described above.

What is not generally known is that the plates for many of the characters of the Toyland Theatres were done by celebrated artists. From 1815 to 1835, Flaxman, the Cruikshanks, Finden and the

Heaths and also Blake, the poet and artist, were responsible for many of the designs. The coloured plates were always noted for the brilliancy of the colours, especially the reds and yellows. The former were produced by carmine mixed with sugar and the latter by gamboge also mixed with sugar.

Many of the characters were actual portraits of famous actors of the time. The St. George was Ducrow of Astley's. The Red Rover was Yates of the Adelphi, and another character in the Red Rover was a portrait of T. P. Cooke, the original Martin Truegold in the famous Surrey drama "True to the Core," and a well-known William in "Black-Eyed Susan." In "The Bottle Imp" the picture of Willibald was a likeness of Oxberry. The best known of all Toyland dramas—"The Miller and His Men"—was originally drawn by George Cruikshank himself. Claudine was probably a portrait of Sally Booth who created the part in the play and the character of Ravina was also the portrait of a very famous actress of her day, but whom I have been unable to identify. For the original plates of all these Toyland Dramas, the artists who were to become so famous in later years were paid at the rate of £2 a plate. Those sold by West were undoubtedly the most brilliantly coloured and they sold for penny plain and twopence coloured. Those of Skelt in the Minories were rather smaller and fetched only a half-penny plain and twopence coloured.

CHAPTER XIX

AUDIENCES OF THE PAST AND AUDIENCES OF THE PRESENT

THEATRE audiences of the Past were constituted very differently from those of the Present. In order to understand this thoroughly, one must take account of the different way in which the auditorium of the theatre was arranged, and of the very different type of person who formed the bulk of the playgoers.

Until the middle of the nineteenth century, the majority of Londoners did not frequent the playhouses as they do now. Fashionable folk went to the Opera Houses and to leading theatres such as the Haymarket, St. James's and the like. The lower classes delighted in the Old Vic, and other outlying houses where they could enjoy the blood and thunder melodramas of the time.

But in early Victorian days there was a numerous middle-class who did not approve of theatres at all, and it was a long time before the example of the better class and even of the Queen herself who, with Prince Consort, used to be a constant visitor at the leading houses, could induce the British bourgeois to become an habitual playgoer.

As regards the Italian Opera, for instance, by which I mean especially the Opera House in the Haymarket, burned down in 1867, it must be remembered that there were only two rows of stalls, and at an earlier date not even these. The pit, which was the fashionable part of the house for those who had not subscribed for a box, extended down nearly as far as the orchestra, and was filled with a company of the " Upper Ten Thousand " in full evening dress. It was in fact, what the stalls are at the present time. Down the centre of the pit ran a passage known as " Fops' Alley," up and down which the beaux and dandies would stroll during the interval, ogling the ladies in all parts of the house, pointing out to friends by name and title the aristocratic folk in the private boxes and showing off their fine clothes. Fine clothes, indeed, were the order of the day for gentlemen visiting the fashionable parts of the Opera House. No law seems to have governed the attire of the ladies : perhaps because it was realized that no law was necessary ! But severe sumptuary regulations were laid down in the early years of the nineteenth century with regard to the correct costume in which a gentleman should appear.

The dress had to consist of a long-tailed coat with ruffles at the wrist, white cravat with stand-up shirt collar, small-clothes with diamond or gold buckles, silk stockings, shoes, a waistcoat open to show the shirt front or frill, and white kid gloves. A cocked hat, called a " chapeau bras," because carried under the arm, and a sword at the side, completed the costume. The hair was always very carefully dressed.

Unwritten rules for gentlemen's dress at the Opera have been in force ever since then up to a few years ago, when the stalls and boxes began to be invaded by persons who, presumably, had plenty of money to pay for them, but who had never been accustomed to change their attire in the evening, and in fact, did " not see the use of it," as I was once told ! They are of that type of person who has never realized the comfort of getting into clean linen and different clothes after the business of the day.

At one time, no one was admitted to the stalls or boxes at the Opera House unless in evening dress, but *nous avons changé tout celà*—and the day may not be far distant on which lounge suits, walking boots, and pipes will be permitted there ; when ladies will not be required to take off their hats and may smoke as many cigarettes as the singers can stand without revolt. I believe that state of affairs has already been reached among the Bolsheviks : why not, then, in a country which contains so many of their admirers ?

As regards the theatres, however, the rules for dress have always been less rigid. In fact, I do not think that regulations have ever been laid down by any manager with regard to the wearing of evening dress. It has never been necessary. Hitherto a frequenter of the stalls would have as soon thought of coming in his dressing-gown as in a morning suit. Moreover, in the first half of last century, the arrangement of the interior of theatres was somewhat different. Stalls were a later innovation. I think Madame Vestris at the Olympic was the first to take away part of the pit which, up to then, had extended right down to the orchestra. The fashionable folk sat in the public boxes (where the dress circle now is), open to each other, but separated by partitions over which you could hold a conversation with your neighbour in the next box.

But Vestris was no doubt compelled to make this change by the increasingly aristocratic character of her audience. All the rank and fashion of London flocked to the theatre in the slums. It is recorded that the Duke of Wellington tried three times in one week unsuccessfully to book a seat, and the house was habitually filled with fashionable people like Lady Blessington and Count D'Orsay— veritable leaders of the mode—and literary celebrities such as Charles Dickens and the Brothers James and Horace Smith.

As early as 1825 it became the custom for families, or parties in which there were ladies, to take private boxes rather than occupy the public ones, where they were liable to be troubled by the proximity of rougher parties or of young men who had drunk " not wisely but too well." Indeed, the public boxes soon fell out of favour altogether and were gradually converted into a continuous circle where people sucked oranges or munched apples and talked across loudly to any acquaintances whom they might descry.

These kinds of " open " boxes lingered on in the provinces some time after they had disappeared from the London theatres—especially in the smaller and less important houses. I well remember them in Vincent Crummles's little old theatre in the Commercial Road, Landport, when I saw " The Red Rover " many, many years agone. They also survived to my day in the little theatre on Richmond Green (vanished for some years now) where Edmund Kean acted, and I feel sure that other provincial playhouses kept them much longer than London.

At nine o'clock, or whatever time the half-price came into force, theatre audiences were always increased by a rougher lot, who had not the means, or did not choose, to pay for the whole entertainment, and who also, maybe, had " been dining." Many disturbances could be traced to the system of " half-price," and theatres benefited much when it was abolished.

I think the old Olympic was the last theatre of importance to continue the habit. I know I went there more than once in my young days at half-time.

Another cause of disturbance to the audience in the past were the men and women laden with large baskets of oranges, apples, nuts, cakes, buns, thick sandwiches of ham, beef and pork, bottles of beer, lemonade and ginger-beer and other comestibles who threaded their way round the house between the jammed rows of spectators, amid the jeers of the wags, and the curses of such as did not want anything to eat or drink and did not like to have their feet walked on by the burly purveyors. In the theatres of the type of the Surrey and Britannia even after the curtailment of the pit, these hefty carriers would go round the stalls as well and do an equally good trade.

Such refreshments were naturally more in demand in the outlying houses of the East End and the transpontine districts than in the fashionable theatres of the West End, though at places like the Adelphi, Princess's and Olympic, the custom lingered for years. Perhaps the patrons of melodrama require more solid sustenance than those who are listening to musical pieces or high comedy. They certainly pay more attention to the play. Even now, I think that the occupiers of the cheaper seats (pit, gallery and upper boxes) are far more attentive and more appreciative of good dramatic fare than those in the stalls and boxes. Although I have seen the best parts of the house literally " rise " at the Lyceum on special occasions in the Irving days, I can't help feeling that the well-dressed stallites think it vulgar to let themselves go !

With the exception of the old Gaiety in the days of the Pas de Quatre where the relations between audience and stage were of a peculiarly intimate kind—it is to the lower class of theatre (if I may so call them) like the Surrey, Britannia, Old Vic, and Standard (in the days of the Douglasses) that we must look for a real entente cordiale between the front and back of the house. The interest with which a play was followed at these theatres was very great, and the appreciation of its good points the more keen accordingly. The audiences listened intently to the piece, judged it on its merits and damned it if they thought it ought to be damned ! Sometimes this result was achieved by groans and hisses, but as often as not by chaff and outbursts of wit that made the rest of the theatre roar with laughter when they ought to have been fumbling for their handkerchiefs. Several good stories are told of plays sent eternally to the rightabout by scathingly witty remarks from the pit or gallery, always keen to discern the weak points and " rub it in " for the players, and mysterious indeed were, on occasion, the impulses that apparently gave rise to these interruptions and remarks.

I can remember two instances when the play was slain outright —dead as mutton—by the remarks of the pit. In one case (" Zillah : or The Scar on the Wrist " produced at the Lyceum by the great actress, Genevieve Ward) the cause was undoubtedly a set made at a certain negro character in the play. In the other, no less a drama than " Monte Cristo " given at the Adelphi by Fechter, the same mortal blow was dealt by the pit on account of an actor of the old, old school of ranters who, it was considered, took too long to die !

This was during the very last engagement of Fechter in London in the late sixties. The Monte Cristo play was not a success, and, curiously enough, no dramatic adaptation of the novel ever has pleased in this country. As an exciting story it ought to have great possibilities for the stage, but it will not, I think, be ever tried again : there seems to be too much ill-luck attached to it. It was the play that the French company from Paris tried to give when disgraceful riots were organized against " foreign actors " in 1848. It failed on another occasion when produced with quite a good cast, and I will now tell you how it failed in spite of the glamour of Fechter in the rôle of the hero.

In the early part of the story, before Dantes escapes from the Château d'If, it will be remembered that he has a long interview with an old Abbé who has discovered the treasures of the Island of

Monte Cristo, in which the old man describes how to get to the grotto with its stores of gold and precious stones, and then dies.

Fechter, of course, was Dantes, and the part of the Abbé was taken by one C. J. Smith. This was an actor of the very pronounced old school who had been at the Adelphi for years and, like all members of stock companies, had to take any part allotted to him. It should be stated that he was invaluable in rôles where there was nothing to say, for he was a particularly clever mime. His earliest appearance of all had been at the old Royalty Theatre in Wellclose Square about the year 1814, but, coming down to 1855, we find him as the Bear in "Valentine and Orson" (one of Keeley's great successes) and very often as Pantaloon in the annual pantomime at the Adelphi. He was also an excellent exponent of the chief Gnome in the Katskill scene of "Rip van Winkle," which required great acting powers but no elocution. It is true that he had been entrusted with the not unimportant part of Corrigan in the first production of " The Colleen Bawn " in 1860, but the chance of playing a scene with such a " star " as Fechter was one of which he determined to take the fullest advantage and to prolong as much as possible. When the time came for him to die, he gasped, took time over every word and kept calling Dantes to his side to administer refreshing draughts of cold water. At last, during one of these pauses, a man in the pit suddenly rose and caught his eye : " If you please, sir," he said, " shall you be *much* longer a-dying ? " That killed the play, for the audience could no longer take anything seriously, and it was laughed out of existence.

The case of " Zillah " was rather more mysterious. The Zillah was Genevieve Ward, a tragic actress of great power, and a favourite with the public. Members of the cast included Barnes, Willie Herbert, Tyars, Mead, Forbes-Robertson and one McIntyre, a popular actor of melodramatic villains who in general could always command the applause of the theatrical public. He was playing the part of a negro, and for some reason the pit, or a portion of it, had its knife into him from the beginning. What his offence was I don't think was ever ascertained. Perhaps it was only a personal matter with some individual in the pit who took advantage of the production of a rather stupid play to " let him have it."

It was a very lurid piece by Palgrave Simpson and a certain " Claude Templar," whose real name was Daugars. Whenever the unfortunate negro appeared on the scene, a gentleman in the pit suggested some means of getting rid of him. He was with a band of robbers plotting a murder. The pit critic called out : " Gentlemen, will you be so good as to shoot the nigger ? " Later on, the villainess of the play was preparing to poison the hero with doctored wine. The negro was eagerly watching her doings. Suddenly the voice from the pit was again heard : " Madame, will you please let the hero alone. If you want to poison anyone, poison the nigger." Finally, in the last act, when virtue was triumphant, the negro was in for a bad time. There was a " practicable well " on the stage, which one of the characters had referred to as being of great depth. A serious quarrel took place with the negro and his fellow-villains, and he was to die a death of some kind. " What shall we do with him ? " cried the band. The pit observer seized the opportunity and called out : " Why not put him in the well ? " As this was the fate the author had intended for him all along, to the great delight of the audience, he *was* put in the well ! The story is told at some length by Mr. Arthur à Beckett in his most amusing book of Recollections, and he was present himself on the occasion.

But, sometimes, interrupters in the audience had more solid grounds for their protests. At the first representation of Charles Reade's drama " It's Never Too Late to Mend," at the Princess's in 1865, a charming young actress, Louisa Moore (sister of the famous Nelly Moore who died at the beginning of her successes), played the boy Josephs in the convict scene, and fainted on the stage from the too realistic treatment of those enacting the prison warders. Mr. Guest Tomlins, the dramatic critic of the *Morning Advertiser*, a much respected journalist, stood up in the stalls and openly protested against the undisguised brutality of the scene. George Vining, the manager of the theatre, was so ill-advised as to remind the critics that they had not paid for their seats, and were the guests of the theatre. The play was not allowed to go on till he had apologized from the stage for his speech.

A more amusing interruption was that which occurred at a Manchester theatre when Mrs. Nisbett was playing Juliana in " The Honeymoon." She wore a large hat with feathers, one of which fell out after her most effective speech. " You're moulting, ma'am," cried a voice from the gallery.

Greville in his Memoirs records a similar incident as reported by Thomas Moore at the theatre in Dublin. Othello was being played. A friend of the gentleman acting the Moor suddenly called out from the audience : " Larry, Larry, Larry, there's the least taste in life of your linen hanging out." These incidents are, however, but trifling in themselves.

For the most famous riot in a London playhouse one must go back to the year 1809, when Covent Garden reopened its doors after having been totally destroyed by fire. It was a much more serious affair than any before or since, and this chapter would not be complete without an account, however short, gathered from the records of the day.

To meet the expenses of rebuilding the theatre, the prices were raised from 3s. 6d. to 4s. for the pit and from 6s. to 7s. for the boxes. This increase in the prices, which was moderate enough, and would not have occasioned any such disturbance in modern times, gave rise to what came to be known as the "O.P. riots," which were continued for some time. When the curtain was raised on the opening night, the pit created such an uproar that not one word of the play could be heard the whole evening. The slogan of the rioters was "Old Prices !" a phrase which they kept up for hours, until some magistrates read the Riot Act from the stage, and a few of the most noisy rioters were arrested. On the next night, the disturbances were still worse and placards with the inscription "Old Prices" were waved aloft in the pit. For no less than sixty-six nights the disturbances were kept up by means of "cat-calls, trumpets, watchman's rattles, hooting, hissing, groaning, imitation of dogs barking, cats mewing, asses braying, cattle lowing and all sorts of animal noises, until at length the actors made no more pretence of doing their parts even in dumb show, but simply walked on to the stage to be spectators of the drama that the audience was providing for their amusement."

The management at length decided to close the house. A financial statement was issued showing that the profits on the capital would be only 3½ per cent., even with the new prices, and that under the old prices, there must be a loss of 15s. per cent. This representation did not satisfy the O.P. rioters, and when the theatre was once more opened the disturbances began anew. Plays were announced but the opponents would not let them be performed.

John Kemble was not exempt from the attacks, in spite of the fact that he was a public favourite. He was assailed with the coarsest epithets ; offensive placards were raised on poles in the pit and thrust in the faces of such actors as were plucky enough to appear. Dustmen's bells were incessantly rung in the galleries and the noise nightly was greater than ever.

Then the mystic letters "O.P." became leaders of fashion in the Town ! "O.P." handkerchiefs, "O.P." waistcoats were in great demand : the latter garments, which were only worn in the theatre, bore an "O" on one flap and a "P" on the other. Hats were inscribed with the same letters and some of the ladies had "O.P." bonnets. Toothpicks, pencils, seals and other articles of common use were manufactured in haste bearing the cabalistic letters. The whole Town went mad on "O.P."

At last, some more sensible rioter realized that, in spite of the uproar, they were really benefiting the management, by filling the theatre every night, and they made a resolution of not coming till half-price time. During the first part of the evening therefore, the performance went off as usual, but on the entry of the mob the war was renewed. On the fall of the curtain, they sang the National Anthem, climbed into the boxes and finally took possession of the stage, and danced what they were pleased to call the " O.P. Dance."

In the end, the management was obliged to yield half their demands. The pit prices were restored to 3s. 6d., but the boxes remained at the higher figure. On the first night after this arrangement was announced, Kemble was received with great applause, each actor was called by name to be cheered, and a large placard several feet long was displayed in front of the pit, bearing the words "We are satisfied."

Thus ended the O.P. Riots, probably unparalleled in the history of the theatre in any country. But it was the age of riots and mob law. Kemble could not escape the fate of so many of the social and political characters of the day.

I have referred to the opposition organized by English managers and playgoers to the advent of the French players at Drury Lane in 1840. The play was " Monte Cristo " and the company from the Théatre Historique in Paris. After " God Save the Queen " had been sung, the audience demanded it again, and then went on halloing, hooting, whistling and shouting for three hours. Persons in the pit put up umbrellas, and an occupant in the boxes was much applauded for wanting to fight some one. It was supposed to be all done in the interests of the British Drama, and had been heralded by a manifesto headed :

" Britons, stand by the British Drama, and help to restore it to its pristine vigour." Macready was incensed with the insult offered to visitors from a friendly country, and took the part of the French company, writing the directors a letter to express his regret at the circumstances. But Matthews, Webster, Kean, Farren, Buckstone and others took exception to this friendly feeling for the French actors, and seem to have shown the narrowest prejudice all through. Macready was actually served with a summons in the names of the above managers to bring him to account for words alleged to have been used by him in a conversation with the French manager, and the case was only dropped by his explaining that he had not actually made use of the words with which he was credited. It was altogether a rather pitiful example of how far British insularity can go, and Macready came out of the quarrel with much credit in the opinion of all fair-minded people. He was, no doubt, far in advance of his time. We have learned long ago to welcome with acclaim the performances of the great artistes of other countries when they do us the honour to pay us a visit, but for a considerable time they had a hard struggle to make their talents appreciated as they ought to be.

The affair of 1840 died a natural death, and the company was permitted to finish its engagement, but the feeling against foreign actors continued for many years, even when such great artistes appeared at the St. James's as Rachel, Judith, Schneider, or Desclée. The people who went to see the "French Players" as they were always called, were sneered at by those who did not understand the language or preferred the more robust acting of the Olympic or Adelphi, while there was yet another section of the Victorian public who were persuaded that everything French must be indelicate if not worse. It was a very long time before the average Londoner would go to opera bouffe (except on the sly and as something rather "naughty"). When the opera bouffe rage did set in, we went to the other extreme and could not have enough of it. This was, however, not till the late sixties and the seventies of the nineteenth century.

When the Bancrofts took over the Haymarket Theatre in January, 1880, they abolished the pit, extending the stalls right up to the back of the house. As a substitute for the pit, a very commodious upper circle was made above the dress circle. The regular pittites, however, were furious and, on a smaller scale got up a one night repetition of the O.P. riots. Bancroft made a speech in which he pointed out that it was a matter of business, that he could not afford to have a pit, and that he was the loser if he did have one. As a matter of fact, he was greatly the gainer by not having one, for he added 150 stalls to the house and they were generally all booked up weeks beforehand, such was the success of his productions. It was a long time ere the audience was really appeased. I think the new arrangement lasted throughout the Bancroft management, but the pit was restored afterwards. I was there myself not so very long ago to see "Mary Rose" (and dreadfully bored I must confess I was with that masterpiece !) but I had to pay 3s. 6d. for the privilege, and I remember much better performances at the same house for a paltry 2s.

I have described in another chapter the anger, the outspoken fury of the Old Vic gallery when, in "Oliver Twist," Bill Sikes drags the unfortunate Nancy round the stage by the hair of her head. Audiences at the Minor Theatres were frequently like that. They seemed to enter far more than those of the fashionable West End houses into the spirit, I might almost say the realities of the action of the play. I think I have also mentioned the instance of Madame Celeste in "The Green Bushes" who shoots the husband who had deserted her. "Serve him right !" called out a woman in the pit. "He's just like my monster !" This lady had her emotions less under control than a Frenchwoman in a Paris theatre who fell from the gallery into the pit. Of course every one supposed she must be dead. But she picked herself up, gave her dress a shake and merely remarked : "Thank goodness, I've at last got a seat where I can see and hear."

An interruption of a later day was noted at a performance of "Drink" with Warner as Coupeau. "Don't give it him, you wretch,"—exclaimed an old lady in the pit when they tried to make Coupeau drink !

Sometimes the interruptions came from the stage and not from the audience.

It is related of Miolhan-Carvalho, the great opera singer, that she used to order hot soup from a neighbouring restaurant for her refreshment between the acts. On one occasion, the delivery of the soup was entrusted to a servant who knew the singer well by sight, and she was specially instructed to see that it got into Carvalho's hands and was not given to anyone else. Wandering down towards the stage, she caught sight of Carvalho singing the finale of the first Act of "Lucia." Ravenswood and Lucy were just about to begin the impassioned finale, when, lo, entered the maid with the soup ! She placed the tureen on a mossy bank, lifted the cover, made a curtsy and said : "Begging your pardon, sir, for interrupting you and the lady, but here's the soup ! "

Modern audiences are much less enthusiastic than those of the past. Either the war has taken all the enthusiasm out of them or, which is more likely, there is considerably less for them to be enthusiastic about. The chief concern of the modern pittite seems to be to spot the various celebrities (actors and actresses for choice) on their entry into the theatre. After the performance, whole queues of members of the audience, gushing young women and long-haired young men, form up to watch for the exit, not only of the chief performers from the stage door, but also of the principal "society items" from the main entrance. The ineffable cheap pictorial press is responsible for much of this, for, thanks to it, the features of women in Society are now as well known as those of the players themselves or the members of the half-world.

Many of the occupants of the stalls, desirous of publicity, will stand up deliberately in order that they may hear the pit remark : "Look ! There's so-and-so ! " Some of these are well-known players themselves, and obtain the public recognition and appreciation of the modern audience in the auditorium which they are not always in a position to get on the stage itself.

The really "business" portion of the audience, the part which has come to see and judge the play, is ensconced in the gallery far away from the frivolities of the stalls and boxes. On a first night, its attention is usually concentrated on finding out the defects of the new piece, and on seizing the occasion to express its august disapproval. One might reasonably suppose that its opinion would not matter very much if the remainder of the audience were favourably disposed. But it is not so. A gallery, whether it understands the play or not, has the power (and frequently exercises it) of damning a production on the first night, regardless of the fact that it perhaps cost thousands of pounds to put on the stage, and that it may not be altogether a bad play if it were given a reasonable chance.

Another feature of modern first nights is the first entrance on the stage of some popular idol (generally of the male sex), a signal for outbursts of loud and prolonged applause from his admirers, which stops the action of the piece for a considerable time.

These favoured gentlemen are now known specifically by the name of " Matinée Idols " and I have already alluded to them in the chapter on the Globe Theatre.

I now make a suggestion that Fechter was the first. His exquisite love-making, his admirable fencing, his deeds of dering-do, and his generally romantic appearance must have made him the pet of the susceptible flappers of his day. After Fechter, I doubt if there was another so adored until Terriss and, after him, Lewis Waller came upon the scene, though Harry Montagu, Henry Neville and Wilson Barrett also had their devoted admirers, and Alexander, at a later date, his. In the present day, the idols " grow on every bush." As our American friends say—" The hedges are full of them." It is quite unnecessary to name the favoured swains, but I have heard that one especial pet is, or was, a member of the Gilbert and Sullivan Opera Co., and that another singer of light opera was known, in his younger days, as the " adorable Adonis " and the " flappers' fancy." It is not a pretty trait in our modern audiences, and certainly does not conduce to an increase in the number of first-class actors.

I have said that special theatres have special audiences. So have special plays and always have had. The audience who sit down to enjoy " The Ticket of Leave Man " would be quite a different one from that which would delight in " Maria Martin," though both these pieces come within the category of melodrama.

I once saw, at the Grecian Theatre I think, a fearsome piece called " Catherine Howard." I cannot remember whether it had anything to do with the fifth wife of bluff King Hal, but what I do distinctly recall is the scene of a burial vault where the heroine is lying in a gruesome coffin most realistically set out on trestles in the centre of the stage, coffin cloth, brass nails and all complete. Her lover (like Romeo of old) gets into the vault, and gives way to grief and long speeches—and anon the coffin lid is pushed up and the lady appears in her shroud. This scene was received with the closest attention. Sighs and groans were audible among the occupants of the pit, and one lady next to me, under the influence of strong emotion, muttered under her breath : " Ah, poor dear, poor dear ! "

I was young myself in those days, and I dare say I was also properly thrilled. Not so, however, in much later years, when in the pit at the Lyceum, during the performance of one of the popular melo-dramas of the brothers Melville, I fear I laughed too audibly at a moment when I ought perhaps to have rather cried. A good lady just in front of me whispered to her neighbour : " What's he laughing at ? " The lady addressed looked me up and down with an air of pitiful scorn and replied : " Poor old man, don't you see he doesn't understand the play ? "

Such audiences as these would be like fish out of water at the Haymarket or His Majesty's in Tree's time, though the play might be exciting and the mounting gorgeous. It would be all a little above their heads. In the same way, I am bound to confess that some of the high-brow (pass me the fearful expression, please) productions of Everyman Theatre or the Stage Societies are above mine. Especi-ally is there one play (in which a row of characters discuss the question of a loathsome disease) which has always seemed to me to be a mis-take, from any point of view even that of propaganda, and is certainly not artistic. Long dialogues without any action may be uplifting and good for one, but give me " The Duke's Motto " or " The Ticket of Leave Man " or " Arrah na Pogue " or even a Drury Lane autumn drama before them any day, and so say the majority of playgoers or I am very much mistaken.

The Britannia, the Great Theatre, Hoxton, had its audience of a very special kind. The company there was a stock one, its personnel changing very little from year to year, and each member of it was hailed by the audience as an old friend. They knew all about them, probably knew much about their personal troubles, and how they managed to scrape along on small salaries, and when the Annual Britannia Festival came along (generally on the Monday before Christmas week) they showed a practical sympathy that could only have been exhibited between friends.

At the risk of repeating a story that has, perhaps, become a little stale, I must give some idea of the Festival as I saw it myself more than once.

The " Old Brit." as every one knows, was presided over for a great many years by Mr. and Mrs. Lane (especially Mrs.) who were known throughout Hoxton and the regions roundabout as wielding the most powerful influence in the neighbourhood—an influence, moreover,

ever for good. It is said that Sara Lane could go alone where police-
men had to go in couples, and she certainly was, through a very,
long life, the good fairy of a particularly nasty, dirty, criminal
district.

About the 18th of December then, each year, the Festival
announced weeks beforehand, would open about 6.30 with a long
drama, followed perhaps by some acrobatic turns, or songs by individuals before front groove scenes while the preparations for the event of
the evening were being made behind. An interval ensued during
which the audience in all parts of the house consumed enormous
stacks of the hugest sandwiches I ever saw, and then the curtain
would go up on a sort of tableau where you saw Mrs. Lane generally
dressed as a " principal boy " (I believe she stuck to this attire for the
Festival till long after she had reached her sixth decade) enthroned in
the centre of the stage, and, grouped around, the members of the
company, each one in the costume of the rôle in which he or she had
succeeded during the past season.

The Queen of Hoxton would say a few words and then some
elder of the company would present to Her Majesty each member
of the troupe in turn, and for each one she had a few words and a
present. That is what my recollection tells me was the beginning
of the Festival. After this, the company would repeat in turn a
couple of lines, making at the same time his or her obeisance to the
audience who would respond with showers of presents of all kinds.
Not bouquets nor even chocolates for the ladies, not buttonholes
for the gentlemen—but joints of meat, petticoats, ties, stays, boots,
stockings, large parcels which might contain anything, umbrellas
and walking sticks, baskets of fruit or vegetables, babies' socks or
ladies' more intimate " undies," in short, whatever the giver might
imagine would be most acceptable. I have seen the time when the
audience in the stalls had to put up umbrellas to avoid the showers
of gifts that poured on to the stage from all parts of the theatre. I
have seen Miss Beatrice Toy—leading lady of the Brit melodramas—
surrounded by ever-increasing piles of parcels, and, alas, on more
than one occasion I have seen poor things say their few words, bow
to the audience and retire with—nothing ! It must have been a
bitter moment for them, but I may hope they got their little gifts
from the Queen all the same.

The Festival audience would certainly be considered a special
one. It filled the huge house (one of the largest in London) from
floor to roof and my goodness ! how all did eat ! I never could have
imagined the amount of food consumed that night if I had not seen
it with my own eyes. Only the household of Gargamelle could be its
parallel. To give some idea of this huge amount of food, I am

tempted to quote from an article by Mr. H. Chance Newton ("Carados" of the *Referee*). He knew the Brit by heart, so to say, and was an old friend of Mrs. Sara Lane herself. Thus he writes of what were mildly spoken of as "Refreshments" :

"The pittite and gallery folk, who, when fortunate enough to be in the front row stuck the long, greasy, blackened, halfpenny bill on the row of spikes put there for safety, would consume, coram populo, masses of thick, chubby ham or, rather, boiled bacon, in penny and twopenny sandwiches, tail and middle pieces of fried fish, or hot saveloys. These provisions were handed round by shouting attendants staggering under huge trays of this solid and savoury fare. These slices of fried fish, these filling sandwiches and saveloys were also consumed with gleeful appetite even by the patrons of those 'private' boxes. The supply and demand of liquid refreshment was wonderfully worked at this Hoxton theatrical gold-mine. Not only were copious draughts of beer pumped up lavishly by strong-armed barmen at the long, pewter-covered counters, with stacks of food thereon, but gills of what Papa Eccles in 'Caste' calls 'cool, refreshing gin' and other spirituous liquors were dispensed in abundance. Moreover, all around the extensive Brit auditorium went shirt-sleeved beer-bearers. Some of these bore the precious 'Pongelo' (local language for IT) in rows of pewter pots, and tin cans on combined shelves, a stand of which they carried in each hand. Some of these heavy wet-bearers were far more ingeniously provided for the purveying of porter, four-ale, &c. They wore around the waist a wide and deep zinc belt divided into porter and ale compartments. Each of these divisions was supplied with a tap from which the walking beer-bearer 'drew off' a pewterful to measure of whichever form of 'Pongelo' was preferred. Do not imagine, however, that only alcoholic liquors were served at the palace of the Queen of Hoxton. Even then, as still more nowadays, the 'temperance' playgoer was found among the east-end toilers and moilers, and the managements of such theatres as the Brit, the Pavilion, Whitechapel and the Surrey were compelled not only to stock non-alcoholic beverages, but provide special temperance bars.........so, in the breezy Bohemian Brit, the cry of the itinerant refreshment caterer all over the house was the judiciously blended 'Ginger-beer, Lemonade, Ale or Stout.'"

The prices at the Brit were suited to the lowest purse. The gallery was threepence, the pit sixpence, and there were some few stalls at a shilling each. The house probably held anything from four to five thousand people. There were some private boxes at a shilling a head. They were not very private, and sometimes over a dozen would squeeze into one box. I am unaware if by payment of a larger sum down, one could reserve the whole box for a party, but perhaps a guinea would have done it.

Such was the audience at the Brit, and at the Grecian it was very much the same, though they seem to have gone in for brandy rather largely at the old Eagle and for a drink called " Capillaire " which I have never tasted but which I seem to remember to have seen in bottles at old-fashioned public-houses. The Surrey, on the south side, was a replica in many ways of the Brit. It was (and is in its later form) an enormous house where in former days melodrama alternated with pantomime. There were also Gargantuan supplies of food and drink, but the prices of admission were, I fancy, a little higher than at the Brit, at any rate after the Conquests came there from the Grecian, for I know I have paid as much as 2s. 6d. for an orchestra stall !

Another special audience is that which attends regularly at the revivals of all the Gilbert and Sullivan Operas. This may be divided fairly into two parts—those who are more or less advanced in years and go to recall past delights and those who are too young to remember the original productions but have assiduously cultivated a furore for the whole lot as they are given to-day. The older part of this very specialized audience enjoy themselves amazingly, they are all *laudatores temporis acti* and, while appreciating the company of to-day, cannot help whispering to the moderns, " Ah, but if you had seen Grossmith, or Rosina Brandram or Mrs. Howard Paul ! " The younger portion of the audience are, as a whole, a very irritating lot. They bring books of the score with them, lie in wait for the various songs and concerted pieces which have always been applauded and hardly allow the singer to finish before they are loudly demanding an encore. The Sentry's song in " Iolanthe " has to be repeated over and over again. It is well known and the pit know they are quite safe in redemanding it ; but after the fifth or sixth encore, the shouting for which begins before the verse is well ended, one is justified in wishing the enthusiasm were shown a little less " according to plan." From the feminine part of these young enthusiasts of Gilbert and Sullivan (a slightly hysterical band) come a large group of " matinée idol worshippers " and the dressing-rooms of the better looking gentlemen of the company are, *on dit*, filled nightly with flowers and *billets doux*.

But the handsome singer or *jeune premier* on the stage has never wanted for excited or neurotic admirers among the other sex. It is related of Mario, the opera tenor, that when he was once singing the second verse of " La Chanson de l'Amoureux," in which occurs the following lines,

> Ah, viens aux bois, folle maîtresse
> Aux bois sombres et mystérieux,
> Ah, viens aux bois

a young lady rose from her seat in the audience and in a dreamy, ecstatic voice exclaimed " Je viens—je viens," showing the fascination Mario exercised over the fair sex.

One of the most annoying kinds of pittites is he or she (generally a lady) who will inform her neighbours all about the play and the actors and actresses and impart secret information with many mysterious nods and winks. Lyceum pittites in the Irving days were famous for this. In the Brocken scene in " Faust " one pittite was heard to say to her next door neighbour :

" You wait to the end and you will see. That's Martha's husband (indicating one of the witches). He'll turn up at the end so as she shan't have to marry the devil."

And in " The Corsican Brothers " :

" That's Irving—see ; he's eating with his knife to show he's a Corsican."

Sometimes the well-informed pittite will go into details as to the home life or private character of the actor. It has been recorded that during the run of " The Harbour Lights " at the Adelphi a good lady in the pit said confidentially to her neighbour when Terriss had taken a call :

" Yes, is he not splendid ? So good-looking, but such a sad life. Years ago fell in love with a young lady in the Louvre, who broke off the match because she said she was not worthy of him. He has never been married, and will never speak to a woman if he can help it. He never acts the day she died."

Sometimes the feelings of the pittites are quite carried away by the dialogue of the play. Once at Dublin in Louis XI, when it is announced " The King is dead," the feelings of a pious Catholic in the pit got the better of him and he was heard to murmur : " And may the Lord have mercy on his soul."

A theatre of the latter years of the nineteenth century which had a very special audience of its own was the Gaiety in the time of Hollingshead, the " Sacred Lamp of Burlesque," and the Pas de Quatre. The stalls were filled night after night by the same young men, many of them young officers of the Guards, and others, the would-be viveurs of the day. These were known by the nickname of " Crutch and Toothpick Brigade " and were generally looked upon as being not too well supplied with brains. But they were a faithful lot as regards the Gaiety company. Some had a passion for little Connie Gilchrist, some for Nelly Farren, some for Tilly Wadman and some for Kate Vaughan, while it is not to be denied that many went for members of the chorus, who profited thereby to get handsomely settled in life. In one burlesque, Kate Vaughan appeared in long black gloves, and her posse of admirers turned up at the theatre next night all with black gloves with which they loudly applauded their favourite.

Nelly Farren's devotees were principally found in the gallery. She called them her " boys," and when after a long absence from sickness she made her reappearance, the galleryites let down a huge placard on which was seen in large letters " The Boys welcome their Nelly." The entente between stage and auditorium at the Gaiety was perfect, as it had been previously at the old Strand Theatre in the early Swanborough days, at the Prince of Wales's when the Bancrofts took it over, and in the Irving reign at the Lyceum, the Alexander reign at the St. James's and the earlier portion of the Thorne and James management at the Vaudeville. Perhaps in most cases the personality of the actor-managers had a great deal to do with it. The performances at these theatres were so to speak *reglés* : the audience knew they were in for something good, though at one time perhaps better than at another. They never went with the intention half-formed of " guying " a piece, and were always more prepared to like than to dislike the entertainment prepared for them.

At other houses, occupied temporarily by one manager after another, there is no doubt that the audience were not so prepared to " be good." Those contretemps that have taken place at several *premières* might have been avoided if the entente between the Front and the Back had been more complete. The behaviour of a first-night audience is always an unknown quantity. The most experienced management can never be absolutely certain how a new play will go ; only I am sure that there is much more chance for it when the house (by which I mean principally the pit and gallery) is favourably disposed towards the Management for what it has done for them in the past.

The stalls of to-day are largely occupied with those who in their young days were, perforce, content with pit or even gallery seats ;

as a witty writer has recently said in a book of sketches on London—
"the curious strata of society vomited up from a volcanic war that
now fills the stalls in the theatres and the restaurants that used to call
themselves exclusive." In the pit of to-day sit the stallites of
pre-war times. The conversation heard before the rise of the
curtain and between the acts speaks for itself and "gives away the
show."

It is one of the penalties of those four years of suffering and trial
that courtesy is now at a discount, and that the mere possession of
much money and a knowledge of "smart" slang are better passports
to Society than the good manners which were once the pride and
boast of Englishmen and Englishwomen.

INDEXES.

I. Places and General Index.   II. Plays.   III. Persons.

I. PLACES AND GENERAL INDEX.

Note :—For names of Theatres see under sub-heading of " Theatres."

Adelaide Gallery 305
Alexandra Palace 297.
Albert Music Hall, Canning Town,
E. 304.
Albert Palace 297.
Amateur Actors 191, 324-5, 336-7,
339 to 345.
Anerley Gardens 290.
Aquarium (see Westminster
Aquarium).
Argyll Rooms 321.
Astley's Piccadilly Hall 55.
Audiences, theatrical 352 to 369.

Barnard's Tavern 315.
Barnum's Circus 183.
Bartholomew Fair 329 *et seq.*
Booths, various theatrical 329 *et seq.*
Brompton theatrical neighbourhood
103-4.
Burlesque 216, 218 to 223, 226 *et
seq.*, 232.

Cancan in England 159, 263-4.
" Canterbury Arms " and Music
Hall 262, 265, 277.
Carlisle House 198.
" Catamarans " Club 282.
Christy Minstrels 286.
Chinese Gallery (Hyde Park Corner)
314.
Church Cottage, Mrs. Bernard Beere
at, 245-6.
Clowns 26 *et seq.*, 61.
Coal-Cellar (Maiden Lane) 264.
Cosmotheca Hall 285.
Craven House 55, 78.
Cremorne Gardens 73.
Cremorne Supper Rooms (Leicester
Square) 73.
Curtis's " Halfpenny Hatch " 52.

Deutscher Theater from Berlin 261.
Dickens's Novels, dramas on, 96-7.

Dilettante Club 267.
Dramatic College Fetes 337.
Drop Scenes and Curtains 118-9.
Drury House 77,-8,-9.
" Duke's Tavern " (see Bower Saloon).

Eagle Tavern Saloon (City Road)
9, 10 *et seq.*, 18, 314. (See also
Grecian Theatre.)
Eagle Tea Gardens and Saloon
(Whitechapel) 47.
East-end Theatres 37 to 51.
Egyptian Hall, Piccadilly 31.
Entertainments by single performers
122.

Flying Fairies 33.
" Fops Alley " 352.
" Forrest Riots " in New York 130.
French players in London 161,
254, 359-60.

Gatti's, Villiers Street 262.
Ginnett's Circus 68, 318.
Grove House (Camberwell) 290.

Hamlet by women 129-30.
Harlequins 30 to 32.
Henglers' Circus 185.
Highbury Barn Gardens 73. (See
also Alexandra Theatre, High-
bury Barn.)
Holywell Street 237, 252-3.

" Independent Theatre " productions 260.

Kean's (Charles) Shakesperian productions 136 *et seq.*

Licensing Act 50-51.
Lyon's Inn 237.

371

" Matinée Idols " 362, 366.
Melodrama 12 et seq., 242-3.
Menken's Poetry 69-70.
" Mogul " Music Hall 300.
" Mulberries " (Club) 283.

Newcastle Street, Strand 63, 237.

Occidental Tavern 162, 196, 266.
" Old Clown " Tavern, Clerkenwell 318.
Olympic Saloon 9, 11, 78,-9. (See also Grecian Theatre.)
Opera Bouffe 193, 238, 242, 254, 262 to 277.
Opera in English, early performances of, 19, 123,-4,-5, 131, 165, 199, 217, 262, 293.
O.P. Riots 358-9.
Oxford Music Hall 228, 230, 264-5.

Panopticon of Science and Art 296.
Pantomime 23 et seq., 131, 285, 298.
Paragon Music Hall 47.
" Patent " Theatres 48 to 51.
Polygraphic Hall 305.

" Queen of Bohemis " Tavern 78.

Radnor Restaurant 73.
Ratcliff Highway 47.
" Rationals " (Club) 283.
Regent Music Hall 73.
Reinagle's Panorama 211.
Richardson's Show 38, 279, 326, 329 to 338.
" Ring " Dramas 57, 60-62.
" Rose and Crown " (Ratcliff) 47.

St. James's Hall 88, 265.
St. Martin's Hall 201.
St. Martin's Lane 90.
Shepherdess Tea Gardens 9.
South London Palace 20.
Southwark Fair 329 et seq.
Stadium (Holborn) 189.
Stall occupiers of to-day 368-9.
Stock Authors 157.
Stock Companies 5, 171, 224.
Strombolo House Tea-Gardens 322.

Theatres :—
Adelphi 1, 2, 16, 30-1, 87, 89, 97, 101, 102, 159, 160,-4,-7, 190, 205, 214, 220,-4, 274, 307, 355, 367.
Albert, Royal (see Garrick, White-Chapel).
Albert Saloon 26, 62, 326-7.
Albion (alias New Queen's) 320.
Alcazar (see Holborn Amphi-theatre).
Alexandra (Camden Town) 247, 291 to 294.
Alexandra (Highbury Barn) 73, 223, 279, 289 to 291, 307.
Alfred (see Marylebone).
Alhambra 58, 93-4, 186, 197, 228,-9, 244, 264,-7, 275,-6, 296.
Argyll (Regent Street) 321.
Argyll (see King's Cross).
Astley's 2, 3, 29, 37, 45, 49, 52 to 76, 97, 275, 314,-6,-7.
Avenue 233, 276.

Bijou (Haymarket) 324-5, 339, 344.
Borough (Tooley Street) 48.
Bower Saloon 21, 68, 151, 201, 274, 301, 314 to 317.
Bowery (New York) 66, 213.
Brighton 67.
Britannia (Hoxton) 2, 10, 14, 39, 96-7, 114, 145, 316, 363 to 366.
Broadway (New York) 215.

Campden House 339 to 343.
Catherine Street 91, 320.
Charing Cross (see Folly and Toole's).
Chatelet (Paris) 68.
China Hall (Rotherhithe) 327-8.
City Theatre (Cripplegate) 39-40, 135, 161, 292.
City of London 26, 37-8, 43, 91, 279.
Coburg 12, 14, 27, 37-8, 41, 59, 212. (See also Old Vic.)
Colosseum (Regents Park) 22, 274, 323.
Comedy 276.
Connaught (see Holborn Amphi-theatre).
Court 170-1, 215, 299.
Covent Garden 1, 23, 25, 30-1, 35, 58, 93, 124, 157, 197, 256, 274, 301, 357,-9.
Criterion 7, 99, 276.
Curtain (see Holborn)

Theatres—*contd.*
   Drury Lane 1, 24, 27, 33-4,-5, 57,
     60, 73, 80,-8,-9, 124, 145, 164,
     171, 189, 196, 205,-8, 256,
     267, 277, 280,-8,-9, 292, 359,-60.
   Dublin 357.
   Duke's (see Holborn Theatre).

   East London 13, 47,-8, 263.
   Edinburgh 228.
   Effingham Saloon 47. (See also
     East London Theatre.)
   Elephant and Castle 285.
   Empire 274.
   English Theatre in Paris 41.
   Exeter 173.

   Folly 3, 223, 231, 241,-8. (See also
     Toole's.)
   Franconi's Cirque (Paris) 25, 54,-8,
     63.

   Gaiety 17, 33,-4, 96, 187,-8, 204,
     219, 220,-6, 274,-6, 300, 355,
     368.
   Garrick (Whitechapel) 19, 38,-9,
     49, 225.
   Globe (Blackfriars Road) 321.
   Globe (Newcastle Street) 2, 3,
     16, 237 to 253, 276, 300, 309.
   Goodman's Fields 39, 48.
   Grand (Islington) 2, 162, 196, 265.
   Grand (Leeds) 171.
   Grecian 3, 9 to 36, 35, 39, 91,-2,
     7, 170,-1, 187, 362,-3, 366. (See
     also Eagle Tavern, City Road.)
   Greenock 15.

   Hanley 167.
   Haymarket 1, 2, 7, 16, 21,-7,
     49, 98, 128,-9, 169, 196, 203,
     215, 225, 235, 244, 280,-1, 286,-8,
     302, 360.
   Her Majesty's 73,-4, 99, 163, 257,
     270, 307,-8, 352,-3. (See also
     Opera House.)
   His Majesty's 7, 275,-6.
   Holborn Amphitheatre 3, 185 to
     189, 275, 339.
   Holborn Theatre (alias Duke's
     Curtain, Mirror, etc.), 162, 188,
     189 to 198, 216, 266.

   Imperial (or Aquarium) 3, 167,
     285, 297 to 305.

Theatres—*contd.*
   James Street Theatre 327.
   Jersey 207.

   Kent Theatre (Kensington) 320.
   King's Cross (alias Panharmonium,
     Regent, Cabinet, Argyll, etc.),
     317.

   Lincoln's Inn Fields 23,-4,-5.
   Liverpool 38.
   Lyceum 1, 7, 17, 21, 34, 59, 84,
     93,-6, 101, 124, 167, 190, 205,
     214,-6, 220,-2, 266,-7, 274, 292,
     319, 355,-6, 363, 367.
   Lyric 178.

   Manor-House, Chelsea 26, 93, 325.
   Marylebone 1, 2, 14, 35,-8, 51,
     73, 87,-9, 160, 191, 222,-8, 278
     to 289, 321.
   Metropole, Camberwell 257.
   Mirror (see Holborn Theatre).

   National (see Holborn Amphi-
     theatre).
   New Royal Sussex (seeMarylebone).
   New Westminster Royal 72, 239,
     292. (See also Astley's.)
   Nottingham 210.
   Novelty 250.

   Olympic 2, 3, 31,-9, 77 to 120,
     149, 167, 171, 190,-2,-4, 202,-9,
     216,-8, 224, 275, 284, 354.
   Opera Comique 2, 3, 223, 231,-2,-3,
     244, 253 to 261.
   Opera House (King's Theatre)
     2, 31, 352,-3. (See also Her
     Majesty's.)
   Orange Street Theatre (Chelsea)
     322.
   Oriental (Poplar) 84.

   Palace Theatre 265
   Palais Royal (Argyll Street) 185.
   Pantheon 20, 198,-9.
   Pavilion Theatre West (see Mary-
     lebone).
   Pavilion (Whitechapel) 2, 26, 38,
     47, 68, 114, 216, 279.
   Park (see Alexandra, Camden
     Town).
   Peckham Theatre 322-3.

Theatres—*contd.*
  Philharmonic 2, 196, 238, 262 to
    277.
  Portman (see Marylebone).
  Porte St. Martin (Paris) 71, 160.
  Portsmouth 354.
  Prince of Wales's 2, 7, 85, 168,
    192, 220,-4,-9, 293,-9, 308.
  Prince of Wales's (Birmingham)
    153.
  Prince's (Coventry Street) 303.
  Princess's 2, 3, 22,-6, 67, 84,-8,
    93, 100, 121 to 184, 190-1,-4,
    205, 225, 248, 264, 316, 357.
  Punch's Playhouse 216,-7. (See
    also Strand Theatre.)

  Queen's (Long Acre) 3, 16, 177,
    188, 201 to 211, 228, 311, 315.
  Queen's, New (see Albion).

  Raynor's New Subscription Theatre
    (see Strand).
  Rotunda (see Globe, Blackfriars
    Road).
  Royal Grove (see Astley's).
  Royalty (Soho) 2, 4, 26, 96,
    211,-6,-9, 221,-3,-5,-9, 254, 267,
    270, 310.
  Royalty (Wells Street, E.) 43
    to 46, 84, 161.

  Sadlers Wells 1, 2, 15, 27, 37, 49,
    51, 68, 88, 139, 150, 166,-7,
    179, 191, 209,-10, 224, 280,-1,-8,
    292,-3.
  St. James's 1, 2, 7, 88, 96, 101,
    192,-7, 203, 235, 243, 275,-6,
    307,-8, 343.
  Sanger's 75,-6. (See also Astley's.)
  Sans Pareil 39, 49, 80. (See also
    Adelphi.)
  Sans Souci (Leicester Place) 324.
  Savoy 256, 275.
  Scala 2.
  Shaftesbury 171,-8.
  Shakespeare (Shoreditch) 46-7.
  Standard (Shoreditch) 2, 37,-8,
    46, 114, 145, 203, 215, 224,
    275, 278, 293, 319.

Theatres—*contd.*
  Stangate (see Bower Saloon).
  Strand 2, 3, 32, 50, 93,-6,-9, 191,-2,
    207, 211 to 236, 256,-7, 274,-6,
    311.
  Stratford Borough Theatre 251.
  Surrey 1, 2, 13, 16, 20, 35,-7,-8.

  Tavistock House Theatre 102, 344.
  Terry's 8.
  Toole's (alias Folly or Charing
    Cross Theatre) 305 to 313.
  Tottenham Street Theatre 40, 81,
    213, 229. (See also Prince of
    Wales's Theatre.)
  Tothill Street Theatre 278, 296,
    319.
  Toyland Theatres 230, 346 to 351.

  Vaudeville 82, 167, 220,-4, 238,-9.
  Vic, Old 1, 2, 12, 13, 29, 97,-9,
    144, 197, 202, 218, 285, 298,
    326. (See also Coburg.)

  Wallack's (New York) 126.
  Westminster Theatre (see Tothill
    Street Theatre).

Theatres, new since 1867, 198.

Vauxhall Gardens 38, 59, 73.
" Via de Aldwych " 77.

Wellington Restaurant (late
  Crockford's) 73.
Westminster Aquarium 186, 291,
  295 to 297.
White Conduit House Tea-Gardens
  29.
Wilkie Collins's Novels, dramas
  on, 102-3.
Willoughby's Tea-Rooms 289.
Wonderland (Hall) 48.
" Wrekin " Tavern 243, 280,-2.
Wych Street 55, 77, 237.

" Yorkshire Stingo "(Lisson Grove)
  315.

INDEX II.—PLAYS.

Abbrev.—Burl., Burlesque ; Op., Opera ; Op. Com., Opera Comique ; Extrav., Extravaganza ; Trag., Tragedy ; Pant., Pantomime ; Bal.,Ballet.

Abu Hassan (op.) 19.
Acrobat (Belphegor) 114-5.
Adam Bede 188.
Adamless Eden 257.
Æsop's Fables 253.
Africaine (burl.) 224.
After Dark 98, 161, 182.
After darkness dawn 210.
Airey Annie (burl.) 232.
Aladdin (burl.) 125.
Aladdin (pant.) 299.
Alarcos (trag.) 74.
Alfred the Great (pant.) 26.
Alfred the Great 280.
Alice in Wonderland 261.
All for Her 194.
Alone in London 111-2, 183.
All the Comforts of Home 249.
Ambassadress (op.) 19.
American, The 260.
Amos Clarke 188, 203.
Amurath IV 45.
Amy Robsart 164.
Angel at Midnight 153.
Anne Blake 140.
Anne Mie 299.
Anna Bolena (op.) 125.
Antipodes, The 191.
Antony and Cleopatra 88, 160, 181.
Arcadia 12.
Ariane 232, 259.
Arrah na Pogue 107, 158, 182.
Artful Cards 311.
As in a Looking-Glass 245, 257.
As You Like It 45, 81, 191, 196, 206, 216, 255, 284, 299, 302.
Atalanta (burl.) 232.
Auntie 312.
Aurora Floyd 190.

Babette 231.
Babil and Bijou 157, 164, 301.
Barbiere de Siviglia (op.) 43.
Barnaby Rudge 159.
Battle of the Alma (ring play) 61.
Battle of Life 37.
Battle of Waterloo (ring play) 39, 60.
Beaux Stratagem 298.
Becket 111.
Beggars' Opera 21, 23, 81, 124, 217.
Behind the Curtain 197.
Bel Demonio 101, 149.
Belle Sauvage 159.
Belle's Stratagem 81.
Bells, The 126.
Belphegor (drama) 33, 114-5, 150, 163.

Belphegor (burl.) 217.
Ben my Chree 115, 180.
Betsy Baker 341
Billee Taylor (op. com.) 301.
Billy Taylor (pant.) 26, 131,-2.
Billy Button's Ride to Brentford (ring play) 53.
Black and White 102, 151.
Black Eyed Susan (drama) 41, 66, 141, 160, 197.
Black Eyed Susan (burl.) 223.
Black Eyed Susan (pant.) 217.
Black Rover 249.
Black Sheep 104.
Bleeding Nun 14.
Bluebeard (extrav.) 85, 240, 307.
Bluebeard (pant.) 141.
Bluebeard (ring play) 126.
Bluff King Hal (pant.) 181.
Bohemian, A 250.
Bohemian Girl (op.) 19.
Bohemians, The (op. com.) 254.
Bohemians of Paris (drama) 160.
Bootle's Baby 248.
Bottle Imp 17.
Boulangere a des ecus (op. com.) 242.
Bound to Succeed 21.
Box and Cox 319.
Branded 170.
Bride's Death Leap 14.
Bride's Tragedy 280.
Brigadier Gerard 304.
Brigands, Les (op. com.) 193.
Brighton 109.
Buckingham 107.

Called Back 303.
Camilla's Husband 98.
Camille 302.
Carina (op. com.) 259.
Carmen (op.) 267.
Caste 225.
Casting the Boomerang 231, 311.
Castle of Como (op.) 260.
Castle of Otranto (pant.) 25.
Cataract of the Ganges 57, 216.
Cattarina (op. com.) 306.
Cerise and Co. 234.
Charley's Aunt 248, 250.
Cherry and Fairstar (extrav.) 125.
Cheval de Bronze (op.) 229.
Chevalier de St. George 131.
Child of the Sun (drama) 66.
Child of the Wreck 214.
Chilperic (op. com.) 238, 263, 266.

Chinese Honeymoon 234.
Churchwarden 112.
Cinderella (op.) 188.
Clari 319 (see also Maid of Milan).
Claude Duval (op. com.) 110.
Claude Duval (ring play) 61.
Claudian 174-5, 180.
Clito 177-8.
Cloches de Corneville (op. com.) 241, 308-9.
Colleen Bawn 157, 356.
Colonel, The 168.
Comedy of Errors 81, 235.
Comical Courtship 328.
Coming of Age 305.
Conquest of Magdala (ring play) 75.
Contrast (extrav.) 75.
Coriolanus 111.
Corsican Brothers 136, 145,-8, 165.
Courier of Lyons 141.
Court Beauties of Charles II 85.
Couteaux d'Or 145.
Creole, The (drama) 190.
Cricket on the Hearth (burl.) 87.
Cricket on the Hearth (drama) 124, 284.
Crociato in Egitto (op.) 81.
Cromwell 203.
Crown Diamonds (op.) 19, 125.
Cupid's Ladder 308.
Cymbeline 203.
Cynic 242.
Cyril's Success 238.

Daisy Farm 105, 167
Damaged Goods 45.
Dame aux Camellias 145.
Dame Blanche (op.) 19.
David Copperfield 20, 109, 284.
Dead Secret 102.
Deaf as a Post 310.
Dean's Daughter 196.
Dearer than Life 202, 301.
Deep, deep Sea 85.
Derby Winner 182.
Der Freischutz (burl.) 224, 348.
Der Freischutz (op.) 19, 124, 217.
Der Freischutz (play) 17.
Devil and the Widow (bal.) 130.
Deal Boatman 190.
Diane de Lys 309.
Dick Whittington (extrav.) 116.
Diplomacy 244, 302.
Diplunacy (burl.) 229.
Dispute in China (pant.) 27.
Doctor in spite of himself (op. com.) 253.
Dog of Montargis 160.
Dolls House 303.

Dombey and Son 97, 284.
Don Cæsar de Bazan (drama) 125, 150.
Don Carlos (burl.) 224.
Don Juan (extrav.) 231.
Don Juan of Austria 151.
Don Pasquale (op.) 19, 123.
Dorothy Gray 179.
Double Marriage 201.
Douglas 88.
Dragons de Villars (op. com.) 309.
Drink 67, 167-8, 182.

East Lynne 89, 108, 111,-3, 191,-9.
Edendale 305.
Edmund Kean 193.
Edwin Drood 96, 293.
Eily O'Connor 40.
Eleanor's Victory 96.
Elfinella 168.
Elisire d'Amore (op.) 19.
Ernani (burl.) 290.

Fair Rosamond 75.
Falsacappa (op. com.) 238.
Far from the Madding Crowd 243,-5.
Fatal Wedding 183.
Faust (drama) 136, 141, 162, 214.
Fazio (trag.) 64, 79, 129, 233.
Festival of Hope (pant.) 45.
Fidelio (op.) 123.
Field of the Cloth of Gold (burl.) 227, 232.
Fille de Madame Angot (op. com.) 239, 254.
Fille de Regiment (op.) 119.
Fille du Tambour Major (op. com.) 193, 265,-6, 277.
First Printer 147.
Fleur de Lys (op. com.) 204.
Flowers of the Forest 123, 214.
Flying Scud 190.
Fool's Revenge 169, 179, 210.
Forced from Home 197.
Forget Me Not 110,-11.
Four Sons of Aymon (op.) 125.
Fowl Play (burl.) 206.
Fra Diavolo (op.) 19, 81, 123,-4.
Fra Diavolo (burl.) 222.
Frankenstein 160.
Fraud and its Victims 158.
Friendship 292.
Frivoli (op. com.) 267.
Frolique 231.
From Village to Court 141.
Frou-Frou 172.
Frozen Deep 102.

Gamblers 14.
Gamester 192.
Gay Lord Quex 252.
Gazza Ladra (op.) 19, 81.
Genevieve de Brabant (op. com.) 263,-7, 293.
Gentleman in Black (burl.) 306.
George Barnwell 14.
Geraldine 123.
Girls and Boys 312.
Giroflé-Girofla (op. com.) 254.
Giselle (bal.) 63, 123.
Glass of Fashion 247.
Gloriana 250.
Gold Craze 181.
Golden Dustman 167.
Golden Ladder 248.
Good Old Times 180.
Good Time, A (extrav.) 261.
Grand Duchess 226 (see also Opera Bouffe, various)
Great City 162.
Great Pink Pearl 111.
Green Bushes 15, 113, 123, 214, 244.
Gretchen 108.
Griselda 163.
Guinea Gold 166.
Gustavus (op.) 131.
Guy Mannering 46, 187.

Hamlet 114, 127, 146,-8, 151,-2, 169, 175,-7, 180.
Hands across the Sea 180.
Harlequin, The 304.
Harlequin Alfred the Great 26.
Harlequin Billy Taylor 26, 131-2.
Harlequin Dr. Faustus 24.
Harlequin Everywhere 327.
Harlequin Hudibras 73.
Harlequin's Invasion 25.
Harlequin King Jamie 131.
Harlequin Lord Dundreary 72.
Harlequin's Return 24.
Harlequin Sorcerer 23.
Harlequin and the Three Wishes 27.
Harlequin XXX 283.
Harvest 178.
Haunted Houses 163.
Hawthorne U.S.A. 304.
Heart of Gold 114.
Heartsease 165.
Heir at Law 191, 235.
Held by the Enemy 112.
Held in Bondage 293.
Henry Dunbar 103,-7.
Henry IV (Part I) 87.
Henry V 115, 208, 301.
Henry VIII 298.
Hidden Hand 100, 194.

Hit and Miss (op. com.) 110.
His Romance 112.
Home Truths 144.
Hoodman Blind 177, 182.
Horrors of War 12.
How London Lives 183.
Hugenot Captain 159.
Hunted Down 96, 101.
Hunchback 100, 206, 222, 230.
Hurly-Burly 311.

Idalia 90.
Idiot of the Mountains 80.
Idle Apprentice 231.
Imp of the Devil's Gorge 328.
Impudence 300.
In Chancery 112.
Ivanhoe (burl.) 194, 241.
Ivy Hall 99, 144.
Ixion (burl.) 106, 306.

Jack Sheppard (burl.) 17.
Jack Sheppard (drama) 17.
Jack Long of Texas 288.
Jane Eyre 247, 293.
Jane Shore 164, 171, 280.
Jealous Wife 81, 143, 280
Jealousy 108.
Jennie Deans 239.
Jezebel or the Dead Reckoning 197.
Jo 241, 300.
Joan of Arc (burl.) 224, 260.
John Gabriel Borkman 234.
Jonathan Bradford 4.
Juana 260.
Junius 177.

Katti the Family Help 231.
Kenilworth (burl.) 216, 221,-2.
King's Butterfly 149.
King of the Castle (pant.) 143.
King Charles II (op.) 131.
King of the Commons 131.
King's Fool 327.
King John 33, 113, 206, 280, 324.
King of the Kingdom (pant.) 131.
King Lear 40.
King's Rival 88, 307.
King Ugly Mug (pant.) 283.
Knights of the Fog 204.

Lady Barter 181.
Lady Audley's Secret 96, 242.
Lady Clancarty 106.
Lady Clare 247.

Lady of Lyons 90, 150, 166, 248, 255, 286.
Lady Slavey 234.
Lancashire Lass 163, 191, 202.
Lancers, The 141.
L'Assommoir 109, 192.
Lass O'Lowrie's 255.
Last Days of Pompeii 124, 204.
La Vivandiere (burl.) 202.
Led Astray 39, 300.
Liar, The 298.
Life 87.
Life in London 50 Years Ago 285.
Life we Live 182.
Lighthouse 97.
Lights o'London 100, 115, 172-3.
Linda Grey 182.
Little Amy Robsart (burl.) 265.
Little Dr. Faust (burl.) 109.
Little Red Riding Hood 300.
Little Tom Tug 254.
Loan of a Lover 349.
London Assurance 103, 160, 173.
London Pride 268.
Lord Harry 178.
Lord of the Manor 30, 300.
Lorna Doone 183.
Lost in London 163.
Louis XI 136, 141.
Love Chase 215.
Love Story 232.
Love in a Village 41, 187, 328.

Mabel 109.
Mabel's Curse 317.
Macbeth 64, 127, 144, 206, 256, 317, 324.
Madame Favart (op. com.) 230.
Madame L'Archiduc (op. com.) 258, 266.
Magic Mistletoe (pant.) 29.
Maid and the Magpie (burl.) 142, 220-1.
Maid of Milan (see also Clari) 43, 139.
Maid's Tragedy 188.
Ma Mie Rosette (op. com.) 250.
Man and Wife 102.
Man Cat, The 14.
Manfred 163.
Manfred (burl.) 212.
Mankind 242.
Manxman 171.
Marco Spada (play) 141.
Marguerite (operetta) 292.
Marie Antoinette 299.
Maria Martin 14, 317.
Marriage of Figaro 165.
Married and unmarried 141.
Martin Chuzzlewit 96, 124, 213, 225.

Mary Queen of Scots 84.
Mary Warner 104, 190, 196.
Masaniello (play) 213.
Masks and Faces 104.
Master and Man 181.
Master of Ravenswood 150, 284.
Mazeppa 62, 64 et seq., 75.
Medea (trag.) 89, 113.
Medea (burl.) 95.
Melusine (op. com.) 188.
Merchant of Venice 22, 40.
Merchant of Venice (burl.) 93, 161
Mermaidens Well 45.
Merry Wives of Windsor 81, 159.
Michael Strogoff 244.
Midsummer Night's Dream 20, 33, 203, 210, 249.
Mighty Dollar 300.
Mignon (op.) 257.
Miller and His Men (play) 12.
Miller and His Men (burl.) 125, 191, 222, 321.
Miller and His Men (pant.) 141.
Mirage 179.
Miss Elizabeth's Prisoner 304.
Miss Gwilt 103, 240.
Miss Multon (East Lynne) 197.
Monastery of St. Just 156.
Money 225, 241.
Monsieur Beaucaire 304.
Monte Christo (drama) 151, 355.
Mont St. Michel 140.
Moonstone 108.
Mormons, The 109.
Mother Goose (pant.) 27.
Mother in Law 251.
Moths 242.
Mountain Sylph (op.) 19.
Mousquetaires du Couvent (op. com.) 242.
Mr. Jekyll and Mr. Hyde 259.
Much Ado about Nothing 101, 106, 303.
Musette (op. com.) 257.
My Awful Dad 255.
Myra 319.
Mysteries of Audley Court 75.
Mystery of a Hansom Cab 179.
My Sweetheart 197, 231.

Nancy and Co. 231.
Naval Cadets (op. com.) 231, 242.
Never too Late to Mend 47, 75, 109, 159, 182, 357.
New Babylon 144.
New Magdalen 103, 106-7.
New Men and Old Acres 196.
Nicholas Nickleby 124, 191, 213, 235.
Night Dancers (op.) 125.

Night Off 231, 311.
Nitocris 88.
Niobe 233.
Noble Vagabond 178-9.
Norma (op.) 262.
No Thoroughfare 97, 102, 151.
Notre Dame 21.
Not Such a Fool as He Looks 238.
Nowadays 180.
Nozze di Figaro (op.) 81.
Number Twenty 166.

Oberon (op.) 124.
Octoroon 158.
Odds, The 195.
Œil Crevé (op. com.) 238, 254.
Old Curiosity Shop 105, 257.
Old Harry 312.
Old London 16, 204.
Oliver Twist 13, 96, 108, 116, 126, 232.
Olivette (op. com.) 230.
Olympic Devils 85.
Olympic Revels 85.
Omnibus, The 341.
On Change 312.
Only a Clod 96.
On the Jury 162.
Oonagh 163.
Opera-Bouffes, various 265 to 267.
Orange Tree and the Humble Bee (burl.) 224.
Oriana 239.
Otello (op.) 125.
Othello (trag.) 74, 88, 111, 130, 148, 153, 169.
Othello (burl.) 214.
Our American Cousin 90.
Our Boys 167, 225, 231.
Our Flat 125, 234, 259.
Ours 252.
Overland Route 159, 225.

Painter of Ghent 213.
Palace of Truth 303.
Panel Picture 259.
Paphian Bower (extrav.) 85.
Paris or Vive Lempriere (burl.) 221.
Passion Flower 111-2.
Paul Pry 309.
Paul Zegers 288.
Peal of Belles 343.
Pedlars Acre 14.
Peep o'Day 162.
People's Idol 114.
Perfect Love 105, 304.
Perichole, La (op. com.) 256, 267.
Petite Mariée (op. com.) 254.

Petit Faust (op. com.) 266.
Philomel 238.
Pickwick 213.
Pilgrim's Progress 116-7.
Pillars of Society 231.
Pilules de Diable (bal.) 25.
Pindee Singh 286.
Pirates de la Savane 68.
Pirates of the Flowery Land 14.
Pizarro 88, 136, 142, 317.
Plot and Passion 93-4, 109, 284.
Pointsman 112.
Poll and Partner Joe 109, 241.
Poor of New York 158.
Porter's Knot 96.
Postillon de Lonjumeau (op.) 19.
Prayer in the Storm 111.
Presumptive Evidence 161.
Pretty Druidess (burl.) 305.
Pride and Poverty 158.
Prima Donna 136, 140.
Princess, The 104.
Princess Toto (op. com.) 229, 257.
Private Secretary 247-8.
Promise of May 245,-6,-7.
Proof 181.
Puritani (op.) 125, 262.
Puss in Boots (extrav.) 85.
Put to the Test 105.

Queen's Favourite 110.

Rachel 110.
Raft, The 24.
Rake's Progress 292.
Rank and Riches 103.
Rapparree, The 162.
Ratto di Proserpina (op.) 81.
Red Rover (drama) 12, 160, 354.
Red Rover (burl.) 230.
Red Vial 97.
Rent Day 213.
Richard III 33, 40, 66, 111, 249, 317.
Richard Cœur de Lion 164.
Richardson's Show (plays) 329 *et seq.*
Richelieu 166, 169.
Rip van Winkle (drama) 164, 356.
Rip van Winkle (op. com.) 307.
Riquet with the Tuft (extrav.) 85.
Rivals 141, 202, 306.
Road to Ruin 167, 215, 224, 260.
Robert Macaire 149, 311.
Robinson Crusoe (pant.) 30.
Romany Rye 173.
Romeo and Juliet (trag.) 128-9, 154-5, 190-1, 293, 304.
Romeo and Juliet (burl.) 222.
Rose of Amiens 341.

Rough Diamond 299, 343.
Round the World in Eighty Days 363-4.
Royal Divorce 14, 181.
Run Wild 232.
Ruth Oakley 284.
Ruy Blas 146, 304.

Salammbo 197.
Salmagundi (pant.) 27.
Sardanapalus 141, 194.
Scapegoat 249.
Scarecrow 233.
Schamyl 141.
School for Coquettes 341.
School for Intrigue 106.
School for Reform 235.
School for Scandal 93,-6, 173, 192, 215, 225, 244.
Scornful Lady 281.
Secret (or Sliding Panel) 16.
Shadow of a Great City 179.
Shadow of the Sword 110.
Shakespeare v. Harlequin (pant.) 25.
Shakespeare's plays produced by Charles Kean Chapter VI passim.
Shaughran 101, 164, 247, 289.
Sheep in Wolf's Clothing 95.
She Stoops to Conquer 241,-9, 255, 298.
Siberia 179.
Sign of the Cross 176,-8.
Silent Witness 114.
Silver King 100, 115,-6, 173,-4,-7.
Siren (op.) 19.
Sixtus V 149.
Society Butterfly 261.
Sonnambula (op.) 19, 293.
Sorcerer (op. com.) 256.
Spectre Knight (op. com.) 256.
Spoiled Child 124.
Squire 243.
St. Cupid 141.
Star of India 183.
Still Alarm 181.
Still Waters run Deep 95, 109, 202, 244.
Stranger (drama) 115, 284.
Stranger, stranger than ever (burl.) 206.
Streets of London 98, 158.
Strike at Arlingford 260.
Struggle for Gold 111, 283.
Such a Good Man 109.
Sugar and Spice (pant.) 26.
Sultan of Mocha (op. com.) 231.
Susan Hopley 14.
Sweeney Todd 14.
Sweet Lavender 8, 21.
Sweet Nell of Old Drury 252.

Taken from Life 243.
Tale of Two Cities 97.
Taming of the Shrew 202.
Tantalus (burl.) 309.
Telemachus (extrav.) 85.
Tempest 189, 203.
Theodora (drama) 89, 116, 181.
Thespis (op. com.) 256.
Three Musketeers 251.
Ticket of Leave Man 12, 97,-8, 89, 107, 113, 168, 193,-4.
Ticklish Times 344.
Time's Triumph 306.
Timour the Tartar 123.
Tom and Jerry 57, 66.
Tomkins the Troubadour (burl.) 206.
Tosca (drama) 245.
To the Death 112.
Toyland Theatres, plays of 346 et seq.
Treasure 292.
Trial of Effie Deans 72.
Trial by Jury (op. com.) 109, 256, 267.
Trial of Love 140.
Trilby (burl.) 260.
True Blue or the Pressgang 327.
True Heart 180.
True to the Core 160,-3.
Turn of the Tide 203.
Turpin's Ride to York (ring play) 61.
Twelfth Night 101,-3, 134.
Twins 111.
Twixt Axe and Crown 164, 206.
Two Gentlemen of Verona 89.
Two Little Vagabonds 183.
Two Orphans 106,-8,-9, 113, 182.
Two Roses 225.

Uncle Dick's Darling 311.
Uncle Tom's Cabin 73.
Undine 104.
Undine, Spirit of the Waters 21.
Under the Earth ("Hard Times") 75.
Unequal Match 286, 301,-6.
Upper Crust 312.
Urgent Private Affairs 341.

Val d'Andorre (op.) 131.
Valentine and Orson (pant.) 266, 356.
Vampire 140, 158, 160.
Venice Preserved (trag.) 280.
Vert-Vert (op. com.) 193.
Vicar of Bray (op. com.) 246.
Vicar of Wakefield 215,-6.
Vice-Versa 231.
Vie Parisienne (op. com.) 193.
Vikings 303.
Village Coquettes 93.

Villainous Squire and the Village Rose (burl.) 310.
Virginius (trag.) 185, 203.
Voyage en Chine 34, 39.
Vulcan (burl.) 257.

Walker, London 312.
Wandering Heir 75, 160, 207.
Wandering Jew (Ring play) 60.
Watch Cry 150.
White Fawn (extrav.) 191.
White Horse of the Peppers 343,-4.
White Maiden of California 60.
Widow Hunt 253, 306.
William Tell (drama) 280.
Winter's Tale 33, 39, 280.
Witch, The 113.
Woman 308.
Woman in White 102,-5.

Woman of No Importance 245.
Wonder, The 328.
Wonderful Duck (op. com.) 254.
World 182

Yellow Dwarf (burl.) 89, 92, 94, 122.

Zaza 252.
Zillah 355.

NOTE.—Many names of plays of Shakespeare not separately indexed are included in the list of Shakespearian productions by Charles Kean —pages 140 to 143 ; and many opera-bouffes not separately indexed will be found in Chapter XII— pages 269 to 277.

INDEX III.—PERSONS.

Abbey, Henry 169.
A'Beckett, A. 324, 336, 357.
Abingdon, W. L. 179.
Abrahams, Morris 47, 263.
Achurch, Janet 113, 232.
Adams, Maude 42, 147.
Addison (the elder) 133, 190.
Addison, Carlotta 109, 239, 242, 298.
Addison, Fanny 201, 293.
Ænea, Mlle. 33.
Agujari (singer) 198.
Albani 265.
Albertazzi, Mme. 125.
Albery, James 239, 256.
Albu, Annette 257
Alexander, G. 102, 362
Alias, Mons. 263.
Amadi, Mme. 242.
Ancrum, Gladys 277.
Anderson, James 145, 205,-6, 224, 286,-8.
Anderson, Mary 156, 281.
Anderson, Professor 31,-3.
Anson, G. W. 106,-8.
Apjohn, Miss (see Mrs. Frank Matthews)
Archer, Frank 103,-6,-8, 170.
Archideckne, A. 145.
Arnold (of the Lyceum) 199.
Arnold, Matthew 174.
Asche, Oscar 260.
Ashley, Hon. Evelyn 341.
Ashton, Gertrude 292.
Ashwell, Lena 260.
Astley, Philip 52 et seq., 77,-8.

Astley, Mrs. 53-5.
Astley, " Young " 57.
Atherton, Alice (Mrs. Edouin) 231.
Atkins, E. 67, 252.
Aubrey, Kate 215.
Auriol, Mme. 131.
Aynesworth, Allan 112.
Azella 185.

Ball, Lewis 243.
Bancroft, Sir Squire 360.
Bancroft, Lady 31, 115, 150, 192, 216,-9, 220,-2,-9, 240,-4, 258, 308, 360.
Barclay, J. P. 68.
Bandmann, Herr, 167, 207, 259.
Bandmann, Mrs. 167, 188, 207, 259 (see also Palmer, Milly).
Barnes, J. 165, 179, 181, 356.
Barnes (pantaloon) 27.
Barrett, George 115, 171 et seq., 248.
Barrett, Wilson, 114, 164, 170, 171 to 180, 248, 252, 362.
Barrett-Lennard, Lady 343.
Barrington, Rutland 106, 112, 256.
Barry (clown) 29, 30.
Barry, Helen 108, 164,-5, 300,-1.
Barry, Shiel 241, 277, 309.
Barrymore, Lord 212.
Bartley, 133, 140.
Basing, Herbert 182.
Bateman, Isabel 155.
Bateman, Jessie 249.
Bateman, Kate 104, 190,-6, 260, 292.

Bateman, Mrs. 292.
Batty (of Astley's) 59.
Baylis, Lilian 12.
Beard, Mrs. T. 22.
Beatrice, Mlle. 115, 150.
Bedford, Paul 16, 122,-3,-5, 164, 223, 274, 286.
Beecham, Sir T. 277.
Beere, Mrs. Bernard 99, 108, 179, 193, 243 et seq., 258,-9.
Beersmann, Mme. 299.
Belford, W. 204.
Bell, Rose 228, 265.
Bellew, Kyrle 240,-2, 293,-8,-9, 300.
Belmore, G. 102,-4,-5, 151, 167, 190,-1.
Benedict, Sir Jules 270.
Bennett, Mrs. 233.
Benson, Sir Frank 5, 249.
Benson, Lady 249.
Bentley, Walter 292.
Beringer, Esme 130, 207.
Berlioz, Hector 42, 147.
Bernhardt, Sarah 245, 258.
Bigelow, Laleah 156.
Bigwood, J. 279.
Billington, J. 16, 102, 151,-7, 164.
Billington, Mrs. 195, 214.
Bilton, Sisters 34.
Bishop, Alfred 257.
Bishop, Kate 247.
Blackwood, Virginia 67, 258.
Blanchard (the elder) 41.
Blanchard, E. L. 12, 19, 33, 88, 93, 131, 148, 155, 259, 274, 282, 319, 325, 339.
Bland, W. 86, 221.
Blewitt, John 321.
Blondin 291.
Boleno, Harry 21, 29, 58.
Boleyn, R. S. 112.
Bologna (clown) 29, 31.
Bolton, G. 87.
Bond, Jessie 112, 250.
Booth, Edwin 169, 176.
Booth, General 23.
" Booth," proprietors, Various 329 et seq.
Booth, Sally 320,-1.
Boucicault, Dion 42, 72, 140, 156 et seq., 239, 247, 292.
Boucicault, Mrs. Dion 134, 156,-7,-8, 182, 247, 250.
Boucicault, Nina 233.
Bouverie, Frances 161.
Bouverie, Nellie 221.
Bowers, Mrs. 129.
Bowles, T. Gibson 336, 341,-2.
Bowman, Isa 249.
Boyle, Hon. Mary 341.

Boyne, Leonard 111, 180, 240, 259, 300.
Bracy, Henry 231, 242, 309.
Bradbury, Alfred 185.
Braham, John 45, 81, 187.
Brandram, Rosina 112, 256.
Brennan, Maggie 238.
Brereton, Stella 247, 293.
Bressant (Com. Fran.) 254.
Brian, Mr. and Mrs. 265.
Bromley, Nelly 107, 223.
Brooke, Gustavus V. 73, 88,-9, 117, 138.
Brough, Fanny 181, 197, 233,-4.
Brough, Lionel 139, 193, 200,-1,-3,-6, 249, 290,-8,-9, 307.
Brough, R. 257.
Brough, W. 97, 227.
Brougham, Sisters 162, 277.
Bruce, Edgar 302.
Bruce, Edith 116.
Brunswick, Duke of 133.
Buchanan, R. 260,-1.
Buckstone, J. B. 41, 222, 235, 319, 359.
Bufton, Eleanor 99, 100, 137, 142, 191, 224, 235, 310.
Bulmer, May 39.
Bunn, Alfred 280.
Burdini 123.
Burford 211.
Burleigh, Mr. 197.
Burnand, F. C. 288, 336.
Bury, Felix 263.
Butler 8, 86,-7.
Byrne, Mrs. 127, 340.
Byron, Henry J. 167, 218,-9, 231,-8, 244, 279, 310.

Calhaem, S. 109, 112.
Calhoun, Miss 302.
Calvert, Charles 194.
Calvert, Mrs. Charles 317.
Cameron, Agnes 73,-5.
Cameron, Violet 162, 231, 242, 277, 307,-9.
Campbell, Herbert 21, 34.
Campbell, Mrs. Patrick 304.
Carlisle 155, 161,-4, 292.
Carlo, Phœbe 248.
Carr, Comyns 243.
Carré Troupe 185.
Carson, Murray 116, 181.
Cartlich, J. 61,-2,-5, 337.
Carton, R. C. 247, 300.
Cathcart, J. F. 133, 140.
Caryll, Ivan 250.
Caulfield, Mr. and Mrs. 21.
Cave, J. A. 278, 285,-6,-7, 298.

Cavendish, Ada 98, 103,-5,-6, 117, 219, 225, 235, 240, 288.
Cecil, Arthur 240, 255.
Celeste, Mme. 15, 111, 123, 130, 161, 213,-5, 244, 286.
Celli 110, 242, 309.
Cellier, Alfred 208, 256.
Chambers, Emma 257, 260, 300.
Chapman, Ella 307.
Chapman, J. K. 39, 40.
Chapman, Mrs. (see Tree, Ann)
Chapman, Miss 142.
Charles, Tom 194.
Charrington, C. 113, 232.
Chart, Nye 167, 325.
Chatterton, F. 85, 162, 326.
Chatterley, Mrs. 80.
Chester, Elsie 260.
Chevalier, Albert 231,-2,-3.
Chippendale 212.
Chippendale, Mrs. 241.
Churchill, Lord 345.
Clarke, Mrs. Cowden 282.
Clarke, John 105, 165, 190, 217, 221,-2,-4, 238.
Clarke, John S. 193, 225, 231,-5, 306.
Claude, Angelina 220,-9.
Clay, Fred 239, 306.
Clay, Lilla 257.
Clayton, John 194,-6, 202,-3.
Clayton, Miss 292.
Clement, Miss 309.
Clifford, Fanny 292.
Clodoche Troupe, 263,-4.
Coffin, Hayden 275.
Coghlan, C. 102, 166, 181, 244, 266, 320.
Coghlan, Rose 294.
Colas, Stella 102, 147, 154, 206, 254.
Cole, Blanche 230.
Coleman, Fanny 259.
Coleman, George 282.
Coleman, John 110,-3, 208.
Collette, Charles 241,-9, 259.
Collins, Wilkie 345.
Colonna Troupe 263,-4.
Colthurst, Lady 341.
Compton 90, 125, 205, 215, 235,-9.
Compton, E. 260.
Compton, Miss (Mrs. Carton), 232-300.
Conquest, B. Oliver 39.
Conquest, G. 16, 19 et seq., 39, 98, 242.
Conquest, Mrs. and family 20.
Conway, Mrs. 129.
Cooke, Alice 114, 191.
Cooke, Aynsley, 267, 275.
Cooke, G. Frederick 328.
Cooke, T. P. 141, 160, 202, 328, 351.
Cooke, W. (of Astley's) 73, 191.

Cooper, Cliffe 114,-5, 248.
Cooper, F. 114, 117.
Cooper, Gladys 219.
Coote, Bert 164.
Copeland, W. 216.
Costa, Sir Michael 270.
Costmethopila 55.
Courtneidge, R. 113.
Coveney, Harriet, 12, 17, 21,-2, 110, 114, 193, 232,-9, 280, 300.
Coveney, Jane 12, 22, 96, 114.
Cowell, Lydia 300.
Cowper, J. C. 60.
Cox, Harry 220,-1,-9.
Craig, Gordon 303.
Craven, H. T. 222, 238.
Cresswell, Helen 299.
Creswick, 33, 114, 131, 160,-3, 203.
Cross, Julian 112.
Crouch, Harry 235.
Crouch, Louie 262.
Croueste (clown) 29.
Crummles, Vincent 36, 296, 319.
Cullen, Rose 309.
Cundy, Mr. 199.
Cushman, Charlotte 110, 127 et seq., 130, 207, 281.
Cushman, Susan 129.
Cushnie, Thérèse, 20, 32, 72.
Cuthbert, Miss (clown) 29, 217

Dacre, Arthur 109, 168, 182, 242, 257, 260.
Dainton, Marie 234.
Dairolles, Adrienne 260.
D'Algua, Mlle. 309.
Dallas, Mr. 86.
Daly's Co. 231, 311,-2.
D'Anka, Cornelie 239, 272,-5.
D'Antigny, Blanche 238.
Danvers, 34, 95, 223, 290, 306.
D'Arville, Camille 231, 259, 275.
D'Aubans, The 265.
Davenport, Fanny 309, 310.
Davenport, A. H. 103.
Davenport, T. D. 296, 319
David, Ferdinand 270.
Davidge, 38, 320.
Davidson, 87.
Davis (of Astley's) 53, 57 et seq.
Davis, Maria 233.
Day, Philip 168, 306, 310.
Debreux, Marguerite 239, 266.
Dejazet (Com. Fran.) 254.
Delaunay (Com. Fran.) 254.
Delavanti (clown) 30, 45.
Délibes, Leo 264 et seq.
Denny, W. H. 298.
Denvil, 320.

Désclée, Aimée (Com. Fran.) 254.
Deulin 20,-1, 32.
Dewar, F. 72, 101,-2, 223, 254
Dibdin, C. 212, 215, 324.
Dickens, Charles 69, 102, 148,-9, 150,-1, 201, 220, 267, 318, 345, 353.
Dietz, Linda 235.
Dillon, Charles 26, 68,-9, 93, 102, 124, 148,-9, 150, 217, 220, 250.
Dillon, Mrs. Charles 115.
Dixey, Henry 258.
Doche, Mme. 146.
Dolaro, Selina, 231, 242, 263,-4, 309.
Donato 33.
Doone, Neville 172.
D'Orsay, Laurence 250.
Dorus-Gras, Mme. 270.
Douglass, John 46, 278, 293, 320.
Dowton 80.
D'Oyley Carte 253.
Drew, John 311.
Drummond, Dolores 113, 136, 166, 179, 241, 300.
" Du Barry," Mme. 113.
Dubois, Camille 266.
Ducrow, Andrew 58 et seq., 351.
Ducrow, Peter 58-9.
Dulcken, Mme. 270.
Dunning, Alice (see Lingard, Alice)
Dyas, Ada 102, 117.
Dyas, Mrs. 202.

Eastlake, Miss 115, 172,-3,-7, 248.
Edgar, E. F. 283, 298, 300.
Edouin, Rose 115.
Edouin, Willie 29, 217, 231,-2,-4, 259, 260, 290, 307.
Edwards, Edward 326,-7.
Eldred, Jos. 277.
Ellar (harlequin) 31.
Ellinger, Desirée 277.
Elliston 41, 79, 80, 127, 199, 279.
Elsie, Lily 234.
Elsworthy, Miss 101, 145,-8,-9, 150.
Emden, Robert 97.
Emery, Sam 67, 95,-6, 101, 115, 149, 150, 160,-8, 190,-1, 215, 278,-9, 284.
Emery, Winifred (Mrs. Cyril Maude) 114,-5, 284.
Emney, Fred 116.
Ernstone, Helena 306.
Esmond, Henry 259.
Eversfield, Harry 232.
Eyre, Sophie 310.
Eytinge, Rose 108.

Fair, H. B. 188.
Falconer, Edmund 144,-6, 157, 162,-3.

Fairbrother, Sidney 183.
Farini 186.
Farnie, H. B. 228, 231, 308.
Farquhar, Gilbert 112, 232.
Farren, Nelly 17, 99, 100,-2,-3,-5,-7, 194, 220, 230, 255, 260, 274,-6, 307.
Farren, W. 80, 90,-1, 169, 241, 298,-9, 312, 359.
Faucit, Helen 13, 90, 155, 206, 281.
Faucit, Savile 13, 97.
Faucit, Mrs. W. 125.
Favart, Mme. (Com. Fran.) 254.
Fawkes (conjuror) 327.
Fawn, James 34, 285.
Fawsitt, Amy 225, 238.
Fearon, Mme. 123,-4, 212, 316.
Fechter, C. 97, 101,-2,-3, 115, 134,-5, 144 et seq., 160,-1, 176,-9, 254, 281,-4, 316, 355,-6, 362.
Fechter, Paul 115.
Felix, Rachel (see Rachel).
Felix, Raphael 34.
" Female Mazeppas " 66,-7.
Fenton, Charles 32, 223,-7.
Fernandez, James 66,-7, 151, 164, 179, 194, 244, 277, 283, 299, 316.
Ferrar, Ada 249.
Ferrer, Mons. 57.
Fiddes, Josephine 67, 190.
Fielding, Henry 329.
Filippi, Rosina 252, 312.
Filon, Auguste 219.
Finette, Mlle. 34, 264.
Fisher, David 104, 133, 157, 238,-9.
Fitzball 97.
Fitzhenry (see Soldene).
Fitzinnan, Miss 275.
Fitzwilliam, Mrs. 89, 215, 317.
Flexmore 20,-1, 26,-7,-9, 33, 131,-3,-4, 285, 325.
Flockton (of the Marionettes) 323.
Flockton, W. 255, 299, 306.
Florence, Mr. and Mrs. 300.
Foote, Lydia 99, 100,-2,-3, 191,-4, 238.
Foote, Miss (with Vestris) 84.
Footitt (clown) 30.
Forbes, Norman 215,-6, 249, 298.
Forbes-Robertson 107, 163, 170, 245, 299, 356.
Formes, Herr 161.
Forrest, Edwin 127,-9, 130, 280.
Forrester, Henry 88, 160, 212, 244, 292.
Forrester, Maude 66.
Fortescue, Miss 118, 252, 260.
Fowler, Emily 106,-7,-8, 117, 208, 223, 306.

Fredericks 82.
Freear, Louie 234.
Fulton, C. 260.
Furtado, Miss 104, 162, 274.
Fuzzi, Mme. 57.

Gainsborough, Miss 194.
Gammon, Barclay 122.
Garcia, Eugenia 121,-3,-5.
Garrick, David 24,-5, 48.
Garrick, Mrs. 215.
Gellert, Theodore de 267.
Georgi (singer) 198,-9.
Geraldine, Grace 249.
Gerard, Miss 149, 169, 244.
Gerrish, Miss 264.
Giddens, George 233.
Gilbert, Mr. and Mrs. 231.
Gilbert, W. S. 34, 108, 202.
Gilbert, Mrs. 311.
Gilchrist, Connie 300, 368.
Gillette 178.
Ginnett 68.
Giovanelli, Edward 279, 290.
Girards, The 264.
Gladstone, W. E. 245.
Glindon, Robert 22.
Glossop 27, 144, 212, 316.
Glover, Mrs. 215.
Glyn, Miss 73, 88, 160.
Godfrey, Dan 342.
Gomersal 60,-1,-2.
Gooch, Walter 168,-9, 170,-2.
Gordon, Walter 96.
Got (Com. Fran.) 254.
Goward, Miss 62 (see Mrs. Keeley).
Goward, Miss Annie 233.
Gowing, Miss Aylmer 324.
Grahame, Cissy 109, 299.
Grain, Corney 122.
Granby, Marquis of 322.
Granier, Jeanne 275.
Grattan, H. P. 293.
Grattan, Mrs. H. P. 43, 125.
Green (aeronaut) 327.
Greet, Ben 5.
Gregory, Willie 243, 267.
Grey, Marie de 110.
Grey, Lennox 21, 266.
Griffiths, Mrs. (of Astley's) 53.
Grigolati Troupe 33, 35.
Grimaldi 25 et seq., 32,-3, 283.
Grisi, Carlotta 64.
Grisi, G. 144, 266, 270, 342.
Grossmith (the elder) 122.
Grossmith, George 250,-6.
Grundy, Sydney 245.
Gunniss, Tessy 20, 32,-3, 265.
Gwynne, Fanny 158.

Hall, Harry 213,-5.
Hall, Mrs. S. C. 342.
Hamilton, Harry 178, 247,-8.
Hamlet (jeweller) 121,-5.
Hanbury, Lily 114,-5.
Hanlon-Lees, 34.
Hanlon-Voltas 185, 265.
Hanway, Jonas 146.
Harcourt, Charles 107, 279, 288, 320.
Hardy, Thomas 243,-5.
Hare, John 107,-9, 245, 252,-5.
Harland, Julia 126.
Harley 57, 133, 140 et seq.
Harris, Augustus (the elder) 122, 144
   et seq., 316.
Harris, Sir Augustus 172.
Harrison, Clifford 131, 208.
Harrison, Frederick 113.
Harrison (tenor) 131.
Harrold (of " the Wrekin ") 282.
Harvey, Frank 108.
Hastings, Gilbert (see Macdermott,
   G.).
Hatton, Bessie 249.
Hawthorne, Grace 116, 179, 180,-1.
Hawtrey, Charles 178, 247,-8.
Hazlewood 97.
Head, Charles 262.
Heath, Caroline 100, 108, 136,-7,
   140 et seq., 164,-6, 171,-9.
Heenan, J. C. 64,-5, 74.
Helmore, Arthur 247
Henderson, Alex 230., 307,-8.
Henderson, John 62.
Henderson, Marie 75, 102, 193.
Hengler, Charles 185.
Henrade, Miss 233, 279, 287.
Herbert, Miss 96, 101, 194,-7, 203.
Herbert, Willie 102, 233, 249, 255,
   356.
Herring, Paul 62, 326.
Hersee, Rose 165, 230, 267.
Hervé, Florimond 241, 266,-8.
Hibbert, Henry 9.
Hicks, Seymour 180.
Hildyard, Wattie (clown) 29, 30.
Hill, Caroline 112, 166, 170, 188,
   194,-5,-6.
Hill, W. J. 108, 255, 309.
Hingston, E. P. 223.
Hinton, A. and J. 290.
Hodson, G. 301, 315.
Hodson, Henrietta 16, 151, 188, 201,
   Chap. IX passim, 228, 287, 301,
   315.
Hodson, Kate 301, 315.
Hodson, Sylvia 299.
Hogarth, G. 267.
Hollingshead, John 13, 109, 188,
   219, 257.

Holloway (clown) 30, 62.
Holme, Myra 300, 312.
Holt, Clarence 194,-6,-7, 279.
Holt, Elise 227.
Honey, George 123, 159, 225.
Honner, Mr. and Mrs. 37.
Hood, Marion 17, 110.
Hook, Theodore 282.
Horton, Priscilla 153
　(see also Reed, Mrs. German).
Howard, Kate 87.
Howe, J. B. 37, 316.
Howell, H. 22.
Howell (harlequin) 27.
Howson, John 277.
Hughes, Annie 250.
Hughes, Fanny 224,-7.
Huline (clown) 72.
Huntley, Grace 232.
Huntley, Mrs. 106,-9, 113, 170,-9,
　181.

Illington, Marie 233.
Irish, R. W. 244.
Irving, Ethel 219.
Irving, Henry 96,-7,-9, 111, 119,
　134,-5,-8, 144, 152, 169, 190,-5,
　202,-8,-9, 216,-9, 225,-8, 235, 287,
　292, 311, 367.
Irving, Mrs. Joseph 105.
Irwin, Kathleen 306.
Ivanowa, Claire 233.
Ivor, Frances, 260.
Isaacs, Rebecca 222, 290.

James, David 17, 189, 220,-4,-5,-7.
Jecks, Clara 99.
Jefferini (clown) 318.
Jeffries, Maud 114.
Jefferson, Jos. 90, 104,-5.
Jerrold, Douglas 128, 137,-8.
Joachim 271.
Johnson (of Richardson's Show) 37.
Johnson, J. T. 2.
Jones, Avonia 89.
Jonghmanns, Herr 265.
Jordan, George 101, 149.
Josephs, Fanny 107,-9, 166, 190,-1,
　-2, 239.
Joy, Algernon 343,-4.
Joyce, Walter 86, 160, 193.
Jullien 283.

Kean, Charles 128,-9, 130, 133
　et seq., 209, 298.
Kean, Mrs. Charles 40,-3, 129,
　133 et seq., 281.

Kean, Edmund 40, 92, 145, 281,
　317,-9, 330, 354.
Keeley, Louise 144.
Keeley, Mary 31, 136, 140.
Keeley, Mrs. 16, 67, 86, 96, 123 et seq.,
　133,-4, 205, 213,-4,-5,-6.
Keeley, Robert 17, 96, 123 et seq.,
　133,-4, 205, 213,-4,-6.
Keegan, Mary 232.
Keene, Doris 152, 171.
Keene, Laura 90.
Keith, Benjamin 183,-4.
Kelly, Fanny 46, 124, 211, 281.
Kemble, Charles 282, 359.
Kemble, Fanny 128, 192.
Kemble, John 145, 358,-9.
Kemble, Stephen 41.
Kendal, W. 109, 240,-3.
Kendal, Mrs. 5, 109, 111, 158, 162,
　171, 196, 240,-3,-7, 255, 279,
　283,-4, 292, 302,-5, 316.
Kennion, Mrs. 231.
Kerr, Orpheus C. 65.
King, Admiral 349..
Kingsale, Lord 341.
Kingston, Gertrude 113.
Kiralfys, The 33, 264,-5.

Lablache 270, 297.
Lablache, Mme. 122.
Labouchere, Henry 201, 228, 299,
　300, 315.
Lacey, H. R. 286.
Lacy, Walter 87, 96, 100, 129, 136,
　140 et seq., 161, 210, 270, 342,
　366,-7.
Lacy, Mrs. Walter 37, 87.
Lafontaine, Annie 306.
Lago, Signor 116, 274.
Lamb, Beatrice 229, 331-4.
Lamb, Charles 46.
Landor, Mrs. ("The Infant Pheno-
　menon") 319, 320.
Lane (conjuror) 323.
Lane, Sara 363.
Langtry, Mrs. 181,-2, 260, 297,-9,
　301,-2,-4.
Larkin, Sophie 203, 235,-9.
Lauri, Charles 116.
Lauri Family 29.
Lawler, Kate, 232.
Lawler, Uniacke 344.
Lawrence, Eweretta 312.
Leamar Sisters 34.
Leathes, Edmund 169.
Leclercq, Carlotta 21,-6, 97, 101,-2,-9,
　115, 134,-7, 140 et seq., 144 et seq.,
　151, 181, 232, 247,-9, 250.
Leclercq Family 20,-1,-9, 37, 131.

Leclercq, Mme. 27.
Leclercq, Pierre 232.
Leclercq, Rose 21, 72, 144,-8, 151, 161,-2, 194, 255.
Lee, Alexander 212.
Lee, Jennie 241, 266, 300.
Lee, Nelson 25, 38, 278,-9, 285, 326, 337,-8.
Lee, Rose 188.
Le Hay, John 249.
Leigh, Mrs. Henry 248.
Leighton, Miss 206,-8.
Lely, Durward 259.
Lemaitre, Frederic 146,-9.
Lemon, Mark 305.
Leno, Dan 34, 258, 285.
Leopold Family 290.
Leslie, Fannie 168, 180,-1.
Leslie, Fred 17, 307.
Le Thiere, Miss 162.
Lever, Sir Ashton 321.
Levey, Florence 231.
Lewes, G. R. 95.
Lewes, Henry 151,-5.
Lewes, Marie 113.
Lewis, Leopold 287.
Lewis, Monk 282.
Linden, Laura 187, 259, 300.
Linden, Marie 232,-3, 265.
Lindo, Frank 280.
Lingard, Alice 20, 103, 247, 302,-3.
Liston 86, 215.
Liston, Mrs. 105.
Litton, Marie 118, 167, 206, 242, 255, 286, 298,-9, 311.
Lloyd, Arthur 265.
Loraine, Henry 88, 160.
Loredan, H. 242, 257, 277.
Loseby, Constance 188, 239, 241, 267.
Lotta 257,-8.
Ludwig, W. 188, 249.
" Lulu " 186.
Lupino Family 29, 32.
Lynd, Edith 306.

Maccabe, Fred 122.
Macdermott, G. H. 20,-1, 96,-7.
Mackinnon, Capt. 341.
Maclagan, Tom 266.
Macready (the elder) 41,-5.
Macready 82,-8, 93, 115, 130,-1,-2, -3,-4, 176, 205,-6,-9, 280, 359.
Maddox 126, 131,-3.
Magloire (clown) 25.
Maitland, Mrs. 274.
Maitland, Lauderdale 193.
Maitland, Lydia 223,-4.
Maitland, W. L. 191,-3, 329, 341.
Majiltons, The 33, 264

Manning, Ambrose 114.
Mansell Brothers 187, 192,-3, 238, 241, 258, 266, 274,-6, 324, 341.
Mansfield, Richard 248,-9.
Marbury, Miss 258.
Marchant, F. 14, 46.
Mario (singer) 104, 270, 342, 366,·7.
Mario Sisters 34.
Marius 229, 230,-1, 259, 264,-6.
Markatchy, Signor 55.
Markby, R. 173, 255.
Markham, Pauline 202, 308.
Marlborough, Miss 203.
Marriott, Miss 129, 153, 288.
Marshall, Frank 107, 336, 343.
Marshall, G. 263.
Marston, Henry 156, 193, 203, 288.
Marston, Mrs. Henry 89, 150,-6, 301, 315.
Maskell, Miss 95.
Maskelyne and Cooke 305.
Mathews, Charles 73, 83, 86, 103, 130, 161, 192,-6, 214, 222, 235,-9, 255, 282, 324, 359.
Mathews, Mrs. Charles (2nd) 103,-4, 161, 235, 324 (for first wife, see Vestris).
Matthews, Frank 80, 96, 151, 203, 214, 275.
Matthews, Mrs. Frank 41, 96, 203, 214.
Matthews, Julia 226, 265, 272,-4, -5,-7.
Matthews, Tom (clown) 27,-8, 87, 283, 318.
Matthison, Arthur 194, 309.
Mattei, Tito 267.
May, Alice 242.
McCord, Mr. and Mrs. 63.
McIntyre, W. 109, 162,-4, 215, 293, 356.
McLeay, Franklin 114.
Mead, T. 88, 208, 356.
Meadows, Drinkwater 133, 140, 279.
Melfort, Mrs. 95.
Melville Bros. 363.
Melville, G. 286.
Meller, Rose 113,-4.
Mellish, Fuller 116.
Mellon, Mrs. Alfred 96,-7, 102,-4, 114, 151,-7, 164, 190, 214, 274.
Mendelssohn 271.
Menken, Adah Isaacs 62 et seq 77, 229, 316, 337.
Merivale, Herman 242.
Mervin, Fred 193, 231.
Merritt, Paul 15, 97, 194, 241,-2.
Milano, 20, 32, 67.
Milano, Mme. (see Cushnie)
Milner, H. H. 62, 97.

Milner-Gibson, Mrs. 341.
Milton, Maud 112, 166, 170.
Miller, Emily 300.
Millward, Dawson 252.
Millward, Jessie 260.
Miolhan-Carvalho 361.
Modjeska 147, 170,-2, 302.
Moffatt, T. 62.
Monckton, Lady 259.
Montagu (of Ginnett's) 318.
Montagu, Harry 102, 161, 224, 239, 240, 362.
Montgomery, Walter 153,-5, 168, 286, 316.
Moodie, Louise, 109, 116, 260.
Moore, Albert 201.
Moore, Eva, 233, 260.
Moore, George 260.
Moore, Louisa 100, 194, 357.
Moore, Mary (see Wyndham, Lady).
Moore, Nelly 101, 203.
Moore, Peter 45.
Morgan, Wilford 309.
Moritz, Mr. 45.
Morley, Henry 88,-9, 93.
Morris, Clara 42.
Mortimer, C. 62.
Mortimer, James 250, 309.
Morton, J. 262,-3, 282,-6.
Moss, Adele 310.
Moss, Hilda 310.
Mowatt, Cora 89.
Muir, Emily 266, 275.
Munden, 282.
Munyard 320.
Munroe, Kate 188, 257, 268, 275,-7.
Murdoch, James 64.
Murray, Ada 67, 163, 197, 293.
Murray, Miss (Mrs. Brandram) 134.
Murray, Alma 191, 248.
Murray, Dominick 102, 159, 161.
Murray, Mrs. Gaston 215.
Murray, Leigh 87, 90, 215.
Murray, Mrs. Leigh 96, 102, 191, 215,-9, 222, 255.
Musgrave, Mrs. 234.

Nash, " Jolly John " 265.
Nation, W. H. C. 96.
Neilson, Adelaide 102, 155,-7, 206, 311.
Neilson, Julia 252.
Nelson, John 156, 204, 307.
Nesville, Juliette 250.
Nethersole, Olga 196.
Neville, G. 102, 149, 190.
Neville, Henry 16, 97 et seq., 101, 113, 117, 151, 170, 180,-1,-2, 194, 238, 241, 251,-9, 260, 320, 362.

Neville, John 16.
Newland, Abraham 289.
Newton, Adelaide 225.
Newton, Chance 209, 365.
Newton, Miss (amateur) 341.
Nicholls, Harry 21, 180, 268.
Nicholson, " Baron " 212.
Norreys, Rose 112, 180.
Northcott, Richard 268, 273.
Norton, Fleming 300.
Nott, Cicely 283, 306.
Novello, Clara 282.
Novello, Vincent 282.

Odell, E. J. 17, 189, 190, 266, 275,-7, 286, 293.
Offenbach, Chapter XII passim.
O'Grady, Hon. Reg. 341.
Olive, Miss 206.
Oliver, Patty 159, 216, 220,-2,-3, 254,-5.
O'Neill, Miss 129.
O'Reilly, Mr. 199.
Orger, Mrs. 215.
Ormesby, Emmeline 173.
Osbaldistone 215.
Outram, Leonard 260.
Oxberry 43, 80, 122,-5, 351.
Oxenford, John 60, 92, 148, 156.

Palmer, John 45.
Palmer, Milly 103, 129, 155 (see also Bandmann, Mrs.).
Palmer, Minnie 197, 231, 257.
Parisian Grotesque Dancers 159.
Parkes, Caroline 20, 32.
Parry, John 96, 122.
Pateman, Bella 107, 181.
Pateman, Robert 81, 107,-8, 181.
Paton, Miss 124.
Patti 265.
Paul, Mrs. Howard 217, 256, 272,-5.
Paulo 26.
Paulton, Harry 228,-9, 234, 242, 257, 275, 309.
Paulus 275
Pede, Thorpe 291.
Pelham-Clinton, Lord Arthur 191.
Penley, W. S. 229, 233, 246,-8, 250.
Pennington, W. 288.
Pereira, Mlle. 185.
Perry, Capt. 341.
Persiani 271.
Pertoldi 267.
Petersham, Lady Caroline 322.
Phelps, Samuel 15, 74, 85, 88, 96, 134,-8, 144, 162,-3, 171, 191, 203,-5,-8,-9, 210, 256, 286,-8, 292,-8,-9.

Phillips, F. C. 258.
Phillips, Kate 208, 306.
Phillips, Miss 205.
Phillips, Phil 314.
Phillips, Stephen 249.
Phillips, Watts 98, 159, 203.
Pigeon, Mr. 314.
Pinero, W. S. 243.
Piozzi 199.
Pitt, Emily 115.
Pitteri, Mlle. 34.
Planché 85 et seq., 97, 214.
Polini, Marie 114.
Poole, Miss 100, 137, 142.
Pope, Mrs. 61.
Porter, R. E., Major 341.
Potter, Mrs. Brown 299.
Pounds, Courtice 276.
Powell, H. 62.
Powell, Mr. 267.
Power, George 110, 256.
Power, Nelly 224.
Pritchard, Mrs. 330.
Pyne, Louisa 131.

Quartermaine, Leon 98, 152, 170.
Queensberry, Marquis of 245.

Rabut, Mlle. 151.
Rachel, 42, 74, 141,-7, 151.
Raleigh, Cecil 97, 112.
Randall, Harry 265.
Ranoe, Rosina 223, 284.
Raymond, Mrs. 22, 191, 235.
Rayne, Lin 193, 256, 293.
Rayner, B. L. 211.
Raynham, Miss 99, 221,-4, 308.
Raynor, Mr. 45.
Reade, Charles 68, 88, 159, 197,
  201,-7, 307, 357.
Rede, Leman 292.
Reed, Mrs. German 305.
Reeve, Mr. 96.
Reeve, Wybert 306.
Reeves, Sims 21, 205, 265.
Rehan, Ada 202, 231, 299, 211,-2.
Reichemberg, Mlle. (Com. Fran.) 254.
Reinagle, R. A. 131, 211.
Reinhardt, Mattie 104.
Réjane 252.
Reynolds (stock author) 97.
Reynolds, G. 282.
Reynolds, Miss 215.
Rich, 23-4.
Richards, Cicely 179.
Richards, Harry 265.
Richardson (of " The Show ") 279,
  329, and Chap. XVI passim.

Righton, Edward 99, 106,-9, 139,
  241, 300.
Rigby, Vernon 290.
Rignold, G. 60, 188, 203.
Rignold, W. 161,-2,-5,-6.
Ristori, 95, 254.
Ritchie, James 9.
Rivers, Frederic 300.
Riviere 208, 274.
Roberts, Arthur 260, 277.
Roberts, Walter 62.
Robertson, Tom 216.
Robins, Elizabeth 260.
Robson, E. F. 21, 90 et seq., 97, 117,-8.
Rodgers, Katharine 159, 162, 195.
Rodney, Frank 102, 113, 232.
Roe, Bassett 112,-6, 179.
Rogers, James 221,-5.
Romer, Miss 131.
Rose, Annie 257.
Roselle, Amy 100, 111, 168, 178,
  182, 260.
Roselle, Percy 168, 292.
Ross, G. H. 264.
Ross, Herbert 249.
Rorke, Kate 249.
Rorke, Mary 180, 249.
Rousby, W. 163, 207.
Rousby, Mrs. 163, 207.
Rouse, J. 12, 17 et seq.
Rowella (clown) 29.
Royce, E. W. 109, 255, 277.
Ryder, John 100, 115, 129, 133,-7,
  140 et seq., 144,-9, 151,-4, 167, 194,
  203 et seq., 241, 254,-5, 286,-8,
  292,-8.

St. Claire, Mme. 129, 293.
St. George, Julia 89.
St. John, Florence 230, 268, 272,-5,-6.
St. Quentin, Lizzie 242.
Saker, Rose 233.
Sala, Charles (see Wynne).
Sala, Mme. 122.
Salvini 208.
Sandy, Little (clown) 30.
Sanger, Rachel 160, 229, 241, 290,
  307.
Sangers 75-6.
Santley, Charles 165.
Santley, Kate 67, 228,-9, 265, 275,
  306.
Sayers, Tom 74.
Schneider 254, 271 et seq.
Schroeder-Devrient, Mme. 123.
Scott, Clement 70,-1, 98, 130, 154,-5,
  279, 324.
Scott-Siddons, Mrs. 196.
Scovel, Chevalier 277.

Searle, Mr. 108.
Sebright, Sir John 191.
Sedgwick, Amy 149, 286.
Selby, Mrs. 88, 216, 222.
Selwyn, Beatrice 250.
Selwyn, George 322.
Senyah, Mme. 185
Serle, T. 281.
Seymour, Katie 260.
Seymour, Mrs. 88.
Shepherd, W. 33, 97, 224.
Sheridan, Amy 66, 220,-7, 274.
Sheridan, Tom 282.
Sherson, Lady Anne 336, 341,-3,-4.
Sherson, Capt. 341.
Shine, J. L. 182, 234, 247, 260.
Shore, J. G. 161.-3.
Siddons, Sarah 15, 135, 145, 281
Sidney, H. C. 203.
Silva, Mme. 309.
Simpson, Palgrave 148, 324, 344, 356.
Sinnett, Charles 289.
Sketchley, Arthur 345.
Smith, Albert 122,-5, 305.
Smith, C. J. 356.
Smith, E. T. 34, 60,-2,-6,-8, 73 et seq.,
  279, 283, 290,-1,-6.
Smith, O. 16,-7, 114, 167.
Smithson, Harriet 41 et seq., 197.
Snazelle, G. 259.
Soldene 28, 230, 255, 263 et seq.,
  293, and Chapt. XII passim.
Solla, Henry de 116.
Solomon, Ed. 110, 246.
Somerset, C. W. 232.
Sothern, Edward 203.
Sothern, Eva 179.
Sothern, Lytton 307.
Sothern, Sam 260.
Spagnoletti 199.
Speakman, Walter 172.
Standing, Herbert 111, 182, 202,
  260, 275.
Stanley, Alma 232,-3,-4, 260.
Stanley, Emma 122,-3, 305.
Stansfield, Clarkson 121, 314.
Stead, W. (The Perfect Cure) 265.
Steinberg, Amy 215, 293.
Stephens, Mrs. 99, 107, 172, 238.
Stephens, Miss 174, 199.
Stephens, Yorke 112, 180.
Stephens, W. H. 202.
Stevens, Victor 116.
Stirling, Arthur 99.
Stirling, Mrs. 41, 87, 90,-3,-5,-
  7, 104,-7, 130, 159, 205, 213,-5,-6,-9,
  222, 278, 286, 298, 306.
Stoepel 12.
Storey, Fred 264.
Stoyle, J. D. 223,-6, 274,-5.

Strange, Frederick 186,-7, 200.
Stuart, Edith 60, 72.
Stuart, Otho 249.
Swanborough, Ada 191, 216,-7, 221,-7.
Swanborough, Miss (Mrs. Lyons) 218,
  220.
Swanborough, Mrs. 218, 221,-3.
Swinbourne, Tom 72, 108, 169, 193,
  292.
Swinburne, Algernon 68,-9.

Taylor, J. (of Astley's) 55,-7.
Taylor, J. G. 302,-7.
Taylor, Tom 88, 97, 207, 284.
Taylor, J. R. 99.
Telbin 201.
Telbin, Rose 215.
Tempest, Marie 267, 277.
Templar, Claude 356.
Temple, G. 257, 306.
Temple, R. 256,-7, 265.
Tenniel, Sir John 345.
Tennyson 245,-6.
Ternan, Fanny 134,-7, 140 et seq.
Ternan, Mrs. 89.
Terris, Ellaline 182, 233.
Terriss, Will 167, 191,-4, 215,-6, 240.
Terry, Daniel 215.
Terry, Edward 97, 109, 112, 220,-8,
  230, 255.
Terry, Ellen 33, 75, 101, 119, 134,-5,
  -6,-7, 140 et seq., 155, 166, 171, 191,
  201,-2,-8, 215,-6, 240,-3, 299, 303,-4.
Terry, Florence 105.
Terry, Fred 110, 231, 252.
Terry, Kate 4, 5, 26, 100 et seq., 103,
  117, 134,-6,-7, 140 et seq,, 149,
  155, 194, 203.
Terry, Marion 106,-8,-9, 259.
Terry, Minnie 248.
Thackeray 244.
Thalberg (actor) 250.
Thillon, Mme. 125, 271.
Thomas, Brandon 112.
Thompson, Augusta 159, 279.
Thompson, Clara 309.
Thompson, Lydia 88, 141, 224,-7,
  230,-1, 290, 307 et seq.
Thorne, Emily 224, 235.
Thorne, Fred 224.
Thorne, Thomas 220,-1,-4,-7.
Thorne, Sarah 5, 224.
Thumb, Tom 215.
Tomlins, G. 357.
Toole, J. L. 30, 88, 115, 202,-3,-6,
  220,-8, 241, 274,-6, 307, 309 et seq.
Townshend, Lady 322.
Townshend, Marquis of, 191, 336,
  341.

Toy, Beatrice 364.
Tree, Ann 40,-1, 43.
Tree, Beerbohm 39, 138, 247, 251, 276,-7, 303.
Tree, Ellen (see Kean, Mrs. Charles).
Tree, Lady 149, 169.
Tree, Maria 43, 139.
Tremaine, Annie 274.
Tully, James 67, 274, 317, 323.
Tunstall, Miss 21.
Turner, H. J. 222,-4,-7.
Turner, J. W. 292.
Turner, Sallie 275.
Tyars, F. 215, 356.
Tyndal, Kate 183.

Usher (clown) 29.

Van Ambergh 59, 60.
Vanbrugh, Irene 233, 252.
Vanbrugh, Violet 219.
Vance, 31.
Vandenhoff 72, 88, 99.
Vangalla, Miss 45.
Vaughan, Kate 23, 187,-8, 249, 255, 260, 273, 300, 368.
Vaughan, Susie 167,-8, 231,-2.
Velluti 81.
Venne, Lottie 193, 220,-1,-9, 247, 276.
Verner, Charles 75.
Vernon, W. H. 104,-6,-9, 161, 238.
Vesey, Clara 267.
Vestris, Armand 80,-1.
Vestris, Eliza 25, 80 et seq., 117, 124, 130, 214, 222, 353.
Vestvali, Felicita 129, 207.
Vezin, Hermann 74, 149, 162,-6, 203, 215, 242,-5,-8, 255, 286, 299, 310.
Vezin, Mrs. Hermann 74, 144, 169, 192,-3, 217, 244.
Victor, Mary Anne 21, 105.
Vining, George 95, 102, 155,-6,-9, 161, 357.
Vining, Mrs. Henry 38.
Vining, James 40, 140, 153, 161.
Vokes, Fred 264.
Vokes Family 32,-3,-4, 228, 299, 326.
Vollaire, J. 190, 204.
Vyner, Mrs. Charles 102,-5.

Wadman, " Tilly " 17, 242, 368.
Walker, Whimsical 30.
Wallack (the elder) 42,-3, 85, 97.
Wallack Family 126, 215.
Wallack, James 95, 125,-6, 131, 279, 282,-4.

Wallerstein 202.
Wallett (clown) 30, 60.
Waller, Lewis 98, 101, 152, 182, 233, 240,-5,-9, 250,-1.
Waller, Mrs. Lewis 112, 233, 250,-1, -2, 266.
Wallis, Miss 155, 188, 203.
Wallis, Bella 310.
Wallscourt, Lord 341.
Walsham, Henry 306.
Ward, Genevieve 110, 194, 234, 283,-8, 299, 355,-6.
Wardes, The 265.
Wardroper, H. 275.
Warner, Charles 104,-5, 155, 162, 176 et seq., 182, 197, 224, 244, 286, 361.
Warner, J. L. 282.
Warner, Mrs. 38, 131, 222, 278 et seq.
Warner (of " The Wrekin ") 244, 280,-2.
Watts, (of the Olympic) 89, 90, 279, 280,-1.
Waylett, Mrs. 21, 42, 212, 293.
Webster, Ben 42,-3, 85, 97, 102,-3,-4, 114, 151, 161, 214-5, 286, 359.
Weir, G. 249.
Welch, James 116, 234.
Wells, Mrs. Sumbel 320.
White, Mrs. Buckingham 255.
Whitty, Dame May 182, 233, 249.
Widdicomb (the elder) 27, 59.
Widdicomb, Fred 59.
Widdicomb, Henry 59, 115, 148,-9.
Wieland 122.
Wigan, Alfred 91 et seq., 96, 117, 131,-3,-6, 201,-2,-9, 214, 325.
Wigan, Mrs. Alfred 91 et seq., 95, 101, 117, 133, 202, 214, 279.
Wigan, Horace 96,-8, 99, 100,-2,-3, 194.
Wild, G. 87-8.
Willard, E. S. 112, 172 et seq., 171, 248.
Willes, Louise 103, 180, 241,-2.
Williams, A. 21, 110, 300, 318.
Williams, Mostyn 125.
Willing, James 293.
Wills, W. G. 197, 215, 247.
Wilton, Marie (see Bancroft, Lady).
Willmott, Charles 162, 194,-6,-7, 266.
Wiseman, Cardinal 325.
Wises, The 264.
Wood, Mrs. John 38, 159, 173, 207, 225, 241.
Woodin, W. S. 305.
Woolford, Miss (Mrs. Ducrow) 59.
Woolgar, Miss (see Mellon, Mrs. Alfred).
Woolley, T. 339 et seq.

Wrench, 30, 211.
Wright 122,-5, 140 *et seq.*
Wright, Haidée 198, 207.
Wright, Sara (" Wiry Sal ") 264.
Wrottesley, Hon. Mrs. 341.
Wyatt, Frank 232, 250.
Wybrow, Mrs. 45.
Wyndham, Sir Charles 4, 109, 201,-2, 219, 223, 245, 309, 321.
Wyndham, Lady (see Moore, Mary).
Wynne (Charles Sala) 132, 320.
Wynstanley, Mrs. 89, 133, 144, 214.

Yates (the elder) 39, 62, 351.

Yates, Edmund 104.
Young, Arthur 22.
Young, Charles 282.
Young, Mrs. Charles (see Vezin, Mrs. Hermann).
Younge (of Astley's) 27.
Younge, Fred 123.
Younge, R. 306.
Younge, W. 224, 277.

Zæo 186.
Zazel 186.
Zerbini, Carlotta 268.
Zuleika the Princess 206